SECOND EDITION

Positive Psychological Assessment

SECOND EDITION

Positive Psychological Assessment

A Handbook of Models and Measures

EDITED BY
Matthew W. Gallagher and Shane J. Lopez

American Psychological Association
Washington, DC

Published by
American Psychological Association
750 First Street, NE
Washington, DC 20002
https://www.apa.org

Order Department
https://www.apa.org/pubs/books
order@apa.org

In the U.K., Europe, Africa, and the Middle East, copies may be ordered from Eurospan
https://www.eurospanbookstore.com/apa
info@eurospangroup.com

Typeset in Meridien and Ortodoxa by Circle Graphics, Inc., Reisterstown, MD

Printer: Sheridan Books, Chelsea, MI
Cover Designer: Naylor Design, Washington, DC

Library of Congress Cataloging-in-Publication Data

Names: Gallagher, Matthew W., editor. | Lopez, Shane J., editor.
Title: Positive psychological assessment : a handbook of models and measures/ edited by Matthew W. Gallagher, Shane J. Lopez.
Description: Second edition. | Washington, DC : American Psychological Association, 2019. | Revised edition of Positive psychological assessment, c2003. | Includes bibliographical references and index.
Identifiers: LCCN 2018050770 (print) | LCCN 2019002690 (ebook) | ISBN 9781433831072 (eBook) | ISBN 1433831074 (eBook) | ISBN 9781433830020 (hardback) | ISBN 1433830027 (hardcover)
Subjects: LCSH: Psychological tests. | BISAC: PSYCHOLOGY / Assessment, Testing& Measurement. | PSYCHOLOGY / Clinical Psychology. | PSYCHOLOGY /Creative Ability.
Classification: LCC BF176 (ebook) | LCC BF176 .P67 2019 (print) | DDC 153.9/3—dc23
LC record available at https://lccn.loc.gov/2018050770

http://dx.doi.org/10.1037/0000138-000

Printed in the United States of America

10 9 8 7 6 5 4 3 2 1

Dedicated to
Shane J. Lopez (April 4, 1970–July 23, 2016)
and
Charles Richard "Rick" Snyder (December 26, 1944–January 17, 2006)

CONTENTS

CONTRIBUTORS

Matthew W. Ashton, PhD, Counseling and Testing Service, Idaho State University, Pocatello

Karen S. Basinger, PhD, Department of Communications and Behavioral Sciences, Urbana University, Urbana, OH

Chad R. Breeden, MS, Seattle, WA

Victoria Bryan, MA, Department of Psychology, University of New Hampshire, Durham

Robert D. Carlisle, PhD, Department of Research, Assessment, and Accountability, Mesa Public Schools, Mesa, AZ

David R. Caruso, PhD, Yale College Dean's Office, Yale University, New Haven, CT

Charles S. Carver, PhD, Department of Psychology, University of Miami, Coral Gables, FL

Brian P. Cole, PhD, Department of Educational Psychology, University of Kansas, Lawrence

Ed Diener, PhD, Department of Psychology, University of Virginia, Charlottesville; Department of Psychology, University of Utah, Salt Lake City

Bryan J. Dik, PhD, Department of Psychology, Colorado State University, Fort Collins

Lisa M. Edwards, PhD, Department of Counselor Education and Counseling Psychology, Marquette University, Milwaukee, WI

Nancy Eisenberg, PhD, Department of Psychology, Arizona State University, Tempe

Robert A. Emmons, PhD, Department of Psychology, University of California, Davis

Ashley Faytol, MS, Department of Counselor Education and Counseling Psychology, Marquette University, Milwaukee, WI

Lisa Y. Flores, PhD, Department of Educational, School, and Counseling Psychology, University of Missouri-Columbia

Jeffrey Froh, PsyD, Department of Psychology, Hofstra University, Hempstead, NY

Matthew W. Gallagher, PhD, Department of Psychology, University of Houston, Houston, TX

John C. Gibbs, PhD, The Ohio State University, Columbus

Benjamin P. Hardy, MS, Clemson University, Clemson, SC

Clyde Hendrick, PhD, Department of Psychology, Texas Tech University, Lubbock

Susan S. Hendrick, PhD, Department of Psychology, Texas Tech University, Lubbock

Mary J. Heppner, PhD, Department of Educational, School, and Counseling Psychology, University of Missouri, Columbia

Puncky Paul Heppner, PhD, Department of Educational, School, and Counseling Psychology, University of Missouri, Columbia

Monica S. Kearney, MS, Department of Psychology, University of Maryland, College Park

Christie L. Kelley, PhD, Activision Blizzard, Santa Monica, CA

Barbara A. Kerr, PhD, Department of Educational Psychology, University of Kansas, Lawrence

Corey L. M. Keyes, PhD, Department of Sociology, Emory College, Atlanta, GA

Randy J. Larsen, PhD, Department of Psychological and Brain Sciences, Washington University in St. Louis, St. Louis, MO

Stephanie Petersen Leachman, PhD, private practice; University of St. Thomas, Houston, TX

Dasom Lee, MA, Department of Psychology, The Ohio State University, Columbus

Dong-Gwi Lee, PhD, Department of Psychology, Yonsei University, Seoul, South Korea

Hang-Shim Lee, PhD, Counseling Psychology Program, Graduate School of Education, Konkuk University, Seoul, Republic of Korea

Bernhard Leipold, PhD, Institut für Psychologie, Humanwissenschaften, Universität der Bundeswehr München, Neubiberg, Germany

Frederick G. Lopez, PhD, Department of Psychological, Health, and Learning Sciences, University of Houston, Houston, TX

Shane J. Lopez, PhD, (deceased), Don Clifton Strengths Institute, Lincoln, NE; Gallup, Omaha, NE; University of Kansas, Lawrence

Richard E. Lucas, PhD, Department of Psychology, Michigan State University, East Lansing

Jeana L. Magyar, PhD, Psychology Department, University of Wisconsin, Stevens Point

Rod A. Martin, PhD, Department of Psychology, Western University Ontario, London, Ontario, Canada

John D. Mayer, PhD, Department of Psychology, University of New Hampshire, Durham

Michael E. McCullough, PhD, Department of Psychology, University of Miami, Coral Gables, FL

Rebecca McDonald, PhD, Psychology Department, Washington & Jefferson College, Washington, PA

Hannah J. Murphy, PhD, Cisco Systems, Dallas, TX

Karen M. O'Brien, PhD, Department of Psychology, University of Maryland, College Park

Kristin Koetting O'Byrne, PhD, Department of Organizational Leadership, School of Graduate and Professional Studies, Abilene Christian University-Dallas, Dallas, TX

Kimberly G. Phillips, PhD, Institute on Disability, University of New Hampshire, Durham

Cynthia L. Pury, PhD, Department of Psychology, Clemson University, Clemson, SC

Heather N. Rasmussen, PhD, Department of Educational Psychology, University of Kansas, Lawrence

Christine Robitschek, PhD, Department of Psychological Sciences, Texas Tech University, Lubbock

Rachel Rose, PsyD, doctoral candidate, School-Community Psychology, Hofstra University, Hempstead, NY

Peter Salovey, PhD, Department of Psychology, Yale University, New Haven, CT

Elizabeth Sauber, MS, Department of Psychology, University of Maryland, College Park

Michael F. Scheier, PhD, Department of Psychology, Carnegie Mellon University, Pittsburgh, PA

Emily S. Shaffer, PhD, Psychology Department, Tulane University, New Orleans, LA

Yerin Shim, PhD, Positive Psychology Center, University of Pennsylvania, Philadelphia

C. R. Snyder, PhD, (deceased), Department of Psychology, University of Kansas, Lawrence

Ursula M. Staudinger, PhD, Robert N. Butler Columbia Aging Center, Columbia University, New York, NY

Michael F. Steger, PhD, Center for Meaning and Purpose, Colorado State University, Fort Collins; North-West University, Vanderbijlpark, South Africa

Olivia A. Stull, MS, Department of Educational Psychology, University of Kansas, Lawrence

Louis Tay, PhD, Department of Psychological Sciences, Purdue University, West Lafayette, IN

Jennifer Teramoto Pedrotti, PhD, Psychology and Child Development Department, California Polytechnic State University, San Luis Obispo

Laura Y. Thompson, PhD, private practice, Phoenix, AZ

Jo-Ann Tsang, PhD, Department of Psychology and Neuroscience, Baylor University, Waco, TX

Carlos Valiente, PhD, T. Denny Sanford School of Social and Family Dynamics, Arizona State University, Tempe

Michael L. Wehmeyer, PhD, Department of Special Education, University of Kansas, Lawrence

Yu-Wei Wang, PhD, University of Maryland Counseling Center, College Park

Carrie L. Wyland, PhD, Psychology Department, Tulane University, New Orleans, LA

Jesse Wynn, PhD, private practice, Centennial, CO

Qing Zhou, PhD, Department of Psychology, University of California, Berkeley

FOREWORD

In the foreword to the first edition of *Positive Psychological Assessment: A Handbook of Models and Measures*, edited by Shane J. Lopez and C. R. (Rick) Snyder (2003), Donald Clifton, the pioneer in strengths assessment, observed that the volume "provides the foundation of concepts and measurement experience to enable social scientists to make a leap forward in presenting a better way of life for future civilizations" (p. xiii). Clifton concluded his remarks by stating that "this is the kind of guide we need to transform our civilization and open the doors to a new, exciting quality of life—perhaps a world of abundance rather than scarcity and a world of peace for all" (p. xiv).

Those are high expectations for any volume. And yet, as I sit here looking at the table of contents for the second edition of this volume, edited by Matthew W. Gallagher and Shane J. Lopez, I can't help but think that perhaps Donald Clifton was right in shooting for the stars in his hopes for the text. Certainly, the times are seemingly more uncertain today than they were 16 years ago when the first edition was published. If anything, the critical need for positive psychology has dramatically increased since 2003. And, of course, so much of what we need to do clinically and in a research context in positive psychology begins with assessment. In this new edition, Gallagher and Lopez again bring together productive, knowledgeable scholars in positive psychology and assessment—some whose chapters appeared in the first edition, others who bring a fresh perspective to this edition.

In reading the original volume again (okay, scanning it . . . it's a large volume!), I'm struck by the fact that in that first edition, from the foreword to the preface to the individual chapters, there were consistent attempts to justify the need for a volume on positive psychology assessment and defend the idea that we should assess and study what is good and right about people. I do not think that this defense is any longer necessary. I am sure that the field will be as hungry for this edition as it was for the first edition and that the fresh perspectives, updates and expansions on assessment, and information about models and tools that can support efforts to promote optimal human performance will be warmly received. I am also sure that there will be no need to justify this volume's publication in the same way that was the case 16 years ago.

Donald Clifton had the authority and credibility to spend much of his foreword exhorting readers to bring the positive of psychology into their practice and to use the volume as a guide to balancing the negative and positive of human action and behavior. I will let the experts who have authored these chapters do that. I will say that I am impressed with the scope and sequence of topics in this second edition, beginning with chapters providing a "search for the positive"; examining cognitive, emotional, and interpersonal models and measures; and examining models and measures of positive processes and outcomes. This is truly a state-of-the art examination of positive psychological assessment. While writing this foreword, I reread the final chapter in the first edition by Shane and Rick that focused on the future of positive psychological assessment. I think they would be pleased with this new volume in that it provides a new milestone that establishes where we are and provides new information for goals and objectives for the future development of the field of positive psychological assessment and, indeed, for the field of positive psychology more generally.

It is hard to beat having Donald Clifton write the foreword to your text on positive psychological assessment because there are a few people in the field whose level of authority and credibility matches his, and you may be wondering why one of them is not writing this foreword. The reason, quite simply, is that Matt Gallagher, whose Herculean efforts are responsible for bringing this volume to fruition, wanted someone who knew both of the editors from the first edition—Shane Lopez and Rick Snyder—to say a few words. My work has been in the application of the self-determination construct to the disability context (and, I might add, I greatly benefitted from information in the first edition and will do so from this edition as well). When I came to the University of Kansas (KU) in the late 1990s, colleagues told me that I needed to get to know an up-and-coming young professor whose work was in the area of hope. Shane Lopez was, at that time, an assistant professor in educational psychology. He and I hit it off immediately, in part because of the shared themes and values in our scholarly work and in part because Shane knew everyone and was everyone's friend. We began talking about shared research and practice interests. Soon after, Shane introduced me to Rick Snyder, who was a distinguished scholar in the Department of Psychology at KU, a pioneer in positive psychology and hope theory, and Shane's mentor. Like Shane, Rick was friendly, supportive, and thoughtful. The ideas that Rick and Shane had regarding the roles of agency and pathways thinking in hope theory influenced how I understood agentic action and self-determination. I had the opportunity to work with both Rick and Shane. Rick and I had interesting conversations about another KU psychologist, Fritz Heider, and the influence Heider's psychology of interpersonal relationships had on hope theory. Shane was a partner with us in moving our work in self-determination forward, better aligning that work with self-determination theory, and positioning our understanding of the construct to enable us to position our work within the growing field of positive psychology.

It still seems surreal to me that neither Rick nor Shane is with us today. Their physical absence leaves a sense of work undone and important projects never undertaken. A sense of enthusiasm, creativity, and, well, hope seems palpably missing with their passing. But, because I had a chance to get to know many of Shane's doctoral students, I know that the work he and Rick started continues through early-career professionals like Matt Gallagher, the lead editor of this volume, and through chapter authors like Jennifer Teramoto Pedrotti, Lisa Edwards, Heather Rasmussen, Jeana Magyar, and Brian Cole. I suspect that the majority of the contributors, particularly early- and midcareer scholars, have a story to tell about how Shane and/or Rick impacted their lives. To that end, Rick and Shane's enthusiasm, optimism, hope, and support emanate through the words and scholarship of the contributors to this volume and through many other scholars and practitioners in positive psychology.

REFERENCES

Clifton, D. (2003). Foreword. In S. J. Lopez & C. R. Snyder (Eds.), *Positive psychological assessment: A handbook of models and measures* (pp. xiii–xiv). Washington, DC: American Psychological Association.

Lopez, S. J., & Snyder, C. R. (2003). *Positive psychological assessment: A handbook of models and measures.* Washington, DC: American Psychological Association.

—Michael L. Wehmeyer
University of Kansas

I

SEARCHING FOR THE POSITIVE

1

Introduction to Positive Psychological Assessment

Matthew W. Gallagher

Imagine walking into a great hall filled with grand wooden tables. On those tables are thousands of weights and hundreds of well-worn scales, some larger than others. Using the scales, all engraved with the names of age-old foibles, measure the success of your life.

Next, imagine a second hall with twice as many scales—all of the scales for human foibles *plus* scales labeled with antiquated names of human strengths. This huge system of scales measures all qualities essential to life and well-being. Now measure the success of your life.

The premise of this handbook is that the system of scales in the second hall would help to strike a vital balance in our measurement of life success. Indeed, psychological science has provided us with many theoretically grounded, psychometrically sound measures of human strength. The goal of the second edition of this text is to provide an update on advances in the operationalization of constructs and developments of measures in positive psychology.

A POSITIVE PSYCHOLOGY PERSPECTIVE

Historically, scholars and counseling theorists have argued about the *natural state of human behavior.* To reveal any implicit theories regarding this state, we encourage readers to think about the assumptions they make about their research participants and their clients, their partners and their children,

http://dx.doi.org/10.1037/0000138-001
Positive Psychological Assessment: A Handbook of Models and Measures, Second Edition,
M. W. Gallagher and S. J. Lopez (Editors)

themselves and who they want to be. *Perspective* on human behavior determines the routes taken in pursuit of psychological data.

The information-gathering routes we take can yield data reflecting psychological weakness, psychological strength, or a combination of the two. It is the combination, the complementary bodies of knowledge, that will help resolve the shortcomings of common psychological assessment practices. It has been well established for decades that negative events may have a greater immediate effect on cognition, affect, and behavior than positive events (Taylor, 1991). For example, the work of Tversky and Kahneman (1981) demonstrated how framing can influence biases in decision making such that people may focus more on potential losses than gain when making decisions. These findings and decades of related research have led psychologists to suggest that "bad is stronger than good" (Baumeister, Bratslavsky, Finkenauer, & Vohs, 2001). Although this evidence, the realities of prevalence rates of mental illness (American Psychiatric Association, 2013), and the negative influences of societal factors such as poverty and discrimination require psychologists to investigate how best to understand and ameliorate negative psychological outcomes, it is important for the field of psychology to maintain balance in how we assess and understand psychological functioning.

Even if bad experiences are more immediately salient, there are numerous reasons to focus on positive aspects of functioning even when trying to understand the impact of negative events (e.g., Sparks & Baumeister, 2008). For example, it is an unfortunate reality that the vast majority of individuals will experience one or more traumatic events, yet despite estimates of lifetime traumatic exposure rates of 89.7%, only 8.3% of those same individuals were found to ever develop posttraumatic stress disorder in their lifetime (Kilpatrick et al., 2013). Resilience is therefore the modal outcome even in the face of terrible tragedy, and most individuals are mentally healthy and functioning well in life despite various stressors (Keyes, 2005). Any attempt to characterize human functioning that fails to quantify or represent the positive aspects of functioning therefore provides an incomplete and inadequate representation of psychological functioning.

After reading this handbook, it should be easier for you to see both the positive and negative aspects of someone's presentation and to be able to switch back and forth between—and to integrate—the complementary views of psychology and bodies of psychological science. Dozens of psychological strengths have been operationalized by psychologists committed to understanding the best in people. In this volume, the authors present their conceptualizations of particular human strengths, and they examine the psychometric properties and clinical utilities of observational techniques, physiological measures, scales, inventories, and interview and narrative techniques. We have asked the authors to elucidate the theoretical underpinnings of their measures and to critique their assessment strategies in light of today's stringent measurement standards.

Many of these measures of strengths are theoretically based, thus lending themselves to inclusion in explanatory models (such as those describing buffering processes that keep illness at bay and those models detailing how strengths facilitate healthy development). Furthermore, advancements in measurement of strength will provide the tools needed to examine the threshold effects (e.g., how much of a strength is enough to produce benefits in someone's life) and exponential effects of the positive (e.g., whether four strengths combined yield more than double the beneficial effects of two strengths combined).

IMPORTANCE OF POSITIVE OUTCOMES

Tremendous progress has been made since the first volume of this handbook was published, not just in the development and refinement of models and measures of positive psychology, but also in demonstrating the importance of measuring these constructs in different contexts. There is increasing evidence that positive mental health is more than just the absence of mental illness, that promoting positive mental health is important across the lifespan (e.g., Keyes, 2013), and that positive mental health predicts health outcomes, functioning, and even mortality above and beyond traditional measures that focus on deficits or psychopathology (Keyes, 2005, 2007; Keyes & Simoes, 2012). Remarkable work has been conducted in developing taxonomies of character strengths (Peterson & Seligman, 2004) and demonstrating how strengths predict and promote many important life outcomes (e.g., Niemiec, 2013). Meta-analytic reviews have demonstrated the robust evidence that positive outcomes not only reflect but promote further positive outcomes (Lyubomirsky, King, & Diener, 2005) and that positive psychological interventions can both promote mental health and decrease mental illness (Sin & Lyubomirsky, 2009).

Although more research is needed to examine positive psychological outcomes in diverse settings, there is increasing evidence that positive factors such as optimism and positive affect have remarkably consistent effects on well-being and health worldwide (Gallagher, Lopez, & Pressman, 2013; Pressman, Gallagher, & Lopez, 2013). The assessment of positive psychological outcomes is also increasingly being used to improve our understanding of how best to predict and promote positive outcomes in the workplace, in educational settings, and in promoting recovery in psychotherapy. For example, the Gallup Student Poll (Gallup, 2017) has been used in recent years to quantify and enhance the hope, engagement, and well-being of more than 5 million American students. The thesis that studying positive outcomes may improve our understanding in research or outcomes in practice is not new (e.g., Menninger, 1959), but all of this work speaks to the value of positive psychological assessment in advancing the science and practice of psychology

OVERVIEW OF THE SECOND EDITION OF *POSITIVE PSYCHOLOGICAL ASSESSMENT*

In planning the second edition of this handbook, we sought to build on what worked well in the first edition of this handbook and to provide an updated overview of many of the most important and widely studies theories, constructs, and measures of positive psychology. A major goal in revising this handbook was to not only provide an update on the science supporting different models and measures of positive psychology, but to also provide more concrete examples of how these tools have been and can be used in clinical practice. In this way, we hope that this handbook will be a valuable resource both for investigators conducting research to further our understanding of positive psychological constructs and also to serve as a useful introduction and guide for practitioners who are interested in incorporating measures of positive psychological functioning in their clinical practice. New to this edition of the handbook is the inclusion of case studies in many chapters to provide more concrete examples of how the constructs covered in this handbook can be applied when working with clients in clinical settings.

The handbook is organized into six sections. The introductory section on searching for the positive includes chapters that establish the importance of broadening assessment in psychology to include a focus on both the positive and negative features of individuals and environments, the influence that positive and negative labels can have on our understanding of functioning in both research and clinical practice, and the importance of ensuring that positive psychological assessment tools are available for and implemented with individuals across cultures and diverse backgrounds. The second section focuses on cognitive models and measures and includes chapters on different forms of positive thinking (i.e., optimism, hope, self-efficacy) that have been shown to be important predictors of functioning in diverse contexts, as well as other cognitive resources and strengths (problem-solving appraisal, creativity, courage, and wisdom) that have extensive empirical support as important factors in promoting flourishing for individuals.

The third section of this handbook includes four chapters focusing on emotional models and outcomes, including best practices for studying positive affect, how to quantify individual levels of self-esteem, and how the presence of love and emotional intelligence can influence both one's individual and social functioning. The fourth section focuses more on positive outcomes in a social or interpersonal context, including how empathy and attachment security can provide a foundation for healthy relationships; how forgiveness, humor, and gratitude can be measured and their role in strengthening social bonds; and how maturity in moral judgments promotes human development. The fifth section focuses on measures and constructs for assessing positive outcomes in diverse contexts such as understanding the role of religious outcomes, the presence of meaning and other positive work outcomes, and the most widely studied model of characterizing positive mental health: subjective well-being. Finally, the handbook concludes with a brief overview of the progress that has been made in the 15 years since the first edition of the handbook was published and how the field can continue to build on this progress to improve our understanding of positive psychological assessment going forward.

Although the second edition of this handbook contains more than two dozen chapters, it represents a selective compilation of many of the most promising and widely studied topics in the field and does not represent an exhaustive compilation of all models and measures in positive psychology. The degree to which the number of models and measures in positive psychology has grown since the first edition of the handbook speaks to the vibrant nature of the field. Constructs such as resilience, curiosity, mindfulness, flow, posttraumatic growth, and others are also important positive psychological traits and processes and their absence in this volume should not be construed as an indication that those topics and others are not also important positive psychological outcomes that researchers and practitioners may want to assess/consider to more fully characterize functioning. Rather, the breadth of topics that have been and continue to be developed in this area speak to the growing understanding of, and excitement for developing, assessment tools to quantify psychological strengths and resources.

THE LEGACY OF C. R. SNYDER AND SHANE J. LOPEZ

Unfortunately, the field of positive psychology has now lost the two individuals who served as editors of the first edition of this handbook and who were leading figures in establishing and growing the field of positive psychology: Charles Richard "Rick" Snyder and Shane J. Lopez. Rick was a distinguished professor at the University of Kansas who published more than 20 edited volumes and books and more than 250 articles and chapters, was a gifted teacher who received dozens of awards for teaching, and was an inspiring and award-winning mentor. As the primary developer of hope theory (Snyder, 2002), Rick conducted seminal work demonstrating the importance of positive cognition in promoting positive outcomes across many domains, as well as extensive work on coping, reality negotiation, forgiveness, and many other topics in positive psychology. Rick passed away in 2006, a few years after the publication of the first edition of this handbook after developing transitional cell carcinoma.

Like Rick, Shane was an award-winning teacher and researcher and was remarkably productive. Shane was Gallup Senior Scientist in Residence and research director for the Clifton Strengths Institute as well as a professor at the University of Kansas. He published over 100 articles and chapters and over a dozen edited volumes and books, many of which were in collaboration with Rick and represented seminal contributions to the field, such as the *Handbook of Positive Psychology* (Snyder & Lopez, 2009). Shane was a leader in the field of hope and was particularly influential in developing tools such as the Gallup Student Poll to help identify strengths and well-being of students. After years of persevering with a number of serious health conditions, Shane passed away in July 2016 as we were finalizing plans for how to revise this edition of the handbook.

Shane and Rick were extraordinary scientists who were also cherished colleagues, mentors, and friends of many of the contributors to this volume, as well as many other scientists and clinicians around the world. They are dearly missed, and this volume is dedicated to their memory.

CONCLUSION

In developing the second edition of this handbook, we were fortunate to once again have so many distinguished researchers contribute overviews of different assessment tools and theories of positive psychology. With the loss of Rick, Shane, and other pillars of positive psychology such as Chris Peterson, the field of positive psychology is transitioning to the second and third generations of researchers in many areas of positive psychology. The work covered in this volume and the ongoing research on these topics and clinical practice using these tools worldwide speaks to the vibrancy of the field and reason for optimism that continued progress will be made in the field of positive psychological assessment. I hope that this volume not only will help researchers and practitioners understand what is currently known about how best to conceptualize and measure many of the most important aspects of positive psychological functioning in both clinical practice and research, but also will help motivate further developments in positive psychological assessment so that we continue to improve our understanding of how to have a more balanced and complete understanding of optimal functioning for individuals and communities worldwide.

REFERENCES

American Psychiatric Association. (2013). *Diagnostic and statistical manual of mental disorders* (5th ed.). Washington, DC: Author.

Baumeister, R. F., Bratslavsky, E., Finkenauer, C., & Vohs, K. D. (2001). Bad is stronger than good. *Review of General Psychology, 5,* 323–370. http://dx.doi.org/10.1037/1089-2680.5.4.323

Gallagher, M. W., Lopez, S. J., & Pressman, S. D. (2013). Optimism is universal: Exploring the presence and benefits of optimism in a representative sample of the world. *Journal of Personality, 81,* 429–440. http://dx.doi.org/10.1111/jopy.12026

Gallup. (2017). *Gallup Student Poll.* Retrieved from http://www.gallupstudentpoll.com/home.aspx?ref=logo

Keyes, C. L. M. (2005). Mental illness and/or mental health? Investigating axioms of the complete state model of health. *Journal of Consulting and Clinical Psychology, 73,* 539–548. http://dx.doi.org/10.1037/0022-006X.73.3.539

Keyes, C. L. M. (2007). Promoting and protecting mental health as flourishing: A complementary strategy for improving national mental health. *American Psychologist, 62,* 95–108. http://dx.doi.org/10.1037/0003-066X.62.2.95

Keyes, C. L. M. (2013). Promoting and protecting positive mental health: Early and often throughout the lifespan. In C. L. M. Keyes (Ed.), *Mental well-being: International contributions to the study of positive mental health* (pp. 3–28). Dordrecht, the Netherlands: Springer.

Keyes, C. L. M., & Simoes, E. J. (2012). To flourish or not: Positive mental health and all-cause mortality. *American Journal of Public Health, 102,* 2164–2172. http://dx.doi.org/10.2105/AJPH.2012.300918

Kilpatrick, D. G., Resnick, H. S., Milanak, M. E., Miller, M. W., Keyes, K. M., & Friedman, M. J. (2013). National estimates of exposure to traumatic events and PTSD prevalence using *DSM–IV* and *DSM–5* criteria. *Journal of Traumatic Stress, 26,* 537–547. http://dx.doi.org/10.1002/jts.21848

Lyubomirsky, S., King, L., & Diener, E. (2005). The benefits of frequent positive affect: Does happiness lead to success? *Psychological Bulletin, 131,* 803–855. http://dx.doi.org/10.1037/0033-2909.131.6.803

Menninger, K. (1959). The academic lecture: Hope. *The American Journal of Psychiatry, 116,* 481–491. http://dx.doi.org/10.1176/ajp.116.6.481

Niemiec, R. M. (2013). VIA character strengths: Research and practice (the first 10 years). In H. H. Knoop & A. D. Fave (Eds.), *Well-being and cultures* (pp. 11–29). Dordrecht, the Netherlands: Springer. http://dx.doi.org/10.1007/978-94-007-4611-4_2

Peterson, C., & Seligman, M. E. (2004). *Character strengths and virtues: A handbook and classification.* New York, NY: Oxford University Press.

Pressman, S. D., Gallagher, M. W., & Lopez, S. J. (2013). Is the emotion-health connection a "first-world problem"? *Psychological Science, 24,* 544–549. http://dx.doi.org/10.1177/0956797612457382

Sin, N. L., & Lyubomirsky, S. (2009). Enhancing well-being and alleviating depressive symptoms with positive psychology interventions: A practice-friendly meta-analysis. *Journal of Clinical Psychology, 65,* 467–487. http://dx.doi.org/10.1002/jclp.20593

Snyder, C. R. (2002). Hope theory: Rainbows in the mind. *Psychological Inquiry, 13,* 249–275. http://dx.doi.org/10.1207/S15327965PLI1304_01

Snyder, C. R., & Lopez, S. J. (Eds.). (2009). *The Oxford handbook of positive psychology* (2nd ed.). New York, NY: Oxford University Press.

Sparks, E. A., & Baumeister, R. F. (2008). If bad is stronger than good, why focus on human strength? In S. J. Lopez (Ed.), *Positive psychology* (1st ed., Vol. 1, pp. 55–79). Westport, CT: Praeger.

Taylor, S. E. (1991). Asymmetrical effects of positive and negative events: The mobilization–minimization hypothesis. *Psychological Bulletin, 110,* 67–85. http://dx.doi.org/10.1037/0033-2909.110.1.67

Tversky, A., & Kahneman, D. (1981). The framing of decisions and the psychology of choice. *Science, 211,* 453–458. http://dx.doi.org/10.1126/science.7455683

2

Striking a Vital Balance

Developing a Complementary Focus on Human Weakness and Strength

Shane J. Lopez, C. R. Snyder, Heather N. Rasmussen, and Brian P. Cole

As behavioral scientists and mental health practitioners craft questions about human behavior, we initiate a process of inquiry into what does and does not work in the lives of people. Determining the presence of weaknesses and strengths, and their existing associations, enables us to frame questions, to develop theories of human functioning, and to make recommendations for care. We contend that scientific and professional psychology have been biased toward identifying psychopathology and problems in everyday living, and thus we know a great deal about how to help people resolve concerns and alleviate symptoms. Although progress has been made, we continue to know less, however, about the anatomy of optimal functioning and the enhancement of human strengths. Therefore, in this chapter, we briefly address conceptual issues related to identifying the human strengths that are considered the building blocks of positive psychology. We argue that such human strengths are "real" and that detecting these strengths is an important part of good science and practice. We also identify the shortcomings in common assessment procedures and provide a model for addressing these shortcomings.

HUMAN STRENGTHS ARE AS REAL AS WEAKNESS

Information about human strengths can be drawn from Eastern and Western philosophy, religious texts, historical accounts, and linguistics (Peterson & Seligman, 2004; Schimmel, 2000). Though verification of the authenticity of

---

http://dx.doi.org/10.1037/0000138-002
Positive Psychological Assessment: A Handbook of Models and Measures, Second Edition, M. W. Gallagher and S. J. Lopez (Editors)

human strengths may be rooted in subjectivity, potency of a human strength may be determined in a more objective manner. Indeed, we can answer questions about potency most directly. For example, do human strengths play an active, potent role in the attainment of health, happiness, and optimal functioning? We believe that this question has been addressed empirically. The vast literature dealing with the potency of human strengths has been summarized elsewhere (see Joseph, 2015; Parks & Schueller, 2014), but three examples may be helpful. First, a randomized, wait-list control trial using hope-based group therapy effectively increased agency, meaning in life, and self-esteem while reducing symptoms of anxiety and depression (Cheavens, Feldman, Gum, Michael, & Snyder, 2006). Second, positive psychotherapy is a 14-session treatment approach that emphasizes exploration of strengths, development of meaningful goals, cultivation of positive emotion, reframing of negative life events, and amplification of positive relationships and has demonstrated effectiveness at improving well-being, social skills, and health behaviors while decreasing depression and anxiety across several studies (see Rashid, 2015a, for a review). Third, multiple studies demonstrated the efficacy of well-being therapy, an eight-to-ten session protocol for enhancing well-being and resilience while reducing symptom distress (Fava, 2016).

Human strengths are as real as human weakness, but assessment of strengths is a neglected competency in psychology. By only focusing on weaknesses, psychologists have perpetuated an assessment process that is out of balance. We next identify shortcomings of psychological assessment and describe the practice model of positive psychological assessment and how-to information to address the imbalance. Thus, we hope to encourage researchers and practitioners to engage in a more balanced view of human life—a vital balance between weakness and strength of the person and the environment.

POSITIVE PSYCHOLOGICAL ASSESSMENT: TOWARD A COMPLEMENTARY FOCUS IN RESEARCH AND PRACTICE

The same approaches and types of tools used to make sense out of the presentation and experiences of mental illness can be used to highlight and measure potent elements of strengths.

Therefore, just as in the assessment of psychopathology, scientists conducting examinations of human strengths must be sensitive to the environmental, or contextual, influences that may determine how strength is manifested. More precisely, researchers should attempt to capture the essence of the interplay between the person and the environment. On this note, Menninger, Mayman, and Pruyser (1963) stated that one measure of success in life is "the satisfactoriness to the individual and his environment of their mutual attempts to adapt themselves to each other" (p. 2). Furthermore, examination of strengths within a cultural context is of the utmost importance (Capielo, Mann, Nevels, & Delgado-Romero, 2014; Owens, Magyar-Moe, & Lopez, 2015).

ENVIRONMENTAL ASSESSMENT

The idea that environmental factors influence how an individual functions is well accepted in psychology. In the early 1900s, this notion was popularized by behaviorists who argued that individual behavior could be explained, predicted, and modified if the mechanisms underlying environmental influences were understood (Conyne & Clack, 1981). Despite knowledge of the principles by which the environment shapes the individual, there continues to be a dearth of scholarship devoted to identifying the specific environmental variables that do the shaping. In the first edition of this text, we advocated for the development of reliable operational definitions of environmental variables and discovery of aspects of environments that promote positive functioning and personal growth. Here, we provide updates on advancements toward these goals in the areas of mental health, home, work, and school environments.

The Four-Front Approach: Attending to Environmental Resources

Wright and Lopez (2002, 2009) posited that environmental factors are neglected in psychological assessment and proposed a four-front approach (the four-front approach is discussed in more detail later in this chapter and in Chapter 3 of this volume) to highlight the environment in individual appraisal. They asserted that clinicians must be committed to examining the person's strengths and weaknesses as well as the resources and stressors present in the environment. In practice, this is difficult because the developers of the *Diagnostic and Statistical Manual of Mental Disorders* (fifth ed. [*DSM–5*]; American Psychiatric Association, 2013) removed the axial system that previously gave weight to environmental considerations through its Axis IV (psychosocial and environmental problems). Instead, the *DSM–5* suggests that environmental and contextual information should be included when making diagnoses, but provides no guidance regarding where or how to do so (Kress, Barrio Minton, Adamson, Paylo, & Pope, 2014). Consistent with previous editions, the *DSM–5* provides an incomplete picture of mental health by focusing exclusively on pathology, weaknesses, and stressors while neglecting assets and resources. Similarly, the ICD–10 (World Health Organization, 1992) provides a widely used and well-established taxonomy and classification system for characterizing various forms of psychopathology and other health disorders, but provides little guidance for how best to define, measure, and understand strengths or positive aspects of mental health.

In congruence with the approach put forth by Wright and Lopez (2002, 2009), we believe that assessing environmental resources and stressors is critical to the conceptualization of any individual. As a result of this belief, all instruments examined in the forthcoming sections about environmental assessment in the home, at work, and at school are selected because of their potential for detecting, measuring, or highlighting the positive aspects of the particular environment that it was designed to assess.

Assessment of the Home Environment

As the primary setting of human development and social interaction, the home and family environment is the primary domain for assessment and change. Research has linked various aspects of the home environment and family functioning to children's cognitive, motor, and social development (Miquelote, Santos, Caçola, Montebelo, & Gabbard, 2012; Moos, 1991) and has shown its influence on the school (Felner, Aber, Primavera, & Cauce, 1985) and work (Repetti, 1987). Assessment of the home–family environment began with measures of socioeconomic status such as the Home Index (Gough, 1954) and the American Home Scale (Kerr, 1942). More complex conceptualizations have many different foci, but there is not a comprehensive, universally accepted conceptualization of the home environment (although a few have produced useful assessment tools).

The Home Observation for Measurement of the Environment (HOME) Inventory (Caldwell & Bradley, 1984) assesses the amount and quality of stimulation and support a child receives in the home environment (Totsika & Sylva, 2004). The HOME is used to identify potential sources of risk in the environment so that appropriate remedial interventions may be provided (Boehm, 1985). The inventory is completed during a home visit with the child and primary caregiver through a combination interview/observation and scored using a yes–no format. Four forms of the inventory exist for use with children from birth to age 15. Each instrument assesses parental responsivity, parental acceptance, and availability of learning materials as well as dimensions unique to the age group, such as language stimulation in early childhood and encouragement of maturity in middle childhood (Totsika & Sylva, 2004).

One of the few assessments specifically designed to measure environmental strengths, the Family Functioning Style Scale (FFSS; Deal, Trivette, & Dunst, 1988), assesses the 12 qualities of strong families (e.g., commitment, coping strategies, flexibility, and communication) by asking family members the extent to which they believe their family possesses different strengths and capabilities. The FFSS was developed for use in family interventions to promote discussion about the ways that particular characteristics function as resources for meeting the family's needs (Deal et al., 1988). By identifying family strengths and resources, clinicians can mobilize these qualities to help the family acquire new competencies and build on existing capabilities (Trivette, Dunst, Deal, Hamer, & Propst, 1990). The scale contains 26 self-report items, measured on a 5-point Likert-type scale, with values ranging from *not at all like my family* to *almost always like my family*. The instrument may be completed individually or by two or more family members together (Deal et al., 1988).

Assessment of Workplace Environments

Self-report questionnaires, observations by trained individuals, in-depth interviews, and reviews of records have all been used as a means to assess workplace environments (Schooler, 1999). Researchers and personnel managers collaborated to assess work environments in an effort to determine which types of environmental workplace conditions were most conducive and detrimental to productivity and employee satisfaction. Schooler (1999) contended that accurate analysis includes a mix of observation, in-depth interviews, review of records, and assessment of individual differences in perceptions of and reactions to the work environment.

Buckingham and Coffman (1999) posed an important question: "What does a strong, vibrant workplace look like?" (p. 25). Their conceptualization of a positive work environment is the result of the Gallup's interviews of more than 2 million individuals working in abroad spectrum of jobs. After analysis of the responses, a limited number of indicators were found to measure the strength of the work environment. They found that pay, benefits, and organizational structure do not significantly affect the way that individuals rate their environment; rather, having the opportunity to develop talents into strengths or being given the chance to do what one does best helps create a positive workplace environment.

The Clifton StrengthsFinder 2.0 (Rath, 2007) represents one of the few instruments available to assess strengths-based development processes in work settings (Asplund, Lopez, Hodges, & Harter, 2007). Researchers were able to identify 34 reoccurring patterns or "themes" that are the substance behind an individual's success. Individuals discover which themes exist most strongly in their lives and learn to build on them. The Clifton StrengthsFinder 2.0 consists of 177 pairs of descriptors that the individual is instructed to choose between. On the basis of their response patterns, an individual's five strongest theme areas are determined. Currently the Clifton StrengthsFinder 2.0 is being used in a variety of workplace environments to increase employee engagement, productivity, and retention (Asplund et al., 2007; Clifton & Harter, 2003). It is important to note, however, that there is less published research currently available examining the reliability validity of the Clifton StrengthsFinder 2.0 as it is a proprietary measure.

Assessment of the School Environment

Assessment of the school environment has perhaps changed the most since the first edition of this text. Traditionally, professionals have relied on methods such as observation, teacher interviews, checklists, task analysis, parent interviews, and social histories to assess the school environment (Ysseldyke & Elliott, 1999). Developers of measures of classroom and school climate also have attempted to identify the climate or ambiance and the effect that it has on the learner. Current approaches to exploring educational environments emphasize the importance of an ecological view of the school context, or "the interface between proximal processes in classrooms and schools and higher level school contexts" (Talbert & McLaughlin, 1999, p. 198; see also McCurdy, Coutts, Sheridan, & Campbell, 2012). The tenets of instructional ecology suggest that learning not only resides in the learner, but rather "is functionally related to the setting in which takes place" (Ysseldyke & Elliott, 1999, p. 500).

Inventory on Learning Climate and Student Well-Being

The Inventory on Learning Climate and Student Well-Being (ILCSWB; Walker, 2006) was developed to examine the psychological well-being of college students by exploring their experiences across seven dimensions of interpersonal and intrapersonal functioning on college campuses. The inventory consists of 48 items, which are answered using a 6-point Likert type scale (1 = *definitely does not apply to me* to 6 = *definitely applies to me*), with higher scores indicating higher levels of well-being (Walker, 2009). The ILCSWB examines a number of domains of functioning that support psychological well-being (e.g., having purpose and goals, autonomy, and self-acceptance) in addition to dimensions specific to adjustment to college (e.g., academic skills; money management; engagement on campus; and relations with students, faculty, and staff).

Gallup Student Poll

The Gallup Student Poll (Gallup, 2017) is a web-based survey developed to assess factors related to positive school culture. More specifically, each year, students in Grades 5 through 12 are asked 24 items addressing their level of engagement (i.e., involvement and enthusiasm for school), hope (i.e., ideas and energy for future goals), entrepreneurial aspirations (i.e., innate talent for building businesses), and career/financial literacy (i.e., knowledge, attitudes, and behaviors related to making economic choices). To date, nearly 5 million students have participated in the Gallup Student Poll, and data from the poll is utilized to enhance student outcomes by providing feedback on ways to develop strength-based educational environments (Gallup, 2017).

Examining the Forces of the Environment

In the 15 years that have passed since the first edition of this text, there have been a number of advancements in the area of environmental assessment. However, there is still much work to be done. Although there is greater understanding of the essential role of environmental variables, there continues to be a focus on individual characteristics. Perhaps this is the result of inherent beliefs that external variables are largely immutable. Others may concede the malleability of external variables but believe that the individual represents the most feasible point of intervention. We continue to hold that a comprehensive understanding of environmental variables has the potential to greatly enhance the understanding of human functioning, thereby allowing for greater sensitivity in research designs and interventions. Next, we outline our attempt at establishing a strategic approach to collecting data about the individual strengths and weaknesses as well as environmental assets and deficits with the hope that it will inspire others to seek to broaden their approaches to assessment.

POSITIVE PSYCHOLOGICAL ASSESSMENT: TOWARD A COMPLEMENTARY FOCUS IN PRACTICE

Professionals in a variety of disciplines have attested to the value of capitalizing on the strengths they have identified in their clients (e.g., Saleebey, 2001; Wright & Fletcher, 1982). Nevertheless, there continue to be inherent problems with the standard assessment process. Indeed, "Two common shortcomings of assessment procedures in agencies that deal with client problems and adjustment are the concentration on negative aspects of functioning, with insufficient attention to environmental aspects" (Wright & Fletcher, 1982, p. 229).

Figure 2.1 depicts the assessment approach that we use when working with clients. This model is based on Pepinsky and Pepinsky's (1954) view of counselor-as-scientist and Spengler, Strohmer, Dixon, and Shivy's (1995) scientist–practitioner model of psychological assessment that is described as a "cognitive map" for practitioners engaging in the assessment process. Similarly, we encourage readers to walk through the model, or map, as we describe each aspect of it. Note that the headings in this section of the chapter correspond to steps of our approach.

FIGURE 2.1. The Practice Model of Psychological Assessment

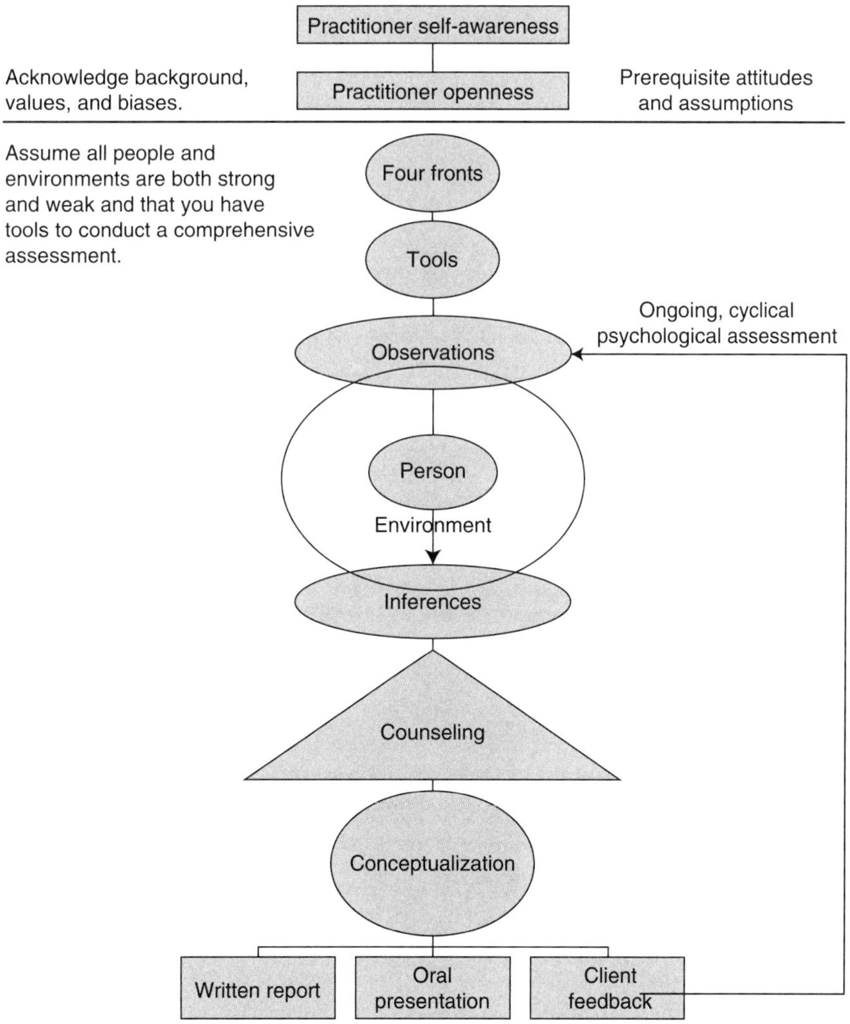

The unique aspects of our model are the focus on complementary hypotheses (on strength and weakness); the attention paid to the environmental influences on client functioning; the framework for collecting balanced, comprehensive client data; and the fact-checking facilitated by sharing balanced data with clients and colleagues. This model also presents counseling and assessment processes as intricately intertwined. The open, flexible, and self-correcting quality of the approach is not unique (see Spengler et al., 1995, for a model with similar flexibility).

Acknowledge Background, Values, and Biases

As established in the beginning of this chapter, experiences influence what is seen. Personal background, values developed over a lifetime, and the biases that are part of all decision-making processes serve as the filters for the information gathered when working with clients. Acknowledging how background, values, and biases affect the assessment process is a goal that all practitioners should pursue. Neutralizing or debiasing the effects of personal experiences and attitudes may serve as an aspirational goal, but it is important to note that we believe all assessments to be inherently flawed. This makes the self-correcting nature of this model valuable. Values and biases that could influence assessment of behavior are made explicit, and implicit theories about personality are more thoroughly operationalized.

Assume All People and Environments Are Both Strong and Weak and That You Have Tools to Conduct a Comprehensive Assessment

Developing a complementary focus in practice requires practitioners to have particular beliefs and an awareness of professional resources. Specifically, practitioners must assume that all people and environments are both strong and weak. The reason for the assumption is simple: People only search for things they believe to exist. Thus, this volume attempts to provide tools designed to detect the best in people. Combining these tools with the tools used for detecting pathology would make it possible to conduct a balanced, comprehensive assessment.

Construct an Implicit Theory of Client Functioning

The assessment process begins the moment a practitioner sees a client's name on a schedule. From this data, guesses about sex and ethnicity are made. Review of intake paperwork yields data that may influence, to some extent, the approach in the first session. These data along with observations of the client's behavior (as positively and negatively affected by the environment) serve as the initial layers of a multilayered, implicit theory of client functioning—a theory that reflects the unconscious, unsubstantiated assumptions about the client's functioning.

Constructing an implicit theory requires practitioners to make observations of the client in the context of the client's environment. Most practitioners do not interact with clients in their homes, schools, or workplaces; however, they do have the capacity to contextualize the client's presentation (determine how the client's functioning is dependent on environmental and cultural variables). Thus, as the model depicts, the practitioners make observations about how the client functions in his or her environment. To do this, practitioners must transcend the boundary of the client's context so that they can become more sensitive to the client's experience of the world.

Contextualizing inferences about a client's psychological status and capacity for change is the next focus in the construction of an implicit theory. These inferences should be focused on all domains of variables that are associated with client functioning. Making inferences along four fronts and gathering data along these fronts are essential aspects of constructing an implicit theory.

Wright's (1991; Wright & Lopez, 2009) four-front approach serves as the data-gathering and organizing method central to positive psychological assessment in practice situations. Practitioners' efforts to make meaningful observations of client status and propensity for growth are initiated by and organized by identifying (a) undermining characteristics of the client, (b) the client's strengths and assets, (c) lacks and destructive factors in the environment, and (d) resources and opportunities in the environment. Practitioners facilitate this approach by garnering responses to four questions: (a) What deficiencies does the person contribute to his or her problems? (b) What strengths does the person bring to deal effectively with his or her life? (c) What environmental factors serve as impediments to healthy functioning? and (d) What environmental resources accentuate positive human functioning? Practitioners informally gathering data along the four fronts tend to generate a more complex set of inferences that ultimately evolve into formal clinical hypotheses to be tested directly.

Gather Complementary Data

Though strict adherence to scientific methodology would preclude the collection of formal data before clearly stating hypotheses, clinical work involves a process that is less of a lockstep approach and more of a simultaneous unfolding of multiple steps. Indeed, we believe that inferences are drawn from clinical data, and an implicit theory about client functioning takes shape. Then, the creation of this theory triggers strategic and formal data collection efforts along the four fronts. Though these efforts at data gathering may not be directly linked to specific hypotheses at the onset, implicit views of clients become more explicit over time (possibly over the course of one session) and formal hypotheses (and disconfirmatory and alternative versions of these hypotheses) are refined and are tested directly (discussed in the section Testing Complementary Hypotheses).

Strategic collection of complementary data involves using standard methods of detecting weakness (semistructured interviews, symptom checklists, objective and projective personality measures) and novel means of seeking out strengths. Also, a balanced, complementary approach to data collection would involve the identification of environmental resources and deficits. Because the detection of human weakness is the topic of most other assessment books, formal measures of strengths are presented throughout this volume, and we will limit our subsequent discussion to the informal assessment of strengths.

"What Are Your Strengths?" and Beyond: Informal Means of Detecting Human Strengths

Wright and Fletcher (1982) noted that practitioners distort reality when they identify only problems without uncovering the positives in clients. In other words, practitioners should strive to uncover strengths along with problems when interviewing clients. Saleebey (2012) argued that all people possess strengths that can be extracted to improve the quality of their lives. In addition, focusing on client strengths helps practitioners and clients discover how clients have managed to survive in even the most inhospitable environments and situations. Finally, Saleebey noted that all environments and clients contain resources; practitioners who engage in collaborative exploration with their clients can discover these strengths.

Unfortunately, few refined protocols for uncovering strengths via interviews are available. Instead, there has been a focus on diagnostic interviewing using pathology, treatment, medical, and dysfunction metaphors (Cowger, 1997). In the past decade, however, attempts have been made to focus on positive aspects of people rather than deficiencies. Cowger (1997) emphasized the need to make assessment of clients and their strengths multidimensional. The focus of the interview should be on uncovering the client's external strengths as well as internal strengths. External strengths may include resources such as family networks, significant others, and community or church groups. The client's internal strengths may include psychological factors such as motivation, coping, and cognitive resources.

De Jong and Miller (1995) suggested using solution-focused interviewing (de Shazer, 1988) to uncover the strengths in clients. They stated that interviewing for solutions helps clients develop (a) well-formed, realistic goals that seek the presence of something rather than the absence and (b) solutions based on exceptions. Exceptions are "those occasions in the client's life when the client's problem could have occurred but did not" (De Jong & Miller, 1995, p. 729). The practitioner seeking out exceptions asks about the client's present and past successes in relation to the goals the client has set to achieve through counseling. Once the exceptions are discovered, the practitioner attempts to clarify the contributions that the client made for the exception to occur. After the practitioner and client uncover an exception, along with the client's strengths, the practitioner aids the client in affirming and amplifying the strengths. The intended consequence of interviewing for strengths is empowerment of the client (De Jong & Miller, 1995; Saleebey, 2012). Thus, hope is stimulated as clients discover that they can create their own solutions and construct more satisfying lives.

Test Complementary Hypotheses in the Context of Counseling

Facets of the implicit model of client functioning serve as the foundation for hypotheses to be tested during counseling. In the practice model of positive psychological assessment, the practitioner should generate parallel hypotheses addressing both strengths and resources and weaknesses and deficits. Moreover, practitioners should use a multiple-hypothesis testing strategy to ensure that she or he is considering all explanations for clinical presentations and life circumstances.

To clarify how this balanced, scientific approach to clinical data may unfold, consider the common initial presentation of a client who is "feeling blue." Of course, despite this being a common presenting complaint, the subtleties of each individual's experience of sadness needs to be carefully considered. Thus, information would be gathered about how symptoms developed and how severe the sadness is day to day. A parallel observation may involve a client's social well-being (i.e., the client has meaningful social interactions irrespective of how he or she is feeling). Both the "sadness" and the "doing well socially" hypotheses need to be put to the test during counseling sessions. Use of a multiple-hypothesis testing strategy (see Figure 2.2 for a detailed breakdown of what occurs during the "counseling" phase of the practice model of positive psychological assessment) would involve being open to and recording data that confirm and disconfirm the hypotheses. Furthermore, the possibility of alternative explanations of the client's mood or level of well-being need to be considered (i.e., alternative hypotheses have to be tested as well). By engaging in the scientific examination of hypotheses about strengths and weaknesses, practitioners can increase the possibility that unbiased, balanced determinations about psychological functioning are being made.

Develop a Flexible, Comprehensive Conceptualization

The scientific examination of complementary hypotheses generates a tremendous amount of data that needs to be organized, analyzed, and interpreted by the practitioner. Sifting through these data is made easier when the practitioner envisions the assessment process as cyclical and self-correcting. There is no "right" answer, but the goal of the process is to develop a conceptualization of how the client's strengths and weaknesses reverberate and contribute to psychological status.

Constructing this flexible, comprehensive conceptualization requires the practitioner to guard against bias entering their decision-making processes. Furthermore, metacognition functions as the scale that balances the information about human strength and human weakness that is incorporated into the working client model. Flexibility and comprehensiveness of the conceptualization are maintained over time by adding clinical information to the scale.

In addition, we believe that a conceptualization is incomplete if it is not accompanied by recommendations for counseling and change tailored for the client. Indeed, balanced descriptions of people still fall flat if they are not associated with relevant, meaningful suggestions for changing and growing.

Share a Balanced Report of the Client's Strengths/ Resources and Weaknesses/Deficits

Fact-checking the information in the working model of a client is facilitated by sharing that information with others. This sharing occurs in different ways,

FIGURE 2.2. Testing Hypotheses in the Context of Counseling

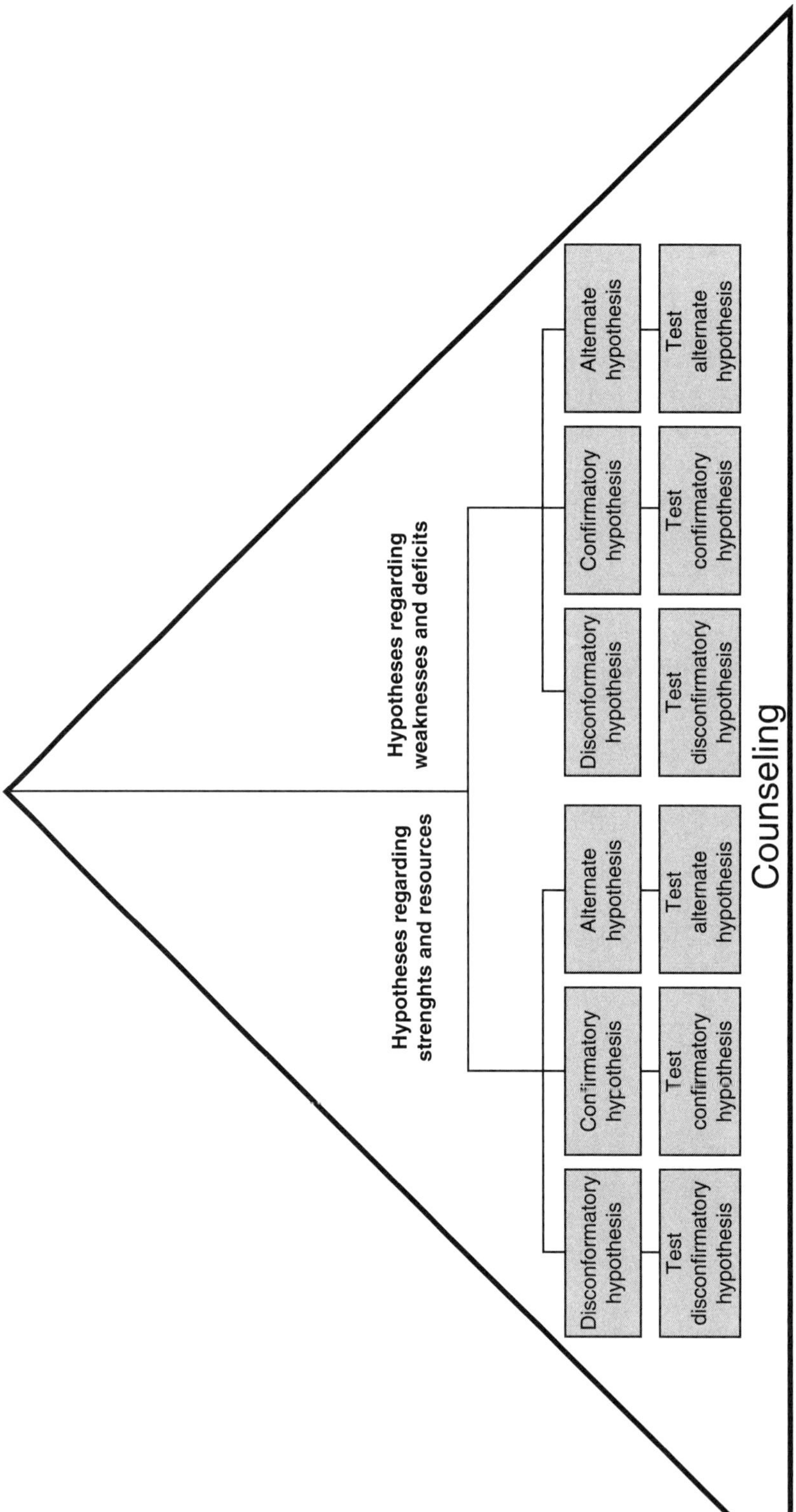

including written reports, case presentations with colleagues, and feedback to the client.

Communicating with colleagues and people who provide support and care to the client can provide invaluable information that can enhance the accuracy of the conceptualization. Also, the conceptualization can become a cognitive map for others working directly with the client—it is hoped that this would result in support that is more sensitive to the needs of a client.

Information about client functioning often has been cloaked in psychological jargon and somewhat hidden from the client. In our approach to assessment, client opinions about the evolving conceptualization are gathered so that continued assessment can be refined by incorporating hypotheses pertinent to the client. Including the client's opinion establishes that his or her views on change are valued and that he or she is expected to be an active self-healer. (Guidelines for the feedback session of the therapeutic assessment model [Finn & Martin, 2013; Finn & Tonsager, 1997] also should be considered. The feedback rule of "equal space, equal time, equal emphasis" should be followed when sharing assessment information with clients, members of the clients' support systems, fellow practitioners, and mental health agencies and related organizations.)

Equal Space, Equal Time, Equal Emphasis

Wright (1991; Wright & Lopez, 2009) recommended that practitioners abide by the rule of giving equal space and equal time to the presentation of strengths and weaknesses (hence equal emphasis). It is important to remember to follow the rule of equal space and equal time when writing progress notes and reports to convey a comprehensive view of the client.

An aspirational goal related to this end might involve devoting half of the clinical-impressions section of a report to psychological weaknesses and half to psychological strengths. For example, if the practitioner is accustomed to writing four-page reports—with one page addressing background information, one page presenting test results, and two pages describing clinical impressions and recommendations (i.e., the flexible, comprehensive conceptualization)—half of the last two pages of information should address client strengths and resources. Accordingly, if a practitioner is in the habit of writing one-page progress notes, half of the page should be devoted to the discussion of strengths and resources and how these can be used to promote change.

Though equal space in a report or progress note is considered the ideal within our model of assessment, we have realized through our clinical work and training of graduate students that initial "best practice" of this rule may involve appending a "strengths" section to a report or note or to provide balanced diagnostic information. For example, the Balanced Diagnostic Impressions Model (DICE-PM; Owens et al., 2015) emphasizes a balanced approach to presenting the client's diagnosis by including: (a) **D**iagnosis, **I**ndividual Strengths and Weaknesses, (b) **C**ultural Assets and Struggles, (c) **E**nvironmental Resources and Deficits, (d) **P**hysical Wellness and Health Concerns, and (e) a **M**ental Health Categorization based on the Complete State Model of Mental Health.

Another important part of any psychological assessment process is reporting test results to clients. Throughout this chapter, we have emphasized the need for psychologists to strive for a more balanced assessment of their clients; thus, test feedback offered to clients also must be balanced (Drummond, 1988). Although models for reporting results in a balanced manor are limited, several models have been proposed (e.g., Levak, Siegel, & Nichols, 2011; Magyar-Moe, 2009). Finn and Martin (2013) suggested that the practitioner should engage the client by sharing test data and hypotheses and asking clients if they fit with the client's experiences and understanding of the presenting problem. By actively involving the client in the feedback session, the practitioner and the client can work together to refine the conceptualization, the client's role of active self-healer is reinforced, and the assessment process facilitates positive change in the client.

A Practice Model of Positive Psychological Assessment Case Example

Michael was a 22-year-old, undecided, college sophomore who was referred to the university counseling center after attending class while intoxicated. He had recently transferred to the university after being dismissed from a prestigious art school in another part of the country. Michael appeared poorly groomed and fatigued, and he was very fidgety as he drank an energy drink throughout the intake interview. When asked about his referral to the counseling center, Michael indicated that he had recently been feeling very depressed and that he had been drinking heavily following the end of a significant romantic relationship. He also reported legal issues related to driving under the influence of alcohol.

I (BPC) began the assessment process by acknowledging my own biases regarding the severity of Michael's substance use as well has his own personal values regarding drinking and driving. Despite the severity of Michael's symptom distress, I made it a point to conduct a comprehensive four-front assessment. In addition to traditional measures of depression and substance use, Michael completed the Adult Trait Hope Scale (Snyder et al., 1991) and the Mental Health Continuum—Short Form (MHC–SF; Keyes et al., 2008). His scores on the depression and substance use inventories indicated that he was experiencing severe depression without thoughts of self-harm as well as alcohol use that met the *DSM–5* criteria for a diagnosis of Alcohol Use Disorder. However, interviews and examination of measures of positive functioning indicated that Michael had a number of personal and environmental assets. Michael was passionate about writing, and he had identified a number of pathways to reach his goal of writing a novel. Examination of his scores on the MHC–SF were reflective of his depressed mood, but they also indicated that he had a number of strengths related to his ability to build and maintain positive relationships with others.

Although the typical protocol when working with clients like Michael was to focus primarily on the problematic classroom behaviors and substance use that led to his referral, I took a balanced approach to the work that emphasized reduction of Michael's symptom distress while improving his hope and well-being. Once the therapeutic alliance was established, I utilized Motivational Interviewing (Miller & Rose, 2009) to explore Michael's alcohol use and worked collaboratively with him to develop goals for improving his safety and health. While working toward these goals, we utilized a solution-focused approach to explore his experiences of depression as well as his passion for writing and the significance of having positive relationships in his life. Michael identified exceptions to his recent experiences of depression, times when he felt less depressed, more connected to others, and more productive in his writing. I highlighted themes of positive functioning and strengths in his narratives each session, provided observations, and sought his feedback about the hypotheses I had developed (i.e., that his substance use was an attempt to cope with intense negative emotions that began with the end of his romantic relationship, his move to a new city where he had no social connections, and his uncharacteristic legal issues). We then worked collaboratively to identify approach-oriented goals to engage in healthier behaviors and enhance his emotional well-being by building and maintaining relationships with friends and family and using his writing as an avenue to meet new people and reduce his social isolation.

ASPIRING TO STRIKE A VITAL BALANCE

The evolution of positive psychological science depends on sound measurement of strengths, healthy processes, and fulfillments. The model of positive psychological assessment provides a cognitive map for detecting the strengths and resources of all clients. Furthermore, the scientific approach provides debiasing techniques that result in hypothesis testing, which in turn reveals meaningful findings. These findings, organized as a conceptualization, are shared with colleagues and the client, and feedback and subsequent interactions with the client serve to enhance the conceptualization.

Self-report measures are the primary means of data collection in positive psychology research and practice, and our reliance on this staid approach to measurement needs to be addressed. Several strength-based assessment techniques have been developed (e.g., Joseph & Wood, 2010; Magyar-Moe, 2009; Rashid, 2015b). Continued development and evaluation of structured approaches for assessment of strengths is sorely needed. Furthermore, existing measures need to be evaluated for cultural equivalence. Perhaps one of the most comprehensive approaches to a culturally sensitive positive psychological assessment is the Comprehensive Model of Positive Psychological Assessment Semistructured Clinical Interview (see Owens et al., 2015, for a review).

The conventional view of mental illness as progressive and refractory was challenged by Karl Menninger (Menninger, Mayman, & Pruyser, 1963) in the book *The Vital Balance*. Menninger and colleagues called for psychiatrists to view mental illness as amenable to change—thus this new view of mental illness would bring the old into balance. We call for a different type of balance—a balanced view of human life that puts weakness and strength in perspective.

REFERENCES

American Psychiatric Association. (2013). *Diagnostic and statistical manual of mental disorders* (5th ed.). Washington, DC: Author.

Asplund, J., Lopez, S. J., Hodges, T., & Harter, J. (2007). *The Clifton StrengthsFinder 2.0 technical report: Development and validation*. Princeton, NJ: The Gallup Organization.

Boehm, A. (1985). Review of Home Observation for the Measurement of the Environment. In J. V. Mitchell (Ed.), *The ninth mental measurements yearbook* (pp. 663–665). Lincoln, NE: Buros Institute of Mental Measurements.

Buckingham, M., & Coffman, C. (1999). *First, break all the rules*. New York, NY: Simon & Schuster.

Caldwell, B., & Bradley, R. (1984). *Home observation for measurement of the environment*. Little Rock: University of Arkansas at Little Rock.

Capielo, C., Mann, L., Nevels, B., & Delgado-Romero, E. (2014). Multicultural considerations in measurement and classification of positive psychology. In J. Teramoto Pedrotti & L. M. Edwards (Eds.), *Perspectives on the intersection multiculturalism and positive psychology* (pp. 31–44). New York, NY: Springer. http://dx.doi.org/10.1007/978-94-017-8654-6_3

Cheavens, J. S., Feldman, D., Gum, A., Michael, S. T., & Snyder, C. R. (2006). Hope therapy in a community sample: A pilot investigation. *Social Indicators Research, 77*, 61–78. http://dx.doi.org/10.1007/s11205-005-5553-0

Clifton, D. O., & Harter, J. K. (2003). Investing in strengths. In A. K. S. Cameron, B. J. E. Dutton, & C. R. E. Quinn (Eds.), *Positive organizational scholarship: Foundations of a new discipline* (pp. 111–121). San Francisco, CA: Berrett-Koehler.

Conyne, R. K., & Clack, J. R. (1981). *Environmental assessment and design: A new tool for the applied behavioral scientist*. New York, NY: Praeger.

Cowger, C. D. (1997). Assessment of client strengths. In D. Saleebey (Ed.), *The strengths perspective in social work practice* (pp. 139–147). New York, NY: Longman.

De Jong, P., & Miller, S. D. (1995). How to interview for client strengths. *Social Work, 40*, 729–736.

de Shazer, S. (1988). *Clues: Investigating solutions in brief therapy*. New York, NY: W. W. Norton.

Deal, A. G., Trivette, C. M., & Dunst, C. J. (1988). Family Functioning Style scale. In C. J. Dunst, C. M. Trivette, & A. G. Deal (Eds.), *Enabling and empowering families: Principles and guidelines for practice* (pp. 179–184). Cambridge, MA: Brookline Books.

Drummond, R. J. (1988). *Appraisal procedures for counselors and helping professionals*. Columbus, OH: Merrill.

Fava, G. A. (2016). *Well-being therapy: Treatment manual and clinical applications*. Basel, Switzerland: Karger. http://dx.doi.org/10.1159/isbn.978-3-318-05822-2

Felner, R. D., Aber, M. S., Primavera, J., & Cauce, A. M. (1985). Adaptation and vulnerability in high-risk adolescents: An examination of environmental mediators. *American Journal of Community Psychology, 13*, 365–379. http://dx.doi.org/10.1007/BF00911214

Finn, S. E., & Martin, H. (2013). Therapeutic assessment: Using psychological testing as brief therapy. In K. F. Geisinger, B. A. Bracken, J. F. Carlson, J.-I. C. Hansen, N. R. Kuncel, S. P. Reise, & M. C. Rodriguez (Eds.), *APA handbook of testing and assessment in psychology: Vol. 2. Testing and assessment in clinical and counseling psychology* (pp. 453–465). Washington, DC: American Psychological Association. http://dx.doi.org/10.1037/14048-026

Finn, S. E., & Tonsager, M. E. (1997). Information-gathering and therapeutic models of assessment: Complementary paradigms. *Psychological Assessment, 9*, 374–385. http://dx.doi.org/10.1037/1040-3590.9.4.374

Gallup. (2017). *Gallup Student Poll*. Retrieved from http://www.gallupstudentpoll.com/home.aspx?ref=logo

Gough, H. G. (1954). *The Home Index.* Berkeley: University of California Press.

Kerr, W. A. (1942). The measurement of home environment and its relationship with certain other variables. *Studies in Higher Education, Purdue University, 45,* 5–43.

Keyes, C. L. M., Wissing, M., Potgieter, J. P., Temane, M., Kruger, A., & van Rooy, S. (2008). Evaluation of the Mental Health Continuum—Short Form (MHC–SF) in Setswana-speaking South Africans. *Clinical Psychology & Psychotherapy, 15,* 181–192. http://dx.doi.org/10.1002/cpp.572

Kress, V. E., Barrio Minton, C. A., Adamson, N. A., Paylo, M. J., & Pope, V. (2014). The removal of the multiaxial system in *DSM–5*: Implications and practice suggestions for counselors. *The Professional Counselor, 4,* 191–201. http://dx.doi.org/10.15241/vek.4.3.191

Joseph, S. (Ed.). (2015). *Positive psychology in practice* (2nd ed.). Hoboken, NJ: Wiley. http://dx.doi.org/10.1002/9781118996874

Joseph, S., & Wood, A. (2010). Assessment of positive functioning in clinical psychology: Theoretical and practical issues. *Clinical Psychology Review, 30,* 830–838. http://dx.doi.org/10.1016/j.cpr.2010.01.002

Levak, R. W., Siegel, L., & Nichols, D. S. (2011). *Therapeutic feedback with the MMPI–2: A positive psychology approach.* New York, NY: Routledge.

Magyar-Moe, J. L. (2009). *Therapist's guide to positive psychological interventions.* Burlington, MA: Academic Press.

McCurdy, M., Coutts, M. J., Sheridan, S. M., & Campbell, L. M. (2012). Ecological variables in school-based assessment and intervention planning. In R. Brown-Chidsey & K. Andren (Eds.), *Assessment for intervention: A problem-solving approach* (2nd ed., pp. 39–61). New York, NY: Guilford Press.

Menninger, K., Mayman, M., & Pruyser, P. W. (1963). *The vital balance.* New York, NY: Viking Press.

Miller, W. R., & Rose, G. S. (2009). Toward a theory of motivational interviewing. *American Psychologist, 64,* 527–537. http://dx.doi.org/10.1037/a0016830

Miquelote, A. F., Santos, D. C., Caçola, P. M., Montebelo, M. I., & Gabbard, C. (2012). Effect of the home environment on motor and cognitive behavior of infants. *Infant Behavior & Development, 35,* 329–334. http://dx.doi.org/10.1016/j.infbeh.2012.02.002

Moos, R. H. (1991). Connection between school, work, and family settings. In B. J. Fraser & H. J. Walberg (Eds.), *Educational environments: Evaluation, antecedents, and consequences* (pp. 29–53). New York, NY: Pergamon Press.

Owens, R. L., Magyar-Moe, J. L., & Lopez, S. J. (2015). Finding balance via positive psychological assessment and conceptualization: Recommendations for practice. *The Counseling Psychologist, 43,* 634–670. http://dx.doi.org/10.1177/0011000015584956

Parks, A. C., & Schueller, S. (Eds.). (2014). *The Wiley-Blackwell handbook of positive psychological interventions.* Oxford, England: Wiley-Blackwell. http://dx.doi.org/10.1002/9781118315927

Pepinsky, H. B., & Pepinsky, N. (1954). *Counseling theory and practice.* New York, NY: Ronald Press. http://dx.doi.org/10.1037/10631-000

Peterson, C., & Seligman, M. E. P. (2004). *Character strengths and virtues: A handbook and classification.* Washington, DC: American Psychological Association and New York, NY: Oxford University Press.

Rath, T. (2007). *StrengthsFinder 2.0.* New York, NY: Gallup Press.

Rashid, T. (2015a). Positive psychotherapy: A strength-based approach. *The Journal of Positive Psychology, 10,* 25–40. http://dx.doi.org/10.1080/17439760.2014.920411

Rashid, T. (2015b). Strength-based assessment. In S. Joseph (Ed.), *Positive psychology in practice* (2nd ed., pp. 519–542). Hoboken, NJ: Wiley. http://dx.doi.org/10.1002/9781118996874.ch31

Repetti, R. L. (1987). Linkages between work and family roles. In S. Oskamp (Ed.), *Applied social psychology annual* (Vol. 7, pp. 98–127). Beverly Hills, CA: Sage.

Saleebey, D. (2001). The diagnostic strengths manual? *Social Work, 46,* 183–187. http://dx.doi.org/10.1093/sw/46.2.183

Saleebey, D. (2012). *The strengths perspective in social work practice* (6th ed.). New York, NY: Pearson.

Schimmel, S. (2000). Vices, virtues and sources of human strength in historical perspective. *Journal of Social and Clinical Psychology, 19,* 137–150. http://dx.doi.org/10.1521/jscp.2000.19.1.137

Schooler, C. (1999). The workplace environment: Measurement, psychological effects, and basic issues. In S. L. Friedman & T. D. Wachs (Eds.), *Measuring environment across the life span: Emerging methods and concepts* (pp. 229–246). Washington, DC: American Psychological Association. http://dx.doi.org/10.1037/10317-008

Snyder, C. R., Harris, C., Anderson, J. R., Holleran, S. A., Irving, L. M., Sigmon, S. T., . . . Harney, P. (1991). The will and the ways: Development and validation of an individual-differences measure of hope. *Journal of Personality and Social Psychology, 60,* 570–585. http://dx.doi.org/10.1037/0022-3514.60.4.570

Spengler, P. M., Strohmer, D. C., Dixon, D. N., & Shivy, V. A. (1995). A scientist-practitioner model of psychological assessment: Implications for training, practice and research. *The Counseling Psychologist, 23,* 506–534. http://dx.doi.org/10.1177/0011000095233009

Talbert, J. E., & McLaughlin, M. W. (1999). Assessing the school environment: Embedded contexts and bottom-up research strategies. In S. L. Friedman & T. D. Wachs (Eds.), *Measuring environment across the life span: Emerging methods and concepts* (pp. 197–227). Washington, DC: American Psychological Association. http://dx.doi.org/10.1037/10317-007

Totsika, V., & Sylva, K. (2004). The Home Observation for Measurement of the Environment revisited. *Child and Adolescent Mental Health, 9,* 25–35.

Trivette, C. M., Dunst, C. J., Deal, A. G., Hamer, A. W., & Propst, S. (1990). Assessing family strengths and family functioning style. *Topics in Early Childhood Special Education, 10,* 16–35. http://dx.doi.org/10.1177/027112149001000103

Walker, C. J. (2006, May). *Using positivity ratios to distinguish languishing from flourishing in college students.* Poster session presented at the national meeting of the Association for Psychological Science, New York, New York.

Walker, C. J. (2009, August). *A longitudinal study on student well-being.* Poster session presented at the national meeting of the American Psychological Association, Toronto, Ontario, Canada.

World Health Organization. (1992). *International classification of diseases and related health problems* (10th rev.). Geneva, Switzerland: Author.

Wright, B. A. (1991). Labeling: The need for greater person-environmental individuation. In C. R. Snyder & D. R. Forsyth (Eds.), *Handbook of social and clinical psychology: The health perspective* (pp. 469–487). New York, NY: Pergamon Press.

Wright, B. A., & Fletcher, B. L. (1982). Uncovering hidden resources: A challenge in assessment. *Professional Psychology, 13,* 229–235. http://dx.doi.org/10.1037/0735-7028.13.2.229

Wright, B. A., & Lopez, S. J. (2002). Widening the diagnostic focus: A case for including human strengths and environmental resources. In C. R. Snyder & S. J. Lopez (Eds.), *Handbook of positive psychology* (pp. 26–44). New York, NY: Oxford University Press.

Wright, B. A., & Lopez, S. J. (2009). Widening the diagnostic focus: A case for including human strengths and environmental resources. In C. R. Snyder & S. J. Lopez (Eds.), *The Oxford handbook of positive psychology* (2nd ed., pp. 71–88). New York, NY: Oxford University Press.

Ysseldyke, J., & Elliott, J. (1999). Effective instructional practices: Implications for assessing educational environments. In C. R. Reynolds & T. B. Gutkin (Eds.), *The handbook of school psychology* (3rd ed., pp. 497–518). New York, NY: Wiley.

3

Measuring and Labeling the Positive and the Negative

Lisa M. Edwards, Jennifer Teramoto Pedrotti, Ashley Faytol,
Jesse Wynn, C. R. Snyder, and Shane J. Lopez

As long as we have applied labels to one another, we probably have spoken of the degrees to which people have more or less of the characteristics reflected in those labels. This focus on labeling became more formal, however, when capitalism began to take root in Great Britain around the 19th century (Buss & Poley, 1976). With the need to quantify the prices of products for ease of sale, so too was there a need to attach value to different human skills or efforts. Work was divided into units, and value was attached to those units. Measurement thus allowed for trading, commerce, and the ensuing placement of value on everything—including what people did. The historical extreme of this process was servitude and slavery, wherein the entire person was priced and sold in a manner similar to that for other "commodities."

What happens when a person's worth is charted by using a pejorative term or negative label rather than a positive descriptor? The stakes are very high with regard to labeling and measuring people. In this chapter, we present our views on the inherent power and limitations in the process of labeling (i.e., naming a person according to a characteristic) and measuring (i.e., identifying the degree to which a person possesses that characteristic). We provide alternative approaches to a pathology model of describing people, including alterations to our current diagnostic system that clinicians can use to develop more balanced conceptualizations of functioning in people.

http://dx.doi.org/10.1037/0000138-003
Positive Psychological Assessment: A Handbook of Models and Measures, Second Edition,
M. W. Gallagher and S. J. Lopez (Editors)

THE POWER IN LABELING

Why are we so impressed with something that is labeled? Several reasons might explain how labels gain such power. First, a name provides a means for two or more people to communicate readily about the "named" entity. When applied to humans, such names represent a shorthand means of conveying an assumed shared meaning. In turn, the term and its meaning shape such interactions. Unfortunately, we often assume that others hold the same definition for the label as we do. In reality, however, there are substantial variabilities in meanings that are ascribed to the same terms. Ask 20 mental health professionals, for example, to define the label *at risk*, and you will get 20 different responses. Undaunted or perhaps oblivious to this caveat, we nevertheless are likely to assume that others share our meanings.

Labels are powerful in that they also serve a gatekeeping role. A child must be labeled to receive "special" educational services, and a client must receive a label for the mental health professional to obtain reimbursement from third parties. Using labels as pathways to resources and treatment ascribes a power to a contrived name that is then reinforced by social institutions.

Psychological labels also form the lexicon mental health professionals, and others, use to talk with each other. Moreover, terms that once were only in psychology textbooks are now common fare in popular magazines and everyday language (e.g., panic attack). These terms believed to be rife with descriptive value often become watered-down versions of their former selves because of their common usage.

A final reason a label has such power is that it facilitates our belief that we "understand" it. Unfortunately, a name only has a surface reality and only initiates the process of understanding that which is labeled. More specifically, when something is given a name, we are explicitly placing it in a category of entities that differ from other categories and their associated entities and often assuming that the name carries with it "deep" meaning. At best, such labels may only serve to differentiate the labeled person from others; even that premise, however, may be questionable when carefully scrutinized (see Wright & Lopez, 2009, for a discussion of deindividuation associated with labeling). For example, consider how the label *depressed* is used in practice parlance as well as in scholarly work. How often do we use the term with precision? When we describe a client as depressed, we evoke thoughts of major depressive disorder, dysthymia, adjustment disorder, or bereavement—when the person may just be "feeling blue" and not experiencing any disorder. Our casual use of labels is commonplace in social science as well. For example, consider researchers who refer to their "depressed" samples, which are made up of individuals who have scored higher than a particular cutoff on a screening measure.

In summary, labels always have represented shorthand phrases for conveying our understanding of others. Labels help sustain our illusions that we comprehend other people and can convey that knowledge in a facile, efficient manner. In truth, the potency of our language is decreasing as we use it with less and less precision, and labels take on even greater power as they supplant phrases and entire sentences of vivid and specific description.

THE POWER IN MEASURING

If we are impressed with something that is labeled, we are even more impressed when some sort of measurement metric is attached to that named entity. Labels reach their greatest power when used in degrees because there is supposedly more communicative information when the label carries a qualifier. The users of such degree-based labels thereby perceive that they are discoursing at a refined level, one that carries a metric of precision that likely does not exist. For example, users of the *Diagnostic and Statistical Manual of Mental Disorders* (fifth ed. [*DSM–5*]; American Psychiatric Association, 2013) label people to two decimal places. Furthermore, once such a measurement device (e.g., a scale, a categorical system such as the *DSM–5*) becomes available and recognized in a field, more professionals are likely to use that device, thereby enhancing its power. Because we readily can apply psychological instruments to measure some personal characteristic, there is the potential for producing large amounts of relatively vacuous research findings. In turn, the users of such instruments become even more enamored of the power of "their" instruments to yield precise measurements and insights about people. This can lead to an acceptance of measurements, without thoughtful consideration of their scientific underpinnings. We do not suggest that measurement-based labels can or should be eliminated, as there are clearly benefits associated with them, but it is important to be mindful of the various problems associated with these types of labels. Whether we are measuring weaknesses or strengths, the validity of our instruments must be scrutinized.

THE LIMITS OF DIAGNOSTIC SYSTEMS

Ironies abound in the diagnostic systems that currently are part of the mental health field. Consider that our complex diagnostic systems, with the *DSM* representing the crown jewel, are not very reliable (see Garb, 1998, 2005, for a related discussion of veracity in clinical judgment; Mullins-Sweatt, Lengel, & DeShong, 2016). Biases, stereotyping, and heuristics often challenge the accuracy of diagnostic decision making, but lack of reliability is not the only problem. Our diagnostic systems also are not well validated. They often have reflected the ideas of the test constructors more so than a meaningful taxonomy for the characteristics of the people whom we seek to help.

This is particularly important when thinking about how cultural context may influence ideas of what is "healthy" versus what is pathological (Pedrotti & Edwards, 2014). When characteristics and traits are viewed from within a singular cultural lens, erroneous labels may be placed on individuals from other cultural contexts. An example of this is shown by the different reactions to the construct of gratitude in different cultures. Whereas in the United States, being grateful is often touted as a beneficial and healthy experience that often leads to increased well-being, studies in some Eastern countries find that listing reasons to be grateful often leads to a decrease in well-being (Layous, Lee, Choi, & Lyubomirsky, 2013). Different experiences with this same construct may lead one culture to tout it as something to be encouraged, but another to count it as problematic, and possibly something to be suppressed.

Perhaps the capstone of myths, however, is that our diagnoses really dictate our treatments. Unfortunately, this typically is not true (Lopez et al., 2006; Maddux, in press; Raskin & Lewandowski, 2000). At best, there is a modest relationship between diagnoses and the subsequent treatments (Snyder & Ingram, 2000). The fact that our labels (otherwise known as diagnoses) are lacking in reliability and validity, and that they are not related to treatments, produces a collaborative illusion. On this point, we should not place the responsibility for this on practitioners, because they are doing that for which they were trained; in turn, the educators are conveying that which the researchers have suggested.

To the mismeasurements that we have described so far in this section, we must add yet another very troubling one: the focus on weaknesses. Clinicians' assessments are generally designed to obtain information relating to symptomatology rather than uncover evidence of optimal or normal functioning. Furthermore, clinicians are often guided by their expectations of observing abnormal behavior to meet *DSM* diagnostic criteria (Lopez et al., 2006). It is true that people come to mental health professionals with problems and practitioners need to be attuned to this, but it is not necessary for weakness to dictate the interventions that are used. If our client conceptualizations are solely based on pathology and weakness, surely we are guilty of yet another mismeasurement in that we have left out half of the human repertoire—*that which entails the strengths of people.*

THE POTENTIAL EFFECTS OF BEING LABELED AND MEASURED

In today's education and mental health care systems, and society more broadly, we focus on labeling behaviors that are troublesome to us. Furthermore, because we sometimes label others to distance ourselves from them, names may carry negative connotations and be stigmatizing. This may happen more often in circumstances where we see someone as different from us in some way. How we are labeled and measured guides the way that we are treated by powerful *other* people, how we come to see ourselves, and how we conduct our lives. Public knowledge of labels can result in reduced social status, social alienation, and loss of employment (Lopez et al., 2006), and it is this power to limit individual potential that we discuss next.

Consider the well-known, self-fulfilling prophecy notion as introduced by sociologist Robert Merton (1957) and refined by psychologist Robert Rosenthal

(Rosenthal & Jacobson, 1968). The major emphasis in the self-fulfilling prophecy literature has been on how the perceiver treats the target of the perception. For example, an eighth-grade teacher perceives that boys are better at math than girls. Therefore, in math class and study sessions, the teacher spends less time with the girls. With the relatively greater attention and instruction, the boys then do better than the girls on math examinations. The girls in this example do not get their fair share of encouragement or instruction from the teacher. This all happens because the teacher has internally labeled the boys as being "very capable" in math, whereas the girls are "not very capable." To compound matters, the teacher probably is unaware of their differential behaviors toward the students. Moreover, if boys are seen as the ideal math student, girls would then be marginalized within a model of deficiency (Sue & Sue, 2016), further contributing to the self-fulfilling prophecy (Capielo, Mann, Nevels, & Delgado-Romero, 2014; Pedrotti, Edwards, & Lopez, 2009). If the girls are also of color or living with a disability, they may be further marginalized, be deemed even less capable, and receive less of the teacher's time and resources—therefore performing at lower levels, further validating the self-fulfilling prophecy.

The aforementioned description of the effect of labeling in the self-fulfilling prophecy is the standard approach to describing the dynamics of how the students' behaviors are shaped by the teacher. A far less explored aspect of this self-fulfilling prophecy, however, involves the processes transpiring among the objects of the labeling—the eighth-grade boys and girls in this math example. With repeated treatments by the teachers as being either "smart" or "dumb" in math, the students come to see themselves in the same manner. They internalize the labels, and those labels influence their motivations and actions. In this sense, the labels have unleashed their full power in shaping both how the teacher treats the students and *how the students' self-views drive their own efforts*.

What makes such labeling even more troublesome is that the particular instantiations are happening in addition to, or on top of, other ongoing societal prejudices. With prejudice there are different rules and behaviors exhibited toward some subset of labeled people. The prejudices and the related "isms" (ageism, racism, sexism, heterosexism) operate via focusing on some dimension of personhood and thereafter ascribing different behaviors to identified subsets of those people. Once named, the target of that prejudicial naming is constrained in what they can do; moreover, that person is not allowed to play the game of life on a level playing field (Snyder & Feldman, 2000). The tragedy in such labeling is that a person can become stuck, unable to escape the powerful grip of the label in determining aspects of life. This may lead to hopelessness or a feeling that one has no control over their life (Sue, 1978; Sue & Sue, 2016). Research on stereotype threat, for example, has confirmed that individuals who prescribe to a specific identity that is associated with negative stereotypes often underperform when faced with the possibility of being judged within that stereotype (Spencer, Logel, & Davies, 2016; Steele, 1997). It is important to note that this experience is not a case of a *self*-fulfilling prophecy, but *society*-fulfilling prophecy and carries with it a series of consequences for individuals labeled as intellectually inferior, regardless of their beliefs about themselves.

Thus, even if one believes that they can accomplish a particular goal, the belief from others that they cannot may impact their ability to actually achieve this goal. It may be that this can sometimes lead to a personal belief of inferiority as well. With the isms, for example, think of the enormous loss of talent when subgroups of the population are told *and come to believe* that they cannot do certain things.

Given the many concerns with the diagnostic system and the implications of psychological measurement and labeling on individuals, what can be done to destigmatize the process? It is not enough to merely criticize without also offering some possible solutions. In the remaining portion of this chapter, we offer such solutions for practitioners who seek to reclaim the positive, enabling power of labels and measurement.

RECLAIMING THE POWER OF LABELS AND MEASUREMENT

A note should be included about the importance of reclaiming the power of labels and measurement for the purpose of social justice. Social justice advocacy recognizes internalized and environmental oppression as stressors that detract from wellness (Greenleaf & Williams, 2009; Williams & Greenleaf, 2012). Traditional counseling and educational models are based on White, majority-culture norms, but often these models are unsuccessful at recognizing the impact of multicultural factors on mental health, such as an individual's age, class, culture, disability, ethnicity, and gender (Zalaquett, Fuerth, Stein, Ivey, & Ivey, 2008). In addition, our field's approaches to addressing diversity have historically pathologized those who are culturally different from White, middle-class individuals and have neglected to identify the unique strengths of members of disenfranchised populations. These *blind spots* (Hays, 2016) toward understanding and conceptualization of non-White individuals, women and transgender individuals, members of the LGBTQ+ community, those who live in poverty, and others underscore the importance of a new, broader perspective of positive functioning.

When we give salience to a strength by explicitly naming it, we are suggesting to the named person, and to those in the surrounding environment, that there is merit in this identified characteristic. It is something to be valued for both its intrinsic and extrinsic worth. On this point, we would suggest that the usual individualistic categories of meritorious behavior—achievements in academics and sports—are worthy of our attention. Perhaps more important, however, are communal characteristics that often make society more livable: sharing, compassion, wisdom, forgiveness, companionship, and love. Strengths that emanate from nonmajority cultures and communities are beginning to be understood by researchers, and we contend that these resources need to be better understood and singled out for our praise. (For a useful list of culturally relevant personal, interpersonal, and environmental strengths, see Hays, 2016.)

Balanced Dimensioning in Conceptualizing Mental Health

In this section we discuss alternative approaches to the labeling and measurement process in the mental health profession. We begin with two foundational premises. First, we strongly believe that normality and abnormality are not constructs that apply only to certain people (Barone, Maddux, & Snyder, 1997), although the way in which they manifest may differ from group to group. Rather, the processes that underlie adaptive and maladaptive functioning are the same for all people. Indeed, maladaptive and adaptive do not yield differences in kind but rather differences of degree (Maddux, 1993a).

Second, we reject the premise that the diagnostic process involves the identification of surface symptoms for the underlying diseases. We believe that the pathology model predisposes the helper to make errors in the subsequent gathering of information, as well as in making clinical decisions (Maddux, 1993b; Salovey & Turk, 1991). For example, the weakness model leads helpers into conceptual flowcharts wherein all options lead to "degree of pathology" inferences (Lopez et al., 2006).

Balanced Dimensions, Conceptualization, and Diagnosis

Consistent with recent recommendations (T. A. Brown & Barlow, 2005, 2009), we suggest a *dimensioning* approach to the labeling and measuring process. Instead of categories with inclusion/noninclusion criteria, as typifies the pathology perspective, we advocate the use of those individual difference dimensions that appear to give a thorough coverage and overview of the specific person. Each individual differences dimension would range from one end of a continuum reflecting very low to very high levels. Various dimensions differ conceptually, but often may be correlated. Researchers already have charted many of these individual difference dimensions, but there is more to be done in terms of adding new ones. This would also assist in taking culture into account in diagnosing and treatment. Healthy locations on these various dimensions might differ depending on context.

Some might argue that this suggested approach amounts to adding positive poles to previously pure pathology conceptualizations; however, we believe that it does not. As the pathology model presently operates, the closest that the diagnostician can come to reporting strength in a client is to note that "no pathologies were evident." Even when such a phrase is used, however, the diagnostician may intimate that the client was "covering up," "faking good," or that the instruments "may not have been sensitive to his particular symptom manifestation of the underlying pathology." (We have seen these phrases mentioned in actual reports.)

Considering various dimensions reveals to professionals that a person can display one or more strengths. This alone would force the diagnostician to consider these strengths. Remember, the pathology model does not allow any strengths to appear in the diagnostic process, and instead builds the diagnostic report on the basis of degree of pathology. Conceptualizing characteristics along dimensions also forces the diagnostician into using multiple inputs when forming ideas about a client. Rarely do people fit discretely into neat categories, and with dimensions the practitioner can use several applicable axes to fully chart the client's characteristics. Dimensions thus free the diagnostician to tailor assessment for the individual.

We suggest that all dimensions would have the inherent capability of yielding information that varies in content from maladaptive to adaptive. In addition to a mental health professional inquiring about weakness or concerns from a dimensional perspective, the helper also would ask the client about their personal strengths. On hearing these, the diagnostician would add dimensions to tap into those strengths, keeping cultural context and other factors in mind. Such assets not only would help to form a more complete diagnostic impression of the client, but also may become very important in the developing and implementing of treatments that are matched to the client's existing strengths. As an example, in addition to asking about strengths and supports, a clinician could also administer a set of brief strengths measures, including hope (Snyder et al., 1991; see also Chapter 6, this volume), optimism (Scheier, Carver, & Bridges, 1994; see also Chapter 5, this volume), personal growth initiative (Robitschek, 1998), and satisfaction with life (Diener, Emmons, Larsen, & Griffin, 1985). Together the information from inquiring about strengths and administering formal scales can be integrated with presenting concerns for a balanced perspective of the client's functioning.

Four-Front Approach

Another means of injecting more balance into a diagnosis is to encourage diagnosticians to venture beyond the realm of personality. The *DSM–IV–TR* (fourth ed., text rev.; American Psychiatric Association, 2000) endorses a system that places the problem within the individual and often ignores the more salient environmental influences (Zalaquett et al., 2008); unfortunately, the *DSM–5* is not significantly different enough for this statement to not continue to ring true. Additionally, most diagnosticians focus on the factors "inside" of a person to form an impression. This focus probably stems from the fundamental attributional error, wherein an observer forming an impression of a target person is prone to explain that target person's actions in terms of traits (Nisbett, Caputo, Legant, & Marecek, 1973). Conversely, we describe our own actions based on situational factors. On the basis of the predilection of diagnosticians to see clients in terms of their underlying personality dynamics, we believe that another necessary means of balancing a diagnosis is to make sure that the environmental contributions are examined. In this regard, we endorse the pioneering thinking of Beatrice Wright in regard to what she called the *four-front approach* to diagnosis (Wright & Lopez, 2009). In this approach, professionals gather information about (a) strengths and assets of the client, (b) deficiencies and undermining characteristics of the client, (c) resources and opportunities in the environment, and (d) lacks and destructive factors in the environment. By assessing each front dimensionally, the focus is broadened, allowing for a more balanced conceptualization of resources and liabilities and helping to counteract deindividuation and other cognitive biases (Lopez et al., 2006).

By taking a four-front approach (Wright & Lopez, 2009) to client conceptualization, practitioners are able to offer more comprehensive descriptions of clients and what they need to make changes in their lives. Determining the psychological liabilities of a person along dimensions might involve examining the client's negative affect, anxiety, depression, rigid thought patterns, functional limitations, physiological symptoms, somatization, social struggles, disengagement with life, and other "problems." Shades of dysfunction will become evident as details of dimensions are revealed. Additionally, the client's psychological assets would need to be explored. Personal characteristics of strength (e.g., wisdom, well-being, resilience), expectations about the future, level of social support, and coping skills should be targets of assessment. By creating dimensions on which to map these assets, the practitioner should have a more balanced view of a client whose makeup was once tightly linked to their presenting problem. Next, environmental liabilities and assets need to be taken into consideration. When first practicing the balanced-dimension approach, practitioners may find filling these cells with dimensions to be challenging. In general, mental health practitioners are not well trained to conduct environmental assessments; however, through self-report scales and focused questioning, the client can describe their view of this context, and through direct observation or collateral reports a more expansive view of the client's environment can be gained.

Once all four fronts are filled with information about the client's liabilities and assets, a data synthesis process begins. In a scientific approach to the data, a practitioner creates hypotheses about any given client and thereafter considers the evidence. As hypotheses and alternative hypotheses are tested and recast, a conceptualization of the client emerges and is refined by considering the diversity stemming from gender identity, race, age, sexual orientation, and so forth (Ridley, Li, & Hill, 1998). This "tentative, working client model" (Spengler, Strohmer, Dixon, & Shivy, 1995, p. 518) incorporates the shades of pathology and of strengths, and the shades of environmental support and deficiencies. Once this conceptualization of the client's strengths and weaknesses is refined, the process of identifying those diagnostic criteria that do and do not align with the model begins.

Developmental Counseling and Therapy System

The developmental counseling and therapy (DCT) system as defined by Ivey and Ivey (1998) endorses a holistic, psychosocial view of clients' strengths and distress within their unique cultural contexts. In contrast to a traditional classification system, DCT moves from diagnosis to case formulation, acknowledging the complexity of multiple influences (particularly those from the environment) on clients' presenting concerns (Lopez et al., 2006). Through case formulation, practitioners can work with clients to understand and make meaning of their unique situations and thereby grow and change (Zalaquett et al., 2008).

When gathering information for client conceptualization, clinicians using DCT (Ivey & Ivey, 1998) should focus more attention on psychological and environmental assets, and less on confirming a diagnosis. Practitioners thus work with clients in a collaborative relationship to improve treatment planning. The focus of pathology is expanded beyond the individual in DCT, thereby allowing for intervention techniques aimed at improving various dimensions of clients' lives (Zalaquett et al., 2008).

New Personality Dimension

Oldham and Morris (1995) described a dimensional approach to conceptualizing personality disorders that serves as an alternative to traditional diagnosis. Although this book refers to *DSM–IV*, the principles relating to personality disorders still apply. The authors argued that each of the 14 personality disorders listed in the *DSM–IV* (and subsequently the *DSM–IV–TR*; note that there are now 10 personality disorders included in the *DSM–5*) can be viewed as existing on a continuum of adaptation, rather than in a categorical nature (Lopez et al., 2006). On one end of these continua are the actual manifestations of the personality disorders (e.g., narcissistic, histrionic) and on the other end are less serious presentations of the personality type (e.g., self-confident, dramatic). For any given individual, personal and environmental stressors may move the person toward the more pathological end of the continuum, leading them to manifest one of the problematic personality styles. Without this type of stress, however, individuals' personality styles might be highly adaptive and may in fact be beneficial characteristics in their interactions with others.

For example, an individual may appear to have avoidant personality disorder in highly stressful situations but may be described as "sensitive" on the lower end of the continuum when less stress is present in their lives. The Oldham and Morris (1995) dimensional approach allows clinicians to be more flexible in their diagnosis by considering the degree of dysfunction as well as strengths. A formal assessment of these personality types, the Personality Self-Portrait (Oldham & Morris, 1996), also exists to aid practitioners in the identification of prominent personality styles in their clients. The theory and assessment of this dimensional typology provides a refreshing alternative language to the pathological labels we frequently use, which do little to elucidate strengths or ways to intervene to improve one's life.

MAKING CHANGES: *DSM–5*

In the *DSM–IV–TR*, the diagnostic framework comprises five axes: clinical disorders and other conditions that may be a focus of clinical attention (Axis I), personality disorders and mental retardation (Axis II), general medical conditions (Axis III), psychosocial and environmental problems (Axis IV), and global assessment of functioning (Axis V). Diagnosis and conceptualization within this framework were grossly incomplete because environmental resources, well-being, and psychological strengths are not addressed, especially for those from diverse cultural backgrounds. The *DSM*'s place in psychology is firm; however, with the publication of the fifth edition, the axis framework has been retired. This decision was made because of the realization that using a nonaxial system would better fit with the understanding that there is no difference in the conceptualization of the disorders that were previously split between the first three axes and, further, to create a thorough conceptualization of a disorder we must take into account the physical or biological factors, including medical conditions, that may have an impact on the behavioral or psychosocial presentations of a client. However, the *DSM* still fails to emphasize the positive side of functioning, which would provide a greater wealth of information for client conceptualization.

AXIS IV TO ICD-10

When addressing psychosocial and environmental problems in previous versions of the *DSM* (Axis IV), clinicians logged the problems that served to add some context to the psychological disorders diagnosed along Axes I and II. However, with the loss of the axial system, the developers of *DSM–5* chose to move to the *International Classification of Diseases and Related Health Problems* (10th rev. [ICD–10]; World Health Organization, 1992) codes, which were developed to code and differentiate mortality data, but still only look at psychosocial and environmental "problems." Considering that the problems that clinicians are coding for might serve as initiating and exacerbating factors of disorder, then everyday resources (e.g., hope, courage, spirituality) can also serve as protective factors that might prevent the development of, and would reduce the impact of, disorder. Listing these resources alongside the "problems" might facilitate the conceptualization of the ways in which the client copes and solves problems in their life. Again, it is important to consider resources that might emerge from community and one's cultural background, as discussed by Hays (2016). Cultural strengths such as ethnic identity, biculturalism, collectivism, and traditional rituals are resources often overlooked by mainstream psychology but are vital strengths that individuals might utilize to experience well-being (Pedrotti, Edwards, & Lopez, 2009). Many of these strengths can be measured with tools described in this volume.

Axis V was incorporated into the *DSM–IV* system to assess client functioning. This is the only axis that did not focus exclusively on pathology, yet it remained limited in its ability to assess strengths. A global assessment of functioning (GAF) score was assigned to a client based off their perceived level of functioning, between 1 and 100, with 100 indicating no symptoms of disorder and superior functioning and 1 indicating a person who was a persistent danger to self or was unable to maintain activities of daily living. The *DSM–5* now advocates the use of the World Health Organization Disability Assessment Schedule

(WHODAS), which provides a global assessment of functioning. However, the WHODAS is still limited in its ability to recognize the strengths of a client. As an alternative, and possibly in connection with the WHODAS, Magyar-Moe (2014) suggested a Global Assessment of Positive Functioning Scale, which would be structured similarly to the GAF (1–100 score) but with 1 signifying an absence of "well-being symptoms" and 100 indicating optimal functioning (p. 238). For example, a score of between 81 and 90 would indicate that a client may experience something like mild anxiety but has the positive coping skills, support system, or resources so it does not impede the client's ability to function positively in many areas of life. The focus is on what is positive and helps clients from receiving a lower score, rather than on the pathological symptoms, which would be assessed by the WHODAS.

STRENGTHS CLASSIFICATION SYSTEMS

As the field of psychology shifts to a balance model focusing on mental illness and mental health, practitioners and researchers must move beyond traditional deficit diagnosis. Specifically, it is important that they are able to tap into the psychological strengths associated with therapeutic change and positive functioning, thus serving the added function of creating a connection between diagnosis and treatment. To help clinicians do this, a classification system, as well as a measurement, was created: Values in Action (VIA) classification system and Gallup's Clifton StrengthsFinder (Asplund, Lopez, Hodges, & Harter, 2007).

The VIA (Peterson & Seligman, 2001, 2004) classification of strengths serves as a complement to the *DSM* system and holds some promise for fostering additional understanding of psychological strengths. Peterson and Seligman made the point that although members of the field of psychology currently have a common language to use in speaking about the negative side of psychology, they have no such equivalent terminology to use in speaking about the strengths of individuals. The VIA classification of strengths provides common language and at the same time encourages a more strengths-based approach to diagnosis and treatment (treatment manuals focused on enhancing strengths will accompany the diagnostic manual). Aside from psychology, it has also been used in the fields of education, management, consulting, coaching, and many others.

In support of a less unilateral classification system, the VIA classification system describes the individual differences of character strengths on continua and not as distinct categories. In this way, the authors contended that their classification approach is sensitive to the developmental differences in which character strengths are displayed and deployed (Peterson & Seligman, 2001, 2004). Six categories are delineated in the VIA classification system: *wisdom*, *courage*, *humanity*, *justice*, *temperance*, and *transcendence*, and these are represented as universal and cross-cultural virtues (Peterson & Seligman, 2001, 2004). This belief in the universality of these constructs as "strengths" raises some concerns, as we know many characteristics may be present in different cultural groups but are not necessarily thought of with the same degree of positivity in all (Lopez, Pedrotti, & Snyder, 2015). When results are interpreted and viewed through the appropriate lens by a culturally competent clinician, however, they may help to guide a client toward a more positive understanding of themselves.

The Clifton StrengthsFinder is a measurement of talent, which Donald Clifton, the founder of strengths-based psychology, believed was a foundational determinant in the development of strengths (S. D. Brown & Lent, 2008). Hodges and Clifton (2004) defined *talent* as "naturally recurring patterns of thought, feeling, or behavior that can be productively applied," whereas strength is being able to attain "consistent, near-perfect performance in a given activity" (p. 257), therefore making strengths a natural extension of talent combined with skills and knowledge, acquired attributes. Once talents are ascertained through the StrengthsFinder measure, to foster behavioral change, the respondent must integrate that talent into their self-concept and continue to foster it (Hodges & Clifton, 2004).

Although this measure is not meant to be used as a mental health screening, it has proven to be very popular within positive psychology because of its exclusive focus on one's strengths. However, further longitudinal research is needed to track the long-term effect of strength-based interventions (Clifton & Harter, 2003). Currently, this measure is primarily used in the business world as well as in educational settings as a way for employers/teachers to identify and foster the unique talents of employees/students.

POWER OF POSITIVE PSYCHOLOGICAL ASSESSMENT

By assessing for strengths, the diagnostician is fostering several positive reactions in the client. First, the client can see that the helper is trying to understand the whole person. Second, the client is shown that they are not being equated with the problem. Third, the client is not reinforced for "having a problem," but rather is encouraged to look at their assets. Fourth, the client can recall and reclaim some of the personal worth that may have been depleted before coming to the mental health professional. Fifth, a consideration of the client's strengths can facilitate an alliance of trust and mutuality with the mental health professional; in turn, the client is open and giving of information that may yield a maximally productive diagnosis. Finally, identifying strengths should be integrated into efforts toward social justice, whereby clients can marshal personal and community resources to cope with oppression and inequities and optimize wellness. When attention is given to cultural context as a natural part of assessment, this last goal can be better achieved. By assessing strengths, therefore, a positive assessment can at once be healing and buoyant in its focus. Positive psychology in general, and positive psychological assessment in particular, offer a perspective for identifying and working with the strengths in people. We owe nothing less to those who ask for our help.

REFERENCES

American Psychiatric Association. (2000). *Diagnostic and statistical manual of mental disorders* (4th ed., Text rev.). Washington, DC: Author.

American Psychiatric Association. (2013). *Diagnostic and statistical manual of mental disorders* (5th ed.). Washington, DC: Author.

Asplund, M. A., Lopez, S. J., Hodges, T., & Harter, J. (2007). *The Clifton StrengthsFinder® 2.0 technical report: Development and validation.* Retrieved from https://www.gallup.com/services/176321/clifton-strengthsfinder-technical-report-development-validation.aspx

Barone, D., Maddux, J., & Snyder, C. R. (1997). The social cognitive construction of difference and disorder. In D. Barone, J. Maddux, & C. R. Snyder (Eds.), *Social cognitive psychology: History and current domains* (pp. 397–426). New York, NY: Plenum Press. http://dx.doi.org/10.1007/978-1-4615-5843-9_14

Brown, S. D., & Lent, R. W. (Eds.). (2008). *Handbook of counseling psychology* (4th ed.). Hoboken, NJ: Wiley.

Brown, T. A., & Barlow, D. H. (2005). Dimensional versus categorical classification of mental disorders in the fifth edition of the *Diagnostic and Statistical Manual of Mental Disorders* and beyond: Comment on the special section. *Journal of Abnormal Psychology, 114,* 551–556. http://dx.doi.org/10.1037/0021-843X.114.4.551

Brown, T. A., & Barlow, D. H. (2009). A proposal for a dimensional classification system based on the shared features of the *DSM–IV* anxiety and mood disorders: Implications for assessment and treatment. *Psychological Assessment, 21,* 256–271. http://dx.doi.org/10.1037/a0016608

Buss, A. R., & Poley, W. (1976). *Individual differences: Traits and factors.* New York, NY: Gardner Press.

Capielo, C., Mann, L., Nevels, B., & Delgado-Romero, E. (2014). Infusing multiculturalism and positive psychology in psychotherapy. In J. T. Pedrotti & L. M. Edwards (Eds.), *Perspectives on the intersection of multiculturalism and positive psychology* (pp. 31–44). New York, NY: Springer. http://dx.doi.org/10.1007/978-94-017-8654-6_3

Clifton, D. O., & Harter, J. K. (2003). Investing in strengths. In A. K. S. Cameron, B. J. E. Dutton, & C. R. E. Quinn (Eds.), *Positive organizational scholarship: Foundations of a new discipline* (pp. 111–121). San Francisco, CA: Berrett-Koehler.

Diener, E., Emmons, R. A., Larsen, R. J., & Griffin, S. (1985). The Satisfaction With Life Scale. *Journal of Personality Assessment, 49,* 71–75. http://dx.doi.org/10.1207/s15327752jpa4901_13

Garb, H. N. (1998). *Studying the clinician: Judgment research and psychological assessment.* Washington, DC: American Psychological Association. http://dx.doi.org/10.1037/10299-000

Garb, H. N. (2005). Clinical judgment and decision making. *Annual Review of Clinical Psychology, 1,* 67–89. http://dx.doi.org/10.1146/annurev.clinpsy.1.102803.143810

Greenleaf, A. T., & Williams, J. M. (2009). Supporting social justice advocacy: A paradigm shift towards an ecological perspective. *Journal for Social Action in Counseling and Psychology, 2,* 1–14.

Hays, P. A. (2016). *Addressing cultural complexities in practice: Assessment, diagnosis, and therapy* (3rd ed.). Washington, DC: American Psychological Association. http://dx.doi.org/10.1037/14801-000

Hodges, T. D., & Clifton, D. O. (2004). Strengths-based development in practice. In A. Linley & S. Joseph (Eds.), *Handbook of positive psychology in practice* (pp. 269–286). Hoboken, NJ: Wiley. http://dx.doi.org/10.1002/9780470939338.ch16

Ivey, A. E., & Ivey, M. B. (1998). Reframing *DSM–IV*: Positive strategies from developmental counseling and therapy. *Journal of Counseling & Development, 76,* 334–350. http://dx.doi.org/10.1002/j.1556-6676.1998.tb02550.x

Layous, K. L., Lee, H., Choi, I., & Lyubomirsky, S. (2013). Culture matters when designing a successful happiness-increasing activity: A comparison of the United States and

South Korea. *Journal of Cross-Cultural Psychology, 44,* 1294–1303. http://dx.doi.org/10.1177/0022022113487591

Lopez, S. J., Edwards, L. M., Pedrotti, J. T., Prosser, E. C., LaRue, S., Spalitto, S. V., & Ulven, J. C. (2006). Beyond the *DSM*: Assumptions, alternatives, and alterations. *Journal of Counseling & Development, 84,* 259–267. http://dx.doi.org/10.1002/j.1556-6678.2006.tb00404.x

Lopez, S. J., Pedrotti, J. T., & Snyder, C. R. (2015). *Positive psychology: The scientific and practical explorations of human strengths* (3rd ed.). Thousand Oaks, CA: Sage.

Maddux, J. E. (1993a). The mythology of psychopathology: A social cognitive view of deviance, difference, and disorder. *The General Psychologist, 29,* 34–45.

Maddux, J. E. (1993b). Social science, social policy, and scientific research. *American Psychologist, 48,* 689–691. http://dx.doi.org/10.1037/0003-066X.48.6.689.b

Maddux, J. E. (in press). Stopping the "madness": Positive psychology and the deconstruction of the illness ideology and the *DSM*. In C. R. Snyder & S. J. Lopez (Eds.), *The handbook of positive psychology* (3rd ed.). New York, NY: Oxford Press.

Magyar-Moe, J. L. (2014). Infusing multiculturalism and positive psychology in psychotherapy. In J. T. Pedrotti & L. M. Edwards (Eds.), *Perspectives on the intersection of multiculturalism and positive psychology* (pp. 235–249). New York, NY: Springer. http://dx.doi.org/10.1007/978-94-017-8654-6_16

Merton, R. (1957). *Social theory and social structure* (Rev. ed.). Glencoe, IL: Free Press.

Mullins-Sweatt, S. N., Lengel, G. J., & DeShong, H. L. (2016). The importance of considering clinical utility in the construction of a diagnostic manual. *Annual Review of Clinical Psychology, 12,* 133–155. http://dx.doi.org/10.1146/annurev-clinpsy-021815-092954

Nisbett, R. E., Caputo, C., Legant, P., & Marecek, J. (1973). Behavior as seen by the actor and as seen by the observer. *Journal of Personality and Social Psychology, 27,* 154–164. http://dx.doi.org/10.1037/h0034779

Oldham, J. M., & Morris, L. B. (1995). *New personality self-portrait: Why you think, work, love, and act the way you do.* New York, NY: Bantam.

Oldham, J. M., & Morris, L. B. (1996). *The Personality Self-Portrait: Interpretation guide.* North Tonawanda, NY: Multi-Health Systems.

Pedrotti, J. T., & Edwards, L. M. (Eds.). (2014). *Perspectives on the intersection of multiculturalism and positive psychology.* New York, NY: Springer. http://dx.doi.org/10.1007/978-94-017-8654-6

Pedrotti, J. T., Edwards, L. M., & Lopez, S. J. (2009). Positive psychology within a cultural context. In S. J. Lopez (Ed.), *Handbook of positive psychology* (2nd ed., pp. 49–58). New York, NY: Oxford University Press.

Peterson, C., & Seligman, M. E. P. (2001). *Values in Action (VIA) classification of strengths.* Retrieved from http://www.psych.upenn.edu/seligman/taxonomy.htm

Peterson, C., & Seligman, M. E. P. (2004). *Character strengths and virtues: A handbook and classification.* Washington, DC: American Psychological Association.

Raskin, J. D., & Lewandowski, A. M. (2000). The construction of disorder as human enterprise. In R. A. Neimeyer & J. D. Raskin (Eds.), *Constructions of disorder: Meaning making frameworks for psychotherapy* (pp. 15–40). Washington, DC: American Psychological Association. http://dx.doi.org/10.1037/10368-002

Ridley, C. R., Li, L. C., & Hill, C. L. (1998). Multicultural assessment: Reexamination, reconceptualization, and practical application. *The Counseling Psychologist, 26,* 827–910. http://dx.doi.org/10.1177/0011000098266005

Robitschek, C. (1998). Personal growth initiative: The construct and its measure. *Measurement and Evaluation in Counseling and Development, 30,* 183–198.

Rosenthal, R., & Jacobson, L. (1968). *Pygmalion in the classroom: Teacher expectation and pupils' intellectual development.* New York, NY: Holt, Rinehart, & Winston.

Salovey, P., & Turk, D. C. (1991). Clinical judgment and decision-making. In C. R. Snyder & D. R. Forsyth (Eds.), *Handbook of social and clinical psychology: The health perspective* (pp. 416–437). New York, NY: Pergamon Press.

Scheier, M. F., Carver, C. S., & Bridges, M. N. (1994). Distinguishing optimism from neuroticism (and trait anxiety, self-mastery, and self-esteem): A reevaluation of the Life Orientation Test. *Journal of Personality and Social Psychology, 67,* 1063–1078. http://dx.doi.org/10.1037/0022-3514.67.6.1063

Snyder, C. R., & Feldman, D. B. (2000). Hope for the many: An empowering social agenda. In C. R. Snyder (Ed.), *Handbook of hope: Theory, measures, and applications* (pp. 389–415). San Diego, CA: Academic Press. http://dx.doi.org/10.1016/B978-012654050-5/50023-3

Snyder, C. R., Harris, C., Anderson, J. R., Holleran, S. A., Irving, L. M., Sigmon, S. T., . . . Harney, P. (1991). The will and the ways: Development and validation of an individual-differences measure of hope. *Journal of Personality and Social Psychology, 60,* 570–585. http://dx.doi.org/10.1037/0022-3514.60.4.570

Snyder, C. R., & Ingram, R. E. (2000). Psychotherapy: Questions for an evolving field. In C. R. Snyder & R. E. Ingram (Eds.), *Handbook of psychological change: Psychotherapy processes and practices for the 21st century* (pp. 707–735). New York, NY: Wiley.

Spencer, S. J., Logel, C., & Davies, P. G. (2016). Stereotype threat. *Annual Review of Psychology, 67,* 415–437. http://dx.doi.org/10.1146/annurev-psych-073115-103235

Spengler, P. M., Strohmer, D. C., Dixon, D. N., & Shivy, V. A. (1995). A scientist-practitioner model of psychological assessment: Implications for training, practice and research. *The Counseling Psychologist, 23,* 506–534. http://dx.doi.org/10.1177/0011000095233009

Steele, C. M. (1997). A threat in the air. How stereotypes shape intellectual identity and performance. *American Psychologist, 52,* 613–629. http://dx.doi.org/10.1037/0003-066X.52.6.613

Sue, D. W. (1978). Eliminating cultural oppression in counseling: Toward a general theory. *Journal of Counseling Psychology, 25,* 419–428. http://dx.doi.org/10.1037/0022-0167.25.5.419

Sue, D. W., & Sue, D. (2016). *Counseling the culturally diverse: Theory and practice* (7th ed.). Hoboken, NJ: Wiley.

Williams, J. M., & Greenleaf, A. T. (2012). Ecological psychology: Potential contributions to social justice and advocacy in school settings. *Journal of Educational & Psychological Consultation, 22*(1–2), 141–157. http://dx.doi.org/10.1080/10474412.2011.649653

World Health Organization. (1992). *International classification of diseases and related health problems* (10th rev.). Geneva, Switzerland: Author.

Wright, B. A., & Lopez, S. J. (2009). Widening the diagnostic focus: A case for including human strengths and environmental resources. In C. R. Snyder & S. J. Lopez (Eds.), *Oxford handbook of positive psychology* (pp. 71–88). New York, NY: Oxford University Press.

Zalaquett, C. P., Fuerth, K. M., Stein, C., Ivey, A. E., & Ivey, M. B. (2008). Reframing the *DSM–IV–TR* from a multicultural/social justice perspective. *Journal of Counseling & Development, 86,* 364–371. http://dx.doi.org/10.1002/j.1556-6678.2008.tb00521.x

4

Assessment of Positive Psychology Constructs Across Cultures

Lisa Y. Flores and Hang-Shim Lee

The demographic landscape in the United States is undergoing a dramatic shift. Today, the U.S. population includes over 300 million people (U.S. Census Bureau, 2016), over a third of whom are racially diverse. Across the diverse racial groups in the United States, 18% are Latino, 13% are African American, 6% are Asian American/Pacific Islanders, 1% are Native American/American Indian, and 3% are multiracial. Looking into the future, Whites are expected to decrease in size, while all other racial groups are projected to grow. By 2045, it is estimated that collectively, people of color will constitute the majority population in the United States. The United States is becoming a true multicultural society, and at the same time, globalization has led to increased interdependence across cultures around the world.

Positive psychology reemerged within psychology during a time when significant shifts were projected in the demographic makeup of the country and during the most recent wave of globalization, and scholars acknowledged that for positive psychology, research and practice must be embedded within a cultural context to remain a viable force (Pedrotti & Edwards, 2014; Pedrotti, Edwards, & Lopez, 2009). Multiculturalism within positive psychology has been characterized as being at the adolescence stage (Downey & Chang, 2014), reflecting some advancements and also suggesting potential for significant growth in this area. It is imperative that researchers in positive psychology consider the cultural applications of positive psychological constructs, models, and theories and extend the external validity of research findings to culturally

http://dx.doi.org/10.1037/0000138-004
Positive Psychological Assessment: A Handbook of Models and Measures, Second Edition,
M. W. Gallagher and S. J. Lopez (Editors)

diverse populations. The inclusion of research samples from underrepresented populations in research will increase the relevance and significance of positive psychology research both domestically and internationally. To understand the extent to which positive psychological models are universal or culturally specific will require (a) increased work in developing culture-specific instruments with demonstrated reliability and validity and/or validating existing positive psychology measures with diverse groups and (b) using professional research guidelines (see American Psychological Association [APA], 2003) in future positive psychology research with diverse groups.

The purpose of this chapter is to assess the current state of multicultural and cross-cultural assessment in positive psychology by evaluating our ability to measure positive characteristics of individuals across diverse populations and to examine the interpretation and generalizability of these findings from one culture to another. Specifically, we review the history of psychological assessment with diverse racial/ethnic groups in the United States and discuss current guidelines for research and practice with diverse populations. Next, we provide an overview of methodological issues in multicultural and cross-cultural measurement and review recent investigations of cultural validity of two positive psychological instruments. Finally, we describe a model for positive psychological assessment with culturally diverse populations and provide recommendations for future developments in multicultural and cross-cultural assessment of positive psychological constructs.

COMPETENT PSYCHOLOGICAL RESEARCH IN AN INCREASINGLY DIVERSE WORLD

Thanks to the pioneering work of Black psychologists in the 1960s and numerous psychologists since who have been committed to an inclusive psychology, we are aware of the importance of the sociocultural context in understanding individual behaviors. Today, there is increasing attention within psychology to conducting multicultural research (Byrne et al., 2009). Recently, scholars renewed a call for more psychological research using a *multicultural approach* with underrepresented cultural groups (Hall, Yip, & Zárate, 2016). These scholars compare and contrast three approaches to psychological research: (a) generalizability, (b) group differences, and (c) the multicultural psychology approaches (Hall et al., 2016). Using a generalizability approach, research validates the assumption that theories are universally applicable. Often, cultural and contextual variables are not included, and when they are, they are often used as control variables and tap into broad, general constructs (i.e., nationality) that mask nuanced differences within cultural groups. When findings do not support the universal assumption, they are often overlooked or minimized. On the other hand, group differences research examines both commonalities and differences across groups. Although this approach extends generalizability research to examine the underlying reasons attributed to group differences when universality is not supported, its main drawbacks include the tendency to use European Americans as the standard reference group and assessing cultural variables that are relevant to all groups. Most research in psychology falls into either the generalizability or group differences approaches, with fewer studies reflecting a true multicultural approach that utilizes *intentional* samples from underrepresented groups and seeks to understand the cultural nuances within a single group without comparison to others. Research on specific cultural groups is valued, and practices and behaviors are understood and interpreted within the context of the culture. Multicultural research aims to explore the psychological processes of individuals from marginalized groups within both cultural and social contexts, and it incorporates psychological and cultural variables that are relevant to the particular group of study. In essence, multicultural research recognizes, accepts, and respects the strengths and values within cultures, a perspective that aligns nicely with the aims and values of positive psychology. Though conducting multicultural research presents some challenges to efficiency and productivity, positive psychology researchers can take an important step in heeding the recommendations of Hall and his colleagues (2016) in applying these principles in future work.

The profession has transformed steadily over the past 50 years to integrate multicultural perspectives in our professional ethical codes (APA, 2017) and to endorse multicultural guidelines that cover broad psychological practices, including research, training, and service delivery (APA, 2003). Specifically, ethical standards for assessment practice require that psychologists administer tests in an individual's preferred language and use assessment instruments with established psychometric properties for the population being tested; when data are not available, psychologists acknowledge the strengths and limitations of the test (APA, 2017). This requires a commitment to training the next generation of psychologists who are fluent in multiple languages and who are knowledgeable of the cultures represented in their communities. In addition, our professional guidelines indicate that regardless of the roles in which we operate as psychologists, we are aware of ourselves as cultural beings, recognize our beliefs about other cultural groups, and gain an understanding of the worldview of other cultural groups in the assessment setting because the cultural awareness of psychologists can have an impact not only on the administration process, but also on the interpretation of the results and the effective ways to deliver the feedback to clients. Thus, it is critical to include multicultural trainings of assessment in our clinical settings. Also, as researchers, we need to engage in studies that are culture centered and to understand how culture (and language) may affect the constructs that we study.

Multicultural and cross-cultural psychology aims to build on individuals' cultural strengths by focusing on the role of culture in explaining human behavior. Positive psychology, with its burgeoning body of science and its focus on promoting optimal human functioning, has the opportunity to acknowledge and strategically address ethnicity and culture while building its scholarly framework, research tools, and intervention practices. Multicultural and cross-cultural research in positive psychology has the potential to positively impact clinical practice with diverse cultural groups by informing psychologists of the cultural nuances in the presentation of strength, healthy processes, and optimal living as experienced within diverse cultural groups.

MULTICULTURAL POSITIVE PSYCHOLOGICAL ASSESSMENT

Several issues must be taken into account in the construction, adaptation, and selection of positive psychological measures for use in research and practice with individuals from culturally diverse groups. (See Table 4.1 for a list of general concerns related to psychological measurement and test construction that influence the validity of positive psychological measures with diverse cultural groups.) To begin, positive psychological researchers must understand the meaning of positive constructs among diverse cultural groups and determine whether the construct is defined similarly across cultures (*etic*) or whether the construct is culturally specific (*emic*). Within psychology, a common assumption is that most psychological instruments are etic, or generalizable to individuals across cultures, without empirical evidence to support this (Dana, 1996). When clients are not represented in the normative data of an instrument, measures can be adapted through translation, incorporating multicultural assessment guidelines, or modifying response options (Dana, 2014).

When selecting measures for psychological assessment and research, it is important to determine if the measure was constructed from the worldview perspective of the cultural group for which it is intended to be used and that

TABLE 4.1. Methodological Issues in Multicultural Assessment

Methodological issue	Definition	Question
Conceptual equivalence	The construct has the same meaning across cultures.	How is this construct defined within this group?
Content equivalence	Item content is relevant across cultures.	Do the items reflect actual occurrences within this group?
Functional equivalence	Characteristic assessed in the instrument are equivalent across groups.	Are the manifestations of the construct captured in the assessment for this group?
Normative equivalence	Standardized data available.	Is psychometric data derived for scores on this measure from a culturally similar sample (i.e., race, education level, age, social class)?
Translation equivalence	The measure is available in the individual's preferred language and has been properly translated.	Do the translated items maintain the same meaning when back-translated to the original language?
Examiner bias	Professional has knowledge of other culture and personal biases that may filter interpretations of responses.	Does professional understand the culture well enough to interpret responses and behaviors?

Note. Definitions for methodological issues are derived from Leong, Leung, and Cheung (2010).

interpretations of the data are communicated in a manner that improves an individual's or a community's current condition in a culturally sensitive way. Moreover, psychologists should recognize variations within cultural groups that may shape one's interpretations of the results. Various factors that contribute to differences within cultural groups (e.g., gender socialization, social class, religious beliefs) should be taken into consideration when conceptualizing studies and interpreting research findings.

Empirical Tests of Measurement Bias

Both traditional and modern approaches can be used to empirically examine measurement bias in existing positive psychological measures. Qualitative methods, particularly focus-group interviews and expert panels, can provide valuable information about cultural meanings of constructs and manifestations of behaviors or attitudes to researchers in the development of an emic instrument or adaptation of an etic instrument (Ramírez, Ford, Stewart, & Teresi, 2005). Traditional psychometric approaches involving evaluations of content and construct validity, as well as reporting internal consistency, test–retest reliability, and factorial validity, can also be used to provide cultural validity support for test scores (Ramírez et al., 2005). Finally, modern psychometric theory, multilevel analysis, and latent variable approaches consist of various statistical applications, such as confirmatory factor analysis, differential item functioning, item response theory, and hierarchical linear modeling, that are gaining prominence in cross-cultural assessment research (Allen, 2007; Byrne et al., 2009; Leong, Leung, & Cheung, 2010).

Cultural Validity Data for Two Positive Psychology Measures

Subjective well-being has been a highly researched area within positive psychology. To assess the cognitive aspect of one's satisfaction in life, Diener, Emmons, Larsen, and Griffin (1985) developed the Satisfaction With Life Scale (SWLS). Even though life satisfaction has been perceived as a global measurement of the well-being of one's life (Pavot & Diener, 1993), individuals' experiences of satisfaction with life is inherently related to culture, meaning, and value, so the cultural validity of SWLS scores is vital to future research in this area. Recently, multicultural and cross-cultural studies of the SWLS have been conducted with Mexican Americans (Edwards, Ong, & Lopez, 2007; Ojeda, Edwards, Hardin, & Piña-Watson, 2014; Ojeda, Flores, & Navarro, 2011), African Americans (Ajibade, Hook, Utsey, Davis, & Van Tongeren, 2016; Constantine, Alleyne, Wallace, & Franklin-Jackson, 2006; Utsey, Ponterotto, Reynolds, & Cancelli, 2000), South Africans (Dodd, 2016; Muzindutsi & Sekhampu, 2014; Westaway & Maluka, 2005), Asians (Bai, Wu, Zheng, & Ren, 2011; Wong, Ho, Li, Shin, & Tsai, 2011; Wu & Yao, 2006), and Europeans (Di Fabio & Gori, 2016; Vittersø, Biswas-Diener, & Diener, 2005; Whisman & Judd, 2016). In addition, measurement invariance of the SWLS have been tested in cross-national studies in countries such as the United States, England, and Japan (Whisman & Judd, 2016).

SWLS scores evidenced acceptable internal consistency reliabilities, ranging from .75 to .92 among these studies, with the exception of a sample from Greenland (Cronbach's alpha = .58). Validity estimates suggested that SWLS is related to positive affect, hope, family support, friend support, optimism, self-efficacy, academic satisfaction, and goal progress among Mexican Americans (Edwards et al., 2007; Ojeda et al., 2011, 2014). Life satisfaction was related to high levels of self-esteem but was not related to perceived social support satisfaction among African American adolescent girls (Constantine et al., 2006). A confirmatory factor analysis of data from Mainland China showed that the only model that had an acceptable fit included items that assess satisfaction with one's past life (Bai et al., 2011). These findings were different from the results from samples in Hong Kong (Sachs, 2003) and Taiwan (Wu & Yao, 2006), possibly suggesting that the economic progress in Mainland China has resulted in expanded time orientations of life satisfaction. Furthermore, relative to the Norwegians, Greenlanders were more likely to use extreme categories in responding to the SWLS (Vittersø et al., 2005). Finally, Singelis et al. (2006) examined the metric equivalence of SWLS scores across Spanish and English Language versions. The reliabilities of the scale scores ranged from .74 to .82 across both language versions. Although metric equivalence was supported, this study highlighted the importance of conceptual, construct, or functional equivalence across cultures as an area for future study.

The Problem-Solving Inventory (PSI; Heppner & Petersen, 1982) has been available for over 35 years to assess how people respond to difficult, often stressful problems. Multicultural and cross-cultural studies of the PSI have included African American college students (Neville, Heppner, & Wang, 1997), African American and Latino college students (Winograd & Tryon, 2009), Latino youth (Huang & Flores, 2011; Flores, Ojeda, Huang, Gee, & Lee, 2006; Schinke, Schwinn, Hopkins, & Wahlstrom, 2016), Italian youth (Nota, Heppner, Soresi, & Heppner, 2009), and South African college students (Heppner, Pretorius, Wei, Lee, & Wang, 2002). Validity estimates indicated that the PSI is related to self-esteem, career decision making, educational goals, learning strategies, Anglo-oriented acculturation, and physical and psychological stress (Flores et al., 2006; Neville et al., 1997; Winograd & Tryon, 2009). PSI scores demonstrated acceptable internal consistency across these samples, with alpha coefficients ranging from .82 to .90, .77 to .85, .76 to .84, and .66 to .76 for the full scale, and problem-solving confidence, approach/avoidance, and personal control subscales, respectively. A three-factor structure was reported with diverse samples in the United States and internationally (Heppner et al., 2002; Huang & Flores, 2011; Nota et al., 2009). PSI means and standard deviations were also comparable to those reported in previous PSI studies conducted with White college students (Heppner et al., 2002; Huang & Flores, 2011). Although statistically significant differences were not reported between men and women on the PSI with most U.S. samples, Italian high school males scored lower or more positively than their female peers on the total scale (Nota et al., 2009). More cross-cultural and multicultural data could enhance the generalizability of some of the findings reported in U.S. samples and can offer additional support for the utility of the PSI in describing problem-solving behaviors across diverse groups.

MULTICULTURAL POSITIVE PSYCHOLOGICAL ASSESSMENT PROCEDURES

Culturally sensitive positive psychological assessment is a multifaceted process. Psychologists administer psychological tests and instruments to better understand people, and they use several methods to gather information to understand individual behavior. Assessment information can be obtained through both formal (i.e., paper-and-pencil tests) and informal (i.e., talking to the person, talking to the person's family and friends) methods and should be comprehensive to include both standardized and nonstandardized (i.e., narratives) measures (Dana, 2014). We ascribe to Allen's (2007) definition of *multicultural assessment* to include a process of gathering information in which the people (i.e., client, practitioner, or researcher) involved in the process differ from one another along the dimensions of race, culture, or ethnicity and/or when the instrument that is being used was developed for use with a different cultural group. We want to underscore the fact that assessment is a process, where hypotheses are formulated and then reformulated on the basis of incoming information and feedback from the person and environment. A continual feedback loop between the individual or cultural group and professional is necessary to validate evidence that is gathered and to support conclusions.

Roysircar (2014) described an ecological approach to multicultural assessment that includes a thorough understanding of an individual's peer, family, school, community, and cultural contexts. Without considering the environmental and cultural contexts in which behaviors occurs, it is difficult to accurately interpret an individual's behaviors. Take as an example a student yelling in the middle of the afternoon while walking around campus. This may not reflect typical or acceptable behavior; however, consider that the school just made it to its first national championship title game. In this circumstance, a student yelling on campus would reflect behaviors of an excited fan on campus who is eagerly anticipating the game later in the day. Obtaining information regarding the environment, cultural explanations for behaviors, and characterizations of behaviors from the perspective of individuals who are part of the culture are essential components of multicultural assessment.

In accordance with professional standards, it is essential that psychologists embrace stringent assessment and research procedures that are designed to maximize the exchange of knowledge between cultural groups and that places culture in the center of all assessment activities. The following are culturally sensitive skills and procedures to incorporate in positive psychology assessment with culturally diverse individuals that have been previously described in the literature (Allen, 2007; Dana, 2005; Flores, Spanierman, & Obasi, 2003; Grieger, 2008; Ridley, Li, & Hill, 1998; Roysircar, 2014; Roysircar-Sodowsky & Kuo, 2001):

1. The development of basic multicultural competencies in assessment and research practices are a critical component to effective assessment with individuals from culturally diverse groups. *Multicultural competencies* have been conceptualized to include awareness of personal beliefs, knowledge, and skills in working with diverse populations (APA, 2003). A psychologist must understand one's cultural frame of reference prior to embarking on the assessment process with culturally different individuals (APA, 2003; Sue & Sue, 2016). As such, psychologists should evaluate personal worldview, values, prejudices, stereotypes, and reference group identity, as these will be influential when formulating research questions or clinical hypotheses for individuals from diverse cultural backgrounds. In addition, psychologists also should take steps to examine the social–political realities, worldview, and values of the cultural groups with whom one works. This knowledge will facilitate the assessment process and decrease problems due to cultural differences, considering that the information gathered from this process will permeate all aspects of the assessment process.

2. *Gathering information* about personal and cultural strengths that an individual can draw on to develop optimal functioning is the first step of the assessment process. In addition to a strengths assessment, psychologists should also conduct a thorough assessment of relevant demographic and cultural factors that may influence responses on a measure, such as racial identity (Helms, 2006) and acculturation (Allen, 2007; Dana, 2014; Roysircar-Sodowsky & Kuo, 2001). Information should also be gathered on the multiple sociocultural contexts in which the individual interacts (Roysircar, 2014), self-identified racial/ethnic categorization, acculturative stress, language preference, worldview, and values.

3. Psychologists use a range of measures—objective and narrative approaches—to gather assessment data. To determine which positive psychology instrument is most appropriate for the individual, psychologists *evaluate available instruments* on the basis of the information that they have gathered on the individual and review normative data that are available for the cultural group with which the individual identifies. Cultural data can be used to select the appropriateness of an etic, adapted etic, or emic assessment measure. When using an etic or adapted etic measure, psychologists should consider the cultural equivalence and other forms of measurement bias described earlier in this chapter to determine if the test will provide the most accurate information or if other methods of assessment should be considered.

4. Cultural considerations should also be taken into account to *facilitate a culturally sensitive administration* of an instrument, including cultural standards

for interpersonal interactions. The psychologist develops rapport and trust with the client and ensures that the instrument is administered in a fashion that is congruent with the client's familiarity with test administration and history with test taking. This is particularly important with individuals from cultural groups that may be highly suspicious of how the data are going to be used.

5. Psychologists *incorporate cultural data when interpreting findings* and acknowledge any limitations of the instrument or assessment process that may contribute to culturally invalid or insensitive assessment decisions. Both examiner bias and test bias must be minimized to ensure negligible error in appropriately interpreting the assessment data and the behaviors of individuals from culturally diverse groups. Finally, the interpretation of the results always should be presented to the individual to solicit feedback regarding the results and can be used to determine whether etic or emic interventions are warranted. Psychologists may recycle back through these procedures to compensate for the new information gathered during the assessment process.

FUTURE RESEARCH AND TRAINING DEVELOPMENTS IN MULTICULTURAL AND CROSS-CULTURAL ASSESSMENT OF POSITIVE PSYCHOLOGY CONSTRUCTS

Researchers in positive psychology have made important contributions to the literature regarding individual strengths. With some exceptions (i.e., subjective well-being, optimism and pessimism, coping), there has been relatively limited research activity to validate positive psychological constructs and related measures among U.S. racial/ethnic groups or cross-culturally (Pedrotti, Edwards, & Lopez, 2009). As a result, exploring the cultural validity of several existing positive psychology measures and designing new (objective and narrative) measures is a research area that is ripe for future examination. In addition, there is a need to develop emic measures to capture positive psychology constructs within cultures (e.g., Heppner et al., 2006; Moore & Constantine, 2005; Ozer & Schotland, 2011). The following research recommendations are provided to further multicultural and cross-cultural research in positive psychology and to provide evidence for the universal applicability of positive psychology constructs, models, and theories: (a) design culture-specific measures to assess positive psychology constructs; (b) generate research that tests the conceptual and methodological equivalence of existing positive psychological measures with U.S. racial/ethnic groups and international samples; (c) when using measures with cultural groups that are not represented in standardization samples, obtain preliminary reliability and validity data on the measure's scores through small pilot studies; (d) use a variety of measures and sources to assess the variable of interest to better represent its cultural complexity; (e) generate more empirical support for positive psychology theories with diverse cultural groups that are underrepresented in research; and (f) collaborate with international psychologists who have expertise and knowledge of particular groups to design emic measures. In terms of training and practice in multicultural assessment within positive psychology, we (a) encourage an increase in the number of graduate students in psychology who express interest in studying positive psychological functioning in culturally diverse populations; (b) incorporate and strengthen multicultural training across graduate coursework in assessment and psychometrics (Allen, 2007), and encourage students to complete advanced-level statistical classes to stay current on modern statistical techniques for validating instruments across cultures; and (c) apply the findings from positive psychology's research within clinical practice to improve the functioning and status of culturally diverse groups by building on the strengths and values within the culture.

CASE STUDY

Ruben, a psychologist at a university counseling center, has an intake session with Bo, a first-year international student studying architecture and design. Bo is from China and reports that this is her first semester in the United States. She has sought guidance for dealing with the stress related to transitioning to living in the United States and the high demands of her major and fears of failing in her courses. She reports spending long hours in the lab working on a design project and feeling high levels of competition among her peers. She dreads having to present her project at the end of the semester because she has heard that "the faculty rip it to shreds." Ruben tries to explore how Bo copes with high levels of stress by using an assessment. Ruben is familiar with an existing coping measure that provides an individual's coping types. However, on the basis of Bo's narratives related to useful coping strategies for dealing with stress in her home country, Ruben questions whether the measure, which was developed in a Western individualistic culture, could accurately assess Bo's coping strategies. To select a culturally appropriate measurement, Ruben reviewed the normative data on the measure, including the normative sample's cultural background as well as reliability and validity estimates for the scale's scores. Normative data were not available for Asian young adults.

After reviewing other coping styles measures, Ruben located the Collectivist Coping Styles (CCS; Heppner et al., 2006) inventory, which was designed by an international research team that included European Americans and Asians to capture Asian values and ways of coping. A series of studies were performed with a large (over 3,000 participants) Asian international sample to validate and provide normative data for CCS scores. The CCS identified five factors: acceptance, reframing, and striving; family support; religion–spirituality; avoidance and detachment; and private emotional outlets. Using this measure, Ruben finds that family support is Bo's main coping strategy among the five factors. In a session where Ruben provided the results of CCS, Ruben realizes that Bo has difficulty utilizing family support after coming to the United States because of the time difference between her home country and the United States. Ruben helps Bo to explore how she can still utilize her effective coping strategies by setting up a regular time to talk with her family and using online technology to make the call. Ruben and Bo discuss how Bo can still use or modify her original coping strategies and her strengths to deal with the stress stemming from her transition and high academic demands.

CONCLUSION

In this chapter, we highlighted the revival of positive psychology during a period of significant demographic shifts in the United States that has resulted in a more culturally diverse society. The production of a culturally informed positive psychology theory, research, and interventions is evidence of how the field has benefited by this timing, but there is room for growth in the integration of multicultural psychology approaches in positive psychology. We reviewed frameworks for multicultural research (Hall et al., 2016) and cultural competencies (APA, 2017) that provide a foundation for expanding conceptual frameworks and measures in positive psychology that are culturally relevant to the diverse members in our society. Next, we featured measurement issues (e.g., conceptual equivalence, normative equivalence) that positive psychology researchers and practitioners should consider in determining the cultural relevance of positive psychological measures with a particular client or group. Our review of the positive psychology assessment research pointed to two constructs, subjective well-being and problem solving, and their related measures that have generated a great deal of research both domestically and internationally to support their use with diverse cultural groups; we provided a sampling of the cultural evidence produced for these respective measurements. Next, we outlined an assessment process beginning with gathering client information in a manner that integrates cultural data, utilizing multiple data sources, and finally communicating the assessment results in a culturally congruent manner. Finally, the chapter concludes by providing research recommendations for advancing multicultural positive psychology assessment and presenting a case study of a psychologist utilizing the recommendations in this chapter when working with a fictional Chinese international student who was seeking help for her adjustment to the United States and reported a fear of failing in a demanding major.

REFERENCES

Ajibade, A., Hook, J. N., Utsey, S. O., Davis, D. E., & Van Tongeren, D. R. (2016). Racial/ethnic identity, religious commitment, and well-being in African Americans. *Journal of Black Psychology, 42,* 244–258. http://dx.doi.org/10.1177/0095798414568115

Allen, J. (2007). A multicultural assessment supervision model to guide research and practice. *Professional Psychology: Research and Practice, 38,* 248–258. http://dx.doi.org/10.1037/0735-7028.38.3.248

American Psychological Association. (2003). Guidelines on multicultural education, training, research, practice, and organizational change for psychologists. *American Psychologist, 58,* 377–402. http://dx.doi.org/10.1037/0003-066X.58.5.377

American Psychological Association. (2017). *Ethical principles of psychologists and code of conduct* (2002, Amended June 1, 2010 and January 1, 2017). Retrieved from http://www.apa.org/ethics/code/index.aspx

Bai, X., Wu, C., Zheng, R., & Ren, X. (2011). The psychometric evaluation of the Satisfaction With Life Scale using a nationally representative sample of China. *Journal of Happiness Studies, 12,* 183–197. http://dx.doi.org/10.1007/s10902-010-9186-x

Byrne, B. M., Oakland, T., Leong, F. T. L., van de Vijver, F. J. R., Hambleton, R. K., Cheung, F. M., & Bartram, D. (2009). A critical analysis of cross-cultural research and testing practices: Implications for improved education and training in psychology. *Training and Education in Professional Psychology, 3,* 94–105. http://dx.doi.org/10.1037/a0014516

Constantine, M. G., Alleyne, V. L., Wallace, B. D., & Franklin-Jackson, D. C. (2006). Africentric cultural values: Their relation to positive mental health in African American adolescent girls. *Journal of Black Psychology, 32,* 141–154. http://dx.doi.org/10.1177/0095798406286801

Dana, R. H. (1996). Culturally competent assessment practice in the United States. *Journal of Personality Assessment, 66,* 472–487. http://dx.doi.org/10.1207/s15327752jpa6603_2

Dana, R. H. (2005). *Multicultural assessment: Principles, applications, and examples.* Mahwah, NJ: Erlbaum. http://dx.doi.org/10.4324/9781410612540

Dana, R. H. (2014). Personality tests and psychological science: Instruments, populations, practice. In F. T. L. Leong, L. Comas-Diaz, G. C. Nagayama Hall, V. C. McLoyd, & J. E. Trimble (Eds.), *APA handbook of multicultural psychology: Vol. 2. Applications and training* (pp. 181–196). Washington, DC: American Psychological Association. http://dx.doi.org/10.1037/14187-011

Diener, E., Emmons, R. A., Larsen, R. J., & Griffin, S. (1985). The Satisfaction With Life Scale. *Journal of Personality Assessment, 49,* 71–75. http://dx.doi.org/10.1207/s15327752jpa4901_13

Di Fabio, A., & Gori, A. (2016). Measuring adolescent life satisfaction: Psychometric properties of the Satisfaction With Life Scale in a sample of Italian adolescents and young adults. *Journal of Psychoeducational Assessment, 34,* 501–506. http://dx.doi.org/10.1177/0734282915621223

Dodd, N. M. (2016). Household hunger, standard of living and satisfaction with life in Alice, South Africa. *Journal of Psychology in Africa, 26,* 284–287. http://dx.doi.org/10.1080/14330237.2016.1185918

Downey, C. A., & Chang, E. C. (2014). Positive psychology: Current knowledge, multicultural considerations, and the future of the movement. In F. T. L. Leong, L. Comas-Diaz, G. C. Nagayama Hall, V. C. McLoyd, & J. E. Trimble (Eds.), *APA handbook of multicultural psychology: Vol. 2. Applications and training* (pp. 133–149). Washington, DC: American Psychological Association. http://dx.doi.org/10.1037/14187-008

Edwards, L. M., Ong, A. D., & Lopez, S. J. (2007). Hope measurement in Mexican American youth. *Hispanic Journal of Behavioral Sciences, 29,* 225–241. http://dx.doi.org/10.1177/0739986307299692

Flores, L. Y., Ojeda, L., Huang, Y., Gee, D., & Lee, S. (2006). The relation of acculturation, problem-solving appraisal, and career decision-making self-efficacy to Mexican American high school students' educational goal. *Journal of Counseling Psychology, 53,* 260–266. http://dx.doi.org/10.1037/0022-0167.53.2.260

Flores, L. Y., Spanierman, L. B., & Obasi, E. M. (2003). Professional and ethical issues in career assessment with diverse racial and ethnic groups. *Journal of Career Assessment, 11,* 76–95. http://dx.doi.org/10.1177/106907202237461

Grieger, I. (2008). A cultural assessment framework and interview protocol. In L. A. Suzuki & J. G. Ponterotto (Eds.), *Handbook of multicultural assessment: Clinical, psychological, and educational applications* (pp. 132–161). San Francisco, CA: Jossey-Bass.

Hall, G. C. N., Yip, T., & Zárate, M. A. (2016). On becoming multicultural in a monocultural research world: A conceptual approach to studying ethnocultural diversity. *American Psychologist, 71,* 40–51. http://dx.doi.org/10.1037/a0039734

Helms, J. E. (2006). Fairness is not validity or cultural bias in racial-group assessment: A quantitative perspective. *American Psychologist, 61,* 845–859. http://dx.doi.org/10.1037/0003-066X.61.8.845

Heppner, P. P., Heppner, M. J., Lee, D.-G., Wang, Y.-W., Park, H.-J., & Wang, L.-F. (2006). Development and validation of a collectivistic coping styles inventory. *Journal of Counseling Psychology, 53,* 107–125. http://dx.doi.org/10.1037/0022-0167.53.1.107

Heppner, P. P., & Petersen, C. H. (1982). The development and implications of a personal problem-solving inventory. *Journal of Counseling Psychology, 29,* 66–75. http://dx.doi.org/10.1037/0022-0167.29.1.66

Heppner, P. P., Pretorius, T. B., Wei, M., Lee, D.-G., & Wang, Y. W. (2002). Examining the generalizability of problem-solving appraisal in black South Africans. *Journal of Counseling Psychology, 49,* 484–498. http://dx.doi.org/10.1037/0022-0167.49.4.484

Huang, Y. P., & Flores, L. Y. (2011). Exploring the validity of the Problem-Solving Inventory with Mexican American high school students. *Journal of Career Assessment, 19,* 431–441. http://dx.doi.org/10.1177/1069072711409720

Leong, F. T. L., Leung, K., & Cheung, F. M. (2010). Integrating cross-cultural psychology research methods into ethnic minority psychology. *Cultural Diversity & Ethnic Minority Psychology, 16,* 590–597. http://dx.doi.org/10.1037/a0020127

Moore, J. L., III, & Constantine, M. G. (2005). Development and initial validation of the collectivistic coping styles measure with African American, Asian, and Latin American international students. *Journal of Mental Health Counseling, 27,* 329–347. http://dx.doi.org/10.17744/mehc.27.4.frcqxuy1we5nwpqe

Muzindutsi, P. F., & Sekhampu, T. J. (2014). Determinants of wellbeing in a South African township. *International Journal of Social Sciences and Humanity Studies, 6,* 47–57.

Neville, H. A., Heppner, P. P., & Wang, L. (1997). Relations among racial identity attitudes, perceived stressors, and coping styles in African American college students. *Journal of Counseling & Development, 75,* 303–311. http://dx.doi.org/10.1002/j.1556-6676.1997.tb02345.x

Nota, L., Heppner, P. P., Soresi, S., & Heppner, M. J. (2009). Examining cultural validity of the Problem-Solving Inventory (PSI) in Italy. *Journal of Career Assessment, 17,* 478–494. http://dx.doi.org/10.1177/1069072709339490

Ojeda, L., Edwards, L. M., Hardin, E. E., & Piña-Watson, B. (2014). The role of behavioral and cognitive cultural orientation on Mexican American college students' life satisfaction. *Journal of Hispanic Higher Education, 13,* 63–74. http://dx.doi.org/10.1177/1538192713513464

Ojeda, L., Flores, L. Y., & Navarro, R. L. (2011). Social cognitive predictors of Mexican American college students' academic and life satisfaction. *Journal of Counseling Psychology, 58,* 61–71. http://dx.doi.org/10.1037/a0021687

Ozer, E. J., & Schotland, M. (2011). Psychological empowerment among urban youth: Measure development and relationship to psychosocial functioning. *Health Education & Behavior, 38,* 348–356. http://dx.doi.org/10.1177/1090198110373734

Pavot, W., & Diener, E. (1993). Review of the Satisfaction With Life Scale. *Psychological Assessment, 5,* 164–172. http://dx.doi.org/10.1037/1040-3590.5.2.164

Pedrotti, J. T., & Edwards, L. M. (Eds.). (2014). *Perspectives on the intersection of multiculturalism and positive psychology.* New York, NY: Springer. http://dx.doi.org/10.1007/978-94-017-8654-6

Pedrotti, J. T., Edwards, L. M., & Lopez, S. J. (2009). Positive psychology within a cultural context. In C. R. Snyder & S. J. Lopez (Eds.), *The Oxford handbook of positive psychology* (pp. 49–57). New York, NY: Oxford University Press.

Ramírez, M., Ford, M. E., Stewart, A. L., & Teresi, J. A. (2005). Measurement issues in health disparities research. *Health Services Research, 40,* 1640–1657. http://dx.doi.org/10.1111/j.1475-6773.2005.00450.x

Ridley, C. R., Li, L. C., & Hill, C. L. (1998). Multicultural assessment: Reexamination, reconceptualization, and practical application. *The Counseling Psychologist, 26,* 827–910. http://dx.doi.org/10.1177/0011000098266001

Roysircar, G. (2014). Multicultural assessment: Individual and contextual dynamic sizing. In F. T. L. Leong, L. Comas-Diaz, G. C. Nagayama Hall, V. C. McLoyd, & J. E. Trimble (Eds.), *APA handbook of multicultural psychology: Vol. 1. Theory and research* (pp. 141–160). Washington, DC: American Psychological Association. http://dx.doi.org/10.1037/14189-008

Roysircar-Sodowsky, G., & Kuo, P. Y. (2001). Determining cultural validity of personality assessment: Some guidelines. In D. Pope-Davis & H. L. K. Coleman (Eds.), *The intersection of race, class, and gender: Implications for multicultural counseling* (pp. 213–240). Thousand Oaks, CA: Sage. http://dx.doi.org/10.4135/9781452231846.n9

Sachs, J. (2003). Validation of the Satisfaction With Life Scale in a sample of Hong Kong University students. *Psychologia, 46,* 225–234.

Schinke, S., Schwinn, T., Hopkins, J., & Wahlstrom, L. (2016). Drug abuse risk and protective factors among Hispanic adolescents. *Preventive Medicine Reports, 3,* 185–188. http://dx.doi.org/10.1016/j.pmedr.2016.01.012

Singelis, T. M., Yamada, A. M., Barrio, C., Laney, J. H., Her, P., Ruiz-Anaya, A., & Lennertz, S. T. (2006). Metric equivalence of the Bidimensional Acculturation Scale, the Satisfaction With Life Scale, and the Self-Construal Scale across Spanish and English language version. *Hispanic Journal of Behavioral Sciences, 28,* 231–244. http://dx.doi.org/10.1177/0739986306286682

Sue, D. W., & Sue, D. (2016). *Counseling the culturally diverse: Theory and practice* (7th ed.). New York, NY: Wiley.

U.S. Census Bureau. (2016). *Current Population Survey.* Retrieved from http://www.census.gov/quickfacts/table/PST045215/00

Utsey, S. O., Ponterotto, J. G., Reynolds, A. L., & Cancelli, A. A. (2000). Racial discrimination, coping, life satisfaction, and self-esteem among African Americans. *Journal of Counseling & Development, 78,* 72–80. http://dx.doi.org/10.1002/j.1556-6676.2000.tb02562.x

Vittersø, J., Biswas-Diener, R., & Diener, E. (2005). The divergent meanings of life satisfaction: Item response modeling of the Satisfaction With Life Scale in Greenland and Norway. *Social Indicators Research, 74,* 327–348. http://dx.doi.org/10.1007/s11205-004-4644-7

Westaway, M. S., & Maluka, C. S. (2005). Are life satisfaction and self-esteem distinct constructs? A black South African perspective. *Psychological Reports, 97,* 567–575. http://dx.doi.org/10.2466/pr0.97.2.567-575

Whisman, M. A., & Judd, C. M. (2016). A cross-national analysis of measurement invariance of the Satisfaction With Life Scale. *Psychological Assessment, 28,* 239–244. http://dx.doi.org/10.1037/pas0000181

Winograd, G., & Tryon, G. S. (2009). Counseling expectations among students in an opportunity program: Dispositional and cultural influences. *Journal of Counseling & Development, 87,* 438–448. http://dx.doi.org/10.1002/j.1556-6678.2009.tb00128.x

Wong, Y. J., Ho, R. M., Li, P., Shin, M., & Tsai, P.-C. (2011). Chinese Singaporean' lay beliefs, adherence to Asian values, and subjective well-being. *Personality and Individual Differences, 50,* 822–827. http://dx.doi.org/10.1016/j.paid.2011.01.003

Wu, D. H., & Yao, G. (2006). Analysis of factorial invariance across gender in the Taiwan version of the Satisfaction With Life Scale. *Personality and Individual Differences, 40,* 1259–1268. http://dx.doi.org/10.1016/j.paid.2005.11.012

II

COGNITIVE MODELS AND MEASURES

5

Optimism

Charles S. Carver and Michael F. Scheier

Optimists are people who expect good things to happen to them; *pessimists* are people who expect bad things to happen to them. Optimists and pessimists differ in several ways that have a big impact on their lives. They differ in how they approach problems and challenges they face, and they differ in the manner and the success with which they cope with life's difficulties.

Definitions of optimism and pessimism rest on people's expectations for the future. This grounding in expectations links optimism and pessimism to a long tradition of expectancy–value models of motivation. The optimism construct thus connects to decades of theory and research on human motives and how they become expressed in behavior. We begin this chapter with a brief outline of the expectancy–value approach to motivation, to make clear the dynamics we think underlie optimism and pessimism.

EXPECTANCY–VALUE MODELS OF MOTIVATION

Expectancy–value theories begin by assuming that behavior is aimed at the pursuit of goals. Goals have a variety of labels, but in this chapter we want to emphasize their commonalities (see Carver & Scheier, 1998, 2013). *Goals* are actions, end states, or values that people see as either desirable or undesirable. People try to fit their behaviors—indeed fit their very selves—to what they see as desirable. They try to stay away from what they see as undesirable (think of the undesirable as "anti-goals"). The more important a goal is, the greater its

http://dx.doi.org/10.1037/0000138-005
Positive Psychological Assessment: A Handbook of Models and Measures, Second Edition,
M. W. Gallagher and S. J. Lopez (Editors)

value in the person's motivation. Without having a goal that matters, there is no reason to act.

The second element in expectancy–value theories is *expectancy*—a sense of confidence or doubt about the attainability of the goal value. If the person lacks confidence, again there will be no action. Doubts can dampen effort before the action starts or while it is ongoing. Only if people have enough confidence will they act and keep acting. When people are confident about an eventual outcome, effort continues even in the face of great adversity.

Goals Vary in Breadth and Abstractness

Goals vary from the very concrete and narrow, to those that pertain to a particular domain of life, to the very general. Expectancies have a comparable range of variation (Armor & Taylor, 1998; Carver & Scheier, 1998, 2013). You can be confident about having a fulfilling life, about making good impressions in social situations, about finding a nice place to vacation, about winning a particular tennis game, or about tying your shoes.

Which expectancies matter? Probably all of them. Expectancy-based theories generally suggest, explicitly or implicitly, that behavior is predicted best when the level of expectancy fits that of the behavior being predicted. Some say that prediction is best when you take into account several levels of specificity that pertain to the behavior (e.g., action-specific, domain-specific, and generalized). Many events in life are new, or evolve over time. In such situations, generalized expectations may be particularly useful in predicting behavior.

The principles that apply to a focused confidence also apply to the generalized sense of confidence: optimism. When we talk about optimism and pessimism, the confidence is diffuse and broad in scope. When confronting a challenge (whatever it is), optimists should tend to approach it with confidence and persistence (even if progress is difficult or slow). Pessimists should be doubtful and hesitant.

Given our view that optimism embodies expectancies that are very broad in scope, it should perhaps come as no surprise that we also assume that optimism is relatively stable. The origins of optimism are rooted in the genetic variation among people (Mosing, Pedersen, Martin, & Wright, 2010; Plomin et al., 1992) and emerge from a lifetime of early and later life experiences (Heinonen et al., 2006). Once established, it should not change so easily. Thus, optimism is best viewed as similar to a personality disposition or trait. The fact that one's level of optimism does remain relatively stable across time is now well documented (Matthews, Räikkönen, Sutton-Tyrrell, & Kuller, 2004), although it is perhaps more labile during times of life transitions (Segerstrom, 2007).

Optimism as Confidence Rather Than Control

Another conceptual issue that arises is the extent to which optimism overlaps with the concept of control or personal efficacy (Bandura, 1986, 1997). These constructs also have strong overtones of expecting desired outcomes to take place. However, they differ in assumptions made about how the outcomes are expected to come to pass. Self-efficacy is a construct in which the self as a causal agent is paramount. The same is true of the concept of control. When people perceive themselves as in control, they are assuming that the desired outcome will occur through their personal efforts (Carver et al., 2000).

In contrast to this, our view of optimism always has been that it is broader than that. People can be optimistic because they believe they are immensely talented, because they are hardworking, because they are blessed, because they have friends in the right places, or any combination of these or other factors that create good outcomes (cf. Murphy et al., 2000). Clearly circumstances exist in which personal efficacy is the key determinant of a desired outcome. However, there are also many cases in which the causal determinant of the outcome is far less important than the occurrence of the outcome. We believe those cases also belong under the umbrella of the optimism construct.

This view has sometimes caused others to question whether optimists can really be expected to exert efforts toward desired goals. Why should optimists not just sit quietly waiting for all good things to happen to them from out of the sky? (As is described shortly, they do not seem to do this.) Our answer is that optimists appear to expect good outcomes contingent on remaining in pursuit of those outcomes. It may be one's own efforts that turn the tide, or it may be that, by remaining involved, the person is able to take advantage of breaks that fall his or her way. In either case, the optimist expects the best but also understands the need to be part of the matrix of influences on the outcome.

Effects of Optimism on Coping Responses and Well-Being

A fairly substantial body of research has investigated various hypotheses that derive from this conceptual analysis (for a broad review, see Carver, Scheier, & Segerstrom, 2010). Optimists differ from pessimists in the subjective well-being they enjoy when experiencing various kinds of adversity. They also differ in the ways they cope with difficulties in their lives (e.g., Carver & Scheier, 1999, 2017; Scheier, Carver, & Bridges, 2001; Solberg Nes & Segerstrom, 2006; see also Chapter 8 in this volume by Heppner et al.). Optimists are quicker to accept the reality of a challenge. They engage in more focused, active coping when such efforts are likely to be productive. They are less likely to show signs of disengagement or giving up pursuit of their goals. Indeed, optimism is related to better health outcomes in certain circumstances (for more information, see Bouchard, Carver, Mens, & Scheier, 2018; Mens, Scheier, & Carver, in press).

ASSESSMENT OF OPTIMISM

Several tools exist to measure individual differences in optimism and pessimism, all of which have roots in expectancy–value models of behavior. The measures have different focuses and characteristics, but in large part they share the same underlying conception.

Life Orientation Test

We began our own work on this topic by developing a measure called the Life Orientation Test, or LOT (Scheier & Carver, 1985). The LOT consists of eight coded items, plus fillers. Half the items are framed in an optimistic manner, half in a pessimistic manner, and respondents indicate their extent of agreement or disagreement with each item on a multipoint scale. The LOT has good psychometric properties. However, an important disadvantage of the scale is that some of the items seem to assess characteristics that are not limited solely to expectations per se (Scheier, Carver, & Bridges, 1994).

To address these issues, we created the Life Orientation Test—Revised (LOT–R; Scheier et al., 1994). The LOT–R (see Appendix 5.1) is briefer than the original (six coded items, three framed in each direction). We omitted or rewrote items that did not focus explicitly on expectancies. The LOT–R has good internal consistency (Cronbach's alpha runs in the high .70s to low .80s) and is stable over time. In factor analyses, the positively worded and negatively worded items tend to load onto separate factors (we have more to say about this later). Because of the extensive item overlap between the original and the revised scale, correlations between the two scales are very high, hovering around .90 (Scheier et al., 1994). Given the improvements in the LOT–R, however, the original LOT is seldom used.

Scores on both the LOT and LOT–R are distributed continuously. Distributions tend to be skewed toward the optimistic, but not greatly so. We often refer to optimists and pessimists as though they were distinct groups, but that is a matter of linguistic convenience. There is no criterion for saying that a person is an optimist or a pessimist. Rather, people range from very optimistic to very pessimistic, with most falling somewhere in between.

Hopelessness Scale

Another measure that assesses an optimistic versus pessimistic orientation to life is the Hopelessness Scale (Beck, Weissman, Lester, & Trexler, 1974). This 20-item scale is similar in some respects to the pessimistic side of the LOT–R. However, it uses a true–false response format and is somewhat broader in its focus. That is, in addition to items concerning pessimism per se, it also includes items that measure affective experiences and giving-up tendencies (which form separate factors but are usually not separated from each other when using the scale). We believe that both of these are important concomitants of pessimism, but we also think they should be distinguished from pessimism per se. In addition, as Chang, D'Zurilla, and Maydeu-Olivares (1994) noted, many of this scale's items are fairly extreme in their expression of pessimism. This may make the measure less sensitive to variations within the less extreme part of the distribution.

In our own early work (Scheier & Carver, 1985), we found that the full scale correlated –.47 with the LOT. Chang et al. (1994) reported correlations between Hopelessness and the two subsets of LOT items of –.53 and –.67, suggesting more convergence. Lucas, Diener, and Suh (1996) also found a correlation of −.53 between the scale and the LOT, but from a variety of other data concluded that the two do not measure the same thing. We are inclined to regard the subset of items from the Hopelessness Scale that focus on expectancies for the future as a reasonable measure of optimism, but to regard the other items as distinct from optimism.

Generalized Expectancy of Success Scale

Another measure that is relevant to the assessment of optimism is the Generalized Expectancy of Success Scale (GESS; Fibel & Hale, 1978). It presents a set of situations, some specific, others more general, and respondents evaluate their likelihood of experiencing a success in each. The stem for each item is "In the future I expect that I will . . ." with response options ranging from *highly improbable* to *highly probable*. Most of the items refer to successful outcomes, with a few (reverse scored) relating to failures. The situations range fairly widely. Perhaps in part for this reason, the GESS has four factors, each focused around one domain (Fibel & Hale, 1978).

One criticism of the GESS is that some of the original items (e.g., "be a good parent," "have a successful marital relationship") don't fit some populations (Mearns, 1989). In part for this reason, the GESS underwent a minor revision (Hale, Fiedler, & Cochran, 1992). In the revision, such items were rewritten, several new ones were created, and the results were distilled to 25 items by examining item–total correlations. Reliance on this procedure rather than factor analysis, however, leaves unclear how many factors the GESS—Revised contains.

Correlations ranging from .55 (Smith, Pope, Rhodewalt, & Poulton, 1989) to .40 (Hale et al., 1992) have been reported between the GESS and the LOT, suggesting that the two assess somewhat different qualities. The original GESS correlated with the Hopelessness Scale −.69 (among men) and −.31 (among women) in two small samples reported by Fibel and Hale (1978).

AN ALTERNATIVE CONCEPTUALIZATION

As indicated previously, we prefer to assess expectancies directly. However, there is also a way to measure them indirectly. This approach relies on the idea that expectancies for the future derive from people's view of the causes of events in the past (Peterson & Seligman, 1984; Seligman, 1991). If explanations for past failures emphasize causes that are stable, internal to the person, and broadly applicable, expectancies for the future (even in different domains) will likely be negative. The opposite combination of explanations should lead to expectancies that are more positive. The terms *explanatory style* and *attributional style* are used to identify the consistent profile of attributions that a person makes (Peterson & Seligman, 1984; Seligman, 1991). People are said to have a more optimistic or pessimistic explanatory style, depending on whether their normative pattern of attributions primes them for holding positive or negative future expectations, respectively.

Attributional style is indexed by a questionnaire, called the Attributional Style Questionnaire or ASQ, which asks people to imagine hypothetical negative and positive events (Peterson et al., 1982). Respondents then write down the likely cause for the event and rate that cause on attributional dimensions, using a 7-point scale to reflect how important each of the attributional dimensions was to producing the cause. Test–retest correlations across a 5-week interval were adequate (ranging from .57 to .69). Peterson et al. (1982) reported adequate internal reliability when all attributional dimensions were combined into an overall index, but lower reliabilities when the attributional dimensions were examined separately. It turns out that the average correlation among the three attributional dimensions was much higher for the positive scenarios (approximately .50) than for the negative scenarios (approximately .30). The average correlation between the two sets of scenarios (positive and negative) hovered close to zero. Because of differences in the psychometric properties of responses to the positive versus negative scenarios, researchers typically ask respondents to respond only to the negative set of scenarios in their studies (Schulman, Seligman, & Amsterdam, 1987).

A second method of assessing attributional style is called Content Analysis of Verbatim Explanations (CAVE; Peterson, Luborsky, & Seligman, 1983; Peterson, Schulman, Castellon, & Seligman, 1992). It involves assembling a sample of written or spoken material from a person—letters, diaries, interviews, speeches, and so on—that contain statements about explanations for outcomes. The statements are then analyzed for their attributional qualities. The CAVE is a flexible assessment tool, inasmuch as it allows inferences to be drawn about attributional style from readily available archival data. It has been used to study how attributional style predicts the longevity of baseball Hall of Famers, using player quotes found in newspapers about why their team might have won or lost a game (Peterson & Seligman, 1987). It was also used to predict the outcome of political elections, using quotes drawn from the acceptance speeches of major party candidates (Zullow, Oettingen, Peterson, & Seligman, 1988).

The direct approach to the assessment of optimism and the indirect approach to assessment via attributional style have led to their own research literatures, each of which sheds light on the nature and function of optimism and pessimism (see also hope, another member of this theoretical family, which is discussed by Snyder, 1994, and by Gallagher et al. in Chapter 6 of this volume). In this chapter, though, we focus largely on optimism as we have operationalized it (Scheier & Carver, 1985, 1992; Scheier et al., 1994)—that is, in terms of self-reports of generalized expectancies. This focus is driven by the observation that use of the attributional approach to the assessment of optimism has diminished significantly over the years.

We would speculate that use of attributional measures has waned in part because of the complex nature of its format and scoring. It is noteworthy that much of the recent research on optimism addresses associations between optimism and health. Increasingly, information about these associations is gathered by large epidemiological studies. Such studies require efficient assessment, the briefer the better. The LOT–R, with only six items, provides a good candidate for such studies. Indeed, the brevity of the LOT–R even makes it preferable to some of the other instruments that capture optimism directly.

CONSTRUCT MEASUREMENT ISSUES

As in the assessment of any psychological construct, several issues have emerged over the years concerning the measurement of optimism and pessimism. Indeed, several issues were raised in the preceding sections.

Operationalization of Generality

One issue that is relevant to the assessment of optimism is how best to operationalize its breadth. That is, optimism is considered to be a generalized expectancy, one that is broad in scope. There are at least two ways in which that generality can be operationalized.

One approach is to survey broadly among specific life domains (e.g., social interaction, professional achievement), assessing expectancies in each domain. One can then aggregate or integrate the expectancies across the domains. If all relevant domains are adequately sampled in this survey, the aggregate index would be a reasonable measure of optimism. This is the approach taken in the GESS (Fibel & Hale, 1978) and in questionnaires on attributional style. The other approach is to frame items not in terms of specific domains, but in terms of the broad generality of life as a whole. Items written using this approach are more abstract.

Each of these approaches has advantages and disadvantages. The aggregation approach asks about specific domains. Respondents must integrate information across at least a few events before making the response, but they do not have to integrate very far. This is a plus, as accuracy should be high. In contrast, the approach using general items requires people to merge expectancies across multiple domains and report accurately on that overall sense of confidence versus doubt about life. It might be harder to think about optimism in general than it is about optimism in specific domains.

The disadvantage of the aggregation approach is that it makes two assumptions that may not be correct: First, it assumes that the generalized sense of optimism is really the summation of a set of specific expectancies. This may not be true. There is evidence that global self-esteem is different from the sum of specific areas of self-esteem (Marsh, 1986), and the same issue can be raised about expectancies. Generalized optimism may instead be an emergent quality, different from the sum of the contributors that lie behind it. There is evidence from several studies that generalized expectancies do not relate strongly to various specific expectancies (Scheier et al., 1989; Taylor et al., 1992), which tends to support this argument.

The other assumption made in the aggregation approach is that different individuals weight the various domains of life in roughly the same way. If, however, a domain matters a lot to one person and not at all to another, confidence of success in that domain should influence the overall sense of optimism more in the person for whom the domain matters a great deal.

Dimensionality of Optimism and Pessimism

Another issue, also alluded to previously in the chapter, may be a methodological issue, but it may also be a conceptual issue. The items of the LOT and LOT–R typically yield two factors, one defined by the positively framed items, the other defined by the negatively framed items (Kubzansky, Kubzansky, & Maselko, 2004; Marshall, Wortman, Kusulas, Hervig, & Vickers, 1992). The two subscales have somewhat different personality correlates (Marshall et al., 1992) and are only moderately correlated (Oreskovic & Goodman, 2013; Scheier & Carver, 1985; Scheier, Carver, & Bridges, 1994). Moreover, some studies (though not all) have found one subscale to be more important than the other in predicting outcomes (Kim, Park, & Peterson, 2011; Robinson-Whelen, Kim, MacCallum, & Kiecolt-Glaser, 1997), though which subscale is more important varies from study to study.

The question is what to make of this difference between the two subsets of items. Some argue that we should reconceptualize optimism as two distinct, albeit correlated, constructs—one reflecting expectations for positive events, and one reflecting expectations for negative events (Marshall et al., 1992). On the other hand, some have argued that this two-factor model merely reflects method artifacts (Rauch, Schweizer, & Moosbrugger, 2007).

Researchers have turned to confirmatory factor analysis to evaluate the possibility that the two factors are due to method artifacts. Several studies found that a model with a single optimism/pessimism factor and a method artifact factor better fit the data than a model with separate optimism and pessimism factors (Monzani, Steca, & Greco, 2014; Rauch et al., 2007; Vautier, Raufaste, & Cariou, 2003). It is worth noting, however, that both models adequately fit the data from these studies, and differences between model fit indices were small. Furthermore, identifying the method artifact that could account for the two-factor model has proven difficult.

Modifications of the LOT have suggested that neither extreme response options nor positive versus negative framing explain the two-factor model (Kubzansky et al., 2004; Segerstrom, Evans, & Eisenlohr-Moul, 2011). Another study suggested that social desirability might explain the two-factor model (Rauch et al., 2007). However, the final model in that study suffered from several limitations, including unexplained correlated errors among several pessimism items, which precludes a solution based on a single factor (Vautier et al., 2003). More recently, researchers have attempted to address the question of dimensionality with item-response theory (Chiesi, Galli, Primi, Innocenti Borgi, & Bonacchi, 2013; Steca, Monzani, Greco, Chiesi, & Primi, 2015), but these results have also been somewhat inconclusive.

In sum, despite several decades of psychometric research, there is still no consensus on whether the distinction between optimism and pessimism is meaningful. It is clear that efforts to answer this question will not abate in the future. Going forward, we would encourage researchers to provide information about how the optimism and pessimism factors each relate to the outcome of interest, as well as information about how the combined scale predicts the outcome. If this policy is followed, studies will accumulate over time that will enable meta-analyses that will provide yet another perspective on whether differences between optimism and pessimism matter.

DISCRIMINANT VALIDITY

Discriminant validity has to do with the extent to which the optimism construct differs from other constructs in personality psychology (cf. Lucas et al., 1996). In this section, we consider potential overlap between optimism/pessimism and several other seemingly similar constructs.

Optimism Versus Negative Affectivity

Pessimism has some resemblance to negative affectivity or neuroticism (Smith et al., 1989), one of the Big Five personality factors. Negative affectivity is defined by a tendency to worry and be anxious, to experience other unpleasant emotions, and to be pessimistic. Smith et al. (1989) found that the LOT related strongly to a negative affectivity scale (see also Marshall & Lang, 1990). Smith et al. (1989) also found that correlations between optimism and outcome variables were sharply reduced when negative affectivity was controlled.

Does this imply that pessimism is essentially the same as negative affectivity? No. When asking about predictive overlap between optimism and negative affectivity, it is just as important to examine the issue the other way around. Negative affectivity is a broad construct. It incorporates the quality of pessimism, but other qualities as well. To ask whether an effect attributed to pessimism is really an effect of negative affectivity also raises the question of whether any aspect of negative affectivity other than its pessimism component matters to such effects (see Scheier et al., 1994, for additional discussion of this point).

Furthermore, subsequent research has made it clear that measures of negative affectivity or neuroticism do not always have such a large effect on associations between optimism and other relevant variables. Scheier et al. (1999) found that optimism predicted disease-related rates of rehospitalization after coronary artery bypass graft surgery, even when the effects of self-esteem, neuroticism, and depression were controlled. Kim, Smith, and Kubzansky (2014) showed that optimism prospectively predicted heart failure, controlling for differences in anxiety, depressive symptoms, and hostility. Tindle et al. (2009) found that optimism prospectively predicted all-cause mortality after controlling for depressive symptoms and hostility. And Scheier et al. (1994) found that optimism retained predictive power after controlling for neuroticism, trait anxiety, self-mastery, and self-esteem (see also Miciuk, Jankowski, & Oleś, 2016; Steptoe, Wright, Kunz-Ebrecht, & Iliffe, 2006).

Optimism Versus Unrealistic Optimism

Another important conceptual distinction to be made is between optimism and what is called *unrealistic optimism* (sometimes called *optimistic bias*). Unrealistic optimism refers to the tendency on the part of people to see their future as more positive than it can be (Shepperd, Klein, Waters, & Weinstein, 2013; Shepperd, Waters, Weinstein, & Klein, 2015). This is reflected in the observation that when people are asked to estimate the occurrence of some future negative event, for example the likelihood of getting heart disease, the averaged group estimate is usually more positive than the group's established risk is known to be (based, for example, on known prevalence data).

How do optimism (as we have discussed it here) and unrealistic optimism relate? Data on this issue are scant, as the two research areas have largely evolved independent of each other. Intuitively, one might assume that optimism and unrealistic optimism are somehow linked. After all, both deal with a kind of positivity in outlook. The fact is, however, that the two constructs are largely unrelated empirically (e.g., Klein & Zajac, 2009). It is uncertain why. Perhaps it is due to the level of generality of the two concepts. Optimism reflects expectancies that are very broad and generalized, whereas unrealistic optimism reflects expectations for very specific events and outcomes. This may lead to the decoupling of the two. Regardless of the cause, it appears that optimism and unrealistic optimism should not be taken as the same or very similar constructs.

FUTURE DEVELOPMENT IN MEASUREMENT

How will efforts to assess optimism evolve in future years? At least three possibilities stand out as likely directions for further work.

Further Discriminant Validity

One never-ending issue, in measuring any construct, is discriminant validity. The theorist–researcher is always fighting a holding action against the potential erosion of confidence in a measure by the challenges of new constructs. Indeed, even if we were absolutely certain that optimism is distinct from every single other construct that now exists, the problem would still remain, because psychologists of the 21st century doubtlessly will develop new constructs. When those constructs arrive, one or more of them may pose a challenge to optimism as a key variable. When that happens, people interested in optimism will have another discrimination to examine.

State Measures of Optimism

Another issue concerning the assessment of optimism that is sure to receive attention derives from the broad issue of state versus trait measures. It has long been recognized in the literature of emotions that people can have transient emotions, but people also vary in chronic tendencies to experience a particular emotion. Thus, there is merit in developing ways to assess both the current level of state anxiety and the normative (trait or dispositional) tendency to be anxious (Spielberger, Gorsuch, & Lushene, 1970). Although the point may have been made first with respect to emotions (and proneness to certain emotional experiences), in principle the same issue can be raised for any characteristic that varies over time and situations and also varies as a disposition. We became interested in optimism as a trait that remains fairly stable across time. However, there is little doubt that even a serious pessimist varies somewhat in his or her pessimism over changing circumstances, as does the optimist. To measure such changes over time and situations requires a state measure.

Relation Between Domain and Generalized Expectancies

A final issue that seems likely to receive additional attention concerns the fact that expectancies exist at multiple levels of abstraction. As noted earlier, there is some reason to believe that these expectancies are not strongly related. An important question is how these levels of abstraction function. Does the best prediction come from taking a combination of expectancies into account? Does the best prediction come from a level of abstraction that is close to that of the outcome? Might the answers to such questions differ from outcome to outcome? These are some of the questions to be addressed in future work.

FUTURE APPLICATIONS

Although the focus of this chapter is on assessment, it seems appropriate to close with a few brief comments on future applications of the LOT–R and the optimism construct more broadly. We are personality and health psychologists. As such, we have been interested primarily in how this basic quality of personality relates to behavior and affect, and how it differentiates people's responses to stressful circumstances. We intend to continue to investigate mechanisms by which these differences between people are manifested in their experiences.

We have devoted less attention to the question of how pessimism might be changed into optimism. There is, however, research evidence that such changes can indeed occur (Antoni et al., 2001), though the magnitude of the change in that study was not great. One avenue for further exploration is whether such recently acquired optimism functions in the same way as optimism that develops by more typical pathways. Investigating such questions will require research that takes place over longer time spans than has been true of past work. Yet the questions invite study. We look forward to finding out how they are answered.

APPENDIX 5.1
ITEMS OF THE LIFE ORIENTATION TEST—REVISED (LOT-R), A MEASURE OF GENERALIZED OPTIMISM VERSUS PESSIMISM

1. In uncertain times, I usually expect the best.
2. It's easy for me to relax. (Filler)
3. If something can go wrong for me, it will.[a]
4. I'm always optimistic about my future.
5. I enjoy my friends a lot. (Filler)
6. It's important for me to keep busy. (Filler)
7. I hardly ever expect things to go my way.[a]
8. I don't get upset too easily. (Filler)
9. I rarely count on good things happening to me.[a]
10. Overall, I expect more good things to happen to me than bad.

Note. Respondents indicate the extent of their agreement with each item using a 5-point scale ranging from *strongly disagree* to *strongly agree*. After reverse coding the negatively worded items (those identified with the superscript "a"), the six nonfiller items are summed to produce an overall score. Reprinted from "Distinguishing Optimism From Neuroticism (and Trait Anxiety, Self-Mastery, and Self-Esteem): A Reevaluation of the Life Orientation Test," by M. F. Scheier, C. S. Carver, and M. W. Bridges, 1994, *Journal of Personality and Social Psychology, 67*, p. 1073. Copyright 1994 by the American Psychological Association.

REFERENCES

Antoni, M. H., Lehman, J. M., Kilbourn, K. M., Boyers, A. E., Culver, J. L., Alferi, S. M., . . . Carver, C. S. (2001). Cognitive-behavioral stress management intervention decreases the prevalence of depression and enhances benefit finding among women under treatment for early-stage breast cancer. *Health Psychology, 20*, 20–32. http://dx.doi.org/10.1037/0278-6133.20.1.20

Armor, D. A., & Taylor, S. E. (1998). Situated optimism: Specific outcome expectancies and self-regulation. In M. P. Zanna (Ed.), *Advances in experimental social psychology* (Vol. 30, pp. 309–379). San Diego, CA: Academic Press.

Bandura, A. (1986). *Social foundations of thought and action: A social cognitive theory.* Englewood Cliffs, NJ: Prentice-Hall.

Bandura, A. (1997). *Self-efficacy: The exercise of control.* New York, NY: Freeman.

Beck, A. T., Weissman, A., Lester, D., & Trexler, L. (1974). The measurement of pessimism: The Hopelessness Scale. *Journal of Consulting and Clinical Psychology, 42*, 861–865. http://dx.doi.org/10.1037/h0037562

Bouchard, L. C., Carver, C. S., Mens, M. G., & Scheier, M. F. (2018). Optimism, health, and well-being. In D. S. Dunn (Ed.), *Positive psychology: Established and emerging issues* (pp. 112–130). New York, NY: Routledge.

Carver, C. S., Harris, S. D., Lehman, J. M., Durel, L. A., Antoni, M. H., Spencer, S. M., & Pozo-Kaderman, C. (2000). How important is the perception of personal control? Studies of early stage breast cancer patients. *Personality and Social Psychology Bulletin, 26*, 139–149. http://dx.doi.org/10.1177/0146167200264001

Carver, C. S., & Scheier, M. F. (1998). *On the self-regulation of behavior.* New York, NY: Cambridge University Press. http://dx.doi.org/10.1017/CBO9781139174794

Carver, C. S., & Scheier, M. F. (1999). Optimism. In C. R. Snyder (Ed.), *Coping: The psychology of what works* (pp. 182–204). New York, NY: Oxford University Press.

Carver, C. S., & Scheier, M. F. (2013). Goals and emotion. In M. D. Robinson, E. R. Watkins, & E. Harmon-Jones (Eds.), *Guilford handbook of cognition and emotion* (pp. 176–194). New York, NY: Guilford Press.

Carver, C. S., & Scheier, M. F. (2017). Optimism, coping, and well-being. In C. Cooper & J. C. Quick (Eds.), *Wiley handbook of stress and health: A guide to research and practice* (pp. 400–414). Chichester, England: Wiley-Blackwell. http://dx.doi.org/10.1002/9781118993811.ch24

Carver, C. S., Scheier, M. F., & Segerstrom, S. C. (2010). Optimism. *Clinical Psychology Review, 30,* 879–889. http://dx.doi.org/10.1016/j.cpr.2010.01.006

Chang, E. C., D'Zurilla, T. J., & Maydeu-Olivares, A. (1994). Assessing the dimensionality of optimism and pessimism using a multimeasure approach. *Cognitive Therapy and Research, 18,* 143–160. http://dx.doi.org/10.1007/BF02357221

Chiesi, F., Galli, S., Primi, C., Innocenti Borgi, P., & Bonacchi, A. (2013). The accuracy of the Life Orientation Test—Revised (LOT–R) in measuring dispositional optimism: Evidence from item response theory analyses. *Journal of Personality Assessment, 95,* 523–529. http://dx.doi.org/10.1080/00223891.2013.781029

Fibel, B., & Hale, W. D. (1978). The Generalized Expectancy for Success Scale—A new measure. *Journal of Consulting and Clinical Psychology, 46,* 924–931. http://dx.doi.org/10.1037/0022-006X.46.5.924

Hale, W. D., Fiedler, L. R., & Cochran, C. D. (1992). The revised Generalized Expectancy for Success Scale: A validity and reliability study. *Journal of Clinical Psychology, 48,* 517–521. http://dx.doi.org/10.1002/1097-4679(199207)48:4<517::AID-JCLP2270480413>3.0.CO;2-Z

Heinonen, K., Räikkönen, K., Matthews, K. A., Scheier, M. F., Raitakari, O. T., Pulkki, L., & Keltikangas-Järvinen, L. (2006). Socioeconomic status in childhood and adulthood: Associations with dispositional optimism and pessimism over a 21-year follow-up. *Journal of Personality, 74,* 1111–1126. http://dx.doi.org/10.1111/j.1467-6494.2006.00404.x

Kim, E. S., Park, N., & Peterson, C. (2011). Dispositional optimism protects older adults from stroke: The Health and Retirement Study. *Stroke, 42,* 2855–2859. http://dx.doi.org/10.1161/STROKEAHA.111.613448

Kim, E. S., Smith, J., & Kubzansky, L. D. (2014). Prospective study of the association between dispositional optimism and incident heart failure. *Circulation: Heart Failure, 7,* 394–400. http://dx.doi.org/10.1161/CIRCHEARTFAILURE.113.000644

Klein, W. P., & Zajac, L. E. (2009). Imagining a rosy future: The psychology of optimism. In K. D. Markman, W. M. Klein, & J. A. Suhr (Eds.), *Handbook of imagination and mental simulation* (pp. 313–329). New York, NY: Psychology Press.

Kubzansky, L. D., Kubzansky, P. E., & Maselko, J. (2004). Optimism and pessimism in the context of health: Bipolar opposites or separate constructs? *Personality and Social Psychology Bulletin, 30,* 943–956. http://dx.doi.org/10.1177/0146167203262086

Lucas, R. E., Diener, E., & Suh, E. (1996). Discriminant validity of well-being measures. *Journal of Personality and Social Psychology, 71,* 616–628. http://dx.doi.org/10.1037/0022-3514.71.3.616

Marsh, H. W. (1986). Global self-esteem: Its relation to specific facets of self-concept and their importance. *Journal of Personality and Social Psychology, 51,* 1224–1236. http://dx.doi.org/10.1037/0022-3514.51.6.1224

Marshall, G. N., & Lang, E. L. (1990). Optimism, self-mastery, and symptoms of depression in women professionals. *Journal of Personality and Social Psychology, 59,* 132–139. http://dx.doi.org/10.1037/0022-3514.59.1.132

Marshall, G. N., Wortman, C. B., Kusulas, J. W., Hervig, L. K., & Vickers, R. R., Jr. (1992). Distinguishing optimism from pessimism: Relations to fundamental dimensions of mood and personality. *Journal of Personality and Social Psychology, 62,* 1067–1074. http://dx.doi.org/10.1037/0022-3514.62.6.1067

Matthews, K. A., Räikkönen, K., Sutton-Tyrrell, K., & Kuller, L. H. (2004). Optimistic attitudes protect against progression of carotid atherosclerosis in healthy middle-aged women. *Psychosomatic Medicine, 66,* 640–644. http://dx.doi.org/10.1097/01.psy.0000139999.99756.a5

Mearns, J. (1989). Measuring self-acceptance: Expectancy for success vs. self-esteem. *Journal of Clinical Psychology, 45,* 390–397. http://dx.doi.org/10.1002/1097-4679(198905)45:3<390::AID-JCLP2270450307>3.0.CO;2-S

Mens, M. G., Scheier, M. F., & Carver, C. S. (in press). Optimism and physical health. In K. Sweeny & M. Robbins (Eds.), *Wiley encyclopedia of health psychology*. New York, NY: Wiley.

Miciuk, L. R., Jankowski, T., & Oleś, P. (2016). Incremental validity of positive orientation: Predictive efficiency beyond the five-factor model. *Health Psychology Report, 4,* 294–302. http://dx.doi.org/10.5114/hpr.2016.59895

Monzani, D., Steca, P., & Greco, A. (2014). Brief report: Assessing dispositional optimism in adolescence—Factor structure and concurrent validity of the Life Orientation Test—Revised. *Journal of Adolescence, 37,* 97–101. http://dx.doi.org/10.1016/j.adolescence.2013.11.006

Mosing, M. A., Pedersen, N. L., Martin, N. G., & Wright, M. J. (2010). Sex differences in the genetic architecture of optimism and health and their interrelation: A study of Australian and Swedish twins. *Twin Research and Human Genetics, 13,* 322–329. http://dx.doi.org/10.1375/twin.13.4.322

Murphy, P. E., Ciarrocchi, J. W., Piedmont, R. L., Cheston, S., Peyrot, M., & Fitchett, G. (2000). The relation of religious belief and practices, depression, and hopelessness in persons with clinical depression. *Journal of Consulting and Clinical Psychology, 68,* 1102–1106. http://dx.doi.org/10.1037/0022-006X.68.6.1102

Oreskovic, N. M., & Goodman, E. (2013). Association of optimism with cardiometabolic risk in adolescents. *Journal of Adolescent Health, 52,* 407–412. http://dx.doi.org/10.1016/j.jadohealth.2012.09.011

Peterson, C., Luborsky, L., & Seligman, M. E. P. (1983). Attributions and depressive mood shifts: A case study using the symptom–context model. *Journal of Abnormal Psychology, 92,* 96–103. http://dx.doi.org/10.1037/0021-843X.92.1.96

Peterson, C., Schulman, P., Castellon, C., & Seligman, M. E. P. (1992). The explanatory style scoring manual. In C. P. Smith (Ed.), *Handbook of thematic analysis* (pp. 383–392). New York, NY: Cambridge University Press.

Peterson, C., & Seligman, M. E. P. (1984). Causal explanations as a risk factor for depression: Theory and evidence. *Psychological Review, 91,* 347–374. http://dx.doi.org/10.1037/0033-295X.91.3.347

Peterson, C., & Seligman, M. E. P. (1987). Explanatory style and illness. *Journal of Personality, 55,* 237–265. http://dx.doi.org/10.1111/j.1467-6494.1987.tb00436.x

Peterson, C., Semmel, A., von Baeyer, C., Abramson, L. Y., Metalsky, G. I., & Seligman, M. E. P. (1982). The Attributional Style Questionnaire. *Cognitive Therapy and Research, 6,* 287–299. http://dx.doi.org/10.1007/BF01173577

Plomin, R., Scheier, M. F., Bergeman, C. S., Pedersen, N. L., Nesselroade, J. R., & McClearn, G. E. (1992). Optimism, pessimism, and mental health: A twin/adoption analysis. *Personality and Individual Differences, 13,* 921–930. http://dx.doi.org/10.1016/0191-8869(92)90009-E

Rauch, W. A., Schweizer, K., & Moosbrugger, H. (2007). Method effects due to social desirability as a parsimonious explanation of the deviation from unidimensionality in LOT–R scores. *Personality and Individual Differences, 42,* 1597–1607. http://dx.doi.org/10.1016/j.paid.2006.10.035

Robinson-Whelen, S., Kim, C., MacCallum, R. C., & Kiecolt-Glaser, J. K. (1997). Distinguishing optimism from pessimism in older adults: Is it more important to be optimistic or not to be pessimistic? *Journal of Personality and Social Psychology, 73,* 1345–1353. http://dx.doi.org/10.1037/0022-3514.73.6.1345

Scheier, M. F., & Carver, C. S. (1985). Optimism, coping, and health: Assessment and implications of generalized outcome expectancies. *Health Psychology, 4,* 219–247. http://dx.doi.org/10.1037/0278-6133.4.3.219

Scheier, M. F., & Carver, C. S. (1992). Effects of optimism on psychological and physical well-being: Theoretical overview and empirical update. *Cognitive Therapy and Research, 16,* 201–228. http://dx.doi.org/10.1007/BF01173489

Scheier, M. F., Carver, C. S., & Bridges, M. W. (1994). Distinguishing optimism from neuroticism (and trait anxiety, self-mastery, and self-esteem): A reevaluation of the Life Orientation Test. *Journal of Personality and Social Psychology, 67,* 1063–1078. http://dx.doi.org/10.1037/0022-3514.67.6.1063

Scheier, M. F., Carver, C. S., & Bridges, M. W. (2001). Optimism, pessimism, and psychological well-being. In E. C. Chang (Ed.), *Optimism and pessimism: Implications for theory, research, and practice* (pp. 189–216). Washington, DC: American Psychological Association. http://dx.doi.org/10.1037/10385-009

Scheier, M. F., Matthews, K. A., Owens, J. F., Magovern, G. J., Sr., Lefebvre, R. C., Abbott, R. A., & Carver, C. S. (1989). Dispositional optimism and recovery from coronary artery bypass surgery: The beneficial effects on physical and psychological well-being. *Journal of Personality and Social Psychology, 57,* 1024–1040. http://dx.doi.org/10.1037/0022-3514.57.6.1024

Scheier, M. F., Matthews, K. A., Owens, J. F., Schulz, R., Bridges, M. W., Magovern, G. J., & Carver, C. S. (1999). Optimism and rehospitalization after coronary artery bypass graft surgery. *Archives of Internal Medicine, 159,* 829–835. http://dx.doi.org/10.1001/archinte.159.8.829

Schulman, P., Seligman, M. E. P., & Amsterdam, D. (1987). The Attributional Style Questionnaire is not transparent. *Behaviour Research and Therapy, 25,* 391–395. http://dx.doi.org/10.1016/0005-7967(87)90016-7

Segerstrom, S. C. (2007). Optimism and resources: Effects on each other and on health over 10 years. *Journal of Research in Personality, 41,* 772–786. http://dx.doi.org/10.1016/j.jrp.2006.09.004

Segerstrom, S. C., Evans, D. R., & Eisenlohr-Moul, T. A. (2011). Optimism and pessimism dimensions in the Life Orientation Test—Revised: Method and meaning. *Journal of Research in Personality, 45,* 126–129. http://dx.doi.org/10.1016/j.jrp.2010.11.007

Seligman, M. E. P. (1991). *Learned optimism.* New York, NY: Knopf.

Shepperd, J. A., Klein, W. M. P., Waters, E. A., & Weinstein, N. D. (2013). Taking stock of unrealistic optimism. *Perspectives on Psychological Science, 8,* 395–411. http://dx.doi.org/10.1177/1745691613485247

Shepperd, J. A., Waters, E., Weinstein, N. D., & Klein, W. M. P. (2015). A primer on unrealistic optimism. *Current Directions in Psychological Science, 24,* 232–237. http://dx.doi.org/10.1177/0963721414568341

Smith, T. W., Pope, M. K., Rhodewalt, F., & Poulton, J. L. (1989). Optimism, neuroticism, coping, and symptom reports: An alternative interpretation of the Life Orientation Test. *Journal of Personality and Social Psychology, 56,* 640–648. http://dx.doi.org/10.1037/0022-3514.56.4.640

Snyder, C. R. (1994). *The psychology of hope: You can get there from here.* New York, NY: Free Press.

Solberg Nes, L. S., & Segerstrom, S. C. (2006). Dispositional optimism and coping: A meta-analytic review. *Personality and Social Psychology Review, 10,* 235–251. http://dx.doi.org/10.1207/s15327957pspr1003_3

Spielberger, C. D., Gorsuch, R. L., & Lushene, R. E. (1970). *Manual for the State–Trait Anxiety Inventory.* Palo Alto, CA: Consulting Psychologists Press.

Steca, P., Monzani, D., Greco, A., Chiesi, F., & Primi, C. (2015). Item response theory analysis of the life orientation test-revised: Age and gender differential item functioning analyses. *Assessment, 22,* 341–350. http://dx.doi.org/10.1177/1073191114544471

Steptoe, A., Wright, C., Kunz-Ebrecht, S. R., & Iliffe, S. (2006). Dispositional optimism and health behaviour in community-dwelling older people: Associations with healthy ageing. *British Journal of Health Psychology, 11,* 71–84. http://dx.doi.org/10.1348/135910705X42850

Taylor, S. E., Kemeny, M. E., Aspinwall, L. G., Schneider, S. G., Rodriguez, R., & Herbert, M. (1992). Optimism, coping, psychological distress, and high-risk sexual behavior among men at risk for acquired immunodeficiency syndrome (AIDS). *Journal of Personality and Social Psychology, 63,* 460–473. http://dx.doi.org/10.1037/0022-3514.63.3.460

Tindle, H. A., Chang, Y. F., Kuller, L. H., Manson, J. E., Robinson, J. G., Rosal, M. C., . . . Matthews, K. A. (2009). Optimism, cynical hostility, and incident coronary heart disease and mortality in the Women's Health Initiative. *Circulation, 120,* 656–662. http://dx.doi.org/10.1161/CIRCULATIONAHA.108.827642

Vautier, S., Raufaste, E., & Cariou, M. (2003). Dimensionality of the Revised Life Orientation Test and the status of filler items. *International Journal of Psychology, 38,* 390–400. http://dx.doi.org/10.1080/00207590344000222

Zullow, H. M., Oettingen, G., Peterson, C., & Seligman, M. E. P. (1988). Pessimistic explanatory style in the historical record: CAVing LBJ, presidential candidates, and East versus West Berlin. *American Psychologist, 43,* 673–682. http://dx.doi.org/10.1037/0003-066X.43.9.673

6

Hope

Matthew W. Gallagher, Jennifer Teramoto Pedrotti,
Shane J. Lopez, and C. R. Snyder

Do you have hope? It is a simple question. If your answer is "yes," then how much hope do you have, and do you have enough? If the answer to the initial question is "no," then would you describe yourself as "hopeless" or have you pursued "false hope" down difficult paths? These questions and many others have been grappled with over the centuries by philosophers, spiritual leaders, psychologists, and each of us as we conduct our individual lives.

In the late 20th century, social scientists turned their attentions to improving our understanding of the psychology of hope. Dozens of theories of hope have been developed in the past century, but the vast majority of hope research is now based on the theory and measures of hope developed by C. R. Snyder, Harris, et al. (1991). In this chapter we provide an overview of the progression of hope theory and measurement in recent decades, including the early debate on whether hope is best conceptualized as an emotion or a cognition, and early theories and measures of hope. We then review Snyder's (1994, 2002) theory of hope and the measures that have been developed to assess hope based on this theory. Snyder's model and measures are now the dominant method of conceptualizing and assessing hope, and the examination of hope using these measures is one of the most active areas of positive psychology. Finally, we highlight some important issues in the measurement of hope such as measuring hope across cultures and distinguishing hope from related constructs such as optimism (see Chapter 5, this volume), before sharing some thoughts about future directions in hope measurement.

---

http://dx.doi.org/10.1037/0000138-006
Positive Psychological Assessment: A Handbook of Models and Measures, Second Edition,
M. W. Gallagher and S. J. Lopez (Editors)

EARLY CONCEPTUALIZATIONS OF HOPE

Most theories and ideas regarding the concept of hope can be grouped into either an emotion-based or a cognition-based category. In popular literature and prose, hope often is treated solely as an emotion, a particular feeling that allows one to sustain belief in dire circumstances. Contrary to what one might intuitively postulate, models that define hope as an emotional construct are fewer in number than those that are more cognitive in nature, and the cognitive side of hope has received considerably more research attention. Furthermore, many of the researchers who put forth emotion-based models include some sort of cognitive component. These two perspectives have merged to some degree, imbuing hope with both affective and cognitive qualities. For the purposes of this portion of the chapter, we briefly discuss early emotion and cognitive theories of hope separately before focusing on Snyder's cognitive model of hope in greater detail.

Averill, Catlin, and Chon (1990) described their theory of hope as an emotion, though governed by cognitions. Environment was named in this theory as having an effect on the development as well as the deterioration of hope. These researchers see hope as most appropriate when goals are (a) reasonably attainable, (b) under control, (c) viewed as important by the individual, and (d) acceptable at a social and moral level. Thus, Averill and colleagues believed that hope only can be understood within a social and cultural context.

Mowrer's (1960) conceptualization of hope is based on a more behavioral point of view, with hope as an affective form of secondary reinforcement. In his research with animals, for example, Mowrer noticed that when working in a stimulus–response paradigm, the emotion of hope seemed to appear in these subjects when a stimulus associated with something pleasurable occurred. Once this affective ingredient was induced, the animals seemed to anticipate the eventual pleasurable occurrence, as shown by increased activity. In this way, hope sustained desirous behavior by contributing to the reinforcement of the original stimulus. In these cases, the emotion of hope seemed to propel animals toward their goal.

The work of Erikson represented one of the earliest cognitive models of hope and suggested that hope is an element of healthy cognitive development. Accordingly, Erikson (1964) defined hope as "the enduring belief in the attainability of fervent wishes, in spite of the dark urges and rages which mark the beginning of existence" (p. 118). Thus, hope is a thought or belief that allows individuals to sustain movement toward goals. Erikson placed hope in a developmental context, positing that we hope from birth; moreover, he discussed the conflicts that arise internally because of hope. Our "fervent wishes" may come into conflict with those of others, especially when we are infants.

Breznitz (1986) also took a cognitive slant in defining hope, suggesting that hope "relates to a fleeting thought or to a description of a cognitive state" (p. 296). For hope to have influence on the individual, he posited that it must be of sufficient strength and persistence to induce a physiological response. In this sense, a momentary thought such as a soothing self-statement ("I will be fine") has less chance of fully invoking the same type of response that the true process of hoping will have on the body. Breznitz also identified hope as an illusion and highlighted the conundrum that is evident in the works of many writers who question the inclusion of hope alongside the evils in Pandora's Box.

Other theorists (e.g., Stotland, Gottschalk) have emphasized how perspective and expectancy are involved in hoping. Stotland (1969) conceptualized hope as "an expectation greater than zero of achieving a goal" (p. 2). If a sufficient level of importance is attached to the particular goal, then hope is ignited, mediating between the desire and the actual movement toward the goal. Gottschalk (1974) viewed hope in terms of positive expectancy, defining it as an amount of optimism that particular favorable outcomes are likely to occur. Hope is thus believed to be a provocative force that impels an individual to move through psychological problems. In Staats's view, hope is seen as "the interaction between wishes and expectations" (1989, p. 367). This view combines tenets of Erikson's view with those of the theorists who emphasized expectancy, and Staats defined hope as having both affective and cognitive aspects.

SNYDER'S MODEL OF HOPE

A theory of hope by Snyder and his colleagues (Snyder, 1994, 2002; Snyder, Harris, et al., 1991) has received considerable attention in the past 3 decades. Originally built almost solely on cognitions, this theory has evolved to include roles for emotions. Within this theory, hope is defined as "a positive motivational state that is based on an interactively derived sense of successful (a) agency (goal-directed energy) and (b) pathways (planning to meet goals)" (Snyder, Irving, & Anderson, 1991, p. 287). Snyder's theory of hope (and the associated measures discussed subsequently) is now the most widely used method of studying hope within psychology and has served as the foundation for a remarkable account of research examining when, how, and why hope can promote positive functioning (Gallagher & Lopez, 2018; Snyder, 2000).

A fundamental premise of Snyder's theory of hope is that human behavior is largely driven by the identification and pursuit of goals. Goals may vary temporally from short to long term; moreover, a given goal must be of sufficient value before a person will pursue it. In addition, goals may be approach oriented in nature (i.e., something positive that we want to happen) or preventative in nature (i.e., something negative that we want to stop from happening). Goals may vary depending on cultural values, and last, goals can vary in difficulty of attainment. Even seemingly "impossible" goals may at times be attained through supreme planning and efforts. Accordingly, Snyder has warned that we should be careful in criticizing goals that seem to be based on "false hopes" (Snyder, Rand, King, Feldman, & Woodward, 2002).

Pathways thought reflects the actual production of alternate routes when impeded, as well as positive self-talk about being able to find routes to desired goals (e.g., "I'll find a way to solve this"; Snyder, LaPointe, Crowson, & Early,

1998). Agency thinking is the motivational component of hope theory. On this point, high-hopers endorse agentic personal self-talk phrases (e.g., "I won't give up"; Snyder, LaPointe, et al., 1998). Such agency thought is especially important in applying the motivation to the appropriate alternate pathway when confronted by impediments.

Hope theory expressly addresses the roles of barriers, stressors, and emotions. When encountering barriers that impede goal pursuits, people appraise such circumstances as stressful. According to the postulates of hope theory, positive emotions result because of perceptions of successful goal pursuit. Conversely, negative emotions typically reflect the perceived lack of success under unimpeded, and especially impeded, circumstances. Thus, the perceptions regarding the success of goal pursuits causally drive subsequent positive and negative emotions (see Snyder et al., 1996). Furthermore, these emotions serve as reinforcing feedback.

Given their histories of successfully dealing with stressors and attaining their desired goals, high-hopers generally have positive emotions, as well as zest and confidence (Snyder, Sympson, Michael, & Cheavens, 2000); conversely, low-hopers have histories of not dealing successfully with stressors, along with negative emotions and affective flatness. Depending on their trait hope levels, and their cultural context, people might bring these emotional sets to their goal-related activities.

To give the reader an overview of the various interactions of the components in hope theory, we have constructed Figure 6.1. To the left, the iterative relationship of pathways and agency thoughts is shown. (For the reader who would like detailed descriptions of the developmental antecedents of the hope process, we recommend Snyder, 1994, pp. 75–114, and Snyder, McDermott, Cook, & Rapoff, 1997, pp. 1–32). Immediately to the right of agency–pathways thoughts, we see the emotional sets that each individual brings to the particular goal-pursuit process. Together, these learning histories and mood predispositions reflect the beginning context for goal-pursuit thinking in regard to specific goals.

Turning our attentions to the preevent analysis phase of Figure 6.1, we see the values related to particular goal pursuits. Assuming that there is sufficient value attached to a given goal pursuit, the person next moves into the event sequence analysis phase. Here, the person initiates behaviors for achieving the desired goal. If the goal pursuit seems to be going well at this stage, the feedback loop involves positive emotions that reinforce the goal-pursuit process. As such, these positive emotions sustain motivation. If the person is not doing well, negative emotions and self-critical ruminations should arise, thereby undermining the goal-pursuit process. It should be noted that Snyder and colleagues adopted a functional view of emotions. On this point, Levenson (1994) wrote, "Emotions serve to establish our position vis-a-vis our environment, pulling us toward certain people, objects, actions, and ideas, and pushing us away from others" (p. 123).

Returning to Figure 6.1, note the point at which a stressor—a barrier to the progression of the actual goal pursuit—is met. High-hope persons interpret

FIGURE 6.1. Hope theory model

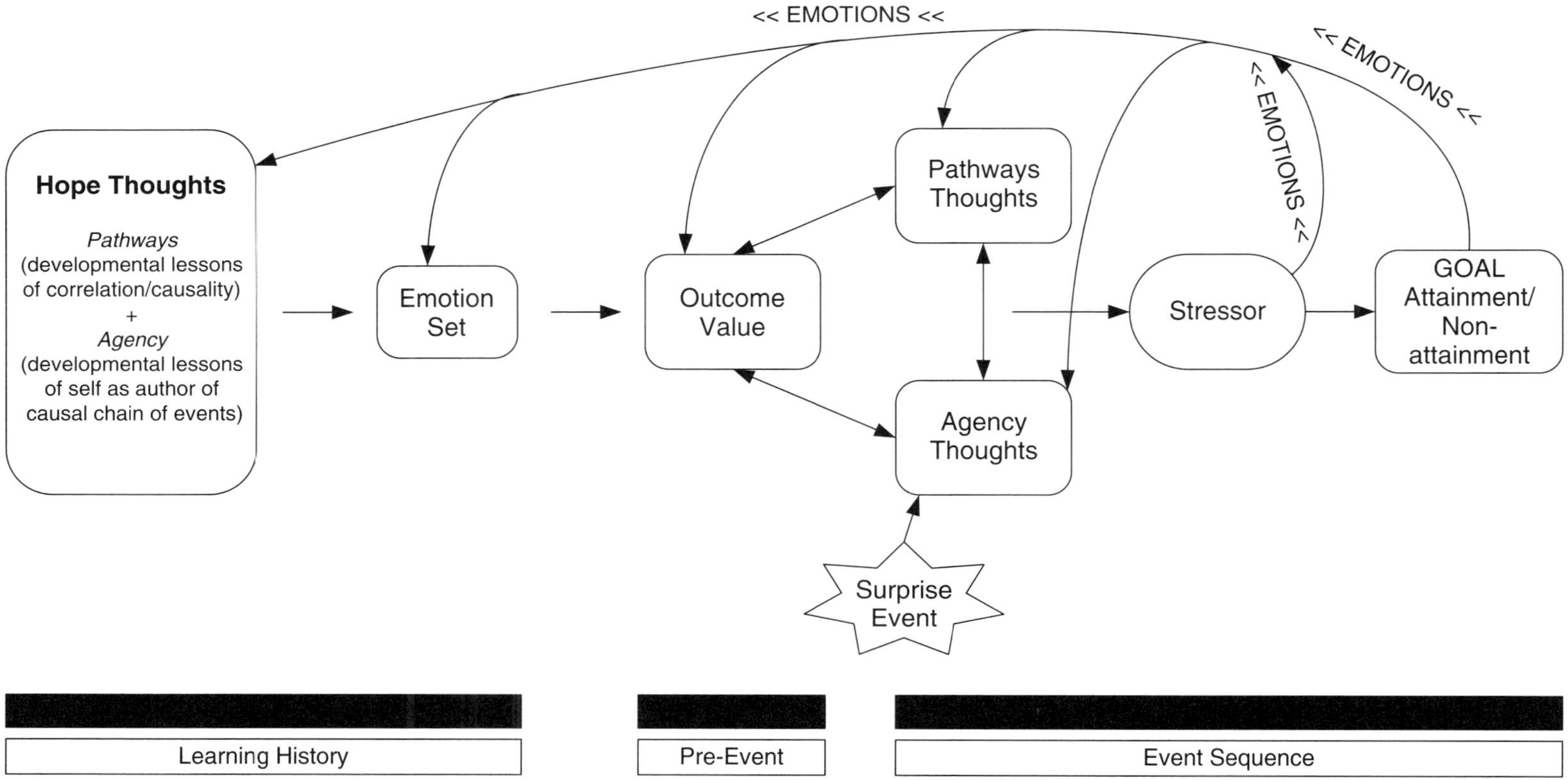

such barriers as challenges and thereafter seek alternate routes and rechannel their motivation to those routes. Often successful in bridging the impeding stressor, positive emotions thus reinforce hopeful thinking. On the other hand, low-hope people typically become "stuck" and experience ruminative thoughts and negative emotions—the result being that they are likely to abandon their goal pursuits.

A later addition to hope theory was the specification of the role of surprise events (see Figure 6.1, lower center). Such surprises may be negative (e.g., watching your 6-year-old bicycle rider hit a bump and fly headfirst over the handlebars) or positive (e.g., watching your child finally learn to ride a bike). Surprises typically are quick to produce emotions because of their sheer contrast (positive or negative) in relation to ongoing events. Such surprise-based emotions elicit arousal that is transformed almost immediately into motivation (i.e., agency). This agency then is "attached" to a goal and pathways that befit the situation (e.g., rushing to the aid of the child who has had an accident). Though such surprise-based emotions begin outside the typical goal-pursuit "corridor," it should be noted how readily they are incorporated into goal pursuits.

In summary, it can be seen that hope theory has both feedforward and feedback emotion-laden mechanisms that modulate the person's success in attaining a given goal. Thus, hope theory is an interrelated system of goal-directed thinking that responds to emotionally laden feedback throughout goal pursuit. As such, although Snyder's hope theory places a greater emphasis on cognitions when it comes to defining and measuring hope, hope theory explicitly identified how thoughts and emotions work hand-in-hand to help the person pursue the coveted goals that are crucial in day-to-day living and that motivate behavior across the life span.

SELF-REPORT MEASURES OF HOPE

Researchers have had different views on the topic of measuring hope. Stotland, for example, did not believe that asking individuals about their levels of hope could provide accurate information. He contended that self-report leads to confusion, or to socially desirable responses, making it more feasible to ask questions regarding such topics as the individual's perceived probability of success. Affective conceptualizations do not easily lend themselves to measurement via self-report. This may be attributed to historical difficulties operationalizing hope and a scholarly neglect of models of positive emotions. Cognitive conceptualizations, however, have been operationalized to produce brief, valid self-report measures of hope. The most validated and widely used measures of hope are measures developed based on Snyder's conceptualization of hope. These measures now include the three original hope measures developed by Snyder and colleagues (Adult Dispositional Hope Scale, State Hope Scale, and Children's Hope Scale) and a variety of domain specific hope scales that have been developed in recent years to identify the role of hope in specific contexts. Given that the majority of hope research now uses one of the measures developed based on Snyder's model, we primarily review those measures in this chapter, but we also highlight a few alternative measurement approaches.

Snyder's Hope Scales

Adult Dispositional Hope Scale

The Adult Hope Scale (AHS; Snyder, Harris, et al., 1991) is a self-report, 12-item inventory designed to tap dispositional hope in adults, ages 15 and older (see Appendix 6.1). The 4-point continuum (from 1 = *definitely false* to 4 = *definitely true*) was used in the original studies, although an 8-point scale is now generally used to encourage diverse responding. Total AHS scores range from 8 to 64 when the 8-point continuum is used. Four items reflect agency, four reflect pathways, and four are distracters. Agency and pathways items can be summed to examine the facets separately or summed to yield a total hope score.

Regarding the psychometric properties of the AHS, a recent review examined the internal consistency of 74 published studies that used the AHS and test–retest reliability in 17 studies (Hellman, Pittman, & Munoz, 2013). The mean reliability estimate for the AHS was high (.82; 95% CI [.79, .85]), and there was no evidence found that the sample characteristics of age, gender, or ethnicity were significant moderators of the internal consistency of the AHS. The mean estimate of test–retest reliability from previous studies was also high (.80; 95% CI [.77, .82]), and there was no evidence that age, gender, or ethnicity moderated the test–retest reliability. These findings are consistent with the first published estimates of the reliability of the AHS (Snyder, Harris, et al., 1991) and provide strong evidence that the AHS has good measurement properties. Studies using confirmatory factor analysis (CFA) have also consistently found support for the hypothesized latent structure of the AHS (e.g., Babyak, Snyder, & Yoshinobu, 1993; Roesch & Vaughn, 2006).

There is now extensive evidence demonstrating the convergent and discriminant validity of the AHS. A series of meta-analytic reviews have demonstrated that hope is associated with a broad range of outcomes in various life domains including academics, work, personality, and mental health (Alarcon, Bowling, & Khazon, 2013; Marques, Gallagher, & Lopez, 2017; Reichard, Avey, Lopez, & Dollwet, 2013). Responses to the AHS are also highly correlated with responses to several scales tapping similar psychological processes (Snyder, Harris, et al., 1991). Many studies have demonstrated that hope as assessed by the AHS is strongly correlated (i.e., *r*s of .50–.60) with related measures of optimism (e.g., the Life Orientation Test—Revised: Scheier, Carver, & Bridges, 1994), self-efficacy, or self-esteem, but that hope is clearly distinct and uniquely predicts various outcomes (e.g., Gallagher & Lopez, 2009; Rand, 2009). Moreover, AHS scores have correlated negatively with Minnesota Multiphasic Personality Inventory subscale scores (Irving, Crenshaw, Snyder, Francis, & Gentry, 1990). As an early test of discriminant validity, the AHS scores were correlated with a measure (the Self-Confidence Scale; Fenigstein, Scheier, & Buss, 1975) in which the content was believed to be unrelated to hope. As predicted, no significant correlations resulted with hope scores and the subscales of Public and Private Self-Consciousness (*r*s of .06 and −.03, respectively; Snyder, Harris, et al., 1991).

Children's Hope Scale

The Children's Hope Scale (CHS; Snyder, Hoza, et al., 1997) is a six-item self-report measure that is based on the premise that children are goal directed and that their goal-directed thoughts can be understood according to agency and pathways. The CHS has been validated for use with children ages 7 to 16. Three of the six items reflect agency, and three reflect pathways thinking. Children respond to a 6-point Likert scale regarding the applicability of each item. Total scores can range from 6 to 36. The administrator can have the child read the scale without guidance or read the items aloud and mark their responses.

Reliabilities for the CHS have been acceptable, with Cronbach alphas for the CHS total score ranging from .72 to .86, with a median alpha of .77 (e.g., Snyder, Hoza, et al., 1997); moreover, the test–retest correlations over the 1-month interval were both positive and significant (*r*s of .70–.80; Snyder, Hoza, et al., 1997). The scores on the CHS correlated positively (with one exception) with the five subscales of the Self-Perception Profile for Children (SPP-C; Harter, 1985) and with overall SPP-C self-worth (ranging from .23 to .55). In correlating responses to the CHS and the Children's Attributional Style Questionnaire (Kaslow, Tanenbaum, & Seligman, 1978), the children scoring higher on the CHS exhibited an attributional attachment to positive outcomes and a slight disposition to distance themselves from negative outcomes. Finally, scores on the Children's Depression Inventory (CDI; Kovacs, 1985) and the CHS correlated negatively (*r*s of −.27 to −.48). CFA examinations of the factor structure of the CHS have supported the hypothesized factor structure (Valle, Huebner, & Suldo, 2004) and there is promising evidence that children's hope is an important predictor of academic outcomes (e.g., Ciarrochi, Heaven, & Davies, 2007) and longitudinal trajectories of well-being in adolescents (Ciarrochi, Parker, Kashdan, Heaven, & Barkus, 2015). Together, these findings offer support for the concurrent validity of the CHS.

Adult State Hope Scale

The State Hope Scale (SHS; Appendix 6.2; Snyder et al., 1996) is a six-item self-report scale (response range of 1 = *definitely true* to 8 = *definitely false*) that assesses goal-directed thinking at a given moment in time. This scale can be administered in 2 to 5 minutes and hand-scored in a minute or less. The scale is written at approximately a sixth-grade reading level and includes the agency and pathways subscales, as well as a total score that is attained by summing responses to all six items. The agency and pathways subscale scores are derived by summing their respective three items, with total scores ranging from 6 to 48.

In four studies involving college students, the alphas for the overall SHS ranged from a low of .79 to a high of .95. Alphas for the agency subscale varied from .76 to .95, and from .59 to .93 for the pathways subscale (Snyder et al.,

1996). Overall, there is strong support for the internal reliability of the SHS. Test–retest correlations, which should vary because of the differing situations in which the SHS is taken, ranged from a low of .48 to a high of .93 comparing any 2 days across a 4-week study (Snyder et al., 1996). CFA examinations of the SHS have supported the hypothesized two-factor structure and have also demonstrated measurement invariance of the SHS across gender and age (Martin-Krumm, Delas, Lafrenière, Fenouillet, & Lopez, 2015).

As with the AHS and CHS, there is extensive evidence demonstrating the convergent and discriminant validity of the SHS and the utility of the SHS in predicting outcomes across many life domains. Over a 1-month period, SHS scores and the daily scores from the State Self-Esteem Scale (Heatherton & Polivy, 1991) correlated positively and significantly (*rs* = .45–.75). Similarly, over the 30-day interval, the daily SHS scores correlated (a) positively (*rs* = .48–.65) with scores on the Positive Affect scale of the State Positive and Negative Affect Schedule (PANAS; Watson, Clark, & Tellegen, 1988) and (b) negatively (*rs* = −.37 to −.50) with the scores on the Negative Affect scale of the PANAS (Snyder et al., 1996). Higher scores on the SHS has also been found to predict anxiety and depression (Cheavens, Feldman, Gum, Michael, & Snyder, 2006), athletic performance (Curry, Snyder, Cook, Ruby, & Rehm, 1997), and resilience (Ong, Edwards, & Bergeman, 2006), and the SHS can detect changes in hope following interventions (e.g., Cheavens et al., 2006).

Domain Specific and Observational Measures of Hope

Although the initial measures of hope developed on the basis of Snyder's model and the majority of subsequent research have focused on generalized hope at either the state or trait level, there has been increasing attention in recent years to the potential utility of domain specific measures of hope. The Domain Specific Hope Scale (DSHS) developed by Sympson (1999) was the first attempt to develop measures of hope in specific domains. The DSHS consists of 48 items that assess pathways and agency in six domains: academics, social relationships, romantic relationships, leisure, family, and work hope. Although not as widely used as the trait measures of hope, there is promising evidence that these measures can be used to better understand the presence and influence of hope in specific domains such as academics (e.g., Feldman & Kubota, 2015; Gallagher, Marques, & Lopez, 2017). Additional domain specific measures of hope developed in recent years include the Math Hope Scale (Robinson & Rose, 2010), the Writing Hope Scale (Sieben, 2013), the Work Hope Scale (Juntunen & Wettersten, 2006), and Employment Hope Scale (Hong, Polanin, & Pigott, 2012). A goal-specific hope scale has also been developed to provide a method of assessing hope in relation to discrete goals (Feldman, Rand, & Kahle-Wrobleski, 2009).

There have also been limited attempts to determine the feasibility and efficacy of assessing hope via written samples and observational methods, with some evidence that there is moderate correspondence between self-ratings and observational ratings generated by someone who knows the client/participant well (Snyder, Harris, et al., 1991). Using hope theory, Snyder and his colleagues have also made suggestions about inferring hope level via a person's writing. Snyder, McDermott, et al. (1997) offered techniques for tapping hope of children through prose. For adults, Snyder (1994) and McDermott and Snyder (1999) described how to extract hope levels from the writing products. Finally, Vance (1996) developed the Narrative Hope Scale to gauge the agency and pathways elements of hope in adults' stories. Using the Vance scale, raters identify hope markers by selecting from a menu of descriptors that reflect high- versus low-hope thoughts and behaviors. Also, Lopez (2013) generated procedures and detailed lists of questions about goals, pathways, agency, and barriers that can be posed to clients and individuals of all backgrounds to find the hope they already possess and identify methods for increasing the presence and benefits of hope in their lives.

Alternative Models of Measuring Hope

Currently, the measures based on Snyder's model are the most widely used approach for studying the presence and benefits of hope, but there are multiple alternatives approaches that are based on different conceptualizations of hope that also have promising support. Hope is one of the 24 strengths included in the widely used Values in Action (VIA) survey of character strengths (Peterson & Seligman, 2004), and multiple studies examining the effects of hope as measured by the VIA survey have indicated that hope is one of strongest predictors of well-being of the various character strengths (Park, Peterson, & Seligman, 2004; Peterson, Ruch, Beermann, Park, & Seligman, 2007). Another commonly used approach for studying hope is based on Herth's model of hope, which identifies temporality and future, positive readiness and expectancy, and interconnectedness as three components of hope. The Herth Hope Scale (Herth, 1991), as well as the Herth Hope Index (Herth, 1992), which was adapted from the original to have a briefer measure suitable for clinical settings, are based on this model and have been used in many studies, particularly in health care settings, to examine the benefits of hope (e.g., Ballard, Green, McCaa, & Logsdon, 1997).

Finally, less widely used measures that nevertheless have some empirical support include the 1975 Hope Scale (Erickson, Post, & Paige, 1975), which consists of a list of 20 focused goals that are not situation-specific in nature and that are intended to span an array of common goals; the Expected Balance scale (EBS; Staats, 1989), which assesses the affective side of the Staats model of hope and consists of 18 items (nine positive and nine negative); and The Hope Index (Staats & Stassen, as cited in Staats, 1989), which assesses the cognitive side of Staats's model of hope and specifically focuses on particular events and outcomes, instead of a more general focus, and contains four subscales: hope-self, hope-other, wish, and expect. Each of these scales has demonstrated some evidence of internal consistency, test–retest reliability, and construct validity.

MEASURING HOPE ACROSS CULTURES AND CONTEXTS

As the field of positive psychology has matured, there has been an increasing recognition of the importance of examining the measurement and promotion of positive psychology constructs like hope within a cultural context (Flores & Lee; see also Chapter 4, this volume; Pedrotti, Edwards, & Lopez, 2009). Although the Snyder hope scales were initially developed and evaluated with relatively racially and ethnically homogenous samples, there has been significant progress in the past decade in our understanding of the utility and equivalence of hope measures when used across different cultures (e.g., hope measurement in Mexican American Youth; Edwards, Ong, & Lopez, 2007) and languages, and how demographic characteristics such as gender may influence the measurement properties of the scale. The AHS has now been translated and validated in many languages including Spanish (Galiana, Oliver, Sancho, & Tomás, 2015), French (Gana, Daigre, & Ledrich, 2013), Portuguese (Marques, Lopez, Fontaine, Coimbra, & Mitchell, 2014), Arabic (Abdel-Khalek & Snyder, 2007), and Chinese (Sun, Ng, & Wang, 2012). The CHS has also been translated into multiple languages, including Spanish (Edwards et al., 2000), Portuguese (Marques, Pais-Ribeiro, & Lopez, 2009), and Serbian (Jovanović, 2013). CFA examinations of the measurement properties of the AHS have demonstrated metric invariance of the AHS across both gender and ethnicity (Roesch & Vaughn, 2006). Despite these positive strides made with regard to linguistic equivalence, issues surrounding construct and functional equivalence (i.e., whether hope is defined, manifested, and utilized the same way in different cultural groups) must be further investigated (Pedrotti & Edwards, 2014). Some researchers have found that positive expectancies for the future might be found across countries and some cultures (Gallagher, Lopez, & Pressman, 2013), yet others have found divergent correlations between optimism and various constructs in some cultural groups (Chang, Downey, Hirsch, & Lin, 2016). As such, it will be important for future work to continue to explore the reliability and validity of hope measures across cultures and contexts.

DISTINGUISHING HOPE FROM RELATED CONSTRUCTS

Another important issue in the measurement of hope that has received increasing attention in recent years is the examination of whether what is measured by hope scales is distinct from related constructs such as optimism and self-efficacy. A complete overview of the conceptual distinctions between hope and related constructs is beyond the scope of this chapter but is presented elsewhere (Rand, 2018). Factor analytic studies that have examined the distinctiveness of hope and related constructs have consistently found that hope is a distinct latent construct and that hope uniquely predicts various outcomes above and beyond related positive thinking constructs. One of the first studies to examine this issue used CFA to demonstrate that hope is distinct from self-efficacy and optimism (Magaletta & Oliver, 1999). Similarly, Bryant and Cvengros (2004) found that the agency and pathways components were distinct from both optimism and pessimism and that specifying distinct higher order latent constructs of hope and optimism better explained the associations among the factors than the specification of just a single globalized positive expectancies construct. Subsequent studies have provided further evidence not only that hope is a distinct latent construct from optimism, but also that hope uniquely predicts components of well-being (Gallagher & Lopez, 2009), academic performance (Rand, 2009), positive work outcomes (Youssef & Luthans, 2007), and posttraumatic growth in cancer survivors (Ho et al., 2011) above and beyond levels of optimism. More research is needed to examine the unique effects and mechanisms of hope in different contexts, but it is clear now that current measures of hope assess a source of psychological resilience that positively and uniquely predicts many aspects of psychosocial functioning.

CONCLUSION

Significant progress has been made in the past 15 years in understanding how best to assess and quantify hope. There is now extensive evidence supporting the reliability, validity, factor structure, and predictive utility of the three primary measures of hope that are based on Snyder's model of hope. The robust evidence supporting the use of these measures demonstrates that hope is no longer a mysterious phenomenon that cannot be measured but that we can now reliably and accurately quantify individual differences in levels of hope and can detect the impact of efforts to increase hope via interventions (e.g., Cheavens et al., 2006). The progress in our ability to assess hope has helped its study to remain one of the most active and promising areas of positive psychology. Although Snyder's model and measures of hope remain the most widely used approach for assessing hope, new models and measures of hope continue to be developed (e.g., Schrank, Woppmann, Sibitz, & Lauber, 2011). It will be important for researchers to continue to examine the unique contributions and relationships among distinct models of hope. It will also be crucial to continue work exploring how hope can be measured and better understood in diverse cultural groups so that we can effectively determine how hope might function in the lives of people everywhere.

APPENDIX 6.1
ADULT DISPOSITIONAL HOPE SCALE ITEMS AND DIRECTIONS FOR ADMINISTERING AND SCORING THE GOALS SCALE

THE GOALS SCALE

Directions

Read each item carefully. Using the scale shown below, please select the number that best describes YOU and put that number in the blank provided.

1 = *definitely false*	2 = *mostly false*	3 = *somewhat false*	4 = *slightly false*
5 = *slightly true*	6 = *somewhat true*	7 = *mostly true*	8 = *definitely true*

1. I can think of many ways to get out of a jam.
2. I energetically pursue my goals.
3. I feel tired most of the time.
4. There are lots of ways around any problem.
5. I am easily downed in an argument.
6. I can think of many ways to get the things in life that are most important to me.
7. I worry about my health.
8. Even when others get discouraged, I know I can find a way to solve the problem.
9. My past experiences have prepared me well for my future.
10. I've been pretty successful in life.
11. I usually find myself worrying about something.
12. I meet the goals that I set for myself.

Notes. When administered, we have called this the "Goals scale" rather than the "Hope scale" because on some initial occasions when giving the scale, people became sufficiently interested in the fact that hope could be measured that they wanted to discuss this rather than taking the scale. No such problems have been encountered with the rather mundane title "Goals scale." Items 3, 5, 7, and 11 are distracters and are not used for scoring. The pathways subscale score is the sum of Items 1, 4, 6, and 8; the agency subscale is the sum of Items 2, 9, 10, and 12. Hope is the sum of the four pathways and four agency items. In our original studies, we used a 4-point response continuum, but to encourage more diversity in scores in our more recent studies, we have used the 8-point scale. Adapted from "The Will and the Ways: Development and Validation of an Individual-Differences Measure of Hope," by C. R. Snyder, C. Harris, J. R. Anderson, S. A. Holleran, L. M. Irving, S. T. Sigmon, . . . P. Harney, 1991, *Journal of Personality and Social Psychology*, *60*, p. 585. Copyright 1991 by the American Psychological Association.

APPENDIX 6.2
THE STATE HOPE SCALE

GOALS SCALE FOR THE PRESENT

Directions: Read each item carefully. Using the scale shown below, please select the number that best describes how you think about yourself right now and put that number in the blank before each sentence. Please take a few moments to focus on yourself and what is going on in your life at this moment. Once you have this "here and now" set, go ahead and answer each item according to the following scale:

1 = *Definitely false*	2 = *Mostly false*	3 = *Somewhat false*	4 = *Slightly false*
5 = *Slightly true*	6 = *Somewhat true*	7 = *Mostly true*	8 = *Definitely true*

_____ 1. If I should find myself in a jam, I could think of many ways to get out of it.

_____ 2. At the present time, I am energetically pursuing my goals.

_____ 3. There are lots of ways around any problem that I am facing now.

_____ 4. Right now, I see myself as being pretty successful.

_____ 5. I can think of many ways to reach my current goals.

_____ 6. At this time, I am meeting the goals that I have set for myself.

Note. The Agency subscale score is derived by summing the three even-numbered items; the Pathways subscale score is derived by adding the three odd-numbered items. The total State Hope Scale score is derived by summing the three Agency and the three Pathways items. Scores can range from a low of 6 to a high of 48. When administering the State Hope Scale, it is labeled as the "Goals Scale for the Present." Reprinted from "Development and Validation of the State Hope Scale," by C. R. Snyder, S. C. Sympson, F. C. Ybasco, T. F. Borders, M. A. Babyak, and R. L. Higgins, 1996, *Journal of Personality and Social Psychology, 70*, p. 335. Copyright 1996 by the American Psychological Association.

REFERENCES

Abdel-Khalek, A., & Snyder, C. R. (2007). Correlates and predictors of an Arabic translation of the Snyder Hope Scale. *The Journal of Positive Psychology, 2*, 228–235. http://dx.doi.org/10.1080/17439760701552337

Alarcon, G. M., Bowling, N. A., & Khazon, S. (2013). Great expectations: A meta-analytic examination of optimism and hope. *Personality and Individual Differences, 54*, 821–827. http://dx.doi.org/10.1016/j.paid.2012.12.004

Averill, J. R., Catlin, G., & Chon, K. K. (1990). *Rules of hope*. New York, NY: Springer-Verlag. http://dx.doi.org/10.1007/978-1-4613-9674-1

Babyak, M. A., Snyder, C. R., & Yoshinobu, L. (1993). Psychometric properties of the Hope Scale: A confirmatory factor analysis. *Journal of Research in Personality, 27*, 154–169. http://dx.doi.org/10.1006/jrpe.1993.1011

Ballard, A., Green, T., McCaa, A., & Logsdon, M. C. (1997, June). A comparison of the level of hope in patients with newly diagnosed and recurrent cancer. *Oncology Nursing Forum, 24,* 899–904.

Breznitz, S. (1986). The effect of hope on coping with stress. In M. H. Appley & P. Trumbull (Eds.), *Dynamics of stress: Physiological, psychological, and social perspectives* (pp. 295–306). New York, NY: Plenum Press. http://dx.doi.org/10.1007/978-1-4684-5122-1_15

Bryant, F. B., & Cvengros, J. A. (2004). Distinguishing hope and optimism: Two sides of a coin, or two separate coins? *Journal of Social and Clinical Psychology, 23,* 273–302. http://dx.doi.org/10.1521/jscp.23.2.273.31018

Chang, E. C., Downey, C. A., Hirsch, J. J., & Lin, N. J. (Eds.). (2016). *Positive psychology in racial and ethnic groups: Theory, research, and practice.* Washington, DC: American Psychological Association. http://dx.doi.org/10.1037/14799-000

Cheavens, J. S., Feldman, D. B., Gum, A., Michael, S. T., & Snyder, C. R. (2006). Hope therapy in a community sample: A pilot investigation. *Social Indicators Research, 77,* 61–78. http://dx.doi.org/10.1007/s11205-005-5553-0

Ciarrochi, J., Heaven, P. C., & Davies, F. (2007). The impact of hope, self-esteem, and attributional style on adolescents' school grades and emotional well-being: A longitudinal study. *Journal of Research in Personality, 41,* 1161–1178. http://dx.doi.org/10.1016/j.jrp.2007.02.001

Ciarrochi, J., Parker, P., Kashdan, T. B., Heaven, P. C., & Barkus, E. (2015). Hope and emotional well-being: A six-year study to distinguish antecedents, correlates, and consequences. *The Journal of Positive Psychology, 10,* 520–532. http://dx.doi.org/10.1080/17439760.2015.1015154

Curry, L. A., Snyder, C. R., Cook, D. L., Ruby, B. C., & Rehm, M. (1997). Role of hope in academic and sport achievement. *Journal of Personality and Social Psychology, 73,* 1257–1267. http://dx.doi.org/10.1037/0022-3514.73.6.1257

Edwards, L. M., McDermott, D., Pedrotti, J. T., LaRue, S., Stone, M. E., Diamond, K. L., & Spalitto, S. V. (2000, August). *Preliminary validation of a Spanish language translation of the Children's Hope Scale.* Paper presented at the annual conference of the American Psychological Association, Washington, DC.

Edwards, L. M., Ong, A. D., & Lopez, S. J. (2007). Hope measurement in Mexican American youth. *Hispanic Journal of Behavioral Sciences, 29,* 225–241. http://dx.doi.org/10.1177/0739986307299692

Erickson, R. C., Post, R. D., & Paige, A. B. (1975). Hope as a psychiatric variable. *Journal of Clinical Psychology, 31,* 324–330. http://dx.doi.org/10.1002/1097-4679(197504)31:2<324::AID-JCLP2270310236>3.0.CO;2-Q

Erikson, E. H. (1964). *Insight and responsibility.* New York, NY: W. W. Norton.

Feldman, D. B., & Kubota, M. (2015). Hope, self-efficacy, optimism, and academic achievement: Distinguishing constructs and levels of specificity in predicting college grade-point average. *Learning and Individual Differences, 37,* 210–216. http://dx.doi.org/10.1016/j.lindif.2014.11.022

Feldman, D. B., Rand, K. L., & Kahle-Wrobleski, K. (2009). Hope and goal attainment: Testing a basic prediction of hope theory. *Journal of Social and Clinical Psychology, 28,* 479–497. http://dx.doi.org/10.1521/jscp.2009.28.4.479

Fenigstein, A., Scheier, M. F., & Buss, A. H. (1975). Public and private self-consciousness: Assessment and theory. *Journal of Consulting and Clinical Psychology, 43,* 522–527. http://dx.doi.org/10.1037/h0076760

Galiana, L., Oliver, A., Sancho, P., & Tomás, J. M. (2015). Dimensionality and validation of the Dispositional Hope Scale in a Spanish sample. *Social Indicators Research, 120,* 297–308. http://dx.doi.org/10.1007/s11205-014-0582-1

Gallagher, M. W., & Lopez, S. J. (2009). Positive expectancies and mental health: Identifying the unique contributions of hope and optimism. *The Journal of Positive Psychology, 4,* 548–556. http://dx.doi.org/10.1080/17439760903157166

Gallagher, M. W., & Lopez, S. J. (Eds.). (2018). *The Oxford handbook of hope*. New York, NY: Oxford University Press. http://dx.doi.org/10.1093/oxfordhb/9780199399314.001.0001

Gallagher, M. W., Lopez, S. J., & Pressman, S. D. (2013). Optimism is universal: Exploring the presence and benefits of optimism in a representative sample of the world. *Journal of Personality, 81*, 429–440. http://dx.doi.org/10.1111/jopy.12026

Gallagher, M. W., Marques, S. C., & Lopez, S. J. (2017). Hope and the academic trajectory of college students. *Journal of Happiness Studies, 18*, 341–352. http://dx.doi.org/10.1007/s10902-016-9727-z

Gana, K., Daigre, S., & Ledrich, J. (2013). Psychometric properties of the French version of the adult dispositional hope scale. *Assessment, 20*, 114–118. http://dx.doi.org/10.1177/1073191112468315

Gottschalk, L. A. (1974). A Hope Scale applicable to verbal samples. *Archives of General Psychiatry, 30*, 779–785. http://dx.doi.org/10.1001/archpsyc.1974.01760120041007

Harter, S. (1985). *Manual for the Self-Perception Profile for Children: Revision of the Perceived Competence Scale Score for Children*. Denver, CO: University of Denver Press.

Heatherton, T. F., & Polivy, J. (1991). Development and validation of a scale for measuring state self-esteem. *Journal of Personality and Social Psychology, 60*, 895–910. http://dx.doi.org/10.1037/0022-3514.60.6.895

Hellman, C. M., Pittman, M. K., & Munoz, R. T. (2013). The first twenty years of the will and the ways: An examination of score reliability distribution on Snyder's Dispositional Hope Scale. *Journal of Happiness Studies, 14*, 723–729. http://dx.doi.org/10.1007/s10902-012-9351-5

Herth, K. (1991). Development and refinement of an instrument to measure hope. *Scholarly Inquiry for Nursing Practice: An International Journal, 5*, 39–51.

Herth, K. (1992). Abbreviated instrument to measure hope: Development and psychometric evaluation. *Journal of Advanced Nursing, 17*, 1251–1259. http://dx.doi.org/10.1111/j.1365-2648.1992.tb01843.x

Ho, S., Rajandram, R. K., Chan, N., Samman, N., McGrath, C., & Zwahlen, R. A. (2011). The roles of hope and optimism on posttraumatic growth in oral cavity cancer patients. *Oral Oncology, 47*, 121–124. http://dx.doi.org/10.1016/j.oraloncology.2010.11.015

Hong, P., Polanin, J. R., & Pigott, T. D. (2012). Empirical explanation of the employment hope measure using exploratory factor analysis. *Research on Social Work Practice, 22*, 322–333.

Irving, L. M., Crenshaw, W., Snyder, C. R., Francis, P., & Gentry, G. (1990, May). *Hope and its correlates in a psychiatric inpatient setting*. Paper presented at the 62nd annual meeting of the Midwestern Psychological Association, Chicago, IL.

Jovanović, V. (2013). Evaluation of the Children's Hope Scale in Serbian adolescents: Dimensionality, measurement invariance across gender, convergent and incremental validity. *Child Indicators Research, 6*, 797–811. http://dx.doi.org/10.1007/s12187-013-9195-5

Juntunen, C. L., & Wettersten, K. B. (2006). Work hope: Development and initial validation of a measure. *Journal of Counseling Psychology, 53*, 94–106. http://dx.doi.org/10.1037/0022-0167.53.1.94

Kaslow, N. J., Tanenbaum, R. L., & Seligman, M. E. P. (1978). *The KASTAN-R: A children's attributional style questionnaire (KASTAN-R-CASQ)*. Unpublished manuscript, University of Pennsylvania, Philadelphia.

Kovacs, M. (1985). The Children's Depression Inventory (CDI). *Psychopharmacology Bulletin, 21*, 995–998.

Levenson, R. W. (1994). Human emotion: A functionalist view. In P. Ekman & R. J. Davidson (Eds.), *The nature of emotion: Fundamental questions* (pp. 123–126). New York, NY: Oxford University Press.

Lopez, S. J. (2013). *Making hope happen: Create the future you want for yourself and others*. New York, NY: Simon and Schuster.

Magaletta, P. R., & Oliver, J. M. (1999). The hope construct, will, and ways: Their relations with self-efficacy, optimism, and general well-being. *Journal of Clinical Psychology, 55,* 539–551. http://dx.doi.org/10.1002/(SICI)1097-4679(199905)55:5<539::AID-JCLP2>3.0.CO;2-G

Marques, S. C., Gallagher, M. W., & Lopez, S. J. (2017). Hope- and academic-related outcomes: A meta-analysis. *School Mental Health, 9,* 1–13. http://dx.doi.org/10.1007/s12310-017-9212-9

Marques, S. C., Lopez, S. J., Fontaine, A. M., Coimbra, S., & Mitchell, J. (2014). Validation of a Portuguese version of the Snyder Hope Scale in a sample of high school students. *Journal of Psychoeducational Assessment, 32,* 781–786. http://dx.doi.org/10.1177/0734282914540865

Marques, S. C., Pais-Ribeiro, J. L., & Lopez, S. J. (2009). Validation of the Portuguese version of the Children's Hope Scale. *School Psychology International, 30,* 538–551. http://dx.doi.org/10.1177/0143034309107069

Martin-Krumm, C., Delas, Y., Lafrenière, M. A., Fenouillet, F., & Lopez, S. J. (2015). The structure of the State Hope Scale. *The Journal of Positive Psychology, 10,* 272–281. http://dx.doi.org/10.1080/17439760.2014.936964

McDermott, D., & Snyder, C. R. (1999). *Making hope happen: A workbook for turning possibilities into reality.* Oakland, CA: New Harbinger Press.

Mowrer, O. H. (1960). *Learning theory and behavior.* New York, NY: Wiley. http://dx.doi.org/10.1037/10802-000

Ong, A. D., Edwards, L. M., & Bergeman, C. S. (2006). Hope as a source of resilience in later adulthood. *Personality and Individual Differences, 41,* 1263–1273. http://dx.doi.org/10.1016/j.paid.2006.03.028

Park, N., Peterson, C., & Seligman, M. E. (2004). Strengths of character and well-being. *Journal of Social and Clinical Psychology, 23,* 603–619. http://dx.doi.org/10.1521/jscp.23.5.603.50748

Pedrotti, J. T., & Edwards, L. M. (Eds.). (2014). *Perspectives on the intersection of multiculturalism and positive psychology.* New York, NY: Springer. http://dx.doi.org/10.1007/978-94-017-8654-6

Pedrotti, J. T., Edwards, L. M., & Lopez, S. J. (2009). Positive psychology within a cultural context. In C. R. Snyder & S. J. Lopez (Eds.), *The Oxford handbook of positive psychology* (pp. 49–57). New York, NY: Oxford University Press.

Peterson, C., Ruch, W., Beermann, U., Park, N., & Seligman, M. E. (2007). Strengths of character, orientations to happiness, and life satisfaction. *The Journal of Positive Psychology, 2,* 149–156. http://dx.doi.org/10.1080/17439760701228938

Peterson, C., & Seligman, M. E. P. (2004). *Character strengths and virtues: A handbook and classification.* New York, NY: Oxford University Press and Washington, DC: American Psychological Association.

Rand, K. L. (2009). Hope and optimism: Latent structures and influences on grade expectancy and academic performance. *Journal of Personality, 77,* 231–260. http://dx.doi.org/10.1111/j.1467-6494.2008.00544.x

Rand, K. L. (2018). Hope, self-efficacy, and optimism: Conceptual and empirical differences. In M. W. Gallagher & S. J. Lopez (Eds.), *The Oxford handbook of hope* (pp. 45–58). New York, NY: Oxford University Press.

Reichard, R. J., Avey, J. B., Lopez, S., & Dollwet, M. (2013). Having the will and finding the way: A review and meta-analysis of hope at work. *The Journal of Positive Psychology, 8,* 292–304. http://dx.doi.org/10.1080/17439760.2013.800903

Robinson, C., & Rose, S. (2010). Predictive, construct, and convergent validity of general and domain-specific measures of hope for college student academic achievement. *Research in the Schools, 17,* 38–52.

Roesch, S. C., & Vaughn, A. A. (2006). Evidence for the factorial validity of the Dispositional Hope Scale. *European Journal of Psychological Assessment, 22,* 78–84. http://dx.doi.org/10.1027/1015-5759.22.2.78

Scheier, M. F., Carver, C. S., & Bridges, M. W. (1994). Distinguishing optimism from neuroticism (and trait anxiety, self-mastery, and self-esteem): A reevaluation of the Life Orientation Test. *Journal of Personality and Social Psychology, 67,* 1063–1078. http://dx.doi.org/10.1037/0022-3514.67.6.1063

Schrank, B., Woppmann, A., Sibitz, I., & Lauber, C. (2011). Development and validation of an integrative scale to assess hope. *Health Expectations, 14,* 417–428. http://dx.doi.org/10.1111/j.1369-7625.2010.00645.x

Sieben, N. (2013). *Writing hope, self-regulation, and self-efficacy as predictors of writing ability in first-year college students.* Unpublished doctoral dissertation, Hofstra University, Hempstead, NY.

Snyder, C. R. (1994). *The psychology of hope: You can get there from here.* New York, NY: Free Press.

Snyder, C. R. (Ed.). (2000). *Handbook of hope: Theory, measures, and applications.* San Diego, CA: Academic Press.

Snyder, C. R. (2002). Hope theory: Rainbows in the mind. *Psychological Inquiry, 13,* 249–275. http://dx.doi.org/10.1207/S15327965PLI1304_01

Snyder, C. R., Harris, C., Anderson, J. R., Holleran, S. A., Irving, L. M., Sigmon, S. T., . . . Harney, P. (1991). The will and the ways: Development and validation of an individual-differences measure of hope. *Journal of Personality and Social Psychology, 60,* 570–585. http://dx.doi.org/10.1037/0022-3514.60.4.570

Snyder, C. R., Hoza, B., Pelham, W. E., Rapoff, M., Ware, L., Danovsky, M., . . . Stahl, K. J. (1997). The development and validation of the Children's Hope Scale. *Journal of Pediatric Psychology, 22,* 399–421. http://dx.doi.org/10.1093/jpepsy/22.3.399

Snyder, C. R., Irving, L. M., & Anderson, J. R. (1991). Hope and health. In C. R. Snyder & D. R. Forsyth (Eds.), *Pergamon general psychology series: Vol. 162. Handbook of social and clinical psychology: The health perspective* (pp. 285–305). Elmsford, NY: Pergamon Press.

Snyder, C. R., LaPointe, A. B., Crowson, J. J., & Early, S. (1998). Preferences of high- and low-hope people for self-referential input. *Cognition and Emotion, 12,* 807–823. http://dx.doi.org/10.1080/026999398379448

Snyder, C. R., McDermott, D., Cook, W., & Rapoff, M. (1997). *Journeys of hope: Giving children stories to grow on.* Boulder, CO: Westview/HarperCollins.

Snyder, C. R., Rand, K. L., King, E. A., Feldman, D. B., & Woodward, J. T. (2002). "False" hope. *Journal of Clinical Psychology, 58,* 1003–1022. http://dx.doi.org/10.1002/jclp.10096

Snyder, C. R., Sympson, S. C., Michael, S. T., & Cheavens, J. (2000). The optimism and hope constructs: Variants on a positive expectancy theme. In E. C. Chang (Ed.), *Optimism and pessimism* (pp. 103–124). Washington, DC: American Psychological Association.

Snyder, C. R., Sympson, S. C., Ybasco, F. C., Borders, T. F., Babyak, M. A., & Higgins, R. L. (1996). Development and validation of the State Hope Scale. *Journal of Personality and Social Psychology, 70,* 321–335. http://dx.doi.org/10.1037/0022-3514.70.2.321

Staats, S. R. (1989). Hope: A comparison of two self-report measures for adults. *Journal of Personality Assessment, 53,* 366–375. http://dx.doi.org/10.1207/s15327752jpa5302_13

Stotland, E. (1969). *The psychology of hope.* San Francisco, CA: Jossey-Bass.

Sun, Q., Ng, K. M., & Wang, C. (2012). A validation study on a new Chinese Version of the Dispositional Hope Scale. *Measurement and Evaluation in Counseling and Development, 45,* 133–148. http://dx.doi.org/10.1177/0748175611429011

Sympson, S. (1999). *Validation of the Domain Specific Hope Scale.* Unpublished doctoral dissertation, Department of Psychology, University of Kansas, Lawrence.

Valle, M. F., Huebner, E. S., & Suldo, S. M. (2004). Further evaluation of the Children's Hope Scale. *Journal of Psychoeducational Assessment, 22,* 320–337. http://dx.doi.org/10.1177/073428290402200403

Vance, M. (1996). *Measuring hope in personal narratives: The development and preliminary validation of the Narrative Hope Scale* (Unpublished doctoral dissertation). University of Kansas, Lawrence.

Watson, D., Clark, L. A., & Tellegen, A. (1988). Development and validation of brief measures of positive and negative affect: The PANAS scales. *Journal of Personality and Social Psychology, 54,* 1063–1070. http://dx.doi.org/10.1037/0022-3514.54.6.1063

Youssef, C. M., & Luthans, F. (2007). Positive organizational behavior in the workplace: The impact of hope, optimism, and resilience. *Journal of Management, 33,* 774–800. http://dx.doi.org/10.1177/0149206307305562

7

Measuring Career and Occupational Self-Efficacy

Karen M. O'Brien, Monica S. Kearney, and Elizabeth Sauber

Freud suggested that healthy functioning could be operationalized as the ability to love and to work. Similarly, social scientists identified love, intimacy, and satisfying work as salient characteristics that contribute to a positive life (Clifton, 2000). For many years, counseling psychologists have assisted individuals in maximizing their ability to select careers that will allow them to succeed and thus lead meaningful and healthy work lives. Hackett and Betz (1981) advanced the work of counseling psychologists when they applied Bandura's (1977, 1997) cognitive theory to the study of vocational development. Specifically, they hypothesized that women who were confident in their ability to pursue career-related tasks (i.e., demonstrated strong levels of career self-efficacy) would be likely to consider a wide range of careers and be satisfied with their vocational choice. Since that time, career-related self-efficacy has been studied extensively and shown to be predictive of variables related to healthy vocational development, occupational success, and life satisfaction (Choi et al., 2012; Flores & O'Brien, 2002; Piña-Watson, Jimenez, & Ojeda, 2014; Spurk & Abele, 2014). To further assist researchers and practitioners in promoting health and success in the workplace, this chapter provides information regarding the measurement of career-related self-efficacy.

http://dx.doi.org/10.1037/0000138-007
Positive Psychological Assessment: A Handbook of Models and Measures, Second Edition,
M. W. Gallagher and S. J. Lopez (Editors)

SELF-EFFICACY: A THEORY UNFOLDS

Bandura (1977) provided researchers and clinicians with a meaningful tool to assist people in pursuit of positive and productive lives when he advanced the self-efficacy component of his social cognitive theory. Self-efficacy, defined as "beliefs in one's capabilities to organize and execute the courses of action required to produce given attainments" (Bandura, 1997, p. 3), leads to initiation of behaviors, effort expended, persistence despite obstacles, and eventual success. Bandura also indicated that self-efficacy beliefs influence resilience when faced with adversity, the presence of helpful or hindering cognitions, and the degree of depression and stress when difficult situations are encountered. Moreover, he suggested that self-efficacy is domain-specific and that "efficacy beliefs should be measured in terms of particularized judgments of capability that may vary across realms of activity, under different levels of task demands within a given activity domain, and under different situational circumstances" (Bandura, 1997, p. 42). The precursors of self-efficacy, according to Bandura, include previous performance accomplishments, vicarious experiences, verbal persuasion, and affective reactions.

CAREER SELF-EFFICACY: MULTIPLE CONSTRUCTS AND MYRIAD MEASURES

The application of Bandura's social cognitive theory and related research to clinical interventions has assisted people to lead healthy and productive lives in myriad ways. For example, researchers have studied the role of career self-efficacy in vocational development and occupational achievement. Career self-efficacy can be broadly defined as confidence in one's ability to manage career development and work-related tasks. This construct has been shown to relate to vocational interests (Nauta, Kahn, Angell, & Cantarelli, 2002), self-esteem (Choi et al., 2012), and career indecision and vocational identity (Betz, Hammond, & Multon, 2005; Choi et al., 2012). Bandura, Barbaranelli, Caprara, and Pastorelli (2001) found that children's perceived occupational self-efficacy was more predictive of career choice than academic performance. Moreover, because this construct is malleable, numerous researchers have developed vocational interventions aimed at enhancing career-related self-efficacy beliefs to promote healthy vocational development and occupational success (e.g., Betz & Schifano, 2000; Grier-Reed & Ganuza, 2012; Isik, 2014; Krieshok, Ulven, Hecox, & Wettersten, 2000; Turner & Lapan, 2005). This chapter focuses on two career-related self-efficacy measures that have great potential to enhance the career functioning of college students and adults.

Career Decision Self-Efficacy: Scale Purpose and Uses

The Career Decision Self-Efficacy Scale—Short Form (CDSE–SF; Betz, Klein, & Taylor, 1996) is a self-report, 25-item inventory developed to assess confidence in making career-related decisions and engaging in tasks related to career decision making (see Appendix 7.1 for several sample items). This instrument can be used to promote confidence and satisfaction in academic or work settings by identifying areas in which college students or adults lack confidence and then developing interventions to increase confidence in the career development process. Individuals who feel confident in pursuing career-related tasks exhibit lower levels of career indecision and feel more confident in exploring careers (Choi et al., 2012), which may, in turn, lead to healthier career choices and eventual success and satisfaction at work.

This scale was formerly known as the Career Decision-Making Self-Efficacy Scale and is widely used. A cursory review of articles published on career self-efficacy revealed that the vast majority of published studies from 2010 until 2015 used the CDSE (Betz et al., 1996; Betz & Taylor, 2000). The instrument was shortened from the original 50-item CDSE developed by Taylor and Betz (1983) through item, split-scale, and factor analyses (Betz et al., 1996). The authors based the development of the original scale (and five subscales) on Crites's (1978) model of career maturity, which identified five career choice competencies believed to underlie healthy career decision making (i.e., accurate self-appraisal, gathering occupational information, goal selection, making future plans, and problem solving). Written permission from the publisher is needed to use this scale (see Appendix 7.1).

Administration and Scoring

The instrument can be administered to individuals or groups and takes fewer than 10 minutes to complete. A 10-level confidence continuum ranging from *no confidence at all* (1) to *complete confidence* (10) or a five-level continuum ranging from *no confidence at all* (1) to *complete confidence* (5) can be used. The five-level response continuum was found to be as reliable and valid as the 10-level continuum (Betz et al., 2005).

All 25 items are summed to obtain the total score on the CDSE–SF. Subscale scores are calculated by summing the scores on the five items for each subscale, and they can range from 5 to 50, or 5 to 25. High scores reflect strong levels of confidence in completing career-related tasks. An average score can be calculated by dividing the total scale sum by 25 or the subscale sum by 5 to allow for ease in interpretation of level of confidence.

Descriptive Statistics

Betz et al. (2005) reported the following descriptive data for a large sample of African American (n = 188), Asian American (n = 71), Latina/Latino (n = 62), and White (n = 1,399) college students. Mean scores ranged from 3.8 (SD = .55) to 3.9 (SD = .73) on the total scale and from 3.7 (SD = .56) to 4.1 (SD = .76) on the subscales (five-level continuum).

Reliability Estimates

According to Betz et al. (2005), the total score (using either the five- or 10-level continuum) was very reliable with large samples of college students, ranging from .93 to .95. Subscale reliabilities ranged from .73 to .81 for self-appraisal, .78 to .82 for occupational information, .83 to .87 for goal selection, .79 to .84 for planning, and .75 to .81 for problem solving (Betz et al., 1996, 2005).

Factor Structure

The research is contradictory regarding the utility of the five-factor structure of the CDSE–SF. In 1996, Betz et al. noted that factor analyses marginally supported the five-factor structure of this measure as the occupational information and goal-selection factors emerged as clear subscales (although planning items were included on each of these factors), the problem-solving and self-appraisal items loaded on two other factors, and only one self-appraisal item made up the fifth factor. More recently, empirical support was found for the five-factor structure with two samples of Asian American students and European American college students (Miller, Sendrowitz Roy, Brown, Thomas, & McDaniel, 2009) and with a large sample of Italian high school students (Lo Presti et al., 2013). Other studies failed to find support for the five-factor model (e.g., Buyukgoze-Kavas, 2014; Chaney, Hammond, Betz, & Multon, 2007; Gaudron, 2011). Nevertheless, Betz and her colleagues suggested using the five-factor solution because of the derivation of these subscales from theory and their usefulness in applied settings (e.g., designing interventions). Alternatively, the total score may be used as an indicator of career decision self-efficacy.

Validity Estimates

Support for the validity of this instrument has been demonstrated through negative correlations with measures of career indecision and positive correlations with vocational identity (Betz et al., 2005; Choi et al., 2012). Scores on the CDSE–SF were related to having stable career goals, being able to set career goals, and knowing how to address career barriers (Betz et al., 2005), as well as self-esteem, peer support, and career-related outcome expectations (Choi et al., 2012).

Use With Diverse Populations

The CDSE–SF has been adapted for use with several international populations, including Chinese, French, Italian, Taiwanese, and Turkish university students (Buyukgoze-Kavas, 2014; Gaudron, 2011; Huang, 2015; Jin, Ye, & Watkins, 2012; Lo Presti et al., 2013). Additionally, the scale has been used with minority American samples, including Asian American (Grier-Reed & Ganuza, 2011; Miller et al., 2009), African American (Chung, 2002; Gushue, Scanlan, Pantzer, & Clarke, 2006), and Latina/o (Gushue, Clarke, Pantzer, & Scanlan, 2006) students. Still, most studies used samples that were majority European Americans; additional research is needed regarding the reliability and validity of the CDSE–SF when used with people of color.

Personal Efficacy Beliefs Scale: Scale Purpose and Uses

The Personal Efficacy Beliefs Scale of the Self-Efficacy and Outcome Expectancy Scales was developed by Riggs, Warka, Babasa, Betancourt, and Hooker (1994) to measure self-efficacy regarding job skills and work-related tasks (see Appendix 7.2). This scale is part of a larger four-scale instrument that assesses personal and collective-worker efficacy as well as personal and collective-worker outcome expectations in varied job fields. Job-related self-efficacy has been linked to general well-being and satisfaction as individuals with high job-related self-efficacy reported strong job performance, positive job-related affectivity, and psychological and physical health (Lubbers, Loughlin, & Zweig, 2005). Moreover, the scale can be used to foster confidence in the workplace by measuring employees' efficacy regarding their job skills and developing interventions to increase confidence in performing work-related tasks.

The measurement of self-efficacy must be domain-specific (Bandura, 1977), which poses challenges for instruments assessing work self-efficacy across different occupations. Riggs et al. (1994) argued that domain specificity in a measure of work self-efficacy could be achieved by instructing respondents to refer to their job skills or job-related outcomes when answering the items rather than describing them within the scale items. Thus, Riggs and colleagues (1994) developed the Personal Efficacy Beliefs Scale with the intention that the scale could be used across various occupations.

Administration and Scoring

The Personal Efficacy Beliefs Scale consists of 10 items and measures confidence in job-related tasks, skills, and abilities. Participants indicate their agreement with the items using the following 6-point Likert scale: *strongly disagree* (1), *disagree* (2), *disagree somewhat* (3), *agree somewhat* (4), *agree* (5), and *strongly agree* (6). Six negatively worded items are reverse coded, and responses to the items are summed. High scores indicate strong job-related self-efficacy.

Descriptive Statistics

Riggs et al. (1994) reported a mean score of 47.29 ($SD = 7.75$) for a sample of 134 employees from diverse jobs. Although the sample consisted of majority White participants, there was approximately equal representation from retail, public education, mental health rehabilitation, and community service occupations. In a more recent study with a sample of 1,966 Korean nurses, a mean score of 35.66 ($SD = 4.54$) was reported (Lee & Ko, 2010). Additionally, a mean score of 38.85 ($SD = 6.56$) was found for a sample of 206 diverse adult workers recruited through Mechanical Turk (Duffy, Bott, Torrey, & Webster, 2013).

Reliability Estimates

Riggs and colleagues (1994) found an internal consistency reliability estimate of .86 for their sample of 134 workers from various job fields for the Personal Efficacy Beliefs Scale. In a more recent study examining the moderating effects of job-related self-efficacy on the relationship between negative affectivity and psychological strain, an internal consistency reliability estimate of .74 was found for a sample of 230 middle- to upper-middle-class Brazilian full-time employees (Zellars, Perrewé, Rossi, Tepper, & Ferris, 2008). Moreover, the internal consistency reliability estimate for a sample of 232 nurses working in acute care in Canada was .82 (Peterson, Hall, O'Brien-Pallas, & Cockerill, 2011).

Factor Structure

Factor analyses revealed a four-factor structure for the entire measure (Riggs et al., 1994), providing support for the items on the Personal Efficacy Beliefs Scale. The Personal Efficacy Beliefs Scale was the most independent factor on the larger measure, correlating from .06 to .28 with the other subscales, suggesting that personal job-related self-efficacy is a unique construct from outcome expectations and collective-worker efficacy.

Validity Estimates

Support for the validity of the Personal Efficacy Beliefs Scale has been demonstrated through positive relationships with measures of satisfaction, job performance, and organization commitment (Riggs et al., 1994). Additionally, in a more recent study, high scores on the Personal Efficacy Beliefs Scale were related to positive mood, task persistence, and task performance (Tsai, Chen, & Liu, 2007). Moreover, job-related self-efficacy predicted general health, such that high scores on the Personal Efficacy Beliefs Scale were related to better general health for employees (Schreurs, van Emmerik, Notelaers, & De Witte, 2010).

Use With Diverse Populations

The Personal Efficacy Beliefs Scale has been used successfully with a number of diverse samples. Internationally, the scale was used with employees in Brazil, Korea, and China (Lee & Ko, 2010; Peng, Schaubroeck, & Xie, 2015; Zellars et al., 2008). The scale also has been used with samples comprised of workers who identified as African American, Asian/Asian American, and Latina/o American (Duffy et al., 2013; Lyons & Schneider, 2009; Pascal & Kurpius, 2012). However, the representation of ethnic minorities within the samples in these studies was low. Therefore, additional research is needed to examine the reliability and validity of the Personal Efficacy Beliefs Scale with racial and ethnic minorities.

CONSTRUCT MEASUREMENT ISSUES

When measuring self-efficacy (or selecting measures of self-efficacy) it is critical to keep the following four points in mind. First, according to Bandura (1997), self-efficacy is domain-specific and must be contextualized:

> Analyses of how efficacy beliefs affect actions rely on microanalytic measures rather than global indices of personality traits or motives of effectance. It is no more informative to speak of self-efficacy in general terms than to speak of nonspecific social behavior. (p. 14)

For example, if a student was asked about her global sense of being able to find a fulfilling career, she may think broadly about her ability to perform well in any job. This overall assessment of career self-efficacy would not take into consideration the student's ability to assess her skills, develop goals, and confront obstacles in the process of identifying careers that match her abilities. Thus, accurate assessment relies on the clear and comprehensive operationalization and measurement of the domain being assessed.

Second, Bandura (1997) indicated that self-efficacy measurement should not be broken down into subskills, but rather assess the person's belief in her or his capability to perform a function (i.e., link a number of subskills) in a variety of challenging situations related to the domain of interest. For example, a career search self-efficacy scale might include items that assess confidence in scheduling an informational interview in a variety of challenging situations. The measurement of this construct should not include items assessing confidence in finding the professional's number or asking to speak to the professional because these items would not assess the construct as a whole, as Bandura (1997) intended. Including challenging items ensures variability in scores and guards against ceiling effects.

Third, as to specific instructions regarding the wording of items, Bandura (1995) indicated that items should not inquire about future plans to complete a task (thus assessing intention), but rather should be phrased to assess thoughts regarding current ability to perform the task. Specifically, items should be written to assess what individuals think they can do now versus what they will do or what they plan to do. Moreover, individuals must understand what they are rating to obtain an accurate assessment of self-efficacy. If a participant does not know what an ophthalmologist is, she cannot accurately rate her ability to complete the tasks necessary for this career. Also, items should be written at the appropriate reading level and should not assess more than one task per item. For example, an item should not read "Rate your confidence in your ability to ask your boss for a raise and to describe your many work accomplishments," because the employee may have different levels of efficacy for asking for a raise versus articulating her successes at work. In addition, Bandura recommended including a sample item and rating self-efficacy on a 100- or 10-point scale to obtain variability in scores.

Fourth, at times the measurement of self-efficacy has been confused with other constructs (e.g., self-esteem, outcome expectations). For example, Bandura (1997) noted that self-efficacy addresses feelings regarding abilities, whereas self-esteem focuses on sense of self-worth. An individual might have low self-efficacy for pursuing a career as a physician, yet these beliefs may not negatively affect one's sense of self if there is no interest in a career in medicine.

FUTURE DIRECTIONS FOR THE MEASUREMENT OF CAREER-RELATED SELF-EFFICACY

Researchers and practitioners have used measures of career-related self-efficacy to facilitate knowledge about, and interventions to enhance, the vocational development of many people. Continued research is needed to develop and use career-related self-efficacy measures with people from varied cultures, backgrounds, and occupations. In addition, the use of these measures in the evaluation of vocational interventions is strongly recommended.

First, many career-related self-efficacy measures have been used without attention to the reliability and validity of these instruments with diverse samples. Given the changing demographics of American society, researchers must attend to the psychometric properties of these instruments with people of color. This call to action presents challenges because self-efficacy measures must be domain-specific. Although it is unlikely that measures of every construct could be developed and tested with every diverse group, attention to the proper development of self-efficacy measures and accurate assessment of the psychometric properties of these instruments with people of color could result in a greater number of measures for use in research and practice. Similarly, Miller and colleagues (2009) emphasized the need to consider conceptual equivalence, or the meaningfulness of a construct across cultural groups, when using career-related self-efficacy measures. Future researchers should investigate potentially universal experiences and culturally specific experiences related to making career decisions with international samples (Miller et al., 2009). Kim (2017) provided an excellent example of investigating the psychometric properties of an often-used instrument across diverse groups.

Second, the research on career-related self-efficacy often reports on the confidence levels of college students. Similar to Brown, Reedy, Fountain, Johnson, and Dichiser (2000) in their investigation of the career decision-making self-efficacy of abused women, researchers must study a wide variety of individuals who may, in fact, need career assistance more than college students. Notable examples include the interventions developed for veterans to strengthen self-efficacy expectations for job searching, decision making, and integrating a new understanding of problems in future vocational decisions and work experiences (Krieshok et al., 2000).

Third, researchers should be encouraged to use self-efficacy measures when evaluating vocational interventions designed to enhance career-related self-efficacy. For example, studies have highlighted effective interventions for improving career self-efficacy using an interest inventory intervention (Isik, 2014), increasing women's self-efficacy in pursuing traditionally male-dominated occupations (Betz & Schifano, 2000) and enhancing career self-efficacy among first-generation, low-income, and underrepresented TRIO students (Grier-Reed & Ganuza, 2012; O'Brien, Dukstein, Jackson, Tomlinson, & Kamatuka, 1999). Continued research is needed to inform the development of career interventions that are based in theory and previous research.

Fourth, the call put forth many years ago that we integrate environmental factors into the study of career self-efficacy (an individually focused construct; Lent, Brown, & Hackett, 1994; Lent & Hackett, 1987) remains salient today. Given that self-efficacy was born from a theory that posits the reciprocal interaction of person, environment, and behavior, it seems timely to echo their call for continued research involving contextual variables.

CASE EXAMPLE

The client, Elena, is a 20-year-old Mexican American woman who is a first-generation college student majoring in chemistry at a prestigious university in Washington, DC. Her reason for seeking counseling was "to figure out who I am and what I value so I can make some important life decisions." She is feeling increasing sadness, difficulty concentrating on her schoolwork, lethargy, loss of motivation, and bursts of anger. Elena is not taking any medication and never sought counseling previously.

In the intake session, Elena presented with career and relationship concerns. She is very successful in school, although she is questioning whether she wants to continue in the chemistry major. Elena does well in her courses, but she does not enjoy the course material. She is uncertain about whether she wants to become a physician—a goal she and her family have had for many years. Elena maintains close relationships with her parents and sister, all of whom live in Kansas City.

In the initial sessions, Elena reported periods of sadness and loss of interest in schoolwork. She forces herself to attend her classes and study as she does not want to disappoint herself or her parents. In counseling, Elena agreed to complete two career inventories and was assigned an interest inventory and the CDSE–SF. Her highest themes on the interest inventory were in the artistic, social, and enterprising areas. On the CDSE–SF, she scored highest on gathering occupational information, accurate self-appraisal, and problem solving. Her scores on goal selection and making future plans were extremely low, indicating that she had very little confidence in her ability to choose a major/career and determine her future career path.

Although Elena enthusiastically participated in the interpretation of the tests, she was disappointed when they did not specifically indicate whether she should continue in chemistry and pursue medical school. The therapist talked with Elena about who she is, what she enjoys, and her feelings about questioning her previous career goals. Elena indicated that she enjoys photography, cycling, hiking, traveling, and volunteering in a soup kitchen. She wants a career where she makes a difference and can be creative, but she does not feel called to be a physician. Not being sure of her path creates much anxiety, and Elena again voiced her fear of disappointing her parents. The foci of therapy, aided by the inventories completed, included (a) normalizing the need for time to figure out what career to pursue, (b) assisting Elena in developing confidence in choosing a major and future career, and (c) role-playing how Elena might discuss her uncertainty about medical school with her parents. In the course of the therapy, Elena successfully talked with her parents about her feelings and began to feel more hopeful and confident about finding a career that matched her interests and abilities. At the conclusion of therapy, Elena was committed to taking a wide range of courses, pursuing several internship and volunteer opportunities, and taking time to decide on her future career path.

CONCLUSION

Career-related self-efficacy is related to success and satisfaction in making vocational decisions and is predictive of both occupational and life satisfaction (Choi et al., 2012; Flores & O'Brien, 2002; Piña-Watson et al., 2014; Spurk & Abele, 2014). Continued attention to the measurement of this construct could assist researchers and practitioners in improving the quality of life for those who seek fulfilling careers, strive to succeed in work, and aspire to lead positive and productive lives.

APPENDIX 7.1
CAREER DECISION SELF-EFFICACY SCALE

EXAMPLE ITEMS:

1. Choose a major or career that will fit your interests.
2. Talk with a person already employed in the field you are interested in.
3. Make a plan of your goals for the next five years.
4. Determine what your ideal job would be.
5. Identify some reasonable major or career alternatives if you are unable to get your first choice.

From "Career Decision Self-Efficacy Scale," by N. E. Betz and K. M. Taylor, 2012, (https://www.mindgarden.com/79-career-decision-self-efficacy-scale).

APPENDIX 7.2
THE PERSONAL EFFICACY BELIEFS SCALE

Think about your ability to do the tasks required by your job. When answering the following questions, answer in reference to your own personal work skills and ability to perform your job.

Strongly Disagree	*Disagree*	*Disagree Somewhat*	*Agree Somewhat*	*Agree*	*Strongly Agree*
1	2	3	4	5	6

1. I have confidence in my ability to do my job.
2. There are some tasks required by my job that I cannot do well.*
3. When my performance is poor, it is due to my lack of ability.*
4. I doubt my ability to do my job.*
5. I have all the skills needed to perform my job well.
6. Most people in my line of work can do this job better than I can.*
7. I am an expert at my job.
8. My future in this job is limited because of my lack of skills.*
9. I am very proud of my job skills and abilities.
10. I feel threatened when other watch me work.*

Note. * = reverse scored. From "Development and Validation of Self-Efficacy and Outcome Expectancy Scales for Job-Related Applications," by M. L. Riggs, J. Warka, B. Babasa, R. Betancourt, and S. Hooker, 1994, *Educational and Psychological Measurement, 54* (p. 797). Copyright 1994 by SAGE. Reprinted with permission.

REFERENCES

Bandura, A. (1977). Self-efficacy: Toward a unifying theory of behavioral change. *Psychological Review, 84,* 191–215. http://dx.doi.org/10.1037/0033-295X.84.2.191

Bandura, A. (1995). *Guide for constructing self-efficacy scales.* Unpublished manuscript, Stanford University, Stanford, California.

Bandura, A. (1997). *Self-efficacy: The exercise of control.* New York, NY: W. H. Freeman.

Bandura, A., Barbaranelli, C., Caprara, G. V., & Pastorelli, C. (2001). Self-efficacy beliefs as shapers of children's aspirations and career trajectories. *Child Development, 72,* 187–206. http://dx.doi.org/10.1111/1467-8624.00273

Betz, N. E., Hammond, M. S., & Multon, K. D. (2005). Reliability and validity of five-level response continua for the Career Decision Self-Efficacy Scale. *Journal of Career Assessment, 13,* 131–149. http://dx.doi.org/10.1177/1069072704273123

Betz, N. E., Klein, K., & Taylor, K. M. (1996). Evaluation of a short form of the Career Decision-Making Self-Efficacy Scale. *Journal of Career Assessment, 4,* 47–57. http://dx.doi.org/10.1177/106907279600400103

Betz, N. E., & Schifano, R. S. (2000). Evaluation of an intervention to increase realistic self-efficacy and interests in college women. *Journal of Vocational Behavior, 56,* 35–52. http://dx.doi.org/10.1006/jvbe.1999.1690

Betz, N. E., & Taylor, K. M. (2000). *Manual for the Career Decision Self-Efficacy Scale and CDMSE—Short Form.* Unpublished instrument, Ohio State University, Columbus.

Betz, N. E., & Taylor, K. M. (2012). *Career Decision Self-Efficacy Scale.* Retrieved from Mind Garden, Inc. website: https://www.mindgarden.com/79-career-decision-self-efficacy-scale

Brown, C., Reedy, D., Fountain, J., Johnson, A., & Dichiser, T. (2000). Battered women's career decision-making self-efficacy: Further insights and contributing factors. *Journal of Career Assessment, 8,* 251–265. http://dx.doi.org/10.1177/106907270000800304

Buyukgoze-Kavas, A. (2014). A psychometric evaluation of the Career Decision Self-Efficacy Scale—Short Form with Turkish university students. *Journal of Career Assessment, 22,* 386–397. http://dx.doi.org/10.1177/1069072713484561

Chaney, D., Hammond, M. S., Betz, N. E., & Multon, K. D. (2007). The reliability and factor structure of the Career Decision Self-Efficacy Scale—SF with African Americans. *Journal of Career Assessment, 15,* 194–205. http://dx.doi.org/10.1177/1069072706298020

Choi, B. Y., Park, H., Yang, E., Lee, S. K., Lee, Y., & Lee, S. M. (2012). Understanding career decision self-efficacy: A meta-analytic approach. *Journal of Career Development, 39,* 443–460. http://dx.doi.org/10.1177/0894845311398042

Chung, Y. B. (2002). Career decision-making self-efficacy and career commitment: Gender and ethnic differences among college students. *Journal of Career Development, 28,* 277–284. http://dx.doi.org/10.1177/089484530202800404

Clifton, D. O. (2000). Mapping the wellsprings of a positive life: The importance of measurement to the movement. *The Gallup Review, 3,* 8–13.

Crites, J. O. (1978). *Career Maturity Inventory.* Monterey, CA: CTB/McGraw Hill.

Duffy, R. D., Bott, E. M., Torrey, C. L., & Webster, G. W. (2013). Work volition as a critical moderator in the prediction of job satisfaction. *Journal of Career Assessment, 21,* 20–31. http://dx.doi.org/10.1177/1069072712453831

Flores, L. Y., & O'Brien, K. M. (2002). The career development of Mexican American adolescent women: A test of social cognitive career theory. *Journal of Counseling Psychology, 49,* 14–27. http://dx.doi.org/10.1037/0022-0167.49.1.14

Gaudron, J. (2011). A psychometric evaluation of the Career Decision Self-Efficacy Scale—Short Form among French university students. *Journal of Career Assessment, 19,* 420–430. http://dx.doi.org/10.1177/1069072711409713

Grier-Reed, T., & Ganuza, Z. M. (2011). Constructivism and career decision self-efficacy for Asian Americans and African Americans. *Journal of Counseling & Development, 89,* 200–205. http://dx.doi.org/10.1002/j.1556-6678.2011.tb00078.x

Grier-Reed, T., & Ganuza, Z. (2012). Using constructivist career development to improve career decision self-efficacy in TRIO students. *Journal of College Student Development, 53,* 464–471. http://dx.doi.org/10.1353/csd.2012.0045

Gushue, G. V., Clarke, C. P., Pantzer, K. M., & Scanlan, K. L. (2006). Self-efficacy, perceptions of barriers, vocational identity, and the career exploration behavior of Latino/a high school students. *The Career Development Quarterly, 54,* 307–317. http://dx.doi.org/10.1002/j.2161-0045.2006.tb00196.x

Gushue, G. V., Scanlan, K. L., Pantzer, K. M., & Clarke, C. P. (2006). The relationship of career decision-making self-efficacy, vocational identity, and career exploration behavior in African American high school students. *Journal of Career Development, 33,* 19–28. http://dx.doi.org/10.1177/0894845305283004

Hackett, G., & Betz, N. E. (1981). A self-efficacy approach to the career development of women. *Journal of Vocational Behavior, 18,* 326–339. http://dx.doi.org/10.1016/0001-8791(81)90019-1

Huang, J. (2015). Hardiness, perceived employability, and career decision self-efficacy among Taiwanese college students. *Journal of Career Development, 42,* 311–324. http://dx.doi.org/10.1177/0894845314562960

Isik, E. (2014). Effects of a brief interest inventory intervention on career decision self-efficacy. *Australian Journal of Guidance and Counselling, 24,* 215–226. http://dx.doi.org/10.1017/jgc.2014.13

Jin, L., Ye, S., & Watkins, D. (2012). The dimensionality of the Career Decision Self-Efficacy Scale—Short Form among Chinese graduate students. *Journal of Career Assessment, 20,* 520–529. http://dx.doi.org/10.1177/1069072712450492

Kim, Y. H. (2017). *Career barriers of college women across racial/ethnic groups: Examination of the Perception of Barriers Scale* (Unpublished doctoral dissertation). University of Maryland, College Park.

Krieshok, T. S., Ulven, J. C., Hecox, J. L., & Wettersten, K. (2000). Resume therapy and vocational test feedback: Tailoring interventions to self-efficacy outcomes. *Journal of Career Assessment, 8,* 267–281. http://dx.doi.org/10.1177/106907270000800305

Lee, T. W., & Ko, Y. K. (2010). Effects of self-efficacy, affectivity and collective efficacy on nursing performance of hospital nurses. *Journal of Advanced Nursing, 66,* 839–848. http://dx.doi.org/10.1111/j.1365-2648.2009.05244.x

Lent, R. W., Brown, S. D., & Hackett, G. (1994). Toward a unifying social cognitive theory of career and academic interest, choice, and performance. *Journal of Vocational Behavior, 45,* 79–122. http://dx.doi.org/10.1006/jvbe.1994.1027

Lent, R. W., & Hackett, G. (1987). Career self-efficacy: Empirical status and future directions. *Journal of Vocational Behavior, 30,* 347–382. http://dx.doi.org/10.1016/0001-8791(87)90010-8

Lo Presti, A., Pace, F., Mondo, M., Nota, L., Casarubia, P., Ferrari, L., & Betz, N. E. (2013). An examination of the structure of the Career Decision Self-Efficacy Scale (short form) among Italian high school students. *Journal of Career Assessment, 21,* 337–347. http://dx.doi.org/10.1177/1069072712471506

Lubbers, R., Loughlin, C., & Zweig, D. (2005). Young workers' job self-efficacy and affect: Pathways to health and performance. *Journal of Vocational Behavior, 67,* 199–214. http://dx.doi.org/10.1016/j.jvb.2004.03.002

Lyons, J. B., & Schneider, T. R. (2009). The effects of leadership style on stress outcomes. *The Leadership Quarterly, 20,* 737–748. http://dx.doi.org/10.1016/j.leaqua.2009.06.010

Miller, M. J., Sendrowitz Roy, K., Brown, S. D., Thomas, J., & McDaniel, C. (2009). A confirmatory test of the factor structure of the short form of the Career Decision Self-Efficacy Scale. *Journal of Career Assessment, 17,* 507–519. http://dx.doi.org/10.1177/1069072709340665

Nauta, M. M., Kahn, J., Angell, J., & Cantarelli, E. A. (2002). Identifying the antecedent in the relation between career interests and self-efficacy: Is it one, the other, or both? *Journal of Counseling Psychology, 49,* 290–301. http://dx.doi.org/10.1037/0022-0167.49.3.290

O'Brien, K. M., Dukstein, R. D., Jackson, S. L., Tomlinson, M. J., & Kamatuka, N. A. (1999). Broadening career horizons for students in at-risk environments. *The Career Development Quarterly, 47,* 215–229. http://dx.doi.org/10.1002/j.2161-0045.1999.tb00732.x

Pascal, B., & Kurpius, S. R. (2012). Perceptions of clients: Influences of client weight and job status. *Professional Psychology: Research and Practice, 43,* 349–355. http://dx.doi.org/10.1037/a0028525

Peng, A. C., Schaubroeck, J. M., & Xie, J. L. (2015). When confidence comes and goes: How variation in self-efficacy moderates stressor-strain relationships. *Journal of Occupational Health Psychology, 20,* 359–376. http://dx.doi.org/10.1037/a0038588

Peterson, J., Hall, L. M., O'Brien-Pallas, L., & Cockerill, R. (2011). Job satisfaction and intentions to leave of new nurses. *Journal of Research in Nursing, 16,* 536–548. http://dx.doi.org/10.1177/1744987111422423

Piña-Watson, B., Jimenez, N., & Ojeda, L. (2014). Self-construal, career decision self-efficacy, and perceived barriers predict Mexican American women's life satisfaction. *The Career Development Quarterly, 62,* 210–223. http://dx.doi.org/10.1002/j.2161-0045.2014.00080.x

Riggs, M. L., Warka, J., Babasa, B., Betancourt, R., & Hooker, S. (1994). Development and validation of self-efficacy and outcome expectancy scales for job-related applications. *Educational and Psychological Measurement, 54,* 793–802. http://dx.doi.org/10.1177/0013164494054003026

Schreurs, B., van Emmerik, H., Notelaers, G., & De Witte, H. (2010). Job insecurity and employee health: The buffering potential of job control and job self-efficacy. *Work & Stress, 24,* 56–72. http://dx.doi.org/10.1080/02678371003718733

Spurk, D., & Abele, A. E. (2014). Synchronous and time-lagged effects between occupational self-efficacy and objective and subjective career success: Findings from a four-wave and 9-year longitudinal study. *Journal of Vocational Behavior, 84,* 119–132. http://dx.doi.org/10.1016/j.jvb.2013.12.002

Taylor, K. M., & Betz, N. E. (1983). Applications of self-efficacy theory to the understanding and treatment of career indecision. *Journal of Vocational Behavior, 22,* 63–81. http://dx.doi.org/10.1016/0001-8791(83)90006-4

Tsai, W. C., Chen, C. C., & Liu, H. L. (2007). Test of a model linking employee positive moods and task performance. *Journal of Applied Psychology, 92,* 1570–1583. http://dx.doi.org/10.1037/0021-9010.92.6.1570

Turner, S. L., & Lapan, R. T. (2005). Evaluation of an intervention to increase non-traditional career interests and career-related self-efficacy among middle-school adolescents. *Journal of Vocational Behavior, 66,* 516–531. http://dx.doi.org/10.1016/j.jvb.2004.02.005

Zellars, K. L., Perrewé, P. L., Rossi, A. M., Tepper, B. J., & Ferris, G. R. (2008). Moderating effects of political skill, perceived control, and job-related self-efficacy on the relationship between negative affectivity and physiological strain. *Journal of Organizational Behavior, 29,* 549–571. http://dx.doi.org/10.1002/job.484

8

Creating a Positive Life

The Role of Problem-Solving Appraisal

Puncky Paul Heppner, Mary J. Heppner, Yu-Wei Wang, and Dong-Gwi Lee

Life comes with problems, but it is how we cope with those inevitable problems that can make the difference between a positive life where we experience a great deal of satisfaction and well-being or one mired in distress and difficulty. An important individual difference that affects how people cope with myriad life problems is how people evaluate their problem-solving capabilities as well as their style of approaching or avoiding problems, which has been identified as a person's *problem-solving appraisal* (P. P. Heppner & Wang, 2003; P. P. Heppner, Witty, & Dixon, 2004). More specifically, over a quarter century of research and practice with the most widely used measure of problem-solving appraisal, the Problem-Solving Inventory (PSI; P. P. Heppner, 1988), clearly indicates that when people (a) have greater confidence in how they deal with inevitable life problems, (b) have a greater proclivity to take a proactive stance in approaching problems, and (c) possess greater control over their emotions as they move through these problems, they are much more likely to experience better psychological and physical health. For example, those with a positive problem-solving appraisal tend to have (a) more positive self-concepts, such as self-esteem and life meaning (Choi & Son, 2007); (b) higher levels of self-efficacy, assertiveness, and personal agency (P. P. Heppner, Witty, & Dixon, 2004); (c) more positive family environments characterized by healthy and supportive relationships (Pretorius, 1993) and perceived social support (Park, 2005); (d) higher levels of optimism and positive emotions (H.-K. Lee, 2008), and (e) a more positive outlook and view of

http://dx.doi.org/10.1037/0000138-008
Positive Psychological Assessment: A Handbook of Models and Measures, Second Edition,
M. W. Gallagher and S. J. Lopez (Editors)

their partners (Larson, Allen, Imao, & Piersel, 1993), their counseling sessions (M. J. Heppner et al., 2004), and their resources within their communities (Neal & Heppner, 1986). Also, they tend to be people who are clearer about their vocational identity (Larson, Toulouse, Ngumba, Fitzpatrick, & Heppner, 1994) and who report more positive outcomes in their career planning (M. J. Heppner et al., 2004). In addition, they are much less likely to suffer from psychological maladjustment, including uneasiness, worry, depression, anxiety, hopelessness, suicidal ideation, or irrational beliefs (see P. P. Heppner, Witty, & Dixon, 2004). In essence, there is a great deal of power in a positive problem-solving appraisal to help individuals pursue and achieve better lives (Larson & Heppner, 1985).

In many cases these are not small or clinically insignificant results; rather, how individuals appraise their problem-solving capability can account for a great deal of variance (see P. P. Heppner et al., 2004). Lopez and Janowski (2004) concluded that the construct of problem-solving appraisal, and the extensive line of supportive programmatic research, was in fact implementing what Super (1955) discussed over 5 decades ago as *hygiology,* or in effect, "locating and developing personal and social resources and adaptive tendencies so that the individual can be assisted in making more effective use of them" (p. 5). Thus, if counselors and educators enhance people's problem-solving appraisal, the existing empirical data strongly suggest that clients and students are likely to lead a much more positive life on a host of indicators.

Most important, one's problem-solving appraisal is changeable, and with appropriate interventions, individuals can be empowered to develop more positive problem-solving appraisal. In fact, at least nine studies have now found that a wide range of interventions—from telephone protocols (Grant, 1999), to career counseling (M. J. Heppner et al., 2004), to motivational courses (Chynoweth, Blankinship, & Parker, 1986), to individual psychotherapy (P. P. Heppner, Cooper, Mulholland, & Wei, 2001)—all significantly improved people's problem-solving appraisal. In short, problem-solving appraisal is a construct that not only has been related to myriad positive life outcomes but also can be learned and enhanced; thus, individuals who have not developed a positive appraisal can be educated to do so and gain greater well-being.

This chapter first describes the construct of problem-solving appraisal in more detail and the related assessment inventory, the PSI (P. P. Heppner, 1988), to measure this construct. We present information regarding the instrument's reliability, validity, norms, and applications. Second, we also provide information on two other instruments that assess other dimensions of applied problem solving, the Problem Resolution Outcome Survey (PROS; P. P. Heppner et al., 2001) and the Problem-Focused Style of Coping (PF–SOC) inventory (P. P. Heppner, Cook, Wright, & Johnson, 1995). Third, we provide a case example of how counselors can work with clients using client's PSI scores in a strengths-based approach. Finally, we suggest strategies integrating the construct of problem-solving appraisal more fully into the positive psychology literature and examine its role in helping people live their best life.

THE PROBLEM-SOLVING INVENTORY

People respond to applied personal problems in different ways. Some people bring a wealth of resources to coping with their problems, whereas others show significant problem-solving deficits. For example, consider Tanya, who had been working for a large, high-tech firm as director of research. Her company was downsized, and she was laid off with little warning. Naturally, she was disappointed, but she was also confident she could find employment, maybe even a position that would be more satisfying. In fact, after a few days Tanya saw this as an opportunity to make a career change. Within a few weeks of her dismissal, Tanya had updated her resume, arranged informational interviews, and was making progress toward resolving career problems.

Conversely, consider Tom, who moved to a new city when his wife was relocated. Tom had worked as an accountant and was experiencing a considerable amount of fear in looking for a new position. He slept and drank more than usual and did other, less important tasks than seeking new employment. Tom found himself applying for jobs well below his experience level in hopes that someone would find him competent. Tom's lack of confidence in his ability to find employment impeded his progress in resolving his career problem. The two contrasting scenarios not only highlight how people respond to personal problems in different ways, but also how one's self-assessment of his or her problem-solving capability affects one's well-being and life satisfaction.

Instrument

The PSI assesses perceptions of one's problem-solving ability, as well as behaviors and attitudes associated with one's problem-solving style (P. P. Heppner, 1988; P. P. Heppner & Baker, 1997). The inventory does not assess actual problem-solving skills (although there is a strong relationship between appraisal and skills; see P. P. Heppner et al., 2004). The term *problem* refers to both intrapersonal and interpersonal issues that many people experience in daily life as well as more stressful and even traumatic life events—in essence, common problems of everyday life that can keep people from living the most satisfying life that they possibly can.

The PSI consists of 35 items (including three filler items) with a 6-point Likert-type scale (1 = *strongly agree* to 6 = *strongly disagree*). This inventory can be completed in 10 to 15 minutes in any location. It can be either hand scored in fewer than 5 minutes or computer scored. The PSI should be administered and interpreted by professionals who have training in assessment, knowledge of the problem-solving literature, and normative information on the scale.

The PSI consists of three factors: (a) Problem-Solving Confidence (PSC, 11 items), (b) Approach–Avoidance Style (AAS, 16 items), and (c) Personal Control (PC, 5 items); the PSI total score is the sum of these three subscales. Specifically, PSC is defined as an individual's self-assurance and a belief and trust in one's ability to effectively cope with a wide range of problems (e.g., "When faced with a novel situation, I have confidence that I can handle problems that may arise"). Lower PSC scores reflect higher levels of problem-solving confidence. AAS refers to a general tendency to approach or avoid different problem-solving activities (e.g., "When making a decision, I weigh the consequences of each alternative and compare them against each other"). Lower AAS scores are associated with approaching rather than avoiding problems. PC is defined as believing one is in control of his or her emotions and behaviors while engaging in problem solving (e.g., "Even though I work on a problem, sometimes I feel like I am groping or wandering, and am not getting down to the real issue"). Lower PC scores indicate more positive individual perception of control in handling problems. The intercorrelations among the three factors typically range from .39 to .69 (see P. P. Heppner, 1988), which suggests that the factors are somewhat interrelated yet distinct.

There are three existing forms of the PSI. The first version (Form A) was published in 1982 and later revised (P. P. Heppner, 1988) as Form B. Eighteen of the original PSI items were reworded to make them easier to understand. Form B is the most widely used version and has a great deal of support for the factor structure using both exploratory and confirmatory factor analyses, which suggests that the PSI factor structure is generalizable across different age groups from various backgrounds such as midwestern high school students (P. P. Heppner, Manley, Perez, & Dixon, 1994); midwestern White college students (e.g., P. P. Heppner, Baumgardner, Larson, & Petty, 1988); military personnel consisting of mostly White Americans and African Americans (Chynoweth, 1987); as well as a similar factor structure across different cultural contexts such as French Canadian adults (Laporte, Sabourin, & Wright, 1988), Turkish college students (Sahin, Sahin, & Heppner, 1993), South African college students (P. P. Heppner, Pretorius, Wei, Lee, & Wang, 2002), and Italian college students (Nota, Heppner, Soresi, & Heppner, 2009). The adolescent version of the PSI was created by reducing the reading levels of the items in Form B from a 9.25 grade to approximately a fourth-grade level (P. P. Heppner et al., 1994). Form B and the adolescent version are available from the first author.

Reliability

The PSI has acceptable internal consistency, which has been demonstrated across a number of populations and cultures (e.g., P. P. Heppner, 1988; P. P. Heppner et al., 1994, 2004): PSI total (high 80s), PSC (mid 80s), AAS (low to mid 80s), and PC (low 70s). Thus, the PSI is internally consistent even with different forms across quite different cultural groups. Five studies provided estimates of stability of the PSI total over various time intervals, from 2 weeks to 2 years (*r*s = .80–.81 over 2 weeks to 4 months and .60 over 2 years) across samples of White college students, Black college students, and French Canadian adults (e.g., P. P. Heppner, 1988). In essence, the results suggest that the PSI scores are stable over time across different populations and cultures.

Validity

A wide range of studies provide a wealth of data supporting the validity of the PSI (see P. P. Heppner, 1988; P. P. Heppner & Baker, 1997; P. P. Heppner & Lee, 2002; P. P. Heppner et al., 2004). A range of studies have supported the concurrent and discriminant validity of problem-solving appraisal. For example, the three subscale scores and the total PSI scores were correlated with students' self-ratings of their levels of problem-solving skills and satisfaction with these skills (P. P. Heppner & Petersen, 1982). Further, raters blind to the research participants' PSI scores independently and successfully differentiated high and low scorers on the PSI (P. P. Heppner & Petersen, 1982), which provided additional support for the construct validity of the PSI. Also, the PSI scores were not strongly correlated with aptitude measures or social desirability (P. P. Heppner & Petersen, 1982), which in turn helped to establish its discriminant validity.

Moreover, a wide range of other studies have related problem-solving appraisal to positive psychological constructs, such as self-esteem and life meaning (Choi & Son, 2007; P. P. Heppner, Reeder, & Larson, 1983); higher levels of self-efficacy, assertiveness, and personal agency (P. P. Heppner et al., 2004); community integration (Rath, Hennessy, & Diller, 2003); positive vocational identity (P. P. Heppner et al., 2004); internal locus of control (Cook & Heppner, 1997); higher levels of optimism and positive emotion (H.-K. Lee, 2008); marital satisfaction (Sabourin, Laporte, & Wright, 1990); social skills (Elliott, Godshall, Herrick, Witty, & Spruell, 1991); and social support (Wright & Heppner, 1991). Although problem-solving appraisal relates in conceptually meaningful ways to several positive psychological constructs, the variance accounted for is typically less than 25% in any of these studies, indicating that problem-solving appraisal is clearly a distinct construct.

Normative Information

In general, nonclinical populations have lower PSI means (i.e., more positive problem-solving appraisal) than do clinical populations. For college students, nonclinical samples had a PSI mean around 88 with a range of 78 to 89 (e.g., P. P. Heppner, 1988), whereas the mean score for the clinical samples tended to be around 100 with a range of 87 to 118 (e.g., Nezu, 1986). Likewise for adults, nonclinical samples had a PSI mean in the low 80s with a range from 65 to 97 (e.g., Sabourin, Laporte, & Wright, 1990), whereas for clinical adult samples the mean tended to be around 100 with a range of 75 to 126 (Reis & Heppner, 1993). Although PSI means represent approximations (i.e., sample sizes were not taken into account), the distributions suggest rather impressive differences between clinical and nonclinical samples (see P. P. Heppner et al., 2004).

Applications

The PSI has a wide range of applications. In terms of working with clients, it can provide an assessment of a client's problem-solving style that may facilitate his or her ability to live a life of health and well-being, which in turn can be used to inform strengths-based interventions. In addition, the PSI can be a very good outcome measure for evaluating service delivery in general, and in particular for problem-solving training interventions.

The PSI has been used successfully as a training tool to enhance participants' awareness of their problem-solving attitudes, knowledge, and skills (e.g., P. P. Heppner & Reeder, 1984). It also has been applied to school settings, such as helping at-risk youth to see the strengths they bring to their situation and helping them use those strengths for their own betterment and life satisfaction (see P. P. Heppner & Baker, 1997). In essence, from a positive psychology perspective, the PSI has great potential to help people identify and utilize their strengths and assets to lead better lives.

RELATED CONCEPTUALIZATIONS OF PROBLEM SOLVING

Two other strategies to assess verbal measures of applied problem solving are briefly discussed next because they are based on related conceptualizations. The first strategy was to examine the degree to which one's problem-solving activities can facilitate progress toward the outcome or resolution of normal stressful problems, which reflects the perceived effectiveness of one's problem solving to alter the problem or stressor (P. P. Heppner et al., 1995). In short, the construct of problem resolution integrates problem-solving constructs with traditional coping constructs such as problem-focused coping and thus straddles both the traditional applied problem solving and coping literatures. The PF–SOC (P. P. Heppner et al., 1995) was designed to assess such construct. The PF–SOC consists of 18 items with a 5-point Likert scale (1 = *almost never*, 5 = *almost all of the time*) and assesses how frequently each item describes one's personal styles of coping. It contains three subscales: (a) Reflective, which emphasizes cognitive activities such as planning, reflection, and causal analyses; (b) Reactive, which emphasizes emotional and cognitive activities that deplete the individual or distort problem-solving activities; and (c) Suppressive, which indicates an avoidance and denial of problem-solving activities (P. P. Heppner et al., 1995). Psychometric information suggests a stable factor structure; acceptable internal consistency; good stability estimates; and very good estimates of discriminant, concurrent, and construct validity (P. P. Heppner et al., 1995). Research has also suggested that the PF–SOC adds a unique dimension to the assessment of applied problem solving (P. P. Heppner et al., 1995).

The construct of problem resolution has been further operationalized within a counseling context. P. P. Heppner et al. (2001) developed a problem-based psychotherapy outcome measure, the PROS, that assesses the extent to which clients have resolved their presenting concerns. The PROS consists of 24 items and four subscales: (a) Problem Solving Strategies (which represents critical strategies for resolving problems with specific goals, plans, and actions), (b) Problem-Solving Self-Efficacy (which represents a motivational component, or agency, in resolving one's presenting problems), (c) Problem Impact on Daily Functioning (which reflects the extent of impairment on a broad range of daily functioning domains), and (d) General Satisfaction with Therapy (which provides an index of satisfaction with how counseling helped the clients resolve their problems). The total score reflects a multidimensional assessment of client resolution of presenting problems, from specific problem-solving strategies to global satisfaction. The validity estimates suggest that the PROS scores were related to other process, outcome, and problem-solving measures in theoretically consistent ways.

In sum, there are a number of strategies to assess verbal reports of applied problem solving. Researchers have used different strategies to measure different aspects of the problem-solving process. Recently, investigators have added a perceived effectiveness component to the items to assess the perceived or implied impact of problem-solving activities on resolution of stress, such as with the PF–SOC and PROS. The multiple assessment strategies reflect the multifaceted nature of assessing applied problem solving as well as the evolution of conceptualizing and measuring applied problem solving.

UTILIZING THE PSI IN COUNSELING: A STRENGTHS-BASED APPROACH

Pauline was an emergency department nurse and highly competent at her challenging job. She had been a nurse for almost 10 years and had performed very well over the years. She had risen quickly within the ranks, as she was always able to "keep her head" and remain calm and productive even under the most trying circumstances. She was now at the manager level within the hospital's emergency unit and had supervisory responsibilities over a large staff. She had trained almost everyone who currently worked in the emergency unit, and they continued to rely on her for mentoring and guidance. Pauline often took the night shift as many of her married work colleagues had families, and she wanted them to be able to be with their children as much as possible. Pauline had many friends and was well liked by her coworkers. She was active with her friends, often dining and doing outdoor activities.

Pauline's mother lived in the same community, and she visited her mother every day just to check up on her and see if she was doing okay in the assisted living community where she resided. Her mother had suffered two small strokes and was continuing to decline. Pauline knew it would be very difficult for her when her mother died because they had been very close for her entire life. In January she received a call that the nursing staff had found her mother dead in her apartment. Pauline was shocked by the suddenness of the death as she had just been talking with her mother the day before, and she seemed stronger than usual.

Pauline took a week off from work to attend to the funeral and clean out her mother's apartment. On the first evening Pauline returned to work, a survivor from a severe car crash was rushed to the emergency room. Pauline's adrenaline kicked in, and she began functioning in her typical competent manner.

The survivor was badly injured; her face was badly cut and bruised. As Pauline began to stabilize the patient's condition, she suddenly realized it was her best friend lying there. Shortly after she made this recognition, her friend died on the emergency room table. Pauline was devastated.

Pauline came in for counseling a month later; she had gone from a happy and active individual to a severely depressed and suicidal person. She refused to go out with friends, and she felt guilty laughing or enjoying her own life when her mother and close friend were gone. She took a leave of absence from her job and grieved alone in her apartment. She spent long periods of time thinking about and looking at pictures of her mom and her friend. She was not shopping or cooking much, but rather relying on the processed and packaged foods she had at her apartment.

When Pauline came in, the therapist talked with her extensively about her life before and after the deaths and asked her to complete a PSI. The therapist knew from the PSI research that poor problem solvers who also feel hopeless are at a greater risk for suicide (e.g., Bonner & Rich, 1987; Dixon, Heppner, & Rudd, 1994; Rudd et al., 1996). The therapist was very interested to see both her PSI total and the specific subscale scores, as well as examine each item to understand her specific approach to cope with personal problems.

Even though Pauline was currently presenting as very passive and depressed, the therapist had a prediction based on her past history and PSI scores. She scored in a very positive manner on all three PSI factors. Clearly, Pauline still viewed herself as having confidence in her problem-solving ability, approaching problems rather than avoiding them, and having emotional control while solving problems. This profile well described how Pauline performed in her challenging work setting before the two deaths she had recently experienced.

The therapist met with Pauline over the course of a number of weeks. They talked about the grieving process—how it is unique to each person, how it takes time, and how most people never feel they "get over" the loss. But while normalizing some of what Pauline was experiencing, the therapist also had to gently let her know that her increasing depression, isolation, and poor self-care were very unhealthy for her and that although it is normal to feel sad, it is not healthy to slide into a deep depression, and they needed to work together to promote her healthy functioning.

Throughout the counseling sessions, the therapist kept emphasizing Pauline's strengths and pointing out that she had handled very difficult situations in her past with great skills and efficacy and in doing so had built a life for herself that she deemed deeply satisfying. However, Pauline would tend to discount the therapist's statement about her strengths and made comments about that being the "old Pauline," before the current tragedies had occurred.

Each week the therapist and Pauline mutually set goals to leave her apartment and interact with her support system. They set goals for her to walk in her neighborhood and eat healthy foods daily. Although she agreed with the goals at the time, she continued to stay in her apartment, ruminating about the losses and not following through on the goals she had set.

The therapist thought a lot about how to handle this lack of engagement in changing her life, her avoidant problem-solving approach, and also her continued spiraling depression. The therapist knew from her PSI scores that at her core, she was a confident and self-assured person who knew how to approach very difficult situations and who typically had great confidence and personal agency. So, after Pauline described how she had stayed in her apartment again all week, mourning her loses and ruminating about the past, the therapist paused and reflected on Pauline's uncharacteristic avoidance detachment: "It sounds to me that you are choosing to continue to live with dead people who cared a great deal about your well-being." In essence, the therapist confronted Pauline about her atypical problem-solving approach in this very difficult situation. Pauline's face visibly changed, and she looked a bit shocked and angry. She left the session in silence.

The following week, Pauline returned. She looked visibly lighter and less depressed. She walked in, sat down, and quickly said: "You were right. I was living with dead people and I came to realize that continuing to live my own life does not mean I am not still grieving their loss; in fact, they would very much want me to keep living my life and that is exactly what I have decided I am going to do."

Without information about Pauline's problem-solving potential reflected in the PSI scores, the therapist would have been far less likely to confront her in this manner. But the therapist knew about Pauline's problem-solving skills and wanted her to continue using those strengths. In the final sessions, the therapist and Pauline focused on how her strengths could help her get through what is still a very sad part of her life. For example, because her friend died after being hit by a drunk driver, Pauline decided to volunteer to fundraise for an organization aimed at reducing the number of drunk drivers on the roads. She expressed a great deal of confidence in her ability to help with this cause and believed it was the best way to honor the death of her friend. Naming Pauline's strengths and helping her see that throughout her life she has been an active, approaching, self-confident person seemed to help her reclaim her previous identity and to continue on with her life course that gave her a great deal of joy and satisfaction.

PROBLEM-SOLVING APPRAISAL AND POSITIVE PSYCHOLOGY: INTO THE FUTURE

As many have pointed out in this handbook, the primary focus of psychology since World War II has been on pathology and repairing damage. Certainly, alleviating distress is a worthy goal, and the overwhelming evidence from the programmatic line of PSI research clearly indicates that there is power in positive problem-solving appraisal to alleviate a host of maladies from depression and suicidal tendencies to eating disorders and alcohol abuse (Etringer, Altmaier, & Bowers, 1989; Godshall & Elliott, 1997, respectively). This evidence is strong and remarkably consistent.

We urge future researchers to apply the same rigor and sustained programmatic research to examine how the construct of problem-solving appraisal relates to helping people thrive and flourish and to understand that "treatment is not just fixing what is broken; it is nurturing what is best" (Seligman & Csikszentmihalyi, 2000, p. 7). We believe that the research already conducted with the PSI clearly underscores that positive problem-solving appraisal has the effect of making people's lives better, but more research is needed to understand how it can help people lead their very best lives.

We strongly echo Lopez and Janowski's (2004) recommendations that researchers "should consider the effects of problems solving interventions on meaningful life outcomes, such as meeting educational goals, sustaining relationships and finding meaning and purpose" in their lives (p. 462). We would also suggest that researchers consider examining the relationship of problem-solving appraisal to both the subjective level of experiences as well as the level of individual traits (Seligman & Csikszentmihalyi, 2000). In the area of subjective experiences, we would recommend investigating the relationship of problem-solving appraisal to such variables as well-being, contentment, and happiness. At the individual traits level, we would recommend an examination of the ability to find greater fulfillment in work and love, to persevere, to forgive, and to act with courage. There is a growing repertoire of psychometrically sound instruments designed to measure various aspects of life satisfaction, positive affectivity, and well-being. Continued advances in such assessments will strengthen the research produced in this area.

In conducting research on the relationships between problem-solving appraisal and positive psychology constructs, we urge researchers to not only examine simple zero-order correlations, but also investigate the potential role of problem-solving appraisal as a mediator or moderator in such relationships, or structural paths between a host of individual variables and positive life outcomes (also see P. P. Heppner, Wei, Neville, & Kanagui-Muñoz, 2014). For example, does one's problem-solving appraisal mediate the relationship between gender role socialization and life satisfaction? Does it moderate the relationship for those who face various forms of discrimination and their psychological well-being? The more we can understand about the mechanisms that produce lives of meaning, purpose, and deep satisfaction, the more we can empower people to access them.

Another promising area of research here is the determination of antecedents or predictors of positive problem-solving appraisal. In conceptualizing the PSI, it was assumed that problem solving resulted from "countless personal experiences" (P. P. Heppner, 1988, p. 16), but there are limited data on the development of an individual's problem-solving appraisal (see P. P. Heppner et al., 2004). For example, is problem-solving appraisal the result of the predominant outcomes with previous attempts to solve life's problems, or is it more complex than that? Do individuals with a positive problem-solving appraisal have different life histories, parental role models, or major defining positive life events? Can we determine what creates a positive problem-solving appraisal, and how we can foster it in our young? In this sense, researchers may consider using mixed methods (i.e., utilizing quantitative and qualitative approaches) to increase our understanding of the core characteristics of positive problem solvers. Another potential useful methodology may be to utilize the concept mapping method (i.e., a combination of a semistructured interview, cluster analysis, and multidimensional scaling; see Trochim & Kane, 2005).

In addition, more creative work is needed to identify best practices in problem-solving training and bring that training to more diverse groups of people. We strongly agree with Lopez and Janowski (2004) when they stated,

> Given that 'problem-solving appraisal is learned and amenable to change, and this provides hope for millions of people to bring positive change in their lives' (P. P. Heppner et al., 2004, p. 413), we believe that effective training methods would be packaged and shared with counselors so that the likelihood of use is increased. (p. 463)

At this point, more sophisticated methods are needed to assess the efficacy of a problem-solving training intervention. We recommend researchers examine change using a longitudinal research design along with advanced statistical methods such as hierarchical linear modeling and longitudinal growth models. For example, D.-G. Lee, Park, and Heppner (2009) reanalyzed M. J. Heppner et al.'s (2004) findings using a cross-lagged panel design to provide further support for the positive role of clients' precounseling problem-solving appraisal in predicting postcounseling career decision-making outcomes. This is meaningful because the results confirmed the directionality of prediction from problem-solving appraisal to career counseling outcome, which is not testable with traditional correlation and regression analysis (Raudenbush & Bryk, 2002). We also strongly agree with O'Neil (2004) when he concluded: "The strength of the data on the PSI made me wonder how problem-solving appraisal could become more accessible to a wider public. How can we give away our problem-solving knowledge and skills?" (p. 448). Isolating best practices and providing them in manualized forms for counselors to use is an important next step in this area.

In essence, we believe that problem-solving appraisal can be a construct that helps people lead richer and more fulfilling lives. At a broader level, we believe that in the future the PSI research will help fulfill Seligman and Csikszentmihalyi's (2000) prediction that "a psychology of positive human functioning will arise that achieves a scientific understanding and effective interventions to build thriving individuals, families and communities" (p. 13).

REFERENCES

Bonner, R. L., & Rich, A. R. (1987). Toward a predictive model of suicidal ideation and behavior: Some preliminary data in college students. *Suicide and Life-Threatening Behavior, 17,* 50–63. http://dx.doi.org/10.1111/j.1943-278X.1987.tb00061.x

Choi, M. S., & Son, J. N. (2007). The effects of purpose in life on self-esteem, problem solving aptitudes, and fear of negative evaluation. *Korean Journal of Health Psychology, 12,* 951–967. http://dx.doi.org/10.17315/kjhp.2007.12.4.017

Chynoweth, G. H. (1987). *Problem solving: A rational process with an emotional matrix.* Unpublished manuscript, Kansas State University, Manhattan.

Chynoweth, G. H., Blankinship, D. A., & Parker, M. W. (1986). The binomial expansion: Simplify the evaluation process. *Journal of Counseling & Development, 64,* 645–647. http://dx.doi.org/10.1002/j.1556-6676.1986.tb01029.x

Cook, S. W., & Heppner, P. P. (1997). A psychometric study of three coping measures. *Educational and Psychological Measurement, 57,* 906–923. http://dx.doi.org/10.1177/0013164497057006002

Dixon, W. A., Heppner, P. P., & Rudd, M. (1994). Problem-solving appraisal, hopelessness, and suicidal ideation: Evidence for meditational model. *Journal of Counseling Psychology, 41,* 91–98. http://dx.doi.org/10.1037/0022-0167.41.1.91

Elliott, T. R., Godshall, F. J., Herrick, S. M., Witty, T. E., & Spruell, M. (1991). Problem solving appraisal and psychological adjustment following spinal cord injury. *Cognitive Therapy and Research, 15,* 387–398. http://dx.doi.org/10.1007/BF01173033

Etringer, B. D., Altmaier, E. M., & Bowers, W. (1989). An investigation into the cognitive functioning of bulimic women. *Journal of Counseling & Development, 68,* 216–219. http://dx.doi.org/10.1002/j.1556-6676.1989.tb01360.x

Godshall, F. J., & Elliott, T. R. (1997). Behavioral correlates of self-appraised problem-solving ability: Problem-solving skills and health compromising behaviors. *Journal of Applied Social Psychology, 27,* 929–944. http://dx.doi.org/10.1111/j.1559-1816.1997.tb00279.x

Grant, J. S. (1999). Social problem-solving partnerships with family caregivers. *Rehabilitation Nursing, 24,* 254–260. http://dx.doi.org/10.1002/j.2048-7940.1999.tb02192.x

Heppner, M. J., Lee, D.-G., Heppner, P. P., McKinnon, L. C., Multon, K. D., & Gysbers, N. C. (2004). The role of problem-solving appraisal in the process and outcome of career counseling. *Journal of Vocational Behavior, 65,* 217–238. http://dx.doi.org/10.1016/S0001-8791(03)00100-3

Heppner, P. P. (1988). *The Problem-Solving Inventory.* Palo Alto, CA: Consulting Psychologist Press.

Heppner, P. P., & Baker, C. E. (1997). Applications of the Problem-Solving Inventory. *Measurement and Evaluation in Counseling and Development, 29,* 229–241.

Heppner, P. P., Baumgardner, A. H., Larson, L. M., & Petty, R. E. (1988). The utility of problem-solving training that emphasizes self-management principles. *Counselling Psychology Quarterly, 1,* 129–143. http://dx.doi.org/10.1080/09515078808254196

Heppner, P. P., Cook, S. W., Wright, D. M., & Johnson, C. (1995). Progress in resolving problems: A problem-focused style of coping. *Journal of Counseling Psychology, 42,* 279–293. http://dx.doi.org/10.1037/0022-0167.42.3.279

Heppner, P. P., Cooper, C., Mulholland, A., & Wei, M. (2001). A brief, multidimensional, problem solving psychotherapy outcome measure. *Journal of Counseling Psychology, 48,* 330–343. http://dx.doi.org/10.1037/0022-0167.48.3.330

Heppner, P. P., & Lee, D.-G. (2002). Problem-solving appraisal and psychological adjustment. In C. R. Snyder & S. J. Lopez (Eds.), *Handbook of positive psychology* (pp. 288–298). New York, NY: Oxford University Press.

Heppner, P. P., Manley, C. M., Perez, R. M., & Dixon, W. A. (1994). *An adolescent version of the Problem-Solving Inventory: Initial reliability and validity estimates.* Unpublished manuscript.

Heppner, P. P., & Petersen, C. H. (1982). The development and implications of a personal problem-solving inventory. *Journal of Counseling Psychology, 29,* 66–75. http://dx.doi.org/10.1037/0022-0167.29.1.66

Heppner, P. P., Pretorius, T., Wei, M., Lee, D., & Wang, Y.-W. (2002). Examining the generalizability of problem-solving appraisal in Black South Africans. *Journal of Counseling Psychology, 49,* 484–498. http://dx.doi.org/10.1037/0022-0167.49.4.484

Heppner, P. P., & Reeder, B. L. (1984). Training in problem-solving for residence hall staff: Who is most satisfied? *Journal of College Student Personnel, 25,* 357–360.

Heppner, P. P., Reeder, B. L., & Larson, L. M. (1983). Cognitive variables associated with personal problem-solving appraisal: Implications for counseling. *Journal of Counseling Psychology, 30,* 537–545. http://dx.doi.org/10.1037/0022-0167.30.4.537

Heppner, P. P., & Wang, Y. (2003). Problem solving appraisal. In S. J. Lopez & C. R. Snyder (Eds.), *Positive psychological assessment: A handbook of models and measures* (pp. 127–138). Washington, DC: American Psychological Association. http://dx.doi.org/10.1037/10612-008

Heppner, P. P., Wei, M., Neville, H. A., & Kanagui-Muñoz, M. (2014). A cultural and contextual model of coping. In F. T. L. Leong, L. Comas-Díaz, G. G. Nagayama Hall, V. C. McLoyd, & J. E. Trimble (Eds.), *APA handbook of multicultural psychology: Vol. 2. Applications and Training* (pp. 83–106). Washington, DC: American Psychological Association.

Heppner, P. P., Witty, T. E., & Dixon, W. A. (2004). Problem-solving appraisal and human adjustment: A review of 20 years of research using the Problem-Solving Inventory. *The Counseling Psychologist, 32,* 334–428. http://dx.doi.org/10.1177/0011000003262793

Laporte, L., Sabourin, S., & Wright, J. (1988). L'Inventaire de resolution de problemes personnels: Une perspective metacognitive [The inventory of the resolution of personal problems: One metacognitive perspective]. *International Journal of Psychology, 23,* 569–581. http://dx.doi.org/10.1080/00207598808247786

Larson, L. M., Allen, S. J., Imao, R. A., & Piersel, W. C. (1993). Self-perceived effective and ineffective problem solvers' differential views of their partners' problem-solving styles. *Journal of Counseling & Development, 71,* 528–532. http://dx.doi.org/10.1002/j.1556-6676.1993.tb02236.x

Larson, L. M., & Heppner, P. P. (1985). The relationship of problem-solving appraisal to career decision and indecision. *Journal of Vocational Behavior, 26,* 55–65. http://dx.doi.org/10.1016/0001-8791(85)90025-9

Larson, L. M., Toulouse, A. L., Ngumba, W. E., Fitzpatrick, L. A., & Heppner, P. P. (1994). The development and validation of Coping with Career Indecision. *Journal of Career Assessment, 2,* 91–110. http://dx.doi.org/10.1177/106907279400200201

Lee, D.-G., Park, H.-J., & Heppner, M. J. (2009). Do clients' problem-solving appraisals predict career counseling outcomes or vice versa? A reanalysis of Heppner et al. *Psychological Reports, 105,* 1159–1166. http://dx.doi.org/10.2466/PR0.105.F.1159-1166

Lee, H.-K. (2008). Testing of the relationships among optimism/pessimism, problem-solving appraisal, and positive/negative affects. *Korean Journal of Health Psychology, 13,* 603–623. http://dx.doi.org/10.17315/kjhp.2008.13.3.004

Lopez, S. J., & Janowski, K. M. (2004). The power of positive problem-solving appraisal: Comments on incremental validity, relationships with adjustment and clinical utility. *The Counseling Psychologist, 32,* 460–465. http://dx.doi.org/10.1177/0011000003262798

Neal, G. W., & Heppner, P. P. (1986). Problem-solving self-appraisal, awareness, and utilization of campus helping resources. *Journal of Counseling Psychology, 33,* 39–44. http://dx.doi.org/10.1037/0022-0167.33.1.39

Nezu, A. M. (1986). Efficacy of a social problem-solving therapy approach for unipolar depression. *Journal of Consulting and Clinical Psychology, 54,* 196–202. http://dx.doi.org/10.1037/0022-006X.54.2.196

Nota, L., Heppner, P. P., Soresi, S., & Heppner, M. J. (2009). Examining cultural validity of the Problem-Solving Inventory (PSI) in Italy. *Journal of Career Assessment, 17,* 478–494. http://dx.doi.org/10.1177/1069072709339490

O'Neil, J. M. (2004). Response to Heppner, Witty, and Dixon: Inspiring and high-level scholarship that can change people's lives. *The Counseling Psychologist, 32,* 439–449. http://dx.doi.org/10.1177/0011000003262796

Park, K. (2005). The moderating effects of problem solving and social support on the relationship between child abuse and suicidal ideation in adolescents. *The Korean Journal of School Psychology, 2,* 131–147.

Pretorius, T. B. (1993). Assessing the problem-solving appraisal of Black South African students. *International Journal of Psychology, 28,* 861–870. http://dx.doi.org/10.1080/00207599308246968

Rath, J. F., Hennessy, J. J., & Diller, L. (2003). Social problem solving and community integration in postacute rehabilitation outpatients with traumatic brain injury. *Rehabilitation Psychology, 48,* 137–144. http://dx.doi.org/10.1037/0090-5550.48.3.137

Raudenbush, S. W., & Bryk, A. S. (2002). *Hierarchical linear models: Applications and data analysis methods* (2nd ed.). Newbury Park, CA: Sage.

Reis, S. D., & Heppner, P. P. (1993). Examination of coping resources and family adaptation in mothers and daughters of incestuous versus nonclinical families. *Journal of Counseling Psychology, 40,* 100–108. http://dx.doi.org/10.1037/0022-0167.40.1.100

Rudd, M. D., Rajab, M. H., Orman, D. T., Joiner, T., Stulman, D. A., Joiner, T., & Dixon, W. (1996). Effectiveness of an outpatient intervention targeting suicidal young adults: Preliminary results. *Journal of Consulting and Clinical Psychology, 64,* 179–190. http://dx.doi.org/10.1037/0022-006X.64.1.179

Sabourin, S., Laporte, L., & Wright, J. (1990). Problem-solving self-appraisal and coping efforts in distressed and non-distressed couples. *Journal of Marital and Family Therapy, 16,* 89–97. http://dx.doi.org/10.1111/j.1752-0606.1990.tb00048.x

Sahin, N., Sahin, N. H., & Heppner, P. P. (1993). Psychometric properties of the Problem-Solving Inventory (PSI) in a group of Turkish university students. *Cognitive Therapy and Research, 17,* 379–396. http://dx.doi.org/10.1007/BF01177661

Seligman, M. E. P., & Csikszentmihalyi, M. (2000). Positive psychology. An introduction. *American Psychologist, 55,* 5–14. http://dx.doi.org/10.1037/0003-066X.55.1.5

Super, D. E. (1955). Transition: From vocational guidance to counseling psychology. *Journal of Counseling Psychology, 2,* 3–9. http://dx.doi.org/10.1037/h0041630

Trochim, W., & Kane, M. (2005). Concept mapping: An introduction to structured conceptualization in health care. *International Journal for Quality in Health Care, 17,* 187–191. http://dx.doi.org/10.1093/intqhc/mzi038

Wright, D. M., & Heppner, P. P. (1991). Coping among nonclinical college students: Is knowledge of the presence of parental alcoholism useful? *Journal of Counseling Psychology, 38,* 565–572.

9

Measuring Creativity in Research and Practice

Barbara A. Kerr and Olivia A. Stull

Although from the beginning of positive psychology, creativity has been acknowledged as a variable of interest to this field (Seligman & Csikszentmihalyi, 2000), surprisingly few positive psychology studies include creativity as a variable related to human strengths and human thriving. Most of the research on creativity takes place within diverse disciplines including educational psychology, gifted education, personality psychology, social psychology, and the psychology of intelligence. Forgeard and Eichner (2014) recommended that creativity should be seen by positive psychologists as both a target and a tool in education and counseling. That is, creativity should be seen as the goal of interventions meant to increase well-being and thriving as well as a tool, through creative problem-solving training. Conceptual issues related to the understanding of the construct of creativity abound, including disagreements about whether it is primarily a cognitive, personality, or behavioral characteristic of individuals and whether it can even be understood as a trait of an individual or a system. To be effective in using creativity as an outcome variable or as an intervention, positive psychologists must be knowledgeable about the conceptual issues related to creativity as well as the methods and instruments available for its assessment.

http://dx.doi.org/10.1037/0000138-009
Positive Psychological Assessment: A Handbook of Models and Measures, Second Edition,
M. W. Gallagher and S. J. Lopez (Editors)

MANY DEFINITIONS, MANY MEASURES

Although most researchers agree upon such aspects of creativity as originality, appropriateness, and the production of works of value to society, they have had difficulty agreeing upon appropriate instruments and methods in operationalizing these concepts. The insufficiency of most creativity measures to capture the complex concept of creativity has been well established.

The proliferation of creativity tests, some of which hold up better under psychometric scrutiny than do others, exacerbates the criterion problem for creative research. These concerns leave us asking an important question: What is it exactly that creativity researchers are studying? Some leading researchers in the field choose to consider the multiplicity of measures as indicative of a viable, dynamic, creative field. Houtz and Krug (1995) suggested that "multiple instruments and methods permit flexibility and adaptability to new problems and situations, maximum theory development, and application to real-world problems" (p. 273). Irrespective of one's position on whether criterion variation is problematic, the evaluation of creativity tests fares much better when considered in light of recent advances in the field and when they are interpreted with the appropriate limitations.

WHAT DO CREATIVITY INSTRUMENTS PREDICT?

Many of the available creativity instruments can identify divergent thinking or ideational fluency but fail to predict future creative behavior. In many cases, children identified by creativity measures have not produced significant creative works as adults. An exception is the Torrance Tests of Creative Thinking (TTCT; Torrance, 1974), which have predicted adult creative accomplishments more effectively than have intelligence tests (Kim, 2006). Of note, recent research suggests development of divergent thinking processes is not complete until later adolescence, with marked changes in content quality during mid-adolescence (Kleibeuker, De Dreu, & Crone, 2013). However, Plucker and Runco (1998), discussing advancements in the predictive validity of the measurements, argued that the "death of creativity measurement has been greatly exaggerated" (p. 36). A meta-analysis by Ma (2009) gave support to Plucker and Runco's belief that creativity assessment was alive and well. Ma studied the mean effect size of variables associated with creative person, process, product, and environment. He gathered 2,013 effect sizes from 111 studies and found that most of the variables did indeed have a relationship with some aspect of creativity, with a grand mean effect size, weighted by sample size, of .72. Problem-solving creativity and verbal creativity were the most powerful predictors. However, prestige of honors and awards, working circumstances favorable for creativity, defining problem, and retrieving knowledge were also highly predictive.

CREATIVITY IN CONTEXT

Measuring creative cognition in isolation from other psychological and contextual variables is also problematic, particularly when creativity is conceptualized as "the interaction among aptitude, process, and environment by which an individual or group produces a perceptible product that is both novel and useful as defined within a social context" (Plucker, Beghetto, & Dow, 2004). In a groundbreaking examination of creative people, Csikszentmihalyi (1996) studied 100 individuals who had produced works that were publicly acknowledged as creative and who had all changed the culture in some important way. In this comprehensive study of scientists, artists, writers, educators, politicians and social activists, engineers, and religious leaders, he found that the first and foremost characteristic of creative individuals is mastery of a domain of knowledge or skill. Without mastery of a domain, diverse thinking or ideational fluency is not likely to lead to creative products. These creative individuals, for the most part, had normal childhoods and families that provided them with a solid set of values. They, however, differed significantly from noncreative people. A high proportion had suffered a parental loss, particularly the loss of a father. Commonly, they had other supportive adults in their lives who encouraged them to use their loss as an opportunity to create their own identities. Creative individuals had little good to say about school; in many ways, general schooling was irrelevant to these profoundly curious and self-guided young people. Only in college and advanced training did they find a match between their interests and those of others, in mentors and significant teachers who provided the knowledge they desired so intensely. As adults, these creative people had circuitous paths to their careers. What was most extraordinary, said Csikszentmihalyi, was that these people seized upon whatever opportunities they had been given and then shaped them to meet their own ends, rather than being shaped by genes or external events.

Finally, environmental variables interact in important ways with cognitive variables to produce creative behavior (Piirto, 1996). It has long been observed that certain communities at certain times in history seemed to give rise to a great many creative individuals: 15th-century Florence, Harlem in the 1920s, and San Francisco in the 1960s are examples. The presence of patrons, the support of a subculture of creative individuals, the possibility of freedom of expression, and the availability of materials and resources necessary for creative products all play a part in the emergence of creative behavior in individuals of talent. Gender, race, and class can all be barriers to the expression of creativity when low expectations and stereotypes discourage otherwise talented individuals from pursuing their ideas and fulfilling their gifts. Moreover, Amabile (1983) encouraged creativity researchers to go beyond the assumption that individual creativity depends primarily on talent and to consider environmental influences. Her componential model of creativity, which posits three major components of creativity—skills specific to the task domain, general creativity relevant skills, and task motivation—provides a useful way to conceptualize the importance of the social environment in creativity, which can support or undermine the intrinsic motivation to create.

USING ASSESSMENTS APPROPRIATELY

Different creativity tests measure different constructs within the complex intellectual and affective concept of creativity; problems arise when one measure is inappropriately used, interpreted, or compared against another measure. Torrance (1984), the inventor of standardized creative tests, as well as others (Julmi & Scherm, 2016), cautioned against exclusivity of objective measurement in assessment. He recommended that creativity not be the sole criterion for decision making, that multiple talents be evaluated, and that culturally different individuals be given tasks that evaluate "the kinds of excellence that are valued by the particular culture or subculture" (Torrance, 1984, pp. 155–156) of the individuals being evaluated, as cultural norms and practices are incredibly influential on an individual's creativity (Lehman, Chiu, & Schaller, 2004). Even within the limited context of objective measurement, using multiple measures helps to ensure that the assessment discriminates between individuals and not against them. Thus, many suggest at least two methods of measurement should be used when assessing creative behavior and potential (Cropley, 2000; Johnson & Fishkin, 1999; Kim, 2006; Treffinger, 1985).

MEASURES OF THE CREATIVE PROCESS: DIVERGENT THINKING

Traditionally, the measurement of a person's intelligence had been used to determine who among the population were gifted. Yet, traditional intelligence tests do not require much creative or divergent-production thinking, which led to the hypothesis that creativity and intelligence are separate constructs, requiring separate measures. Traditional intelligence tests primarily measure convergent thinking, the kind of thinking used when a person must "converge" on one right answer to a question or problem. Divergent thinking, in contrast, is the sort of thinking that produces multiple responses to a question and that produces novel ideas and unusual responses to questions. Divergent thinking is cognition that leads in various directions, some conventional and some original. As explained by Runco (1999), "Because some of the resulting ideas are original, divergent thinking represents the potential for creative thinking and problem solving" (p. 577). Thus, to the degree that these tests are reliable and valid for the individuals they are assessing, they can be taken as estimates of the potential for creative thinking; however, caution should be taken when inferring estimates of future creative production, as divergent thinking is not entirely synonymous with creativity (Runco, 2008).

THE TORRANCE TESTS

In the 1960s, E. Paul Torrance developed and employed batteries of divergent thinking tests used in the early study of creativity, which are widely used today. Although Torrance would later acknowledge that creativity "defies precise definition" (Parkhurst, 1999, p. 13), his early attempts at operationalizing creativity for research purposes centered on problem-solving. The TTCT was developed by Torrance in 1966. It has been renormed 4 times: in 1974, 1984, 1990, and 1998. There are two forms (A and B) of the TTCT—Verbal and two forms (A and B) of the TTCT—Figural. The TTCT has been translated into more than 35 languages (Kim, 2006). It is the most widely used test of creativity and is the most cited. The TTCT is a timed test. The sections Thinking Creatively with Pictures and Thinking Creatively with Words are useful for grades kindergarten through graduate school to assess four creative abilities: fluency, flexibility, originality, and elaboration. The nonverbal forms are three sets of activities: drawing lines to elaborate on a single shape, drawing lines to complete a picture, and drawing as many different pictures as possible using the same shape. These are scored for fluency, originality, elaboration, abstractness of titles, and resistance to premature closure. The verbal forms consist of six activities that involve generating questions, describing alternative uses, and making guesses about a picture. Each of the verbal sections is scored for fluency, flexibility, and originality.

Not only are the Torrance Tests the most widely used measure of creativity (Kim, 2006), but they offer more evidence for validity than does any other creativity test. Data on the TTCT have been gathered on an international scale and critically reviewed. Treffinger's (1985) analysis of several studies of test–retest reliability attest to moderate to high reliability and posit a range extending from .50 to .93. Torrance (1988) reported on a 22-year longitudinal study in which scores were correlated with accomplishments in adulthood with validity coefficients of .62 for males and .57 for females. Although these coefficients demonstrate only moderate predictive validity, Torrance noted that they are sometimes even higher than coefficients for intelligence in predicting adult achievement. In a 50-year follow-up of students identified as creative, Runco, Millar, Acar, and Cramond (2010) found that the TTCT predicted creative adult lives in both personal and public domains.

CREATIVE PERSONALITY ASSESSMENT

Some researchers view creativity entirely as a cognitive process, whereas others see it as a set of personality traits. When individuals are evaluated as creative thinkers but do not manifest such characteristics as endurance and independence, they may not become creatively productive. A valid assessment procedure should consider both cognitive and personality components.

Research into creative personality has been one of the most productive areas of assessment research. The relationship of Big Five personality factors (Neuroticism, Extraversion, Openness to Experience, Agreeability, and

Conscientiousness) has been studied in depth. Early reviews consistently found core personality traits that are reasonably stable across domains (Barron & Harrington, 1981). These traits include broad interests, independence of judgment, autonomy, and openness to experience. Openness to experience is consistently correlated with measures of creativity. In a meta-analysis that explored personality traits in scientific and artistic creativity, Feist (1999) linked personality findings to the Big Five personality factors. Feist found that across both artistic and scientific domains, creative individuals were characterized by high openness to new experiences, low agreeability (nonconforming), and low conscientiousness. Personality facets of the Big Five personality factors, including three facets of Openness to Experience (Aesthetics, Actions, and Ideas), two of Neuroticism (Angry Hostility and negative Vulnerability), and two of Conscientiousness (Competence and negative Deliberation), provided a nuanced profile of the personality of creative individuals in a study by Batey, Chamorro-Premuzic, and Furnham (2010). Openness to experience appears to be a domain-general trait. Extraversion, in contrast, seems to be a domain-specific trait: People in performing arts class score higher in extraversion than do those in visual arts class (Silvia, Kaufman, & Pretz, 2009). Similarly, in Kerr and McKay's (2013) factor analysis and cluster analyses of personalities of creative adolescents, openness to experience was characteristic of creative students in general, but extraversion was characteristic only of students in performing domains.

The personality characteristic of openness to experience seems to cut across domains of ability, but there may be differences in creative personality related to the domain of talent. The personality trait of openness to experience is moderately heritable. It may, therefore, have evolutionary roots as well as neurophysiological correlates.

PERSONALITY INVENTORIES: NEO-PI-R, NEO-PI-3, AND THE SFPQ

The NEO Personality Inventory—Revised (NEO-PI-R; Costa & McCrae, 1992) is a comprehensive personality inventory based on the leading theory of personality, the five-factor model. The NEO-PI-R is a well-established measure that yields five dimensions of personality and is appropriate for older adolescents. This 240-item assessment has coefficient alphas of .92 (Neuroticism), .89 (Extraversion), .87 (Openness), .86 (Agreeableness), and .90 (Conscientiousness). Numerous studies have supported the construct validity and reliability of the instrument. From factor analyses of hundreds of personality tests, Costa and McCrae derived basic personality dimensions: conscientiousness, agreeableness, openness to experience, extraversion, and neuroticism. This self-report personality inventory requires subjects to rate themselves on nine-step bipolar scales using adjective pairs. Whereas the Openness to Experience scale is consistently, positively correlated with intelligence ($r = .30$; Ackerman & Heggestad, 1997; DeYoung, Quilty, Peterson, & Gray, 2014), it, as well as the (reversed) Conscientiousness scale, was more predictive of ideational behavior than was intelligence alone (Batey et al., 2010). The NEO-PI-3 (Costa & McCrae, 2010) is an updated, more readable form of the NEO-PI that has both youth (ages 12–20) and adult (ages 21–80) forms. It adds 38 new items and provides new norms, while maintaining similar or better validity and reliability.

The Six Factor Personality Questionnaire (SFPQ; Jackson, Paunonen, Fraboni, & Goffin, 1996) measures the same five personality traits and comprises 108 items that assess six personality factors: Extraversion, Agreeableness, Openness to Experience, Methodicalness, Industriousness, and Independence. These factors correspond to the factors of the NEO-PI-R with the exception that the NEO-PI-R dimension of Conscientiousness was subdivided into two factors, Methodicalness and Industriousness, and the NEO-PI-R Neuroticism factor was renamed as Independence (corresponding to a low level of Neuroticism). Jackson et al. (1996) showed that both tests have high reliability and validity; however, the SFPQ, because of its being validated with normal, educated populations, is more appropriate for creativity assessment.

CONSENSUAL ASSESSMENT TECHNIQUES

Amabile (1982) circumvented the problems of both the definition and the measurement of creativity with what she called the Consensual Assessment Technique (CAT), by which experts assess creative products using their own individual criteria and their own definitions of creativity. A typical item is "On a scale of 1 to 5, and using your own subjective definition of creativity, rate the degree to which this painting is creative." It is simply not possible, according to Amabile, to articulate clear, objective criteria for a creative product, whereas, if appropriate judges independently agree that a given product is creative, then it can and must be accepted as such. By extension, the person who created the product is also creative. The CAT has been used in many studies with many activities with people across the lifespan. Independent expert ratings with the CAT have moderate to high interrater reliabilities (e.g., Amabile, 1982, 1996; Baer, Kaufman, & Gentile, 2004).

CHECKLISTS AND BEHAVIOR QUESTIONNAIRES

Developed by Carson, Peterson, and Higgins (2005), the Creative Achievement Questionnaire (CAQ) is a self-report measure of creative achievement that assesses achievement across 10 domains of creativity. The items are visual arts, music, dance, individual sports, team sports, architectural design, entrepreneurial ventures, creative writing, humor, inventions, scientific inquiry, theater and film, and culinary arts. On each item, an individual rates him- or herself from 1, a level of having had training, through various levels of recognition to 7, having achieved national recognition. It has good test–retest reliability ($r = .81$, $p < .0001$) and internal consistency reliability ($\alpha = .96$).

The CAQ has moderate predictive validity for artistic products and convergent validity with divergent thinking tests, the Creative Personality Scale (Gough, 1979), and Openness to Experience. It discriminates between intelligence and creativity well. An examination of the factor structure of the CAQ found a three-factor solution identified as Expressive, Scientific, and Performance factors of creative achievement (Julmi & Scherm, 2016), and a two-factor solution identified an Arts factor and a Science factor.

The Runco Ideational Behavior Scale (RIBS; Runco, Plucker, & Lim, 2001) was developed according to the theory that a wide variety of motives, interests, and behaviors related to having ideas could be considered the product of creativity. On this 23-item scale, subjects are asked to rate the degree to which the item describes one of their behaviors that reflect their use of, appreciation of, and skill with ideas. Items include such statements as "I come up with an idea or solution other people have never thought of." The RIBS has very good internal consistency and moderate construct validity. It has been found to correlate with divergent thinking and other measures of creativity but to discriminate between creative ideation and grade point average (Plucker, Runco, & Lim, 2006).

PROFILING

Profiling is an assessment method that combines cognitive, personality, and behavioral characteristics that have been found to be related to creative productivity. Kerr and McKay (2013) surveyed the biographies of eminent individuals to determine those abilities, traits, and behaviors that were characteristic of adults eminent in five domains of accomplishments when these eminent people were 16 years old. The profiles were used by teachers to identify a group of 400 adolescents in the midwest United States who matched the characteristics. The group of adolescents was found, upon assessment, to score very high in openness to experience and to have accomplishments that were similar to those of adolescents assessed as creatively achieving. Profiling appears to select groups of students that reflect the gender and ethnic makeup of the school population from which they are drawn. The profiles have been further refined and are used to identify adolescents who can benefit from specialized counseling to guide them toward creative career pathways as well as to promote well-being (Kerr & Vuyk, 2013).

USING CREATIVITY ASSESSMENT IN POSITIVE PSYCHOLOGY

Given the importance of creativity and innovation to the global economy, The National Science Foundation (2007) has called for research on the people and processes that bring about innovation in science, technology, engineering, and mathematics (STEM) fields. The group of innovators necessary to the future of society comprises not only scientists and engineers. People in design, education, arts, music, and entertainment interact in creative communities that encourage innovation across the spectrum of human activity (Florida, 2002). If creative people and the innovations they produce are critical to the future, how do educators and psychologists find them? How do counselors guide them toward positions in STEM, the arts, and entrepreneurship?

If a client has been referred for educational assessment, for example, for the purpose of placement in gifted classes or for a special program, then the therapist should investigate the nature of the program for which the client is being assessed. The method should always match the program. That is, if the curriculum emphasizes the ability to brainstorm ideas and to use creative problem-solving, then the Torrance Tests may be very appropriate. If, on the other hand, the curriculum focuses upon a particular domain, such as art, music, or creative writing, then it may be more effective to use consensual assessment techniques, such as having art teachers judge the creative artwork of students. Unfortunately, most personality tests are not appropriate for children because they may not be ready developmentally for self-report of personality characteristics.

What does it mean if a client who has been referred for educational testing scores very high on the Torrance Tests? It means that the client thinks creatively but not necessarily that the client has produced creative works. It does mean that the individual has the cognitive "building blocks" of creativity: ideational fluency, flexibility, and originality; however, these must be combined with motivation to achieve, above-average intelligence, and endurance as well as a great number of other characteristics in order to predict creative behavior. If the client is to be placed in a program that will require creative writing and artwork as well as creative problem-solving, then the TTCT may help support that placement if it is used in combination with tests of ability in the critical domains and personality tests that yield information about the need for achievement and the need for endurance. The child who is a creative thinker but lacks intelligence, motivation to achieve, and persistence may have many interesting ideas but be unable to carry them through or to evaluate them critically. Even the very intelligent creative thinker is likely to become an academic dilettante without the personality characteristics that permit intense concentration in the pursuit of a goal. In addition, girls and minority populations may not have the social and cultural capital necessary to achieve their creative goals (Kerr, Vuyk, & Rea, 2012).

By adolescence, personality tests may be the assessment of choice, in the absence of knowledge of and data on creative accomplishments. The TTCT is expensive to administer and score and may not be appropriate to the needs of adolescents. If the client is requesting career guidance, then a much broader approach to creativity assessment may be appropriate. The Openness to Experience scales of Big Five personality inventories that are correlated with creativity may be used to identify creative potential. The CAQ may be very effective in identifying creative productivity in a wide variety of domains. These tests can be combined with vocational interest tests and values inventories to yield a profile of the particular domains in which the client might be most creative. Together with vocational interests and values, these scores were very useful to clients in determining the probability of satisfaction and success in creative fields.

Profiling, a simple, inexpensive method that combines qualitative and quantitative assessment in holistic profiles, may have promise for identifying adolescents who are most likely to thrive in creative careers (Kerr & McKay, 2013). Using their research-based profiles, teachers and counselors can screen those students who can benefit most by specialized career and talent development for creative occupations. Following profiling, students are given a combination of vocational interest tests, personality tests, creative accomplishment questionnaires, and values inventories to create an individualized profile with specific suggestions for ways of climbing the "invisible career ladders" of creative occupations. The following is an example of how profiling works.

CASE STUDY

Robert, a 20-year-old sophomore at a prestigious and challenging art university, is questioning his decision to pursue a degree and career in a creative field. Robert finds the workload of classes overwhelming, is feeling marginally depressed, and is unsure about how he can develop a career with his art degree. Robert seeks counseling services for his depression and to assist in making a decision regarding whether he should stay at his current art university or transfer to a state school to pursue a more generalized degree (e.g., business, psychology).

Upon meeting Robert for the first time, his counselor, Jerry, decides to give him a variety of assessments to better understand Robert and his unique worldview. Jerry proctors the NEO-PI-R, CAQ, the Vocational Preference Inventory (VPI), and the Rokeach Value Survey (RVS).

For their second session, Jerry helps to interpret Robert's scores while using valuable input from Robert to complete a holistic image of Robert's creativity (e.g., creative achievements, interests, openness) within the frame of his overarching personality. Starting with Robert's Holland code, as indicated by his VPI scores, Jerry asks Robert to read aloud his top three scores (Artistic, Social, and Investigative) and their subsequent descriptions, then describe how this may or may not "fit" with how he views himself.

Next, Jerry ties in Robert's interpretations and acceptance of VPI score into his NEO-PI-R scores, focusing on his high openness to experience (99%) and extraversion (87%) scores. Knowing that scoring that highly on openness is a major theme of highly creative individuals, as well as a potential risk factor for increased difficulty when making major life decisions, such as career choices, Jerry utilizes Robert's feedback to identify historical patterns of similar behavior. During this discussion, Jerry notices a theme: Many of Robert's interests are creative in some way, and many involve being around people (i.e., not spent alone in studio, working for long hours, which is what Robert had been doing much of the year).

Robert's scores on the CAQ indicate he has already achieved a lot within visual arts, creative writing, theater and film, and humor domains. Jerry points out Robert's successes are primarily in the realm of his current major and/or social domains, two aspects of Robert that have already been established as essential in understanding his worldview, to which Robert replies he used to work on film projects with a close group of friends back in his hometown and that this is what inspired him to seek his current degree.

Finally, Jerry and Robert review Robert's top three scores on the terminal values subsection of the RVS. Robert states that his top value, True Friendship, is something that he has struggled with since moving to a new city to attend this art university and is likely a factor in his depression. Robert's second and third highest values, A World of Beauty and Equality, prompt Jerry to ask Robert more about the art he has been working on lately. Robert states he has mostly been working on basic short animations because he is learning a new and very complicated program and that he has not worked on any of his personal (nonacademic) illustrations or films because he does not feel as though he has the time to do so anymore.

It is clear to Jerry that Robert is stressed, lonely, and not exactly enjoying the work he is doing for school, and with Robert's picturesque creative person's profile, it does not surprise Jerry that Robert is contemplating transferring to a less intense program. Focusing in on Robert's values, however, Jerry and Robert discuss ways to align his long-term goals with some of the things that mean the most to Robert: friendship, equality, and a beautiful world. It becomes clear to Robert that although it is not necessarily easy or fun to practice the basics of a new, complex program, it will allow him to create his dream movie, an interstellar animation that focuses on controversial social topics from a futuristic time traveler's point of view. Not only has this been his dream for many years, but it satisfies two of his top values simultaneously with his interests and natural talent domains. Jerry's use of creativity assessments in conjunction with career development assessments helped reaffirm Robert's wavering confidence in himself and his creativity, while identifying long-term career goals as well as current areas where Jerry and Robert can work together to help alleviate some of Robert's symptoms of depression.

REFERENCES

Ackerman, P. L., & Heggestad, E. D. (1997). Intelligence, personality, and interests: Evidence for overlapping traits. *Psychological Bulletin, 121,* 219–245. http://dx.doi.org/10.1037/0033-2909.121.2.219

Amabile, T. M. (1982). Social psychology of creativity: A consensual assessment technique. *Journal of Personality and Social Psychology, 43,* 997–1013. http://dx.doi.org/10.1037/0022-3514.43.5.997

Amabile, T. M. (1983). The social psychology of creativity: A componential conceptualization. *Journal of Personality and Social Psychology, 45,* 357–376. http://dx.doi.org/10.1037/0022-3514.45.2.357

Amabile, T. M. (1996). *Creativity in context.* Boulder, CO: Westview Press.

Baer, J., Kaufman, J. C., & Gentile, C. A. (2004). Extension of the consensual assessment technique to nonparallel creative products. *Creativity Research Journal, 16,* 113–117. http://dx.doi.org/10.1207/s15326934crj1601_11

Barron, F., & Harrington, D. M. (1981). Creativity, intelligence, and personality. *Annual Review of Psychology, 32,* 439–476. http://dx.doi.org/10.1146/annurev.ps.32.020181.002255

Batey, M., Chamorro-Premuzic, T., & Furnham, A. (2010). Individual differences in ideational behavior: Can the big five and psychometric intelligence predict creativity scores? *Creativity Research Journal, 22,* 90–97.

Carson, S. H., Peterson, J. B., & Higgins, D. M. (2005). Reliability, validity, and factor structure of the Creative Achievement Questionnaire. *Creativity Research Journal, 17,* 37–50. http://dx.doi.org/10.1207/s15326934crj1701_4

Costa, P. T., Jr., & McCrae, R. R. (1992). Four ways five factors are basic. *Personality and Individual Differences, 13,* 653–665. http://dx.doi.org/10.1016/0191-8869(92)90236-I

Costa, P. T., & McCrae, R. R. (2010). *The NEO Personality Inventory 3.* Odessa, FL: Psychological Assessment Resources.

Cropley, A. J. (2000). Defining and measuring creativity: Are creativity tests worth using? *Roeper Review: A Journal on Gifted Education, 23,* 72–79. http://dx.doi.org/10.1080/02783190009554069

Csikszentmihalyi, M. (1996). *Creativity: Flow and the psychology of discovery and invention.* New York, NY: Harper-Collins.

DeYoung, C. G., Quilty, L. C., Peterson, J. B., & Gray, J. R. (2014). Openness to experience, intellect, and cognitive ability. *Journal of Personality Assessment, 96,* 46–52. http://dx.doi.org/10.1080/00223891.2013.806327

Feist, G. J. (1999). Autonomy and independence. In M. A. Runco & S. Pritzker (Eds.), *Encyclopedia of creativity* (Vol. 1, pp. 157–163). San Diego, CA: Academic Press.

Florida, R. (2002). *The rise of the creative class: How it's transforming work, leisure, community and everyday life.* New York, NY: Perseus Book Group.

Forgeard, M. J., & Eichner, K. V. (2014). Creativity as a target and tool for positive interventions. In A. C. Parks & S. M. Schueller (Eds.), *The Wiley Blackwell handbook of positive psychological interventions* (pp. 135–154). Chichester, England: John Wiley & Sons.

Gough, H. G. (1979). A creative personality scale for the adjective check list. *Journal of Personality and Social Psychology, 37,* 1398–1405. http://dx.doi.org/10.1037/0022-3514.37.8.1398

Houtz, J. C., & Krug, D. (1995). Assessment of creativity: Resolving a mid-life crisis. *Educational Psychology Review, 7,* 269–300. http://dx.doi.org/10.1007/BF02213374

Jackson, D. N., Paunonen, S. V., Fraboni, M., & Goffin, R. D. (1996). A five-factor versus six factor model of personality structure. *Personality and Individual Differences, 20*(1), 33–45. http://dx.doi.org/10.1016/0191 8869(95)00143-T

Johnson, A. S., & Fishkin, A. S. (1999). Assessment of cognitive and affective behaviors related to creativity. In A. S. Fishkin, B. Cramond, & P. Olszewski-Kubilius (Eds.), *Investigating creativity in youth: Research and methods* (pp. 265–306). Cresskill, NJ: Hampton.

Julmi, C., & Scherm, E. (2016). *Measuring the domain-specificity of creativity* (Working Paper No. 502). Hagen, Germany: University of Hagen. Retrieved from https://www.researchgate.net/profile/Christian_Julmi/publication/311649673_Measuring_the_Domain-Specificity_of_Creativity/links/58524c4608ae0c0f32223557.pdf

Kerr, B. A., & McKay, R. A. (2013). Searching for tomorrow's innovators: Profiling creative adolescents. *Creativity Research Journal, 25,* 21–32. http://dx.doi.org/10.1080/10400419.2013.752180

Kerr, B. A., & Vuyk, M. A. (2013). Career development for creatively gifted students. In S. Sriraman (Series Ed.) & K. H. Kim, J. C. Kaufman, J. Baer, & B. Sriraman (Vol. Eds.), *Creatively gifted students are not like other gifted students: Research, theory, and practice* (Vol. 4, pp. 137–152). Rotterdam, The Netherlands: Sense.

Kerr, B. A., Vuyk, M. A., & Rea, C. (2012). Gendered practices in the education of gifted girls and boys. *Psychology in the Schools, 49,* 647–655. http://dx.doi.org/10.1002/pits.21627

Kim, K. H. (2006). Can we trust creativity tests? A review of the Torrance Tests of Creative Thinking (TTCT). *Creativity Research Journal, 18,* 3–14. http://dx.doi.org/10.1207/s15326934crj1801_2

Kleibeuker, S. W., De Dreu, C. K. W., & Crone, E. A. (2013). The development of creative cognition across adolescence: Distinct trajectories for insight and divergent thinking. *Developmental Science, 16*(1), 2–12. http://dx.doi.org/10.1111/j.1467-7687.2012.01176.x

Lehman, D. R., Chiu, C.-Y., & Schaller, M. (2004). Psychology and culture. *Annual Review of Psychology, 55,* 689–714. http://dx.doi.org/10.1146/annurev.psych.55.090902.141927

Ma, H. H. (2009). The effect size of variables associated with creativity: A meta-analysis. *Creativity Research Journal, 21,* 30–42. http://dx.doi.org/10.1080/10400410802633400

National Science Foundation. (2007). *Final report from the NSF Innovation and Discovery Workshop: The scientific basis of individual and team innovation and discovery.* Washington, DC: Author.

Parkhurst, H. B. (1999). Confusion, lack of consensus, and the definition of creativity as a construct. *The Journal of Creative Behavior, 33,* 1–21. http://dx.doi.org/10.1002/j.2162-6057.1999.tb01035.x

Piirto, J. (1996). *Understanding those who create.* Scottsdale, AZ: Gifted Psychology Press.

Plucker, J. A., Beghetto, R. A., & Dow, G. T. (2004). Why isn't creativity more important to educational psychologists? Potentials, pitfalls, and future directions in creativity research. *Educational Psychologist, 39,* 83–96. http://dx.doi.org/10.1207/s15326985ep3902_1

Plucker, J. A., & Runco, M. A. (1998). The death of creativity measurement has been greatly exaggerated: Current issues, recent advances, and future directions in creativity assessment. *Roeper Review: A Journal on Gifted Education, 21,* 36–39. http://dx.doi.org/10.1080/02783199809553924

Plucker, J. A., Runco, M. A., & Lim, W. (2006). Predicting ideational behavior from divergent thinking and discretionary time on task. *Creativity Research Journal, 18,* 55–63. http://dx.doi.org/10.1207/s15326934crj1801_7

Runco, M. A. (1999). Divergent thinking. In M. A. Runco & S. R. Pritzker (Eds.), *Encyclopedia of creativity* (Vol. 1, pp. 577–582). San Diego, CA: Academic Press.

Runco, M. A. (2008). Commentary: Divergent thinking is not synonymous with creativity. *Psychology of Aesthetics, Creativity, and the Arts, 2,* 93–96. http://dx.doi.org/10.1037/1931-3896.2.2.93

Runco, M. A., Millar, G., Acar, S., & Cramond, B. (2010). Torrance Tests of Creative Thinking as predictors of personal and public achievement: A fifty-year follow-up. *Creativity Research Journal, 22,* 361–368. http://dx.doi.org/10.1080/10400419.2010.523393

Runco, M. A., Plucker, J. A., & Lim, W. (2001). Development and psychometric integrity of a measure of ideational behavior. *Creativity Research Journal, 13,* 393–400. http://dx.doi.org/10.1207/S15326934CRJ1334_16

Seligman, M. E., & Csikszentmihalyi, M. (Eds.). (2000). Positive psychology [Special issue]. *American Psychologist, 55*(1). http://dx.doi.org/10.1037/0003-066X.55.1.5

Silvia, P. J., Kaufman, J. C., & Pretz, J. E. (2009). Is creativity domain-specific? Latent class models of creative accomplishments and creative self-descriptions. *Psychology of Aesthetics, Creativity, and the Arts, 3,* 139–148. http://dx.doi.org/10.1037/a0014940

Torrance, E. P. (1974). *The Torrance Tests of Creative Thinking: Norms-technical manual (Research ed.). Verbal Tests, Forms A and B. Figural Tests, Forms A and B.* Princeton, NJ: Personnel Press.

Torrance, E. P. (1984). The role of creativity in identification of the gifted and talented. *Gifted Child Quarterly, 28,* 153–156. http://dx.doi.org/10.1177/001698628402800403

Torrance, E. P. (1988). The nature of creativity as manifest in its testing. In R. J. Sternberg (Ed.), *The nature of creativity: Contemporary psychological perspectives* (pp. 43–75). New York, NY: Cambridge University Press.

Treffinger, D. J. (1985). Review of the Torrance Tests for Creative Thinking. In J. Mitchell (Ed.), *Ninth mental measurements yearbook* (pp. 1633–1634). Lincoln, NE: Buros Institute of Mental Measurement.

10

The Assessment of Wisdom-Related Performance

Ursula M. Staudinger and Bernhard Leipold

Since the beginning of human culture, wisdom has been viewed as the ideal endpoint of human development. The identification of wisdom in individuals (such as wise persons), the predominant approach in psychology, is but one of the ways by which wisdom is instantiated. In the Western world, the question of whether wisdom is divine or human was at the center of wisdom-related discourse during the Middle Ages and the Renaissance. A conclusion to this debate was reached during the later phases of the Enlightenment, when worldly wisdom took center stage. Archaeological–cultural work dealing with the origins of religious and secular bodies of wisdom-related texts in China, India, Egypt, Old Mesopotamia, and the like has revealed many similarities in the definition of wisdom across cultures and historical time.

In the general historical wisdom literature, however, the identification of wisdom with the mind and character (knowledge and virtue) of individuals is not the preferred mode of analysis. More often (cf. Staudinger & Glück, 2011) wisdom is described as a system of insights and heuristics that is instantiated in religious and constitutional texts or collections of proverbs. Wisdom includes knowledge about the limits of knowledge and the uncertainties of the world. Wisdom not only is an increase in insight and judgment but also includes personality growth (in contrast to increases in personality adjustment; Staudinger & Kessler, 2009). As the perfect integration of mind and

http://dx.doi.org/10.1037/0000138-010
Positive Psychological Assessment: A Handbook of Models and Measures, Second Edition,
M. W. Gallagher and S. J. Lopez (Editors)

character, wisdom concerns the dialectic between poles of human existence such as good and bad, intimacy and autonomy, certainty and doubt, or selfishness and altruism. Wisdom addresses important and difficult questions and strategies about the conduct and meaning of life and represents knowledge used for one's own good or well-being and that of others. Wisdom can be observed, for instance, as truly superior level of judgment, advice with an appreciation of the context, and knowledge with extraordinary scope, depth, measure, and balance.

It has been argued that wisdom in this sense has been culturally selected because of its adaptive value for humankind (e.g., Staudinger, 1996; Staudinger & Glück, 2011). Wisdom in its full sense is considered more a utopian ideal than a realistic goal for individual development. Given that Western industrialized societies have become pluralistic, how to lead a good life is no longer obvious. A need for guidance and orientation has emerged. The concept of wisdom seems ideally suited to fulfilling such needs.

PSYCHOLOGICAL DEFINITIONS OF WISDOM

Psychologists who define *wisdom* must specify the content and formal properties of wisdom-related judgment and advice in terms of psychological categories; moreover, they must describe the characteristics of persons who have approached a state of wisdom and are capable of transmitting such wisdom to others. For the most part, initial efforts by psychologists were theoretical and speculative. In his pioneering piece on senescence, G. Stanley Hall (1922) associated wisdom with the emergence of a meditative attitude, philosophical calmness, impartiality, and the desire to draw moral lessons that emerge in later adulthood. Furthermore, writers emphasized that wisdom involved the search for the moderate course between extremes, a dynamic between knowledge and doubt, a sufficient detachment from the problem at hand, and a well-balanced coordination of emotion, motivation, and thought (e.g., Hartshorne, 1987; Labouvie-Vief, 1990; Staudinger & Glück, 2011). Psychological definitions typically include that wisdom is knowledge about (a) the human condition at its frontier, (b) the most difficult questions of the meaning and conduct of life, and (c) the uncertainties of life and what cannot be known as well as dealing with that limited knowledge. Although wisdom has been described for millennia as the ideal integration of mind and virtue, only recently has it been investigated empirically. One reason for this dearth of empirical conceptualization and study may indicate the existence of serious doubts as to whether a concept so rich in ideational history and connotations is even amenable to scientific study. Admittedly, the current empirical attempts capture only parts of this highly complex phenomenon. Yet we believe that the current operationalizations of wisdom have demonstrated that it can be studied and is worth the effort.

MAJOR APPROACHES TO THE PSYCHOLOGICAL STUDY OF WISDOM

Two major approaches to the psychological study of wisdom can be distinguished: the implicit and the explicit theories of wisdom. *Implicit* theories focus on the assessment of subjective, commonsense beliefs about wisdom or wise persons (e.g., Bluck & Glück, 2005; Clayton & Birren, 1980; Holliday & Chandler, 1986; Sternberg, 1985). *Explicit* theories address how to empirically investigate expressions of wisdom. Within the explicit approach, it is useful to distinguish general wisdom from personal wisdom (i.e., wisdom about one's own life; e.g., Mickler & Staudinger, 2008; Staudinger, 2013; Staudinger, Dörner, & Mickler, 2005). A further distinction might be helpful to organize the different operationalizations of wisdom. Two types of assessment have been identified: measuring wisdom as an aspect of personality in the traditional view with self-report measures and measuring it as an aspect of cognitive–emotional expertise that requires performance measures (see Table 10.1).

Implicit Theories of Wisdom

Implicit or subjective theories of wisdom investigate the nature of everyday beliefs and folk conceptions and pursue answers to what is wisdom or what are characteristics of wise people or wise acts (Staudinger & Baltes, 1994; Staudinger & Glück, 2011). Thus, the criteria for wisdom are by definition consensual. Most studies of implicit wisdom theories have used descriptor-rating methods (Bluck & Glück, 2005). Wisdom in these studies is assessed in several ways. Participants are asked to sort adjectives according to either the degree to which they reflect wisdom (Clayton, 1975) or their probability of co-occurring in one person (Sternberg, 1985). In other studies, participants rated the degree to which items reflected their prototype of a wise person, a nonwise person, and

TABLE 10.1. Assessment of Wisdom in Implicit and Explicit Theories of Wisdom

	Explicit theories of wisdom		
Implicit theories	General wisdom	Personal wisdom	
Structure-analytical methods	Performance measures	Performance measures	Self-report measures
Lists of attributes, ratings, interviews (multidimensional scaling, factor analysis, classifications)	Open-ended questions, sentence completions, think-aloud method, scenarios with possible options		Questionnaires, self-ratings
Clayton; Holliday & Chandler; Sternberg	Berlin wisdom paradigm; Grossmann; Neo-Piagetian perspectives; Sternberg	Dörner & Staudinger; Labouvie-Vief; Loevinger; Mickler & Staudinger	Ardelt; Levenson; Ryff; Webster; Wink & Helson

nonrelevant characteristics (Holliday & Chandler, 1986). Structure-analytical methods such as multidimensional scaling or factor analysis can be used to extract underlying components from these ratings. Clayton (1975), for instance, identified three dimensions of wisdom: affective (e.g., empathy, compassion), reflective (e.g., intuition, introspection), and cognitive (e.g., experience, intelligence). She found that the concept of wisdom became more differentiated with increasing age of respondents.

From a series of studies, Sternberg (1985) concluded that investigating implicit theories was useful for studying the meaning of wisdom. Laypersons (nonacademicians) as well as academicians from several disciplines were asked to rate the prototypicality of each of the behaviors with respect to their own conception of an ideally wise person. The results suggested that the listed items were quite characteristic for wise persons in each of the groups. Furthermore, the ratings were highly consistent across participants (.86–.96) and items (.89–.97).

Bluck and Glück (2005) reviewed the empirical work on implicit theories of wisdom and grouped the components into general categories: cognitive ability, insight, reflective attitude, concern for others, and real-world skills. The content and the quality of the adjective lists and categories used in the content analysis affected the results in the studies reviewed.

From the research on implicit theories of wisdom and wise persons, it is evident that Westerners apparently hold fairly clear-cut images of the nature of wisdom. Four findings are especially noteworthy. First, wisdom seems to be closely related to wise persons and their acts as "carriers" of wisdom. Second, wise people integrate positive features of mind and character and are able to balance multiple interests and choices. Third, wisdom contains a very strong interpersonal and social aspect in both its application (advice) and the consensual recognition of its occurrence. Fourth, wisdom exhibits overlap with other related concepts such as intelligence, but in aspects such as sagacity, prudence, and the integration of cognition, emotion, and motivation, it also carries unique variance. In the Eastern tradition, studies focus on processes of mental attention, consciousness, and meditation, which contribute to the emergence of wisdom (e.g., Pascual-Leone, 2000).

Cross-cultural studies emphasize the differences between two broad modes of wisdom: an analytic mode prevalent in Western cultures that emphasizes cognitive complexity and knowledge and a synthesizing Eastern mode that focuses on the integration of cognition and affect (Takahashi & Overton, 2005). To date, very few studies (and unfortunately of questionable scientific quality) compare implicit theories of wisdom between cultures.

Explicit Theories of General and Personal Wisdom

In contrast to the implicit theories, the other approach to the psychological study of wisdom involves explicit theories. They are grounded in theoretical conceptions of wisdom that subsequently are operationalized and tested. Behavioral expressions of wisdom are the unit of analysis in this tradition. Within the explicit approaches, one can distinguish between general wisdom and personal wisdom (Staudinger, 2013). According to this distinction, general wisdom is concerned with insights into life in general. What does an individual know about life in general from an observer's point of view, that is, when she/he is not personally concerned? Personal wisdom refers to individuals' insights into their own lives. What does a person know about her- or himself? This distinction is loosely related to the philosophical separation between the ontology of the first and the third person (Searle, 1992) and points out that a person can be prudent with regard to other people's problems, but not necessarily to their own problems.

Within this dichotomy, that for heuristic purposes admittedly oversimplifies the differences between the existing approaches to wisdom, general wisdom has been investigated through three lines of work: the balance theory (e.g., Sternberg, 1998, 2001), the neo-Piagetian tradition (e.g., Kramer & Woodruff, 1986; Labouvie-Vief, 1990), and the assessment of wisdom as an expert system (e.g., Baltes & Staudinger, 2000; Kunzmann & Baltes, 2003).

Sternberg integrated his work on implicit theories of wisdom and practical intelligence and tacit knowledge and suggested that the notion of balance was central in defining wisdom (Sternberg, 1998; Sternberg, Reznitskaya, & Jarvin, 2007). Wisdom is seen as being inherently linked to the interaction between the individual and the situation. It is defined as the application of tacit knowledge with the goal of achieving a common good. In particular, tacit knowledge is applied to balance interests (intrapersonal, interpersonal, extrapersonal) as well as responses to environmental context (adaptation, shaping, selection). Wisdom in this sense is a special form of practical intelligence that requires balancing of interests to achieve a common good.

Informed by the Piagetian tradition of studying cognitive development, several investigators have proposed a postformal stage of adult thinking. In these theories of postformal thought, wisdom is conceptualized as increasingly complex and dialectic thinking that integrates the social and the emotional logics (cf. Labouvie-Vief, 2005, 2015). Criteria for postformal thinking include awareness of multiple causes and solutions, awareness of paradoxes and contradictions, and the ability to deal with uncertainty, imperfection, and compromise (Sinnott, 1998, 2014). Finally, wisdom also has been conceptualized as a special kind of expert-level insight and heuristics (Staudinger & Glück, 2011). Consistent with the idea that expertise is grounded in years of acquiring domain-specific experiences, research within this framework demonstrates that experts excel mainly in a special domain—namely, the "fundamental pragmatics of life" (e.g., Baltes & Staudinger, 2000).

Within theories of personality development, wisdom usually is conceptualized as an advanced, if not the final, stage of development. For Erikson (1959), wisdom implied accepting one's life without major regrets and accepting death as the inevitable end. Whereas integrity versus despair constitutes the final psychosocial crisis of human existence, integrity can be attained only in a dynamic balance with despair. A related aspect of personality development is transcendence (Levenson, Jennings, Aldwin, & Shiraishi, 2005; Orwoll &

Perlmutter, 1990), or moving beyond individualistic concerns to more collective or universal issues. Personal wisdom is closely linked with notions of "maturity" and "personal growth" (for an overview, see Staudinger & Glück, 2011).

INDIVIDUAL-DIFFERENCES MEASURES OF GENERAL AND PERSONAL WISDOM

As described, general wisdom is assessed using performance measures. Personal wisdom can be measured employing both methods. In this section, the self-report measures as well as the performance measures related to the explicit approaches to the study of wisdom are presented in more detail.

Assessment of General Wisdom

Assessment of Wisdom in the Balance Theory

In a series of studies on practical intelligence, Sternberg (2001) developed assessments of tacit knowledge. Participants were asked to use Likert scales to solve problems (scenarios), and the response profile for all problems was scored against a profile of a nominated expert group. Reliability coefficients typically ranged between .60 and .90.

Assessment of Wisdom as Postformal Thinking

Central to neo-Piagetian theories of adult thought is the transcendence of the universal truth criterion that characterizes formal logic. This transcendence is common to conceptions such as dialectical, complementary, and relativistic thinking. Such tolerance of multiple truths—that is, tolerance of ambiguity—also has been mentioned as a crucial feature of wisdom. A number of different approaches all linked to this basic understanding can be distinguished: dialectical thinking, complementary thinking, relativistic thinking, and reflective judgment. Usually, these kinds of mature thoughts are assessed as performances. Thus, participants are asked to respond to a fictitious problem. The answers subsequently are coded according to respective coding schemes reflecting ascending levels of mature thought (e.g., Blanchard-Fields, 1986; Kitchener & Brenner, 1990; Kramer & Woodruff, 1986). Reported interrater agreements usually range between Cronbach's alpha .75 and .85.

Kramer (1983) suggested the following three features of mature thinking to summarize a number of models of postformal thinking: awareness of the relativistic nature of knowledge, acceptance of contradiction, and integration of contradiction into the dialectical whole. In a study by Kramer and Woodruff (1986), these features were operationalized as sequentially ordered levels of mature thinking and, at the same time, as coding categories for the analysis of response protocols. To assess postformal thinking, participants were each presented with two dilemmas (e.g., a woman's decision about whether to enter the workforce for the first time full-time). Coders rated each protocol for instances of responses that revealed each of the categories of thought. On the basis of coding, each participant was assigned a frequency score and a rating score that indicated the quality of the responses with regard to dialectical thinking.

Ill-structured social dilemmas usually are used to examine postformal thought. In another study, the role of emotions in social reasoning was investigated (Blanchard-Fields, 1986). Three age groups were presented with three fictitious situations, each of which offered two opposing accounts. The tasks varied in emotional saliency and the degree of interpersonal conflict. Participants were asked to give their accounts of the situation, and then they were asked some probing questions (e.g., Who was at fault in this situation? How was the conflict resolved?). Responses were scored according to levels of dialectical thinking and judgment under uncertainty (Kitchener & King, 1981). Interrater reliability ranged from .92 to .94.

Assessment of Wisdom as Expert-Level Knowledge and Judgment in the Fundamental Pragmatics of Life

In addition to these measures of wisdom as a feature of mature thought, there also is work that attempts to assess wisdom-related performance in tasks dealing with the interpretation, conduct, and management of life. This approach is based on lifespan theory, the developmental study of the aging mind and aging personality, research on expert systems, and cultural–historical definitions of wisdom (Baltes, Smith, & Staudinger, 1992). Integrating these perspectives, wisdom is defined as an expert knowledge system in the fundamental pragmatics of life, permitting exceptional insight, judgment, and advice involving complex and uncertain matters of the human condition.

The body of knowledge and skills associated with wisdom as an expertise in the fundamental pragmatics of life entails insights into the quintessential aspects of the human condition, including its biological finitude and cultural conditioning. Wisdom involves a fine-tuned and well-balanced coordination of cognition, motivation, and emotion (Kunzmann & Baltes, 2003). More specifically, wisdom-related knowledge and skills can be characterized by a family of five criteria: (a) rich factual knowledge about life, (b) rich procedural knowledge about life, (c) lifespan contextualism, (d) value relativism, and (e) awareness and management of uncertainty (see Baltes & Staudinger, 2000, for an extensive definition).

To elicit and measure wisdom-related knowledge and skills in this approach, participants are presented with difficult life dilemmas such as "Imagine someone receives a call from a good friend who tells him/her that he/she can't go on anymore and has decided to commit suicide. What would the person/what would you do and consider in this situation?" Participants then are asked to "think aloud" about such dilemmas. The five wisdom-related criteria are used to evaluate these protocols. To do so, an age-heterogeneous expert panel of raters is selected based on their life experience, and every rater is trained on only one criterion to avoid halo affects. Two raters always apply the same criterion to establish interrater reliability. The reliabilities of the five criteria have ranged between .72 and .93, and the reliability of the wisdom scores averaged across the five criteria even reached a Cronbach's alpha of .98. The exact training procedure and the calibration protocols are described and included in the *Rater Manual*, which can be obtained from the authors (Staudinger, Smith, & Baltes, 1994).

When using this wisdom paradigm to study people who were nominated as wise according to nominators' subjective beliefs about wisdom, it was found that wisdom nominees also received higher wisdom scores than did comparable control samples of various ages and professional backgrounds (Baltes & Staudinger, 2000). Convergent and discriminant validity was established with regard to extant measures of cognitive and personality functioning. In line with the historical wisdom literature that portrays wisdom as the ideal combination of mind and virtue, it was found that wisdom-related performance was best predicted by measures located at the interface of cognition and personality, such as a judicious cognitive style, creativity, and moral reasoning. Neither intelligence (fluid, crystallized) nor personality (Big Five, psychological-mindedness) made a significant independent contribution to wisdom-related knowledge and judgment (Staudinger, Lopez, & Baltes, 1997).

Wisdom is related to affective involvement (being interested, inspired) but weakly and negatively related to positive and negative affect (Kunzmann & Baltes, 2003). Results showed that individuals higher on wisdom-related knowledge reported a value orientation that focused conjointly on other-enhancing values and personal growth combined with a lower tendency toward values revolving around a pleasurable life. In addition, a preference for cooperative conflict management strategies combined with a lower tendency to adopt submissive, avoidant, or dominant conflict strategies was found in this study.

Another more recently introduced performance measure of wisdom is the wise reasoning measure developed by Grossmann et al. (2010). It uses an empirical paradigm similar to the Berlin wisdom approach by presenting participants with a social dilemma situation of either a real-life or a fictitious nature. Participants are asked to think aloud about the dilemma, and the transcribed responses are content-analyzed to determine the degree to which each of the four criteria of wise reasoning is met (Grossmann, 2017). The four criteria are (a) intellectual humility or the recognition of limits of one's own knowledge, (b) recognition of others' perspective or the broader contexts than the issue at hand, (c) recognition of uncertainty and change, and (d) integration of different opinions or preferences and compromise. As with the empirical paradigm, the wisdom criteria also bear similarity to some of the Berlin wisdom criteria such as lifespan contextualism, recognition and management of uncertainty, and value relativism.

Assessment of Personal Wisdom

Within personality theories, wisdom usually is conceptualized as an advanced if not the final stage of personality development. In this context, wisdom is comparable to "optimal maturity." A wise person is characterized, for instance, as integrating rather than ignoring or repressing self-related information by coordinating opposites and by transcending personal agendas in favor of collective or universal issues. Because "optimal maturity" is highly desirable, most self-reports are skewed toward the socially desirable end of the scale. Glück et al. (2013) compared extant self-report measures of wisdom and found that they were significantly correlated with each other.

Assessment of Personal Wisdom With Self-Report Measures

Ryff and Heincke (1983), for instance, developed self-report questionnaires based on the Eriksonian notions of personality development, especially integrity or wisdom. Their Integrity scale consists of 16 items. A high scorer is described as adapting to triumphs and disappointments of being; accepting personal life as something that had to be; viewing past life as inevitable, appropriate, and meaningful; being emotionally integrated; having resolved past conflicts; and having a sense of having taken care of things.

Other approaches have used recombinations of extant personality questionnaires to operationalize wisdom in the sense of self-development and maturity. For instance, Wink and Helson (1997) used a personality measure and open-ended responses to assess practical (e.g., interpersonal skill and interest, insight, clear thinking, reflectiveness, tolerance) and transcendent wisdom (e.g., transcending the personal, recognizing the complexities and limits of knowledge, integrating thought and effort, spiritual depth). The Practical Wisdom scale, for example, consists of 14 indicative items (e.g., mature, insightful, tolerant) and four contraindicative items (e.g., immature, reckless, shallow). In addition to self-reported wisdom, participants also are asked, "Many people hope to become wiser as they grow older. Would you give an example of wisdom you have acquired and how you came by it?" A panel of trained judges evaluates the answers using a 5-point scale.

Ardelt's Wisdom Scale. On the basis of earlier research by Clayton and Birren (1980), Ardelt (2003) defined wisdom as an integration of cognitive, reflective, and affective personality characteristics. The final version of the Three-Dimensional Wisdom Scale consists of 14 items for the cognitive, 12 for the reflective, and 13 for the affective components of wisdom. Cronbach's alpha ranged from .71 to .85.

Webster's Wisdom Scale. Webster (2003) developed a 30-item scale assessing five interrelated dimensions of wisdom (experience, emotions, reminiscence, openness, and humor). The Self-Assessed Wisdom Scale (SAWS) appears to be a reliable scale with Cronbach's alphas of .77 and .87 and shows significant relationships with measures of generativity and ego integrity. A 40-item version of the SAWS has excellent reliability (test–retest = .83; Cronbach's alpha = .90; Webster, 2007).

Levenson's Wisdom Scale. Levenson et al. (2005) developed the Adult Self-Transcendence questionnaire that identifies learning that goes beyond narrow self-interest. This measure includes items associated with spiritual transcendence and the psychopathology of depression. According to the authors, self-transcendence is equivalent to wisdom and implies the dissolution of (self-based) obstacles to empathy, understanding, and integrity.

Assessment of Personal Wisdom With Performance Measures

Similar to the methods used to assess general wisdom, performance measures can also be used to measure personal wisdom or related constructs reliably. In contrast to self-ratings, performance-based answers are compared with defined standards that allow the assessment of expertise, but they are more time-consuming to score.

Loevinger's Ego Development. Jane Loevinger's model (e.g., Loevinger, 1993) conceptualizes personality development as a successive progression toward psychological maturity. The eight postulated stages can be measured by content coding of standardized self-descriptions with regard to four characteristics (impulse control, interpersonal style, conscious preoccupations, and cognitive styles). The sentence completion test consists of 36 items, and the rater is required to assign every response to a specific level.

Labouvie-Vief's Approach to Personal Wisdom. Labouvie-Vief (e.g., 2005, 2015) developed a concept of maturity that combines the tendency to constrain affect to the positive (affect optimization) with the amplification of affect in a search for differentiation (affect complexity). Her model is rooted in the theories of postformal thought. She has coded brief narratives from individuals about their emotions and their selves into five qualitative levels demonstrating good interrater reliabilities for differing cognitive–affective complexity. The assumption that structural (differentiation, complexity) and dynamic (affect, happiness) aspects of life are interconnected is stated in the dynamic integration theory (e.g., Labouvie-Vief, 2005).

The Bremen Measure of Personal Wisdom. Mickler and Staudinger suggested that it might be useful to distinguish between wisdom about life in general and wisdom about one's own life (Mickler & Staudinger, 2008; Staudinger, Dörner, & Mickler, 2005). Personal wisdom refers to insight into one's own life based on personal experience (see Appendix 10.1). On the basis of the Berlin wisdom paradigm and growth models of personality, five criteria of personal wisdom were developed. More specifically, personal wisdom is characterized by two basic criteria—(a) self-knowledge and (b) growth and self-regulation—and three metacriteria—(c) interrelating the self to circumstances/context, (d) self-relativism, and (e) tolerance of ambiguity. The interrater reliability was high (.84). Personal wisdom was more strongly related to indicators of personality maturity than was general wisdom. Life events that led to new self-insights were the second most important predictor of personal wisdom. In contrast to the findings for general wisdom, personal wisdom was not facilitated by the opportunity to exchange ideas with a familiar person. Staudinger, Kessler, and Dörner (2006) found that instruction about how to infer insight from personal experiences significantly increased personal wisdom scores.

ONTOGENESIS OF WISDOM

A working model of the development of wisdom-related knowledge specifies a set of conditions and processes that need to "cooperate" for wisdom to develop (e.g., Baltes et al., 1992; Staudinger et al., 1997). The development of wisdom is dependent on *general person factors* (e.g., cognitive mechanics, openness to experience, social competence), *expertise-specific factors* (e.g., experience in life matters, receiving mentorship, motivational dispositions such as striving for excellence), and *facilitative experiential contexts* (e.g., age, education, profession, period). Furthermore, three processes have been specified that may support the acquisition of wisdom: *life review, life management,* and *life planning*. These processes refer to the threefold perception of time, organize the experiences and impressions, and provide an avenue to measure wisdom-related knowledge. An effective constellation of context-related, person-related, and expertise-specific factors is assumed to maximize the likelihood of attaining expertise in the fundamental pragmatics of life.

Tests of this ontogenetic model demonstrated that age-related increases of wisdom-related performance occur only between the ages of 14 and approximately 25 years of age (Pasupathi, Staudinger, & Baltes, 2001). Thereafter, until later adulthood (approximately 75 years), it is not enough to grow older to become wiser (Staudinger, 1999). During adulthood, factors other than chronological age predict wisdom performance. Empirical studies supported the important role of experiential settings as well as guidance and mentorship in dealing with difficult life issues (e.g., Smith, Staudinger, & Baltes, 1994; Staudinger, Smith, & Baltes, 1992). In the same vein, it was found that wisdom-related knowledge and judgment does not follow a simple cumulative function, but rather it is related to the contexts of everyday life. It was demonstrated that young and old respondents gave best responses when asked about a problem relevant to their own life phase (for a review, see Staudinger, 1999).

In a comparison of these findings on general wisdom with evidence regarding correlates of personal wisdom, similarities and differences emerge. Neither general nor personal wisdom has a linear positive relationship to age. For example, a recent study presented evidence from a 34-year longitudinal study on personal wisdom in an Eriksonian sense (Sneed & Whitbourne, 2003). With considerable interindividual differences, integrity scores increased in young adulthood, dropped somewhat around age 40, and then began to increase again. Many aging adults may focus on stabilizing previous self-perceptions to maintain well-being, rather than engaging in deep life reflection (Mickler & Staudinger, 2008; Sneed & Whitbourne, 2003), which is consistent with the idea that in old age, wisdom, unlike well-being, is a rare quality (Staudinger & Kessler, 2009). Research with the Bremen measure of personal wisdom found that age is not only unrelated (as is the case for general wisdom) to personal wisdom but even also negatively related for the three metacriteria, that is, self-relativism, interrelating the self, and tolerance of ambiguity (Mickler & Staudinger, 2008). Declining cognitive resources may make abstract thinking, which is required more to satisfy the meta- than the basic wisdom criteria, more difficult for older adults. Also, younger adults' higher level of openness to experience may be an added advantage when it comes to testing established self-related insights against new evidence, which is prerequisite to further developing self-insight. Further, self-criticism is less crucial for general wisdom-related performance than it is for personal wisdom. Similarly, personal growth is generally negatively related to age (Ryff & Keyes, 1995), and ego development peaks in early midlife and declines thereafter (Cohn & Westenberg, 2004). When such findings are being interpreted, contemporaneous societal restrictions of growth opportunities in old age need to be taken into account (e.g., Ryff & Singer, 2006; Staudinger & Kessler, 2009).

Second, personal wisdom shows a significantly smaller relationship with indicators of subjective well-being than does general wisdom. Third, personal life events did not contribute to the prediction of general wisdom-related performance, but they played an important role when predicting personal wisdom scores (Mickler & Staudinger, 2008). This is in line with the finding that traumatic life experiences can be conducive to the development of (personal) wisdom (e.g., Baltes, Staudinger, Maercker, & Smith, 1995). After negative experiences such as accidents, life-threatening illness, or the death of a close other person, many people report self-perceived increases in aspects of personal characteristics such as compassion, affect regulation, self-understanding, honesty and reliability, spirituality, and self-reported wisdom itself (cf. Park, 2004). Although such self-perceptions of growth may be delusional (Maercker & Zoellner, 2004), it seems plausible that personal wisdom is fostered by the experience of fundamental changes that "force" individuals to grow (Nolen-Hoeksema & Larson, 1999) by challenging them to reorganize their assumptions about life and priorities but not completely destroying them.

FACILITATING WISDOM-RELATED PERFORMANCE

Besides finding evidence for the ontogenetic model, it also was shown that wisdom-related performance can be facilitated. Wisdom-related performance was enhanced by one standard deviation if participants had a chance to discuss the life problem with a self-selected partner before responding (Staudinger & Baltes, 1996). In a second study, teaching participants a thinking strategy that encouraged switching between perspectives resulted in significant increases in wisdom-related performances (Böhmig-Krumhaar, Staudinger, & Baltes, 2002). However, activation of abstract conceptions about wisdom (by means of the instruction to "try to give a wise response") does not lead to increases in performance (Glück & Baltes, 2006).

Similarly, a first intervention study using the Bremen measure of personal wisdom was successful but also once more proved different from general wisdom. In contrast to the findings for general wisdom (Staudinger & Baltes, 1996), personal wisdom was not facilitated by the opportunity to exchange ideas with a familiar person before responding to a personal wisdom task. Rather, it was found that instruction about how to infer insight from personal experiences (cf. life review; Staudinger, 2001) significantly increased personal wisdom scores (cf. Staudinger et al., 2006). The authors interpreted this finding such that in the case of personal wisdom, the exchange with a well-known other person may be less helpful, as relationships tend to develop in ways that partners get along well without touching upon sensitive issues. Thus, for personal wisdom to be facilitated it seems more useful to seek support from someone unknown and trained to support the life-reflection process, such as a psychotherapist. In sum, experimental studies have yielded encouraging evidence that both general and personal wisdom can be facilitated. Consequently, we may ask how such wisdom-conducive conditions can be implemented in everyday life.

CLINICAL CASE STUDY

Mary, a 50-year-old woman, has been diagnosed with cancer. The doctors told her that she has only 1 year to live. This diagnosis prompts her to review the life she has led so far. In thinking about what she should do and consider in making her plans, she went for counseling. Should she, as much as possible, continue living the way she has been, or should she make a drastic change in her life? Familiar with the criteria of the Berlin and Bremen wisdom research, the psychologist made sure of Mary's knowledge about the disease-related changes and adequate pain therapy to optimize her quality of life in these last months (factual knowledge and self-regulation). In addition, he encouraged her to reflect upon questions concerning what has been important in her life and how successful she may have been realizing these values (personal values and their relativistic nature). Do these values maintain their importance in the new life situation of hers? Also, he alerted her to the fact that nothing in life is ever certain. Things might turn out differently than expected but nevertheless she needed to go ahead and act as if her lifetime would be ending after 1 year. During the counseling sessions he directed Mary's attention to the biographical contexts and idiosyncratic decisions to gain a better understanding of why certain things happened the way they did in her life (the interrelations between the self and circumstances/lifespan contextualism). In short, psychological wisdom-related counseling and therapy pertain to virtues and competences and should prepare Mary to review her life and come to grips with her life as lived (or not lived) as well as to support her in making plans and setting priorities for the remaining months.

CONCLUSION

The concept of wisdom represents a fruitful topic for psychological research because (a) the study of wisdom emphasizes the search for continued optimization and the additional evolution of the human condition, and (b) in a prototypical fashion, it allows the study of collaboration among cognitive, emotional, and motivational processes. The results show that wisdom can be reliably assessed with different measures and through different avenues; however, in terms of validity (e.g., Mickler & Staudinger, 2008), we need more studies that compare wisdom-related "inventories."

Future research on wisdom will be expanded in at least four ways: (a) identifying more social and personality factors as well as life processes relevant to the ontogeny of wisdom, (b) attempting to further develop less labor-intensive assessment tools, (c) gaining better understanding of the interplay between self-related wisdom and wisdom about others, and (d) comparing antecedents and correlates of wise judgment or wise advice as compared with wise acts. Within the field of positive psychology, wisdom may be considered one of the central human strengths, and attempts will be made to facilitate its development.

APPENDIX 10.1
PERSONAL WISDOM: ILLUSTRATION OF A WISDOM-RELATED TASK WITH EXAMPLES OF HIGH-LEVEL RESPONSES[1]

Please think aloud about yourself as a friend. What are your typical behaviors? How do you act in difficult situations? Can you think of examples? Can you think of reasons for your behavior? What are your strengths and weaknesses? What would you like to change?

I've learned many things through my friendships. I think others could say the same. Moreover, I think it is very stimulating to be different from each other; especially when friends can view things from their own individual stance—that can be quite enriching. I once had a friend when I was in kindergarten. Back then, my family had to move to another city. Was that the reason for our friendship falling apart? Probably, yes. But even with the earliest of friendships, it often happens that you grow apart from each other as you mature. I actually had friends even when it was especially difficult under the social conditions and circumstances, such as when my father passed away early in my childhood and we had to move to my grandparents' home. Of course, it may also have had to do with me that some friendships fell apart. I would naturally have some influence, but the other person carries part of the responsibility as well. One other very

[1]Abbreviated; cf. Mickler & Staudinger (2007).

good friend of mine back then got married quickly—that's the way things go. . . . But because I love him, I was ready to accept his friends, even if I didn't like them all too much. When I look back to all of my friendships, I remember one very good friend of mine who passed away. That's something we all will one day have to come to terms with. For some, it comes sooner than others. In the meantime, it's something that belongs to life, placing all of our fears into context. How I am as a friend depends completely on the degree of the friendship.

REFERENCES

Ardelt, M. (2003). Empirical assessment of a three-dimensional wisdom scale. *Research on Aging, 25,* 275–324. http://dx.doi.org/10.1177/0164027503025003004

Baltes, P. B., Smith, J., & Staudinger, U. M. (1992). Wisdom and successful aging. In T. Sonderegger (Ed.), *Nebraska symposium on motivation* (Vol. 39, pp. 123–167). Lincoln: University of Nebraska Press.

Baltes, P. B., & Staudinger, U. M. (2000). Wisdom. A metaheuristic (pragmatic) to orchestrate mind and virtue toward excellence. *American Psychologist, 55,* 122–136. http://dx.doi.org/10.1037/0003-066X.55.1.122

Baltes, P. B., Staudinger, U. M., Maercker, A., & Smith, J. (1995). People nominated as wise: A comparative study of wisdom-related knowledge. *Psychology and Aging, 10,* 155–166. http://dx.doi.org/10.1037/0882-7974.10.2.155

Blanchard-Fields, F. (1986). Reasoning on social dilemmas varying in emotional saliency: An adult developmental perspective. *Psychology and Aging, 1,* 325–333. http://dx.doi.org/10.1037/0882-7974.1.4.325

Bluck, S., & Glück, J. (2005). From the inside out: People's implicit theories of wisdom. In R. J. Sternberg & J. Jordan (Eds.), *A handbook of wisdom: Psychological perspectives* (pp. 84–109). Cambridge, England: Cambridge University Press. http://dx.doi.org/10.1017/CBO9780511610486.005

Böhmig-Krumhaar, S., Staudinger, U. M., & Baltes, P. B. (2002). Mehr Toleranz tut Not: Läβt sich wert-relativierendes Denken und Urteilen verbessern? [In need of more tolerance: Is it possible to facilitate value relativism?]. *Zeitschrift für Entwicklungspsychologie und Pädagogische Psychologie, 36,* 30–43.

Clayton, V. (1975). Erikson's theory of human development as it applies to the aged: Wisdom as contradictive cognition. *Human Development, 18,* 119–128. http://dx.doi.org/10.1159/000271479

Clayton, V. P., & Birren, J. E. (1980). The development of wisdom across the life span: A reexamination of an ancient topic. In P. B. Baltes & J. O. G. Brim (Eds.), *Life-span development and behavior* (Vol. 3, pp. 103–135). New York, NY: Academic Press.

Cohn, L. D., & Westenberg, P. M. (2004). Intelligence and maturity: Meta-analytic evidence for the incremental and discriminant validity of Loevinger's measure of ego development. *Journal of Personality and Social Psychology, 86,* 760–772. http://dx.doi.org/10.1037/0022-3514.86.5.760

Erikson, E. H. (1959). *Identity and the life cycle.* New York, NY: International University Press.

Glück, J., & Baltes, P. B. (2006). Using the concept of wisdom to enhance the expression of wisdom knowledge: Not the philosopher's dream but differential effects of developmental preparedness. *Psychology and Aging, 21,* 679–690. http://dx.doi.org/10.1037/0882-7974.21.4.679

Glück, J., König, S., Naschenweng, K., Redzanowski, U., Dorner, L., Straβer, I., & Wiedermann, W. (2013). How to measure wisdom: Content, reliability, and validity of five measures. *Frontiers in Psychology, 4,* 405.

Grossmann, I. (2017). Wisdom in context. *Perspectives on Psychological Science, 12,* 233–257. http://dx.doi.org/10.1177/1745691616672066

Grossmann, I., Na, J., Varnum, M. E. W., Park, D. C., Kitayama, S., & Nisbett, R. E. (2010). Reasoning about social conflicts improves into old age. *Proceedings of the National Academy of Sciences of the United States of America, 107,* 7246–7250. http://dx.doi.org/10.1073/pnas.1001715107

Hall, G. S. (1922). *Senescence: The last half of life.* New York, NY: Appleton. http://dx.doi.org/10.1037/10896-000

Hartshorne, C. (1987). *Wisdom as moderation: A philosophy of the middle way.* Albany: State University of New York Press.

Holliday, S. G., & Chandler, M. J. (1986). Wisdom: Explorations in adult competence. In J. A. Meacham (Ed.), *Contributions to human development* (Vol. 17, pp. 1–96). Basel, Switzerland: Karger.

Kitchener, K. S., & Brenner, H. G. (1990). Wisdom and reflective judgement: Knowing in the face of uncertainty. In R. J. Sternberg (Ed.), *Wisdom: Its nature, origins, and development* (pp. 212–229). New York, NY: Cambridge University Press. http://dx.doi.org/10.1017/CBO9781139173704.011

Kitchener, K. S., & King, P. M. (1981). Reflective judgment: Concepts of justification and their relationship to age and education. *Journal of Applied Developmental Psychology, 2,* 89–116. http://dx.doi.org/10.1016/0193-3973(81)90032-0

Kramer, D. A. (1983). Postformal operations? A need for further conceptualization. *Human Development, 26,* 91–105. http://dx.doi.org/10.1159/000272873

Kramer, D. A., & Woodruff, D. S. (1986). Relativistic and dialectical thought in three adult age groups. *Human Development, 29,* 280–290. http://dx.doi.org/10.1159/000273064

Kunzmann, U., & Baltes, P. B. (2003). Wisdom-related knowledge: Affective, motivational, and interpersonal correlates. *Personality and Social Psychology Bulletin, 29,* 1104–1119. http://dx.doi.org/10.1177/0146167203254506

Labouvie-Vief, G. (1990). Wisdom as integrated thought: Historical and developmental perspectives. In R. J. Sternberg (Ed.), *Wisdom: Its nature, origins, and development* (pp. 52–84). New York, NY: Cambridge University Press. http://dx.doi.org/10.1017/CBO9781139173704.005

Labouvie-Vief, G. (2005). Self-with-other representations and the organization of the self. *Journal of Research in Personality, 39,* 185–205. http://dx.doi.org/10.1016/j.jrp.2004.09.007

Labouvie-Vief, G. (2015). *Integrating emotions and cognition throughout the lifespan.* New York, NY: Springer. http://dx.doi.org/10.1007/978-3-319-09822-7

Levenson, M. R., Jennings, P. A., Aldwin, C. M., & Shiraishi, R. W. (2005). Self-transcendence: Conceptualization and measurement. *The International Journal of Aging & Human Development, 60,* 127–143. http://dx.doi.org/10.2190/XRXM-FYRA-7U0X-GRC0

Loevinger, J. (1993). Measurement of personality: True of false. *Psychological Inquiry, 4,* 1–16. http://dx.doi.org/10.1207/s15327965pli0401_1

Maercker, A., & Zoellner, T. (2004). The Janus face of self-perceived growth: Toward a two-component model of posttraumatic growth. *Psychological Inquiry, 14,* 41–48.

Mickler, C., & Staudinger, U. M. (2007). *Personal wisdom: Assessment and evaluation* (Technical report). Bremen, Germany: Jacobs University Bremen.

Mickler, C., & Staudinger, U. M. (2008). Personal wisdom: Validation and age-related differences of a performance measure. *Psychology and Aging, 23,* 787–799. http://dx.doi.org/10.1037/a0013928

Nolen-Hoeksema, S., & Larson, J. (1999). *Coping with loss.* Mahwah, NJ: Erlbaum.

Orwoll, L., & Perlmutter, M. (1990). The study of wise persons: Integrating a personality perspective. In R. J. Sternberg (Ed.), *Wisdom: Its nature, origins, and development* (pp. 160–178). New York, NY: Cambridge University Press. http://dx.doi.org/10.1017/CBO9781139173704.009

Park, C. L. (2004). The notion of growth following stressful life experiences: Problems and prospects. *Psychological Inquiry, 15,* 69–76.

Pascual-Leone, J. (2000). Mental attention, consciousness, and the progressive emergence of wisdom. *Journal of Adult Development, 7,* 241–254. http://dx.doi.org/10.1023/A:1009563428260

Pasupathi, M., Staudinger, U. M., & Baltes, P. B. (2001). Seeds of wisdom: Adolescents' knowledge and judgment about difficult life problems. *Developmental Psychology, 37,* 351–361. http://dx.doi.org/10.1037/0012-1649.37.3.351

Ryff, C. D., & Heincke, S. G. (1983). The subjective organization of personality in adulthood and aging. *Journal of Personality and Social Psychology, 44,* 807–816. http://dx.doi.org/10.1037/0022-3514.44.4.807

Ryff, C. D., & Keyes, C. L. M. (1995). The structure of psychological well-being revisited. *Journal of Personality and Social Psychology, 69,* 719–727. http://dx.doi.org/10.1037/0022-3514.69.4.719

Ryff, C. D., & Singer, B. H. (2006). Best news yet on the six-factor model of well-being. *Social Science Research, 35,* 1103–1119. http://dx.doi.org/10.1016/j.ssresearch.2006.01.002

Searle, J. R. (1992). *The rediscovery of the mind.* Cambridge, MA: MIT Press.

Sinnott, J. D. (1998). *The development of logic in adulthood: Postformal thought and its applications.* New York, NY: Plenum. http://dx.doi.org/10.1007/978-1-4757-2911-5

Sinnott, J. D. (2014). *Adult development: Cognitive aspects of thriving close relationships.* Oxford, England: Oxford University Press. http://dx.doi.org/10.1093/acprof:oso/9780199892815.001.0001

Smith, J., Staudinger, U. M., & Baltes, P. B. (1994). Occupational settings facilitating wisdom-related knowledge: The sample case of clinical psychologists. *Journal of Consulting and Clinical Psychology, 62,* 989–999. http://dx.doi.org/10.1037/0022-006X.62.5.989

Sneed, J. R., & Whitbourne, S. K. (2003). Identity processing and self-consciousness in middle and later adulthood. *The Journals of Gerontology: Series B. Psychological Sciences and Social Sciences, 58,* P313–P319. http://dx.doi.org/10.1093/geronb/58.6.P313

Staudinger, U. M. (1996). Wisdom and the social-interactive foundation of the mind. In P. B. Baltes & U. M. Staudinger (Eds.), *Interactive minds* (pp. 276–315). New York, NY: Cambridge University Press.

Staudinger, U. M. (1999). Older and wiser? Integrating results on the relationship between age and wisdom-related performance. *International Journal of Behavioral Development, 23,* 641–664. http://dx.doi.org/10.1080/016502599383739

Staudinger, U. M. (2001). Life reflection: A social-cognitive analysis of life review. *Review of General Psychology, 5,* 148–160. http://dx.doi.org/10.1037/1089-2680.5.2.148

Staudinger, U. M. (2013). The need to distinguish personal from general wisdom: A short history and empirical evidence. In M. Ferrari & N. Westrate (Eds.), *The scientific study of personal wisdom* (pp. 3–19). Dordrecht, The Netherlands: Springer.

Staudinger, U. M., & Baltes, P. B. (1994). The psychology of wisdom. In R. J. Sternberg (Ed.), *Encyclopedia of intelligence* (pp. 1143–1152). New York, NY: Macmillan.

Staudinger, U. M., & Baltes, P. B. (1996). Interactive minds: A facilitative setting for wisdom-related performance? *Journal of Personality and Social Psychology, 71,* 746–762. http://dx.doi.org/10.1037/0022-3514.71.4.746

Staudinger, U. M., Dörner, J., & Mickler, C. (2005). Wisdom and personality. In R. Sternberg & J. Jordan (Eds.), *Handbook of wisdom* (pp. 191–219). New York, NY: Cambridge University Press. http://dx.doi.org/10.1017/CBO9780511610486.009

Staudinger, U. M., & Glück, J. (2011). Psychological wisdom research: Commonalities and differences in a growing field. *Annual Review of Psychology, 62,* 215–241. http://dx.doi.org/10.1146/annurev.psych.121208.131659

Staudinger, U. M., & Kessler, E.-M. (2009). Adjustment and growth: Two trajectories of positive personality development across adulthood. In M. C. Smith &

N. DeFrates-Densch (Eds.), *Handbook of research on adult learning and development* (pp. 241–268). New York, NY: Routledge.

Staudinger, U. M., Kessler, E.-M., & Dörner, J. (2006). Wisdom in social context. In K. W. Schaie & L. Carstensen (Eds.), *Social structures, aging, and self-regulation in the elderly* (pp. 33–54). New York, NY: Springer.

Staudinger, U. M., Lopez, D., & Baltes, P. B. (1997). The psychometric location of wisdom-related performance: Intelligence, personality, and more? *Personality and Social Psychology Bulletin, 23,* 1200–1214. http://dx.doi.org/10.1177/01461672972311007

Staudinger, U. M., Smith, J., & Baltes, P. B. (1992). Wisdom-related knowledge in a life review task: Age differences and the role of professional specialization. *Psychology and Aging, 7,* 271–281. http://dx.doi.org/10.1037/0882-7974.7.2.271

Staudinger, U. M., Smith, J., & Baltes, P. B. (1994). *Manual for the assessment of wisdom-related knowledge* (Technical report). Berlin, Germany: Max Planck Institute for Human Development.

Sternberg, R. J. (1985). Implicit theories of intelligence, creativity, and wisdom. *Journal of Personality and Social Psychology, 49,* 607–627. http://dx.doi.org/10.1037/0022-3514.49.3.607

Sternberg, R. J. (1998). A balance theory of wisdom. *Review of General Psychology, 2,* 347–365. http://dx.doi.org/10.1037/1089-2680.2.4.347

Sternberg, R. J. (2001). Why schools should teach for wisdom: The balance theory of wisdom in educational settings. *Educational Psychologist, 36,* 227–245. http://dx.doi.org/10.1207/S15326985EP3604_2

Sternberg, R. J., Reznitskaya, A., & Jarvin, L. (2007). Teaching for wisdom: What matters is not just what students know, but how they use it. *London Review of Education, 5,* 143–158. http://dx.doi.org/10.1080/14748460701440830

Takahashi, M., & Overton, W. F. (2005). Cultural foundations of wisdom. An integrated developmental approach. In R. Sternberg & J. Jordan (Eds.), *Handbook of wisdom* (pp. 32–60). New York, NY: Cambridge University Press. http://dx.doi.org/10.1017/CBO9780511610486.003

Webster, J. D. (2003). An exploratory analysis of a self-assessed wisdom scale. *Journal of Adult Development, 10,* 13–22. http://dx.doi.org/10.1023/A:1020782619051

Webster, J. D. (2007). Measuring the character strength of wisdom. *The International Journal of Aging & Human Development, 65,* 163–183. http://dx.doi.org/10.2190/AG.65.2.d

Wink, P., & Helson, R. (1997). Practical and transcendent wisdom: Their nature and some longitudinal findings. *Journal of Adult Development, 4,* 1–15. http://dx.doi.org/10.1007/BF02511845

11

Conceptualizing Courage

Christie L. Kelley, Hannah J. Murphy, Chad R. Breeden, Benjamin P. Hardy, Shane J. Lopez, Kristin Koetting O'Byrne, Stephanie Petersen Leachman, and Cynthia L. Pury

Courage is difficult to operationalize but not hard to find. Acts of courage are often easy to recognize, but exactly what makes an act courageous is less obvious. It can reflect extraordinary acts in extraordinary circumstances (thus rendering it a rare occurrence), or it can occur in more commonplace situations, reflecting subjective perceptions of risk (Pury, Kowalski, & Spearman, 2007).

In Plato's *Laches*, written more than 2,000 years ago, Socrates discusses the nature of courage with the Athenian generals Nicias and Laches. They consider a range of potentially courageous actions, then focus on intellectual qualities and endurance in their respective views of courage. Likewise, we begin with a discussion of the range of common types of courageous action, then discuss the shared features common among all forms of courage. Finally, we discuss the implications of these distinct and common features for existing and future measures of courage.

CASE STUDY

Faye is a 34-year-old client from a major metropolitan area. She is in a significant long-term relationship with a live-in boyfriend and has a well-paying career she enjoys. Furthermore, she has an 8-month history with a clinic due to panic attacks; she often has one or two full-blown attacks per day. She also

http://dx.doi.org/10.1037/0000138-011
Positive Psychological Assessment: A Handbook of Models and Measures, Second Edition,
M. W. Gallagher and S. J. Lopez (Editors)

has significant fear, but not avoidance, of her nightly drive home on the interstate in rush-hour traffic.

Faye's panic attacks began quite suddenly after hearing a traffic report about a car that had run off an overpass and was stuck in a tree. She reported thinking, "That could be me!" and began to panic. Soon she was developing panic symptoms when driving home over bridges. Then she started having uncued panic attacks at home, often when her spouse was away for the evening. Fearing she was having a heart attack (like her uncle did), she sought medical help and was diagnosed with panic disorder. Her most prominent panic symptoms are racing heart, smothering sensations, dizziness, fear of going crazy, and fear of dying. She also complained of muscle tension.

Faye describes her home environment as "a good, solid relationship," and she expresses a high level of love of and trust in her spouse. Her relationships with her family of origin and extended family are also positive and supportive. Her work environment, however, is "tense." As an information technology (IT) professional, she hears every complaint when systems perform at less than 100% but no comments when things work well. She describes receiving little support from her colleagues in the IT department, instead describing a system of mutual blame and continued fault-finding.

Faye was treated with cognitive behavior therapy, including elements of relaxation training, cognitive restructuring, and exposure to feared body sensations and environmental triggers. Faye approached the exposure exercises with great courage and determination. For example, she asked to start exposure exercises at a higher Subjective Units of Distress Scale level than do most clients. Her weekly records of panic attacks showed an increase in panic during weeks with exposure exercises, commensurate with this greater challenge. Yet she improved rapidly and markedly as she stayed in each exercise until panic symptoms subsided, and, in her own words, "it got boring."

During treatment, it became apparent that Faye had a significant amount of unacknowledged anger about the conflicts she faced daily at work. It was likely her panic symptoms were exacerbated by her experiencing the physical sensations of anger but misattributing them to fear. In particular, she reported several incidents in which she disagreed with her workgroup about the appropriate action but felt she could not speak up. As part of treatment, Faye was encouraged to find the voice to express professional views assertively but appropriately. Faye successfully completed treatment and at 6-month follow up, reported high well-being and was nearly symptom free.

COMMON TYPES OF COURAGEOUS BEHAVIOR

A variety of different types of courageous behavior have been proposed, including physical courage, moral courage, and psychological or vital courage (Putman, 1997, 2010). *Physical courage*, or valor, has been identified as the ability to maintain societal good through physical acts that are socially valuable (Lopez et al., 2010). *Moral courage* is the behavioral demonstration of authenticity in the face of disapproval and rejection. Though Putman acknowledged all courage stemming from a psychological process, *psychological courage* focuses on the strength to face inner fears and other barriers to growth. Psychological evidence for different types comes from studies of people's folk conceptions of courage (Lopez, O'Byrne, & Petersen, 2003; Lopez et al., 2010) and from first-person accounts of taking a self-nominated courageous action (Pury, Kowalski, & Spearman, 2007). Both methodologies find evidence for three types of courage: physical courage, moral courage, and a third type, which is characterized by Pury et al. (2007) as Putman's psychological courage, whereas it is characterized by Lopez et al. (2003) as the closely related construct of vital courage. *Vital courage* is the act of facing a personal turmoil or struggle, such as cancer or depression, and persevering even when the outcome is unclear (Finfgeld, 1995, 1999). Vital courage appears to overlap with Putman's psychological courage as discussed below.

Physical Courage: The Battlefield and Beyond

Physical courage can be characterized as the overcoming of fear of physical harm or even death in the face of risk (Lopez et al., 2003). The study of physical courage is not a recent undertaking. As early as the 4th century B.C., Aristotle analyzed courage in his writings on ethics. He talked about courage as a necessity to protect one's self and one's family from harm's way, emphasizing a difference made through physical action (Putman, 2010). People have always admired and valued physical courage. *Andreia*, or military courage, defined the "brave soldier" in ancient Greece. Finding the rugged path between cowardice and foolhardiness distinguished a Greek soldier as courageous and hence more valuable to the force. That disposition to act appropriately in situations involving fear and confidence on the battlefield seems to be universally valued—from ancient times to present day (Rorty, 1988).

Fear became the focus of Jack Rachman's research after he realized physical courage was the mirror image of the fear associated with physical jeopardy, and some people deal with the perceived danger better than do others. Rachman (1984) worked with paratroopers, decorated soldiers, and bomb squad members to gather information on the nature of courage. He found that the courageous persevere and can make a quick physiological recovery. He also suggested courageous acts are not necessarily confined to a special few, nor do they always take place in public. In regard to this latter point, he became intrigued by the inner battles and private courage displayed by his psychotherapy clients. Rachman concluded there clearly was more to courage than *andreia* and related physical conquests over danger.

The move beyond *andreia*, even in soldiers headed to combat, is highlighted in McGurk and Castro's (2010) mental health training system for U.S. army soldiers called *Battlemind.* Battlemind was designed to teach soldiers to face combat and unpleasant situations with courage. This training system is based on the belief that courage is not something you must be born with but is a dynamic, evolving force that can be developed through experience and personal motivation. Their approach, as well as other investigations of courage in the military, suggests that courage in combat is greater than having physical courage. Rather, moral courage may be a building block of military courage. Thus, physical and moral courage may be highly correlated, but they have differing effects on soldiers' mental health (see also Ozkaptan, Fiero, & Saint, 2007).

Moral Courage: Doing What Is Best and Authentic

Plato's writing on Socrates makes the ancient distinction between moral and physical courage apparent. As Putman (1997) noted, Socrates endured in the fight to protect Athens from conquest, but he fought a more difficult battle when he defended "a greater moral good *against* society" (p. 1).

Other writers and laypersons have noted that summoning and sustaining moral courage requires incredible strength. For example, John F. Kennedy was fascinated by courage. He spent years gathering stories of statesmen who followed their hearts and principles when determining what was "best" for the American people—even when constituents did not agree with their decision making or value their representation. Although Kennedy himself was a military hero, he lauded moral rather than physical triumphs in his *Profiles in Courage* (Kennedy, 1956/2006).

Authenticity and integrity may be the fulfillments most closely associated with the expression of personal views and values in the face of dissension and rejection. Though they are valued as aspects of "the good life," there is no guide for doing what is best or most authentic. Exactly when should one take a stand? Rosa Parks said she took a seat at the front of a bus to protest racial segregation because it was time to do so. Others value the moral courage needed to face prejudice and hold firm to ideas when situations demanded such (O'Byrne, Lopez, & Peterson, 2000).

Regarding health care, some argue courage should be facilitated by health care providers in part by being truthful and straightforward (Finfgeld, 1998; Shelp, 1984). Not only does it take courage to speak the truth, but it also takes courage to hear the truth. Moral courage can take on still another face when an individual stands up to someone with power over him or her (e.g., boss) for the greater good, and individuals displaying moral courage often are at risk for social disapproval (Putman, 1997). Similarly, Osswald, Greitemeyer, Fischer, and Frey (2010) defined moral courage as "a prosocial behavior with high social costs and no (or rare) direct rewards for the actor," specifically showing "brave behavior accompanied by anger and indignation, which intends to enforce societal and ethical norms without considering one's own social costs" (p. 150). Osswald et al. (2010) further described social costs and the distinguishing factor of moral courage. Thus, moral courage includes, but goes beyond and is distinctive from, acts of heroism and other helping behaviors (Kastenmüller, Greitemeyer, Fischer, & Frey, 2007).

Becker and Eagly (2004) investigated moral courage in the form of heroism focusing on extremely dangerous actions—including the actions of non-Jews aiding potential victims of the Holocaust—or in moderately dangerous actions such as donating a kidney or volunteering for the Peace Corps or Doctors of the World. Using a list of Carnegie Hero Medal winners, they found men to be more likely to engage in traditionally heralded physical courage required to rescue others from immediate danger, whereas women are more likely to engage in courageous acts involving physical harm for a cause they believe in.

Likewise, Fagin-Jones and Midlarsky (2007) examined positive personality variables in relations to character strengths of courage. Their research on courageous altruism suggests that social responsibility, altruistic moral reasoning, empathic concern, and risk taking were characteristics of rescuers but not bystanders. Fagin-Jones and Midlarsky (2007) successfully linked personality traits to the decision to engage in actions of moral courage.

Moral courage also appears in the workplace (Worline, 2004, 2010). As examples, whistleblowing, challenging subjectively wrong decisions, and conducting difficult performance evaluations each require workers to do the right thing despite opposing social pressure. Client Faye's efforts to be more assertive at work fall under this category.

Vital and Psychological Courage: The Fight for Life and for the Quality of Life

Hospitals are akin to the battlefields of old. Well-trained, well-equipped professionals face the enemy alongside their wounded brethren, fighting both physical and mental sicknesses. *Vital courage* is at work as the patient struggles against surgery, medication, and treatment regimens. Physicians, nurses, and other allied health professionals use their expertise to save lives or to improve quality of life of those they serve. Many researchers have examined vital courage, and their work highlights the mental strength and conviction it takes to face these challenges.

Haase (1987) used a phenomenological approach to study the subjective experiences of courage in nine chronically ill adolescents. An eight-step process of analysis was used to address the answer to the question "What is the essential structure of the lived-experience of courage in chronically ill adolescents?" and to uncover the essential structure of courage in the face of illness. To Haase, the "lived experience" (p. 69) of courage is an interpersonally assigned attribute from living a specific way through a negative health condition. Initially, the lived experience involves a struggle for personal awareness of the nature and impact of the situation. Through daily encounters with "minisituations" of courage (e.g., treatment, procedures, and physical changes resulting from this illness), the adolescent comes to awareness and resolution of the experience as one of courage. Increasingly, the situation is viewed as difficult but not impossible. Coping strategies are developed, and other aspects of life unrelated to the illness are actively pursued. Through resolution of the situation of courage, the adolescent develops a sense of mastery, competence, and accomplishment and a feeling of growth.

After interviewing middle-aged adults with illnesses, Finfgeld (1998) determined that courage involves becoming aware of and accepting of the threat of a long-term health condition, solving problems through insight, and developing enhanced sensitivities to self and others. Finfgeld (1995) also interviewed older adults who demonstrated courage in the face of chronic illness, concluding courage is a lifelong process involving significant others, values, and hope. These participants also indicated that struggle or threat elicited courage in their lives. Finfgeld purports that courageous behaviors take place following the identification of a threat and problem solving, which lead one to shift from struggle to challenge. Behavioral expectations, the existence of role models, and value systems also appear to determine if and how courage unfolds. This courageous behavior may result in a sense of equanimity and absence of regret about one's life, along with a sense of personal integrity.

Finfgeld (1995, 1998) and Shelp (1984) both discussed courage in health care and being facilitated by health care providers. According to Shelp (1984), courage—among other virtues such as competence and compassion—is prerequisite for physicians to effectively treat patients. Moreover, instilling courage through "encouragement" (p. 358) is required of anyone in a profession exemplifying care and concern. Shelp (1984) further argued the specific aspects of such courage include (a) freedom of choice, (b) fear of a situation, and (c) the willingness to take risks in an uncertain situation toward a morally worthy end.

According to Putman (2004), *psychological courage* is facing inner fears, including the idea that we have a particular problem or that we may become unhappy. This form of vital courage is quite common as we all struggle with psychological challenges in the forms of stress, sadness, and dysfunctional relationships. In light of these threats to our psychological stability, many psychotherapies encourage us to stand up to our dysfunction by restructuring our beliefs or systematically desensitizing ourselves to the fears. Faye's full-on participation in exposure exercises is an excellent example of psychological courage.

Psychological courage also can be enacted for other reasons beyond getting well, including moving away from familiar people and places for career or education or other instances of stepping outside one's comfort zone (Pury et al., 2007). One of Putman's (2010) arguments about psychological courage is that there is a paucity of training for psychological courage compared with that for physical and moral courage. In pop culture, we have many physically courageous and morally courageous icons presented in literary works and movies, but exemplars of psychologically courageous individuals are few and far between. Perhaps this is a result of the negative stigma surrounding mental health problems and destructive behaviors, particularly for soldiers returning from the battlefield. However, it is also possible that the language surrounding vital courage is new relative to moral and physical courage, which have been acknowledged since the time of Plato and Aristotle. Ultimately, all people must deal with the troubles of life, and the individual response to those challenges requires courage.

COMMON STRENGTHS OF COURAGE

Another way to parse courage is to consider the character strengths one needs to behave courageously. As part of their larger Values in Action (VIA) system, Peterson and Seligman (2004b) classified courage as a core human virtue made up of four strengths. Those strengths include bravery or valor, persistence or perseverance, integrity or authenticity, and vitality or zest. *Bravery* involves standing up to threat or risks. *Persistence* involves continuing efforts toward a goal until it is reached. *Integrity* is a combination of taking responsibility for what one does and feels and ensuring that one's outer actions match one's inner convictions. Finally, *vitality* involves doing things wholeheartedly and enthusiastically.

The extent to which the component strengths of courage are an inherent part of courageous action was investigated by Pury and Kowalski (2007), who asked people to rate the extent to which a courageous action they actually performed was characterized by each of the 24 VIA strengths. They found that people described their own courageous actions as characterized by three of the four strengths of courage: persistence, integrity, and bravery. Courageous actions were not particularly characterized by vitality. However, they were strongly characterized by two additional VIA strengths: (a) *hope*, or believing in a good future and working to bring it about; and (b) *kindness*, or doing something good for the benefit of another.

CORE FEATURES OF COURAGE

Psychologists and other scholars since Plato have had a difficult time arriving at a consensus definition of courage. Rate, Clarke, Lindsay, and Sternberg (2007) explained that this problem may stem from the focus on differing "brands of courage" and creating multiple definitions that are reliant on context. The optimal resolution is to find a set of core features that does not depend on context but could be applied to any situation.

To more closely examine how laypersons view courage, O'Byrne et al. (2000) queried 97 people and found that people's views of this virtue varied considerably. For example, some individuals perceived courage as an attitude (e.g., optimism), others as a behavior (e.g., saving someone's life). Some referred to mental strength, while others wrote of physical strength. Participants discussed scenarios that could be classified as vital courage, moral courage, and physical courage, all providing some support for the multidimensional nature of this virtue. Some claimed that courage involves taking a risk, whereas others mentioned fear. However, neither of these components was found in all responses.

Shelp (1984) defined courage as having four key components: free choice to accept or reject the consequences of acting, risk or danger, a worthy end, and the uncertainty of outcome. Fear was excluded as a necessary component of courage.

In the most comprehensive set of studies to date, Rate et al. (2007) investigated the core components of courage in multiple ways. Through a series of empirical studies, they compared the features of an ideally courageous person, examined the behaviors of an ideally courageous person, sorted prototypical courageous behaviors, and responded to vignettes. These data were combined with an expert analysis of multiple published definitions of courage, both from the psychological literature and from other sources. Rate et al. concluded that courage is characterized by being

> a) a willful, intentional act, b) executed after mindful deliberation, c) involving objective substantial risk to the actor, d) primarily motivated to bring about a noble good or worthy end, e) despite, *perhaps*, the presence of the emotion of fear. (p. 95)

These features can be distilled into three core features: (a) circumstances (most notably, those that lead to risk to the actor), (b) motivation toward excellence, and (c) volition (Rate, 2010). As we will see, Rate et al.'s possible inclusion of fear is reflected in measures of courage: Some require the presence of fear whereas others do not.

Rate's (2010) definition also suggests a way to understand different brands of courage. Pury, Britt, Zinzow, and Raymond (2014) suggested that different types of courage might arise from the nonrandom distribution of risks associated with pursuing particular types of goals. For example, saving someone from physical danger often involves risking that same danger oneself. Standing up to others for what is right commonly involves risking social rejection by those same people. Improving one's emotional response to a traumatic event commonly involves facing the emotional discomfort generated by examining that event. Thus, as Pury and colleagues argued, different types of courage emerge. Yet these types are not absolute: Blended courage is proposed to occur when the goals of one type of courage are pursued by facing the risks of other types of courage. For example, active-duty soldiers seeking treatment for mental illness—a goal typical of psychological courage—commonly need to face the social risks more commonly associated with moral courage (Pury et al., 2014). Those demonstrating for civil and human rights worldwide—a goal of moral courage—often risk their physical safety and their lives in doing so. Keeping an intoxicated friend and others on the road safe from a possible horrific car accident—a goal more typical of physical courage—might be best accomplished by taking the social risks of moral courage incurred by taking the keys.

Finally, Pury and Starkey (2010) proposed that there is an important distinction between measuring *courage as a process*, or the psychological experience of voluntarily taking a noble action despite risk, and *courage as an accolade*, or the way in which people determine if an action is courageous or not. In both cases, the more voluntary the action and the nobler the goal, the more likely the action is to be taken or the more courageous it seems. The more risky the action, the more likely it is to be seen as courageous but the less likely it is to be taken.

Moreover, both the riskiness of the action and the value of the goal have strong subjective components. Subjective, rather than objective, risk assessment leads to two additional types of courage. *General courage* describes actions in which the risks would be seen as risky to most people, whereas *personal courage* (Pury et al., 2007) occurs when the risks are unique to the individual. Faye's individual fear of driving and fear of panic symptoms characterize her actions during exposure therapy as personal courage; her learning to speak up at work may have both general and personal courage components to it.

MEASURING COURAGE

Researchers and clinicians have used many different means for measuring courage. Although a few scales are specific to the different types of courage (e.g., moral courage; Kastenmüller et al., 2007), the majority of these scales measure general courage in different situations. Beginning with Rachman, a pioneer in courage research, physiological responses associated with courageous responses to fear or stress were measured (e.g., Cox, Hallam, O'Connor, & Rachman, 1983; McMillan & Rachman, 1987, 1988; Rachman, 1983, 2010). Finfgeld (1995, 1998) developed a system of interviews highlighting the process of becoming and being courageous in the face of chronic illness.

Further, Buss and Craik's (1983) act–frequency approach and related sociometric procedures lend themselves to identifying courage exemplars and their qualities. More recently, courage has been measured as a life data approach (Becker & Eagly, 2004; Fagin-Jones & Midlarsky, 2007) and as a self-reported willingness to act despite fear (Norton & Weiss, 2009) or in a wide variety of risky situations (Woodard & Pury, 2007). Finally, researchers have begun to focus on workplace courage (e.g., Kilmann, O'Hara, & Strauss, 2010). The following sections discuss each of these approaches.

Measuring Physiological Responses Associated With Courage

Rachman (1984) questioned the link between fearlessness and courage, asserting that frightened people can perform courageous acts. Although courage and fearlessness often are regarded as synonymous, many (e.g., Muris, 2009; Norton & Weiss, 2009; Rachman, 1984) have argued perseverance despite fear is the purest form of courage. This approach to courage proposes that true courage is being willing and able to approach a fearful situation despite the presence of subjective fear. In this case, physiological responses may be measured to assess the presence of fear or stress in a given situation to determine how the courageous respond.

Rachman's (1978) research before his work on courage focused on subjective fear and one's bodily responses. When he became interested in courage, he and his colleagues (Cox et al., 1983; O'Connor, Hallam, & Rachman, 1985) studied the distinction between courage and fearlessness with bomb operators as well as the distinction between courageous acts and courageous actors. Operators who had received decorations for "gallantry" were compared with undecorated operators with comparable training and years of service. The decoration served as a method of identifying individuals with the experience of a courageous act. The individuals' performance under stress was determined by various subjective, behavioral, and psychophysiological measures. Experimental results (Cox et al., 1983) provided indications of distinctive physiological responses under stress for decorated and nondecorated bomb operators, though no subjective differences were found. The identified courageous actors (i.e., decorated bomb operators) reported that bodily sensations under stress were similar to those of other participants.

In a replication, O'Connor et al. (1985) demonstrated that decorated operators maintained a lower cardiac rate under stress than did other participants. Moreover, Rachman (1984) found that paratroopers reported a moderate amount of fear at the beginning of their program, but this fear subsided within five jumps. The execution of a jump despite the presence of fear (i.e., courage) was followed by a reduction of fear.

Becoming and Being Courageous

Several researchers have attempted to measure and determine how people "become" courageous through a phenomenological, descriptive method of assessment by asking individuals to describe a situation involving courage. In an unstructured interview format with chronically ill adolescents, each participant responded to the following prompt: "Describe a situation in which you were courageous. Describe your experience as you remember it, include your thoughts, feelings, and perceptions as you remember experiencing them. Continue to describe the experience until you feel it is fully described" (Haase, 1987, p. 66). This statement assumes all individuals have the capacity for and past experience with courage. Haase's findings regarding courage point to the development of attitudes and coping methods rather than descriptions of so-called "born heroes."

Regarding younger children's conceptualizations of courage, Szagun (1992) studied 5- to 12-year-olds using structured individual interviews asking them to rate the degree of courage for 12 different risks (on a 5-point scale ranging from not courageous to very courageous) and judge courage vignettes. Unsurprisingly, younger children (5- to 6-year-olds) likened courage to the difficulty of the task at hand and being fearless, whereas older children (8- to 9-year-olds) likened courage to subjective risk taking and overcoming fear. Even still, the oldest children (11- to 12-year-olds) reported that being fully aware of a risk at the time of acting is a necessary component of courage. Not surprisingly given their developmental stage, the younger group rated physical risks as more courageous than other risks (e.g., psychological risks). Muris (2009) found that young children (8–13 years old) are quite capable of distinguishing between courage and fear. Thus, even at a young age, people internalize courage as a distinct quality and value, which strengthens the potential for training or instilling courage.

The Battlemind Training System (Castro, Hoge, & Cox, 2006) trains soldiers to face the unpleasant and fear-laden situations of combat and to act in spite of being aware of these dangers. This encourages a positive outlook and emphasizes the ability of all service members to act in a courageous manner in combat. Data from Iraq following the implementation of the Battlemind system indicated that developing courage in individuals was dependent upon organization, group, and leader. In addition, individual levels of self-discipline or religiosity may play an important role of influencing courage (McGurk & Castro, 2010).

In recent years, research on courage has led to more questions on its development, but strictly empirical research is limited. Lester, Vogelgesang, Hannah, and Kimmey (2010) proposed courage can be developed through learning skills that increase the likelihood of courageous behavior. Particularly important is the relationship and influence that mentors and transformational leadership can elicit on courage. When role models provide successful, competent examples of courage, they can improve development of courage vicariously; when individuals guided by these role models are exposed to mock situations eliciting fear that require courage, their development may also see augmentation (Bandura, 1997; Hannah, Sweeney, & Lester, 2010).

May, Luth, and Schwoerer (2014) sought to determine whether taking a course on ethical decision making in business could positively influence students to, among other things, be more morally courageous in raising ethical problems at work even if it is unpopular. They measured moral courage using four items based on the work of Gibbs and colleagues (1986), who studied the relation between moral judgments and moral courage among high school students. A sampling of these items includes "I would stand up for a just or rightful cause even if the cause is unpopular and it would mean criticizing important others," and "I would prefer to remain in the background even if a friend is being taunted or talked about unfairly." Compared with the control group that did not take the business ethics treatment course, the experimental group that took the course experienced a significantly positive increase in moral courage.

Graupmann and Frey (2014) examined the effect of watching a documentary film about Milgram's obedience experiment on personal responsibility, civil courage, and societal engagement among a student sample. Civil courage is similar to moral courage and is defined as a propensity to intervene and/or oppose a majority opinion in a situation based on one's authentic values while considering disapproval by authorities and social rejection (Lopez et al., 2003). Whereas civil courage is associated with high negative social consequences, helping behavior is associated with low negative social consequences (Kastenmüller et al., 2007). Graupmann and Frey measured civil courage before or after the students watched the documentary using a scale developed by Kastenmüller and colleagues (2007) that examines how likely an individual would intervene in 13 situations requiring civil courage (e.g., While riding on a train, you witness a group of youngsters loudly exchanging racist jokes). After watching the film, participants were more likely to exhibit civil courage.

The Act-Frequency Approach and Sociometric Methodology

Buss and Craik's (1983) act–frequency approach has individuals nominate others who demonstrate a particular trait and support that nomination with details of the behaviors the nominee has engaged in consistent with the state or trait. This process is valuable because it identifies exemplars of courage and the structure of their courage. A modification of this approach might be used with Faye, reminding her of her courage during difficult exposure exercises to help her gain the courage to speak out at work. For example, she approached her exposure exercises with increasing self-efficacy and in fact took many of them beyond the original assignment, making them more difficult when they "got boring" by no longer provoking a fear response. Given this observation, the therapist might ask her to write out her thought process the most recent time she made an exercise more difficult, then ask her what that same person would say about speaking out at work.

Sociometric methodology may also be instrumental in detecting people with courage who are part of a particular group (e.g., a family, team, and firm). This is a simple approach in which all members of a group are asked choice (e.g., "Whom would you recruit to join you in a demonstration against a company's unfair hiring practices?") and rejection (e.g., "Whom would you not look to when seeking support in a dispute?") questions. Via this interview process (see Hale, 1985, for details), group members use their interpersonal experiences to collectively determine who might possess the courage necessary to occupy a leadership role in the group.

Narrative Data

Pury, Starkey, Kulik, Skjerning, and Sullivan (2015) examined the possibility of nonvirtuous courage, which can occur when an actor voluntarily assumes personal risk for a goal he or she believes is noble but society views as a wrong. To measure nonvirtuous courage, Pury et al. (2015) used narrative data from suicide attempts and terrorist attacks and coded for the three elements of courage (e.g., volition, risk, and value of the goal) as found by Rate (2010). Pury et al. (2015) found that volition was in 75% of the narratives, risk in 50%, and value of the goal in 80%. Moreover, each of these three types of statements was present in 40% of all narratives, evidencing that bad courage can and does occur. Thus, from a measurement perspective, future narrative data can be coded using the three elements of Rate's (2010) definition.

Life Data Approach

Becker and Eagly (2004) studied courage as a life data approach, using information collected from public activities and actual events in a person's life. In this study, those life events were the relatively unusual actions of winning a Carnegie medal, non-Jewish people saving victims of the Holocaust, donating kidneys, and volunteering for the Peace Corps and Doctors of the World.

Gender differences in types of heroism were explored based on differences between the specific actions studied.

Brief Self-Report Scales

In the context of the positive psychology initiative, efforts are being made to measure aspects of a positive life. Brief questionnaires are being developed or revised to effectively tap the strengths within every individual. This psychometric work, as suggested in other chapters in this volume, has been going on for decades. Specifically regarding measures of courage, efforts to devise a brief scale have been somewhat sporadic. In 1976, Larsen and Giles developed a scale to measure two types of courage: existential (akin to moral courage) and social (related to physical courage). Twenty-two items tap the social-courage domain, and 28 examine existential courage. Psychometric support for this measure is limited, and little if any work has been done to refine the scale.

The self-report measures associated with the VIA Inventory of Strengths (VIA-IS; Peterson & Seligman, 2004a) include scales for measuring each of the four strengths they associate with courage: bravery, integrity, persistence, and vitality. The VIA-IS also contains scales to measure the two other strengths associated with courageous action, hope, and kindness (see Pury & Kowalski, 2007). The scales are part of a much larger measure with hundreds of items that are discussed elsewhere in this volume. Faye's therapist might use the VIA-IS to help her define her core strengths to draw on during therapy.

Woodard (2004) measured courage using four dimensions: endurance for positive outcomes, dealings with groups, acting alone, and physical pain/breaking social norms. In 2007 the scale was further validated and revised by first defining courage as "the voluntary willingness to act, with or without varying levels of fear, in response to a threat to achieve an important, perhaps moral, outcome or goal" (Woodard & Pury, 2007, p. 135). A notable difference between this conceptualization and the original is that fear is considered a voluntary variable not necessary for courageous actions. Factor analysis of this scale revealed that three items from the original scale did not load on any factors, and characterization of the factors shifted to include the following factors: work courage, belief-based physical courage, social–moral courage, and independent courage (WPCS-23; Woodard & Pury, 2007). Generally, however, the replication of the original scale provided information that the WPCS-23 has a relatively stable factor structure. If used in the case study, Faye's scores on this scale may indicate she would be relatively more willing to experience exposure exercises than to speak out at work. Conversely, Faye strongly valued her professional role, so she might score higher on work courage.

Norton and Weiss (2009) developed the courage measure (CM) and validated it by exposing people with arachnophobia to taxidermied spiders in a two-phase study. Phase 1 prescreened participants for elevated fear of spiders, and Phase 2 included an individual experimental session in which participants were shown the spiders. Before being shown the spiders, participants were informed the purpose of the study was to examine how close arachnophobic individuals can get to spiders. The participants were shown a definition of courage and then given a questionnaire including Norton and Weiss's 12-item measure of courage. The CM measures courage as a "persistence or perseverance despite having fear" (Norton & Weiss, 2009, p. 214) and thus explicitly defines courage as requiring fear. The questionnaire includes items indicating a willingness to face fear in general, without reference to the goals of the action, such as "I tend to face my fears" and "If I am worried or anxious about something, I will do or face it anyway." The measure is unidimensional and psychometrically sound. Interestingly, results from the original study proposed that the scale may be context-specific: CM scores predicted behavioral approach when the questionnaire was given a few minutes before participants knew they would be asked to approach spiders; it did not predict behavioral approach when it was given in the context of a general screening questionnaire without reference to the upcoming spider-approach challenge. Thus, if this measure were to be used with Faye, it is likely she might have scored differently if asked to think about completing exposure exercises and if asked to think about speaking out at work.

Howard and Alipour (2014) performed a theoretical, psychometric, and empirical analysis of the CM to confirm the strength of findings drawn from the scale. The results of their examination suggest the CM has theoretical concerns stemming from the operational definition of courage, which may not actually measure courage. As stated previously, the CM measures courage as a "persistence or perseverance despite having fear" (Norton & Weiss, 2009, p. 214) and thus explicitly defines courage as requiring fear. This fear-based definition is problematic in two ways in light of Rate's (2010) definition: (a) fear is considered essential and (b) the definition focuses almost exclusively on risk taking and does not fully encapsulate courage.

Regarding the first challenge of the CM definition of courage, according to Rate's (2010) empirically derived definition, courage includes (a) an intentional act (b) primarily motivated to bring about a noble or worthy outcome (c) involving substantial risk to the actor. Thus, according to Rate (2010), the presence of the emotion is extraneous for classifying courageous behaviors, and those who experience fear during a behavior are no more courageous than are those who do not (Howard & Alipour, 2014).

Regarding the second challenge of the CM definition of courage, Howard and Alipour (2014) further argued that Norton and Weiss's (2009) definition used in the CM more accurately describes risk taking, which does not fully encapsulate the construct of courage. Indeed, simply taking risks, such as jumping in front of an oncoming car for the thrill of risk taking, does not necessarily make the act courageous. Thus, after analyzing Norton and Weiss's measure, Howard and Alipour (2014) determined the scale may measure only risk taking.

Regarding psychometric concerns of the CM, Howard and Alipour (2014) determined that the interpretation of Norton and Weiss's (2009) factor analysis warrants attention. Specifically, the explanation of their determined number of factors was brief. Although it is best practice to report the eigenvalues to defend any judgments, Norton and Weiss left these values unreported. Thus, the number of factors within the CM is still uncertain. To determine the appropriate number of factors to extract, Howard and Alipour (2014) used a parallel analysis and found that most of the reverse-coded scale items did not load onto the primary factor. Once those items were removed, the scale went from being two-dimensional to being unidimensional.

Regarding construct validity concerns of the CM, Howard and Alipour (2014) pointed out that although Norton and Weiss (2009) provided ample evidence for their scale's criterion-related validity, no other types of validity were explored. When comparing the CM to a risk-taking scale and the Big Five personality measure, the CM was most related to risk taking. However, the CM did not have a large enough correlation with risk taking to argue for the scale's convergent validity. Thus, it appears the scale measures something other than risk taking, but whether it measures courage should still be considered, according to Howard and Alipour.

In Faye's case, a clinician might utilize the CM in a more motivational rather than diagnostic way. Taking the scale and discussing the items during a session might help her reimagine herself as quite courageous, given her demonstrated wiliness to face her fears.

Kilmann et al. (2010) developed an organizational measure of courage. This measure is used to describe a theory of organizational change in which courage is a segue to a supreme organizational climate where employees can act without fear. In four stages, Kilmann et al. described a courageous organization in which there are a large number of courageous behaviors and a large amount of fear, a fearful organization in which there is a low number of courageous behaviors and a high amount of fear, a bureaucratic organization in which there is a low number of courageous behaviors and a low amount of fear, and finally the supreme quantum organization in which there is a high number of courageous behaviors and a low amount of fear. Thus, the type of organization is decided upon by a measure of fear and a two-factor (observed acts and feared acts) 40-item measure of courage. This scale might be used with Faye to help identify areas at work she finds particularly intimidating and those in which she feels freer to speak her mind.

Observational Data

Whereas most laboratory studies of courage include observations of specific behaviors that differ in courageousness (e.g., Fischer, Greitemeyer, Pollozek, & Frey, 2006; Niesta Kayser, Greitemeyer, Fischer, & Frey, 2010), a final approach to measuring courage is in the form of observations made by those who know the target or their actions well. It could be argued that samples who have won awards for courage (e.g., Becker & Eagly, 2004; Cox et al., 1983) utilize the outcome of observational data. Parental ratings of children's courage have been used as external validation of the self-report CM for children (Muris, Mayer, & Schubert, 2010).

Observations of courage in the workplace have also been measured using more psychometrically derived observational scales. In a factor analysis of the Executive Dimensions scale (Center for Creative Leadership, 2009), Sosik, Gentry, and Chun (2012) created a four-item bravery scale (e.g., "Takes the lead on unpopular though necessary actions") with an alpha of .87. Palanski, Cullen, Gentry, and Nichols (2015) relabeled this scale as measuring *behavioral courage*, or "the perceived consistency of action under adverse conditions" (p. 2). As with other forms of accolade courage (Pury & Starkey, 2010), Palanski et al. pointed out that such measures are influenced by observer characteristics as well as the directly observable action. Such cautions may be true for all observational measurement of courage.

CONCLUSION

The psychology of courage is in its infancy. Although consensus is limited, it appears this ancient virtue involves a voluntary and risky action motivated by a noble goal. This core can have many different permutations, including the three most common types of courage: physical, moral, and vital/psychological courage. It can be aided by several character strengths, including persistence, bravery, and integrity and possibly including vitality, hope, and (depending on the situation) kindness.

This multidimensional nature suggests a multidimensional approach to measurement and study. Psychologists seeking to measure courage should first examine what particular features of courage they are most interested in before selecting measures. In addition, the likely differences between looking at courage as a process and courage as an accolade (Pury & Starkey, 2010) indicate that researchers should intentionally target one or the other. For example, courage in entrepreneurs is likely to be most similar to psychological courage, in which the individual may need to overcome emotional risks more than physical harm or social rejection. Norton and Weiss's (2009) measure may be an appropriate test to examine an individual's internal response to risk and fear. Conversely, psychologists studying fairness in the distribution of citations for valor in emergency responders are examining physical courage as an accolade, and measures examining the internal fear of the actor are likely to be of limited use. Instead, courage should be measured based on the perceived goodness of the goal, perceived physical danger, and perceived voluntariness.

Faye's case illustrates two different types of courage in treatment: psychological courage and moral courage. Although the measures presented here have not been tested in therapy, many could be used in an exploratory fashion as described above.

Any new measure development should be based on an understanding of the underlying constructs constituting courage in the particular context of the research. For example, a researcher may need to consider what types of risks are encountered by a student who stands up to bullies on behalf of others and what that commitment to the other person may look like. This measure of courage may look very different than does a measure of courage in cancer patients or a measure of courage in combat soldiers. Research to date, however (e.g., Rate, 2010; Rate et al., 2007), suggests all should include measures of voluntariness, risk, and goodness of the goal.

REFERENCES

Bandura, A. (1997). *Self-efficacy: The exercise of control.* New York, NY: W. H. Freeman/Times Books/Henry Holt & Co.

Becker, S. W., & Eagly, A. H. (2004). The heroism of women and men. *American Psychologist, 59,* 163–178. http://dx.doi.org/10.1037/0003-066X.59.3.163

Buss, D. M., & Craik, K. H. (1983). The act frequency approach to personality. *Psychological Review, 90,* 105–126. http://dx.doi.org/10.1037/0033-295X.90.2.105

Castro, C. A., Hoge, C. W., & Cox, A. L. (2006, April). Battlemind training: Building soldier resiliency. In *Human dimensions in military operations–Military leaders' strategies for addressing stress and psychological support.* Symposium conducted at the meeting of the NATO Research and Technology Organisation (No. RTO-MP-HFM-134-42), Neuilly-sur-Seine, France. Retrieved from https://www.sto.nato.int/publications/STO%20Meeting%20Proceedings/RTO-MP-HFM-134/MP-HFM-134-42.pdf

Center for Creative Leadership. (2009). *Executive dimensions technical manual.* Greensboro, NC: Author.

Cox, D., Hallam, R., O'Connor, K., & Rachman, S. (1983). An experimental analysis of fearlessness and courage. *British Journal of Psychology, 74,* 107–117. http://dx.doi.org/10.1111/j.2044-8295.1983.tb01847.x

Fagin-Jones, S., & Midlarsky, E. (2007). Courageous altruism: Personal and situational correlates of rescue during the Holocaust. *The Journal of Positive Psychology, 2,* 136–147. http://dx.doi.org/10.1080/17439760701228979

Finfgeld, D. L. (1995). Becoming and being courageous in the chronically ill elderly. *Issues in Mental Health Nursing, 16,* 1–11. http://dx.doi.org/10.3109/01612849509042959

Finfgeld, D. L. (1998). Courage in middle-aged adults with long-term health concerns. *The Canadian Journal of Nursing Research, 30*(1), 153–169.

Finfgeld, D. L. (1999). Courage as a process of pushing beyond the struggle. *Qualitative Health Research, 9,* 803–814. http://dx.doi.org/10.1177/104973299129122298

Fischer, P., Greitemeyer, T., Pollozek, F., & Frey, D. (2006). The unresponsive bystander: Are bystanders more responsive in dangerous emergencies? *European Journal of Social Psychology, 36,* 267–278. http://dx.doi.org/10.1002/ejsp.297

Gibbs, J. C., Clark, P. M., Joseph, J. A., Green, J. L., Goodrick, T. S., & Makowski, D. G. (1986). Relations between moral judgment, moral courage, and field independence. *Child Development, 57,* 185–193. http://dx.doi.org/10.2307/1130650

Graupmann, V., & Frey, D. (2014). Bad examples: How thinking about blind obedience can induce responsibility and courage. *Peace and Conflict: Journal of Peace Psychology, 20*(2), 124–134. http://dx.doi.org/10.1037/pac0000021

Haase, J. E. (1987). Components of courage in chronically ill adolescents: A phenomenological study. *Advances in Nursing Science, 9*(2), 64–80. http://dx.doi.org/10.1097/00012272-198701000-00010

Hale, A. E. (1985). *Conducting clinical sociometric explorations. A manual for psychodramatists and sociometrists.* Roanoke, VA: Royal.

Hannah, S. T., Sweeney, P. J., & Lester, P. B. (2010). The courageous mind-set: A dynamic personality system approach to courage. In C. L. S. Pury & S. J. Lopez (Eds.), *The psychology of courage: Modern research on an ancient virtue* (pp. 125–148). Washington, DC: American Psychological Association. http://dx.doi.org/10.1037/12168-007

Howard, M. C., & Alipour, K. K. (2014). Does the courage measure really measure courage? A theoretical and empirical evaluation. *The Journal of Positive Psychology, 9,* 449–459. http://dx.doi.org/10.1080/17439760.2014.910828

Kastenmüller, A., Greitemeyer, T., Fischer, P., & Frey, D. (2007). Das Münchner Zivilcourage-Instrument (MüZI) [The Munich Civil Courage Instrument]. *Diagnostica, 53,* 205–217. http://dx.doi.org/10.1026/0012-1924.53.4.205

Kennedy, J. F. (2006). *Profiles in courage.* New York, NY: Harper Perennial Modern Classics. (Original work published 1956)

Kilmann, R. H., O'Hara, L. A., & Strauss, J. P. (2010). Developing and validating a quantitative measure of organizational courage. *Journal of Business and Psychology, 25*(1), 15–23. http://dx.doi.org/10.1007/s10869-009-9125-1

Larsen, K. S., & Giles, H. (1976). Survival or courage as human motivation: Development of an attitude scale. *Psychological Reports, 39,* 299–302. http://dx.doi.org/10.2466/pr0.1976.39.1.299

Lester, P. B., Vogelgesang, G. R., Hannah, S. T., & Kimmey, T., Jr. (2010). Developing courage in followers: Theoretical and applied perspectives. In C. L. S. Pury & S. J. Lopez (Eds.), *The psychology of courage: Modern research on an ancient virtue* (pp. 187–207). Washington, DC: American Psychological Association.

Lopez, S. J., O'Byrne, K. K., & Petersen, S. (2003). Profiling courage. In S. J. Lopez & C. R. Snyder (Eds.), *Positive psychological assessment: A handbook of models and measures* (pp. 185–197). Washington, DC: American Psychological Association. http://dx.doi.org/10.1037/10612-012

Lopez, S. J., Rasmussen, H. N., Skorupski, W. P., Koetting, K., Petersen, S. E., & Yang, Y.-T. (2010). Folk conceptualizations of courage. In C. L. S. Pury & S. J. Lopez (Eds.), *The psychology of courage: Modern research on an ancient virtue* (pp. 23–45). Washington, DC: American Psychological Association. http://dx.doi.org/10.1037/12168-002

May, D., Luth, M., & Schwoerer, C. (2014). The influence of business ethics education on moral efficacy, moral meaningfulness, and moral courage: A quasi-experimental study. *Journal of Business Ethics, 124*(1), 67–80. http://dx.doi.org/10.1007/s10551-013-1860-6

McGurk, D., & Castro, C. A. (2010). Courage in combat. In C. L. S. Pury & S. J. Lopez (Eds.), *The psychology of courage: Modern research on an ancient virtue* (pp. 167–185). Washington, DC: American Psychological Association. http://dx.doi.org/10.1037/12168-009

McMillan, T. M., & Rachman, S. J. (1987). Fearlessness and courage: A laboratory study of paratrooper veterans of the Falklands War. *British Journal of Psychology, 78,* 375–383. http://dx.doi.org/10.1111/j.2044-8295.1987.tb02255.x

McMillan, T. M., & Rachman, S. J. (1988). Fearlessness and courage in paratroopers undergoing training. *Personality and Individual Differences, 9,* 373–378. http://dx.doi.org/10.1016/0191-8869(88)90100-6

Muris, P. (2009). Fear and courage in children: Two sides of the same coin? *Journal of Child and Family Studies, 18,* 486–490. http://dx.doi.org/10.1007/s10826-009-9271-0

Muris, P., Mayer, B., & Schubert, T. (2010). "You might belong in Gryffindor": Children's courage and its relationships to anxiety symptoms, big five personality traits, and sex roles. *Child Psychiatry and Human Development, 41,* 204–213. http://dx.doi.org/10.1007/s10578-009-0161-x

Niesta Kayser, D., Greitemeyer, T., Fischer, P., & Frey, D. (2010). Why mood affects help giving, but not moral courage: Comparing two types of prosocial behaviour. *European Journal of Social Psychology, 40,* 1136–1157. http://dx.doi.org/10.1002/ejsp.717

Norton, P. J., & Weiss, B. J. (2009). The role of courage on behavioral approach in a fear-eliciting situation: A proof-of-concept pilot study. *Journal of Anxiety Disorders, 23,* 212–217. http://dx.doi.org/10.1016/j.janxdis.2008.07.002

O'Byrne, K. K., Lopez, S. J., & Peterson, S. (2000, August). *Building a theory of courage: A precursor to change?* Paper presented at the 108th Annual Convention of the American Psychological Association, Washington, DC.

O'Connor, K., Hallam, R. S., & Rachman, S. (1985). Fearlessness and courage: A replication experiment. *British Journal of Psychology, 76,* 187–197. http://dx.doi.org/10.1111/j.2044-8295.1985.tb01942.x

Osswald, S., Greitemeyer, T., Fischer, P., & Frey, D. (2010). Moral prototypes and moral behavior: Specific effects on emotional precursors of moral behavior and on moral behavior by the activation of moral prototypes. *European Journal of Social Psychology, 40,* 1078–1094. http://dx.doi.org/10.1002/ejsp.728

Ozkaptan, H., Fiero, R. S., & Saint, C. E. (2007). *Conquering fear: Development of courage in soldiers and other high risk occupations.* Raleigh, NC: Lulu.com.

Palanski, M., Cullen, K., Gentry, W., & Nichols, C. (2015). Virtuous leadership: Exploring the effects of leader courage and behavioral integrity on leader performance and image. *Journal of Business Ethics, 132,* 297–310. http://dx.doi.org/10.1007/s10551-014-2317-2

Peterson, C., & Seligman, M. E. P. (2004a). *Character strengths and virtues: A handbook and classification.* New York, NY: Oxford University Press and Washington, DC: American Psychological Association.

Peterson, C., & Seligman, M. E. P. (2004b). Introduction to a "Manual of the Sanities." In C. Peterson & M. E. P. Seligman (Eds.), *Character strengths and virtues: A handbook and classification* (pp. 3–32). New York, NY: Oxford University Press and Washington, DC: American Psychological Association.

Pury, C. L. S., Britt, T. W., Zinzow, H. M., & Raymond, M. A. (2014). Blended courage: Moral and psychological courage elements in mental health treatment seeking by active duty military personnel. *The Journal of Positive Psychology, 9,* 30–41. http://dx.doi.org/10.1080/17439760.2013.831466

Pury, C. L. S., & Kowalski, R. M. (2007). Human strengths, courageous actions, and general and personal courage. *The Journal of Positive Psychology, 2,* 120–128. http://dx.doi.org/10.1080/17439760701228813

Pury, C. L. S., Kowalski, R. M., & Spearman, J. (2007). Distinctions between general and personal courage. *The Journal of Positive Psychology, 2,* 99–114. http://dx.doi.org/10.1080/17439760701237962

Pury, C. L. S., & Starkey, C. B. (2010). Is courage an accolade or a process? A fundamental question for courage research. In C. L. S. Pury & S. J. Lopez (Eds.), *The psychology of courage: Modern research on an ancient virtue* (pp. 67–87). Washington, DC: American Psychological Association. http://dx.doi.org/10.1037/12168-004

Pury, C. L. S., Starkey, C. B., Kulik, R. E., Skjerning, K. L., & Sullivan, E. A. (2015). Is courage always a virtue? Suicide, killing, and bad courage. *The Journal of Positive Psychology, 10,* 383–388. http://dx.doi.org/10.1080/17439760.2015.1004552

Putman, D. (1997). Psychological courage. *Philosophy, Psychiatry, & Psychology, 4*(1), 1–11. http://dx.doi.org/10.1353/ppp.1997.0008

Putman, D. (2004). *Psychological courage.* Lanham, MD: University Press of America.

Putman, D. (2010). Philosophical roots of the concept of courage. In C. L. S. Pury & S. J. Lopez (Eds.), *The psychology of courage: Modern research on an ancient virtue* (pp. 9–22). Washington, DC: American Psychological Association. http://dx.doi.org/10.1037/12168-001

Rachman, S. J. (1978). Human fears: A three systems analysis. *Scandinavian Journal of Behaviour Therapy, 7,* 237–245. http://dx.doi.org/10.1080/16506077809456104

Rachman, S. J. (1983). Part I—Overview: Fearlessness and courage in bomb-disposal operators. *Advances in Behaviour Research and Therapy, 4,* 99–104. http://dx.doi.org/10.1016/0146-6402(83)90020-6

Rachman, S. J. (1984). Fear and courage. *Behavior Therapy, 15,* 109–120. http://dx.doi.org/10.1016/S0005-7894(84)80045-3

Rachman, S. J. (2010). Courage: A psychological perspective. In C. L. S. Pury & S. J. Lopez (Eds.), *The psychology of courage: Modern research on an ancient virtue* (pp. 91–107). Washington, DC: American Psychological Association. http://dx.doi.org/10.1037/12168-005

Rate, C. R. (2010). Defining the features of courage: A search for meaning. In C. L. S. Pury & S. J. Lopez (Eds.), *The psychology of courage: Modern research on an ancient virtue* (pp. 47–66). Washington, DC: American Psychological Association. http://dx.doi.org/10.1037/12168-003

Rate, C. R., Clarke, J. A., Lindsay, D. R., & Sternberg, R. J. (2007). Implicit theories of courage. *The Journal of Positive Psychology, 2,* 80–98. http://dx.doi.org/10.1080/17439760701228755

Rorty, A. O. (1988). *Mind in action: Essays in the philosophy of mind.* Boston, MA: Beacon Press.

Shelp, E. E. (1984). Courage: A neglected virtue in the patient-physician relationship. *Social Science & Medicine, 18,* 351–360. http://dx.doi.org/10.1016/0277-9536(84)90125-4

Sosik, J. J., Gentry, W. A., & Chun, J. U. (2012). The value of virtue in the upper echelons: A multisource examination of executive character strengths and performance. *The Leadership Quarterly, 23,* 367–382. http://dx.doi.org/10.1016/j.leaqua.2011.08.010

Szagun, G. (1992). Age-related changes in children's understanding of courage. *The Journal of Genetic Psychology: Research and Theory on Human Development, 153,* 405–420. http://dx.doi.org/10.1080/00221325.1992.10753736

Woodard, C. R. (2004). Hardiness and the concept of courage. *Consulting Psychology Journal: Practice and Research, 56,* 173–185. http://dx.doi.org/10.1037/1065-9293.56.3.173

Woodard, C. R., & Pury, C. L. S. (2007). The construct of courage: Categorization and measurement. *Consulting Psychology Journal: Practice and Research, 59,* 135–147. http://dx.doi.org/10.1037/1065-9293.59.2.135

Worline, M. C. (2004). *Dancing the cliff edge: The place of courage in social life* (Doctoral dissertation, University of Michigan). Retrieved from https://search.proquest.com/docview/305183048

Worline, M. C. (2010). Understanding the role of courage in social life. In C. L. S. Pury & S. J. Lopez (Eds.), *The psychology of courage: Modern research on an ancient virtue* (pp. 209–226). Washington, DC: American Psychological Association. http://dx.doi.org/10.1037/12168-011

III

EMOTIONAL MODELS AND MEASURES

12

Measuring Positive Emotions

Louis Tay, Ed Diener, Richard E. Lucas, and Randy J. Larsen

One of the central aspects of positive psychology is the emphasis on positive characteristics in individuals and organizations, which include the cultivation of strengths and enhancing of positive experiences (Seligman & Csikszentmihalyi, 2000). Among these positive experiences, the experience of positive emotions is core because it subjectively signals that one is leading a flourishing life (Diener, 1984). Judgments of happiness and life satisfaction are consistently and moderately to strongly correlated with the frequency with which one experiences pleasant emotions such as joy, contentment, excitement, affection, and energy (Diener & Lucas, 2000). Positive emotions are also functional, and there is growing evidence that they lead to positive life outcomes such as health, success, and positive social relations (De Neve, Diener, Tay, & Xuereb, 2013). Furthermore, individual differences in the tendency to experience positive emotions have implications for personality traits: Some researchers claim that positive emotionality forms the core of the extraversion personality dimension (Lucas, Diener, Grob, Suh, & Shao, 2000). As an individual difference variable, it has the potential to moderate outcomes of interest. It should also be noted that another important subjective well-being variable that is highly relevant to positive psychology, life satisfaction, is not covered here, and readers are referred to Diener, Inglehart, and Tay (2013) and Pavot and Diener (1993) for discussions of it. Life satisfaction is often correlated with positive emotions but shows a degree of independence from them (Lucas, Diener, & Suh, 1996).

http://dx.doi.org/10.1037/0000138-012
Positive Psychological Assessment: A Handbook of Models and Measures, Second Edition, M. W. Gallagher and S. J. Lopez (Editors)

Given that positive emotions can serve as outcome, predictors or mechanisms, or moderators, it is essential to consider them in an integrative account of positive psychology. To understand positive emotions, it is essential that our measures of positive emotions are adequate. However, it is not enough simply to examine the reliability and validity of our emotion scales. Emotions are complex phenomena with a broad array of components that range from purely subjective feelings to action tendencies and from observable behaviors to specific physiological changes. Often, these various components are only modestly related, and by measuring only one or two of these components, researchers may miss part of the picture. In this chapter, we discuss some of the issues surrounding the measurement of positive emotions, which will enable psychologists to understand, evaluate, and select positive emotion measures.

DEFINITIONS OF (POSITIVE) EMOTIONS

To answer the question, What is a positive emotion? we first need to address the question, What is an *emotion*? There is no single, widely agreed-on answer to this question (Frijda, 1999; Ortony & Turner, 1990; Russell, 2003), and so our focus will be on presenting several different perspectives to positive emotions and highlighting their assessment implications. To provide a road map for understanding how these different perspectives are distinguished and related, we propose that the differences occur for several overarching reasons seen across different perspectives. First, one may seek to understand and analyze emotions at different levels (i.e., as concept labels vs. underlying components vs. episodes). Second, there may be an emphasis on the adaptive function of the emotions rather than the experience of the emotions themselves in defining the goodness of emotions. Third, there may be differences in the extent to which emotions are directed by the self (i.e., self-regulated), and there is a differential emphasis on regulatory versus experiential aspects. Finally, there may be an emphasis on emotions either as biologically based (i.e., reducible to neuroscience and biology) or socially constructed (i.e., reducible to sociology). To highlight these emphases and their measurement implications, we present them in a simplified form while recognizing that many of these perspectives overlap.

One perspective is that emotions are defined by concept labels through language, and they should be the primary unit of analysis (Izard, 1992). This would include labels such as fear, happiness, anger, and so forth. This is commonly the basis of discrete and/or basic emotions (e.g., happy, angry, sad) where these labels are fundamental concepts by which emotions are defined, with less emphasis on explaining emotions in terms of their underlying components (e.g., Ekman, 1992). For example, researchers may be interested in understanding positive emotions such as awe or gratitude. In this case, the assessment of positive emotions would simply comprise these specific labels or related statements or labels that are believed to be subordinate to these concepts. For example, the awe scale comprises statements such as "I often feel awe" and "I feel almost wonder every day" (Shiota, Keltner, & Mossman, 2007). This perspective is also popularly used in sentiment analysis of texts (i.e., positive and negative vs. neutral), and concept labels are assumed to be psychologically meaningful (Tausczik & Pennebaker, 2010).

Another perspective concerns how to explain emotions from their underlying conceptual components. On this basis, a multicomponent account of emotions was proposed by Frijda (1999) who argued that emotions are made up of the following components: (a) affect, or the experience of pleasure or pain; (b) appraisal of an object or event as good or bad; (c) action readiness, or the readiness for changes in behavior toward the environment; (d) autonomic arousal; and (e) cognitive activity changes. Although this covers many important components, not all theorists think that positive emotions have to have all components. For example, it has been argued that not all positive emotions have identifiable action tendencies (Fredrickson, 1998). In terms of *affect*—or the experience of pleasure or pain—it has been argued that some kinds of positive emotions, such as surprise, interest, and desire, can be affectively pleasant, unpleasant, or neutral (Ortony & Turner, 1990). This perspective implies that the assessment of positive emotions may comprise all or some of the specific underlying components.

One increasingly popular perspective concerns the adaptive function of emotions, where positive emotions are those that are linked to positive outcomes (Keltner & Gross, 1999). In this regard, positivity is not so much a feature of the experience of emotions but an evaluation of the outcomes it produces. Positivity may be dependent on the blend of positive and negative emotions in producing greater psychological health outcomes (Gruber, Kogan, Quoidbach, & Mauss, 2013). Similarly, from a moral emotions perspective, there are unpleasant emotions (e.g., shame, guilt) that can bring about positive change in character and actions (Haidt, 2003). On this account, the focus of assessment may also include negative emotions as well.

Emotions may also be defined as an episode. The idea behind this is that emotions are complex and unlikely reducible to a basic primitive or conceptual label (Oatley & Johnson-Laird, 1987); instead, they have to be understood as having different components that underlie prototypical episodes of emotions—these include components described by Frijda (1999) but also other aspects that would help individuals subjectively define an emotion (e.g., meta-experience and emotional regulation; Russell, 2009). Although the focus is on how emotions are psychologically defined, the operational implication is that emotions should be understood in a temporally dynamic manner. In terms of assessment, it is important to consider how positive emotions unfold over time through experience sampling (Schimmack, 2003).

There is a growing interest in the understanding of emotions that includes an emotion regulation component, which is in line with an episodic view of emotions (Tugade & Fredrickson, 2007). This approach highlights methods of maintaining, harnessing, and using emotions (e.g., savoring, positive rumination; Quoidbach, Berry, Hansenne, & Mikolajczak, 2010). Given this perspective, the focus of assessments may be on positive emotion strategies rather than the experience of positive emotions itself (e.g., Sheldon & Lyubomirsky, 2006). Because emotion regulation is often situational within the context of emotional intelligence (Salovey & Grewal, 2005), the underlying components can potentially be assessed through a test format (e.g., The Mayer-Salovey-Caruso Emotional Intelligence Test; Mayer, Salovey, & Caruso, 2002) rather than self-report.

Although the aforementioned perspectives emphasize a more social constructive approach to emotions, there are also more neurobiological approaches to understanding and defining emotions; that is, emotions are consonant with, or generated by, neurobiological components (Panksepp, 2004). Therefore, one can assess positive emotions by directly assessing components such as subcortical brain regions, physiological aspects (e.g., hormones), or facial expressions (see Burgdorf & Panksepp, 2006).

STRUCTURE OF (POSITIVE) EMOTIONS

Emotion theorists have not only sought to define (positive) emotions but have also sought to understand the associations among emotions to create models of emotions that account for the variety of emotions observed. There are four primary classes of models that are most relevant to positive psychology: (a) dimensional models of emotions, (b) basic models of emotions, (c) hierarchical models of emotions, and (d) discrete emotions. We discuss these models and their assessment implications next.

Dimensional Models

Dimensional models of emotions seek to understand the different varieties of emotions by positing underlying dimensions that are common to these emotions (Russell, 1980). The dimensions represent the affective core and, in combination with other cognitive–motivational–physiological–situational aspects (e.g., conceptual knowledge, exteroceptive sensation, appraisal, attribution), form specific emotions (e.g., fear, anger; Russell, 2003). The number of dimensions posited to account for emotions has varied, ranging from one to three dimensions. Historically, a dimensional model of *valence* (or positivity–negativity, pleasure–displeasure, happy–sad; Titchener, 1908) was proposed. Although the positivity–negativity dimension of affect is one of the most robust dimensions (Barrett, 2006) and holds across all the different models, it alone does not seem to be able to differentiate a wide variety of emotions. For example, it is difficult to distinguish between calm and excited because they are both positively valenced.

Another dimensional model of emotion is the two-dimensional model of emotion (Russell, 2003; Tellegen, Watson, & Clark, 1999), also known as the

FIGURE 12.1. Illustration of Dimensions within Dimensional Models of Affect

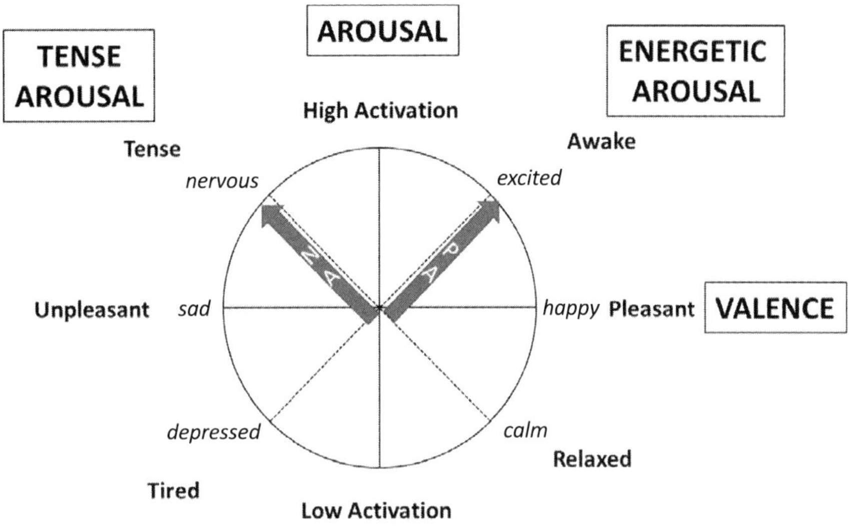

circumplex model of emotion (Russell, 1980), where orthogonal to the valence dimension is the *arousal* dimension (or activated–deactivated, high energy–low energy, intense–mild). The emotions are thought to be equally spaced in a circle around a point formed from the intersection of the two independent emotion dimensions (for a review, see Larsen & Diener, 1992). As shown in Figure 12.1, the two-dimensional model of emotion captures the range of emotions, and the emotions calm and excited can be differentiated according to the valence and arousal dimension. This three-dimensional model has found some empirical support (Schimmack & Grob, 2000), although it has not been widely adopted because there are questions as to whether three dimensions (i.e., valence, tense arousal, energetic arousal) overparameterize a two-dimensional space.

Although the three-dimensional model of affect has not been widely adopted, it has been influential in underpinning conversations about how affect dimensions should be rotated. Among the two-dimensional models of emotion, there are alternative approaches to understanding the specific dimensions that emerge. Specifically, within any factorial representation of mood terms, the factors can be rotated differently, and the dimensions that emerge will have different interpretations. Russell (1980) and Russell and Barrett (1999), for example, argued that the factor space can be described well by independent valence and arousal dimensions, as shown in Figure 12.1. Watson, Tellegen, and their colleagues (Watson & Tellegen, 1985; Watson, Wiese, Vaidya, & Tellegen, 1999), however, argued that these dimensions should be rotated 45 degrees along energetic arousal and tense arousal to create independent positive affect or positive activation and negative affect or negative activation dimensions. As shown in Figure 12.1, positive affect is a combination of high pleasantness and high arousal and includes such emotions as interested, engaged, and active; negative affect is a combination of high unpleasantness and high arousal and includes such emotions as nervous, distressed, and afraid. These researchers contended that these rotated dimensions are aligned with the major clusters of emotions and that they represent fundamental emotional systems.

With the use of dimensional models, one implication for assessing positive emotions is that one has to consider whether the indicators of positive emotions align with the desired dimensions. One should evaluate whether selected instruments or indicators assess specific dimensions more than others. For example, using the Positive and Negative Affect Schedule (PANAS; Watson, Clark, & Tellegen, 1988), one primarily captures the positive activated and negative activated dimension; it may be appropriate for examining valence because it does not have indicators such as "happy" or "sad."

Another implication of dimensional models is that the dimensions posited are fundamentally bipolar. Among the different dimensions, whether the valence dimension is bipolar is one of the long-standing controversies in psychology. There are multiple issues to consider, such as (a) whether truly bipolar indicators are selected, (b) whether emotions are assessed in the moment or over a longer period, (c) the bipolarity of the scale response, and (d) the degree of measurement error (Diener & Iran-Nejad, 1986; Green, Goldman, & Salovey, 1993; Green, Salovey, & Truax, 1999; Russell & Carroll, 1999). More recently, it has been shown that the lack of bipolarity is an artifact of scale responding because individuals tend to endorse scale indicators close to their affective state; having a normal distribution of affective states within a bipolar continuum would lead to co-endorsements of both slightly happy and slightly sad, but endorsements of extreme happiness and sadness are unlikely (Tay & Drasgow, 2012; Tay & Kuykendall, 2017). If valence is bipolar, the assessment of only negative (or positive) emotions will be only covering half the affective space. Researchers should consider whether the assessment of only positive emotions, or both positive and negative emotions, will be more helpful for the research at hand.

Basic Emotion Models

Although dimensional models seek to describe what is in common among the varieties of emotions, models of basic emotions focus on the elemental types of emotions. Basic emotions may also be viewed as classes, or families, of emotions and can be potentially viewed as an organizing framework or building blocks for other types of more "complex" emotions (Ekman & Cordaro, 2011; Ortony & Turner, 1990). The idea of basic emotions was developed from Ekman's research on facial expressions of emotions (see the review by Ekman, 2016). There was cross-cultural recognition and production of these facial expressions (Ekman, 1993). From this work, six basic emotions were identified: anger, disgust, fear, happiness, sadness, and surprise. In general, basic emotions have two main characteristics: (a) they are discrete emotional states that stem from a common event that elicits a unique pattern of facial, vocal, physiological, and behavioral responses, and (b) they were honed through evolutionary history in seeking to overcome fundamental life tasks (Ekman, 1992). There is some disagreement about what constitutes a basic emotion and which emotions satisfy these requirements, resulting in different lists of basic emotions (Ekman, 1992, 1993; Izard, 1992; Ortony & Turner, 1990; Panksepp, 1992).

What are the implications of a basic emotions approach to modeling emotions? In Ortony and Turner's (1990) review, most theorists only included a single general pleasant emotion (e.g., joy, happiness, elation, pleasure). More specific emotions such as courage, hope, love, and wonder (along with the questionably positive emotions of interest, surprise, and desire) were included as basic emotions less frequently. Basic positive emotions seem to be fewer in number than basic negative emotions.

Hierarchical Models

Another approach to organizing the varieties of emotions is through a hierarchical framework. Early work seeking to comprehensively represent the different types of emotions using a hierarchical model was developed by Shaver, Schwartz, Kirson, and O'Connor (1987). On the basis of similarity sorting of about 130 prototypical emotion words, hierarchical cluster analysis revealed six distinct clusters: love, joy, surprise, anger, sadness, and fear. These higher order clusters of emotions comprised the specific emotion words. Therefore, love and joy were the two primary clusters of positive emotions. This was further confirmed by Diener, Smith, and Fujita (1995) who, through a systematic, empirical approach and selected emotion terms from a variety of research traditions (including cognitive approaches to emotion, biological and evolutionary approaches, and empirical approaches), found that two distinct types of positive emotion were necessary to account for the variability: love and joy.

Apart from comprehensive hierarchical accounts of emotions, there are also hierarchical accounts of emotions that are related to specific aspects of positivity. As noted earlier in regard to dimensional models, the positive and negative affect model of emotions focuses on positive activated and negative activated emotions (Watson & Clark, 1997; Watson et al., 1988; Watson & Tellegen, 1985). In this model, it is also possible to construe positive and negative affect as two higher level factors in a hierarchy, with a larger number of correlated lower order factors needed to describe emotion structure fully (Watson, 2000). Specifically, positive affect can be broken down into three distinct facets: joviality, self-assuredness, and attention.

The assessment implication of these hierarchical models is that researchers who desire to assess higher order clusters (or constructs) of positive emotions have an established basis for doing so. Love (which contains emotion descriptors *like, fondness, caring,* and *tenderness*) and joy (which contains emotion descriptors *contentment, pleasure, enjoyment,* and *hope*) are the two primary positive clusters across positive emotions; joviality, self-assuredness, and attention are the three positive affect clusters that are narrower than love and joy. Researchers should refer to the specific emotion indicators used for establishing the higher order clusters in past research for consistency and a valid assessment of these higher order clusters (Diener et al., 1995; Shaver et al., 1987; Watson, 2000).

Discrete Emotions

Discrete emotions share similarities with basic emotions in that they are often construed as stemming from a common event that elicits a unique pattern of facial, vocal, physiological, and behavioral responses. However, discrete emotions differ from basic emotions in that they do not seek to provide an integrative account of all the varieties of positive and negative emotions, and they do necessarily claim universality. Instead of seeking an expansive taxonomy of emotions, organizing discrete emotions frequently focuses on a specific domain of emotions with an emphasis on their prototypes. There are two relevant taxonomies of discrete emotions in positive psychology. First, in the broaden-and-build theory of positive emotions (Fredrickson, 1998, 2004), it is posited that there are four discrete emotions: joy, interest, contentment, and love. The basis for the choice of the emotions was the maximal distinctiveness of these emotions (except for love) and anecdotal evidence for their recognizability and frequency across cultures. Second, Haidt (2003) proposed a taxonomy of moral emotions that comprises discrete emotions under four emotion families: (a) the other-condemning family (contempt, anger, and disgust), (b) the self-conscious family (shame, embarrassment, and guilt), (c) the other-suffering family (compassion), and (d) the other-praising family (gratitude and elevation).

In positive psychology, there has been increased interest in these different positive discrete emotions (e.g., interest, contentment, gratitude, elevation) from these two models of emotions. A focus on discrete emotions is useful when one seeks to understand a specific emotion. At the same time, this has to be balanced with the recognition that in self-reports of emotion terms, positive emotions are often strongly correlated and relatively undifferentiated (Diener et al., 1995; Fredrickson, 1998; Watson, 2000). Therefore, it may be more useful to assess these discrete emotions with specific scales, rather than adjectives, to integratively assess the events and responses that pertain to each discrete emotion term.

METHODS FOR ASSESSING POSITIVE EMOTIONS

On the basis of the different definitions and structures of emotions, one can quickly see that the assessment of emotions requires multiple approaches. Next, we discuss the different methods used for assessing positive emotions and specific conceptual and methodological considerations.

Self-Reports of Positive Emotions

Self-report emotion scales generally ask respondents to indicate how frequently or intensely they are experiencing or have experienced different positive emotions or endorse statements that capture certain positive feelings. There are several aspects to consider in using self-reports of positive emotions.

Number of Items

The simplest way to assess positive emotions is to ask how a respondent feels using a single, broad positive emotion. For example, he or she could be asked, "How pleasant are you feeling in general?" or "How happy do you feel in general?" Alternatively, if a psychologist was interested in a specific positive emotion such as excitement, he or she could ask, "How excited do you feel right now?" Scales such as these have some amount of validity and have the advantage of brevity. Unfortunately, they might have low reliability.

Multiple-item scales offer the advantage of greater reliability and, in many cases, greater breadth of coverage. Multiple aspects of a single basic emotion can be assessed (e.g., contentment, happiness, joy, and elation all reflect various intensities of a single basic emotion), or multiple basic emotions can be included so that a broad range of positive emotions is sampled.

Although emotion scales can run as long as 132 items (e.g., the Multiple Affect Adjective Checklist-Revised; Zuckerman & Lubin, 1985), most scales are much shorter. Because the various positive emotions are highly correlated, even scales as short as three to five items often exhibit strong reliability (e.g., Diener et al., 1995; Su, Tay, & Diener, 2014; Watson & Clark, 1994; Watson et al., 1988).

Response Scale

A variety of response scales have been used to measure positive emotions. Many instruments use a simple checklist approach in which participants are presented with a list of emotions and asked to check the ones they are experiencing or have experienced during some discrete period (e.g., Zuckerman & Lubin, 1985). A variation of this approach asks participants to indicate, using a yes–no response scale, whether they agree with various statements that describe their emotional states in the moment or over a specific period (e.g., Tay & Diener, 2011). Checks or "yes" responses can be summed for an overall positive emotion score. Checklists may be more likely than other response scales to be influenced by certain response sets, and some researchers caution against their use (Green et al., 1993).

An alternative to the checklist is the Likert-type response scale (e.g., *strongly agree–strongly disagree*). Participants are presented with a list of emotion terms or statements describing their emotional states. They are then asked to indicate how strongly they feel the emotion (i.e., intensity), how frequently they have felt the emotion in the past (i.e., frequency), or how much they agree with the statement using a numbered Likert-type scale (i.e., agreement). The number of points on the scales varies and the specific anchors change depending on the focus of the measure. Some scales assess the strength with which a respondent has experienced an emotion, and these scales often use labels that range from *not at all* or *slightly, a little, moderately, quite a bit,* to *very much* (e.g., Watson et al., 1988). Other scales assess the frequency with which a respondent has experienced an emotion, and these scales may use anchors that refer to specific percentages of time (e.g., *0% of the time, 10% of the time*) or general frequency descriptors (e.g., *never, about half the time, always*; Diener et al., 1995). Frequency and intensity are separable components of emotional experience, and they may reflect different processes (Diener, Larsen, Levine, & Emmons, 1985). Diener, Sandvik, and Pavot (2009) argued that overall happiness reflects the frequency—but not intensity—of positive versus negative affect over time. Because these components are separable, we recommend using response scales that refer to the frequency or intensity of emotion (or both measured separately) and to avoid response scales that ambiguously measure both (e.g., *not much* or *a lot*). See also other types of measures (e.g., scenario rating test) for assessing emotion intensity (Schimmack & Diener, 1997).

A variation of the Likert response scale is the visual analog scale. This approach uses a visual representation of the response options on the Likert scale. For example, participants may be presented with a series of faces that range from frowning to neutral to smiling. They can then circle the face that best reflected their feeling state. Similarly, participants may be presented with a line separating two opposing adjectives or a thermometer indicating the intensity of an emotion. Participants can indicate how they feel by dragging a cursor (or pointing) somewhere on the visual analog. Visual analog scales are a useful alternative to traditional emotion measures when participants are likely to have difficulty understanding the words on a scale. For example, research with young children (Bieri, Reeve, Champion, Addicoat, & Ziegler, 1990) or those who have cognitive impairments (Stern, Arruda, Hooper, Wolfner, & Morey, 1997) can benefit from the use of visual analog scales.

It is also important to consider the bipolarity of the response format in emotions—for example, bipolar response format (e.g., *very sad–very happy*), ambiguous-likely bipolar (e.g., *strongly disagree–strongly agree*), and unipolar (e.g., *slightly–extremely*; see the review by Russell & Carroll, 1999). In many different response formats, people often construe response categories such as *not at all* happy or *strong disagreement* with happy as sad. When seeking to examine the distinctions between positive and negative emotions, one can seek to reduce the overlap by ensuring one uses more unipolar response formats, combinations of response scales (e.g., Did you experience happiness at all? [yes/no] If "yes," then rate yourself on *slightly* to *extremely* happy; Russell & Carroll, 1999), or even endorsements on different levels of emotion indicators (e.g., yes/no for "slightly happy"; yes/no for "very happy"; Tay & Kuykendall, 2017).

Time Frame

Another important feature to consider when deciding how to assess emotion is the time frame of the instructions. As noted previously, most theorists distinguish between the short-lived reactions to specific stimuli (emotions) and the long-lasting feelings that tend to be unrelated to specific objects and events (moods). Furthermore, long-term individual differences in emotions and moods may reflect one's underlying personality dispositions. Indeed, in the clinical literature, mood-related disorders show strong relations to personality (Kotov, Gamez, Schmidt, & Watson, 2010). The processes that underlie moods, emotions, and temperament may differ and may be differentially related to other phenomena. Therefore, it is essential for researchers and clinicians to decide which aspect of emotional experience they wish to study and to select appropriate measures.

Many emotion questionnaires have different instructions for measuring different types of emotional experiences. For example, Watson et al. (1988) noted that their PANAS scale can be administered with instructions that ask participants to indicate how they feel "right now," "today," "in the last week," "in the last month," or "in the last few months." The shorter the time frame, the more likely one is to capture emotional responses; the longer the time frame, the more likely one is to capture mood or personality differences in emotionality. The instructions for most emotion questionnaires can be altered to assess various aspects of emotional experience. Past research has shown that longer time frames exhibit greater orthogonality between positive and negative feelings, whereas those in the moment demonstrate more bipolarity (Diener & Emmons, 1984; Russell & Carroll, 1999).

Online Versus Retrospective Reports

The issue of time frame naturally brings up another consideration in emotion assessment: the dynamic nature of emotional experience as alluded to in the definition of emotions. Asking participants to retrospectively evaluate their emotions requires participants to remember their feelings and accurately aggregate across this dynamic experience, a task that may be difficult because individuals neglect durations and averages but instead are swayed more by the peak or end of an experience in their subjective summary of an emotional episode (Fredrickson & Kahneman, 1993; Redelmeier, Katz, & Kahneman, 2003).

Given the heuristics individuals use in their subjective summary of emotions over time, researchers who seek to capture fine-grained changes use methods that tap into online (or moment-by-moment) measures of emotions. There are generally three types of methods.

- The goal of *experience sampling methodology* (ESM) is to capture representative activities and experiences through multiple repeated randomized signal-based surveys (Csikszentmihalyi & Larson, 1987). The application of this method for assessing positive emotions would be to obtain prototypical levels of positive emotions across and within situations. ESM generally uses signals (via pagers, messaging, or app notifications) that are randomized to capture a variety of activities.
- Although the terms *ESM* and *ecological momentary assessment* (EMA) are often used interchangeably, EMA is less concerned with the representativeness

of activities but seeks to capture dynamic changes in experiences over time (Stone, Shiffman, & DeVries, 1999). It uses different types of signal scheduling and includes randomized, fixed-interval, stratified random (e.g., random from 9 a.m. to 10 a.m.), or event-contingent (e.g., whenever one gets into work) depending on the phenomena of interest. Both ESM and EMA are now frequently assessed using a smartphone, and according to a 2017 Pew Survey, about 77% of Americans own one, so it is expected that these methods will be more widely adopted. A full review of ESM and EMA is beyond the scope of the chapter and we refer readers to a review by Scollon, Kim-Prieto, and Diener (2003)

- As both ESM and EMA are intensive and costly, the *day reconstruction method* (DRM) was proposed as a means of capturing more online emotional experiences (Kahneman, Krueger, Schkade, Schwarz, & Stone, 2004). The implicit goals are similar to ESM: It asks respondents to break down the day (or previous day) into the different activities and has respondents rate their emotional experiences related to those activities. See the review of DRM by Diener and Tay (2014).

By assessing emotions over time, psychologists can examine several features of emotional experience. Multiple emotion reports can be decomposed into distinct components. For example, separate frequency and intensity scores can be calculated, and emotional reactivity can be examined by calculating variability in emotions or peak levels of emotional experience. Similarly, different sampling strategies can be used to emphasize emotions versus mood. An event sampling strategy, where participants are asked to complete a report any time a significant emotional event takes place, is likely to capture emotional reactions to specific events.

Online emotions can also be compared with retrospective judgments of positive emotions to assess how well participants can remember and report the emotions they experienced. Online emotion assessment is becoming an increasingly important part of a comprehensive study of positive emotional experience. It is important to note that although online emotions can more precisely describe actual experienced emotions, the in-the-moment experiences may be less related to life outcomes (unless aggregated to reflect trait-like affect) as opposed to recalled or remembered emotions as they reflect personal processing. For example, ESM reports of experiencing a vacation were unrelated to wanting to have a similar spring break experience, unlike global or retrospective reports (Wirtz, Kruger, Scollon, & Diener, 2003).

Specific Positive Emotion Measures

Table 12.1 presents a list of 15 widely used self-report positive emotion scales. Most are embedded in larger emotion questionnaires that assess a broad range of emotional experiences. Some were designed specifically to measure individual differences in emotionality (e.g., Tellegen & Waller's, 1994, Multidimensional

TABLE 12.1. Summary of Positive Emotion Measures

Measure	Subscales	Items	Positive emotions subscales
Activation–Deactivation Adjective checklist (Thayer, 1967)	2	28	Energetic arousal
Affect Balance Scale (Bradburn & Caplovitz, 1965)	2	10	Positive emotions
Affect Grid (Russell, Weiss, & Mendelsohn, 1989)	2	1	Pleasantness
Comprehensive Inventory of Thriving (Su, Tay, & Diener, 2014)	18	54	Positive emotions
Differential Emotions Scale (Izard, Dougherty, Bloxom, & Kotsch, 1974)	10	30	Interest, surprise, enjoyment
Dispositional Positive Emotion Scales (Shiota, Keltner, & John, 2006)	7	38	Joy, contentment, pride, love, compassion, amusement, awe
Modified Differential Emotions Scale (Fredrickson, Tugade, Waugh, & Larkin, 2003)	20	20	Amusement, awe, gratefulness, hopefulness, inspiration, interest, joy, love, pride, serenity
Mood Adjective Checklist (Nowlis & Green, 1957)	12	190	Surgency, elation, social affection, vigor
Multiple Affect Adjective Checklist (Zuckerman & Lubin, 1985)	5	132	Positive affect
Multidimensional Personality Questionnaire (Tellegen & Waller, 1994)	11	300	Positive emotionality
Positive and Negative Affect Schedule (Watson, Clark, & Tellegen, 1988)	2	20	Positive affect
Positive and Negative Affect Schedule (Expanded) (Watson & Clark, 1994)	11	55	Joviality, self-assurance, attentiveness
Profile of Mood States (McNair, Lorr, & Droppleman, 1971)	6	72	Vigor
Satisfaction With Life Scale (Diener, Emmons, Larsen, & Griffin, 1985)	1	5	Life satisfaction
Scale of Positive and Negative Affect Experience (Diener et al., 2010)	2	12	Positive emotions

Personality Questionnaire), whereas most can be used to measure individual differences or momentary experiences of emotion depending on the specific instructions and response scales. As noted previously, theories about the structure of positive emotions differ, and the measures described in Table 12.1 reflect these differences. Some measures focus on basic positive emotions or lower level facets of positive emotional experience, whereas others focus on broad pleasantness or activated positive emotion dimensions. Most lower order scales can be combined to form a single higher order positive emotion scale. Because most positive emotions are highly intercorrelated (especially at an individual difference level; see Zelenski & Larsen, 2000), all the scales listed in Table 12.1 exhibit strong internal consistency and strong evidence of validity (with the possible exception of the Affect Balance Scale; see Larsen, Diener, & Emmons, 1985). Also included is a measure of cognitive well-being, the Satisfaction With Life Scale (Diener, Emmons, Larsen, & Griffin, 1985). Measures of cognitive well-being are moderately correlated with the experience of positive emotions (Lucas et al., 1996).

Non-Self-Report Measures

Most non-self-report measures of positive emotions assume that an emotion—because of its biological and/or social nature—is recognizable. Therefore, informant reports of emotional experience can provide a useful alternative to self-reports. Further, positive emotions comprise multiple components (e.g., brain activity, physiology, meta-experience, regulation), as described in our earlier sections. By assessing these different components, researchers may be able to tap into aspects of emotions that cannot be easily recognized by the person who is experiencing the emotion.

Observer Reports

One simple and easily administered alternative to self-reports is the observer report. Most current self-report positive emotion measures can be easily altered to create reliable and valid observer measures of emotion. By asking friends, family, or colleagues to rate how frequently or intensely a target participant has experienced an emotion, researchers can get additional information about emotional experience. Informants likely have different response sets, response styles, and memory biases, and the combination of self- and informant reports of emotion may provide more valid assessments of positive emotions (Diener et al., 1995). A meta-analysis conducted by Schneider and Schimmack (2009) showed that the average correlation between self- and target ratings was $r = .42$; correspondence was highest for global ratings of happiness, followed by positive emotions and then by negative emotions.

An alternative to the known-informant approach is the expert-rater approach. Using this technique, informants who do not know the target can be trained to interpret and code specific signs of emotional experience (e.g., Gottman, 1993). Alternatively, untrained judges can simply be asked to judge a person's emotion after observing the target in an emotion-provoking situation. The former approach involves extensive training of raters but provides more valid and reliable emotion reports than the latter.

Facial Measures

In addition to training raters to judge emotional experience holistically, it is possible to train raters to look for specific signs of emotions in the facial expressions that targets exhibit. The Facial Action Coding System (FACS; Ekman & Friesen, 1978) has been foundational for describing different facial expressions of emotions and guides raters to make judgments about emotions on both type and intensity according to specific muscle movements in the face. By using FACS, reliable and valid measures of individual differences in positive emotions can be obtained from static pictures such as yearbook photos (e.g., Harker & Keltner, 2001). However, substantial training is required, and facial coding of temporal sequences can be time consuming. To overcome this, there have been algorithms and commercial programs developed using FACS and other coding schemes to automatically capture the types and intensity of emotions even in real time (see the survey by Fasel & Luettin, 2003).

Apart from visual cues from facial expressions, the measurement of facial expressions can be automated using electromyographical techniques (Cacioppo, Berntson, Larsen, Poehlmann, & Ito, 2000). These techniques measure muscle contractions in the face and compare these muscle contractions to known changes that occur when emotions are expressed. Electromyography has the added advantage of being able to capture muscle changes that may be too small to be noticed by the naked eye. We should note that although facial measures of positive emotions offer a promising alternative to self-reports, it may be difficult to differentiate measures of positive emotions from facial measures (Fredrickson, 1998). For example, key visual facial cues of the mouth and eyes convey the degree of happiness (Calvo, Álvarez-Plaza, & Fernández-Martín, 2017). However, these techniques can probably only reliably measure general pleasantness or happiness, although a more recent review suggested that measures of arousal can also be obtained (Calvo & Nummenmaa, 2016).

Physiological Measures

Other psychophysiological measures have been used to measure emotion, but again, these tend to distinguish general happiness from negative emotions or distinguish among various negative emotions. Cacioppo et al. (2000) presented a meta-analysis of the literature examining the physiological correlates of different emotional experiences. The studies they reviewed measured such variables as heart rate, heart rate acceleration, blood pressure, body temperature, finger temperature, respiration amplitude, skin conductance, and many others. Several of these variables were able to distinguish positive from negative emotions, but they had limited success in discriminating among discrete emotions.

Neuroimaging

The techniques of neuroimaging (i.e., functional imaging magnetic resonance imaging and positron emission tomography) can address the question of whether certain brain regions underpin positive emotions. From a basic emotions perspective, one may seek to examine different types of emotions (e.g., fear, anger, happiness) as localized within a specific brain region. In other words, what parts of our brain generate happiness? One meta-analysis found that happiness was associated with brain activation of the basal ganglia (Phan, Wager, Taylor, & Liberzon, 2002), whereas another meta-analysis found brain activation of the rostral supracallosal anterior cingulate cortex (RSACC) and dorsomedial prefrontal cortex (DMPFC; Murphy, Nimmo-Smith, & Lawrence, 2003). Yet these same brain regions have also been implicated in other types of basic emotions in the meta-analyses. For example, the basal ganglia were also associated with disgust (Phan et al., 2002), and the RSACC and DMPFC were also associated with sadness (Murphy et al., 2003).

The lack of consistency for basic emotions has prompted other researchers to question whether there are basic emotion circuits in the brain or whether discrete experiences of emotions are constructed from more basic fundamental "dimensions" of emotions (as seen in the earlier section—e.g., valence, arousal, positive affect, negative affect, approach or withdrawal; Barrett & Wager, 2006). On this front, Barrett and Wager (2006) noted that there seems to be more consistent evidence for the dimension of approach-type emotions (i.e., interest, enjoyment, anger) to be associated with left-side brain activations in the frontal cortex (Wager, Phan, Liberzon, & Taylor, 2003). Other reviews and studies seem to be consistent with this. For example, Davidson (1992) reviewed evidence that the left anterior region of the brain may be responsible for positive emotions due to the left hemisphere processing more approach-related behaviors and emotions. Left superior frontal activation is also related to higher well-being in general (Urry et al., 2004). Overall, this suggests that neuroimaging may not be able to capture specific types of discrete emotions, although it may be able to assess more fundamental processes underlying experienced emotions.

Emotion Tasks

Because cognitive processes and action tendencies are implicated in emotions, researchers can seek out ways to assess these aspects to measure emotions. Using a memory task, Sandvik, Diener, and Seidlitz (1993) asked people to recall as many happy experiences from their lives within 2 minutes, followed by recalling as many unhappy experiences from their lives in the next 2 minutes. The balance of happy to unhappy experiences was positively correlated with happiness reports. Other memory tasks have also shown that happy people tend to falsely remember *happiness* in a word list (Koo & Oishi, 2009).

Other studies have used other cognitive processing tasks such as word-completion and word-recognition tasks. Happy participants are quicker than participants in neutral states to identify positive words as words, and happy participants are more likely than unhappy participants to complete word stems to form positive words. Some studies have used the idea that happier people have tighter associations in happy concepts to show greater explicit linkages (Koo & Oishi, 2009) or faster reaction times compared with unhappy people (Robinson & Kirkeby, 2005). When researchers are concerned about social desirability or other issues that may make respondents answer in untruthful ways, cognitive tasks such as these may help identify how happy the respondent is. Rusting (1998) reviewed evidence that these cognitive tasks are sensitive to both individual differences in positive emotions as well as positive emotional states.

Social Media and Other Sources

Social media is also a growing source of data for assessing positive emotions. Many social media sites such as Facebook and Twitter can analyze the language of unstructured text posts for positive or negative sentiment. For example, analysis can be based on the occurrence of specific lexicons (e.g., *happy*) as a measure of positive emotions, and there are different lexicons one can use (e.g., LIWC; Tausczik & Pennebaker, 2010). Alternatively, positive emotion predictive models can be created by anchoring the linguistic features (e.g., words, phrases) of text posts to self-reported ratings of happiness from a sample of social media users (see Schwartz et al., 2013). This predictive model can then be generalized to the general population of social media users who did not provide survey data. In general, the massive amount of data that is generated from social media can be used to great effect to assess the happiness of different geographic regions—for example, examining county-level happiness using Twitter data (Eichstaedt et al., 2015).

With the growth in technology use, there are also many other sources of data, such as images and videos, that can be harnessed for assessing positive emotions. For example, images from Facebook can be obtained to assess happiness (Seder & Oishi, 2012). Automated procedures can also be used to examine happiness in photos from Twitter as well (Abdullah, Murnane, Costa, & Choudhury, 2015). Further, there is also increasing availability of various types of video data that can be harnessed for assessing human behaviors such as emotions (Tay, Jebb, & Woo, 2017). For instance, public video camera data were used to count the number of smiles on a college campus and found seasonal effects, such as more smiles on weekends; further there were event-based changes too, such as fewer smiles during examinations and most smiles after graduation day (Hernandez, Hoque, Drevo, & Picard, 2012).

NEW CHALLENGES

The rise of positive psychology, alongside greater attention to societal well-being by governments and intergovernmental organizations, has led to a rise in well-being assessments—and positive emotions—for nations around the globe (Diener & Seligman, 2004; Diener & Tov, 2012). Apart from the important issues of reliability and validity of positive emotion measures, researchers also have to carefully consider the comparability of these measures across cultures through measurement equivalence procedures (Tay, Meade, & Cao, 2015). Another issue to consider is that the variability attributable to national conditions is substantially smaller than evaluative well-being indicators. For example, past research on 123 nations has shown that less than 6% of the variability is attributable to the nation level compared with evaluative well-being where 24% of variability was attributable to the nation level (Tay & Diener, 2011). This suggests that emotion indicators likely reflect more personalized conditions than national conditions. Researchers seeking to compare national differences in positive emotions will have to be aware of the drawbacks on this front.

CONCLUSION

In conclusion, our review of positive emotions assessments shows that positive psychologists can confidently assess positive emotions using a variety of well-validated measurement techniques. The simplest and most flexible are self-reports of emotions, and self-reports probably provide the best insight into the experience of emotion within individuals over time and across nations. However, new methodologies, such as using data from social media, may be harnessed to great effect, though more research will have to be done to establish their reliability and validity for cross-national comparisons. We encourage researchers to consider the use of non-self-report measures as well as informant reports, physiological measures, neuroimaging, facial expressions, emotion tasks, and social media data for a multimethod approach to understanding positive emotions and the components that underpin these experiences.

REFERENCES

Abdullah, S., Murnane, E. L., Costa, J. M. R., & Choudhury, T. (2015, March). *Collective smile: Measuring societal happiness from geolocated images.* Paper presented at the ACM Conference on Computer Supported Cooperative Work and Social Computing.

Barrett, L. F. (2006). Valence is a basic building block of emotional life. *Journal of Research in Personality, 40,* 35–55. http://dx.doi.org/10.1016/j.jrp.2005.08.006

Barrett, L. F., & Wager, T. D. (2006). The structure of emotion: Evidence from neuroimaging studies. *Current Directions in Psychological Science, 15,* 79–83. http://dx.doi.org/10.1111/j.0963-7214.2006.00411.x

Bieri, D., Reeve, R. A., Champion, G. D., Addicoat, L., & Ziegler, J. B. (1990). The Faces Pain Scale for the self-assessment of the severity of pain experienced by children: Development, initial validation, and preliminary investigation for ratio scale properties. *Pain, 41,* 139–150. http://dx.doi.org/10.1016/0304-3959(90)90018-9

Bradburn, N. M., & Caplovitz, D. (1965). *Reports on happiness.* Chicago, IL: Aldine.

Burgdorf, J., & Panksepp, J. (2006). The neurobiology of positive emotions. *Neuroscience and Biobehavioral Reviews, 30,* 173–187. http://dx.doi.org/10.1016/j.neubiorev.2005.06.001

Cacioppo, J. T., Berntson, G. G., Larsen, J. T., Poehlmann, K. M., & Ito, T. A. (2000). The psychophysiology of emotion. In M. Lewis & J. M. Haviland-Janes (Eds.), *Handbook of emotions* (pp. 173–191). New York, NY: Guilford Press.

Calvo, M. G., Álvarez-Plaza, P., & Fernández-Martín, A. (2017). The contribution of facial regions to judgements of happiness and trustworthiness from dynamic expressions. *Journal of Cognitive Psychology, 29,* 618–625. http://dx.doi.org/10.1080/20445911.2017.1302450

Calvo, M. G., & Nummenmaa, L. (2016). Perceptual and affective mechanisms in facial expression recognition: An integrative review. *Cognition and Emotion, 30,* 1081–1106. http://dx.doi.org/10.1080/02699931.2015.1049124

Csikszentmihalyi, M., & Larson, R. (1987). Validity and reliability of the experience-sampling method. *Journal of Nervous and Mental Disease, 175,* 526–536. http://dx.doi.org/10.1097/00005053-198709000-00004

Davidson, R. J. (1992). Anterior cerebral asymmetry and the nature of emotion. *Brain and Cognition, 20,* 125–151. http://dx.doi.org/10.1016/0278-2626(92)90065-T

De Neve, J.-E., Diener, E., Tay, L., & Xuereb, C. (2013). The objective benefits of subjective well-being. In J. Helliwell, R. Layard, & J. Sachs (Eds.), *World Happiness Report 2013* (Vol. 2, pp. 54–79). New York, NY: UN Sustainable Development Solutions Network.

Diener, E. (1984). Subjective well-being. *Psychological Bulletin, 95,* 542–575. http://dx.doi.org/10.1037/0033-2909.95.3.542

Diener, E., & Emmons, R. A. (1984). The independence of positive and negative affect. *Journal of Personality and Social Psychology, 47,* 1105–1117. http://dx.doi.org/10.1037/0022-3514.47.5.1105

Diener, E., Emmons, R. A., Larsen, R. J., & Griffin, S. (1985). The Satisfaction With Life Scale. *Journal of Personality Assessment, 49,* 71–75. http://dx.doi.org/10.1207/s15327752jpa4901_13

Diener, E., Inglehart, R., & Tay, L. (2013). Theory and validity of life satisfaction scales. *Social Indicators Research, 112,* 497–527. http://dx.doi.org/10.1007/s11205-012-0076-y

Diener, E., & Iran-Nejad, A. (1986). The relationship in experience between various types of affect. *Journal of Personality and Social Psychology, 50,* 1031–1038. http://dx.doi.org/10.1037/0022-3514.50.5.1031

Diener, E., Larsen, R. J., Levine, S., & Emmons, R. A. (1985). Intensity and frequency: Dimensions underlying positive and negative affect. *Journal of Personality and Social Psychology, 48,* 1253–1265. http://dx.doi.org/10.1037/0022-3514.48.5.1253

Diener, E., & Lucas, R. E. (2000). Subjective emotional well-being. In M. Lewis & J. M. Haviland (Eds.), *Handbook of emotions* (2nd ed., pp. 325–337). New York, NY: Guilford Press.

Diener, E., Sandvik, E., & Pavot, W. (2009). Happiness is the frequency, not the intensity, of positive versus negative affect. In F. Strack, M. Argyle, & N. Schwarz (Eds.), *Subjective well-being: An interdisciplinary perspective* (pp. 119–140). New York, NY: Pergamon Press.

Diener, E., & Seligman, M. E. P. (2004). Beyond money: Toward an economy of well-being. *Psychological Science in the Public Interest, 5,* 1–31. http://dx.doi.org/10.1111/j.0963-7214.2004.00501001.x

Diener, E., Smith, H., & Fujita, F. (1995). The personality structure of affect. *Journal of Personality and Social Psychology, 69,* 130–141. http://dx.doi.org/10.1037/0022-3514.69.1.130

Diener, E., & Tay, L. (2014). Review of the Day Reconstruction Method (DRM). *Social Indicators Research, 116,* 255–267. http://dx.doi.org/10.1007/s11205-013-0279-x

Diener, E., & Tov, W. (2012). National accounts of well-being. In K. C. Land, A. C. Michalos, & M. J. Sirgy (Eds.), *Handbook of social indicators and quality of life research* (pp. 137–157). New York, NY: Springer. http://dx.doi.org/10.1007/978-94-007-2421-1_7

Diener, E., Wirtz, D., Tov, W., Kim-Prieto, C., Choi, D., Oishi, S., & Biswas-Diener, R. (2010). New well-being measures: Short scales to assess flourishing and positive and negative feelings. *Social Indicators Research, 97,* 143–156. http://dx.doi.org/10.1007/s11205-009-9493-y

Eichstaedt, J. C., Schwartz, H. A., Kern, M. L., Park, G., Labarthe, D. R., Merchant, R. M., . . . Seligman, M. E. (2015). Psychological language on Twitter predicts county-level heart disease mortality. *Psychological Science, 26,* 159–169. http://dx.doi.org/10.1177/0956797614557867

Ekman, P. (1992). An argument for basic emotions. *Cognition and Emotion, 6,* 169–200. http://dx.doi.org/10.1080/02699939208411068

Ekman, P. (1993). Facial expression and emotion. *American Psychologist, 48,* 384–392. http://dx.doi.org/10.1037/0003-066X.48.4.384

Ekman, P. (2016). What scientists who study emotion agree about. *Perspectives on Psychological Science, 11,* 31–34. http://dx.doi.org/10.1177/1745691615596992

Ekman, P., & Cordaro, D. (2011). What is meant by calling emotions basic. *Emotion Review, 3,* 364–370. http://dx.doi.org/10.1177/1754073911410740

Ekman, P., & Friesen, W. (1978). *Facial action coding system.* Palo Alto, CA: Consulting Psychologists Press.

Fasel, B., & Luettin, J. (2003). Automatic facial expression analysis: A survey. *Pattern Recognition, 36,* 259–275. http://dx.doi.org/10.1016/S0031-3203(02)00052-3

Fredrickson, B. L. (1998). What good are positive emotions? *Review of General Psychology, 2,* 300–319. http://dx.doi.org/10.1037/1089-2680.2.3.300

Fredrickson, B. L. (2004). The broaden-and-build theory of positive emotions. *Philosophical Transactions of the Royal Society of London B: Biological Sciences, 359,* 1367–1377. http://dx.doi.org/10.1098/rstb.2004.1512

Fredrickson, B. L., & Kahneman, D. (1993). Duration neglect in retrospective evaluations of affective episodes. *Journal of Personality and Social Psychology, 65,* 45–55. http://dx.doi.org/10.1037/0022-3514.65.1.45

Fredrickson, B. L., Tugade, M. M., Waugh, C. E., & Larkin, G. R. (2003). What good are positive emotions in crises? A prospective study of resilience and emotions following the terrorist attacks on the United States on September 11th, 2001. *Journal of Personality and Social Psychology, 84,* 365–376. http://dx.doi.org/10.1037/0022-3514.84.2.365

Frijda, N. H. (1999). Emotions and hedonic experience. In D. Kahneman, E. Diener, & N. Schwarz (Eds.), *Well being: The foundations of hedonic psychology* (pp. 190–210). New York, NY: Russell Sage Foundation.

Gottman, J. M. (1993). Studying emotion in social interaction. In M. Lewis & J. M. Haviland (Eds.), *Handbook of emotions* (pp. 475–487). New York, NY: Guilford Press.

Green, D. P., Goldman, S. L., & Salovey, P. (1993). Measurement error masks bipolarity in affect ratings. *Journal of Personality and Social Psychology, 64,* 1029–1041. http://dx.doi.org/10.1037/0022-3514.64.6.1029

Green, D. P., Salovey, P., & Truax, K. M. (1999). Static, dynamic, and causative bipolarity of affect. *Journal of Personality and Social Psychology, 76,* 856–867. http://dx.doi.org/10.1037/0022-3514.76.5.856

Gruber, J., Kogan, A., Quoidbach, J., & Mauss, I. B. (2013). Happiness is best kept stable: Positive emotion variability is associated with poorer psychological health. *Emotion, 13,* 1–6. http://dx.doi.org/10.1037/a0030262

Haidt, J. (2003). The moral emotions. In R. J. Davidson, K. R. Scherer, & H. H. Goldsmith (Eds.), *Handbook of affective sciences* (pp. 852–870). Oxford, England: Oxford University Press.

Harker, L., & Keltner, D. (2001). Expressions of positive emotion in women's college yearbook pictures and their relationship to personality and life outcomes across adulthood. *Journal of Personality and Social Psychology, 80,* 112–124. http://dx.doi.org/10.1037/0022-3514.80.1.112

Hernandez, J., Hoque, M., Drevo, W., & Picard, R. W. (2012, September). *Mood meter: Counting smiles in the wild.* Paper presented at the ACM Conference on Ubiquitous Computing.

Izard, C. E. (1992). Basic emotions, relations among emotions, and emotion-cognition relations. *Psychological Review, 99,* 561–565. http://dx.doi.org/10.1037/0033-295X.99.3.561

Izard, C. E., Dougherty, F. E., Bloxom, B. M., & Kotsch, W. W. (1974). *The differential emotions scale: A method of measuring the subjective experience of discrete emotions.* Unpublished manuscript.

Kahneman, D., Krueger, A. B., Schkade, D. A., Schwarz, N., & Stone, A. A. (2004, December 3). A survey method for characterizing daily life experience: The day reconstruction method. *Science, 306,* 1776–1780. http://dx.doi.org/10.1126/science.1103572

Keltner, D., & Gross, J. J. (1999). Functional accounts of emotions. *Cognition and Emotion, 13*, 467–480. http://dx.doi.org/10.1080/026999399379140

Koo, M., & Oishi, S. (2009). False memory and the associative network of happiness. *Personality and Social Psychology Bulletin, 35*, 212–220. http://dx.doi.org/10.1177/0146167208327191

Kotov, R., Gamez, W., Schmidt, F., & Watson, D. (2010). Linking "big" personality traits to anxiety, depressive, and substance use disorders: A meta-analysis. *Psychological Bulletin, 136*, 768–821. http://dx.doi.org/10.1037/a0020327

Larsen, R. J., & Diener, E. (1992). Promises and problems with the circumplex model of emotion. In M. S. Clark (Ed.), *Review of personality and social psychology: Emotion* (Vol. 13, pp. 25–59). Newbury Park, CA: Sage.

Larsen, R. J., Diener, E., & Emmons, R. A. (1985). An evaluation of subjective well-being measures. *Social Indicators Research, 17*, 1–7. http://dx.doi.org/10.1007/BF00354108

Lucas, R. E., Diener, E., Grob, A., Suh, E. M., & Shao, L. (2000). Cross-cultural evidence for the fundamental features of extraversion. *Journal of Personality and Social Psychology, 79*, 452–468. http://dx.doi.org/10.1037/0022-3514.79.3.452

Lucas, R. E., Diener, E., & Suh, E. (1996). Discriminant validity of well-being measures. *Journal of Personality and Social Psychology, 71*, 616–628. http://dx.doi.org/10.1037/0022-3514.71.3.616

Mayer, J. D., Salovey, P., & Caruso, D. (2002). *The Mayer-Salovey-Caruso Emotional Intelligence Test (MSCEIT)*. Toronto, Ontario, Canada: Multi-Health Systems.

McNair, D. M., Lorr, M., & Droppleman, L. F. (1971). *Manual: Profile of mood states*. San Diego, CA: Educational and Industrial Testing Service.

Murphy, F. C., Nimmo-Smith, I., & Lawrence, A. D. (2003). Functional neuroanatomy of emotions: A meta-analysis. *Cognitive, Affective & Behavioral Neuroscience, 3*, 207–233. http://dx.doi.org/10.3758/CABN.3.3.207

Nowlis, V., & Green, R. (1957). *The experimental analysis of mood*. Washington, DC: Office of Naval Research.

Oatley, K., & Johnson-Laird, P. N. (1987). Towards a cognitive theory of emotions. *Cognition and Emotion, 1*, 29–50. http://dx.doi.org/10.1080/02699938708408362

Ortony, A., & Turner, T. J. (1990). What's basic about basic emotions? *Psychological Review, 97*, 315–331. http://dx.doi.org/10.1037/0033-295X.97.3.315

Panksepp, J. (1992). A critical role for "affective neuroscience" in resolving what is basic about basic emotions. *Psychological Review, 99*, 554–560. http://dx.doi.org/10.1037/0033-295X.99.3.554

Panksepp, J. (2004). *Affective neuroscience: The foundations of human and animal emotions*. New York, NY: Oxford University Press.

Pavot, W., & Diener, E. (1993). Review of the Satisfaction With Life Scale. *Psychological Assessment, 5*, 164–172. http://dx.doi.org/10.1037/1040-3590.5.2.164

Phan, K. L., Wager, T., Taylor, S. F., & Liberzon, I. (2002). Functional neuroanatomy of emotion: A meta-analysis of emotion activation studies in PET and fMRI. *NeuroImage, 16*, 331–348. http://dx.doi.org/10.1006/nimg.2002.1087

Quoidbach, J., Berry, E. V., Hansenne, M., & Mikolajczak, M. (2010). Positive emotion regulation and well-being: Comparing the impact of eight savoring and dampening strategies. *Personality and Individual Differences, 49*, 368–373. http://dx.doi.org/10.1016/j.paid.2010.03.048

Redelmeier, D. A., Katz, J., & Kahneman, D. (2003). Memories of colonoscopy: A randomized trial. *Pain, 104*, 187–194. http://dx.doi.org/10.1016/S0304-3959(03)00003-4

Robinson, M. D., & Kirkeby, B. S. (2005). Happiness as a belief system: Individual differences and priming in emotion judgments. *Personality and Social Psychology Bulletin, 31*, 1134–1144. http://dx.doi.org/10.1177/0146167204274081

Russell, J. A. (1980). A circumplex model of affect. *Journal of Personality and Social Psychology, 39*, 1161–1178. http://dx.doi.org/10.1037/h0077714

Russell, J. A. (2003). Core affect and the psychological construction of emotion. *Psychological Review, 110,* 145–172. http://dx.doi.org/10.1037/0033-295X.110.1.145

Russell, J. A. (2009). Emotion, core affect, and psychological construction. *Cognition and Emotion, 23,* 1259–1283. http://dx.doi.org/10.1080/02699930902809375

Russell, J. A., & Barrett, L. F. (1999). Core affect, prototypical emotional episodes, and other things called emotion: Dissecting the elephant. *Journal of Personality and Social Psychology, 76,* 805–819. http://dx.doi.org/10.1037/0022-3514.76.5.805

Russell, J. A., & Carroll, J. M. (1999). On the bipolarity of positive and negative affect. *Psychological Bulletin, 125,* 3–30. http://dx.doi.org/10.1037/0033-2909.125.1.3

Russell, J. A., Weiss, A., & Mendelsohn, G. A. (1989). Affect Grid: A single-item scale of pleasure and arousal. *Journal of Personality and Social Psychology, 57,* 493–502. http://dx.doi.org/10.1037/0022-3514.57.3.493

Rusting, C. L. (1998). Personality, mood, and cognitive processing of emotional information: Three conceptual frameworks. *Psychological Bulletin, 124,* 165–196. http://dx.doi.org/10.1037/0033-2909.124.2.165

Salovey, P., & Grewal, D. (2005). The science of emotional intelligence. *Current Directions in Psychological Science, 14,* 281–285. http://dx.doi.org/10.1111/j.0963-7214.2005.00381.x

Sandvik, E., Diener, E., & Seidlitz, L. (1993). Subjective well-being: The convergence and stability of self-report and non-self-report measures. *Journal of Personality, 61,* 317–342. http://dx.doi.org/10.1111/j.1467-6494.1993.tb00283.x

Schimmack, U. (2003). Affect measurement in experience sampling research. *Journal of Happiness Studies, 4,* 79–106. http://dx.doi.org/10.1023/A:1023661322862

Schimmack, U., & Diener, E. (1997). Affect intensity: Separating intensity and frequency in repeatedly measured affect. *Journal of Personality and Social Psychology, 73,* 1313–1329. http://dx.doi.org/10.1037/0022-3514.73.6.1313

Schimmack, U., & Grob, A. (2000). Dimensional models of core affect: A quantitative comparison by means of structural equation modeling. *European Journal of Personality, 14,* 325–345. http://dx.doi.org/10.1002/1099-0984(200007/08)14:4<325::AID-PER380>3.0.CO;2-I

Schneider, L., & Schimmack, U. (2009). Self-informant agreement in well-being ratings: A meta-analysis. *Social Indicators Research, 94,* 363–376. http://dx.doi.org/10.1007/s11205-009-9440-y

Schwartz, H. A., Eichstaedt, J. C., Kern, M. L., Dziurzynski, L., Ramones, S. M., Agrawal, M., . . . Ungar, L. H. (2013). Personality, gender, and age in the language of social media: The open-vocabulary approach. *PLoS One, 8*(9), e73791. http://dx.doi.org/10.1371/journal.pone.0073791

Scollon, C. N., Kim-Prieto, C., & Diener, E. (2003). Experience sampling: Promises and pitfalls, strengths and weaknesses. *Journal of Happiness Studies, 4,* 5–34. http://dx.doi.org/10.1023/A:1023605205115

Seder, J. P., & Oishi, S. (2012). Intensity of smiling in Facebook photos predicts future life satisfaction. *Social Psychological and Personality Science, 3,* 407–413. http://dx.doi.org/10.1177/1948550611424968

Seligman, M. E. P., & Csikszentmihalyi, M. (2000). Positive psychology. An introduction. *American Psychologist, 55,* 5–14. http://dx.doi.org/10.1037/0003-066X.55.1.5

Shaver, P., Schwartz, J., Kirson, D., & O'Connor, C. (1987). Emotion knowledge: Further exploration of a prototype approach. *Journal of Personality and Social Psychology, 52,* 1061–1086. http://dx.doi.org/10.1037/0022-3514.52.6.1061

Sheldon, K. M., & Lyubomirsky, S. (2006). How to increase and sustain positive emotion: The effects of expressing gratitude and visualizing best possible selves. *The Journal of Positive Psychology, 1,* 73–82. http://dx.doi.org/10.1080/17439760500510676

Shiota, M. N., Keltner, D., & John, O. P. (2006). Positive emotion dispositions differentially associated with Big Five personality and attachment style. *The Journal of Positive Psychology, 1,* 61–71. http://dx.doi.org/10.1080/17439760500510833

Shiota, M. N., Keltner, D., & Mossman, A. (2007). The nature of awe: Elicitors, appraisals, and effects on self-concept. *Cognition and Emotion, 21,* 944–963. http://dx.doi.org/10.1080/02699930600923668

Stern, R. A., Arruda, J. E., Hooper, C. R., Wolfner, G. D., & Morey, C. E. (1997). Visual analogue mood scales to measure internal mood state in neurologically impaired patients: Description and initial validity evidence. *Aphasiology, 11,* 59–71. http://dx.doi.org/10.1080/02687039708248455

Stone, A. A., Shiffman, S. S., & DeVries, M. W. (1999). Ecological momentary assessment. In D. Kahneman, E. Diener, & N. Schwarz (Eds.), *Well-being: The foundations of hedonic psychology* (pp. 26–39). New York, NY: Russell Sage Foundation.

Su, R., Tay, L., & Diener, E. (2014). The development and validation of the Comprehensive Inventory of Thriving (CIT) and the Brief Inventory of Thriving (BIT). *Applied Psychology: Health and Well-Being, 6,* 251–279. http://dx.doi.org/10.1111/aphw.12027

Tausczik, Y. R., & Pennebaker, J. W. (2010). The psychological meaning of works: LIWC and computerized text analysis methods. *Journal of Language and Social Psychology, 29,* 24–54. http://dx.doi.org/10.1177/0261927X09351676

Tay, L., & Diener, E. (2011). Needs and subjective well-being around the world. *Journal of Personality and Social Psychology, 101,* 354–365. http://dx.doi.org/10.1037/a0023779

Tay, L., & Drasgow, F. (2012). Theoretical, statistical, and substantive issues in the assessment of construct dimensionality: Accounting for the item response process. *Organizational Research Methods, 15,* 363–384. http://dx.doi.org/10.1177/1094428112439709

Tay, L., Jebb, A. T., & Woo, S. E. (2017). Video capture of human behaviors: Toward a Big Data approach. *Current Opinion in Behavioral Sciences, 18,* 17–22. http://dx.doi.org/10.1016/j.cobeha.2017.05.026

Tay, L., & Kuykendall, L. (2017). Why self-reports of happiness and sadness may not necessarily contradict bipolarity: A psychometric review and proposal. *Emotion Review, 9,* 146–154. http://dx.doi.org/10.1177/1754073916637656

Tay, L., Meade, A. W., & Cao, M. (2015). An overview and practical guide to IRT measurement equivalence analysis. *Organizational Research Methods, 18,* 3–46. http://dx.doi.org/10.1177/1094428114553062

Tellegen, A., & Waller, N. G. (1994). Exploring personality through test construction: Development of the Multidimensional Personality Questionnaire. In S. R. Briggs & J. M. Cheek (Eds.), *Personality measures: Development and evaluation* (Vol. 1, pp. 133–161). Greenwich, CT: JAI Press.

Tellegen, A., Watson, D., & Clark, L. A. (1999). On the dimensional and hierarchical structure of affect. *Psychological Science, 10,* 297–303. http://dx.doi.org/10.1111/1467-9280.00157

Thayer, R. E. (1967). Measurement of activation through self-report. *Psychological Reports, 20,* 663–678. http://dx.doi.org/10.2466/pr0.1967.20.2.663

Titchener, E. B. (1908). *Lectures on the elementary psychology of feeling and attention.* New York, NY: Macmillan. http://dx.doi.org/10.1037/10867-000

Tugade, M. M., & Fredrickson, B. L. (2007). Regulation of positive emotions: Emotion regulation strategies that promote resilience. *Journal of Happiness Studies, 8,* 311–333. http://dx.doi.org/10.1007/s10902-006-9015-4

Urry, H. L., Nitschke, J. B., Dolski, I., Jackson, D. C., Dalton, K. M., Mueller, C. J., . . . Davidson, R. J. (2004). Making a life worth living: Neural correlates of well-being. *Psychological Science, 15,* 367–372. http://dx.doi.org/10.1111/j.0956-7976.2004.00686.x

Wager, T. D., Phan, K. L., Liberzon, I., & Taylor, S. F. (2003). Valence, gender, and lateralization of functional brain anatomy in emotion: A meta-analysis of findings from neuroimaging. *NeuroImage, 19,* 513–531. http://dx.doi.org/10.1016/S1053-8119(03)00078-8

Watson, D. (2000). *Mood and temperament.* New York, NY: Guilford Press.

Watson, D., & Clark, L. A. (1994). *The PANAS-X: Manual for the Positive and Negative Affect Schedule—Expanded Form.* Unpublished manuscript.

Watson, D., & Clark, L. A. (1997). Measurement and mismeasurement of mood: Recurrent and emergent issues. *Journal of Personality Assessment, 68,* 267–296. http://dx.doi.org/10.1207/s15327752jpa6802_4

Watson, D., Clark, L. A., & Tellegen, A. (1988). Development and validation of brief measures of positive and negative affect: The PANAS scales. *Journal of Personality and Social Psychology, 54,* 1063–1070. http://dx.doi.org/10.1037/0022-3514.54.6.1063

Watson, D., & Tellegen, A. (1985). Toward a consensual structure of mood. *Psychological Bulletin, 98,* 219–235. http://dx.doi.org/10.1037/0033-2909.98.2.219

Watson, D., Wiese, D., Vaidya, J., & Tellegen, A. (1999). The two general activation systems of affect: Structural findings, evolutionary considerations, and psychobiological evidence. *Journal of Personality and Social Psychology, 76,* 820–838. http://dx.doi.org/10.1037/0022-3514.76.5.820

Wirtz, D., Kruger, A., Scollon, C. N., & Diener, E. (2003). What to do on spring break? The role of predicted, on-line, and remembered experience in future choice. *Psychological Science, 14,* 520–524. http://dx.doi.org/10.1111/1467-9280.03455

Zelenski, J. M., & Larsen, R. J. (2000). The distribution of basic emotions in everyday life: A state and trait perspective from experience sampling data. *Journal of Research in Personality, 34,* 178–197. http://dx.doi.org/10.1006/jrpe.1999.2275

Zuckerman, M., & Lubin, B. (1985). *Manual for the Revised Multiple Affect Adjective Check List.* San Diego, CA: Educational and Industrial Testing Service.

13

Assessing Self-Esteem

Carrie L. Wyland and Emily S. Shaffer

There are many benefits to having a positive view of the self. Those who have high self-esteem are presumed to be psychologically happy and healthy (Branden, 1994; Taylor & Brown, 1988), whereas those with low self-esteem are believed to be psychologically distressed and perhaps even depressed (Tennen & Affleck, 1993). Having high self-esteem provides benefits to those who possess it: They feel good about themselves, they are able to cope effectively with challenges and negative feedback, and they live in a social world in which they believe that people value and respect them. By contrast, people with low self-esteem see the world through a more negative filter, and their general dislike for themselves colors their perceptions of everything around them. Substantial evidence shows a link between self-esteem and depression, shyness, loneliness, and alienation, indicating that low self-esteem is aversive for those who have it.

In fact, there is evidence that self-esteem may be one of the strongest predictors of well-being. In a study of more than 13,000 university students across 31 countries, Diener and Diener (1995) found that self-esteem was one of the strongest predictors of happiness, although this relationship held stronger in individualistic cultures, compared with collectivist ones. In an extensive literature review, Baumeister, Campbell, Krueger, and Vohs (2003) noted that although low self-esteem is consistently associated with depression, it is unclear what moderators or mediators might play a role (e.g., by making stressful times more challenging or by creating a negative lens that hinders positive experiences). Further, although they concluded that the data do not indicate that

http://dx.doi.org/10.1037/0000138-013
Positive Psychological Assessment: A Handbook of Models and Measures, Second Edition,
M. W. Gallagher and S. J. Lopez (Editors)

self-esteem has a positive impact on most objective measures, including academic and career success, relationship outcomes, and antisocial behaviors, the data do predict subjective measures of well-being, such as the experience of happiness and pleasure in life. In fact, some have seen well-being measures as criteria for assessing the predictive validity of self-esteem measures (see Schimmack & Diener, 2003), reinforcing the belief that well-being and happiness are linked to high self-esteem.

Although societal ills are not caused by low self-esteem, it is easy to understand why clinicians, policymakers, and educators are consistently concerned with the emotional consequences of negative self-views. Those who perceive themselves to be socially ostracized experience a variety of negative reactions, including physical illness, emotional problems, and negative affective states. Furthermore, social support is known to be a key ingredient of mental and physical health (Cohen & Wills, 1985), and people who feel disliked may be less likely to receive support from others. Thus, even if the benefits of having high self-esteem have been exaggerated (e.g., Baumeister et al., 2003; Dawes, 1994), there is little doubt that low self-esteem is problematic for those who have it. But what exactly is self-esteem and how is it measured? This chapter examines the various ways in which self-esteem is measured and the implications that these methods have on our understanding of what it means for a person to have high or low self-esteem.

UNDERSTANDING THE CONSTRUCT OF SELF-ESTEEM

Self-esteem is the evaluative aspect of the self-concept that corresponds to an overall view of the self as worthy or unworthy (Baumeister, 1998). This is embodied in Coopersmith's (1967) classic definition of self-esteem:

> The evaluation which the individual makes and customarily maintains with regard to himself: it expresses an attitude of approval and indicates the extent to which an individual believes himself to be capable, significant, successful and worthy. In short, self-esteem is a personal judgment of the worthiness that is expressed in the attitudes the individual holds towards himself. (pp. 4–5)

In short, self-esteem is an attitude about the self and is related to personal beliefs about skills, abilities, social relationships, and future outcomes.

It is important to distinguish *self-esteem* from the more general term *self-concept* because the two terms often are used interchangeably. Self-concept refers to the totality of cognitive beliefs that people have about themselves; it is everything that is known about the self and includes things such as name, race, likes, dislikes, beliefs, values, and appearance descriptions, such as height and weight. By contrast, self-esteem is the emotional response that people experience as they contemplate and evaluate different aspects of themselves. Although self-esteem is related to self-concept, it is possible for people to believe objectively positive things (such as acknowledging skills in academics, athletics, or arts) but continue to not really like themselves. Conversely, it is possible for people to like themselves and therefore hold high self-esteem, in spite of their lacking any objective indicators that support such positive self-views.

Throughout the history of research on self-esteem, there have been concerns that the concept was poorly defined and therefore badly measured (Blascovich & Tomaka, 1991). Jackson (1984) noted that "after thirty years of intensive effort . . . what has emerged . . . is a confusion of results that defies interpretation" (p. 2). Wylie (1974), one of the chief critics of self-esteem research, blamed the area's difficulties on a lack of rigor in experimentation and a proliferation of instruments to measure self-esteem. For example, there are a large number of self-esteem instruments, and many of the scales correlate poorly with one another. Indeed, in reviewing the history of the measurement of self-esteem, Briggs and Cheek (1986) stated, "It was obvious by the mid-1970s that the status of self-esteem measurement research had become something of an embarrassment to the field of personality research" (p. 131).

How a construct is defined has obvious implications for how it is measured. In light of the fact that the term *self-esteem* is widely used in everyday language and heavily laden with social value, perhaps it should not be surprising that idiosyncratic and casual definitions have contributed to the challenge of defining and measuring self-esteem. There is not nearly enough space in this chapter to consider all of the various ways in which self-esteem has been defined, but we touch on some of the central conceptual issues that are relevant to the measure of self-esteem, including the proposed sources of self-esteem and differential views of the dimensionality and stability of self-esteem.

Sources of Self-Esteem

There are many theories about the source of self-esteem. For instance, William James (1890) argued that self-esteem developed from the accumulation of experiences in which people's outcomes exceeded their goals on some important dimension, under the general rule that self-esteem = success/pretensions. From this perspective, assessment has to examine possible discrepancies between current appraisals and personal goals and motives. Moreover, self-perceived skills that allow people to reach goals are also important to assess. Thus, measures ought to include some reference to personal beliefs about competency and ability.

Many of the most popular theories of self-esteem are based on Cooley's (1902) notion of the *looking-glass self*, in which self-appraisals are viewed as inseparable from social milieu. Mead's (1934) *symbolic interactionism* outlined a process by which people internalize ideas and attitudes expressed by significant figures in their lives. In effect, individuals come to respond to themselves in a manner consistent with the ways of those around him. Low self-esteem is likely to result when key figures reject, ignore, demean, or devalue the person. Subsequent thinking by Coopersmith (1967) and Rosenberg (1965, 1979, 1989), as well as most contemporary self-esteem research, is well in accord with the basic tenets of symbolic interactionism. According to this perspective, it is important to assess how people perceive themselves to be viewed by significant others, such as friends, classmates, and family members. Some recent theories of self-esteem have emphasized the norms and values of the cultures and societies in which people are raised. For instance, Crocker and her colleagues have argued that some people experience collective self-esteem because they are especially likely to base their self-esteem on their social identities as belonging to certain groups (Luhtanen & Crocker, 1992).

Leary, Tambor, Terdal, and Downs (1995) proposed a novel and important social account of self-esteem. Sociometer theory begins with the assumption that humans have a fundamental need to belong that is rooted in our evolutionary history and the importance of social groups for survival (Baumeister & Leary, 1995). According to sociometer theory, self-esteem functions as a monitor of the likelihood of social exclusion. When people behave in ways that increase the likelihood they will be rejected, they experience a reduction in state self-esteem. Thus, self-esteem serves as a monitor, or sociometer, of social acceptance–rejection. At the trait level, those with high self-esteem have sociometers that indicate a low probability of rejection, and therefore such individuals do not worry about how they are being perceived by others. By contrast, those with low self-esteem have sociometers that indicate the imminent possibility of rejection, and therefore they are highly motivated to manage their public impressions. An abundance of evidence supports the sociometer theory, including the finding that low self-esteem is highly correlated with social anxiety. Although the sociometer links self-esteem to an evolved need to belong rather than to symbolic interactions, it shares with the earlier theories the idea that social situations need to be examined to assess self-esteem.

Terror management theory (Greenberg, Pyszczynski, & Solomon, 1986), on the other hand, proposes that the purpose of self-esteem is to buffer or manage the existential fear or anxiety related to one's own death. From a developmental perspective, anxiety is experienced throughout the lifespan, beginning with infants who need caregivers to provide protection. As children develop, they begin to understand what is culturally valued and that living up to those cultural standards provides a buffer from anxiety (e.g., Arndt, 2012; Greenberg & Arndt, 2012). With development also comes the realization that death is inevitable. By living up to cultural standards or subscribing to a cultural worldview, one may believe that one is able to escape death by creating a legacy, for example, or even by the continuation of the soul after death. The purpose of self-esteem then, is to provide a buffer from death-related anxiety. Indeed, a large body of work supports this idea, showing that reminders of death motivate individuals to perform in ways that enhance their self-esteem, those with high self-esteem experience less anxiety related to death than do those with lower self-esteem, and threats related to self-esteem increase mortality salience (Greenberg, 2012).

Although these theories clearly differ in their focus on the roots and sources of self-esteem, overall, they all emphasize the strong drive humans have to maintain feelings of self-worth and therefore the importance of self-esteem.

Dimensionality of Self-Esteem

Self-esteem can refer to the overall self or to specific aspects of the self, such as how people feel about their social standing, racial or ethnic group, physical features, athletic skills, job or school performance, and so on. An important issue in the self-esteem literature is whether self-esteem is best conceptualized as a unitary global trait or as a multidimensional trait with independent subcomponents. According to the global approach, self-esteem is considered an overall self-attitude that permeates all aspects of people's lives.

Self-esteem also can be conceptualized as a hierarchical construct such that it can be broken down into its constituent parts. From this perspective, there are three major components: performance self-esteem, social self-esteem, and physical self-esteem (Heatherton & Polivy, 1991). *Performance self-esteem* refers to one's sense of general competence and includes intellectual abilities, school performance, self-regulatory capacities, self-confidence, efficacy, and agency. *Social self-esteem* refers to how people believe others perceive them. Note that it is perception rather than reality that is most critical. If people believe that others, especially significant others, value and respect them, they will experience high social self-esteem. This occurs even if others truly hold them in contempt. People who are low in social self-esteem often experience social anxiety and are high in public self-consciousness. They are highly attentive to their image and they worry about how others view them. Finally, *physical self-esteem* refers to how people view their physical bodies and includes such things as athletic skills, physical attractiveness, and body image, as well as physical stigmas and feelings about race and ethnicity.

How are these subcomponents of self-esteem related to global self-esteem? William James (1892) proposed that global self-esteem was the summation of specific components of self-esteem, each of which is weighted by its importance to one's self-concept. In other words, people have high self-esteem to the extent that they feel good about those things that matter to them. Not being good at tennis is irrelevant to the self-concept of the nonathlete, and doing poorly in school may have little impact on an individual who has disidentified from mainstream values (e.g.; Steele, 1997). On this point, Pelham (1995) and Marsh (1995) have debated the value of global versus specific component models. Pelham's research has generally supported the Jamesian view that the centrality of self-views is an important predictor of the emotional response to self (i.e., one's feelings of self-esteem), whereas Marsh has claimed that domain importance does not relate strongly to self-esteem. Although the jury is still out on this issue, the concept of domain importance is a central feature of most theories of self-esteem.

Stability of Self-Esteem

Another issue in the measurement and definition of self-esteem is whether it is best conceptualized as a stable personality trait or as a context-specific state. Most theories of self-esteem view it as a relatively stable trait: if you have high self-esteem today, you will probably have high self-esteem tomorrow. From this perspective, self-esteem is stable because it slowly builds over time through personal experiences, such as repeatedly succeeding at various tasks or continually being valued by significant others. A number of studies, however, suggest self-esteem serves as the dependent rather than the independent or classification variable (Wells & Marwell, 1976). These studies assume that self-esteem can be momentarily manipulated or affected.

According to some views, self-esteem can be viewed as a state as well as a trait (Heatherton & Polivy, 1991). Around a stable baseline are fluctuations: Although we might generally feel good about ourselves, there are times when we may experience self-doubt and even dislike. Fluctuations in state self-esteem are associated with increased sensitivity to and reliance on social evaluations, increased concern about how one views the self, and even anger and hostility (Kernis, 1993). Further, Paradise and Kernis (2002) showed that in addition to just high self-esteem, stability of self-esteem positively predicts positive psychological functioning. In fact, stability is one of the key ingredients in what Kernis (2003) termed "optimal" self-esteem.

INDIVIDUAL DIFFERENCE MEASURES OF SELF-ESTEEM

Given the importance attached to self-esteem by many people and the fact that it also has defied consensual definition, it is not surprising that there are many measures of self-esteem. Unfortunately, the majority of these measures have not performed adequately, and it is likely that many of them measure very different constructs because the correlations between these scales range from zero to .8, with an average of .4 (Wylie, 1974).

Some self-esteem measures are better than others. Crandall (1973) reviewed 33 self-esteem measures in detail and judged four to be superior: Rosenberg's Self-Esteem Scale (RSES; Rosenberg, 1965, 1989), the Janis–Field Feelings of Inadequacy Scale (JFS; Janis & Field, 1959), the Coopersmith Self-Esteem Inventory (Coopersmith, 1967), and the Tennessee Self-Concept Scale (Fitts, 1964). Except for the Rosenberg, which measures global self-esteem, these scales are multidimensional and measure various affective qualities of self-concept. In a test of eight measures of self-esteem (including projectives, interviews, self-report, and peer ratings), Demo (1985) found that the Rosenberg and Coopersmith scales performed best in factor analysis.

Blascovich and Tomaka's (1991) careful examination of numerous measures of self-esteem led them to conclude that no perfect measure exists and that few of the conceptual and methodological criticisms had been answered. They recommended a revision of the Janis–Field scale as one of the better measures of trait self-esteem. They noted, however, that the Rosenberg scale is the most widely used in research. We next describe both measures as well as the Single-Item Self-Esteem Scale (SISE; Robins, Hendin, & Trzesniewski, 2001) and the State Self-Esteem Scale (SSES; Heatherton & Polivy, 1991).

Revised Janis–Field Feelings of Inadequacy

The original JFS was a 23-item test developed in 1959 to be used in attitude change research (Janis & Field, 1959). This multidimensional scale measures self-regard, academic abilities, social confidence, and appearance (Fleming & Watts, 1980). The split-half reliability estimate by Janis and Field was .83, and the reliability was .91.

The items from the JFS have been modified a number of times (e.g., Fleming & Courtney, 1984; Fleming & Watts, 1980), such as changing the format of the responses (5- or 7-point scales, etc.) or adding questions for other dimensions of self-esteem, such as academic ability (Fleming & Courtney, 1984). A thorough review by Robinson and Shaver (1973) identified the JFS as one of the best for use with adults, and Blascovich and Tomaka (1991) selected the Fleming and Courtney (1984) version as one of the best measures to use. We recommend it for studies in which researchers wish to examine multiple components of self-esteem (see Appendix 13.1).

Rosenberg Self-Esteem Scale

The RSES is the most widely used measure of global self-esteem (Demo, 1985). It is a 10-item scale with high internal reliability (alpha = .92). Rosenberg (1979) reported that the scale is correlated modestly with mood measures. Carmines and Zeller (1974) identified one potential problem with the RSES; they identified separate "positive" and "negative" factors. Unfortunately, those questions that were worded in a negative direction loaded on the negative factor and those that were worded in a positive manner loaded most heavily on the positive factor, thereby suggesting a response set. Because both factors correlated almost identically with a criterion variable (in strength, direction, and consistency), however, they seem to be tapping the same general construct (Rosenberg, 1979; see the RSES in Appendix 13.2).

Single-Item Self-Esteem Scale

The SISE is a single item—"I have high self-esteem"—on a 1-to-5 Likert scale. This measure was developed as a way to measure self-esteem in research contexts that would benefit from a brief measure, such as large-scale surveys. Robins et al. (2001) found that the SISE was reliable with stability across time similar to that of the RSES ($r = .61$ for the SISE and $r = .69$) and that the SISE had high convergent validity with the RSES, ranging from $r = .71$ to $r = .80$ in adult samples. Further, the SISE and the RSES showed similar correlations with multiple criterion variables, including domain-specific evaluations, personality, psychological well-being, and academic outcomes. The researchers concluded that this overlap indicates that the SISE should yield patterns similar to those yielded by the RSES. The fact that individuals are able to accurately respond to this single item suggests that most adults may hold a well-defined schema for self-esteem.

State Self-Esteem Scale

The SSES (Heatherton & Polivy, 1991) is a commonly used measure that is sensitive to laboratory manipulations of self-esteem. The SSES consists of 20 items that tap momentary fluctuations in self-esteem. The scale (see Appendix 13.3) has acceptable internal consistency (alpha = .92), and it is responsive to temporary changes in self-evaluation (see Crocker, Cornwell, & Major, 1993). Psychometric studies show the SSES to be separable from mood (Bagozzi & Heatherton, 1994). Confirmatory factor analysis reveals that the SSES is made up of three factors: performance, social, and appearance self-esteem (Bagozzi & Heatherton, 1994). Of course, measures of trait and state self-esteem are highly correlated, and therefore in neutral settings scores on the SSES will be highly related to trait measures. The decision to use a trait or state measure of self-esteem, therefore, depends on whether one is interested in predicting long-term outcomes or in the immediate effects associated with feelings about the self.

ALTERNATIVE CONCEPTUALIZATIONS: IMPLICIT SELF-ESTEEM

The validity of explicit measures increasingly has come under challenge because, by definition, such measures rely on individuals' potentially biased capacity to accurately report their attitudes and feelings. As a result, implicit measures of attitudes, including self-esteem, attempt to tap into the unconscious, automatic aspects of self. People do not necessarily have access to their internal mental states, and therefore self-presentational motives or other beliefs may produce bias or distortion, both intended and unintended. Greenwald and Banaji (1995) defined *implicit self-esteem* as "the introspectively unidentified (or inaccurately identified) effect of the self-attitude on evaluation of self-associated and self-dissociated object" (p. 10), though recently the concept has been defined more broadly as a "global self-evaluation that people are unable or unwilling to report" (Buhrmester, Blanton, & Swann, 2011, p. 366). A variety of evidence supports the idea of implicit positive attitudes about the self. For instance, people show a positive bias for information about the self, such as preferring their own initials (Koole, Dijksterhuis, & van Knippenberg, 2001) and preferring members of their in-group more than those from an out-group, even when the groups are determined arbitrarily (Greenwald & Banaji, 1995). In essence, anything associated with the self is generally viewed as being especially positive.

A number of different methods have been developed or adapted to assess implicit self-esteem (Bosson, Swann, & Pennebaker, 2000), such as subliminal priming tasks (e.g., Spalding & Hardin, 1999) and the Stroop task (Stroop, 1935); however, the most widely known and used are the Implicit Association Test (IAT; Greenwald, McGhee, & Schwartz, 1998) and the Name-Letter Test (NLT; Greenwald & Banaji, 1995; Nuttin, 1987). It has been suggested that the latter two methods have received the most use as a result of the findings of Bosson and colleagues (2000) showing that the IAT and NLT were the most reliable measures of implicit self-esteem (Buhrmester et al., 2011).

The IAT involves making paired-word associations; when used to measure self-esteem, the distinctions are between self-related words, such as *me*, and other-related words, such as *your*, and between pleasant words, such as *sunshine*, and unpleasant ones, such as *death*. Self-esteem is a function of difference between the reaction time to make self-pleasant (and other-unpleasant) associations and the reaction time to make self-unpleasant (and other-pleasant) associations. The NLT asks participants to rate each letter of the alphabet, and scores are computed by comparing a participant's ratings of their own initials with the average rating of those same letters given by other participants without those letters as initials. It is reasoned that participants who rate the letters in their own name more positively than they rate the letters in the names of other participants have higher implicit self-esteem as a result of the tendency for individuals to like objects associated with themselves (Greenwald & Banaji, 1995).

Though research has consistently shown that implicit self-esteem is a construct independent from explicit self-esteem (e.g., Bosson et al., 2000; Greenwald & Farnham, 2000), there is some concern over the reliability and validity of implicit measures. Buhrmester and colleagues (2011) posited that the finding that test–retest correlations for implicit self-esteem were lower than those for explicit self-esteem, together with the sensitivity of implicit self-esteem to manipulations within the laboratory, indicates that results of these tests may be tapping into state versus trait self-esteem. In addition, their meta-analysis showed that scores on the IAT were unrelated to outcomes typically associated with explicit self-esteem, such as well-being and physical health, though the relation between the NLT and these variables was stronger. Convergent validity between the IAT and NLT was also quite low. However, as noted by Banaji (1999), low convergent validity between implicit self-esteem measures may simply suggest that the construct is a complex one.

As noted earlier, the shift toward measures of implicit self-esteem from those of explicit self-esteem was due in part to self-presentational biases that may influence explicit measures. However, implicit associations regarding self-esteem may not be as inaccessible or nonconscious as previously thought. If individuals do not have insight into their implicit associations, it would be expected that measures of implicit and explicit self-esteem should remain relatively uncorrelated. However, Olson, Fazio, and Hermann (2007) showed that merely prompting participants to respond honestly and to avoid overpresenting themselves on measures of explicit self-esteem resulted in higher correlations between implicit and explicit measures. Furthermore, depending on one's definition of self-esteem—of which there are many—eliminating the self-reflection may call into question whether implicit measures of self-esteem are truly a measure of self-esteem (Buhrmester et al., 2011).

FUTURE DEVELOPMENTS

Despite the popularity of the self-esteem construct and its potential value to understanding the positive aspects of human nature, the measurement of self-esteem does pose some interesting problems for researchers. A major problem inherent in the measure of self-esteem is the extent to which self-reports are influenced by self-presentational concerns. One strategy to combat this might be to use measures of defensiveness or social desirability to tease out the variance associated with self-report biases. Although some researchers have pursued this approach, no single method has established itself to be empirically useful. Further, it is unclear how implicit measures may overcome potential biases inherent to explicit measures; although these newer measures are theoretically promising, their utility is still unclear, specifically due to uncertainty in regard to their validity. At minimum, research on implicit self-esteem has forced researchers to reflect on what exactly a good measure of self-esteem ought to predict in terms of behavioral or cognitive outcomes. This reassessment of the basic definitional issues related to the construct of self-esteem will be important as researchers continue to explore not just issues of measurement but also the underlying nature of self-esteem.

APPENDIX 13.1
REVISED JANIS–FIELD SCALE

Each item is scored on a scale from 1 to 5 using sets of terms such as *"very often, fairly often," "sometimes," "once in a great while,"* and *"practically never"* or *"very confident," "fairly confident," "slightly confident," "not very confident,"* and *"not at all confident."* Most items are reverse-scored so that a high self-esteem response leads to higher scores. Items with (R) are not reverse-scored. Some researchers use 7-point scales with different anchors, depending on the wording of the item.

1. How often do you feel inferior to most of the people you know?
2. How often do you have the feeling that there is nothing you can do well?
3. When in a group of people, do you have trouble thinking of the right things to talk about?
4. How often do you feel worried or bothered about what other people think of you?
5. In turning in a major assignment such as a term paper, how often do you feel you did an excellent job on it? (R)
6. How confident are you that others see you as being physically appealing? (R)
7. Do you ever think that you are a worthless individual?
8. How much do you worry about how well you get along with other people?
9. When you make an embarrassing mistake or have done something that makes you look foolish, how long does it take you to get over it?

10. When you have to read an essay and understand it for a class assignment, how worried or concerned do you feel about it?
11. Compared with classmates, how often do you feel you must study more than they do to get the same grades?
12. Have you ever thought of yourself as physically uncoordinated?
13. How confident do you feel that someday the people you know will look up to you and respect you? (R)
14. How often do you worry about criticisms that might be made of your work by your teacher or employer?
15. Do you often feel uncomfortable meeting new people?
16. When you have to write an argument to convince your teacher, who may disagree with your ideas, how concerned or worried do you feel about it?
17. Have you ever felt ashamed of your physique or figure?
18. Have you ever felt inferior to most other people in athletic ability?
19. Do you ever feel so discouraged with yourself that you wonder whether you are a worthwhile person?
20. Do you ever feel afraid or anxious when you are going into a room by yourself where other people have already gathered and are talking?
21. How often do you worry whether other people like to be with you?
22. How often do you have trouble expressing your ideas when you have to put them into writing as an assignment?
23. Do you often feel that most of your friends or peers are more physically attractive than yourself?
24. When involved in sports requiring physical coordination, are you often concerned that you will not do well?
25. How often do you dislike yourself?
26. How often do you feel self-conscious?
27. How often are you troubled with shyness?
28. How often do you have trouble understanding things you read for class assignments?
29. Do you often wish or fantasize that you were better looking?
30. Have you ever thought that you lacked the ability to be a good dancer or do well at recreational activities involving coordination?
31. In general, how confident do you feel about your abilities? (R)

32. How much do you worry about whether other people regard you as a success or failure in your job or at school?

33. When you think that some of the people you meet might have an unfavorable opinion of you, how concerned or worried do you feel about it?

34. How often do you imagine that you have less scholastic ability than your classmates?

35. Have you ever been concerned or worried about your ability to attract members of the opposite sex?

36. When trying to do well at a sport and you know other people are watching, how rattled or flustered do you get?

Note. Adapted from "The Dimensionality of Self-Esteem: II. Hierarchical Facet Model for Revised Measurement Scales," by J. S. Fleming and B. E. Courtney, 1984, *Journal of Personality and Social Psychology, 46,* pp. 412–413.

APPENDIX 13.2
ROSENBERG SELF-ESTEEM SCALE

3	2	1	0
strongly agree	*agree*	*disagree*	*strongly disagree*

1. I feel that I am a person of worth, at least on an equal plane with others.
2. I feel that I have a number of good qualities.
3. All in all, I am inclined to feel that I am a failure. (R)
4. I am able to do things as well as most people.
5. I feel I do not have much to be proud of. (R)
6. I take a positive attitude toward myself.
7. On the whole, I am satisfied with myself.
8. I wish I could have more respect for myself. (R)
9. I certainly feel useless at times. (R)
10. At times I think that I am no good at all. (R)

For the items marked with an (R), reverse the scoring (0 = 3, 1 = 2, 2 = 1, 3 = 0). For those items without an (R) next to them, simply add the score. Add the scores. Typical scores on the Rosenberg scale are around 22, with most people scoring between 15 and 25.

Note. From *Society and the Adolescent Self-Image* (Rev. ed., pp. 305–307), by M. Rosenberg, 1989, Middletown, CT: Wesleyan University Press.

APPENDIX 13.3
CURRENT THOUGHTS

This is a questionnaire designed to measure what you are thinking at this moment. There is, of course, no right answer for any statement. The best answer is what you feel is true of yourself at this moment. Be sure to answer all of the items, even if you are not certain of the best answer. Again, answer these questions as they are true for you RIGHT NOW.

1 = *not at all* 2 = *a little bit* 3 = *somewhat* 4 = *very much* 5 = *extremely*

1. I feel confident about my abilities.
2. I am worried about whether I am regarded as a success or failure. (R)
3. I feel satisfied with the way my body looks right now.
4. I feel frustrated or rattled about my performance. (R)
5. I feel that I am having trouble understanding things that I read. (R)
6. I feel that others respect and admire me.
7. I am dissatisfied with my weight. (R)
8. I feel self-conscious. (R)
9. I feel as smart as others.
10. I feel displeased with myself. (R)
11. I feel good about myself.
12. I am pleased with my appearance right now.
13. I am worried about what other people think of me. (R)
14. I feel confident that I understand things.
15. I feel inferior to others at this moment. (R)
16. I feel unattractive. (R)
17. I feel concerned about the impression I am making. (R)
18. I feel that I have less scholastic ability right now than others. (R)
19. I feel like I'm not doing well. (R)
20. I am worried about looking foolish. (R)

Note. (R) indicates reverse scoring. Adapted from "Development and Validation of a Scale for Measuring State Self-Esteem," by T. F. Heatherton and J. Polivy, 1991, *Journal of Personality and Social Psychology, 60,* pp. 898. Copyright 1991 by the American Psychological Association.

REFERENCES

Arndt, J. (2012). A significant contributor to a meaningful cultural drama: Terror management research on the functions and implications of self-esteem. In P. R. Shaver & M. Mikulincer (Eds.), *Meaning, mortality, and choice: The social psychology of existential concerns* (pp. 55–73). Washington, DC: American Psychological Association. http://dx.doi.org/10.1037/13748-003

Bagozzi, R. P., & Heatherton, T. F. (1994). A general approach to representing multifaceted personality constructs: Application to state self-esteem. *Structural Equation Modeling, 1,* 35–67. http://dx.doi.org/10.1080/10705519409539961

Banaji, M. R. (1999, June). *Implicit attitudes can be measured.* Paper presented at the Society for Personality and Social Psychology Preconference of the 11th Annual Convention of the American Psychological Society, Denver, CO.

Baumeister, R. F. (1998). The self. In D. Gilbert, S. Fiske, & G. Lindzey (Eds.), *The handbook of social psychology* (Vol. 1, pp. 680–740). New York, NY: Oxford University Press.

Baumeister, R. F., Campbell, J. D., Krueger, J. I., & Vohs, K. D. (2003). Does high self-esteem cause better performance, interpersonal success, happiness, or healthier lifestyles? *Psychological Science in the Public Interest, 4,* 1–44. http://dx.doi.org/10.1111/1529-1006.01431

Baumeister, R. F., & Leary, M. R. (1995). The need to belong: Desire for interpersonal attachments as a fundamental human motivation. *Psychological Bulletin, 117,* 497–529. http://dx.doi.org/10.1037/0033-2909.117.3.497

Blascovich, J., & Tomaka, J. (1991). Measures of self-esteem. In J. P. Robinson & P. R. Shaver (Eds.), *Measures of personality and social psychological attitudes* (pp. 115–160). San Diego, CA: Academic Press. http://dx.doi.org/10.1016/B978-0-12-590241-0.50008-3

Bosson, J. K., Swann, W. B., Jr., & Pennebaker, J. W. (2000). Stalking the perfect measure of implicit self-esteem: The blind men and the elephant revisited? *Journal of Personality and Social Psychology, 79,* 631–643. http://dx.doi.org/10.1037/0022-3514.79.4.631

Branden, N. (1994). *The six pillars of self-esteem.* New York, NY: Bantam Books.

Briggs, S. R., & Cheek, J. M. (1986). The role of factor analysis in the development and evaluation of personality scales. *Journal of Personality, 54,* 106–148. http://dx.doi.org/10.1111/j.1467-6494.1986.tb00391.x

Buhrmester, M. D., Blanton, H., & Swann, W. B., Jr. (2011). Implicit self-esteem: Nature, measurement, and a new way forward. *Journal of Personality and Social Psychology, 100*(2), 365–385. http://dx.doi.org/10.1037/a0021341

Carmines, E. G., & Zeller, R. A. (1974). On establishing the empirical dimensionality of theoretical terms: An analytical example. *Political Methodology, 1*(4), 75–96. https://www.jstor.org/stable/25791395

Cohen, S., & Wills, T. A. (1985). Stress, social support, and the buffering hypothesis. *Psychological Bulletin, 98,* 310–357. http://dx.doi.org/10.1037/0033-2909.98.2.310

Cooley, C. H. (1902). *Human nature and social order.* New York, NY: Charles Scribner & Sons.

Coopersmith, S. (1967). *The antecedents of self-esteem.* San Francisco, CA: Freeman.

Crandall, R. (1973). The measurement of self-esteem and related constructs. In J. P. Robinson & P. Shaver (Eds.), *Measurements of social psychological attitudes* (pp. 45–167). Ann Arbor, MI: Institute for Social Research.

Crocker, J., Cornwell, B., & Major, B. (1993). The stigma of overweight: Affective consequences of attributional ambiguity. *Journal of Personality and Social Psychology, 64,* 60–70. http://dx.doi.org/10.1037/0022-3514.64.1.60

Dawes, R. (1994). Psychological measurement. *Psychological Review, 101,* 278–281. http://dx.doi.org/10.1037/0033-295X.101.2.278

Demo, D. H. (1985). The measurement of self-esteem: Refining our methods. *Journal of Personality and Social Psychology, 48,* 1490–1502. http://dx.doi.org/10.1037/0022-3514.48.6.1490

Diener, E., & Diener, M. (1995). Cross-cultural correlates of life satisfaction and self-esteem. *Journal of Personality and Social Psychology, 68,* 653–663. http://dx.doi.org/10.1037/0022-3514.68.4.653

Fitts, W. H. (1964). *Tennessee Self-Concept Scale.* Los Angeles, CA: Western Psychological Services.

Fleming, J. S., & Courtney, B. E. (1984). The dimensionality of self-esteem: II. Hierarchical facet model for revised measurement scales. *Journal of Personality and Social Psychology, 46,* 404–421. http://dx.doi.org/10.1037/0022-3514.46.2.404

Fleming, J. S., & Watts, W. A. (1980). The dimensionality of self-esteem: Some results for a college sample. *Journal of Personality and Social Psychology, 39,* 921–929. http://dx.doi.org/10.1037/0022-3514.39.5.921

Greenberg, J. (2012). Terror management theory: From genesis to revelations. In P. R. Shaver & M. Mikulincer (Eds.), *Meaning, mortality, and choice: The social psychology of existential concerns* (pp. 17–35). Washington, DC: American Psychological Association. http://dx.doi.org/10.1037/13748-001

Greenberg, J., & Arndt, J. (2012). Terror management theory. In A. W. Kruglanski, E. T. Higgins, & P. A. M. van Lange (Eds.), *Handbook of theories of social psychology* (Vol. 1, pp. 398–415). Thousand Oaks, CA: Sage.

Greenberg, J., Pyszczynski, T., & Solomon, S. (1986). The causes and consequences of a need for self-esteem: A terror management theory. In R. F. Baumeister (Ed.), *Public self and private self* (pp. 189–212). New York, NY: Springer-Verlag. http://dx.doi.org/10.1007/978-1-4613-9564-5_10

Greenwald, A. G., & Banaji, M. R. (1995). Implicit social cognition: Attitudes, self-esteem, and stereotypes. *Psychological Review, 102,* 4–27. http://dx.doi.org/10.1037/0033-295X.102.1.4

Greenwald, A. G., & Farnham, S. D. (2000). Using the implicit association test to measure self-esteem and self-concept. *Journal of Personality and Social Psychology, 79,* 1022–1038. http://dx.doi.org/10.1037/0022-3514.79.6.1022

Greenwald, A. G., McGhee, D. E., & Schwartz, J. L. (1998). Measuring individual differences in implicit cognition: The implicit association test. *Journal of Personality and Social Psychology, 74,* 1464–1480. http://dx.doi.org/10.1037/0022-3514.74.6.1464

Heatherton, T. F., & Polivy, J. (1991). Development and validation of a scale for measuring state self-esteem. *Journal of Personality and Social Psychology, 60,* 895–910. http://dx.doi.org/10.1037/0022-3514.60.6.895

Jackson, M. R. (1984). *Self-esteem and meaning.* Albany: State University of New York Press.

James, W. (1890). *Principles of psychology* (Vol. 1). New York, NY: Henry Holt.

James, W. (1892). *Psychology: The briefer course.* New York, NY: Henry Holt. http://dx.doi.org/10.1037/11060-000

Janis, I. L., & Field, P. B. (1959). Sex differences and factors related to persuasibility. In C. I. Hovland & I. L. Janis (Eds.), *Personality and persuasibility* (pp. 55–68). New Haven, CT: Yale University Press.

Kernis, M. H. (1993). The roles of stability and level of self-esteem in psychological functioning. In R. F. Baumeister (Ed.), *Self-esteem: The puzzle of low self-regard* (pp. 167–182). New York, NY: Plenum Press. http://dx.doi.org/10.1007/978-1-4684-8956-9_9

Kernis, M. H. (2003). Toward a conceptualization of optimal self-esteem. *Psychological Inquiry, 14,* 1–26. http://dx.doi.org/10.1207/S15327965PLI1401_01

Koole, S. L., Dijksterhuis, A., & van Knippenberg, A. (2001). What's in a name: Implicit self-esteem and the automatic self. *Journal of Personality and Social Psychology, 80,* 669–685. http://dx.doi.org/10.1037/0022-3514.80.4.669

Leary, M. R., Tambor, E. S., Terdal, S. K., & Downs, D. L. (1995). Self-esteem as an interpersonal monitor: The sociometer hypothesis. *Journal of Personality and Social Psychology, 68,* 518–530. http://dx.doi.org/10.1037/0022-3514.68.3.518

Luhtanen, R., & Crocker, J. (1992). A collective self-esteem scale: Self-evaluation of one's social identity. *Personality and Social Psychology Bulletin, 18,* 302–318. http://dx.doi.org/10.1177/0146167292183006

Marsh, H. W. (1995). A Jamesian model of self-investment and self-esteem: Comment on Pelham. *Journal of Personality and Social Psychology, 69,* 1151–1160. http://dx.doi.org/10.1037/0022-3514.69.6.1151

Mead, G. H. (1934). *Mind, self, and society.* Chicago, IL: University of Chicago Press.

Nuttin, J. (1987). Affective consequences of mere ownership: The name letter effect in twelve European languages. *European Journal of Social Psychology, 17,* 381–402. http://dx.doi.org/10.1002/ejsp.2420170402

Olson, M. A., Fazio, R. H., & Hermann, A. D. (2007). Reporting tendencies underlie discrepancies between implicit and explicit measures of self-esteem. *Psychological Science, 18,* 287–291. http://dx.doi.org/10.1111/j.1467-9280.2007.01890.x

Paradise, A. W., & Kernis, M. H. (2002). Self-esteem and psychological well-being: Implications of fragile self-esteem. *Journal of Social and Clinical Psychology, 21,* 345–361. http://dx.doi.org/10.1521/jscp.21.4.345.22598

Pelham, B. W. (1995). Self-investment and self-esteem: Evidence for a Jamesian model of selfworth. *Journal of Personality and Social Psychology, 69,* 1141–1150. http://dx.doi.org/10.1037/0022-3514.69.6.1141

Robins, R. W., Hendin, H. M., & Trzesniewski, K. H. (2001). Measuring global self-esteem: Construct validation of a single-item measure and the Rosenberg Self-esteem Scale. *Personality and Social Psychology Bulletin, 27,* 151–161. http://dx.doi.org/10.1177/0146167201272002

Robinson, J., & Shaver, P. R. (1973). *Measures of social psychological attitudes.* Ann Arbor, MI: Institute for Social Research.

Rosenberg, M. (1965). *Society and the adolescent self-image.* Princeton, NJ: Princeton University Press. http://dx.doi.org/10.1515/9781400876136

Rosenberg, M. (1979). *Conceiving the self.* New York, NY: Basic Books.

Rosenberg, M. (1989). *Society and the adolescent self-image* (Rev. ed.). Middletown, CT: Wesleyan University Press.

Schimmack, U., & Diener, E. (2003). Predictive validity of implicit and explicit self-esteem for subjective well-being. *Journal of Research in Personality, 37,* 100–106. http://dx.doi.org/10.1016/S0092-6566(02)00532-9

Spalding, L. R., & Hardin, C. D. (1999). Unconscious unease and self-handicapping: Behavioral consequences of individual differences in implicit and explicit self-esteem. *Psychological Science, 10,* 535–539. http://dx.doi.org/10.1111/1467-9280.00202

Steele, C. M. (1997). Race and the schooling of Black Americans. In L. A. Peplau & S. E. Taylor (Eds.), *Sociocultural perspectives in social psychology: Current readings* (pp. 359–371). Upper Saddle River, NJ: Prentice-Hall.

Stroop, J. R. (1935). Studies of interference in serial verbal reactions. *Journal of Experimental Psychology, 18,* 643–662. http://dx.doi.org/10.1037/h0054651

Taylor, S. E., & Brown, J. D. (1988). Illusion and well-being: A social psychological perspective on mental health. *Psychological Bulletin, 103,* 193–210. http://dx.doi.org/10.1037/0033-2909.103.2.193

Tennen, H., & Affleck, G. (1993). The puzzles of self-esteem: A clinical perspective. In R. F. Baumeister (Ed.), *Self-esteem: The puzzle of low self-regard* (pp. 241–262). New York, NY: Plenum Press. http://dx.doi.org/10.1007/978-1-4684-8956-9_13

Wells, L. E., & Marwell, G. (1976). *Self-esteem: Its conceptualization and measurement.* Beverly Hills, CA: Sage.

Wylie, R. C. (1974). *The self-concept: A review of methodological considerations and measuring instruments.* Lincoln: University of Nebraska Press.

14

Measuring Love

Susan S. Hendrick and Clyde Hendrick

Love is a central characteristic of positive psychology, and it is linked in a dynamic system with other core concepts. As Seligman and Csikszentmihalyi (2000) noted, positive psychology is concerned with "valued subjective experiences: well-being, contentment, and satisfaction . . . flow and happiness . . . the capacity for love and vocation" (p. 5). Love is centrally important to human society. Although this chapter focuses primarily on the measurement of romantic love, we recognize the importance of all forms of love.

We initially discuss historical conceptions of love and love as a societal construction shaped and nuanced by historical period and prevailing culture. We consider love as a primary emotion, an evolutionary imperative, and exemplified most clearly in its romantic form as passionate love and in the corollary of companionate love. We review briefly several psychological conceptions and measures of love. Finally, we mention selected future directions in the study of love.

HISTORICAL CONSIDERATIONS

Philosopher Irving Singer's (e.g., 1984) comprehensive history of love proposed four primary conceptual traditions: *Eros* (the search for the beautiful), *Philia* (love in friendship), *Nomos* (submission and obedience), and *Agape* (bestowal of love by the divine). Such conceptual–philosophical perspectives

http://dx.doi.org/10.1037/0000138-014
Positive Psychological Assessment: A Handbook of Models and Measures, Second Edition,
M. W. Gallagher and S. J. Lopez (Editors)

on love generally take little note that romantic love developed only in recent centuries as an accompaniment to marriage by choice (Gadlin, 1977). Until people developed a sense of a unique "self" that was capable of loving another self, romantic love was perhaps less common than it is today (S. S. Hendrick & Hendrick, 1992). Other scholars, however, view romantic love as existing in all cultures and across all historical periods (Hatfield & Rapson, 1996). Indeed, Cho and Cross (1995) found that both passionate love and free mate choice dated back several thousand years in Chinese literature. Doherty, Hatfield, Thompson, and Choo (1994) compared Japanese American, European American, and Pacific Islander residents of Hawaii and found them to be similar in both passionate and companionate love.

Although there may well be universal aspects to love, the impact of culture and historical period is undeniable. Sprecher and colleagues (1994) compared Russian, Japanese, and American approaches to romantic love, finding both similarities and differences. Furthermore, cultural norms, such as individual mate selection versus arranged marriages, may accompany other cultural differences in love and romantic beliefs (deMunck, 1998). Therefore, even though love may be a cultural universal, it is expressed differently depending on culture and historical era.

APPROACHES TO LOVE

As noted, the emotion of love has many manifestations, including romantic love. Indeed, Shaver, Morgan, and Wu (1996) argued convincingly that love should be considered a "basic emotion," one that is fundamental to all the more complex and nuanced emotions. Shaver et al. noted that emotions are trait-like but also have state-like or "surge" qualities that reflect"moments when we feel especially in-love or loving" (p. 86).

> What all love surges have in common, however, is that they move the person toward proximity, touch, and openness to intimacy. These common behavioral tendencies . . . cause people in many different cultures to use the same term, "love," for all such instances. (Shaver et al., 1996, p. 93)

Whether love is a primary emotion or not, it should be considered fundamental and foundational to human experience. Consistent with the perspective on the centrality of love, Baumeister and Leary (1995) described the fundamental need to belong as a need for attachment and connection that is part of our evolutionary heritage.

It is likely that there is a bonding phenomenon in primates that is designed to facilitate effective mating, infant survival, and group defense (e.g., Hrdy, 2009). That bonding is expressed in human experience as the emotion we call *love*. Thus, the romantic–partnered love elaborated in this chapter is rooted in the emotions and behaviors that sustain our very survival. This latter statement may sound dramatic, but love is dramatic—at least in some forms. Drama is, in fact, one differentiating characteristic between types or styles of love, and this point is clearly drawn in the contrast between passionate and companionate love.

Passionate and Companionate Love

Ancient Chinese, Egyptian, Hebrew, and other writings contain evocative descriptions of passionate sentiments. The social scientific categorization of romantic love into passionate and companionate forms, however, is relatively recent. Berscheid and Walster (1978) organized love into the primary categories of *passionate love* (the intense arousal that fuels the beginning of a romantic union) and *companionate love* (the steady, quiet, glowing embers that sustain a relationship over time). These were conceptualized as two "stages" of love, with passionate love blazing brightly and consuming itself but only in some cases ripening into companionate love. We have referred to this perspective as the "either/or theory of love" (S. S. Hendrick & Hendrick, 2000, p. 204).

Hatfield (1988) envisioned passionate and companionate love as simultaneous rather than necessarily sequential, noting that people "are *capable* [emphasis in original] of passionate/companionate love and are likely to experience such feelings intermittently throughout their lives" (p. 193). In support of this perspective, we (S. S. Hendrick & Hendrick, 1993) found that friendship love was the most frequent theme in respondents' written accounts of their romantic relationships. In addition, nearly half of college students named their romantic partners as their closest friend. Thus, even in the early stages of their relationships, when passion was presumably high, respondents highlighted the friendship aspects of their love. So, both passion and companionship coexist in many (perhaps most?) romantic, partnered relationships.

This dual perspective on passion and friendship has informed considerable research and has strong empirical underpinnings (e.g., C. Hendrick & Hendrick, 1989). It is unlikely, however, that current romantic relationships can be conceptualized in terms of just two love orientations. We consider next a multidimensional approach that offers six different orientations to or "styles" of love.

The Love Styles

Sociologist John Alan Lee (1973) used the metaphor of a color wheel to develop his conception of love as available in different and equally beautiful colors—similar to colors on a color wheel. Lee developed these styles from extensive research using varied methods. Out of this research came Lee's concept of six love styles, described subsequently as ideal types. It is expected that no person matches the ideal and that most people have some of each love style in their love profile.

Eros is intense, passionate love. The erotic lover prefers specific physical attributes in a partner, becomes involved quickly, wants to communicate and "know" the loved one on all levels, and is both self-confident and willing to make a commitment. *Ludus* is love played as a game. The ludic lover wants love to be a pleasant pastime for everyone involved, may "balance" several love relationships at the same time, and avoids emotional intensity and commitment. *Storge* is love based in friendship, much like the companionate love discussed previously. A storgic lover wants a steady, secure, and comfortable relationship with a love partner who has similar attitudes and values and who can be both lover and "best friend." *Pragma* is a love that "goes shopping" for an appropriate partner. A pragmatic lover wants to make a good match and thus might seek help from a computer dating site. *Mania* is a love characterized by emotional ups and downs. A manic lover is obsessive, dependent, and insecure (the downside) and supportive, loving, and devoted to the partner (the upside). *Agape* is a spiritual love that reflects selflessness and altruism. The agapic lover is concerned for the partner's welfare, solicitous of the partner's needs, and relatively undemanding. Some degree of agapic qualities may be necessary if a relationship is to endure successfully (for fuller descriptions, see S. S. Hendrick & Hendrick, 1992).

These six love styles offer a broader set of options for conceptualizing romantic love than was previously available, and they provide the basis for one of the measures of love discussed in the next section.

MEASUREMENT OF LOVE

As noted, there are several approaches to the study of love, each with its own approach to measurement. We consider that statistical measurement of love began with Rubin's (1970) attempt to measure and distinguish between liking and loving. Rubin developed two 13-item rating scales to measure liking and loving, and these scales were used widely. Kelley (1983) pointed out that the liking scale appeared to measure respect, and the love scale appeared to measure the concepts of needing, caring, trust, and tolerance. Experimental work confirmed these four constructs in Rubin's love scale (Steck, Levitan, McLane, & Kelley, 1982).

The complexity discovered in Rubin's (1970) scale also characterizes most of the subsequent love measures. Love is a complicated concept, and thus measurement instruments are often multidimensional. For example, two love scales commonly used, the Love Attitudes Scale (LAS; C. Hendrick & Hendrick, 1986) and the Passionate Love Scale (PLS; Hatfield & Sprecher, 1986) differ widely; the PLS measures the single construct of passionate erotic love, whereas the LAS measures five other constructs in addition to passionate love. We first consider these two different approaches to the measurement of love and then review additional scales.

Love Attitudes Scale

The LAS was developed as a rating measure of Lee's (1973) six love styles. Lee's approach was a typology measured qualitatively. Our quantitative approach construed the love styles as six variables. On the basis of initial measurement work by Lasswell and Lasswell (1976), we developed 42 items to measure the six constructs of *Eros*, *Ludus*, *Storge*, *Pragma*, *Mania*, and *Agape* (C. Hendrick & Hendrick, 1986). Six factors, representing the six love constructs, were extracted from the items, accounting for nearly 45% of the variance. Each factor comprised a scale, with alphas ranging from .69 for *Storge* to .83 for *Agape* and test–retest reliabilities ranging from .70 for *Mania* to .82 for *Ludus* (based on a 4- to 6-week interval; see C. Hendrick & Hendrick, 1986, for more details). With the variable approach, each person obtains six scores on the LAS that can be correlated with relevant relationship and personality constructs.

Many researchers used the LAS, sometimes dropping items from each subscale to create an even briefer total scale. Thus, we decided to develop our own brief LAS. Examining several of our large data collections, we selected the best four items from each of the six scales, thereby creating a 24-item short form of the LAS (C. Hendrick, Hendrick, & Dicke, 1998). The psychometrics on the four-item subscales were excellent, in some cases superior to the seven-item subscales. Coefficient alphas ranged from .75 for *Mania* to .88 for *Agape* and test–retest correlations from .63 for *Pragma* to .76 for *Storge* (an approximately 7-week interval).

The LAS and its briefer version have been used by many researchers and translated into several languages. One version was used in an interesting way in which a scale measuring satisfaction with one's love life was used with a cross-section of adults ranging from young adults to much older adults. Some differences and many similarities were shown across the different age groups in terms of positive correlations between particular love attitudes and satisfaction with one's love life (Neto & da Conceicao Pinto, 2015).

Passionate Love Scale

Hatfield and Sprecher (1986), construing passionate love as an intense longing for union with another specific person, developed a 30-item PLS to tap cognitive and emotional components of this longing. The authors also validated a 15-item PLS with half the original items. The PLS was exceptionally well-constructed. It factored as a unidimensional scale with coefficient alphas of .94 for the 30-item version and .91 for the 15-item version. Hatfield and Rapson (1987) reviewed data supporting the validity of the PLS. They made a powerful case that passionate love occurs across cultures and even in children before puberty. Furthermore, passionate love appears to have existed from the beginning of recorded history. The authors suggested that the experience of passionate love is a human universal.

Independent research supports the quality and validity of the PLS (e.g., C. Hendrick & Hendrick, 1989). It is used widely and in a variety of ways. Van Steenbergen, Langeslag, Band, and Hommel (2014) assessed people who were in a new love relationship. Passionate love (as measured by the PLS) was correlated with reduced cognitive control efficiency. Thus, passionate love clearly is a powerful force. Good measurement of passionate love is necessary for the study of romantic love. Because there appear to be types of romantic love other than passion (or *Eros*), however, numerous other scales have been developed.

Triangular Theory of Love

Sternberg (1986) proposed that romantic love is a mix of three components: passion, intimacy, and commitment. Various mixes (or even absence) of the three components yield eight kinds of love ranging from nonlove (absence of all three components) to consummate love (full combination of all three components). This theory is elegant and simple; many implications can be derived from it. Sternberg (1997) reported an extensive validation study of an early version of the scale, including the revision of several items. The study found that three orthogonal factors fit the data. These factors were best interpreted as representing passion, intimacy, and commitment. Even with the revised scale, however, subscale correlations remained quite high (ranging from .46 to .73). More recently, a shorter version of Sternberg's scale was used with adolescents and adults. Some age and gender differences were found (as is typical in such research), and the measure had acceptable psychometric properties (Sumter, Valkenburg, & Peter, 2013).

Prototype Theory

The prototype approach involves finding a representation or "best case" of a particular entity. In numerous studies, Beverly Fehr (e.g., 1988) developed a prototype theory of love, using various measurement devices. Research participants typically listed types of love, resulting in about 15 types (e.g., friendship, sexual, mother, romantic). In other studies, participants listed attributes for each kind of love (e.g., candlelight dinners, taking walks, caring). Still other studies required ratings of these attributes on characteristics such as similarity, importance, and agreement. Fehr's research found that companionate love was more prototypical of love than passion (e.g., Fehr, 1988). Regan, Kocan, and Whitlock (1998) had one group list features of romantic love and another group rate the centrality of those features. Sexual attraction and passion were indeed on the list of features; however, these features ranked well below other features such as trust, honesty, and happiness. One would expect that for romantic love, passionate features would rank highest, but results showed otherwise. A. Aron and Westbay (1996) factor-analyzed all 68 features originally used by Fehr (1988). They identified three underlying dimensions of passion, intimacy, and commitment; moreover, they found that the features on the intimacy factor were rated as more central to love than features on the other two factors.

A. Aron and Westbay's (1996) research on the prototype perspective suggests a convergence between Fehr's (1988) work and Sternberg's (1986) triangular theory. The approaches of Fehr and Sternberg differ widely in concepts and even more so in methods. Thus, the convergence found by A. Aron and Westbay is all the more interesting.

Self-Expansion Theory

On the basis of a metaphor from Eastern traditions, A. Aron and Aron (1986) proposed that humans have a basic motivation to expand the self. "The idea is that the self expands toward knowing or becoming that which includes everything and everyone, the Self. The steps along the way are ones of including one person or thing, then another, then still another" (E. N. Aron & Aron, 1996, pp. 45–46). Romantic love derives from the basic motivation for self-expansion and the reciprocal inclusion of other in self and, usually, self in other.

Research using the self-expansion metaphor has been fruitful. A variety of measures has been used, including free descriptions, self-efficacy ratings, and various types of questionnaires. An interesting approach to scaling was developed by A. Aron, Aron, and Smollan (1992), who had people rate a relationship by the degree of overlap of two circles representing the two persons in the relationship. This scale—the Inclusion of Other in Self scale—is an effective measure of closeness, and it at least equals and often surpasses more traditional questionnaires in psychometric properties. Additional research found that self-expansion is related to passionate love (Sheets, 2014). Self-expansion theory appears to have a prosperous future and, in fact, has been used to study intergroup relations (Davies & Aron, 2016).

Attachment Processes

Bowlby (1969) developed attachment theory in studying mother–infant relationships. He noted three types of infant attachment: secure, anxious, and avoidant. Hazan and Shaver (1987) extended attachment theory to adult romantic relationships. The literature on attachment is massive, and just the literature on self-report scales for adult romantic attachment is now voluminous. An excellent summary of the many issues involved in adult attachment measures is given in Crowell, Fraley, and Shaver (1999) and Chapter 17 (this volume).

Compassionate Love

Compassionate love was originally highlighted in the social science literature by Underwood (2002), and Sprecher and Fehr (2005) proposed that compassionate (or altruistic) love had been relatively ignored in love research specifically. Compassionate love is a complex concept, overlapping other concepts such as empathy and sympathy. Sprecher and Fehr threaded their way carefully in developing a 21-item Compassionate Love Scale in three versions that could apply to a specific close other, close other generally (e.g., family members or friends), and strangers or humanity in general. In their scale, the authors tried to capture phenomena such as "caring, concern, tenderness, and an orientation toward supporting, helping the other" (p. 630). Despite this wide variety of attributes, the scale was best interpreted as unifactorial.

A great deal of research has been conducted on compassionate love, with some of the initial research summarized in an edited volume by Fehr, Sprecher, and Underwood (2009). Perhaps we should note that calling this large new area "compassionate love" is an act of social construction. Only one item on the scale mentions compassionate love. The item/total correlation for this item was lower than the item/total correlation for an item on "caring and tenderness" for all three versions of the scale. Thus, the item set might equally well have been titled "Caring and Tenderness Scale." However, compassionate love is probably more memorable and is linked naturally to an ongoing research tradition (see also Fehr & Sprecher, 2009).

Neff and Karney (2005) took a somewhat different approach to compassionate love, emphasizing such behaviors as trying to promote the well-being of or attempting to understand and then accept a person for whom one has compassionate love.

More recent research on compassionate love has focused on creating bridges between same-race and cross-race individuals using high self-disclosure (Welker, Slatcher, Baker, & Aron, 2014). The complex research design yielded positive but not fully uniform results. The study broadened the focus of compassionate love from close others to the originally intended "strangers," as articulated originally by Sprecher and Fehr (2005).

Although research is clearly conducted in the "real world," this world is not typically the day-to-day world of relationship formation, maintenance, and dissolution. How might some of the love scales be used in daily life—for example, in counseling a couple who is examining and reconstructing their marriage after challenge and change?

USING LOVE SCALES IN COUPLE COUNSELING

Katherine and Brian are in their mid-40s and have been married for nearly 20 years. They went to see a marital therapist because they have undergone challenges and are continuing to undergo change, even as they feel some of their marriage slipping away. Katherine was diagnosed with early-stage breast cancer at age 41, but with vigorous treatment, she has been cancer-free for several years. Throughout that experience, Brian supported Katherine, was attentive to the needs of their two children (now teenagers), and both Brian and Katherine faced each step together. Now that their children have become more independent, and college is not far in the future, Katherine and Brian wonder what their lives—really, their marriage—might be like in the years ahead, when it is just the two of them again. They do not believe their marriage is at any risk, yet they also do not feel vitality in the relationship.

After interviewing the partners separately and together and having them complete various relationship measures, the therapist decided that Katherine and Brian are perfect candidates for positive couples therapy. This is a general strengths-based approach that builds on basic counseling psychology wellness approaches, Fredrickson's (2001) broaden-and-build approach, and other positive psychology theories. Katherine and Brian separately completed the Love Attitudes Scale: Short Form (C. Hendrick et al., 1998) and the Compassionate Love Scale (Sprecher & Fehr, 2005), and the therapist then scored the scales. Katherine and Brian could see their own scores on the two scales and wanted to see each other's scores so that they could compare and contrast their love styles (*Eros, Storge, Agape*) and compassionate love for each other. (Because this is a positive, strengths-based approach, scales such as *Mania, Pragma*, and *Ludus* were not deemed useful.)

The spouses sat close together so they could compare and contrast their love styles. Using the customary approach of developing a love profile of scores from highest to lowest for each partner, Brian's ranked highest on *Storge* (friendship love), next on *Agape* (altruistic love), and lowest on *Eros* (passionate love). Katherine's scores from highest to lowest were *Eros, Storge*, and *Agape*. Both partners are quite compassionate in their love toward each other and close others. As they discussed their results, Katherine mentioned that she wished there was more passion in their relationship, and Brian expressed surprise. He said he is still attracted to Katherine but is also always concerned about her physical comfort and her health. She, in turn, expressed surprise. The therapist pointed to an empty corner in the room and identified the missing entity, the one they had not discussed so far: cancer. Katherine teared up, and Brian put his arm around her. That is when therapy really began.

This couple is easy to work with, given their commitment, caring, and intelligence, but cancer is a lingering shadow over their relationship, if not their daily lives. Just "naming" the shadow seems to lessen its importance. The therapist can then focus on allowing Brian to ease up on the agapic and storgic attitudes and behaviors so important when Katherine was ill, whereas Katherine can initiate more passion and let Brian know that she is "back" into that part of their relationship. It is a process of communicating, realigning, and then building on their strengths, with the therapist helping the two in this process. They remembered some of the things they did with each other before cancer—date night, evening walks, monthly art trail browsing (walking hand in hand)—and they committed to resuming some or all of these activities. Communicating openly was essential for this couple to broaden and then build on the life-changing emotional experience of Katherine's cancer that was over but still a lingering shadow. If they had not been so open with their feelings, an empty chair technique with each of them addressing the cancer sitting in the empty chair might have been useful.

Of course, this couple is an ideal, yet they are constructed from my (SSH's) real therapy experiences as a counseling psychologist. If other issues had been the presenting ones, other love measures and/or attachment measures could have been used. Because communication is so important in relationships, any vehicle—a scale, a homework assignment, a role plan—that can stimulate communication is a positive tool to be used. Thus, love scales and other positive psychology scales and interventions are potentially useful in helping people improve their lives.

EMERGING APPROACHES TO MEASURING LOVE

Although the various love measurement instruments already discussed are validated and used widely, other assessment techniques are useful also. A. Aron, Fisher, Mashek, Strong, Li, and Brown (2005) used functional magnetic resonance imaging (fMRI) to study brain activity in persons in the early stages of romantic love, when intensity is presumably strong. The researchers did indeed find increased neural activity in the pleasure/reward centers of the brain, where dopamine receptors are plentiful. To follow up, Acevedo, Aron, Fisher, and Brown (2012) also used fMRI methods, this time to measure neural activity of persons stating that they had intense love for their spouses of over 20 years. Results showed neural activity similar to that found in the A. Aron et al. (2005) research, plus neural activity in brain areas correlated with long-term pair bonding. It appears that intensity and pair-bonding can both exist in longer term relationships.

Although the correlates of love have been studied for decades, the effects of love are newer to the love research arena. For example, Stanton, Campbell, and Loving (2014) found that participants who reflected on their romantic partner increased their blood glucose levels, though reflections on other things, such as daily routines, did not affect blood glucose. Such findings point the way for research on love and physical health (see Paxson & Shapiro, 2013), as well as mental health (see Magyar-Moe, 2013).

FUTURE DIRECTIONS

As scholars pursue new directions for the study of love (Hojjat & Cramer, 2013), we also will have to develop and validate new measures. Many research programs emphasize the process of love (e.g., expanding the self to include another). Other research, such as the love styles and passionate love, are more concerned with the content of love, or at least romantic love. Both types of research are valuable and should continue and grow. There is also the new and exciting research on the effects of love, such as the work using fMRI as well as that focusing on mental health and physical health (e.g., Stanton et al., 2014).

Although love research has broadened in some ways, much remains as we get out of our traditional research bubbles and explore attitudes, values, and behaviors of a broad range of ethnic, racial, immigrant, age, and sexual identity groups. As immigrants and transgendered persons have become more visible, it is important to include them in our work without "otherizing" them. We are so much more the same than we are different.

If romantic love is a cultural universal, then scholars should study love across societies, within societies, and across groups within societies. And they are. Love may indeed be biologically hardwired, yet it is culturally expressed. For example, predictors of love attitudes have been studied in Hong Kong and the United Kingdom (Smith & Klases, 2016) and among Chinese college students (Zeng, Pan, Zhou, Yu, & Liu, 2016). And other international scholars developed infatuation and attachment scales for a Dutch-speaking sample (Langeslag, Muris, & Franken, 2013).

Finally, love has to be studied in the context of other positive psychology concepts, such as hope. It is interesting that both "Saint Paul and Martin Luther held hope, along with love, as the essence of what is good in life" (Snyder, 2000, p. 3). The study and measurement of love and the other positive psychology constructs are alive, well, and growing.

The following are questions about the future of research on love:

- Will the varied disciplines which constitute the positive psychology community come to recognize the power and centrality of love for human relationships?
- Will research on love and related physical health and mental health phenomena perhaps extend to medical research, fostering a partnering for scholarship and grant funding?
- How will the continuing expansion of love research across borders and continents continue to influence and expand our conceptions of love?

REFERENCES

Acevedo, B. P., Aron, A., Fisher, H. E., & Brown, L. L. (2012). Neural correlates of long-term intense romantic love. *Social Cognitive and Affective Neuroscience, 7,* 145–159. http://dx.doi.org/10.1093/scan/nsq092

Aron, A., & Aron, E. N. (1986). *Love and the expansion of self: Understanding attraction and satisfaction.* New York, NY: Hemisphere.

Aron, A., Aron, E. N., & Smollan, D. (1992). Inclusion of Other in the Self scale and the structure of interpersonal closeness. *Journal of Personality and Social Psychology, 63,* 596–612. http://dx.doi.org/10.1037/0022-3514.63.4.596

Aron, A., Fisher, H., Mashek, D. J., Strong, G., Li, H., & Brown, L. L. (2005). Reward, motivation, and emotion systems associated with early-stage intense romantic love. *Journal of Neurophysiology, 94,* 327–337. http://dx.doi.org/10.1152/jn.00838.2004

Aron, A., & Westbay, L. (1996). Dimensions of the prototype of love. *Journal of Personality and Social Psychology, 70,* 535–551. http://dx.doi.org/10.1037/0022-3514.70.3.535

Aron, E. N., & Aron, A. (1996). Love and expansion of the self: The state of the model. *Personal Relationships, 3,* 45–58. http://dx.doi.org/10.1111/j.1475-6811.1996.tb00103.x

Baumeister, R. F., & Leary, M. R. (1995). The need to belong: Desire for interpersonal attachments as a fundamental human motivation. *Psychological Bulletin, 117,* 497–529. http://dx.doi.org/10.1037/0033-2909.117.3.497

Berscheid, E., & Walster, E. (1978). *Interpersonal attraction* (2nd ed.). Reading, MA: Addison-Wesley.

Bowlby, J. (1969). *Attachment and loss: Vol. 1. Attachment.* New York, NY: Basic Books.

Cho, W., & Cross, S. E. (1995). Taiwanese love styles and their association with self-esteem and relationship quality. *Genetic, Social, and General Psychology Monographs, 121*, 281–309.

Crowell, J. A., Fraley, R. C., & Shaver, P. R. (1999). Measurement of individual differences in adolescent and adult attachment. In J. Cassidy & P. R. Shaver (Eds.), *Handbook of attachment: Theory, research, and clinical applications* (pp. 434–465). New York, NY: Guilford Press.

Davies, K., & Aron, A. (2016). Friendship development and intergroup attitudes: The role of interpersonal and intergroup friendship processes. *Journal of Social Issues, 72*, 489–510. http://dx.doi.org/10.1111/josi.12178

deMunck, V. C. (1998). Lust, love, and arranged marriages in Sri Lanka. In V. C. deMunck (Ed.), *Romantic love and sexual behavior: Perspectives from the social sciences* (pp. 285–300). Westport, CT: Praeger.

Doherty, R. W., Hatfield, E., Thompson, K., & Choo, P. (1994). Cultural and ethnic influences on love and attachment. *Personal Relationships, 1*, 391–398. http://dx.doi.org/10.1111/j.1475-6811.1994.tb00072.x

Fehr, B. (1988). Prototype analysis of the concepts of love and commitment. *Journal of Personality and Social Psychology, 55*, 557–579. http://dx.doi.org/10.1037/0022-3514.55.4.557

Fehr, B., & Sprecher, S. (2009). Prototype analysis of the concept of compassionate love. *Personal Relationships, 16*, 343–364. http://dx.doi.org/10.1111/j.1475-6811.2009.01227.x

Fehr, B., Sprecher, S., & Underwood, L. G. (Eds.). (2009). *The science of compassionate love: Theory, research, and applications*. Malden, MA: Blackwell.

Fredrickson, B. L. (2001). The role of positive emotions in positive psychology. The broaden-and-build theory of positive emotions. *American Psychologist, 56*, 218–226. http://dx.doi.org/10.1037/0003-066X.56.3.218

Gadlin, H. (1977). Private lives and public order: A critical view of the history of intimate relations in the United States. In G. Levinger & H. L. Raush (Eds.), *Close relationships: Perspectives on the meaning of intimacy* (pp. 33–72). Amherst: University of Massachusetts Press.

Hatfield, E. (1988). Passionate and companionate love. In R. J. Sternberg & M. L. Barnes (Eds.), *The psychology of love* (pp. 191–217). New Haven, CT: Yale University Press.

Hatfield, E., & Rapson, R. L. (1987). Passionate love: New directions in research. In W. H. Jones & D. Perlman (Eds.), *Advances in personal relationships* (Vol. 1, pp. 109–139). Greenwich, CT: JAI Press.

Hatfield, E., & Rapson, R. L. (1996). *Love and sex: Cross-cultural perspectives*. Boston, MA: Allyn & Bacon.

Hatfield, E., & Sprecher, S. (1986). Measuring passionate love in intimate relationships. *Journal of Adolescence, 9*, 383–410. http://dx.doi.org/10.1016/S0140-1971(86)80043-4

Hazan, C., & Shaver, P. (1987). Romantic love conceptualized as an attachment process. *Journal of Personality and Social Psychology, 52*, 511–524. http://dx.doi.org/10.1037/0022-3514.52.3.511

Hendrick, C., & Hendrick, S. S. (1986). A theory and method of love. *Journal of Personality and Social Psychology, 50*, 392–402. http://dx.doi.org/10.1037/0022-3514.50.2.392

Hendrick, C., & Hendrick, S. S. (1989). Research on love: Does it measure up? *Journal of Personality and Social Psychology, 56*, 784–794. http://dx.doi.org/10.1037/0022-3514.56.5.784

Hendrick, C., Hendrick, S. S., & Dicke, A. (1998). The Love Attitudes Scale: Short Form. *Journal of Social and Personal Relationships, 15*, 147–159. http://dx.doi.org/10.1177/0265407598152001

Hendrick, S. S., & Hendrick, C. (1992). *Romantic love*. Newbury Park, CA: Sage.

Hendrick, S. S., & Hendrick, C. (1993). Lovers as friends. *Journal of Social and Personal Relationships, 10,* 459–466. http://dx.doi.org/10.1177/0265407593103011

Hendrick, S. S., & Hendrick, C. (2000). Romantic love. In C. Hendrick & S. S. Hendrick (Eds.), *Close relationships: A sourcebook* (pp. 202–215). Thousand Oaks, CA: Sage. http://dx.doi.org/10.4135/9781452220437.n15

Hojjat, M., & Cramer, D. (Eds.). (2013). *Positive psychology of love.* New York, NY: Oxford University Press. http://dx.doi.org/10.1093/acprof:oso/9780199791064.001.0001

Hrdy, S. B. (2009). *Mothers and others.* Cambridge, MA: The Belknap Press of Harvard University Press.

Kelley, H. H. (1983). Love and commitment. In H. H. Kelley, E. Berscheid, A. Christensen, J. H. Harvey, T. L. Huston, G. Levinger, . . . D. R. Peterson (Eds.), *Close relationships* (pp. 265–314). New York, NY: Freeman.

Langeslag, S. J. E., Muris, P., & Franken, I. H. A. (2013). Measuring romantic love: Psychometric properties of the infatuation and attachment scales. *Journal of Sex Research, 50,* 739–747. http://dx.doi.org/10.1080/00224499.2012.714011

Lasswell, T. E., & Lasswell, M. E. (1976). I love you but I'm not in love with you. *Journal of Marriage and Family Counseling, 2,* 211–224. http://dx.doi.org/10.1111/j.1752-0606.1976.tb00413.x

Lee, J. A. (1973). *The colors of love: An exploration of the ways of loving.* Don Mills, Canada: New Press.

Magyar-Moe, J. L. (2013). Positive psychology and mental health. In M. Hojjat & D. Cramer (Eds.), *Positive psychology of love* (pp. 177–190). New York, NY: Oxford University Press. http://dx.doi.org/10.1093/acprof:oso/9780199791064.003.0013

Neff, L. A., & Karney, B. R. (2005). To know you is to love you: The implications of global adoration and specific accuracy for marital relationships. *Journal of Personality and Social Psychology, 88,* 480–497. http://dx.doi.org/10.1037/0022-3514.88.3.480

Neto, F., & da Conceicao Pinto, M. (2015). Satisfaction with love life across the adult life span. *Applied Research in Quality of Life, 10,* 289–304. http://dx.doi.org/10.1007/s11482-014-9314-6

Paxson, A. A., & Shapiro, S. L. (2013). Love and physical health. In M. Hojjat & D. Cramer (Eds.), *Positive psychology of love* (pp. 191–202). New York, NY: Oxford University Press. http://dx.doi.org/10.1093/acprof:oso/9780199791064.003.0014

Regan, P. C., Kocan, E. R., & Whitlock, T. (1998). Ain't love grand! A prototype analysis of the concept of romantic love. *Journal of Social and Personal Relationships, 15,* 411–420. http://dx.doi.org/10.1177/0265407598153006

Rubin, Z. (1970). Measurement of romantic love. *Journal of Personality and Social Psychology, 16,* 265–273. http://dx.doi.org/10.1037/h0029841

Seligman, M. E. P., & Csikszentmihalyi, M. (2000). Positive psychology. An introduction. *American Psychologist, 55,* 5–14. http://dx.doi.org/10.1037/0003-066X.55.1.5

Shaver, P. R., Morgan, H. J., & Wu, S. (1996). Is love a "basic" emotion? *Personal Relationships, 3,* 81–96. http://dx.doi.org/10.1111/j.1475-6811.1996.tb00105.x

Sheets, V. L. (2014). Passion for life: Self-expansion and passionate love across the life span. *Journal of Social and Personal Relationships, 31,* 958–974. http://dx.doi.org/10.1177/0265407513515618

Singer, I. (1984). *The nature of love: Vol. 1. Plato to Luther* (2nd ed.). Chicago, IL: University of Chicago Press.

Smith, R., & Klases, A. (2016). Predictors of love attitudes: The contribution of cultural orientation, gender attachment style, relationship length and age in participants from the UK and Hong Kong. *Interpersona, 10,* 90–108. http://dx.doi.org/10.5964/ijpr.v10i1.204

Snyder, C. R. (2000). Hypothesis: There is hope. In C. R. Snyder (Ed.), *Handbook of hope: Theory, measures, and applications* (pp. 3–21). San Diego, CA: Academic Press. http://dx.doi.org/10.1016/B978-012654050-5/50003-8

Sprecher, S., Aron, A., Hatfield, E., Cortese, A., Potapova, E., & Levitskaya, A. (1994). Love: American style, Russian style, and Japanese style. *Personal Relationships, 1,* 349–369. http://dx.doi.org/10.1111/j.1475-6811.1994.tb00070.x

Sprecher, S., & Fehr, B. (2005). Compassionate love for close others and humanity. *Journal of Social and Personal Relationships, 22,* 629–651. http://dx.doi.org/10.1177/0265407505056439

Stanton, S. C. E., Campbell, L., & Loving, T. J. (2014). Energized by love: Thinking about romantic relationships increases positive affect and blood glucose levels. *Psychophysiology, 51,* 990–995. http://dx.doi.org/10.1111/psyp.12249

Steck, L., Levitan, D., McLane, D., & Kelley, H. H. (1982). Care, need, and conceptions of love. *Journal of Personality and Social Psychology, 43,* 481–491. http://dx.doi.org/10.1037/0022-3514.43.3.481

Sternberg, R. J. (1986). A triangular theory of love. *Psychological Review, 93,* 119–135. http://dx.doi.org/10.1037/0033-295X.93.2.119

Sternberg, R. J. (1997). Construct validation of a triangular love scale. *European Journal of Social Psychology, 27,* 313–335. http://dx.doi.org/10.1002/(SICI)1099-0992(199705)27:3<313::AID-EJSP824>3.0.CO;2-4

Sumter, S. R., Valkenburg, P. M., & Peter, J. (2013). Perceptions of love across the lifespan: Differences in intimacy, passion, and commitment. *International Journal of Behavioral Development, 37,* 417–427. http://dx.doi.org/10.1177/0165025413492486

Underwood, L. G. (2002). The human experience of compassionate love: Conceptual mapping and data from selected studies. In S. G. Post, L. G. Underwood, J. P. Schloss, & W. B. Hurlbut (Eds.), *Altruism and altruistic love: Science, philosophy, and religion* (pp. 72–88). New York, NY: Oxford University Press.

van Steenbergen, H., Langeslag, S. J. E., Band, G. P. H., & Hommel, B. (2014). Reduced cognitive control in passionate lovers. *Motivation and Emotion, 38,* 444–450. http://dx.doi.org/10.1007/s11031-013-9380-3

Welker, K. M., Slatcher, R. B., Baker, L., & Aron, A. (2014). Creating positive out-group attitudes through intergroup couple friendships and implications for compassionate love. *Journal of Social and Personal Relationships, 31,* 706–725. http://dx.doi.org/10.1177/0265407514522369

Zeng, X., Pan, Y., Zhou, H., Yu, S., & Liu, X. (2016). Exploring different patterns of love attitudes among Chinese college students. *PLoS ONE, 11*(11), e0166410. http://dx.doi.org/10.1371/journal.pone.0166410

15

Measuring Emotional and Personal Intelligence

David R. Caruso, John D. Mayer, Victoria Bryan,
Kimberly G. Phillips, and Peter Salovey

In this chapter, we describe two types of intelligence centered on reasoning about people that we regard as important elements of individuals' positive psychology. Emotional intelligence and personal intelligence are mental abilities related to but partially distinct from general mental ability (i.e., IQ). People use their *emotional intelligence* (EI) to understand people's emotions and the emotional information around them and their *personal intelligence* (PI) to understand personality-related information. We begin by placing EI and PI within the pantheon of other forms of intelligence and at the same time distinguish them from other forms of intelligence, such as spatial or quantitative. We classify EI and PI as "people-centered" intelligences versus more traditional "thing-oriented" intelligences (Mayer, 2018; Mayer & Skimmyhorn, 2017). We also explore how EI and PI are measured and provide examples of how they can be applied in our lives.

INTELLIGENCE

The measure of intelligence is arguably one of the greatest success stories in psychological research (Fancher, 1987). The creation of intelligence tests replaced the less valid assessments of teachers as to who among their students could and could not learn (Fancher, 1987). In addition, people with higher levels of intelligence arguably live more positive lives: Individuals' general mental ability predicts their school grades in the $r = 0.45$ to 0.55 range, and

http://dx.doi.org/10.1037/0000138-015
Positive Psychological Assessment: A Handbook of Models and Measures, Second Edition,
M. W. Gallagher and S. J. Lopez (Editors)

their performance at work at the same r = .45 to .55 level (Deary, 2012; Salgado, Anderson, Moscoso, Bertua, & de Fruyt, 2003; Schmidt & Hunter, 2004). People with higher general intelligence also maintain more stable marital relationships and live longer lives than those with lower intelligence (Roberts, Kuncel, Shiner, Caspi, & Goldberg, 2007).

However, the 20th century has seen a debate as to whether *general intelligence*—the capacity to reason abstractly and acquire knowledge—is more important than an intelligence with a narrower focus, a type of intelligence called *broad intelligence*. The concept of general and broad intelligences comes from the Cattell–Horn–Carroll model, which posits three levels or "strata" of intelligence. Stratum 3 is general intelligence, labeled *g*, followed by a series of what are labeled *broad intelligences* (e.g., fluid reasoning, processing speed); last, Stratum 1 consists of *narrow intelligences* (e.g., memory span, reading speed; Schipolowski, Wilhelm, & Schroeders, 2014). To be considered a form of intelligence, a mental ability has to be both related to other such abilities but also be different enough to warrant calling it a separate form of intelligence. In our view, EI and PI are broad intelligences—occupying the "just right" space where they are both related to and distinct enough from general intelligence.

Broad intelligences are a focus of research for three reasons. First, mathematical models that include both general and broad intelligences fit data better than models that use general intelligence alone (Carroll, 1993; McGrew, 2009; Schneider & Newman, 2015). Second, general intelligence itself is estimated from measures of broad intelligences; it is, therefore, possible to measure, model, and use both at once (Schneider & Newman, 2015). Third, broad intelligences modestly enhance prediction of performance over general intelligence alone (Mayer & Skimmyhorn, 2015; Schneider & Newman, 2015).

Understandably, some intelligence researchers ask whether there are too many intelligences (Hedlund & Sternberg, 2000), and the introduction of PI and EI exacerbates this issue. One way to address this problem is to speak of *people-centered intelligence* and *thing-centered intelligence*, where EI and PI are a form of people-centered intelligence and more traditional broad intelligences are characterized as involving "things," such as visual-processing and quantitative reasoning. Data exist to suggest empirical evidence of the differential prediction of these two classes of mental ability (Mayer, 2018; Mayer & Skimmyhorn, 2017).

EMOTIONAL AND PERSONAL INTELLIGENCES

When two speculative articles were published in 1990 proposing the existence of an emotional intelligence (Salovey & Mayer, 1990), much was unknown about this new intelligence, and the idea did not receive much attention. However, the idea of emotional intelligence entered the public sphere in 1995 when a book aimed at the general public by that name was published (Goleman, 1995). The book received a great deal of press (e.g., Gibbs, 1995). This attention has not waned: A Google search for *emotional intelligence* at the time this chapter was written resulted in 243 million hits (*intelligence* had 446 million hits). Although the popular press is responsible for the outsized interest in EI, this attention has resulted in unsupported claims for the predictive power of EI, and EI itself has been defined as anything from standard personality traits (e.g., optimism and assertiveness) to the opposite of IQ. We caution you to review definitions of EI and cast an especially wary eye on claims regarding "EQ" (emotional quotient). Our focus in this chapter is on EI, which is defined and measured as an ability, or a broad intelligence. We also introduce the related intelligence, PI.

The model of EI proposed in 1990 was updated in 1997 to include four related EI abilities: perceiving emotions, using emotions to facilitate thinking, understanding emotions, and managing emotions. EI described abilities which processed emotional data, data concerning people. In 2008, PI, the ability to reason about personality in oneself and others, was introduced (Mayer, 2008).

ASSESSMENT OF PEOPLE INTELLIGENCES

As research progressed in these areas, the main questions we and others tried to answer were as follows: Could these broad intelligences be measured? What did they predict? Were they truly an intelligence, and if so, were they different from other forms of intelligence? A host of issues arose regarding developing measures of EI and, later, PI. A key assumption for the work on measurement was that if EI was defined as an intelligence, it had to be measured like other intelligences and that required objective or performance-based measures. Scoring objective EI assessments requires a scoring key. Different scoring methods were developed—target, general consensus, expert consensus, and veridical—and it now appears that an objective measure of EI can be objectively scored. For example, veridical, or "true," scoring starts by compiling relevant literature in a field and writing questions based on that research so that a correct answer is determined from the literature.

About the Mayer, Salovey, Caruso Emotional Intelligence Test

The Mayer, Salovey, Caruso Emotional Intelligence Test (MSCEIT)[1] consists of two sets of items measuring each of the four abilities (i.e., perceiving emotions, using emotions to facilitate thinking, understanding emotions, and managing emotions) with a total of 141 items. Scores include a total EI score, four Ability scores, and eight Task scores, as well as two supplementary scales. The Faces Task (Perceive Emotions), for example, shows someone's face and the test taker indicates how much of several emotions are present using a five-point scale. The Blends Task (Understand Emotions) includes multiple-choice items that

[1]Disclosure: Caruso, Mayer, and Salovey receive royalties from the sale of the Mayer, Salovey, Caruso Emotional Intelligence Test described in this chapter.

ask the test taker to define complex emotion words. The scoring key for the MSCEIT is based on the ratings of 21 international emotions researchers, which has resulted in an expert consensus scoring method. A youth version for ages 10 to 17 used a veridical scoring method, where an expert panel created a set of references for each item in the scale and then assigned correct points to each response. We have found that people are not accurate at estimating their level of EI, with the correlation between a self-report measure and the MSCEIT about .20 (Brackett & Mayer, 2003), and many people overestimate their level of EI (Sheldon, Dunning, & Ames, 2014).

Other Measures of Emotional Intelligence

Although the MSCEIT was initially one of the only ability-based measures of EI, several other recently developed tests have demonstrated promise. The Situational Test of Emotional Understanding (STEU) was developed by MacCann and Roberts (2008) and uses 42 items to explore emotional understanding following the appraisal theory of emotions. Participants are presented with scenarios and asked to select which emotion is the most likely result among five options—for example, "An unwanted situation becomes less likely or stops altogether. The person involved is most likely to feel: (a) regret, (b) hope, (c) joy, (d) sadness, (e) relief" (MacCann & Roberts, 2008, p. 542). The STEU is scored veridically, and attempts to explore the factor structure of the test have suggested it is best represented by a single factor of emotional understanding (Ferguson & Austin, 2011). Reliability of the STEU in its initial development ranged from $r = .43$ to .71, with higher reliability in college undergraduate samples than in community samples. The STEU demonstrated a moderate correlation with the MSCEIT ($r = .33$; Austin, 2010).

The Situational Test of Emotion Management (STEM) is an ability-based measure of emotion management. The STEM uses both rate-the-extent and multiple-choice response formats and instructs participants to select the choice that would be the most effective response for the individual in 44 different scenarios (e.g., "Rhea has left her job to be a full-time mother, which she loves, but she misses the company and companionship of her workmates. What action would be the most effective for Rhea?"; MacCann & Roberts, 2008). Like the MSCEIT, the STEM uses expert consensus scoring to create a composite score of emotion management. Reliability of the STEM ranges from .68 (multiple choice) to .92 (rate the extent) in the initial undergraduate sample. Research has suggested that the STEM correlates $r = .36$ with the MSCEIT (Austin, 2010). Once more, research exploring the factor structure of the STEM has suggested that it is best represented by one factor pertaining to emotion management (Ferguson & Austin, 2011).

Finally, the Reading the Mind in the Eyes Test was developed as a measure of theory of mind that explores one's ability to put oneself in the mental state of another individual (Baron-Cohen, Wheelwright, Hill, Raste, & Plumb, 2001). Test-takers are asked to indicate an individual's intentions on the basis of a photograph of their eyes. The test may also be a promising measure of emotional understanding and perception (Mayer, Panter, & Caruso, 2012; Olderbak et al., 2015).

Test of Personal Intelligence

Although the concept of PI is still relatively new in the field of intelligence, work is underway exploring how we can appropriately measure the construct. The Test of Personal Intelligence (TOPI; Mayer, Caruso, & Panter, 2015) consists of a number of multiple-choice items, each of which was derived from research articles on personality. For example, test questions as to which traits go together were based on empirical research on the Big Five. In addition, the Self-Estimated Personal Intelligence scale consists of 16 items and gauges individuals' estimates of their PI. Like the results concerning the MSCEIT, the correlation between self-reported PI and the TOPI (using a 12-item version) was just $r = .11$ (Mayer et al., 2015). Another assessment measuring an ability similar to PI examines individuals' accuracy in forming judgments of others' personalities. Christiansen, Wolcott-Burnam, Janovics, Burns, and Quirk (2005) developed a 45-item multiple-choice measure they called *dispositional intelligence*, defined as "knowledge of personality and how it manifests in behavior" (p. 139).

IMPORTANCE OF EMOTIONAL AND PERSONAL INTELLIGENCE

Research using an ability-based measure of EI has suggested that it can predict positive individual outcomes. Across the lifespan, from children to adults, higher ability-based EI is associated, often through increases in positive affect and decreases in negative affect, with higher life satisfaction (Extremera & Rey, 2016) and greater subjective well-being (Chen, Peng, & Fang, 2016; Gallagher & Vella-Brodrick, 2008). Research findings from 2 decades of EI studies have shown that it relates to better interpersonal functioning, both in everyday contexts and at work, higher student performance, and better social outcomes for children and adults. Furthermore, it is also related to lower social deviance and overall psychological well-being (Mayer, Caruso, Panter, & Salovey, 2012, p. 503; Mayer, Roberts, & Barsade, 2008).

ASSESSMENT OF PEOPLE-CENTERED INTELLIGENCES: APPLICATIONS

Using Emotional Intelligence in Emotional Intelligence Feedback

Providing feedback to a client on people-centered measures of intelligence is challenging, as it is with intelligence more generally. The correlation between people's belief about their intelligence and their actual intelligence is generally low—typically $r = .20$—and this is also true of EI and PI (Brackett & Mayer, 2003; Mayer, Panter, & Caruso, 2017). Given those low correlations, the results of this testing can often be a surprise to the test taker.

Let us use the example of EI. If a person has a low estimate of his or her measured EI, the test administrator's job is relatively easy because there is no need to manage the test taker's disappointment, disbelief, or irritation. However, consider a client who comes to have his EI evaluated because he is considering a career change from compensation analyst in financial services to an executive coaching role. Though expecting to do well, his overall scores on the MSCEIT (shown in Table 15.1) were lower than he anticipated. Using the EI ability model, one can predict the client's reaction, particularly given his low score on Emotion Management and especially on the task that measures self-management. In other words, when someone with poor self-management ability is dealt a setback, they are less likely to bounce back quickly and therefore may not be open to hearing difficult feedback.

Using the ability model of EI as a framework to shape feedback to the client, it seems apparent that starting with his total score would disappoint him, and he would likely not manage this well or be open to further feedback. Instead, one might temper the client's expectations by sharing the results in such a way as to allow him to self-interpret with appropriate background information and to focus first on his strengths. In fact, we strongly recommend that test professionals provide an overview of the ability model of EI, how the abilities are measured, and limitations of assessment and then apply a strengths-based approach to sharing feedback if there is a significant discrepancy between expectations and actual scores or if the scores are low.

In this case, the client was indeed defensive at first, and he pushed back a bit on some of the scores. By following a strengths-based feedback approach and providing the client with suggestions on how to create and maintain openness (e.g., "Consider whether it is possible the results are correct," stating the results as hypotheses to be tested) the client became more open and less resistant. Perhaps the main indication that he understood the feedback and the scores was that he informed the test professional some weeks later that he had abandoned the idea of going into the executive coaching field and decided to stay in compensation where he would make more money.

Emotional Intelligence Assessment and Coaching

Executive coaching is an area of applied psychology in which a trained professional provides feedback focused on enhancing the performance of executives

TABLE 15.1 Client Mayer, Salovey, Caruso Emotional Intelligence Test Scores

Score	Standard Score	Level
Total	80	Consider developing
Perceive	73	Improve
Facilitate	96	Competent
Understand	107	Competent
Manage	89	Consider developing
Self	81	Develop
Other	97	Competent

at work. Here, we provide a case study from my (DRC's) practice along those lines to illustrate how what we have discussed in the chapter relates to an individual's successful performance at work.

Jean was assigned to manage a major IT project for a large health care organization. Over budget and behind schedule, Jean was up for the challenge even though she knew the team had major morale issues. Jean took charge right away, revised the project plan, and called a team meeting first thing Monday morning. She walked into the meeting and asked for introductions. People launched into a well-practiced litany of grievances. Credit was taken where it could be by individuals, and blame was generously apportioned to other team members. She wrestled control of the meeting, walked through her critical agenda items, assigned tasks, and ended the meeting 5 minutes early. The next meeting was on Friday, and the first agenda item was updates on the project by the lead project managers. Again, the meeting descended into chaos, with the same grievances and blaming. Jean's manager got wind of the disaster in the making and referred her for coaching.

The coach included the MSCEIT in an assessment battery along with a Big Five personality assessment and an interpersonal style measure. Scores—see Figure 15.1—ranged from 89 (consider developing) for Facilitate to 111 (skilled) for Understand, with an total competent score of 101. Jean picked up emotion cues, understood the underlying causes of emotions, and was able to stay open to emotions and manage them effectively. However, she did not leverage moods and emotions, failing to connect people's emotions with how they think and make decisions. She struggled to facilitate thinking with emotions. This explained why the team meetings were so unproductive. The bitterness, sadness, and frustration were understandable, but they focused the group's thoughts on what was wrong—a necessary step in problem diagnosis but not helpful to facilitate a team approach to problem solving.

FIGURE 15.1. Mayer, Salovey, Caruso Emotional Intelligence Test Scores for Coaching Client

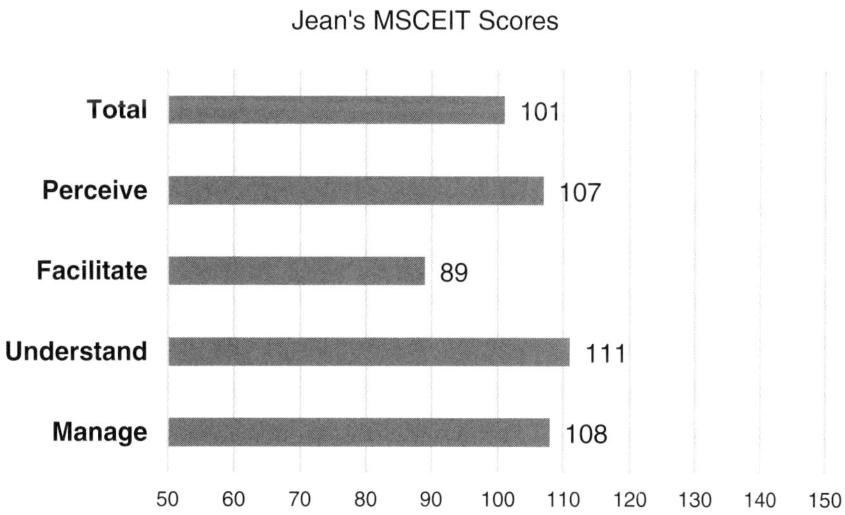

With this insight, Jean kept the concrete items on the meeting agenda as is, but she added two new items: a discussion of members' experience and skills and a list of what the team had accomplished to date. Yes, they were over budget and behind schedule, but they did have some accomplishments. Jean followed up with her own comments, in a quiet tone of confidence and determination, creating a more positive tenor for the meeting. The effect was not noticeable to most of the people in the room, but the manner of participants shifted slightly, and Jean kept the low-key tone of confidence going, redirecting a few nasty comments. Succeeding meetings began with updates and were followed by challenges. Her one-on-one meetings followed a similar agenda. By matching the underlying cognitive task with an emotion that facilitated the thinking processes required, Jean turned things around. She did not do this with ease: She had to carefully analyze each agenda item and consciously plan out the tone it required. Without objective assessment, Jean and her coach may never have diagnosed the issue nor devised a reasonable work-around and compensatory strategy.

INTELLIGENCE ASSESSMENT AND POSITIVE PSYCHOLOGY

One drawback to including mental ability as part of the pantheon of traits associated with positive psychology is that these mental abilities are viewed as relatively fixed. People conclude, with some reason, that because intelligence is strongly influenced by genetics, it is fixed at birth—although, many other personality traits have genetically determined foundations as well (Plomin, DeFries, Knopik, & Neiderhiser, 2016). Regardless, the preponderance of evidence has suggested, with some kernel of truth, that intelligence levels are difficult to modify (Marks, 2014, 2016).

Yet there is reason for some positive thinking as to the possible development of intellectual functioning on three fronts. First, intelligence at a societal level can be enhanced through public health and education; second, intelligence is not quite so fixed as some research would suggest; and third, educational training can improve a person's intellectual performance.

Just because a mental ability has considerable biological bases does not mean it cannot be strengthened or preserved. Government health officials and neuropsychologists have tracked down causes of low intelligence such as lead poisoning, malnutrition, and genetic disorders by looking at intelligence scores across communities at risk and have found that all the aforementioned influences and a number of others put intelligence at risk in a population. By implementing public health initiatives to ameliorate these malicious influences, governments have succeeded in removing neurotoxins such as lead from the environment, supplemented poor nutrition, and monitored genetic abnormalities, benefiting many people who would otherwise have been afflicted by lower intelligence levels over their lives (Martorell, 1998; Rauh & Margolis, 2016; Steen, 2009). Current public health efforts to promote good nutrition and exercise in adulthood promise to preserve better brain health during aging (Jackson et al., 2016).

Second, the idea that intelligence is "relatively fixed" is itself relative. True, people with severe mental disabilities will generally not become super-intelligent individuals, and vice versa. That said, people in the middle of the intelligence spectrum—those with IQs between 85 and 115 and nearby—may shift their intellectual capacities over time in ways that they and the people around them find meaningful. Evidence has suggested that during adolescence, a student may add as much as 3.5 IQ points for each additional year he or she remains in a good school system (Brinch & Galloway, 2012). Although this may not seem like much compared with the near 200-point range of IQ scores along which human beings fall, the effects can be meaningful for an individual who can move from average to somewhat above average.

Third, regardless of whether IQ itself can be altered, educational effects can improve a person's intellectual performance even without a change in intelligence (Ericsson, 2007, 2017; Ericsson & Ward, 2007). For example, no matter how bright students in a high school may be, few of them would be likely to come up with calculus from first principles. Rather, their teachers educate them as to what already is known about an area. Once the students learn the math most of them can operate with calculus effectively, even though they would have been highly unlikely to have developed it themselves. In other words, educating people in a particular area can influence their positive functioning, mostly regardless of their intelligence level.

How Many Emotional Intelligence Abilities?

Ability-based EI, as measured by the MSCEIT, was originally proposed as a four-branch model, where each of the four branches corresponded to the four different ability factors: managing emotions, facilitating thought and using emotions, perceiving emotions, and understanding emotions (Mayer & Salovey, 1997). However, the four-branch model has not been well-supported. For example, MacCann, Joseph, Newman, and Roberts (2014) aimed to address the issues surrounding EI's status as a broad ability factor by modeling EI, as represented by the three-factor MSCEIT, with several other mental abilities. Results of their study demonstrated that three factors of EI fit well within the second stratum of the Cattell–Horn–Carroll model of intelligence. However, a reanalysis of the same data by Legree and colleagues (2014), although lending further support for EI as a second stratum factor, suggested that EI was best represented by a single factor. Although research has suggested that the Using Emotions to Facilitate Thought branch does not emerge as a discrete factor, these four branches represent areas of emotional problem solving and that being able to use our emotions to facilitate thought is an integral part of EI (Mayer, Caruso, & Salovey, 2016).

How Many People Intelligences?

Despite the gains made in terms of exploring EI in relation to other intelligences, the factor structure remains largely uncertain at this time (Legree et al., 2014; MacCann et al., 2014). With advances in our understanding of personal and social intelligences, we may discover that EI is a part of a larger group of people-centered intelligences. Our research has suggested that the broad intelligences vary significantly in the degree to which they correlate with one another. For example, we have found that PI correlates $r = .30$ with quantitative reasoning and $r = .69$ with strategic EI, suggesting that the two constructs are more closely related (Mayer & Skimmyhorn, 2017). Further exploration of the relationship between the broad intelligences may shed additional light on whether EI is a distinct intelligence or whether it is part of a larger group of person-centered intelligences.

CONCLUSION

EI and PI—defined and measured as an ability—may be considered to be broad intelligences along with other intelligences such as verbal or spatial. These new intelligences can assist us in identifying abilities that are related to "people" outcomes such as relationship quality and well-being. The future of people-centered intelligence holds a great deal of promise as the concept is developed further and advances in measurement are achieved.

REFERENCES

Austin, E. J. (2010). Measurement of ability emotional intelligence: Results for two new tests. *British Journal of Psychology, 101,* 563–578. http://dx.doi.org/10.1348/000712609X474370

Baron-Cohen, S., Wheelwright, S., Hill, J., Raste, Y., & Plumb, I. (2001). The "Reading the Mind in the Eyes" Test revised version: A study with normal adults, and adults with Asperger syndrome or high-functioning autism. *Journal of Child Psychology and Psychiatry, 42,* 241–251. http://dx.doi.org/10.1111/1469-7610.00715

Brackett, M. A., & Mayer, J. D. (2003). Convergent, discriminant, and incremental validity of competing measures of emotional intelligence. *Personality and Social Psychology Bulletin, 29,* 1147–1158. http://dx.doi.org/10.1177/0146167203254596

Brinch, C. N., & Galloway, T. A. (2012). Schooling in adolescence raises IQ scores. *PNAS, 109,* 425–430. http://dx.doi.org/10.1073/pnas.1106077109

Carroll, J. B. (1993). *Human cognitive abilities: A survey of factor-analytic studies.* New York, NY: Cambridge University Press. http://dx.doi.org/10.1017/CBO9780511571312

Chen, Y., Peng, Y., & Fang, P. (2016). Emotional intelligence mediates the relationship between age and subjective well-being. *The International Journal of Aging & Human Development, 83,* 91–107. http://dx.doi.org/10.1177/0091415016648705

Christiansen, N. D., Wolcott-Burnam, S., Janovics, J. E., Burns, G. N., & Quirk, S. W. (2005). The good judge revisited: Individual differences in the accuracy of personality judgments. *Human Performance, 18,* 123–149. http://dx.doi.org/10.1207/s15327043hup1802_2

Deary, I. J. (2012). Intelligence. *Annual Review of Psychology, 63,* 453–482. http://dx.doi.org/10.1146/annurev-psych-120710-100353

Ericsson, K. A. (2007). An expert-performance perspective of research on medical expertise: The study of clinical performance. *Medical Education, 41,* 1124–1130. http://dx.doi.org/10.1111/j.1365-2923.2007.02946.x

Ericsson, K. A. (2017). Expertise and individual differences: The search for the structure and acquisition of experts' superior performance. *WIREs Cognitive Science, 8,* e1382. http://dx.doi.org/10.1002/wcs.1382

Ericsson, K. A., & Ward, P. (2007). Capturing the naturally occurring superior performance of experts in the laboratory: Toward a science of expert and exceptional performance. *Current Directions in Psychological Science, 16,* 346–350. http://dx.doi.org/10.1111/j.1467-8721.2007.00533.x

Extremera, N., & Rey, L. (2016). Ability emotional intelligence and life satisfaction: Positive and negative affect as mediators. *Personality and Individual Differences, 102,* 98–101. http://dx.doi.org/10.1016/j.paid.2016.06.051

Fancher, R. E. (1987). *The intelligence men: Makers of the I.Q. controversy.* New York, NY: Norton.

Ferguson, F. J., & Austin, E. J. (2011). The factor structures of the STEM and the STEU. *Personality and Individual Differences, 51,* 791–794. http://dx.doi.org/10.1016/j.paid.2011.07.002

Gallagher, E. N., & Vella-Brodrick, D. A. (2008). Social support and emotional intelligence as predictors of subjective well-being. *Personality and Individual Differences, 44,* 1551–1561. http://dx.doi.org/10.1016/j.paid.2008.01.011

Gibbs, N. (1995, October 2). The EQ factor. *Time, 146,* 60–68.

Goleman, D. (1995). *Emotional intelligence.* New York, NY: Bantam Books.

Hedlund, J., & Sternberg, R. J. (2000). Too many intelligences? integrating social, emotional, and practical intelligence. In J. D. A. Parker (Ed.), *The handbook of emotional intelligence: Theory, development, assessment, and application at home, school, and in the workplace* (pp. 136–167). San Francisco, CA: Jossey-Bass.

Jackson, P. A., Pialoux, V., Corbett, D., Drogos, L., Erickson, K. I., Eskes, G. A., & Poulin, M. J. (2016). Promoting brain health through exercise and diet in older adults: A physiological perspective. *The Journal of Physiology, 594,* 4485–4498. http://dx.doi.org/10.1113/JP271270

Legree, P. J., Psotka, J., Robbins, J., Roberts, R. D., Putka, D. J., & Mullins, H. M. (2014). Profile similarity metrics as an alternate framework to score rating-based tests: MSCEIT reanalyses. *Intelligence, 47,* 159–174. http://dx.doi.org/10.1016/j.intell.2014.09.005

MacCann, C., Joseph, D. L., Newman, D. A., & Roberts, R. D. (2014). Emotional intelligence is a second-stratum factor of intelligence: Evidence from hierarchical and bifactor models. *Emotion, 14,* 358–374. http://dx.doi.org/10.1037/a0034755

MacCann, C., & Roberts, R. D. (2008). New paradigms for assessing emotional intelligence: Theory and data. *Emotion, 8,* 540–551. http://dx.doi.org/10.1037/a0012746

Marks, G. N. (2014). *Education, social background and cognitive ability: The decline of the social.* New York, NY: Routledge/Taylor & Francis.

Marks, G. N. (2016). Explaining the substantial inter-domain and over-time correlations in student achievement: The importance of stable student attributes. *Educational Research and Evaluation, 22,* 45–64. http://dx.doi.org/10.1080/13803611.2016.1191359

Martorell, R. (1998). Nutrition and the worldwide rise in IQ scores. In U. Neisser (Ed.), *The rising curve: Long-term gains in IQ and related measures* (pp. 183–206). Washington, DC: American Psychological Association.

Mayer, J. D. (2008). Personal intelligence. *Imagination, Cognition and Personality, 27,* 209–232. http://dx.doi.org/10.2190/IC.27.3.b

Mayer, J. D. (2018). Intelligences about things and intelligences about people. In R. J. Sternberg (Ed.), *The nature of human intelligence* (pp. 270–286). Cambridge, England: Cambridge University Press.

Mayer, J. D., Caruso, D. R., & Panter, A. T. (2015). Personal intelligence and competencies. In J. D. Wright (Ed.), *International encyclopedia of the social & behavioral sciences* (2nd ed., pp. 750–756). Oxford, England: Elsevier. http://dx.doi.org/10.1016/B978-0-08-097086-8.25073-3

Mayer, J. D., Caruso, D. R., Panter, A. T., & Salovey, P. (2012). The growing significance of hot intelligences. *American Psychologist, 67,* 502–503. http://dx.doi.org/10.1037/a0029456

Mayer, J. D., Caruso, D. R., & Salovey, P. (2016). The ability model of emotional intelligence: Principles and updates. *Emotion Review, 8,* 290–300. http://dx.doi.org/10.1177/1754073916639667

Mayer, J. D., Panter, A. T., & Caruso, D. R. (2012). Does personal intelligence exist? Evidence from a new ability-based measure. *Journal of Personality Assessment, 94,* 124–140. http://dx.doi.org/10.1080/00223891.2011.646108

Mayer, J. D., Panter, A. T., & Caruso, D. R. (2017). A closer look at the Test of Personal Intelligence (TOPI). *Personality and Individual Differences, 111,* 301–311.

Mayer, J. D., Roberts, R. D., & Barsade, S. G. (2008). Human abilities: Emotional intelligence. *Annual Review of Psychology, 59,* 507–536. http://dx.doi.org/10.1146/annurev.psych.59.103006.093646

Mayer, J. D., & Salovey, P. (1997). What is emotional intelligence? In P. Salovey & D. Sluyter (Eds.), *Emotional development and emotional intelligence: Implications for educators* (pp. 3–31). New York, NY: Basic Books.

Mayer, J. D., & Skimmyhorn, W. (2015, June). *Psychological predictors of cadet performance at West Point.* Paper presented at the meeting of the Association for Research in Personality, St. Louis, MO.

Mayer, J. D., & Skimmyhorn, W. (2017). Personality attributes that predict cadet performance West Point. *Journal of Research in Personality, 66,* 14–26. http://dx.doi.org/10.1016/j.jrp.2016.10.012

McGrew, K. S. (2009). CHC theory and the human cognitive abilities project: Standing on the shoulders of the giants of psychometric intelligence research. *Intelligence, 37,* 1–10. http://dx.doi.org/10.1016/j.intell.2008.08.004

Olderbak, S., Wilhelm, O., Olaru, G., Geiger, M., Brenneman, M. W., & Roberts, R. D. (2015). A psychometric analysis of the reading the mind in the eyes test: Toward a brief form for research and applied settings. *Frontiers in Psychology, 6,* 1503. http://dx.doi.org/10.3389/fpsyg.2015.01503

Plomin, R., DeFries, J. C., Knopik, V. S., & Neiderhiser, J. M. (2016). Top 10 replicated findings from behavioral genetics. *Perspectives on Psychological Science, 11,* 3–23. http://dx.doi.org/10.1177/1745691615617439

Rauh, V. A., & Margolis, A. E. (2016). Research review: Environmental exposures, neurodevelopment, and child mental health—new paradigms for the study of brain and behavioral effects. *Journal of Child Psychology and Psychiatry, 57,* 775–793. http://dx.doi.org/10.1111/jcpp.12537

Roberts, B. W., Kuncel, N. R., Shiner, R., Caspi, A., & Goldberg, L. R. (2007). The power of personality: The comparative validity of personality traits, socioeconomic status, and cognitive ability for predicting important life outcomes. *Perspectives on Psychological Science, 2,* 313–345. http://dx.doi.org/10.1111/j.1745-6916.2007.00047.x

Salgado, J. F., Anderson, N., Moscoso, S., Bertua, C., & de Fruyt, F. (2003). International validity generalization of GMA and cognitive abilities: A European community meta-analysis. *Personnel Psychology, 56,* 573–605. http://dx.doi.org/10.1111/j.1744-6570.2003.tb00751.x

Salovey, P., & Mayer, J. D. (1990). Emotional intelligence. *Imagination, Cognition and Personality, 9,* 185–211. http://dx.doi.org/10.2190/DUGG-P24E-52WK-6CDG

Schipolowski, S., Wilhelm, O., & Schroeders, U. (2014). On the nature of crystallized intelligence: The relationship between verbal ability and factual knowledge. *Intelligence, 46,* 156–168. http://dx.doi.org/10.1016/j.intell.2014.05.014

Schmidt, F. L., & Hunter, J. (2004). General mental ability in the world of work: Occupational attainment and job performance. *Journal of Personality and Social Psychology, 86,* 162–173. http://dx.doi.org/10.1037/0022-3514.86.1.162

Schneider, W. J., & Newman, D. A. (2015). Intelligence is multidimensional: Theoretical review and implications of specific cognitive abilities. *Human Resource Management Review, 25,* 12–27. http://dx.doi.org/10.1016/j.hrmr.2014.09.004

Sheldon, O. J., Dunning, D., & Ames, D. R. (2014). Emotionally unskilled, unaware, and uninterested in learning more: Reactions to feedback about deficits in emotional intelligence. *Journal of Applied Psychology, 99,* 125–137. http://dx.doi.org/10.1037/a0034138

Steen, R. G. (2009). *Human intelligence and medical illness: Assessing the Flynn effect.* New York, NY: Springer Science + Business Media. http://dx.doi.org/10.1007/978-1-4419-0092-0

IV

INTERPERSONAL MODELS AND MEASURES

16

Empathy

Qing Zhou, Nancy Eisenberg, and Carlos Valiente

Empathy is an aspect of human responding that is critical for understanding positive development. Empathy motivates helping others and the desire for justice for others, as well as inhibits aggression toward others (Batson, 1991; Hoffman, 2000; Miller & Eisenberg, 1988). Moreover, empathy also facilitates people's socially competent interactions (Eisenberg et al., 1996; Saarni, 1990) and provides a sense of connection among people. Empathy has, and continues to be, defined in various ways. In social and developmental psychology, empathy-related responding is defined as an affective response to the cognitive processing of information about another's state or condition. Similar to Feshbach (1978) and Hoffman (1982), Eisenberg and colleagues have defined empathy as a state of emotional arousal that stems from the apprehension or comprehension of another's affective state. Moreover, it is similar to, or congruent with, the feeling of other people (Eisenberg, Shea, Carlo, & Knight, 1991). For instance, if an observer sees another person who is sad and in response feels sad, that observer is experiencing empathy. Empathy can occur in response to cues of positive as well as negative emotion. Thus, to qualify as empathy, the empathizer must recognize, at least on some level, that the emotion she or he is experiencing is a reflection of the other's emotional, psychological, or physical state.

Work on this chapter was supported by grants from the National Institutes of Mental Health (R01 HH55052 and R01 MH 60838), as well as a Research Scientist Award to Nancy Eisenberg.

http://dx.doi.org/10.1037/0000138-016
Positive Psychological Assessment: A Handbook of Models and Measures, Second Edition,
M. W. Gallagher and S. J. Lopez (Editors)

In early work, most relevant research pertained to global empathy or a combination of various empathy-related processes (Bryant, 1982; Mehrabian & Epstein, 1972). The more recent research has suggested that empathy is a multidimensional construct consisting of multiple processes (e.g., cognitive, affective, and motor empathy; Davis, 1994). For example, *affective empathy* refers to the vicarious experience of emotions consistent with those of the observed person (Hoffman, 2000). *Cognitive empathy* (or perspective taking, empathic accuracy) refers to the ability to understand or infer the feelings of others (Davis, 1983; Ickes, 1993). *Motor empathy* refers to the automatic mimicking of others' facial expressions, voices, and gestures (Dimberg, 1990). The multidimensional view of empathy demonstrated some utility in clinical research (e.g., Derntl et al., 2009; Dziobek et al., 2008).

Furthermore, it is useful to distinguish, at least at a conceptual level, between pure empathy and other empathy-related responses such as sympathy and personal distress (Batson, 1991). *Sympathy* refers to other-oriented emotional responses that are based on the apprehension or comprehension of another's negative emotional condition; it involves feelings of concern and the desire to alleviate the other's negative emotion. Sympathy stems from the experience of empathy, or from cognitive processes such as perspective taking, mental associations, and accessing information about the other's situation from memory (Eisenberg, Shea, et al., 1991). By contrast, *personal distress* involves a negative reaction such as anxiety or discomfort on perceiving cues related to another's distress (Batson, 1991). Scholars have suggested that empathic overarousal (Hoffman, 1982) or personal distress (Batson, 1991) is associated with a self- rather than other-focus. Indeed, researchers have found evidence that aversive emotional arousal induces self-focused attention (Wood, Saltzberg, & Goldsamt, 1990).

In empirical research, it is often difficult to distinguish between different processes of empathy (e.g., cognitive, affective, or motor empathy) or between different modes of empathy-related responding (e.g., empathy, personal distress, or sympathy). Measures of empathy or empathy-related responding could assess more than one construct, especially if they are assessed by the same method (e.g., self-report). Thus, researchers should keep in mind that definitions of empathy, as well as its correlates, vary as a function of the operational notion of the construct. In this chapter, we briefly review and discuss the advantages and disadvantages of commonly used methods for assessing empathy-related responding.

SELF-REPORTED SITUATIONAL OR STATE EMPATHY MEASURES

Situational or state empathy measures usually use emotion-evoking stimuli presented via picture–story procedures, audios, slides, videos, or realistic enactments depicting others experiencing certain emotions (e.g., happiness, sadness). After the exposure to the evoking stimuli, participants are asked to report their emotional reactions by means of self-ratings on a mood scale with adjectives reflecting empathy (e.g., empathic, concerned, warm, softhearted, compassionate; Batson, 1991), positive and negative affect, or other empathy-related responses such as sympathy and personal distress (e.g., Batson, 1991; Holmgren, Eisenberg, & Fabes, 1998; Zahn-Waxler, Friedman, & Cummings, 1983). Depending on the age of the participants, the responses may be obtained with paper-and-pencil measures or verbal reports, or by pointing to pictorial scales indicating how much an adjective applies. In general, moderate associations have been found between prosocial behaviors and self-reported empathy in empathy-evoking situations for adolescents and adults (Eisenberg & Miller, 1987); however, weak relations have been found for children (Eisenberg & Fabes, 1990, 1998).

Picture–story measures of empathy were commonly used for assessing empathy-related responding in young children. With these measures, the child typically is told brief stories while being shown pictures (usually photos or drawings) depicting hypothetical protagonists in emotion-eliciting situations. The most frequently used measure of this type is the Feshbach and Roe Affective Situations Test for Empathy (FASTE; Feshbach, 1978), which was designed to assess empathy in preschool-age and school-age children. The FASTE consists of a series of eight stories (each accompanied by three slides) depicting events that would be expected to make the story protagonist happy, sad, fearful, or angry (there are two stories for each of these emotions). After exposure to each scenario, the child is asked to rate his or her own emotional states. Empathic responsiveness is operationalized as the degree of match between the child's and the story character's emotional states. The FASTE has been modified by many researchers to fit their studies (e.g., Eisenberg-Berg & Lennon, 1980; Iannotti, 1985). There have been some concerns about the psychometric properties of picture–story measures. First, the stories typically are so short that they may not induce sufficient affect to evoke empathy, especially over repeated trials; using longer stories, however, did not improve the validity of the measure in one study (Eisenberg-Berg & Lennon, 1980). Second, children's self-reports of empathy in reaction to picture–story indexes have related positively to public and requested prosocial behavior, but negatively to spontaneous prosocial behavior (e.g., Eisenberg-Berg & Lennon, 1980), which suggests that self-reported empathy is generally affected by social demands (i.e., the need to behave in a socially approved manner).

Strayer and Schroeder (1989; see also Strayer, 1993) developed a set of procedures to measure children's empathic responding to a series of videotaped emotionally evocative vignettes. Van der Graaff et al. (2016) used a lab-based protocol to assess adolescents' empathic responses to emotional film clips. Instead of using hypothetical scenarios, Gleason, Jensen-Campbell, and Ickes (2009) developed a lab protocol to assess adolescents' empathic accuracy using videos of spontaneous teacher–student interactions.

Performance-based state empathy measures have also been developed for adults. For example, Derntl et al. (2009) developed a set of tasks to assess adults' emotion recognition, emotional perspective taking, and affective empathy, respectively. Dziobek et al. (2008) developed the Multifaceted Empathy Test

(MET), a naturalistic measure of empathy that allows separate assessment of cognitive and emotional aspects of empathy. The MET consists of 23 pairs of stimuli (context and person pictures), many of which depict people in emotionally charged situations. To assess cognitive empathy, participants are required to infer the mental state of the individuals shown in the pictures. After those inferences, participants are given feedback about the correct answer. Then, to assess emotional empathy, participants are asked to rate their level of arousal for the person in the picture, as well as to rate the degree of empathic concern they feel for the person in the picture. Cronbach's alphas for the MET subscales ranged from .71 to .92. The MET's emotional subscales were positively and highly correlated (r = .61 to .63) with the Empathic Concern subscale of the Interpersonal Reactivity Index (IRI; Davis, 1983), whereas the cognitive empathy subscale of the MET was positively correlated with (r = .28) the Perspective Taking subscale of the IRI (Dziobek et al., 2008).

Similarly to the procedures used with adolescents by Gleason et al. (2009), Hodges, Kiel, Kramer, Veach, and Villanueva (2010) assessed women's (perceivers') empathic accuracy using videos of new-mother targets describing their experience of new motherhood. After watching the video, participants were asked to complete a self-reported empathy scale, write down their best guess as to what the target was thinking, and write a letter to the target. Perceivers' empathic accuracy was rated by the target and independent coders using a 3-point scale (Ickes, 1993). The alpha reliability among coders was .88 and coders' and targets' ratings of empathic accuracy were moderately correlated (r = .35; Hodges et al., 2010).

Erbas, Sels, Ceulemans, and Kuppens (2016) used an experience-sampling approach to assess cognitive empathy (or empathic accuracy) in couples. For 7 days, participants carried a preprogrammed smartphone during their daily activities and responded to the questions when signaled. The smartphones were programed to signal 10 times a day according to a stratified random-interval scheme, with each day being divided into 10 equal intervals (between 10 a.m. and 10 p.m.). At each signal, the participants are prompted to indicate how angry, depressed, anxious, sad, relaxed, happy, satisfied, and excited they felt at that moment using a slider scale ranging from 1 (*not at all*) to 100 (*very much*). In addition, they rated how they thought their partner felt at the same moment using the same grid. Empathic accuracy was estimated by calculating how well the perceivers' ratings of their partners' affect matched the partners' ratings of their own affect for each assessed time point.

SELF-REPORTED TRAIT EMPATHY QUESTIONNAIRES

Different from situational empathy measures, trait empathy measures assess individuals' empathic responding across a range of situations or settings. One commonly used trait empathy questionnaire is Mehrabian and Epstein's (1972) scale of Emotional Tendency, which has been used mostly with older adolescents and adults. The measure consists of 33 items requiring a response to each item on a 9-point Likert scale. The items pertain to susceptibility to emotional contagion, appreciation of the feelings of unfamiliar and distant others, extreme emotional responsiveness, the tendency to be moved by others' positive emotional experiences, sympathetic tendencies, and willingness to have contact with others who have problems. The internal consistency of the Mehrabian and Epstein measure is .79 among adults (Kalliopuska, 1983) and .48 among seventh graders (Bryant, 1982). A split-half reliability of .84 has been reported (Mehrabian & Epstein, 1972).

Bryant (1982) modified the Mehrabian and Epstein scale for children. Bryant's empathy scale consists of 22 items assessing global sympathy. Seventeen of the items were adapted from Mehrabian and Epstein's (1972) scale. Three formats have been used in administering the resulting children's version of empathy assessment (Bryant, 1987). Younger children place cards (one empathy item per card) in a "me" or "not me" box; older children circle "yes" or "no" in response to each item; and adolescents or adults respond to the Mehrabian and Epstein 9-point format. The alpha of Bryant's (1982) measure was .54 for first graders, .68 for fourth graders, and .79 for the seventh graders.

A major problem with Mehrabian and Epstein's and Bryant's self-report measures is that items seem to tap various aspects of empathy-related responding such as sympathy, susceptibility to emotional arousal, perspective taking, and personal distress. Davis's (1983, 1994) Interpersonal Reactivity scale resolves this concern because it contains separate scales designed to differentiate among empathic concern (i.e., sympathy), personal distress, fantasy empathy (i.e., vicarious responding to characters in books or film), and perspective taking. This measure has been used primarily with adolescents and adults. Internal reliabilities for the four subscales ranged from .70 to .78, and test–retest reliabilities over two months range from .61 to .81 in research with adults (Davis, 1983, 1994). Test–retest reliabilities over 2 years in adolescence ranged from .50 to .62 (Davis & Franzoi, 1991).

Eisenberg and colleagues developed a simplified three-item scale of dispositional sympathy for use with children (Eisenberg, Fabes, Schaller, Carlo, & Miller, 1991; alpha = .67). This scale was enlarged to seven items in Eisenberg et al. (1996; alpha =.73 with kindergarten to second graders) and six items in Spinrad et al. (1999; alpha =.63 with children aged 5 to just turning 8; see Appendix 16.1).

More recently, new trait empathy questionnaires were developed to differentiate various components of empathic responding in adolescents and/or adults. For example, Jolliffe and Farrington (2006) developed the Basic Empathy Scale (BES), a self-reported measure of affective and cognitive empathy for adolescents. In a sample of adolescents (Jolliffe & Farrington, 2006), the alphas of the BES subscales were .79 and .85, and a confirmatory factor analysis supported the two-factor solution. The BES affective and cognitive subscales were positively correlated with the Empathic Concern and Perspective Taking subscales of the IRI (Davis, 1983). In addition, Jordan, Amir, and Bloom (2016) developed the Empathy Index (EI), which was designed to differentiate empathy or emotion contagion (i.e., the tendency to feel what others are feeling) from behavioral contagion (i.e., the tendency to do what others are doing) in adults. The EI has two subscales: empathy, and behavioral contagion (with alphas > .71). Both subscales were positively correlated with the *personal distress* subscale of IRI but were uncorrelated with the *empathic concern* or *perspective taking* subscales of the IRI.

Compared with situational empathy measures, trait empathy measures are more convenient and economical to administer. Because trait measures tap individuals' empathy-related responding over a broad range of behaviors and situations, they likely provide more stable and consistent estimates of empathic responding than situational measures (Eisenberg & Miller, 1987). Indeed, trait measures of empathy have been consistently found to relate positively to participants' prosocial behavior, and negatively to aggression in middle childhood to adulthood (see Eisenberg & Fabes, 1998; Eisenberg & Miller, 1987; Eisenberg, Spinrad, & Knafo-Noam, 2015; Miller & Eisenberg, 1988).

However, a disadvantage of self-reported trait empathy measures is that it is often associated with social desirability in children (e.g., Eisenberg, Fabes, Schaller, Miller, et al., 1991). In adulthood, the desire to see oneself in ways consistent with one's own values, needs, and self-perceptions, including those stemming from one's same-sex gender role (e.g., men might prefer to present themselves as unemotional to others, whereas women might not be concerned about being viewed as emotional) may be more likely than social desirability to influence participants' reports of empathy and sympathy (Losoya & Eisenberg, 2001).

OTHER-REPORTS OF EMPATHY-RELATED RESPONDING

To obtain information about participants' empathy-related responding from parents, teachers, or peers, researchers often adapt items from the self-reported measures reviewed above for other-reports measures. For example, Eisenberg, Fabes, et al. (1998) used a parent- or teacher-reported children's trait empathy/sympathy measure (see Appendix 16.2). As suggested by Losoya and Eisenberg (2001), there are several benefits of using other-report measures. First, other-reports can be used to obtain data on children too young to provide accurate self-reports. Second, other-reports are less likely than self-reports to be biased by social desirability, especially if someone other than a family member is the respondent. Third, it is possible to use multiple reporters to obtain information about participants' empathy-related responding in a variety of settings, which is likely to provide more reliable data than that obtained from a single reporter. There is modest agreement between parents' and teachers' reports of children's sympathy, although this agreement appears to be lower in adolescent samples (Eisenberg, Fabes, et al., 1996, 1998; Murphy, Shepard, Eisenberg, Fabes, & Guthrie, 1999; Vaughan, Eisenberg, French, Purwono, Suryanti, & Pidada, 2009). This may be because junior high teachers do not know their students as well as do elementary school teachers, or because adolescents may be more private or guarded about their emotional experience. In a sample of school-age children from Chinese American immigrant families, Main et al. (2016) found no significant cross-reporter correlations among parent-, teacher-, and child-rated sympathy, which might be due to cultural differences in the perception or evaluation of children's sympathy across reporters.

FACIAL, GESTURAL, AND VOCAL INDICES OF EMPATHY-RELATED RESPONDING

Researchers can collect and code participants' facial, gestural, and vocal reactions to experimentally induced empathy-evoking stimulus as markers of empathy-related reactions (e.g., Holmgren et al., 1998; Zahn-Waxler et al., 1983). A variety of emotions and behaviors can be coded. For example, in Zahn-Waxler and colleagues' study (1992), participants' reactions to naturally occurring instances of another's distress were coded for (a) empathic concern (i.e., emotional arousal that appeared to reflect sympathetic concern for the victim), (b) self-distress (i.e., emotions evoked by the other's distress that were more intense, negative, and reflective of personal distress), and (c) positive affect when viewing another's distress. When coding individuals' facial and gestural reactions to empathy-inducing films, Eisenberg and colleagues tried to differentiate among facial expressions that likely reflect sympathy, empathy, and personal distress. Expressions of concerned attention (e.g., eyebrows pulled down and inward over the nose, head forward, intense interest in evocative events in the film) are believed to indicate sympathy; signs of empathic sadness (sad expressions) likely tap empathy and may be likely to engender sympathy; fearful and anxious expression and lip biting are likely to indicate personal distress (Eisenberg & Fabes, 1990; Eisenberg, Schaller, et al., 1988). Van der Graaff et al. (2016) collected facial electromyography while adult participants viewed emotional film clips, and found that the motor empathy correlated positively with self-reported affective empathy but was uncorrelated with self-reported cognitive empathy or perspective taking.

A clear strength of facial, gestural, and vocal indexes of empathy is that they are less subject to the self-presentational biases inherent in self-report measures, particularly for younger children who have yet to learn socially appropriate facial display rules (Cole, 1986). Therefore, facial, gestural, and vocal measures of empathy-related responding have been used with children from as young as 15 months old through elementary school (e.g., Miller, Eisenberg, Fabes, & Shell, 1996; Zahn-Waxler et al., 1992), as well as with adults (Eisenberg et al., 1994).

However, the facial, vocal, and gestural measures also have limitations. First, the facial expressions in situations involving vicarious emotion reflect not only empathy but also emotional expressivity. Moreover, as children age, they increasingly become able to mask their expression of negative emotion (Cole, 1986), and to do so in a variety of situations (Eisenberg, Fabes, et al., 1988). Thus, as in the case of self-reports, self-presentational biases and demand characteristics may affect older children's and adults' willingness to display negative emotions (Losoya & Eisenberg, 2001). Therefore, facial indexes may not be accurate markers of empathy-related responding for older children and adults, especially if facial expressions are assessed when individuals are in view of others. Likely because of this weakness, researchers found inconsistent associations between facial, gestural, and vocal indexes of empathy and participants' prosocial behavior and aggression. Eisenberg and Miller (1987) conducted a meta-analysis of the available studies and found that the associations between empathy and prosocial behaviors varied by the methods of measuring empathy measures: there was no association between picture–story indices of empathy and prosocial behavior, whereas the associations between other indices of empathy (e.g., parent and teacher ratings, facial or vocal responses to films) and prosocial behaviors. However, no consistent relations were found between facial, gestural, and vocal reactions of empathy (both to pictures–stories and to films) and aggression across studies (Miller & Eisenberg, 1988). In studies since 1988, however, facial indices of empathy, sympathy, and personal distress frequently have been related in theoretically consistent ways with prosocial behavior, externalizing problems, and/or prosocial behavior (e.g., Eisenberg et al., 1989, 1994, 2015; Eisenberg & Fabes, 1998; Zhou et al., 2002).

PHYSIOLOGICAL MEASURES OF EMPATHY-RELATED RESPONSES

Researchers increasingly have used physiological indexes, such as heart rate (HR) and skin conductance (SC), as markers of empathy-related responses (e.g., Eisenberg, Fabes, Schaller, Carlo, & Miller, 1991; Liew et al., 2003, 2011; Taylor, Eisenberg, & Spinrad, 2015; Zahn-Waxler, Cole, Welsh, & Fox, 1995). Although these measures have distinct advantages, they also have some disadvantages regarding ease of use and interpretation. Furthermore, although there has been extensive research on neural mechanisms of empathic concern, including the controversy on the possible role of the mirror neuron system in empathy and sympathy (e.g., Decety, 2010, 2011), it is beyond the scope of this chapter to discuss this literature.

Heart Rate

There is growing evidence that differential patterns of HR are related to empathy-related responses. In psychophysiological studies, HR deceleration has been associated with the intake of information and the outward focus of attention (Cacioppo & Sandman, 1978; Lacey, Kagan, Lacey, & Moss, 1963). Therefore, when individuals exhibit HR deceleration in an empathy-inducing context, they are likely to be focusing on information about another's emotional state or situation and experiencing sympathy. In contrast, acceleration of HR is likely to occur when individuals experience anxiety, distress, and active coping (Cacioppo & Sandman, 1978; Lazarus, 1975). Thus, HR acceleration is believed to be associated with personal distress.

In initial studies, investigators examined whether HR varied when individuals were exposed to sympathy-inducing films (or were talking about sympathy-inducing events) and when they were watching or discussing events that were likely to be more distressing. In general, HR deceleration has occurred in situations likely to evoke sympathy (e.g., during exposure to sympathy-inducing films), whereas HR acceleration has been associated with activities likely to evoke distress (e.g., during a scary film; Eisenberg, Fabes, et al., 1988; Eisenberg, Schaller, et al., 1988). Moreover, consistent with theory on the relation of sympathy to altruism, HR deceleration generally has been positively associated with prosocial behavior (in circumstances where it is likely to be motivated by altruism), whereas HR acceleration sometimes has been negatively related to prosocial behavior (see Eisenberg & Fabes, 1990). For example, in a sample of 4- to 5-year-old children at risk for behavior problems, HR deceleration was associated with prosocial behaviors and empathetic concern (Zahn-Waxler et al., 1995). Liew et al. (2003) found that 9-year-old boys who exhibited higher HR acceleration (or less deceleration) in reaction to slides depicting negative emotions were better regulated, less emotionally intense, and better adjusted than their less responsive peers. Fewer findings were obtained for girls or for positive slides. Importantly, the stimuli used were much less evocative than in other studies, so any response at all might have been indicative of mild empathy. It is important to note that it is HR deceleration during the evocative period, not mean HR over a longer period, that tends to be associated with prosocial tendencies (Eisenberg, personal communication, January 2017; e.g., Zahn-Waxler et al., 1995).

Skin Conductance

Skin conductance (SC) has been used as a marker of empathy-related responding (Eisenberg, Fabes, Schaller, Miller, et al., 1991; Fabes, Eisenberg, & Eisenbud, 1993) and tends to be associated with the experience of anxious or fearful emotion (MacDowell & Mandler, 1989; Wallbott & Scherer, 1991). Because SC is often associated with physiological arousal, SC is believed to be a marker of personal distress rather than sympathy, at least when using fairly evocative eliciting stimuli (Eisenberg & Fabes, 1990). In fact, adults and children tend to exhibit high levels of SC to films likely to induce vicarious distress (Eisenberg, Fabes, Schaller, Carlo, & Miller, 1991; Eisenberg, Fabes, Schaller, Miller, et al., 1991). SC has been related to prosocial and antisocial behavior in ways consistent with theory. For example, Fabes et al. (1993) found an inverse relation between girls' dispositional helpfulness and SC to response to an empathy-inducing film, and their reports of general distress were positively related to SC. Moreover, preschool girls classified as having the most problem behaviors (both externalizing and internalizing) experienced the greatest increase in SC in response to an empathy-inducing stimulus (Zahn-Waxler et al., 1995).

Collecting physiological data to assess empathy-related responses offers a number of advantages. First, because it is unlikely that most individuals will consciously control their physiological reactions, such data probably are relatively free from social-desirability biases. Second, given that children tend to have difficulty reporting their vicariously induced emotional reactions (Eisenberg & Lennon, 1983; Eisenberg & Miller, 1987), physiological data provide an alternative way to tap their empathy-related reactions. Third, including physiological data in the study allows one to overcome the disadvantages of using the same reporter to report on empathy-related responses and other variables included in the study.

Physiological measures also have methodological and practical disadvantages. First, a potentially serious drawback to the use of physiological data is that individuals can experience both personal distress and sympathy concurrently, and presently it is unclear how these reactions would be reflected physiologically. Second, analyses with physiological data can be complicated: The investigator must decide whether the data points just after the evocative event are of most interest, or the mean levels across a longer period of time. Third, age can influence children's physiological reactions, which makes examining physiological data longitudinally more difficult.

At a practical level, the participants, especially young children, may react to the use of the physiological equipment (see Wilson & Cantor, 1985). Even after familiarizing children with the electrodes, they may feel uncomfortable. Gottman, Katz, and Hooven (1997) and their colleagues, however, have developed a creative way to minimize this problem. In their lab, children put on a space suit, which contains the electrodes, and they are then strapped into a space capsule. Using such a procedure has the added advantage of minimizing the child's movement, which is known to interfere with the collection of physiological data. Because speaking also influences physiological reactions, it is necessary to have participants refrain from speaking when collecting data (or somehow covary the effects of amount of speech). It also is necessary to have the laboratory somewhat isolated, because unexpected sounds as well as changes in temperature can affect physiological reactions.

CONCLUSION

In this chapter we have outlined four methods (self-report, other-report, facial, and physiological) for assessing empathy-related responses. There is a need for more information about how these methods relate to one another. In some studies, the measures tend to be modestly positively related (e.g., Eisenberg, Fabes, et al., 1988); however, other data suggest that there are few relations among the measures (Eisenberg, Fabes, Schaller, Carlo, & Miller, 1991; Zahn-Waxler et al., 1995; see also Cacioppo et al., 1992). HR and SC may be more likely to relate to one another when the emotion-eliciting stimulus is relatively evocative (Eisenberg et al., 1996). To explain the lack of correspondence, some theorists have discussed the differential role socialization may play in influencing external (e.g., self-reports and facial expressions) versus internal (physiological responding) expressions of emotion (Cacioppo et al., 1992). Others have hypothesized that some individuals mainly express emotion externally, whereas others tend to express emotion internally (Buck, 1984). However, more data are needed to directly examine the nature and determinants of individual differences in expressing empathy-related emotional responses.

If some people tend to show their emotion (including empathy-related responding) whereas others tend to keep it inside, it is important to use a multimethod approach to assessing empathy-related responding when possible. Such an approach also is important because every measure of empathy-related responding has strengths and weaknesses. In addition, because sympathy and personal distress related differently to prosocial behavior, it is important to move beyond global measures of empathy-related responding if one is interested in positive development. Sympathy, but not personal distress, appears to be related to optimal emotional regulation (Eisenberg et al., 1994, 1996, 1998; see Eisenberg, 2010; Eisenberg et al., 2015, for reviews) and therefore is more likely to be linked to optimal social functioning, including general social competence in childhood (Eisenberg et al., 1996; Murphy et al., 1999), higher levels of moral reasoning (Carlo, Eisenberg, & Knight, 1992; see Eisenberg & Fabes, 1998), and low hostility toward other people (Davis, 1994). Global empathy is probably most useful to study when one is interested in emotional arousal or young children's emotional responding to others, whereas sympathy and personal distress are probably more closely linked (positively and negatively, respectively) to positive social and emotional development and behavior.

Most measures of empathy-related responding measure either dispositional responding (e.g., other- and self-report questionnaires) or situational responding in experimental contexts in which study participants are exposed to empathy-inducing films or enactments. Because empathy-related responding may differ somewhat in real-life and experimental settings, more information on empathy-related reactions in everyday life is needed. Zahn-Waxler et al.'s (1992) approach of having parents report on young children's real-life reactions to others' distresses is very promising; similar techniques could be used to assess children's or adults' vicarious emotional responses. The use of diaries or experience sampling to collect older children's and adults' reports on their empathy-related experiences on multiple days or at multiple times during a day would be useful in learning more about how individuals process and respond to empathy-related emotional experiences. Data of this sort might also provide information on the factors in real-life situations that sometimes inhibit individuals from assisting others when they do experience empathy and sympathy.

In summary, because empathy-related responding is a process that occurs inside people, it is difficult to measure. A multimethod approach generally is recommended because different measures may tap different aspects of empathy-related responding and have different strengths and weaknesses. In addition, there is a need for additional work on assessment tools and procedures, especially regarding measures used to assess empathy, sympathy, and personal distress in children. Because empathy and its related responding plays a significant role in promoting interpersonal understanding and positive behaviors such as helping, as well as in inhibiting aggression and antisocial behaviors, improvements in the measurement of empathy will benefit the research on optimal functioning.

APPENDIX 16.1
EISENBERG ET AL. CHILD-REPORT SYMPATHY SCALE

1. I feel sorry for other kids who don't have toys and clothes.
2. When I see someone being picked on, I feel kind of sorry for them.
3. I feel sorry for people who don't have the things that I have.
4. When I see another child who is hurt or upset, I feel sorry for them.
5. I often feel sorry for other children who are sad or in trouble.
6. I *don't* feel sorry for other children who are being teased or picked on.

Note. Directions for the measure are: "I'll read you some sentences, and you tell me if they are like you or not like you. There are no right or wrong answers. For example, 'I like to go to the movies.'" The child is first asked if the sentence is like him/her or not, and then if it is, if it is *really* (scored 1) or *sort of* like him/her (scored 2; *not like* is scored 3). To make a 3 high for most items, reverse items. Adapted from "Empathy and Its Measurement," by Q. Zhou, C. Valiente, & N. Eisenberg, 2003. In S. J. Lopez & C. R. Snyder (Eds.), *Positive Psychological Assessment: The Handbook of Models and Measures* (p. 280).

APPENDIX 16.2
PARENTS' (OR TEACHERS') REPORTS OF CHILDREN'S SYMPATHY/EMPATHY

Really true	Sort of true				Sort of true	Really true
		1. My child often feels sorry for those who are less fortunate.	Or	My child does not often feel sorry for those who are less fortunate.		
		2. My child usually feels sympathy for others.	Or	My child rarely feels sympathy for others.		
		3. My child usually feels sorry for other children who are being teased.	Or	My child rarely feels sorry for other children who are being teased.		
		4. My child usually feels sympathy for other children upset or sad.	Or	My child rarely feels sympathy for other children who are upset or sad.		
		5. My child gets upset when she/he sees another child being hurt.	Or	My child does not get upset when she/he sees another child hurt.		

Note. Directions read, "Please indicate what you feel to be your child's actual tendencies in response to each question, in your opinion. First, decide what kind of child your child is like, the one described on the left or the one described on the right, and then indicate whether this is just *sort of true* or *really true* for your child. Thus, for each item, put a check in one of the four slots." Change wording from *my child* to *this child* for use with teachers. This scale was used in Eisenberg, Fabes, et al. (1998), where it also included a rating, "In general, to what degree does this child feel sympathetic?" (rated from 1 = *not at all* to 5 = *extremely*). Items were standardized and combined after reversing items so they were all in the same direction. Adapted from "Empathy and Its Measurement," by Q. Zhou, C. Valiente, and N. Eisenberg, in S. J. Lopez and C. R. Snyder (Eds.), *Positive Psychological Assessment: A Handbook of Models and Measures* (p. 281), 2003, Washington, DC: American Psychological Association. Copyright 2003 by the American Psychological Association.

REFERENCES

Batson, C. D. (1991). *The altruism question: Toward a social-psychological answer*. Hillsdale, NJ: Erlbaum.

Bryant, B. (1982). An index of empathy for children and adolescents. *Child Development, 53,* 413–425. http://dx.doi.org/10.2307/1128984

Bryant, B. (1987). Critique of comparable questionnaire methods in use to assess empathy in children and adults. In N. Eisenberg & J. Strayer (Eds.), *Empathy and its development* (pp. 361–373). New York, NY: Cambridge University Press.

Buck, R. (1984). *The communication of emotion*. New York, NY: Guilford Press.

Cacioppo, J. T., & Sandman, C. A. (1978). Physiological differentiation of sensory and cognitive tasks as a function of warning, processing demands, and reported unpleasantness. *Biological Psychology, 6,* 181–192. http://dx.doi.org/10.1016/0301-0511(78)90020-0

Cacioppo, J. T., Uchino, B. N., Crites, S. L., Snydersmith, M. A., Smith, G., Berntson, G. G., & Lang, P. J. (1992). Relationship between facial expressiveness and sympathetic activation in emotion: A critical review, with emphasis on modeling underlying mechanisms and individual differences. *Journal of Personality and Social Psychology, 62,* 110–128. http://dx.doi.org/10.1037/0022-3514.62.1.110

Carlo, G., Eisenberg, N., & Knight, G. P. (1992). An objective measure of adolescents' prosocial moral reasoning. *Journal of Research on Adolescence, 2,* 331–349. http://dx.doi.org/10.1207/s15327795jra0204_3

Cole, P. M. (1986). Children's spontaneous control of facial expression. *Child Development, 57,* 1309–1321. http://dx.doi.org/10.2307/1130411

Davis, M. H. (1983). Measuring individual differences in empathy: Evidence for a multidimensional approach. *Journal of Personality and Social Psychology, 44,* 113–126. http://dx.doi.org/10.1037/0022-3514.44.1.113

Davis, M. H. (1994). *Empathy: A social psychological approach*. Madison, WI: Brown & Benchmark.

Davis, M. H., & Franzoi, S. L. (1991). Stability and change in adolescent self-consciousness and empathy. *Journal of Research in Personality, 25,* 70–87. http://dx.doi.org/10.1016/0092-6566(91)90006-C

Decety, J. (2010). To what extent is the experience of empathy mediated by shared neural circuits? *Emotion Review, 2,* 204–207. http://dx.doi.org/10.1177/1754073910361981

Decety, J. (2011). Dissecting the neural mechanisms mediating empathy. *Emotion Review, 3*(1), 92–108. http://dx.doi.org/10.1177/1754073910374662

Derntl, B., Finkelmeyer, A., Toygar, T. K., Hülsmann, A., Schneider, F., Falkenberg, D. I., & Habel, U. (2009). Generalized deficit in all core components of empathy in schizophrenia. *Schizophrenia Research, 108,* 197–206. http://dx.doi.org/10.1016/j.schres.2008.11.009

Dimberg, U. (1990). Facial electromyography and emotional reactions. *Psychophysiology, 27,* 481–494. http://dx.doi.org/10.1111/j.1469-8986.1990.tb01962.x

Dziobek, I., Rogers, K., Fleck, S., Bahnemann, M., Heekeren, H. R., Wolf, O. T., & Convit, A. (2008). Dissociation of cognitive and emotional empathy in adults with Asperger syndrome using the Multifaceted Empathy Test (MET). *Journal of Autism and Developmental Disorders, 38,* 464–473. http://dx.doi.org/10.1007/s10803-007-0486-x

Eisenberg, N. (2010). Empathy-related responding: Links with self-regulation, moral judgment, and moral behavior. In M. Mikulincer & P. R. Shaver (Eds.), *Prosocial motives, emotions, and behavior: The better angels of our nature* (pp. 129–148). Washington, DC: American Psychological Association.

Eisenberg, N., & Fabes, R. A. (1990). Empathy: Conceptualization, measurement, and relation to prosocial behavior. *Motivation and Emotion, 14,* 131–149. http://dx.doi.org/10.1007/BF00991640

Eisenberg, N., & Fabes, R. A. (1998). Prosocial development. In W. Damon (Series Ed.) & N. Eisenberg (Vol. Ed.), *Handbook of child psychology: Vol. 3. Social, emotional, and personality development* (5th ed., pp. 701–778). New York, NY: Wiley.

Eisenberg, N., Fabes, R. A., Bustamante, D., Mathy, R. M., Miller, P. A., & Lindholm, E. (1988). Differentiation of vicariously induced emotional reactions in children. *Developmental Psychology, 24,* 237–246. http://dx.doi.org/10.1037/0012-1649.24.2.237

Eisenberg, N., Fabes, R. A., Murphy, B., Karbon, M., Maszk, P., Smith, M., . . . Suh, K. (1994). The relations of emotionality and regulation to dispositional and situational empathy-related responding. *Journal of Personality and Social Psychology, 66,* 776–797. http://dx.doi.org/10.1037/0022-3514.66.4.776

Eisenberg, N., Fabes, R. A., Murphy, B., Karbon, M., Smith, M., & Maszk, P. (1996). The relations of children's dispositional empathy-related responding to their emotionality, regulation, and social functioning. *Developmental Psychology, 32,* 195–209. http://dx.doi.org/10.1037/0012-1649.32.2.195

Eisenberg, N., Fabes, R. A., Schaller, M., Carlo, G., & Miller, P. A. (1991). The relations of parental characteristics and practices to children's vicarious emotional responding. *Child Development, 62,* 1393–1408. http://dx.doi.org/10.2307/1130814

Eisenberg, N., Fabes, R. A., Schaller, M., & Miller, P. A. (1989). Sympathy and personal distress: Development, gender differences, and interrelations of indexes. *New Directions for Child Development, 44,* 107–126. http://dx.doi.org/10.1002/cd.23219894408

Eisenberg, N., Fabes, R. A., Schaller, M., Miller, P., Carlo, G., Poulin, R., . . . Shell, R. (1991). Personality and socialization correlates of vicarious emotional responding. *Journal of Personality and Social Psychology, 61,* 459–470. http://dx.doi.org/10.1037/0022-3514.61.3.459

Eisenberg, N., Fabes, R. A., Shepard, S. A., Murphy, B. C., Jones, S., & Guthrie, I. K. (1998). Contemporaneous and longitudinal prediction of children's sympathy from dispositional regulation and emotionality. *Developmental Psychology, 34,* 910–924. http://dx.doi.org/10.1037/0012-1649.34.5.910

Eisenberg, N., & Lennon, R. (1983). Sex differences in empathy and related capacities. *Psychological Bulletin, 94*(1), 100–131. http://dx.doi.org/10.1037/0033-2909.94.1.100

Eisenberg, N., & Miller, P. A. (1987). The relation of empathy to prosocial and related behaviors. *Psychological Bulletin, 101,* 91–119. http://dx.doi.org/10.1037/0033-2909.101.1.91

Eisenberg, N., Schaller, M., Fabes, R. A., Bustamante, D., Mathy, R. M., Shell, R., & Rhodes, K. (1988). Differentiation of personal distress and sympathy in children and adults. *Developmental Psychology, 24,* 766–775. http://dx.doi.org/10.1037/0012-1649.24.6.766

Eisenberg, N., Shea, C. L., Carlo, G., & Knight, G. (1991). Empathy-related responding and cognition: A "chicken and the egg" dilemma. In W. Kurtines & J. L. Gewirtz (Eds.), *Handbook of moral behavior and development. Vol. 2. Research* (pp. 63–88). Hillsdale, NJ: Erlbaum.

Eisenberg, N., Spinrad, T. L., & Knafo-Noam, A. (2015). Prosocial development. In M. Lamb (Vol. Ed.) and R. M. Lerner (Series Ed.), *Handbook of child psychology and developmental science* (7th ed., Vol. 3, pp. 610–656). New York, NY: Wiley. http://dx.doi.org/10.1002/9781118963418.childpsy315

Eisenberg-Berg, N., & Lennon, R. (1980). Altruism and the assessment of empathy in the preschool years. *Child Development, 51,* 552–557. http://dx.doi.org/10.2307/1129290

Erbas, Y., Sels, L., Ceulemans, E., & Kuppens, P. (2016). Feeling me, feeling you: The relation between emotion differentiation and empathic accuracy. *Social Psychological and Personality Science, 7,* 240–247. http://dx.doi.org/10.1177/1948550616633504

Fabes, R. A., Eisenberg, N., & Eisenbud, L. (1993). Behavioral and physiological correlates of children's reactions to others in distress. *Developmental Psychology, 29,* 655–663. http://dx.doi.org/10.1037/0012-1649.29.4.655

Feshbach, N. D. (1978). Studies of empathic behavior in children. In B. A. Maher (Ed.), *Progress in experimental personality research* (Vol. 8, pp. 1–47). New York, NY: Academic Press.

Gleason, K. A., Jensen-Campbell, L. A., & Ickes, W. (2009). The role of empathic accuracy in adolescents' peer relations and adjustment. *Personality and Social Psychology Bulletin, 35,* 997–1011. http://dx.doi.org/10.1177/0146167209336605

Gottman, J. M., Katz, L. F., & Hooven, C. (1997). *Meta-emotion: How families communicate emotionally*. Hillsdale, NJ: Erlbaum.

Hoffman, M. L. (1982). The measurement of empathy. In C. E. Izard (Ed.), *Measuring emotions in infants and children* (pp. 279–296). Cambridge, England: Cambridge University Press.

Hoffman, M. L. (2000). *Empathy and moral development: Implications for caring and justice*. Cambridge, England: Cambridge University Press. http://dx.doi.org/10.1017/CBO9780511805851

Hodges, S. D., Kiel, K. J., Kramer, A. D. I., Veach, D., & Villanueva, B. R. (2010). Giving birth to empathy: The effects of similar experience on empathic accuracy, empathic concern, and perceived empathy. *Personality and Social Psychology Bulletin, 36,* 398–409. http://dx.doi.org/10.1177/0146167209350326

Holmgren, R. A., Eisenberg, N., & Fabes, R. A. (1998). The relations of children's situational empathy-related emotions to dispositional prosocial behavior. *International Journal of Behavioral Development, 22,* 169–193. http://dx.doi.org/10.1080/016502598384568

Iannotti, R. J. (1985). Naturalistic and structured assessments of prosocial behavior in preschool children: The influence of empathy and perspective taking. *Developmental Psychology, 21,* 46–55. http://dx.doi.org/10.1037/0012-1649.21.1.46

Ickes, W. (1993). Empathic accuracy. *Journal of Personality, 61,* 587–610. http://dx.doi.org/10.1111/j.1467-6494.1993.tb00783.x

Jolliffe, D., & Farrington, D. P. (2006). Development and validation of the Basic Empathy Scale. *Journal of Adolescence, 29,* 589–611. http://dx.doi.org/10.1016/j.adolescence.2005.08.010

Jordan, M. R., Amir, D., & Bloom, P. (2016). Are empathy and concern psychologically distinct? *Emotion, 16,* 1107–1116. http://dx.doi.org/10.1037/emo0000228

Kalliopuska, M. (1983). Verbal components of emotional empathy. *Perceptual and Motor Skills, 56,* 487–496. http://dx.doi.org/10.2466/pms.1983.56.2.487

Lacey, J. I., Kagan, J., Lacey, B. C., & Moss, H. A. (1963). The visceral level: Situational determinants and behavioral correlates of autonomic response patterns. In P. H. Knapp (Ed.), *Expression of the emotions in man* (pp. 161–196). New York, NY: International Universities Press.

Lazarus, R. S. (1975). A cognitively oriented psychologist looks at biofeedback. *American Psychologist, 30,* 553–561. http://dx.doi.org/10.1037/h0076649

Liew, J., Eisenberg, N., Losoya, S. H., Fabes, R. A., Guthrie, I. K., & Murphy, B. C. (2003). Children's physiological indices of empathy and their socioemotional adjustment: Does caregivers' expressivity matter? *Journal of Family Psychology, 17,* 584–597. http://dx.doi.org/10.1037/0893-3200.17.4.584

Liew, J., Eisenberg, N., Spinrad, T. L., Eggum, N. D., Haugen, R. G., Kupfer, A., . . . Baham, M. E. (2011). Physiological regulation and fearfulness as predictors of young children's empathy-related reactions. *Social Development, 20,* 111–134. http://dx.doi.org/10.1111/j.1467-9507.2010.00575.x

Losoya, S. H., & Eisenberg, N. (2001). Affective empathy. In J. A. Hall & F. J. Bernieri (Eds.), *Interpersonal sensitivity: Theory and measurement. The LEA series in personality and clinical psychology* (pp. 21–43). Mahwah, NJ: Erlbaum.

MacDowell, K. A., & Mandler, G. (1989). Constructions of emotion: Discrepancy, arousal, and mood. *Motivation and Emotion, 13,* 105–124. http://dx.doi.org/10.1007/BF00992957

Main, A., Zhou, Q., Liew, J., & Lee, C. (2016). Prosocial tendencies among Chinese American children in immigrant families: Links to cultural and socio-demographic factors and psychological adjustment. *Social Development, 26,* 165–184. http://dx.doi.org/10.1111/sode.12182

Mehrabian, A., & Epstein, N. (1972). A measure of emotional empathy. *Journal of Personality, 40,* 525–543. http://dx.doi.org/10.1111/j.1467-6494.1972.tb00078.x

Miller, P. A., & Eisenberg, N. (1988). The relation of empathy to aggressive and externalizing/antisocial behavior. *Psychological Bulletin, 103,* 324–344. http://dx.doi.org/10.1037/0033-2909.103.3.324

Miller, P. A., Eisenberg, N., Fabes, R. A., & Shell, R. (1996). Relations of moral reasoning and vicarious emotion to young children's prosocial behavior toward peers and adults. *Developmental Psychology, 32,* 210–219. http://dx.doi.org/10.1037/0012-1649.32.2.210

Murphy, B. C., Shepard, S. A., Eisenberg, N., Fabes, R. A., & Guthrie, I. K. (1999). Contemporaneous and longitudinal relations of dispositional sympathy to emotionality, regulation, and social functioning. *The Journal of Early Adolescence, 19,* 66–97. http://dx.doi.org/10.1177/0272431699019001004

Saarni, C. (1990). Emotional competence: How emotions and relationships become integrated. In R. A. Thompson (Ed.), *Socioemotional development* (pp. 115–182). Lincoln: University of Nebraska Press.

Spinrad, T. L., Losoya, S. H., Eisenberg, N., Fabes, R. A., Shepard, S. A., Cumberland, A., . . . Murphy, B. C. (1999). The relations of parental affect and encouragement to children's moral emotions and behavior. *Journal of Moral Education, 28,* 323–337. http://dx.doi.org/10.1080/030572499103115

Strayer, J. (1993). Children's concordant emotions and cognitions in response to observed emotions. *Child Development, 64,* 188–201. http://dx.doi.org/10.2307/1131445

Strayer, J., & Schroeder, M. (1989). Children's helping strategies: Influences of emotion, empathy, and age. *New Directions for Child Development, 44,* 85–105. http://dx.doi.org/10.1002/cd.23219894407

Taylor, Z. E., Eisenberg, N., & Spinrad, T. L. (2015). Respiratory sinus arrhythmia, effortful control, and parenting as predictors of children's sympathy across early childhood. *Developmental Psychology, 51,* 17–25. http://dx.doi.org/10.1037/a0038189

Van der Graaff, J., Meeus, W., de Wied, M., van Boxtel, A., van Lier, P. A. C., Koot, H. M., & Branje, S. (2016). Motor, affective and cognitive empathy in adolescence: Interrelations between facial electromyography and self-reported trait and state measures. *Cognition and Emotion, 30,* 745–761. http://dx.doi.org/10.1080/02699931.2015.1027665

Vaughan, J., Eisenberg, N., French, D. C., Purwono, U., Suryanti, T. A., & Pidada, S. (2009). Testing aspects of compassionate love in a sample of Indonesian adolescents. In L. Underwood, S. Sprecher, & B. Fehr (Eds.). *The science of compassionate love: Theory, research, and applications* (pp. 405–430). Chichester, England: Wiley-Blackwell.

Wallbott, H. G., & Scherer, K. R. (1991). Stress specificities: Differential effects of coping style, gender, and type of stressor on autonomic arousal, facial expression, and subjective feeling. *Journal of Personality and Social Psychology, 61,* 147–156. http://dx.doi.org/10.1037/0022-3514.61.1.147

Wilson, B. J., & Cantor, J. (1985). Developmental differences in empathy with a television protagonist's fear. *Journal of Experimental Child Psychology, 39,* 284–299. http://dx.doi.org/10.1016/0022-0965(85)90042-6

Wood, J. V., Saltzberg, J. A., & Goldsamt, L. A. (1990). Does affect induce self-focused attention? *Journal of Personality and Social Psychology, 58,* 899–908. http://dx.doi.org/10.1037/0022-3514.58.5.899

Zahn-Waxler, C., Cole, P. M., Welsh, J. D., & Fox, N. A. (1995). Psychophysiological correlates of empathy and prosocial behaviors in preschool children with behavior problems. *Development and Psychopathology, 7,* 27–48. http://dx.doi.org/10.1017/S0954579400006325

Zahn-Waxler, C., Friedman, S. L., & Cummings, E. M. (1983). Children's emotions and behaviors in response to infants' cries. *Child Development, 54,* 1522–1528. http://dx.doi.org/10.2307/1129815

Zahn-Waxler, C., Radke-Yarrow, M., Wagner, E., & Chapman, M. (1992). Development of concern for others. *Developmental Psychology, 28,* 126–136. http://dx.doi.org/10.1037/0012-1649.28.1.126

Zhou, Q., Eisenberg, N., Losoya, S. H., Fabes, R. A., Reiser, M., Guthrie, I. K., . . . Shepard, S. A. (2002). The relations of parental warmth and positive expressiveness to children's empathy-related responding and social functioning: A longitudinal study. *Child Development, 73,* 893–915. http://dx.doi.org/10.1111/1467-8624.00446

Zhou, Q., Valiente, C., & Eisenberg, N. (2003). Empathy and its measurement. In S. J. Lopez & C. R. Snyder (Eds.), *Positive psychological assessment: A handbook of models and measures* (pp. 269–284). Washington, DC: American Psychological Association. http://dx.doi.org/10.1037/10612-017

17

Adult Attachment Security

Frederick G. Lopez

In the past decade, the robust pace of research on adult attachment has been unabated, efforts to develop and refine assessment methods have continued, and several significant reviews of this literature have been published (Cassidy & Shaver, 2008; Dykas & Cassidy, 2011; Mikulincer & Shaver, 2007; Rholes & Simpson, 2004), including noteworthy conceptual and empirical work more directly connecting the construct of adult attachment security to indicators of optimal functioning and therapeutic change (Daniel, 2006; Lopez, 2009a; Obegi & Berant, 2009; Smith, Msetfi, & Golding, 2010). Therefore, my goals for this chapter are to (a) highlight important instrument developments and measurement-related comparisons, (b) update the reader on new findings and integrative reviews of this literature relevant to earlier assessment issues and controversies, and (c) emphasize how the careful assessment of adult attachment security can promote a strengths-based approach to research and clinical work. I begin by briefly reviewing several core tenets of attachment theory and by calling attention to recent work that has more clearly extended theory and research on adult attachment to the domain of positive psychological functioning and adaptive development.

http://dx.doi.org/10.1037/0000138-017
Positive Psychological Assessment: A Handbook of Models and Measures, Second Edition, M. W. Gallagher and S. J. Lopez (Editors)

"BROADENING AND BUILDING" THROUGH THE LENS OF ATTACHMENT THEORY

Positive psychology is principally concerned with the assessment and development of human traits, virtues, and competencies that enhance and enrich the quality of human life (Sheldon & King, 2001). Generally regarded as one of the most comprehensive theories of personality development, attachment theory (Bowlby, 1969/1982, 1988) provides a broad, lifespan, and heuristic conceptual framework that is intrinsically harmonious with positive psychology's ambitious goals.

Attachment theory posits that human beings are innately programmed to form close emotional bonds (or attachments) with others, as such dispositions were naturally selected as crucial to human survival and reproduction. More specifically, Bowlby (1969/82) argued that early infant–caregiver interactions around the former's experiences of discomfort, fatigue, or threat activated a unique and goal-corrected dynamic (the *attachment* [behavioral] *system*) that, when optimally functioning, coordinated these interactions to restore the infant's experience of felt security. In so doing, these recurring interactions also furnished relational experiences and resources for advancing both the infant's psychological development and his or her environmental mastery. In short, to the extent that early caregivers were competently attuned and responsive to the child's bids for safety and comfort, these adult figures capably served as early external regulators of distress, thus providing the child with vital sensorimotor experiences of security and predictability. Moreover, Bowlby (1969/82) conjectured that within the first year of life, the child would cognitively represent these experiences within a favorable "internal working model of self and other" (IWM)—a model behaviorally expressed as a secure *attachment style* or interactional pattern with the caregiver(s).

In contrast to traditional psychoanalytic views regarding infantile need gratification, Bowlby (1988) further argued that, rather than fostering dependency, the formation of a secure IWM and relational orientation advanced the development of healthy self-reliance by supporting the autonomous functioning and exploratory behavior crucial for the child's acquisition of self-regulatory skills. Finally, and in keeping with his lifespan perspective, Bowlby believed that the relational appraisals and expectations embedded within the IWM exerted confirmatory biases on one's later relationship experiences, thus enabling it to function as a relatively stable template for organizing one's subsequent relationships. Indeed, this hypothesis launched attachment theory's eventual extension to the domain of adult functioning (Hazan & Shaver, 1987).

These core ideas and assumptions mesh well with Fredrickson's (2001) *broaden and build* perspective. According to Fredrickson, positive emotions (e.g., contentment, love) not only serve to buffer the experience of negative or stressful life events; just as importantly, they also "broaden people's momentary thought–action repertoires, which in turn serves to build their enduring personal resources, ranging from physical and intellectual resources to social and psychological resources" (p. 218). In the adult attachment literature, Mikulincer and Shaver (2004) were the first to propose that because the repeated experience of security-based interactions with others shapes the formation of positive, accessible, and mutually nested representational models of self and other, attachment security contributes to broaden and build cycles that progressively enhance the quality of affect regulation and relationship competence in adulthood. Elsewhere, across a series of four studies, Elliot and Reis (2003) found that "attachment security facilitates optimal achievement motivation because it enables individuals to view achievement contexts in terms of personal gains, and to fully focus on effectance pursuits" (p. 327). Similarly, my recent review of findings from attachment theory–driven studies specifically examining indicators of positive and adaptive adult functioning in different life domains yielded a remarkably convergent pattern of findings, leading me to conclude that adult attachment security be considered as the relational scaffolding of positive psychology (Lopez, 2009a). Before commenting further on these findings, however, it is important to note that the continuing expansion of inquiry on adult attachment has been accompanied by new scale developments, refinements, and cross-method (interview vs. self-report) comparisons as well as by enhanced design-related strategies. These advances have both fueled this expanding inquiry and yielded findings that prompt a reconsideration of earlier measurement-related issues and controversies surrounding the assessment of adult attachment security.

THE MEASUREMENT OF ADULT ATTACHMENT SECURITY: A REVIEW AND UPDATE

Researchers continue to use both interview-based and self-report methods for assessing adult attachment security. As I noted in my earlier chapter (Lopez, 2003), interview-based methods such as the Adult Attachment Interview (AAI; George, Kaplan, & Main, 1996) rely on careful discourse analyses of the interview transcripts (conducted by independent raters trained in the use of established coding schemes) of participants' responses to a standard set of questions probing their experiences with early caregivers. The quality of interviewees' narrative responses to these questions are then used to classify them into one of several states of mind regarding attachment (i.e., secure-autonomous, dismissing, preoccupied, unresolved/disorganized). These classification efforts can also be supplemented by rater agreement on several continuous scales assessing, for example, whether these disclosures reflected narrative coherence or whether their emotional tone conveyed either the excessive arousal (*hyperactivation*) or suppression (*deactivation*) of attachment-related affects (see Hesse, 2008, for a detailed discussion of these AAI-related coding and classification methods). In general, however, respondents classified as "secure" are judged as providing complete, thoughtful, and emotionally well-modulated responses to interview questions, whereas those assigned to one of the remaining "insecure" classifications exhibit distinct attentional, memory retrieval, and reporting difficulties when answering these same questions. Although, as noted later, other interview-based methods for assessing adult attachment have been developed, the AAI remains the most frequently used protocol within this measurement tradition.

Self-report methods of assessing adult attachment security, on the other hand, rely on respondents' more direct appraisals of their expectations of, and experiences within intimate relationships. Whereas some early self-report instruments similarly used prototype self-descriptions to classify respondents into one of three (secure, anxious, avoidant) or four (secure, preoccupied, dismissing, fearful) groups (Bartholomew & Horowitz, 1991; Hazan & Shaver, 1987), other instruments containing multiple, continuously scaled items were developed to yield dimensional scores indicative of either secure or insecure adult attachment orientations (Brennan, Clark, & Shaver, 1998; Collins & Read, 1990; Simpson, 1990). Of these, the Experiences in Close Relationships Scale (ECR; Brennan et al., 1998), developed via a factor analysis of items from some 60 attachment scales administered to a large (> 1,000) sample of participants, has emerged as an especially popular self-report measure. The 36-item ECR provides subscale scores on each of the two orthogonal dimensions identified in this factor analysis: Anxiety, or excessive concerns about interpersonal rejection and partner abandonment, and Avoidance, or expressed discomfort with interpersonal closeness and intimacy. Indeed, Brennan et al. (1998) showed that prototype classification based on a four-group model (Bartholomew & Horowitz, 1991) appropriately maps onto the two-dimensional space created by these ECR dimensional scores. More specifically, "secure" individuals evidence low scores on both dimensions; "preoccupied" persons are characterized by high Anxiety and low Avoidance scores; "dismissing" respondents by high Avoidance and low Anxiety scores, and "fearful" individuals by high scores on both dimensions.

Measurement Refinements and New Scale Developments

Recent years have witnessed important refinements of both existing interview-based and self-report measures of adult attachment security, as well as the development of new instruments in each tradition.

Interview-Based Measures

Studies using the AAI have increasingly drawn upon continuous ratings of interviewee responses to assess particular features of adult attachment security. Of note, there has been the more frequent use of scores obtained from reliable rating scales measuring *narrative coherence* (the scale most strongly correlated with the overall classification of attachment security), *hyperactivating* vs. *deactivating* strategies, and *reflective functioning*. The latter index, defined as the interviewees' ability to *mentalize*, or accurately perceive their own and others' (i.e., their parents', their interviewers') mental states (Fonagy, 2006), appears to tap respondents' capacities to contextualize their attachment-related memories and affects when responding to AAI questions. In addition, two alternative interview-based methods inspired by the AAI—the Adult Attachment Projective (AAP; George & West, 2001) and the Current Relationship Interview (CRI; Crowell & Owens, 1996)—have stimulated some recent inquiry. Unlike the AAI, the AAP relies on the coding of interpretive responses to eight projective drawings (one neutral, and seven scenes depicting attachment-related situations) to classify participants into one of the four major adult attachment groups. George and West (2001) reported high interrater reliability for these judgments (kappa = .86, $p < .0001$) as well as strong four-group classification correspondence between AAP and AAI (kappa = .84, $p < .0001$). The CRI, a semistructured interview protocol patterned after the AAI but specifically assessing the discourse quality of one's attachment-related experiences with a current romantic partner, has been used in studies of adult attachment security in couple relationships (Crowell, Treboux, & Waters, 2002; Treboux, Crowell, & Waters, 2004). These investigations have found that CRI classifications were relatively stable over an 18-month interval and showed good correspondence with AAI-derived classifications, and that secure CRI classification significantly predicted relationship quality and satisfaction.

Self-Report Measures

Among important instrument developments in this measurement tradition have been two modifications of the popular ECR (Fraley, Waller, & Brennan, 2000; Wei, Russell, Mallinckrodt, & Vogel, 2007) and the creation of a new state measure of adult attachment security (Gillath, Hart, Noftle, & Stockdale, 2009). Based on findings from an item response theory analysis of three self-report measures of adult attachment suggesting that these measures could be improved by increasing measurement precision at the low (i.e., secure) end of subscale scores, Fraley et al. (2000) replaced some items on the original ECR to create the ECR-R (*revised form*). Like the original measure, the ECR-R contains 36 items and provides subscale scores on the Anxiety and Avoidance dimensions. Not surprisingly, ECR-R- and ECR-derived scores on these dimensions are highly correlated, and the reliability and stability estimates of the two-factor structure across both measures have been found to be comparable (Mikulincer & Shaver, 2007). Taking a different tack, Wei et al. (2007) created the 12-item Experiences in Close Relationships—Short Form (ECR–S) by demonstrating that the original ECR could be substantially shortened without compromising its reliability, validity, and factor structure. Finally, Gillath et al. (2009) developed and validated the State Adult Attachment Measure (SAAM), a 21-item self-report measure capable of assessing situational fluctuations in the experience of adult attachment security. The three factor-analytically-derived subscale scores on the SAAM (Security, Anxiety, and Avoidance) demonstrated acceptable to strong internal consistency reliabilities across seven studies (range of Cronbach alphas: .71–.87) as well as expected (moderate) correlations with ECR subscale scores and with independent measures of positive and negative affect, state anxiety, and relationship satisfaction.

Research Design–Related Advances in the Study of Adult Attachment Security

Paralleling these instrument developments and refinements have been important new longitudinal studies respectively examining the stability of interview-based and self-report methods (Allen, McElhaney, Kuperminc, & Jodl, 2004; Zhang & Labouvie-Vief, 2004), a proliferation of lab-based experiments examining the effects of contextually activated experiences of adult attachment security using subliminal and supraliminal priming methods as well as implicit response measures (Dykas & Cassidy, 2011; Mikulincer & Shaver, 2007), a continuation of adult attachment–related inquiry within culturally diverse samples (Schmitt et al., 2004; van IJzendoorn & Bakermans-Kranenburg, 2010; Wang & Mallinckrodt, 2006; Wang & Scalise, 2010; Wei, Russell, Mallinckrodt, & Zakalik, 2004), and cross-method studies of findings derived from both self-report and interview-based attachment measures (Creasey & Ladd, 2005; Ravitz, Maunder, Hunter, Sthankiya, & Lancee, 2010; Roisman et al., 2007).

A NEW LOOK AT OLD CONTROVERSIES REGARDING THE ASSESSMENT OF ADULT ATTACHMENT SECURITY

Taken together, the continuing instrument refinements, developments, and methodological pluralism of research on adult attachment prompt a reconsideration of earlier assessment-related issues and controversies noted in my previous chapter (Lopez, 2003). These include (a) questions regarding the stability and discriminant validity of available measures, (b) whether interview and self-report measures are assessing the same thing, (c) debate concerning if adult attachment security is better understood as a general (i.e., global) or relationship-specific construct, and (d) whether available measures demonstrate important cross-cultural similarity or variability.

Stability and Discriminant Validity of Measures

In line with earlier findings, the evidence accumulating in the past decade affirms that, whether assessed using interview-based or self-report methods, adult attachment security represents a relatively stable and distinctive personality construct. For example, AAI ratings of attachment security demonstrated noteworthy stability over a 2-year interval (range of test–retest *r*s = .51–.61) within adolescent samples in the United States and Europe (Allen et al., 2004). Similarly, in a study of young women first assessed on the AAI when they were pregnant, and again 5 years later, investigators reported an 86% stability rate for adult attachment classification (Steele &

Steele, 2007, as cited in Hesse, 2008). Controlling for the contributions of Big Five personality traits, Roisman (2006) further showed that AAI classifications of dyadic participants in a lab-based study significantly and independently predicted their contributions to a puzzle-building task; more specifically, unlike their insecure peers, secure participants demonstrated positive and collaborative problem-solving strategies.

Within the self-report tradition, Zhang and Labouvie-Vief (2004) found that adult attachment security, as assessed by continuous indicators on the Relationship Questionnaire (Bartholomew & Horowitz, 1991), was relatively stable over intervals up to 6 years and that observed fluctuations in security were also reliably associated with theoretically predicted changes in respondents' coping and well-being. In addition, studies by Noftle and Shaver (2006) and Picardi, Caroppo, Toni, Bitetti, and Di Maria (2005) provided further evidence that associations between self-reported adult attachment security and adjustment outcomes were largely independent of the contributions of more global personality traits.

Correspondence Between Interview-Based and Self-Report Measures

A relatively recent meta-analytic review of 10 empirical studies comparing adult attachment classifications derived from interview-based and self-report measures confirmed earlier observations that these distinct assessment methods yield only weakly correspondent findings, although assessments derived from each method nonetheless demonstrated similar associations with theoretically predicted aspects of adult relationship functioning (Roisman et al., 2007). In another cross-method study, Creasey and Ladd (2005) observed that college students' AAI classifications moderated the ability of their self-reported attachment security to predict their relationship conflict behaviors. Elsewhere, studies contextually activating attachment security through various priming methods, as well as other investigations examining associations between self-reported attachment security and participant responses to implicit measures of cognitive and emotional processes such as the Stroop Color-Naming Test, the Implicit Associations Test, and standard projective personality measures, have been conducted (Mikulincer & Shaver, 2007). In general, they have found that self-reported attachment security to be related to these processes, thus challenging earlier arguments that between-method correspondence is low because self-report measures are less capable than interview-based methods in tapping unconscious features of adult attachment.

Organization of Adult Attachment Models

Literature indicating persons endorsed different attachment styles in different relationships (e.g., parent, friend, intimate partner) had generated debates about the organization of adult attachment models and about whether attachment security was more appropriately conceptualized as a global or relationship-specific construct. Findings from more recent studies (a) affirm that persons hold both generalized and relationship-specific models, and (b) lend support for the view that relationship-specific models are hierarchically nested below general (i.e., more abstracted) models (Collins, Guichard, Ford, & Feeney, 2004; Overall, Fletcher, & Friesen, 2003). Moreover, whereas both general and relationship-specific models have been found to explain unique variance on indicators of well-being, only relationship-specific models significantly predicted outcomes pertaining to that particular relationship (Klohnen, Weller, Luo, & Choe, 2005). In the latter study, attachment anxiety was more consistently observed across relationships than was attachment avoidance. In another investigation, Barry, Lakey, and Orehek (2007) had samples of undergraduates complete a modified form of the ECR-R that permitted separate assessments of students' relationships with mother, father, and romantic partner, as well as of generalized (cross-relationships) assessment of attachment security. Using multivariate generalizability analyses, Barry et al. found that when attachment dimensions reflected specific bonds, both Anxiety and Avoidance scores were strongly related to perceived support as well as to indices of positive and negative affect; however, associations between attachment and affect were inconclusive when the attachment dimensions reflected generalized styles.

Cross-Cultural Studies of Adult Attachment

Although Bowlby (1988) emphasized the universal influence of attachment security in guiding development and adaptation across the lifespan, Rothbaum, Weisz, Pott, Miyake, and Morelli (2000) questioned this assumption—a challenge that sparked both debate and greater inquiry on cross-cultural patterns in adult attachment security obtained via self-report and interview-based methods. In one particularly impressive study, Schmitt et al. (2004) had over 17,000 participants representing 62 cultural regions around the world complete the original (English-language) or a translated version of the Relationship Questionnaire (Bartholomew & Horowitz, 1991) along with measures of self-esteem and prosociality. Their findings revealed general support for the validity of the two-factor structure of adult attachment organization as well as evidence that secure attachment was normative across 79% of all surveyed cultural groups. However, they also found some evidence of cross-cultural variability; most notably, participants from East Asian cultures reported higher levels of preoccupied attachment than did other cultural groups. Interestingly, however, in a similar large-scale investigation of AAI studies conducted across different countries (Bakermans-Kranenburg & van IJzendoorn, 2009), AAI classification distributions were found to be largely independent of language and cultural origin, thus lending stronger support to Bowlby's universality hypothesis (van IJzendoorn & Bakermans-Kranenburg, 2010).

Cultural studies using the ECR have also produced somewhat mixed findings. For instance, although the ECR factor structure was found to be invariant across four racial/ethnic groups of U.S. college students, Asian Americans reported significantly higher Anxiety scores than did their European American peers, suggesting the presence of cultural variability (Wei et al., 2004). Further probing this possibility, Wang and Mallinckrodt (2006) explored whether samples of U.S. and Taiwanese undergraduates differed in the conceptualizations of *ideal attachment*. In this study, participants were instructed to complete the ECR or the ECR-C (Mallinckrodt & Wang, 2004), a Chinese version of this instrument, as they thought "an ideally emotionally and healthy person of your gender in your culture would answer" (p. 195). These investigators found that, relative to their U.S. counterparts, both Taiwanese men and women reported higher Avoidance scores as indicative of ideal attachment. Taiwanese men also conceptualized ideal attachment as involving higher Anxiety levels than did U.S. men. Although no gender differences in Anxiety and Avoidance ratings of ideal attachment were observed in the Taiwanese sample, U.S. men conceptualized ideal attachment as involving higher Avoidance levels that did U.S. women. The authors interpreted these findings as likely reflecting Chinese interpersonal cultural norms, including more gender-neutral socialization practices. Nonetheless, and like patterns observed in U.S. samples, a follow-up study (Wang & Scalise, 2010) found that when Taiwanese students' actual ECR scores were adjusted for their ideal attachment ratings, participants with low scores on both the Anxiety and Avoidance dimensions (i.e., scores indicative of adult attachment security) reported fewer interpersonal problems, thus supporting the universality hypothesis.

Assessing Adult Attachment Security: Toward a "Rapprochement"

In sum, earlier contentious debates regarding the relative value (and validity) of interview-based and self-report methods of assessing adult attachment security have been softening, with some scholars now proposing that the rich data generated by each investigative tradition support *rapprochement*-related efforts aimed at integrating and synthesizing their respective findings. For example, Collins et al. (2004) concluded that interview-based methods, which emphasize more implicit forms of assessment, and self-report methods, which capture more conscious forms of adult attachment security, are likely to "shape attachment behavior through different yet *equally valid* [original italics] streams of influence" (p. 209). In line with this perspective, Roisman (2009) similarly noted that, despite continuing evidence of between-method divergence in prototype classifications of adult attachment, both methods have yielded findings demonstrating remarkable conceptual convergence and suggesting that the "underlying structure of adult attachment . . . may be best captured by two continuously distributed, albeit correlated dimensions tapping anxiety and avoidance" (p. 122). Arguing that the accumulating evidence made it "no longer reasonable to conceptualize attachment security as a monolithic construct" (p. 125), he also urged future researchers to make greater use of continuously scaled measures of attachment security, to be more specific about what aspects of construct variability they were most interested in assessing, and to use methods appropriate for those inquiry purposes.

ADULT ATTACHMENT SECURITY AS A GUIDE TO STRENGTHS-BASED RESEARCH AND CLINICAL WORK

Having noted recent studies using and evaluating (and sometimes comparing) interview-based and self-report measures of adult attachment, I return to my argument that the careful assessment of attachment security may serve as a powerful, theory-grounded means for advancing the strengths-based research agenda of positive psychology. In this closing section, I buttress this argument by calling particular attention to (a) studies linking adult attachment security to key positive psychology concepts, processes, and outcomes; and (b) studies examining the contribution of attachment-related dynamics to the formation of effective therapeutic relationships and to the restoration of healthy client functioning.

Redux: Adult Attachment Security and the Broaden and Build Perspective

There is now considerable evidence that, whether assessed via interview-based or self-report methods, adult attachment security is significantly related to a wide range of adaptive and constructive virtues and dynamic processes associated with Fredrickson's (2001) broaden and build perspective in positive psychology. For example, adult attachment security has been empirically linked to such key positive psychology concepts as happiness, optimism, stable self-esteem, hope, altruism, compassion, authenticity, posttrauma resilience, and life satisfaction (Lopez, 2009a; Mikulincer & Shaver, 2007; Wright & Perrone, 2010). In addition, relative to their less securely attached peers, secure adults have demonstrated more favorable outcomes and adaptations across a wide array of performance arenas such as academic, work, and parenting contexts, as well as in novel social encounters with strangers (Feeney, Cassidy, & Ramos-Marcuse, 2008; Lopez, 2009a; Mikulincer & Shaver, 2007). Finally, adult attachment security has been consistently associated with more competent adjustments to normative transitional processes like the separation–individuation tasks of emerging adulthood (Scharf, Mayseless, & Kivenson-Baron, 2004), accommodations to "empty nest" experiences (Hobdy et al., 2007), and to optimal caregiving toward aging parents (Steele, Phibbs, & Woods, 2004).

Taken together, these findings suggest that the experience of adult attachment security, whether chronically accessible or situationally primed, activates a *secure base script* (Dykas & Cassidy, 2011; Mikulincer, Shaver, Sapir-Lavid, & Avihou-Kanza, 2009), or an ensemble of favorable cognitive, behavioral, and social information processing biases that synergistically construct realistic appraisals of and collaborative engagements with others and thus create self-propagating (i.e., broaden and build) cycles that sustain positive human functioning. It is not surprising then that the assessment of adult attachment security is increasingly guiding research on how therapeutic processes and interventions operate to promote positive mental health.

Adult Attachment Security as a Guide to Research on Therapeutic Processes

In his final book on attachment theory, Bowlby (1988) argued that by sensitively probing and challenging clients' internalized attachment models, effective therapeutic relationships furnished corrective emotional experiences that restored positive mental health. In essence, he viewed many client problems as the products of insecure attachment models and interactional strategies that obstructed optimal functioning by interfering with adaptive coping and healthy social engagements. He further emphasized the critical role of the therapist in fashioning a secure base relationship that supportively guided the client's self-exploration and revision of these problematic models while concurrently reinforcing his or her vital experience of attachment security.

Because Bowlby did not live long enough to elaborate upon these ideas, researchers and practitioners were initially slow to draw upon his theory as a guide to clinical work (Obegi & Berant, 2009). Now, however, this work is blossoming. These emergent studies have generally used either existing interview-based or self-report measures of adult attachment to examine how the attachment-related dispositions of clients (and, to a lesser extent, therapists) contribute to therapeutic work. In addition, studies using more context-specific measures of client–therapist attachment such as the Client Attachment to Therapist Scale (CATS; Mallinckrodt, Gantt, & Coble, 1995) and the Patient–Therapist Adult Attachment Interview (PT-AAI; Diamond et al., 2003) are complementing these efforts.

For example, in her review of individual psychotherapy studies using either self-report or interview-based attachment measures, Daniel (2006) concluded that patterns of adult attachment were clearly relevant to multiple indicators of therapeutic process and outcome, including client in-treatment behaviors and therapist responsiveness to these behaviors, and to the formation of effective working alliances. In an independent review of studies assessing client attachment security (as indexed by either general or context-specific self-report measures) and working alliance ratings, Smith et al. (2010) similarly found that secure clients were more likely to rate the alliance as stronger, and that relative to general attachment measures, context-specific measures of client-therapist attachment security demonstrated larger effect sizes. A review of clinical studies using the AAI also concluded that this instrument proved useful not only in gauging clients' capacities to form effective alliances but also in promoting these developments (Steele, Steele, & Murphy, 2009).

Elsewhere, relative to their more avoidant counterparts, clients with anxious attachments to therapists (as measured by the CATS) evidenced higher therapist-rated levels of negative (but not positive) transference indicative of weaker alliances (Woodhouse, Schlosser, Crook, Ligiero, & Gelso, 2003). In other studies using the CATS, clients with secure attachments to their therapists demonstrated greater depth of self-exploration during the middle phases of time-limited counseling (Mallinckrodt, Porter, & Kivlighan, 2005; Romano, Fitzpatrick, & Janzen, 2008). In a study using the AAI as an outcome measure, the majority of clients demonstrating positive therapeutic change correspondingly exhibited a consistent pattern of improvement in their "reflective functioning" scores (Diamond et al., 2003).

More recent studies and conceptual papers continue to advance understanding of how the experience of adult attachment security or insecurity may regulate constructive therapeutic processes. For instance, Sutin and Gillath (2009) found that when primed to consider images associated with attachment security, distressed individuals were more able to retrieve coherent autobiographical memories. In a qualitative study of how experienced therapists envisioned working with clients described (in vignettes) as either highly anxious or highly avoidant, therapists proposed initially differentially gratifying these clients' distinctive attachment needs for greater closeness and greater distance, respectively, but later adopting an interpersonal stance that challenged the anxious client to tolerate greater distance and the avoidant client to tolerate greater closeness and intimacy (Daly & Mallinckrodt, 2009). These findings are in line with conceptual arguments (Farber & Metzger, 2009; Lopez, 2009b; Slade, 2009) that careful assessments of clients' adult attachment characteristics can illuminate the scriptedness that organizes their problem behavior both within and outside of the therapeutic context. These conceptualizations, in turn, can inform the appropriate timing and selection of strategies for maximizing client engagement, for productively managing ruptures in the working alliance, and for collaboratively identifying and revising clients' problematic attachment models.

CASE STUDY

Joan, a single, 29-year-old woman, entered counseling reporting considerable distress over her romantic partner's recent decision to end their intense 3-month relationship. A review of her dating history revealed that her prior relationships were also of relatively short duration, marked by her rapidly developing emotional investment in, and idealization of, the partner, and by her increasing doubts about his interest and commitment. These partners would soon express (either verbally or interactionally) their discomfort with this intensity and attempt to slow the pace of intimacy development by limiting their contacts and conversations with her. Joan, however, typically responded to these behaviors by escalating her demands for the partner's availability, a cycle that eventually precipitated his decision to terminate the relationship. Early sessions with the therapist revealed a parallel pattern: Joan would engage in excessive and indiscriminate self-disclosures that were often irrelevant or tangential to the therapist's specific inquiries. She repeatedly sought reassurance of the therapist's availability and support, and was angered by his rescheduling of a session due to an unexpected professional obligation. Familiar with the basic assumptions and tenets of attachment theory, the therapist reasoned that Joan's preoccupied attachment style was obstructing her abilities to cooperatively manage the intimacy-related demands of her close relationships. He reasoned further that if she were to develop these positive relational competencies, she would need to experience a secure therapeutic encounter that both acknowledged her intimacy needs and progressively introduced boundary-setting exchanges aimed at strengthening her tolerance for interpersonal distance. Accordingly, during the difficult working phase of their relationship, the therapist consistently directed Joan's attention to the impact of her attachment style during these exchanges, encouraged her to reflect upon its associations with her earlier family experiences, and challenged her to consider and practice less reactive ways of communicating her attachment needs to him and (by extension) to her intimate partners.

CONCLUSION

The research evidence that has accumulated in the past decade lends further support to the argument that adult attachment security, whether assessed via interview-based or self-report measures, or situationally activated in experimental settings, operates as a distinctive psychological resource with uniquely salubrious impacts on human functioning. Indeed, these convergent findings are in line with Bowlby's (1988) core assumption that the essential nature of attachment security—that is, the concurrent experience of loveworthiness and connection to accessible and responsive others—optimizes lifespan development by coordinating a broad array of positive affects, attitudes, and relational competencies that enhance the construction of adaptive, meaningful, and productive human lives. Moreover, the thoughtful measurement and study of adult attachment security dynamics in therapeutic settings is now enriching our understanding of how therapeutic conversations and exchanges can free distressed clients from the painful and constraining grip of insecure attachment histories and models, activate their experience of attachment security, and thus facilitate transformative and sustainable change.

REFERENCES

Allen, J. P., McElhaney, K. B., Kuperminc, G. P., & Jodl, K. M. (2004). Stability and change in attachment security across adolescence. *Child Development, 75*, 1792–1805. http://dx.doi.org/10.1111/j.1467-8624.2004.00817.x

Bakermans-Kranenburg, M. J., & van IJzendoorn, M. H. (2009). The first 10,000 Adult Attachment Interviews: Distributions of adult attachment representations in clinical and non-clinical groups. *Attachment & Human Development, 11*, 223–263. http://dx.doi.org/10.1080/14616730902814762

Barry, R. A., Lakey, B., & Orehek, E. (2007). Links among attachment dimensions, affect, the self, and perceived support for broadly generalized attachment styles and specific bonds. *Personality and Social Psychology Bulletin, 33*, 340–353. http://dx.doi.org/10.1177/0146167206296102

Bartholomew, K., & Horowitz, L. M. (1991). Attachment styles among young adults: A test of a four-category model. *Journal of Personality and Social Psychology, 61*, 226–244. http://dx.doi.org/10.1037/0022-3514.61.2.226

Bowlby, J. (1982). *Attachment and loss: Vol. 1. Attachment* (2nd ed.). New York, NY: Basic Books. (Original work published 1969)

Bowlby, J. (1988). *A secure base: Parent-child attachment and healthy human development.* New York, NY: Basic Books.

Brennan, K. A., Clark, C. L., & Shaver, P. R. (1998). Self-report measurement of adult attachment: An integrative overview. In J. A. Simpson & W. S. Rholes (Eds.), *Attachment theory and close relationships* (pp. 46–76). New York, NY: Guilford Press.

Cassidy, J., & Shaver, P. R. (Eds.) (2008). *Handbook of attachment: Theory, research, and clinical applications* (2nd ed.). New York, NY: Guilford Press.

Collins, N. L., Guichard, A. C., Ford, M. B., & Feeney, B. C. (2004). Working models of attachment: New developments and emerging themes. In W. S. Rholes & J. A. Simpson (Eds.), *Adult attachment: Theory, research, and clinical applications* (pp. 196–239). New York, NY: Guilford Press.

Collins, N. L., & Read, S. J. (1990). Adult attachment, working models, and relationship quality in dating couples. *Journal of Personality and Social Psychology, 58,* 644–663. http://dx.doi.org/10.1037/0022-3514.58.4.644

Creasey, G., & Ladd, A. (2005). Generalized and specific attachment representations: Unique and interactive roles in predicting conflict behaviors in close relationships. *Personality and Social Psychology Bulletin, 31,* 1026–1038. http://dx.doi.org/10.1177/0146167204274096

Crowell, J. A., & Owens, G. (1996). *Current Relationship Interview and scoring system.* Unpublished manuscript, State University of New York, Stony Brook.

Crowell, J. A., Treboux, D., & Waters, E. (2002). Stability of attachment representations: The transition to marriage. *Developmental Psychology, 38,* 467–479. http://dx.doi.org/10.1037/0012-1649.38.4.467

Daly, K. D., & Mallinckrodt, B. (2009). Experienced therapists' approach to psychotherapy for adults with attachment avoidance or attachment anxiety. *Journal of Counseling Psychology, 56,* 549–563. http://dx.doi.org/10.1037/a0016695

Daniel, S. I. (2006). Adult attachment patterns and individual psychotherapy: A review. *Clinical Psychology Review, 26,* 968–984. http://dx.doi.org/10.1016/j.cpr.2006.02.001

Diamond, D., Clarkin, J. F., Stovall-McClough, K. C., Levy, K. N., Foelsch, P. A., Levine, H., & Yeomans, F. E. (2003). Patient–therapist attachment: Impact on the therapeutic process and outcome. In M. Cortina & M. Marrone (Eds.), *Attachment theory and the psychoanalytic process* (pp. 127–178). London: Whurr.

Dykas, M. J., & Cassidy, J. (2011). Attachment and the processing of social information across the life span: Theory and evidence. *Psychological Bulletin, 137,* 19–46. http://dx.doi.org/10.1037/a0021367

Elliot, A. J., & Reis, H. T. (2003). Attachment and exploration in adulthood. *Journal of Personality and Social Psychology, 85,* 317–331. http://dx.doi.org/10.1037/0022-3514.85.2.317

Farber, B. A., & Metzger, J. A. (2009). The therapist as secure base. In J. Obegi & E. Berant (Eds.), *Attachment theory and research in clinical work with adults* (pp. 46–70). New York, NY: Guilford Press.

Feeney, B. C., Cassidy, J., & Ramos-Marcuse, F. (2008). The generalization of attachment representations to new social situations: Predicting behavior during initial interactions with strangers. *Journal of Personality and Social Psychology, 95,* 1481–1498. http://dx.doi.org/10.1037/a0012635

Fonagy, P. (2006). The mentalization-focused approach to social development. In G. Allen & P. Fonagy (Eds.), *Handbook of mentalization-based treatment* (pp. 51–101). Hoboken, NJ: Wiley. http://dx.doi.org/10.1002/9780470712986.ch3

Fraley, R. C., Waller, N. G., & Brennan, K. A. (2000). An item response theory analysis of self-report measures of adult attachment. *Journal of Personality and Social Psychology, 78,* 350–365. http://dx.doi.org/10.1037/0022-3514.78.2.350

Fredrickson, B. L. (2001). The role of positive emotions in positive psychology: The broaden-and-build theory of positive emotions. *American Psychologist, 56,* 218–226. http://dx.doi.org/10.1037/0003-066X.56.3.218

George, C., Kaplan, N., & Main, M. (1996). *Adult Attachment Interview protocol* (3rd ed.). Unpublished manuscript, University of California at Berkeley.

George, C., & West, M. (2001). The development and preliminary validation of a new measure of adult attachment: The Adult Attachment Projective. *Attachment & Human Development, 3*(1), 30–61. http://dx.doi.org/10.1080/14616730010024771

Gillath, O., Hart, J., Noftle, E. E., & Stockdale, G. D. (2009). Development and validation of a state adult attachment measure (SAAM). *Journal of Research in Personality, 43,* 362–373. http://dx.doi.org/10.1016/j.jrp.2008.12.009

Hazan, C., & Shaver, P. (1987). Romantic love conceptualized as an attachment process. *Journal of Personality and Social Psychology, 52,* 511–524. http://dx.doi.org/10.1037/0022-3514.52.3.511

Hesse, E. (2008). The Adult Attachment Interview: Protocol, method of analysis, and empirical studies. In J. Cassidy & P. R. Shaver (Eds.), *Handbook of attachment: Theory, research, and clinical applications* (2nd ed., pp. 552–598). New York, NY: Guilford Press.

Hobdy, J., Hayslip, B., Jr., Kaminski, P. L., Crowley, B. J., Riggs, S., & York, C. (2007). The role of attachment style in coping with job loss and the empty nest in adulthood. *The International Journal of Aging and Human Development, 65,* 335–371. http://dx.doi.org/10.2190/AG.65.4.d

Klohnen, E. C., Weller, J. A., Luo, S., & Choe, M. (2005). Organization and predictive power of general and relationship-specific attachment models: One for all, and all for one? *Personality and Social Psychology Bulletin, 31,* 1665–1682. http://dx.doi.org/10.1177/0146167205278307

Lopez, F. G. (2003). The assessment of adult attachment security. In S. J. Lopez & C. R. Snyder (Eds.), *Positive psychological assessment: A handbook of models and measures* (pp. 285–299). Washington, DC: American Psychological Association. http://dx.doi.org/10.1037/10612-018

Lopez, F. G. (2009a). Adult attachment security: The relational scaffolding of positive psychology. In S. J. Lopez & C. R. Snyder (Eds.), *Oxford handbook of positive psychology* (2nd ed., pp. 405–415). New York, NY: Oxford University Press.

Lopez, F. G. (2009b). Clinical correlates of adult attachment organization. In J. H. Obegi & E. Berant (Eds.), *Attachment theory and research in clinical work with adults* (pp. 94–117). New York, NY: Guilford Press.

Mallinckrodt, B., Gantt, D. L., & Coble, H. M. (1995). Attachment patterns in the psychotherapy relationship: Development of the Client Attachment to Therapist Scale. *Journal of Counseling Psychology, 42,* 307–317. http://dx.doi.org/10.1037/0022-0167.42.3.307

Mallinckrodt, B., Porter, M. J., & Kivlighan, D. M. (2005). Client attachment to therapist, depth of in-session exploration, and object relations in brief psychotherapy. *Psychotherapy: Theory, Research, Practice, Training, 42,* 85–100. http://dx.doi.org/10.1037/0033-3204.42.1.85

Mallinckrodt, B., & Wang, C. D. (2004). Quantitative methods for verifying semantic equivalence of translated research instruments: A Chinese version of the Experiences in Close Relationships Scale. *Journal of Counseling Psychology, 51,* 368–379. http://dx.doi.org/10.1037/0022-0167.51.3.368

Mikulincer, M., & Shaver, P. R. (2004). Security-based self-representations in adulthood: Contents and processes. In W. S. Rholes & J. A. Simpson (Eds.), *Adult attachment: Theory, research, and clinical implications* (pp. 159–195). New York, NY: Guilford Press.

Mikulincer, M., & Shaver, P. R. (2007). *Attachment in adulthood: Structure, dynamics, and change.* New York, NY: Guilford Press.

Mikulincer, M., Shaver, P. R., Sapir-Lavid, Y., & Avihou-Kanza, N. (2009). What's inside the minds of securely and insecurely attached people? The secure-base script and its associations with attachment-style dimensions. *Journal of Personality and Social Psychology, 97,* 615–633. http://dx.doi.org/10.1037/a0015649

Noftle, E. E., & Shaver, P. R. (2006). Attachment dimensions and the big five personality traits: Associations and comparative ability to predict relationship quality. *Journal of Research in Personality, 40,* 179–208. http://dx.doi.org/10.1016/j.jrp.2004.11.003

Obegi, J. H., & Berant, E. (2009). *Attachment theory and research in clinical work with adults.* New York, NY: Guilford Press.

Overall, N. C., Fletcher, G. J. O., & Friesen, M. D. (2003). Mapping the intimate relationship mind: Comparisons between three models of attachment representations. *Personality and Social Psychology Bulletin, 29,* 1479–1493. http://dx.doi.org/10.1177/0146167203251519

Picardi, A., Caroppo, E., Toni, A., Bitetti, D., & Di Maria, G. (2005). Stability of attachment-related anxiety and avoidance and their relationships with the five-factor model and the psychobiological model of personality. *Psychology and Psychotherapy: Theory, Research and Practice, 78,* 327–345. http://dx.doi.org/10.1348/147608305X26882

Ravitz, P., Maunder, R., Hunter, J., Sthankiya, B., & Lancee, W. (2010). Adult attachment measures: A 25-year review. *Journal of Psychosomatic Research, 69,* 419–432. http://dx.doi.org/10.1016/j.jpsychores.2009.08.006

Rholes, W. S., & Simpson, J. A. (Eds.) (2004). *Adult attachment: Theory, research, and clinical implications.* New York, NY: Guilford Press.

Roisman, G. I. (2006). The role of adult attachment security in non-romantic, non-attachment-related first interactions between same-sex strangers. *Attachment & Human Development, 8,* 341–352. http://dx.doi.org/10.1080/14616730601048217

Roisman, G. I. (2009). Adult attachment: Toward a rapprochement of methodological cultures. *Current Directions in Psychological Science, 18,* 122–126. http://dx.doi.org/10.1111/j.1467-8721.2009.01621.x

Roisman, G. I., Holland, A., Fortuna, K., Fraley, R. C., Clausell, E., & Clarke, A. (2007). The Adult Attachment Interview and self-reports of attachment style: An empirical rapprochement. *Journal of Personality and Social Psychology, 92,* 678–697. http://dx.doi.org/10.1037/0022-3514.92.4.678

Romano, V., Fitzpatrick, M., & Janzen, J. (2008). The secure-base hypothesis: Global attachment, attachment to counselor, and session exploration in psychotherapy. *Journal of Counseling Psychology, 55,* 495–504. http://dx.doi.org/10.1037/a0013721

Rothbaum, F., Weisz, J., Pott, M., Miyake, K., & Morelli, G. (2000). Attachment and culture: Security in the United States and Japan. *American Psychologist, 55,* 1093–1104. http://dx.doi.org/10.1037/0003-066X.55.10.1093

Scharf, M., Mayseless, O., & Kivenson-Baron, I. (2004). Adolescents' attachment representations and developmental tasks in emerging adulthood. *Developmental Psychology, 40,* 430–444. http://dx.doi.org/10.1037/0012-1649.40.3.430

Schmitt, D. P., Diniz, G., Alcalay, L., Durkin, K., Allensworth, M., Echegaray, M., . . . Zupaneie, A. (2004). Patterns and universals of adult romantic attachment across 62 cultural regions: Are models of self and of other pancultural constructs? *Journal of Cross-Cultural Psychology, 35,* 367–402. http://dx.doi.org/10.1177/0022022104266105

Sheldon, K. M., & King, L. (2001). Why positive psychology is necessary. *American Psychologist, 56,* 216–217. http://dx.doi.org/10.1037/0003-066X.56.3.216

Simpson, J. A. (1990). Influence of attachment styles on romantic relationships. *Journal of Personality and Social Psychology, 59,* 971–980. http://dx.doi.org/10.1037/0022-3514.59.5.971

Slade, A. (2009). The implications of attachment theory and research for adult psychotherapy: Research and clinical perspectives. In J. Cassidy & P. R. Shaver (Eds.), *Handbook of attachment* (2nd ed., pp. 762–782). New York: Guilford Press.

Smith, A. E. M., Msetfi, R. M., & Golding, L. (2010). Client self rated adult attachment patterns and the therapeutic alliance: A systematic review. *Clinical Psychology Review, 30,* 326–337. http://dx.doi.org/10.1016/j.cpr.2009.12.007

Steele, H., Phibbs, E., & Woods, R. (2004). Coherence of mind in daughter caregivers of mothers with dementia: Links with their mothers' joy and relatedness on reunion in a strange situation. *Attachment & Human Development, 6,* 439–450. http://dx.doi.org/10.1080/14616730412331323415

Steele, H., & Steele, M. (2007, July). *Intergenerational patterns of attachment: From pregnancy in one generation to adolescence in the next.* Paper presented at the International Attachment Conference, Changing Troubled Attachment Relations: Views from Research and Clinical Work. Braga, Portugal.

Steele, H., Steele, M., & Murphy, A. (2009). Use of the Adult Attachment Interview to measure process and change in psychotherapy. *Psychotherapy Research, 19,* 633–643. http://dx.doi.org/10.1080/10503300802609698

Sutin, A. R., & Gillath, O. (2009). Autobiographical memory phenomenology and content mediate attachment style and psychological distress. *Journal of Counseling Psychology, 56,* 351–364. http://dx.doi.org/10.1037/a0014917

Treboux, D., Crowell, J. A., & Waters, E. (2004). When "new" meets "old": Configurations of adult attachment representations and their implications for marital functioning. *Developmental Psychology, 40,* 295–314. http://dx.doi.org/10.1037/0012-1649.40.2.295

Wang, C. D., & Mallinckrodt, B. (2006). Differences between Taiwanese and U.S. cultural beliefs about ideal adult attachment. *Journal of Counseling Psychology, 53,* 192–204. http://dx.doi.org/10.1037/0022-0167.53.2.192

Wang, C. D., & Scalise, D. A. (2010). Adult attachment, culturally adjusted attachment, and interpersonal difficulties of Taiwanese adults. *The Counseling Psychologist, 38,* 6–31. http://dx.doi.org/10.1177/0011000009338950

Wei, M., Russell, D. W., Mallinckrodt, B., & Vogel, D. L. (2007). The Experiences in Close Relationships (ECR)—Short Form: Reliability, validity, and factor structure. *Journal of Personality Assessment, 88,* 187–204. http://dx.doi.org/10.1080/00223890701268041

Wei, M., Russell, D. W., Mallinckrodt, B., & Zakalik, R. A. (2004). Cultural equivalence of adult attachment across four ethnic groups: Factor structure, structured means, and associations with negative mood. *Journal of Counseling Psychology, 51,* 408–417. http://dx.doi.org/10.1037/0022-0167.51.4.408

Woodhouse, S. S., Schlosser, L. Z., Crook, R. E., Ligiero, D. P., & Gelso, C. J. (2003). Client attachment to therapist: Relations to transference and client recollections of parental caregiving. *Journal of Counseling Psychology, 50,* 395–408. http://dx.doi.org/10.1037/0022-0167.50.4.395

Wright, S. L., & Perrone, K. M. (2010). An examination of the role of attachment and efficacy in life satisfaction. *The Counseling Psychologist, 38,* 796–823. http://dx.doi.org/10.1177/0011000009359204

van IJzendoorn, M. H., & Bakermans-Kranenburg, M. J. (2010). Invariance of adult attachment across gender, culture, and socioeconomic status? *Journal of Social and Personal Relationships, 27,* 200–208. http://dx.doi.org/10.1177/0265407509360908

Zhang, F., & Labouvie-Vief, G. (2004). Stability and fluctuation in adult attachment style over a 6-year period. *Attachment and Human Development, 6,* 419–437. http://dx.doi.org/10.1080/1461673042000303127

18

Forgiveness

Laura Y. Thompson and C. R. Snyder

Forgiveness-related scholarly publications have increased more than five-fold since the first edition of this book was published in 2003, and the number of forgiveness measures has outgrown the original format of this chapter. Rather than address a few measures in detail, this update presents the most widely used trait and state measures of forgiveness of others, self, and situations, as well as measures in the growing area of intergroup forgiveness. The most frequently used forgiveness measures are self-report, but recently implicit measures of forgiveness have been developed, and these are discussed briefly. Other non–self-report measures used to indirectly assess forgiveness are not reviewed, such as behavioral measures (e.g., prisoner's dilemma), chemical markers (e.g., cortisol), and physiological measures (e.g., heart rate variability).

TRANSGRESSIONS AND FORGIVENESS

The opportunity for forgiveness arises only in the context of transgressions. Broadly defined, *transgressions* are "events that people perceive as violating their expectations and assumptions about how they, other people, or the world 'ought' to be" (Thompson et al., 2005, p. 317). In the early stages of each area of forgiveness research (e.g., other-, self-, and intergroup- forgiveness), there was typically little consensus regarding how forgiveness should

http://dx.doi.org/10.1037/0000138-018
Positive Psychological Assessment: A Handbook of Models and Measures, Second Edition,
M. W. Gallagher and S. J. Lopez (Editors)

be defined. Currently, however, most scholars agree that *forgiveness* can be generally defined as a prosocial, intrapersonal process whereby negative thoughts, feelings, behaviors and/or motivations regarding the transgressor(s) and transgression(s) change to become at least neutral and perhaps positive (e.g., McCullough et al., 1998; Subkoviak et al., 1995; Thompson et al., 2005; Voci, Hewstone, Swart, & Veneziani, 2015; Wohl, DeShea, & Wahkinney, 2008). Most definitions used by researchers differentiate forgiveness from constructs such as *reconciling, excusing, pardoning, condoning,* and *justifying.* Dictionary and lay definitions may conflate forgiveness with these constructs.

MEASURES OF TRAIT FORGIVENESS

Trait, or *dispositional,* forgiveness is the degree to which a person tends to forgive across time, situations, and relationships. The Heartland Forgiveness Scale (HFS; Thompson et al., 2005) is the most widely used measure of trait forgiveness. The HFS is three measures in one. Its subscales (HFS Self, HFS Other, and HFS Situation) yield scores that are reported separately as measures of trait forgiveness of self, trait forgiveness of others, and trait forgiveness of situations.

Trait Forgiveness of Self, Others, and Situations: HFS Self, HFS Other, and HFS Situation

HFS Self is the most used measure of forgiveness of self, either state or trait, and HFS Other is the most used measure of trait forgiveness of other people. HFS Situation is the only measure of forgiveness of situations.

Thompson et al. (2005) defined forgiveness as:

> the framing of a perceived transgression such that one's responses to the transgressor, transgression, and sequelae of the transgression are transformed from negative to neutral or positive. The source of a transgression, and therefore the object of forgiveness, may be oneself, another person or persons, or a situation that one views as being beyond anyone's control (e.g., an illness, "fate," or a natural disaster). (p. 318)

These responses include thoughts, feelings, behaviors, and/or motivations. Thompson et al. (2005) proposed that responses have two components, both of which may change—valence and strength. *Valence* refers to whether the responses are negative, neutral, or positive; *strength* refers to the intensity and intrusiveness of the responses. Forgiveness can result from transformation of the negative responses by (a) changing the valence from negative to either neutral or positive, or (b) changing both the valence and the strength of the responses.

Description

The HFS is an 18-item measure with three six-item subscales (HFS Self, HFS Other, and HFS Situation). Half of the items on each subscale are positively worded, and half are negatively worded. Items are endorsed using a 7-point Likert-type scale ranging from 1 (*Almost Always False of Me*) to 7 (*Almost Always True of Me*). Six studies regarding the development of the HFS and its psychometric properties were published in 2005 (Thompson et al., 2005). The HFS was first published as an appendix to the 2003 version of this chapter (Thompson & Snyder, 2003), and for continuity, the HFS is included here (Appendix 18.1).

Psychometric Properties

A general description of the HFS and its subscales, as well as their internal consistency and test–retest reliability estimates, is given in Table 18.1. There is evidence to support HFS and HFS subscale construct validity with university

TABLE 18.1. Internal Consistency and Test-Retest Reliability Estimates of Trait and State Forgiveness Measures

Measure	Forgiveness type	Total items	Positive, negative items	Internal consistency reliability	Test-retest reliability
HFS[a]		18	9+, 9−	$\alpha = .86 - .87$[b]	$r = .78$[c], $r = .83$[d]
Other	Trait Other	6	3+, 3−	$\alpha = .78 - .81$[b]	$r = .69$[c], $r = .73$[d]
Self	Trait Self	6	3+, 3−	$\alpha = .72 - .76$[b]	$r = .69$[c], $r = .72$[d]
Situation	Trait Situation	6	3+, 3−	$\alpha = .77 - .82$[b]	$r = .68$[c], $r = .77$[d]
EFI[e]	State Other	60	30+, 30−	$\alpha = .98 - .99$[f]	$r = .86$[g]
Affect		20	10+, 10−	$\alpha = .96 - .98$[f]	$r = .81$[g]
Behavior		20	10+, 10−	$\alpha = .96 - .97$[f]	$r = .79$[g]
Cognition		20	10+, 10−	$\alpha = .97 - .98$[f]	$r = .91$[g]
TRIM[h]-12	State Other	12	0+, 12−	—	—
Avoidance		7	0+, 7−	$\alpha = .86 - .94$[i]	$r = .86$[j] $r = .44$[k], $r = .64$[l]
Revenge		5	0+, 5−	$\alpha = .90$[i]	$r = .79$[j], $r = .53$[k], $r = .65$[l]
TRIM[h]-18	State Other	18	6+, 12−	person separation reliability = .92[m]	—
Avoidance		7	0+, 7	—	—
Revenge		5	0+, 5−	—	—
Benevolence		6	6+, 0−	—	—
SSFS[n]	State Self	17	8+, 9−	—	—
Feelings & Actions		8	4+, 4−	$\alpha = .86 - .89$[o]	—
Behaviors		9	4+, 5−	$\alpha = .74 - .91$[o]	—

[a]Heartland Forgiveness Scale. [b]University student and adult nonstudent samples (Thompson et al., 2005). [c]9-month test-retest with adult nonstudent sample (Thompson et al., 2005). [d]3-week test-retest with university student sample (Thompson et al., 2005). [e]Enright Forgiveness Inventory. [f]High school student, university student, and adult nonstudent samples (Enright & Rique, 2004). [g]4-week test-retest with university student sample (Subkoviak et al., 1995). [h]Transgression-Related Interpersonal Motivations Inventory. [i]University student samples (McCullough et al., 1998). [j]3-week test-retest with university student sample (McCullough et al., 1998). [k]8-week test-retest with university student sample (McCullough et al., 1998). [l]9-week test-retest with university student sample (McCullough et al., 1998). [m]University student sample (McCullough et al., 2010). [n]State Self-Forgiveness Scale. [o]University student samples (Wohl et al., 2008).

student and nonstudent samples (e.g., Shepherd & Belicki, 2008; Thompson et al., 2005), as well as predictive validity with university student, nonstudent, clinical, and geriatric samples (e.g., Cheavens, Cukrowicz, Hansen, & Mitchell, 2016; Thompson et al., 2005; Weinberg, Gil, & Gilbar, 2014). Although HFS subscales have correlated positively with the Marlowe-Crowne Social Desirability Scale (Crowne & Marlowe, 1960), the overlap of only 9% to 10% (as R^2 for shared variance; Thompson et al., 2005) indicates that these constructs are distinct and that participants' scores on the HFS are not unduly affected by their desire to endorse socially desirable behaviors.

Confirmatory factor analyses of the HFS items indicated that a three-factor solution corresponding only to type of forgiveness (i.e., self, other, and situation) did not fit adequately. Adding uncorrelated method factors related to item wording (i.e., positive and negative wording) did result in an acceptably fitting model, and factor loadings related to forgiveness type were greater than those related to wording (Thompson et al., 2005). Thus, the HFS measures three aspects of forgiveness through two methods of wording. It is therefore recommended that HFS subscale scores be reported. This finding also suggests that it may be important for forgiveness measures to contain items worded in both a forgiving and an unforgiving manner. The HFS has been translated into at least 17 languages (see http://www.heartlandforgiveness.com).

The Concept of Forgiving Situations

Only the HFS assesses forgiveness of situations beyond one's control (e.g., illness, natural disaster). Some (e.g., Enright & Zell, 1989) have suggested that one can forgive only people, and thus would question the validity of forgiveness of situations. Nevertheless, forgiveness of the sacred is an accepted concept within forgiveness research. Witvliet, Van Tongeren, and Luna (2015) recommended considering forgiveness in health care settings across three levels of analysis: self, others, and the sacred. In situations such as illness or natural disaster, one person might have difficulty forgiving the sacred, or God, whereas another person might struggle to forgive the situation, which they may think of as *fate, life,* or *the world.* Forgiveness is a multidimensional construct, and people may have several subjects to forgive for a transgression. For example, people injured by explosives in combat contexts might forgive their commanding officers (other), the people against whom their group is fighting (intergroup), themselves for how they behaved (self), and fate or the sacred for having been in harm's way (situation, or the sacred).

Research indicates that it is important to measure forgiveness as a multidimensional construct and that in some instances forgiveness of situations or the sacred contributes unique information. Exline, Yali, and Lobel (1999) found that, even after accounting for difficulty forgiving the self and others, difficulty forgiving God accounted for unique variance in depressed and anxious mood. Weinberg et al. (2014) found that for victims of terrorist attacks forgiveness of situations had a stronger relationship with posttraumatic stress disorder symptoms than either forgiveness of others or forgiveness of self.

Weinberg et al. proposed that "when dealing with traumatic experiences in which the perpetrator cannot be identified as a specific individual, such as terror attacks, natural disasters, and technological disasters, situational forgiveness should be addressed in addition to self and other forgiveness" (p. 700). Thus, in certain circumstances, it seems advisable to use measures to assess both forgiveness of situations (i.e., HFS Situation subscale) and forgiveness of the sacred, or God (e.g., Attitudes Toward God Scale; Wood et al., 2010), in addition to forgiveness of self, others, and/or groups.

MEASURES OF STATE FORGIVENESS

State forgiveness is the degree to which a person forgives a transgressor (or transgressors) for a transgression at a particular moment in time. The Transgression-Related Interpersonal Motivations Inventory (TRIM; McCullough et al., 1998) and the Enright Forgiveness Inventory (EFI; Subkoviak et al., 1995) are the two most widely used measures of state forgiveness of another person. The State Self-Forgiveness Scale (SSFS; Wohl et al., 2008) is the most widely used measure of state self-forgiveness.

State Forgiveness of Others: EFI

The EFI was one of the first measures of state forgiveness developed, and it has been used extensively with clinical populations. Enright and Rique (2004) defined forgiveness as "a willingness to abandon one's right to resentment, negative judgment, and indifferent behavior toward one who unjustly injured us, while fostering the undeserved qualities of compassion, generosity, and even love toward him or her" (p. 1).

Description

The EFI (Subkoviak et al., 1995) is a 60-item self-report instrument composed of three subscales (Affect, Behavior, and Cognition). Half the items on each subscale are positive, and half are negative (i.e., forgiving and unforgiving). Items are endorsed using a 6-point Likert-type scale ranging from 1 (*strongly disagree*) to 6 (*strongly agree*). There is a five-item pseudo-forgiveness scale used to assess whether the respondent is engaging in something other than forgiveness. Five other items on the EFI assess the degree of hurt, agent of the hurt (i.e., the relationship to the person who caused the hurt), whether the offender is still alive, time since the injury, and an open-ended description of the offense. A single-item forgiveness measure that uses the word *forgiven* is administered at the end of the EFI to check construct validity.

Psychometric Properties

A general description of the EFI and its internal consistency and test–retest reliability estimates are listed in Table 18.1. There is evidence to support convergent, discriminant, and predictive validity of the EFI (Enright & Rique, 2004). Items on the EFI were selected based on the criteria of having moderate correlations with their respective subscale scores and low correlations with the Marlowe-Crowne Social Desirability scale (Crowne & Marlowe, 1960). Thus, the EFI is not generally correlated significantly with the Marlowe-Crowne Social Desirability scale. Enright and Rique (2004) recommended administering a measure of social desirability with the EFI in situations in which there are reasons to expect that respondents will "fake good." Factor analyses indicated that one factor accounted for approximately 58% of the total variance (Subkoviak et al., 1995). Thus, total scores on the EFI, rather than subscale scores, are the most meaningful. The EFI has been translated into at least seven languages and has demonstrated sensitivity to changes in forgiveness with clinical samples (Enright & Rique, 2004). The EFI must be purchased and can be accessed online (see https://www.mindgarden.com).

State Forgiveness of Others: TRIM

The TRIM is the most widely used state measure of forgiveness of another person. McCullough et al. (1998) defined forgiveness as prosocial changes in interpersonal motivations such that one experiences (a) decreased motivation to avoid personal and psychological contact with the offender, (b) decreased motivation to seek revenge or see harm come to the offender, and (c) increased motivation toward benevolence.

Description

The TRIM is based on the work of Wade (1990), and there are several versions. The first and most widely used version is the TRIM-12 (McCullough et al., 1998), which has two subscales: A five-item Revenge subscale assesses revenge motivations (e.g., "I want to see him/her hurt and miserable") and a seven-item Avoidance subscale assesses avoidance motivations (e.g., "I'd keep as much distance between us as possible"). Items are endorsed using a 5-point Likert-type scale ranging from 1 (*strongly disagree*) to 5 (*strongly agree*).

The TRIM-12 measures revenge and avoidance motivations, which are the two unforgiving components of McCullough et al.'s (1998) definition of forgiveness; it does not measure benevolent motivations. In 2010, McCullough and colleagues developed the TRIM-18 (McCullough, Luna, Berry, Tabak, & Bono, 2010), which consists of the TRIM-12 plus a six-item subscale that assesses benevolent motivations toward the offender (e.g., "Even though his/her actions hurt me, I still have goodwill for him/her"). The TRIM-12 could be considered a measure of state unforgiveness of another person for a specific offense, and the TRIM-18 could be considered a measure of state forgiveness of another person for a specific offense.

Psychometric Properties

General descriptions of the TRIM-12 and TRIM-18 are given in Table 18.1, along with their internal consistency and test–retest reliability estimates. There is evidence to support convergent, discriminant, and predictive validity of the TRIM-12 (e.g., McCullough & Hoyt, 2002; McCullough et al., 1998). Confirmatory factor analyses of the TRIM-12 revealed that a two-factor model was superior to a one-factor model and that the two factors (i.e., the Avoidance and Revenge subscales) were correlated. Thus, subscale scores of the TRIM-12 are more meaningful than full-scale scores. The TRIM-12 has been translated into at least 10 languages (see http://www.psy.miami.edu/faculty/mmccullough).

Using Rasch model analyses, McCullough et al. (2010) found that the item separation reliability was acceptable and indicated that the TRIM-18 measures a unidimensional construct (i.e., forgiveness). Thus, it is meaningful to report total scale scores, versus subscale scores, of the TRIM-18. Rasch model analyses also indicated that the five revenge items were the most difficult to endorse, and that a benevolence item was one of the least difficult to endorse. Thus, it may be beneficial for forgiveness measures to use both forgiving and unforgiving wording.

State Forgiveness of Others in Specific Relationships

Measures have been developed to assess forgiveness in specific types of relationships, but due to space limitations these will not be reviewed here. Examples include the Marital Offense-Specific Forgiveness Scale (MOFS; Paleari, Regalia, & Fincham, 2009), the Family Forgiveness Questionnaire (FFQ; Maio, Thomas, Fincham, & Carnelley, 2008), the Forgiveness subscale of the Interpersonal Relationship Resolution Scale (IRRS; Hargrave & Sells, 1997), and the Workplace Forgiveness Scale (Boonyarit, Chuawanlee, Macaskill, & Supparerkchaisakul, 2013).

State Forgiveness of Self: SSFS

Wohl and colleagues used a definition of *self-forgiveness* proposed by Enright and the Human Development Study Group (1996), which Wohl et al. (2008) summarized as "a positive attitudinal shift in the feelings, actions, and beliefs about the self following a self-perceived transgression or wrongdoing committed by the self" (p. 2).

Description

The SSFS is a 17-item self-report measure of state self-forgiveness with two subscales: Self-Forgiving Feelings and Actions (eight items) and Self-Forgiving Beliefs (nine items). Items are rated on a 4-point Likert-type scale ranging from 1 (*not at all*) to 4 (*completely*). All items begin with the stem "As I consider what I did that was wrong, I" and are followed by forgiving or unforgiving feelings, actions, and beliefs about the self (e.g., "As I consider what I did that was wrong, I feel accepting of myself"). Similar to the single-item forgiveness measure that is administered at the end of the EFI, an 18th item is used as a validity check for the measure (i.e., "As I consider what I did that was wrong, I have forgiven myself").

Psychometric Properties

Table 18.1 describes the SSFS and its internal consistency. There is evidence to support convergent and discriminant validity of the SSFS (Wohl et al., 2008).

Wohl et al. (2008; Wohl & McLaughlin, 2014) shared the concern raised by many researchers regarding the potential for measures to erroneously assess constructs other than forgiveness. Wohl et al. (2008) stated, "Granting the self-forgiveness necessarily entails perceiving the self to have committed a wrong. If an individual shifts blame for a given transgression to another party, there is no basis for self-forgiveness" (p. 2). Although they did not explicitly state so, it appears that the stem used to begin each SSFS item is designed to ensure that the SSFS does not tap forms of "pseudo-forgiveness," such as shifting blame or downplaying the offense.

INTERGROUP FORGIVENESS

An area of research that has grown remarkably since the first edition of this book is the study of intergroup forgiveness. In *intergroup forgiveness*, a person who considers him- or herself to be part of a particular sociodemographic group forgives another person or people from a different sociodemographic group. For intergroup forgiveness, there is no single measure that is most widely used. Scholars have developed and tailored their measures to fit particular contexts or projects. Therefore, rather than review one or two measures, this chapter compares and contrasts many intergroup measures and identifies eight types of items found in these measures.

Background

Much of the early intergroup forgiveness research was conducted in Northern Ireland. McLernon, Cairns, and Hewstone (2002) explored conceptualizations of forgiveness based on responses from eight focus groups composed of eight to 12 Northern Irish citizens from different religious and social backgrounds. Many intergroup forgiveness measures contain items based on these focus group responses (see Table 18.2).

In addition, some intergroup forgiveness measures are adaptations of interpersonal forgiveness measures (top half of Table 18.3), and others are adaptations of intergroup forgiveness measures or are measures constructed for specific studies (bottom half of Table 18.3).

Eight Main Concepts Assessed by Intergroup Forgiveness Measures

A review of items on the intergroup forgiveness measures listed in Tables 18.2 and 18.3 reveals that most items assess one or more of eight main concepts: (a) mutual forgiveness, (b) unilateral forgiveness, (c) seeking forgiveness from the other group, (d) willingness to forgive, or support of forgiveness,

TABLE 18.2. Examples of Intergroup Forgiveness Measures Based on McLernon et al. (2002) Focus Group Responses

Citation	Measure	Source(s)	Total items	Forgive items	Forget items	Mutual forgiveness items
Hewstone et al. (2006) Study 2	intergroup forgiveness	McLernon et al. (2002)	7	4	2	3
Hewstone et al. (2004)	Intergroup Forgiveness Scale for Northern Ireland	McLernon et al. (2002); Roe, Pegg, Hodges, & Trimm (1999)				
Survey 1			8	5	2	3
Survey 3			10	5	2	4
Klar & Schori-Eyal (2015)[a]	support for mutual forgiveness	Hewstone et al. (2004)	4	1	1	4
Leach, Baker, & Zielger-Hill et al. (2011)[b]	Modified Intergroup Forgiveness Scale	Moeschberger et al. (2005)	8	5	2	3
Leonard, Yung, & Cairns (2015)	intergroup forgiveness	Myers, Hewstone, & Cairns (2009); Hewstone et al. (2006)	5	3	1	2
Moeschberger et al. (2005)	Northern Ireland Intergroup Forgiveness Scale	McLernon et al. (2002)	8	5	2	3
Myers et al. (2009)	intergroup forgiveness	Hewstone et al. (2006); McLernon et al. (2002); Roe et al. (1999)	4	1	2	2
Tam et al. (2007)	intergroup forgiveness	Hewstone et al. (2004, 2006)	4	2	1	3
Voci, Hewstone, Swart, & Veneziani (2015)	intergroup forgiveness	McLernon et al. (2002); same measure as Hewstone et al. (2006), Study 2	7	4	2	3

Note. All measures are of intergroup forgiveness of Protestants and Catholics in Northern Ireland, except as noted.
[a]Study of Israelis and Palestinians. [b]Study of Blacks and Whites in the United States.

TABLE 18.3. Examples of Intergroup Forgiveness Measures Adapted From Interpersonal Forgiveness Measures and Other Measures Constructed for Intergroup Forgiveness Studies

Citation	Measure adapted from; [target groups]	Measure	Total items	Forgive items
Measures adapted from interpersonal forgiveness measures				
Berndsen et al. (2015)	Rye et al. (2001); [rival Australian Universities]	IFS[a]	15	1
Davis, DeBlaere, et al. (2015)	TRIM-12[b] (McCullough et al., 1998) & DTFS[c] (Davis, Hook, et al., 2015); [various groups]	GFS[d]	17	4
Kira et al. (2009)	ATF[e] (Mullet, Houdbine, Laumonier, & Girard, 1998); [Iraqi refugees & Saddam/his regime]	FRFS[f]	10	10
McLernon et al. (2004)	EFI[g] (Subkoviak et al., 1995); [Protestants & Catholics in N. Ireland]	GEFI-SF[h]	22	0
Philpot & Hornsey (2008)[i]	EFI[g] (Subkoviak et al., 1995) 20 EFI[g] and 10 original items; [scenarios with Australians]	IFS[a]	30	0
Wohl et al. (2015) Study 3	Brown & Phillips (2005); [rival Canadian Universities]	intergroup forgiveness	7	1
Other measures constructed for intergroup forgiveness studies				
Noor, Brown, Gonzalez, et al. (2008) Study 1	not an adaptation; [Chileans from political Right and Left]	intergroup forgiveness	4	2
Study 2	same as Study 1 plus 2 items; [Protestants & Catholics in N. Ireland]	intergroup forgiveness	6	2
Study 3	same as Study 2 plus 1 item and changed wording	IFS[a]	7	2
Regalia, Pelucchi, Paleari, Manzi, & Brambilla. (2015)	Cehajic, Brown, & Castano (2008); Noor, Brown, & Prentice (2008); Tam et al. (2007); [Italians & Years of Lead terrorists]	forgiveness towards the terrorists	9	1[j]

TABLE 18.3. (continued)

Citation	Measure adapted from; [target groups]	Measure	Total items	Forgive items
Strelan & Lawani (2010)	Bilewicz (2007); Sahdra & Ross (2007); [Muslims and Westerners in Australia]	forgiveness of past conflicts	4	2
Wohl & Branscombe (2005)[k]	not an adaptation; [various groups]	willingness to forgive	4	3
Wohl et al. (2012)	Wohl & Branscombe (2005); [Afghanistan National Police & Canadian Soldiers]	forgiveness (of transgressing group)	10	4

[a]Intergroup Forgiveness Scale (3 different measures). [b]Transgression-Related Interpersonal Motivations Scale. [c]Decision To Forgive Scale. [d]Group Forgiveness Scale. [e]Attitudes Toward Forgiveness. [f]Forgiveness Versus Refusal to Forgive Scale. [g]Enright Forgiveness Inventory. [h]Group Enright Forgiveness Inventory-Short Form. [i]Later adapted by Okimoto, Wenzel, and Hornsey (2015) for Australian POWs and Japanese during WWII. [j]Only two of nine items provided. [k]Later adapted by Greenaway, Quinn, & Louis (2011) for Indigenous and White Australians.

(e) state forgiveness, (f) whether forgiveness is necessary to break the cycle of intergroup conflict, (g) respondents' personal conceptualizations of forgiveness (by using some form of forgive), and/or (h) the concept of forgetting as related to forgiveness.

Mutual Forgiveness, Seeking Forgiveness, or Unilateral Forgiveness

Klar and Schori-Eyal (2015) noted that many intergroup and ethno-political conflicts are bilateral, with both groups filling the role of victim and perpetrator. Approximately half of the items on each of the measures derived from McLernon et al. (2002; see Table 18.2) assess mutual forgiveness. For example, "Only when Israelis and Palestinians learn to forgive each other, can we be free of political violence" (Klar & Schori-Eyal, 2015). Additionally, most of the measures derived from McLernon et al. (2002; Table 18.2), include an item regarding seeking forgiveness, such as "My community should, as a group, seek forgiveness from the other community for past paramilitary activities" (Moeschberger, Dixon, Niens, & Cairns, 2005). In contrast, the measures in Table 18.3 assess unilateral intergroup forgiveness.

Willingness to Forgive, Support of Forgiveness, or State Forgiveness

All of the measures based on McLernon et al.'s (2002) focus groups (Table 18.2) and six of the seven measures that are adaptations of intergroup forgiveness measures or measures constructed for specific studies (bottom half of Table 18.3) have items that assess whether respondents are supportive of, or willing to forgive. Examples of these items are "Germans today should be forgiven for what their group did to Jews during World War II" (Wohl & Branscombe, 2005) and "I would like to ask my community to forgive the other community for their acts of violence" (Noor, Brown, Gonzalez, Manzi, & Lewis, 2008, Study 3). A few intergroup measures assess respondents' current level of forgiveness (i.e., state intergroup forgiveness). These assessments include the measures based on interpersonal forgiveness measures (top half of Table 18.3) as well as on Wohl, Hornsey, and Bennett's (2012) measure (Table 18.3). Items on these assessments typically operationalize forgiveness as positive and negative thoughts, feelings, behaviors, and/or motivations.

Whether Forgiveness is Necessary to Break the Cycle of Intergroup Conflict

Most of the measures based on McLernon et al.'s (2002) focus groups (Table 18.2) have items that assess whether respondents view forgiveness as necessary to break the cycle of intergroup conflict. An example is: "Only when the two communities of Northern Ireland learn to forgive each other can we be free of political violence" (Hewstone et al., 2004).

Respondents' Personal Conceptualizations of Forgiveness, or Forgetting

All of the intergroup measures (Tables 18.2 and 18.3) contain at least one item using a form of *forgive*, except the two measures that are adaptations of the EFI (Subkoviak et al., 1995). Like the EFI, these two adaptations (McLernon, Cairns, Hewstone, & Smith, 2004; Philpot & Hornsey, 2008) are administered with an additional, single-item forgiveness-validity-check that includes "forgiven." The items that include forms of forgive tend to assess respondents' personal definitions of forgiveness. All of the measures based on McLernon et al.'s (2002) focus groups (Table 18.2), and one measure in Table 18.3 (Strelan & Lawani, 2010), include the concept of forgetting—for example, "Northern Ireland will never move from the past to the future, until the two communities learn to forget about the past" (Hewstone et al., 2004).

IMPLICIT MEASURES OF FORGIVENESS

Recently, researchers have developed implicit measures to assess forgiveness of self and others. For example: the Implicit Relational Assessment Procedure (IRAP; e.g., Bast & Barnes-Holmes, 2014), the Forgiveness Implicit Association Test (Forgiveness IAT; Goldring & Strelan, 2017), and the Implicit Association Test of forgiveness (Forgiveness IAT; Fatfouta, Schröder-Abé, & Merkl, 2014). Implicit measures are administered via computer, and they use response latency as an indicator of dispositional inclinations and attitudinal preferences that respondents are unwilling or unable to report explicitly. Goldring and Strelan (2017) stated that "the term 'implicit' reflects the idea that individuals' preference decisions operate outside of conscious awareness. As such, the IAT has the potential to address shortcomings of self-report [measures], particularly in relation to forgiveness" (p. 69). Implicit measures are an alternative to explicit self-report measures and may be useful as complimentary measures when used with explicit measures.

CONCLUSION

This chapter reviewed the most-used trait and state measures of forgiveness of others, the self, and situations. Intergroup forgiveness measures were compared and contrasted, with a focus on eight main concepts assessed by most intergroup measures. Implicit measures of forgiveness of self and others were reviewed briefly. In the process of reviewing existing measures, five possible issues in the measurement of forgiveness were noted.

First, in the areas of other- and self-forgiveness, some have expressed concerns that forgiveness measures may not differentiate forgiveness from other responses such as shifting blame for a transgression to another person, or downplaying the offense (e.g., see Hall & Fincham, 2005; Subkoviak et al., 1995). Some researchers have addressed this concern by administering validity-check measures along with their forgiveness measures (e.g., EFI) and by using item wording that acknowledges the "wrongness" of the transgression (e.g., SSFS). Others have developed measures that assess forgiveness as a process rather than as an end state. Measures that operationalize a specific forgiveness process, however, define forgiveness in narrow terms and are likely to unintentionally exclude forms of genuine forgiveness that do not fit the specific process model. This type of process measure may be useful in certain situations, such as studies to assess respondents' current stage of forgiveness within a specific process model of forgiveness (e.g., Gordon & Baucom, 2003).

Second, people may have several subjects to forgive for a transgression (e.g., others, the self, groups, and situations), and thus it seems advisable to measure multiple dimensions of forgiveness. Third, assessment items that use versions of the word *forgive* may tap respondents' own conceptualizations of forgiveness, which could include concepts that are excluded by most research definitions (e.g., reconciling, excusing). Fourth, research suggests that it may be important for forgiveness measures to contain items with both forgiving and unforgiving wording because, although these are part of the larger construct of forgiveness, people appear to respond differently to positively versus negatively worded items. Fifth, because forgiveness is generally regarded as socially desirable, in certain circumstances one may administer a measure of social desirability in combination with forgiveness measures to facilitate controlling for this.

Although all the measures reviewed assess a person's propensity to grant forgiveness, there are differences among the measures. Those who want to assess forgiveness for clinical or research purposes might consider using the measures reviewed and issues raised in this chapter to identify a measure, or combination of measures, that would best match their needs.

APPENDIX 18.1
HFS

Directions: In the course of our lives negative things may occur because of our own actions, the actions of others, or circumstances beyond our control. For some time after these events, we may have negative thoughts or feelings about ourselves, others, or the situation. Think about how you **typically** respond to such negative events. Next to each of the following items write the number (from the 7-point scale below) that best describes how you **typically** respond to the type of negative situation described. There are no right or wrong answers. Please be as open as possible in your answers.

1	2	3	4	5	6	7
Almost Always False of Me		*More Often* False of Me		*More Often* True of Me		*Almost Always* True of Me

____ 1. Although I feel badly at first when I mess up, over time I can give myself some slack.

____ 2. I hold grudges against myself for negative things I've done.

____ 3. Learning from bad things that I've done helps me get over them.

____ 4. It is really hard for me to accept myself once I've messed up.

____ 5. With time I am understanding of myself for mistakes I've made.

____ 6. I don't stop criticizing myself for negative things I've felt, thought, said, or done.

____ 7. I continue to punish a person who has done something that I think is wrong.

____ 8. With time I am understanding of others for the mistakes they've made.

____ 9. I continue to be hard on others who have hurt me.

____ 10. Although others have hurt me in the past, I have eventually been able to see them as good people.

____ 11. If others mistreat me, I continue to think badly of them.

____ 12. When someone disappoints me, I can eventually move past it.

____ 13. When things go wrong for reasons that can't be controlled, I get stuck in negative thoughts about it.

____ 14. With time I can be understanding of bad circumstances in my life.

____ 15. If I am disappointed by uncontrollable circumstances in my life, I continue to think negatively about them.

____ 16. I eventually make peace with bad situations in my life.

____ 17. It's really hard for me to accept negative situations that aren't anybody's fault.

____ 18. Eventually I let go of negative thoughts about bad circumstances that are beyond anyone's control.

Scoring Instructions

To calculate the scores for the HFS and its three subscales, first reverse score items 2, 4, 6, 7, 9, 11, 13, 15, and 17. Then, sum the values for the items that compose each scale (with appropriate items being reverse scored): HFS (Items 1–18), HFS Self subscale (Items 1–6), HFS Other subscale (Items 7–12), HFS Situation subscale (Items 13–18). Note: Scoring instructions should not be included on the HFS when it is administered. The full title of the HFS should not be included when the measure is administered, because the word *forgiveness* should not appear on the measure.

REFERENCES

Bast, D. F., & Barnes-Holmes, D. (2014). A first test of the implicit relational assessment procedure as a measure of forgiveness of self and others. *The Psychological Record, 64,* 253–260. http://dx.doi.org/10.1007/s40732-014-0022-2

Berndsen, M., Hornsey, M. J., & Wohl, M. J. A. (2015). The impact of a victim-focused apology on forgiveness in an intergroup context. *Group Processes & Intergroup Relations, 18,* 726–739. http://dx.doi.org/10.1177/1368430215586275

Bilewicz, M. (2007). History as an obstacle: Impact of temporal-based social categorizations on Polish–Jewish intergroup contact. *Group Processes & Intergroup Relations, 10,* 551–563. http://dx.doi.org/10.1177/1368430207081540

Boonyarit, I., Chuawanlee, W., Macaskill, A., & Supparerkchaisakul, N. (2013). A psychometric analysis of the Workplace Forgiveness Scale. *Europe's Journal of Psychology, 9,* 319–338. http://dx.doi.org/10.5964/ejop.v9i2.551

Brown, R. P., & Phillips, A. (2005). Letting bygones be bygones: Further evidence for the validity of the Tendency to Forgive scale. *Personality and Individual Differences, 38,* 627–638. http://dx.doi.org/10.1016/j.paid.2004.05.017

Cehajic, S., Brown, R., & Castano, E. (2008). Forgive and forget? Antecedents and consequences of intergroup forgiveness in Bosnia and Herzegovina. *Political Psychology, 29,* 351–367. http://dx.doi.org/10.1111/j.1467-9221.2008.00634.x

Cheavens, J. S., Cukrowicz, K. C., Hansen, R., & Mitchell, S. M. (2016). Incorporating resilience factors into the interpersonal theory of suicide: The role of hope and self-forgiveness in an older adult sample. *Journal of Clinical Psychology, 72,* 58–69. http://dx.doi.org/10.1002/jclp.22230

Crowne, D. P., & Marlowe, D. (1960). A new scale of social desirability independent of psychopathology. *Journal of Consulting Psychology, 24,* 349–354. http://dx.doi.org/10.1037/h0047358

Davis, D. E., DeBlaere, C., Hook, J. N., Burnette, J. N., Van Tongeren, D. R., Rice, K. G., & Worthington, E. L., Jr. (2015). Intergroup forgiveness of race-related offenses. *Journal of Counseling Psychology, 62,* 402–412. http://dx.doi.org/10.1037/cou0000081

Davis, D. E., Hook, J. N., Van Tongeren, D. R., DeBlaere, C., Rice, K. G., & Worthington, E. L., Jr. (2015). Making a decision to forgive. *Journal of Counseling Psychology, 62,* 280–288. http://dx.doi.org/10.1037/cou0000054

Enright, R. D., & the Human Development Study Group. (1996). Counseling within the forgiveness triad: On forgiving, receiving forgiveness, and self-forgiveness. *Counseling and Values, 40,* 107–126. http://dx.doi.org/10.1002/j.2161-007X.1996.tb00844.x

Enright, R. D., & Rique, J. (2004). *The Enright Forgiveness Inventory: Sampler set, manual, instrument, and scoring guide.* Menlo Park, CA: Mind Garden.

Enright, R. D., & Zell, R. L. (1989). Problems encountered when we forgive another. *Journal of Psychology and Christianity, 8,* 52–60.

Exline, J. J., Yali, A. M., & Lobel, M. (1999). When god disappoints: Difficulty forgiving god and its role in negative emotion. *Journal of Health Psychology, 4,* 365–379. http://dx.doi.org/10.1177/135910539900400306

Fatfouta, R., Schröder-Abé, M., & Merkl, A. (2014). Forgiving, fast and slow: Validity of the implicit association test for predicting differential response latencies in a transgression-recall paradigm. *Frontiers in Psychology, 5,* 728. http://dx.doi.org/10.3389/fpsyg.2014.00728

Goldring, J., & Strelan, P. (2017). The Forgiveness Implicit Association Test. *Personality and Individual Differences, 108,* 69–78. http://dx.doi.org/10.1016/j.paid.2016.12.006

Gordon, K. C., & Baucom, D. H. (2003). Forgiveness and marriage: Preliminary support for a measure based on a model of recovery from a marital betrayal. *American Journal of Family Therapy, 31,* 179–199. http://dx.doi.org/10.1080/01926180301115

Greenaway, K. H., Quinn, E. A., & Louis, W. R. (2011). Appealing to common humanity increases forgiveness but reduces collective action among victims of historical atrocities. *European Journal of Social Psychology, 41,* 569–573. http://dx.doi.org/10.1002/ejsp.802

Hall, J. H., & Fincham, F. D. (2005). Self-forgiveness: The stepchild of forgiveness research. *Journal of Social and Clinical Psychology, 24,* 621–637. http://dx.doi.org/10.1521/jscp.2005.24.5.621

Hargrave, T. D., & Sells, J. N. (1997). The development of a forgiveness scale. *Journal of Marital and Family Therapy, 23,* 41–62. http://dx.doi.org/10.1111/j.1752-0606.1997.tb00230.x

Hewstone, M., Cairns, E., Voci, A., Hamberger, J., & Niens, U. (2006). Intergroup contact, forgiveness, and experience of "The Troubles" in Northern Ireland. *Journal of Social Issues, 62*(1), 99–120. http://dx.doi.org/10.1111/j.1540-4560.2006.00441.x

Hewstone, M., Cairns, E., Voci, A., McLernon, F., Niens, U., & Noor, M. (2004). Intergroup forgiveness and guilt in Northern Ireland: Social psychological dimensions of "The Troubles." In N. R. Branscombe & B. Doosje (Eds.), *Collective guilt: International perspectives* (pp. 193–215). New York, NY: Cambridge University Press. http://dx.doi.org/10.1017/CBO9781139106931.013

Kira, I. A., Lewandowski, L. A., Templin, T. N., Ramaswamy, V., Ozkan, B., & Mohanesh, J. (2009). The effects of post-retribution inter-group forgiveness: The case of Iraqi refugees. *Peace and Conflict: Journal of Peace Psychology, 15,* 385–413. http://dx.doi.org/10.1080/10781910903158669

Klar, Y., & Schori-Eyal, N. (2015). Gazing at suffering Gaza from suffering Sderot: Seeds of forgiveness and reconciliation amidst the turmoil? *Group Processes & Intergroup Relations, 18,* 624–643. http://dx.doi.org/10.1177/1368430215570502

Leach, M. M., Baker, A., & Zeigler-Hill, V. (2011). The influence of Black racial identity on the forgiveness of Whites. *Journal of Black Psychology, 37,* 185–209. http://dx.doi.org/10.1177/0095798410380201

Leonard, M. A., Yung, S. M., & Cairns, E. (2015). Predicting intergroup forgiveness from in-group identification and collective guilt in adolescent and adult affiliates of a Northern Irish cross-community organization. *Peace and Conflict: Journal of Peace Psychology, 21,* 155–167. http://dx.doi.org/10.1037/pac0000055

Maio, G. R., Thomas, G., Fincham, F. D., & Carnelley, K. B. (2008). Unraveling the role of forgiveness in family relationships. *Journal of Personality and Social Psychology, 94,* 307–319. http://dx.doi.org/10.1037/0022-3514.94.2.307

McCullough, M. E., & Hoyt, W. T. (2002). Transgression-related motivational dispositions: Personality substrates of forgiveness and their links to the Big Five. *Personality and Social Psychology Bulletin, 28,* 1556–1573. http://dx.doi.org/10.1177/014616702237583

McCullough, M. E., Luna, L. R., Berry, J. W., Tabak, B. A., & Bono, G. (2010). On the form and function of forgiving: Modeling the time-forgiveness relationship and testing the valuable relationships hypothesis. *Emotion, 10,* 358–376. http://dx.doi.org/10.1037/a0019349

McCullough, M. E., Rachal, K. C., Sandage, S. J., Worthington, E. L., Jr., Brown, S. W., & Hight, T. L. (1998). Interpersonal forgiving in close relationships: II. Theoretical elaboration and measurement. *Journal of Personality and Social Psychology, 75,* 1586–1603. http://dx.doi.org/10.1037/0022-3514.75.6.1586

McLernon, F., Cairns, E., & Hewstone, M. (2002). Views on forgiveness in Northern Ireland. *Peace Review, 14,* 285–290. http://dx.doi.org/10.1080/1367886022000016839

McLernon, F., Cairns, E., Hewstone, M., & Smith, R. (2004). The development of intergroup forgiveness in Northern Ireland. *Journal of Social Issues, 60,* 587–601. http://dx.doi.org/10.1111/j.0022-4537.2004.00373.x

Moeschberger, S. L., Dixon, D. N., Niens, U., & Cairns, E. (2005). Forgiveness in Northern Ireland: A model for peace in the midst of the 'Troubles.' *Peace and Conflict: Journal of Peace Psychology, 11,* 199–214. http://dx.doi.org/10.1207/s15327949pac1102_5

Mullet, E., Houdbine, A., Laumonier, S., & Girard, M. (1998). "Forgivingness": Factor structure in a sample of young, middle-aged, and elderly adults. *European Psychologist, 3,* 289–297. http://dx.doi.org/10.1027/1016-9040.3.4.289

Myers, E., Hewstone, M., & Cairns, E. (2009). Impact of conflict on mental health in Northern Ireland: The mediating role of intergroup forgiveness and collective guilt. *Political Psychology, 30,* 269–290. http://dx.doi.org/10.1111/j.1467-9221.2008.00691.x

Noor, M., Brown, R., Gonzalez, R., Manzi, J., & Lewis, C. A. (2008). On positive psychological outcomes: What helps groups with a history of conflict to forgive and reconcile with each other? *Personality and Social Psychology Bulletin, 34,* 819–832. http://dx.doi.org/10.1177/0146167208315555

Noor, M., Brown, R., & Prentice, G. (2008). Prospects for intergroup reconciliation: Social-psychological predictors of intergroup forgiveness and reparation in Northern Ireland and Chile. In A. Nadler, T. E. Malloy, & J. D. Fisher (Eds.), *The social psychology of intergroup reconciliation* (pp. 97–114). New York, NY: Oxford University Press. http://dx.doi.org/10.1093/acprof:oso/9780195300314.003.0006

Okimoto, T. G., Wenzel, M., & Hornsey, M. J. (2015). Apologies demanded yet devalued: Normative dilution in the age of apology. *Journal of Experimental Social Psychology, 60,* 133–136. http://dx.doi.org/10.1016/j.jesp.2015.05.008

Paleari, F. G., Regalia, C., & Fincham, F. D. (2009). Measuring offence-specific forgiveness in marriage: The Marital Offence-Specific Forgiveness Scale (MOFS). *Psychological Assessment, 21,* 194–209. http://dx.doi.org/10.1037/a0016068

Philpot, C. R., & Hornsey, M. J. (2008). What happens when groups say sorry: The effect of intergroup apologies on their recipients. *Personality and Social Psychology Bulletin, 34,* 474–487. http://dx.doi.org/10.1177/0146167207311283

Regalia, C., Pelucchi, S., Paleari, F. G., Manzi, C., & Brambilla, M. (2015). Forgiving the terrorists of the Years of Lead in Italy: The role of restorative justice beliefs and sociocognitive determinants. *Group Processes & Intergroup Relations, 18,* 609–623. http://dx.doi.org/10.1177/1368430215570503

Roe, M. D., Pegg, W., Hodges, K., & Trimm, R. A. (1999). Forgiving the other side: Social identity and ethnic memories in Northern Ireland. In J. P. Harrington & E. Mitchell (Eds.), *Politics and performance in contemporary Northern Ireland* (pp. 122–156). Amherst: University of Massachusetts.

Rye, M. S., Loiacono, D. M., Folck, C. D., Olszewski, B. T., Heim, T. A., & Madia, B. P. (2001). Evaluation of the psychometric properties of two forgiveness scales.

Current Psychology: A Journal for Diverse Perspectives on Diverse Psychological Issues, 20, 260–277. http://dx.doi.org/10.1007/s12144-001-1011-6

Sahdra, B., & Ross, M. (2007). Group identification and historical memory. *Personality and Social Psychology Bulletin, 33,* 384–395. http://dx.doi.org/10.1177/0146167206296103

Shepherd, S., & Belicki, K. (2008). Trait forgiveness and traitedness within the HEXACO model of personality. *Personality and Individual Differences, 45,* 389–394. http://dx.doi.org/10.1016/j.paid.2008.05.011

Strelan, P., & Lawani, A. (2010). Muslim and Westerner responses to terrorism: The influence of group identity on attitudes toward forgiveness and reconciliation. *Peace and Conflict: Journal of Peace Psychology, 16,* 59–79. http://dx.doi.org/10.1080/10781910903485294

Subkoviak, M. J., Enright, R. D., Wu, C. R., Gassin, E. A., Freedman, S., Olson, L. M., & Sarinopoulos, I. (1995). Measuring interpersonal forgiveness in late adolescence and middle adulthood. *Journal of Adolescence, 18,* 641–655. http://dx.doi.org/10.1006/jado.1995.1045

Tam, T., Hewstone, M., Cairns, E., Tausch, N., Maio, G., & Kenworthy, J. (2007). The impact of intergroup emotions on forgiveness in Northern Ireland. *Group Processes & Intergroup Relations, 10,* 119–136. http://dx.doi.org/10.1177/1368430207071345

Thompson, L. Y., & Snyder, C. R. (2003). Measuring forgiveness. In S. J. Lopez & C. R. Snyder (Eds.), *Positive psychological assessment: A handbook of models and measures* (pp. 301–312). Washington, DC: American Psychological Association. http://dx.doi.org/10.1037/10612-019

Thompson, L. Y., Snyder, C. R., Hoffman, L., Michael, S. T., Rasmussen, H. N., Billings, L. S., . . . Roberts, D. E. (2005). Dispositional forgiveness of self, others, and situations. *Journal of Personality, 73,* 313–360. http://dx.doi.org/10.1111/j.1467-6494.2005.00311.x

Voci, A., Hewstone, M., Swart, H., & Veneziani, C. A. (2015). Refining the association between intergroup contact and intergroup forgiveness in Northern Ireland: Type of contact, prior conflict experience, and group identification. *Group Processes & Intergroup Relations, 18,* 589–608. http://dx.doi.org/10.1177/1368430215577001

Wade, S. H. (1990). The development of a scale to measure forgiveness. *Dissertational Abstracts International, 50,* 5338B.

Weinberg, M., Gil, S., & Gilbar, O. (2014). Forgiveness, coping, and terrorism: Do tendency to forgive and coping strategies associate with the level of posttraumatic symptoms of injured victims of terror attacks? *Journal of Clinical Psychology, 70,* 693–703. http://dx.doi.org/10.1002/jclp.22056

Witvliet, C. V. O., Van Tongeren, D. R., & Luna, L. R. (2015). Measuring forgiveness in health-related contexts. In L. L. Toussaint, E. L. Worthington, Jr., & D. R. Williams (Eds.), *Forgiveness and health: Scientific evidence and theories relating forgiveness to better health* (pp. 43–58). Dordrecht, Netherlands: Springer. http://dx.doi.org/10.1007/978-94-017-9993-5_4

Wohl, M. J. A., & Branscombe, N. R. (2005). Forgiveness and collective guilt assignment to historical perpetrator groups depend on level of social category inclusiveness. *Journal of Personality and Social Psychology, 88,* 288–303. http://dx.doi.org/10.1037/0022-3514.88.2.288

Wohl, M. J. A., Cohen-Chen, S., Halperin, E., Caouette, J., Hayes, N., & Hornsey, M. J. (2015). Belief in the malleability of groups strengthens the tenuous link between a collective apology and intergroup forgiveness. *Personality and Social Psychology Bulletin, 41,* 714–725. http://dx.doi.org/10.1177/0146167215576721

Wohl, M. J. A., DeShea, L., & Wahkinney, R. L. (2008). Looking within: Measuring state self-forgiveness and its relationship to psychological well-being. *Canadian Journal of Behavioural Science, 40*(1), 1–10. http://dx.doi.org/10.1037/0008-400x.40.1.1.1

Wohl, M. J. A., Hornsey, M. J., & Bennett, S. H. (2012). Why group apologies succeed and fail: Intergroup forgiveness and the role of primary and secondary emotions.

Journal of Personality and Social Psychology, 102, 306–322. http://dx.doi.org/10.1037/a0024838

Wohl, M. J. A., & McLaughlin, K. J. (2014). Self-forgiveness: The good, the bad, and the ugly. *Social and Personality Psychology Compass, 8*, 422–435. http://dx.doi.org/10.1111/spc3.12119

Wood, B. T., Worthington, E. L., Jr., Everett, L., Exline, J. J., Yali, A. M., Aten, J. D., & McMinn, M. R. (2010). Development, refinement, and psychometric properties of the Attitudes Toward God scale (ATGS-9). *Psychology of Religion and Spirituality, 2*, 148–167. http://dx.doi.org/10.1037/a0018753

19

Humor

Rod A. Martin

Although a sense of humor is generally seen as a positive and desirable personality characteristic, it is not always clear what is meant by this concept. Unlike many other constructs in positive psychology, humor has a range of meanings and refers to a variety of cognitions and behaviors, some of which may be conducive to psychological health and well-being, whereas others may be unrelated or even detrimental.

Today it is generally assumed that individuals with a greater sense of humor are better able to cope with stress, to get along well with others, and to enjoy better mental and even physical health (e.g., Martin, 2016; Wheeler, 2013). Humor, however, has not always been viewed so positively. Indeed, the earliest theories of laughter, dating to Aristotle and Plato and continuing in some form to the present day (e.g., Billig, 2005), view it as essentially a form of aggression, a way of asserting one's superiority by making fun of others. Consequently, it is important when considering humor in the context of positive psychology to define it carefully and to use measures that focus on the relevant dimensions. The existence of such conflicting points of view may be understood by examining the ways in which the conceptualization of humor has evolved over several centuries.

http://dx.doi.org/10.1037/0000138-019
Positive Psychological Assessment: A Handbook of Models and Measures, Second Edition,
M. W. Gallagher and S. J. Lopez (Editors)

EVOLUTION OF THE CONCEPT OF HUMOR

Wickberg (1998) provided a fascinating history of the concept of humor (see also Ruch, 1998a). The word itself originated in the classical Greek theory of four humors or bodily fluids (blood, phlegm, black bile, and yellow bile) that were thought to influence all aspects of bodily and psychic function. Over time, *humor* came to refer to mood (a meaning still present when we speak of someone being in good or bad humor), and eventually, in the English language, it evolved into a connotation of wittiness, funniness, and laughableness, although not necessarily in a benevolent sense. During the 18th century, the word *ridicule* was used in much the same way that we use the word *humor* today, that is, as a generic term for anything that causes laughter and mirth. However, it had a much more negative and aggressive connotation than humor has today. At that time, it was socially acceptable to laugh at individuals who were deformed or mentally ill, and the exchange of hostile witty remarks was a popular form of interaction in fashionable society.

Under the influence of 18th-century social reform movements, however, these aggressive forms of laughter began to be viewed as unrefined and vulgar. A new sensibility among middle-class British society emphasized the importance of benevolence, kindness, civility, and sympathy. In keeping with this general outlook, social reformers began to argue in favor of a more humanitarian form of laughter based on sympathy rather than aggression. This led to the need for a new word to describe this benevolent basis of laughter, and *humor* was co-opted to serve this purpose and given a restricted and specialized meaning. Distinct from other laughter-related phenomena (e.g., wit, comedy, sarcasm, irony, satire, ridicule), *humor* was used to refer exclusively to a sympathetic, tolerant, and benevolent amusement at the imperfections of the world and the foibles of human nature in general. Humor also acquired a connotation of not taking oneself too seriously, being able to poke fun at oneself, and maintaining a philosophical detachment in one's outlook. Thus, humor was distinguished from other sources of laughter, such as wit, which was viewed as more sarcastic, biting, and cruel. Individuals who expressed the benevolent, nonhostile, philosophical forms of amusement encompassed by this revised conception of humor were considered refined and noble, in contrast to those who engaged in coarse joking, witty repartee, and laughter at the expense of others. By the Victorian era, a sense of humor (in this restricted meaning) had become a virtue, along with common sense, tolerance, and compromise.

This distinction between humor and other sources of laughter was adopted by Freud (1928), who viewed humor (in this narrow sense) as one of the healthiest defense mechanisms, as distinct from wit or joking, which he viewed as a means of expressing unacceptable aggressive and sexual impulses. According to Freud, humor allows one to maintain a detached perspective in the face of misfortune and adversity, thus sparing oneself the depression, anxiety, and anger that might normally arise, while maintaining a realistic view of oneself and the world. Thus, Freud accepted the virtuous and humanitarian meanings of this restricted definition of *humor* and added a psychological connotation of mental health and well-being. Interestingly, whereas jokes and the comic are typically enjoyed by most people, Freud viewed humor (in this narrow sense) as a "rare and precious gift" (p. 220) that is possessed only by the lucky few.

Subsequent psychological theorists, such as Maslow (1954) and Allport (1961), have echoed these themes, suggesting that a healthy or mature personality is characterized by a particular style of humor that is nonhostile, philosophical, and self-deprecating yet self-accepting. Like Freud, these authors viewed this healthy form of humor as relatively rare, in contrast with the majority of everyday joking and the type of comedy typically found in the media. In addition, they suggested that healthy forms of humor are more likely to be accompanied by a chuckle than by hearty laughter. These formulations suggest that psychological health relates not only to the presence of certain kinds of adaptive humor but also to the absence of more maladaptive forms of humor. Contemporary views of humor as a component of positive psychology can be traced to these ideas (e.g., Edwards & Martin, 2014; Ruch, 2004).

This conceptualization of humor as a positive character strength has become somewhat confused over the past century, however, because the term *humor*, as used both by the layperson and the psychological researcher, generally has lost its narrow focus and has evolved to become a broad umbrella term for all laughter-related phenomena. Humor now refers to all forms of laughter, including jokes, stand-up comedy, television sitcoms, political satire, and ridicule. In this sense, humor now can be aggressive and hostile, as well as benevolent and philosophical. Thus, while retaining its positive connotation, humor now refers to laughter-related phenomena that may not be so positive and healthy.

Consequently, when conceptualizing and measuring sense of humor in relation to positive psychology, it is important to distinguish between healthy and beneficial forms of humor (consistent with the earlier narrow use of the term) and aspects of humor (using the modern, broader meaning) that may be less relevant or potentially even detrimental to well-being.

HUMOR AND PSYCHOLOGICAL WELL-BEING

When considering the more beneficial aspects of humor and its role in positive psychology, there are two general ways it is thought to be beneficial: (a) as a means of coping with stress and regulating emotions and (b) as a way of enhancing personal relationships and thereby contributing to social support (Martin, 2007). The conceptualization of humor as a form of coping and emotion regulation is consistent with the Freudian view of it as a healthy defense mechanism. In this view, a humorous perspective on life mitigates the negative consequences of adversity. Based on Lazarus and Folkman's (1984) transactional model of stress, humor may be viewed as a form of cognitive appraisal that involves perceiving potentially stressful situations in a more benign, less-threatening manner (Maiolino & Kuiper, 2016). Contemporary theories suggest that humor is based on "bisociation" (Koestler, 1964) or "cognitive synergy" (Apter, 2001), which involves the bringing together of two normally unrelated ideas, concepts, or situations in a surprising and playful manner. The shifts in perspective accompanying humor have been seen by a number of writers as the basis for its hypothesized effectiveness as an appraisal-focused coping strategy (e.g., Geisler & Weber, 2010).

Second, humor may contribute to psychological health and resistance to stress by enhancing social support. Humor is essentially a form of communication, which can be used in everyday social interactions to reduce tension, engage in play, and enhance cohesiveness (Martin, 2007). Individuals with a healthy sense of humor tend to be more socially competent (Yip & Martin, 2006) and able to resolve conflicts in relationships (Campbell, Martin, & Ward, 2008); in turn, it may be easier for such persons to attract and maintain friendships and develop a rich social support network, and consequently to obtain the mental and physical health benefits of social support (Berscheid & Reis, 1998).

CONCEPTUALIZING AND MEASURING SENSE OF HUMOR

The term *sense of humor* is used in contemporary psychology to refer to stable individual differences in humor-related cognitions and behaviors (Martin, 2007; Ruch, 1998b). Research on this construct indicates that it is a multifaceted concept, comprising a number of different dimensions. For example, sense of humor may be conceptualized as a habitual behavior pattern (e.g., tendency to laugh frequently, to tell jokes and amuse others), an ability (e.g., to create humor, to amuse others), or an aesthetic response (e.g., enjoyment of particular types of humorous material). These various aspects of sense of humor are not highly intercorrelated, and not all are likely to be relevant to positive psychology.

During the 1980s and 1990s, researchers developed a number of self-report measures of sense of humor to investigate associations with various aspects of psychosocial and physical health and well-being (for reviews, see Martin, 2007; Ruch, 1998b). These measures were designed to assess such aspects of humor as the degree to which individuals smile and laugh in a wide variety of situations (Situational Humor Response Questionnaire—SHRQ; Martin & Lefcourt, 1984), use humor as a coping strategy (Coping Humor Scale—CHS; Martin & Lefcourt, 1983), notice and enjoy humor (Sense of Humor Questionnaire—SHQ; Svebak, 1996), and so on.

Research using these humor measures, however, produced surprisingly weak and inconsistent evidence for associations with psychosocial well-being. For example, Kuiper and Martin (1998) presented a series of five studies examining relations between several of these humor measures (CHS, SHRQ, and SHQ) and various measures relating to aspects of mental health and "positive personality" (e.g., dispositional optimism, psychological well-being, self-esteem, depression, anxiety, social avoidance). On the basis of their findings, they concluded that the humor scales were relatively weak indicators of mental health, in contrast with other measures associated with positive psychology such as dispositional optimism (Carver & Scheier, 2005).

A possible explanation for these weak findings relates to the historical distinctions between potentially adaptive and maladaptive forms of humor discussed previously. As we have seen, past theorists noted that healthy psychological functioning is associated with distinctive styles of humor (e.g., perspective-taking, affiliative) and that other forms of humor (e.g., sarcastic, defensively avoidant) may actually be deleterious to well-being (Allport, 1961; Freud, 1928; Maslow, 1954). Thus, in studying the relationship between humor and psychological health, it seems important to examine the ways in which individuals employ humor, both interpersonally and intrapsychically, in their daily lives. Moreover, the absence of certain potentially detrimental uses of humor may be as important to psychological well-being as is the presence of more beneficial uses. Unfortunately, this distinction between healthy and unhealthy uses of humor was largely ignored in earlier humor research.

HUMOR STYLES QUESTIONNAIRE

The Humor Styles Questionnaire (HSQ) is a newer measure that was designed to correct the perceived weaknesses of earlier scales, by distinguishing between potentially beneficial and detrimental humor styles (Martin, Puhlik-Doris, Larsen, Gray, & Weir, 2003). The focus of this measure is on the ways people use humor in their everyday lives, particularly in the domains of social interaction and coping with life stress. Based on a review of past theoretical and empirical literature, the authors hypothesized four main dimensions, two of which were considered to be relatively healthy or adaptive (affiliative and self-enhancing humor) and two relatively unhealthy and potentially detrimental (aggressive and self-defeating humor).

Affiliative humor refers to the tendency to say funny things, to tell jokes, and to engage in spontaneous witty banter in order to amuse others, to facilitate relationships, and to reduce interpersonal tensions (e.g., "I enjoy making people laugh"). This is hypothesized to be an essentially nonhostile, tolerant use of humor that is affirming of self and others and presumably enhances interpersonal cohesiveness. *Self-enhancing humor* refers to the tendency to be frequently amused by the incongruities of life, to maintain a humorous perspective even in the face of stress or adversity, and to use humor in coping (e.g., "My humorous outlook on life keeps me from getting overly upset or depressed about things"). This humor style is closely related to the construct assessed by the earlier Coping Humor Scale.

In contrast, *aggressive humor* is the tendency to use humor for the purpose of criticizing or manipulating others, as in sarcasm, teasing, ridicule, derision, or disparagement humor, as well as the use of potentially offensive (e.g., racist, sexist) forms of humor (e.g., "If someone makes a mistake, I will often tease them about it"). This type of humor is viewed as a means of enhancing the self at the expense of one's relationships with others. Finally, *self-defeating humor* involves the use of excessively self-disparaging humor, attempts to amuse others by doing or saying funny things at one's own expense, and laughing along with others when being ridiculed or disparaged (e.g., "I often try to make people like or accept me more by saying something funny about my own weaknesses, blunders, or faults"). It also involves the use of humor as a form of defensive denial, to hide one's underlying negative feelings or avoid dealing constructively with problems. This style of humor is seen as an attempt to gain the attention and approval of others at one's own expense.

Although the HSQ assesses the way people "use" humor in their everyday lives, no assumption was made that these uses are consciously or strategically directed. Instead, the authors assumed that people tend to engage in humor quite spontaneously and are often unaware of its social or psychological functions in a given situation. The HSQ was developed using construct-based test-construction procedures over a series of studies with fairly large samples of participants ranging in age from 14 to 87 years (Martin et al., 2003). This methodology resulted in four stable factors that were corroborated by means of confirmatory factor analysis. The final measure contains four eight-item scales, each of which has demonstrated good internal and test-retest reliability. The HSQ has been translated into more than 30 languages and administered to participants in numerous countries throughout the world, and the four-factor structure has been replicated in all cultures studied to date (Chen & Martin, 2007; Kazarian & Martin, 2004, 2006; Saroglou & Scariot, 2002). In addition to the original self-report trait version, 12-item "daily" versions have been created for use in longitudinal diary studies, one assessing general humor use (Edwards, 2013) and another focusing on humor in romantic relationships (Caird & Martin, 2014). A peer-report version has also been developed (Caird, 2015), as well as an observational rating approach (Campbell et al., 2008) and a version for children (Fox, Dean, & Lyford, 2013).

With regard to relationships among the scales themselves, moderate correlations are typically found between self-enhancing and affiliative humor and between aggressive and self-defeating humor, indicating that the two positive and the two negative styles of humor, while conceptually and empirically distinguishable, tend to covary. In addition, aggressive humor tends to be weakly positively correlated with both affiliative and self-enhancing humor, suggesting that even positive styles of humor may include some aggressive elements (e.g., friendly teasing).

Research conducted to date has provided considerable evidence for the construct validity of each scale, as well as discriminant validity among the four scales. For example, scores on each of the scales have been found to correlate significantly with peer ratings of the corresponding dimensions (Martin et al., 2003; Saroglou, Lacour, & Demeure, 2010) and with self-reports of corresponding everyday humor-related behaviors (Heintz, 2017). The affiliative and self-enhancing humor scales tend to be positively correlated with other well-validated self-report humor measures, indicating convergent validity for these scales. The aggressive and self-defeating humor scales, although unrelated to some previous humor measures, have also been found to be positively correlated with some others, indicating that these past humor scales may have failed to distinguish between beneficial and detrimental styles of humor (Martin et al., 2003). In addition, each of the four scales has been shown to be positively correlated with a measure of humor creation ability, indicating that they all involve an ability to generate humor and amuse others (Edwards & Martin, 2010).

Correlational studies also support the view that these four humor styles are differentially related to various aspects of psychosocial well-being. *Affiliative humor* has been found to be positively associated with self-esteem, well-being, positive moods, emotional intelligence, extraversion, and openness (Dyck & Holtzman, 2013; Gignac, Karatamoglou, Wee, & Palacios, 2014; Martin et al., 2003; Mendiburo-Seguel, Páez, & Martínez-Sánchez, 2015; Saroglou & Scariot, 2002). It is also positively related to intimacy, secure attachment, social support, and relationship satisfaction, and negatively related to loneliness and interpersonal anxiety (Cann, Norman, Welbourne, & Calhoun, 2008; Cann, Zapata, & Davis, 2011; Hampes, 2005). Individuals with high scores on this measure have better conflict resolution and social skills, and more satisfying relationships (Campbell et al., 2008; Saroglou et al., 2010; Yip & Martin, 2006). Overall, this style of humor appears to be particularly relevant to forming and maintaining healthy interpersonal relationships, one of the beneficial functions of humor discussed previously.

Self-enhancing humor has been shown to be positively correlated with measures of psychological well-being, such as self-esteem, positive moods, cheerfulness, optimism, hope, mental toughness, emotional intelligence, and mature coping skills, and negatively correlated with anxiety, depression, and stress (Gignac et al., 2014; Kazarian & Martin, 2006; Leist & Müller, 2013; Martin et al., 2003; Vernon et al., 2009; Veselka, Schermer, Martin, & Vernon, 2010a). With regard to the Big Five personality dimensions, this humor style is related to extraversion, openness, and agreeableness (Mendiburo-Seguel et al., 2015; Vernon, Martin, Schermer, & Mackie, 2008). Overall, this style of humor seems to be particularly relevant to emotion regulation and coping, the other potential benefit of humor noted earlier.

Self-defeating humor, in contrast, is consistently *negatively* related to measures of emotional well-being, such as self-esteem, optimism, emotional intelligence, and positive moods, and is positively associated with anxiety, depression, psychiatric symptoms, loneliness, hostility, and aggression (Dozois, Martin, & Bieling, 2009; Fitts, Sebby, & Zlokovich, 2009; Frewen, Brinker, Martin, & Dozois, 2008; Gignac et al., 2014). Individuals with high scores on this measure tend to have more anxious and insecure attachment styles and poorer social skills (Kuiper, Grimshaw, Leite, & Kirsh, 2004). On the Big Five, they tend to be high on neuroticism and low on agreeableness and conscientiousness (Mendiburo-Seguel et al., 2015; Vernon et al., 2008). Thus, this could be described as a particularly "neurotic" humor style.

Finally, *aggressive humor*, while unrelated to emotional well-being variables such as self-esteem, anxiety, and depression, tends to be positively correlated with hostility, aggression, psychopathy, and Machiavellianism (Martin et al., 2003; Veselka, Schermer, Martin, & Vernon, 2010b). Individuals with high scores on this measure tend to have lower emotional intelligence, poorer social skills, poorer conflict resolution abilities, and less satisfying and enduring relationships (Gignac et al., 2014; Saroglou et al., 2010; Yip & Martin, 2006). On the Big Five, these individuals tend to be high on extraversion, openness, and neuroticism, and low on agreeableness and conscientiousness (Mendiburo-Seguel et al., 2015; Vernon et al., 2008). Overall, this style of humor seems to be particularly negatively related to relationship satisfaction.

Several studies have found that these positive and negative humor styles mediate the relationships between certain resiliency or vulnerability factors and various well-being-related outcomes. For example, Dozois and colleagues (2009) found significant mediating effects of both self-enhancing and self-defeating humor on the relationship between early maladaptive schemas and the development of depressed moods. Similarly, Cann and colleagues (2008) found that affiliative humor significantly mediated the association between attachment security and relationship satisfaction. These findings suggest that healthy humor styles may be one way in which individuals with greater resiliency achieve higher levels of emotional and social well-being, whereas unhealthy humor styles may be one mechanism through which vulnerable individuals develop distress and dysfunction (see also Besser, Luyten, & Mayes, 2012; Fitts et al., 2009; Kazarian, Moghnie, & Martin, 2010).

In summary, these findings support the view that the different humor styles, while all involving the ability to be funny and make others laugh, are differentially related to aspects of psychosocial well-being. Self-enhancing humor is positively associated with emotion regulation and adaptive coping, whereas self-defeating humor is negatively correlated with these aspects of well-being. Affiliative humor, in turn, is positively related to relationship satisfaction, intimacy, interpersonal competence, and social support, whereas aggressive humor is negatively related to these interpersonal aspects of well-being. Based on these findings, it seems safe to conclude that both positive and negative styles of humor need to be assessed when examining the role of humor in positive psychology (see also Edwards & Martin, 2014).

STATE–TRAIT CHEERFULNESS INVENTORY

In addition to the HSQ, the State–Trait Cheerfulness Inventory (STCI) is an alternative approach to assessing sense of humor that may be of relevance to positive psychology, although it has received less research attention in this regard. This measure is based on a temperament approach, in which dispositions to cheerfulness, seriousness, and bad mood are viewed as traits forming the temperamental basis of humor (Ruch & Köhler, 1998). Trait and state forms of the STCI were developed to assess individual differences in these traits as well as related states (Ruch, Köhler, & Van Thriel, 1996). In a series of studies, Ruch and colleagues have found that individuals with higher trait scores on this measure are more likely to maintain positive emotions in situations that are normally conducive to negative emotion. This may be a useful alternative approach to conceptualizing and measuring individual differences in humor relevant to positive psychology. The state scale (with day, week, month instructions) also is well-suited for pre–post measures in intervention studies.

CONCLUSION

A sense of humor would seem to be an important characteristic of relevance to positive psychology. The ability to maintain a humorous outlook in the face of stress and to "see the funny side" of life's problems and challenges is an important coping skill, leading to greater resilience and emotional well-being. Furthermore, the ability to make others laugh and to use humor to facilitate relationships and reduce interpersonal tension is a valuable social skill, contributing to social cohesiveness and support. However, it is important to recognize that humor can also be used in ways that are potentially detrimental to psychosocial well-being. Although individuals who frequently engage in aggressive, sarcastic forms of humor can be very witty and entertaining, their humor may interfere with their ability to maintain close relationships. Similarly, those who use humor in excessively self-disparaging ways or as a form of defensive denial can also be very funny, but their humor may contribute to low self-esteem and emotional distress.

Prior to the 20th century, the word *humor* was used exclusively to refer to more positive and healthy forms of mirthful amusement and distinguished from other ways of making people laugh. Over the past century, however, it has taken on a broader meaning, incorporating all sources of amusement and laughter, some of which are less healthy and potentially even detrimental. When conceptualizing and measuring sense of humor in the context of positive psychology, it is therefore important to define clearly the type of humor to which one is referring, and to make a distinction between potentially beneficial and detrimental styles (see Ruch & Heintz, 2016). Consistent with this recommendation, the HSQ was designed to assess two styles of humor that are potentially beneficial for psychosocial well-being and two that are potentially detrimental. Research using this measure has provided support for the view that the *absence* of maladaptive humor styles is at least as important to well-being as is the *presence* of adaptive styles.

REFERENCES

Allport, G. W. (1961). *Pattern and growth in personality*. New York, NY: Holt, Reinhart & Winston.

Apter, M. J. (Ed.). (2001). *Motivational styles in everyday life: A guide to reversal theory*. Washington, DC: American Psychological Association. http://dx.doi.org/10.1037/10427-000

Berscheid, E., & Reis, H. T. (1998). Attraction and close relationships. In D. T. Gilbert, S. T. Fiske, & G. Lindzey (Eds.), *The handbook of social psychology* (4th ed., Vol. 2, pp. 193–281). Boston, MA: McGraw-Hill.

Besser, A., Luyten, P., & Mayes, L. C. (2012). Adult attachment and distress: The mediating role of humor styles. *Individual Differences Research, 10,* 153–164.

Billig, M. (2005). *Laughter and ridicule: Towards a social critique of humour*. Thousand Oaks, CA: Sage.

Caird, S. (2015). *An examination of daily humour styles and relationship satisfaction in dating couples* (Unpublished doctoral dissertation). University of Western Ontario, Canada.

Caird, S., & Martin, R. A. (2014). Relationship-focused humor styles and relationship satisfaction in dating couples: A repeated-measures design. *Humor: International Journal of Humor Research, 27,* 227–247. http://dx.doi.org/10.1515/humor-2014-0015

Campbell, L., Martin, R. A., & Ward, J. R. (2008). An observational study of humor use while resolving conflict in dating couples. *Personal Relationships, 15,* 41–55. http://dx.doi.org/10.1111/j.1475-6811.2007.00183.x

Cann, A., Norman, M. A., Welbourne, J. L., & Calhoun, L. G. (2008). Attachment styles, conflict styles and humour styles: Interrelationships and associations with relationship satisfaction. *European Journal of Personality, 22,* 131–146. http://dx.doi.org/10.1002/per.666

Cann, A., Zapata, C. L., & Davis, H. B. (2011). Humor style and relationship satisfaction in dating couples: Perceived versus self-reported humor styles as predictors of satisfaction. *Humor: International Journal of Humor Research, 24,* 1–20. http://dx.doi.org/10.1515/humr.2011.001

Carver, C. S., & Scheier, M. F. (2005). Optimism. In C. R. Snyder & S. J. Lopez (Eds.), *Handbook of positive psychology* (pp. 231–243). New York, NY: Oxford University Press.

Chen, G. H., & Martin, R. A. (2007). A comparison of humor styles, coping humor, and mental health between Chinese and Canadian university students. *Humor: International Journal of Humor Research, 20,* 215–234. http://dx.doi.org/10.1515/HUMOR.2007.011

Dozois, D. J. A., Martin, R. A., & Bieling, P. J. (2009). Early maladaptive schemas and adaptive/maladaptive styles of humor. *Cognitive Therapy and Research, 33,* 585–596. http://dx.doi.org/10.1007/s10608-008-9223-9

Dyck, K. T. H., & Holtzman, S. (2013). Understanding humor styles and well-being: The importance of social relationships and gender. *Personality and Individual Differences, 55,* 53–58. http://dx.doi.org/10.1016/j.paid.2013.01.023

Edwards, K. R. (2013). *The role of humor as a character strength in positive psychology* (Unpublished doctoral thesis). University of Western Ontario, Canada.

Edwards, K. R., & Martin, R. A. (2010). Humor creation ability and mental health: Are funny people more psychologically healthy? *Europe's Journal of Psychology, 3,* 196–212.

Edwards, K. R., & Martin, R. A. (2014). The conceptualization, measurement, and role of humor as a character strength in positive psychology. *Europe's Journal of Psychology, 10,* 505–519. http://dx.doi.org/10.5964/ejop.v10i3.759

Fitts, S. D., Sebby, R. A., & Zlokovich, M. S. (2009). Humor styles as mediators of the shyness-loneliness relationship. *North American Journal of Psychology, 11,* 257–272.

Fox, C. L., Dean, S., & Lyford, K. (2013). Development of a Humor Styles Questionnaire for children. *Humor: International Journal of Humor Research, 26,* 295–319. http://dx.doi.org/10.1515/humor-2013-0018

Freud, S. (1928). Humour. *The International Journal of Psychoanalysis, 9,* 1–6.

Frewen, P. A., Brinker, J., Martin, R. A., & Dozois, D. J. A. (2008). Humor styles and personality-vulnerability to depression. *Humor: International Journal of Humor Research, 21,* 179–195. http://dx.doi.org/10.1515/HUMOR.2008.009

Geisler, F. C. M., & Weber, H. (2010). Harm that does not hurt: Humour in coping with self-threat. *Motivation and Emotion, 34,* 446–456. http://dx.doi.org/10.1007/s11031-010-9185-6

Gignac, G. E., Karatamoglou, A., Wee, S., & Palacios, G. (2014). Emotional intelligence as a unique predictor of individual differences in humour styles and humour appreciation. *Personality and Individual Differences, 56,* 34–39. http://dx.doi.org/10.1016/j.paid.2013.08.020

Hampes, W. P. (2005). Correlations between humor styles and loneliness. *Psychological Reports, 96,* 747–750. http://dx.doi.org/10.2466/pr0.96.3.747-750

Heintz, S. (2017). Putting a spotlight on daily humor behaviors: Dimensionality and relationships with personality, subjective well-being, and humor styles. *Personality and Individual Differences, 104,* 407–412. http://dx.doi.org/10.1016/j.paid.2016.08.042

Kazarian, S. S., & Martin, R. A. (2004). Humor styles, personality, and well-being among Lebanese university students. *European Journal of Personality, 18,* 209–219. http://dx.doi.org/10.1002/per.505

Kazarian, S. S., & Martin, R. A. (2006). Humor styles, culture-related personality, well-being, and family adjustment among Armenians in Lebanon. *Humor: International Journal of Humor Research, 19,* 405–423. http://dx.doi.org/10.1515/HUMOR.2006.020

Kazarian, S. S., Moghnie, L., & Martin, R. A. (2010). Perceived parental warmth and rejection in childhood as predictors of humor styles and subjective happiness. *Europe's Journal of Psychology, 3,* 71–93.

Koestler, A. (1964). *The act of creation.* London, England: Hutchinson.

Kuiper, N. A., Grimshaw, M., Leite, C., & Kirsh, G. A. (2004). Humor is not always the best medicine: Specific components of sense of humor and psychological well-being. *Humor: International Journal of Humor Research, 17,* 135–168. http://dx.doi.org/10.1515/humr.2004.002

Kuiper, N. A., & Martin, R. A. (1998). Is sense of humor a positive personality characteristic? In W. Ruch (Ed.), *The sense of humor: Explorations of a personality characteristic* (pp. 159–178). Berlin, Germany: Walter de Gruyter. http://dx.doi.org/10.1515/9783110804607.159

Lazarus, R. S., & Folkman, S. (1984). *Stress, appraisal, and coping.* New York, NY: Springer.

Leist, A. K., & Müller, D. (2013). Humor types show different patterns of self-regulation, self-esteem, and well-being. *Journal of Happiness Studies, 14,* 551–569. http://dx.doi.org/10.1007/s10902-012-9342-6

Maiolino, N., & Kuiper, N. A. (2016). Examining the impact of a brief humor exercise on psychological well-being. *Translational Issues in Psychological Science, 2,* 4–13. http://dx.doi.org/10.1037/tps0000065

Martin, R. A. (2007). *The psychology of humor: An integrative approach.* Burlington, MA: Elsevier Academic Press. http://dx.doi.org/10.1016/B978-012372564-6/50024-1

Martin, R. A. (2016). Humor and mental health. In H. S. Friedman (Ed.), *Encyclopedia of mental health* (2nd ed., Vol. 2, pp. 350–353). Waltham, MA: Academic Press. http://dx.doi.org/10.1016/B978-0-12-397045-9.00044-6

Martin, R. A., & Lefcourt, H. M. (1983). Sense of humor as a moderator of the relation between stressors and moods. *Journal of Personality and Social Psychology, 45,* 1313–1324. http://dx.doi.org/10.1037/0022-3514.45.6.1313

Martin, R. A., & Lefcourt, H. M. (1984). Situational Humor Response Questionnaire: Quantitative measure of sense of humor. *Journal of Personality and Social Psychology, 47,* 145–155. http://dx.doi.org/10.1037/0022-3514.47.1.145

Martin, R. A., Puhlik-Doris, P., Larsen, G., Gray, J., & Weir, K. (2003). Individual differences in uses of humor and their relation to psychological well-being: Development of the Humor Styles Questionnaire. *Journal of Research in Personality, 37,* 48–75. http://dx.doi.org/10.1016/S0092-6566(02)00534-2

Maslow, A. H. (1954). *Motivation and personality.* New York, NY: Harper.

Mendiburo-Seguel, A., Páez, D., & Martínez-Sánchez, F. (2015). Humor styles and personality: A meta-analysis of the relation between humor styles and the Big Five personality traits. *Scandinavian Journal of Psychology, 56,* 335–340. http://dx.doi.org/10.1111/sjop.12209

Ruch, W. (1998a). Sense of humor: A new look at an old concept. In W. Ruch (Ed.), *The sense of humor: Explorations of a personality characteristic* (pp. 3–14). Berlin, Germany: Mouton de Gruyter. http://dx.doi.org/10.1515/9783110804607.3

Ruch, W. (1998b). *The sense of humor: Explorations of a personality characteristic.* Berlin, Germany: Mouton de Gruyter.

Ruch, W. (2004). Humor [playfulness]. In C. Peterson & M. E. P. Seligman (Eds.), *Character strengths and virtues: A handbook and classification* (pp. 583–598). Washington, DC: American Psychological Association.

Ruch, W., & Heintz, S. (2016). The virtue gap in humor: Exploring benevolent and corrective humor. *Translational Issues in Psychological Science, 2,* 35–45. http://dx.doi.org/10.1037/tps0000063

Ruch, W., & Köhler, G. (1998). A temperament approach to humor. In W. Ruch (Ed.), *The sense of humor: Explorations of a personality characteristic* (pp. 203–228). Berlin, Germany: Walter de Gruyter. http://dx.doi.org/10.1515/9783110804607.203

Ruch, W., Köhler, G., & Van Thriel, C. (1996). Assessing the "humorous temperament": Construction of the facet and standard trait forms of the State–Trait-Cheerfulness-Inventory—STCI. *Humor: International Journal of Humor Research, 9,* 303–339. http://dx.doi.org/10.1515/humr.1996.9.3-4.303

Saroglou, V., Lacour, C., & Demeure, M.-E. (2010). Bad humor, bad marriage: Humor styles in divorced and married couples. *Europe's Journal of Psychology, 3,* 94–121.

Saroglou, V., & Scariot, C. (2002). Humor Styles Questionnaire: Personality and educational correlates in Belgian high school and college students. *European Journal of Personality, 16,* 43–54. http://dx.doi.org/10.1002/per.430

Svebak, S. (1996). The development of the Sense of Humor Questionnaire: From SHQ to SHQ-6. *Humor: International Journal of Humor Research, 9,* 341–361. http://dx.doi.org/10.1515/humr.1996.9.3-4.341

Vernon, P. A., Martin, R. A., Schermer, J. A., & Mackie, A. (2008). A behavioral genetic investigation of humor styles and their correlations with the Big-5 personality dimensions. *Personality and Individual Differences, 44,* 1116–1125. http://dx.doi.org/10.1016/j.paid.2007.11.003

Vernon, P. A., Villani, V. C., Schermer, J. A., Kirilovic, S., Martin, R. A., Petrides, K. V., . . . Cherkas, L. F. (2009). Genetic and environmental correlations between trait emotional intelligence and humor styles. *Journal of Individual Differences, 30,* 130–137. http://dx.doi.org/10.1027/1614-0001.30.3.130

Veselka, L., Schermer, J. A., Martin, R. A., & Vernon, P. A. (2010a). Laughter and resiliency: A behavioral genetic study of humor styles and mental toughness. *Twin Research and Human Genetics, 13,* 442–449. http://dx.doi.org/10.1375/twin.13.5.442

Veselka, L., Schermer, J. A., Martin, R. A., & Vernon, P. A. (2010b). Relations between humor styles and the Dark Triad traits of personality. *Personality and Individual Differences, 48,* 772–774. http://dx.doi.org/10.1016/j.paid.2010.01.017

Wheeler, E. A. (2013). Amusing ourselves to health: A selected review of lab findings. In J. D. Sinnott (Ed.), *Positive psychology: Advances in understanding adult motivation* (pp. 79–94). New York, NY: Springer. http://dx.doi.org/10.1007/978-1-4614-7282-7_6

Wickberg, D. (1998). *The senses of humor: Self and laughter in modern America.* Ithaca, NY: Cornell University Press.

Yip, J. A., & Martin, R. A. (2006). Sense of humor, emotional intelligence, and social competence. *Journal of Research in Personality, 40,* 1202–1208. http://dx.doi.org/10.1016/j.jrp.2005.08.005

20

Gratitude

Robert A. Emmons, Jeffrey Froh, and Rachel Rose

Since the first edition of this handbook was published, rapid progress has been made in the science of gratitude, due in large part to advances in measurement. In this chapter we describe these recent developments in the measurement of gratitude across the lifespan. We emphasize self-reported gratitude measures, since these have dominated research.

Efforts to develop measures of gratitude have increased as accumulating research has demonstrated that gratitude is foundational to well-being and mental health throughout the lifespan. From childhood to old age, a wide array of psychological, physical, and relational benefits are associated with gratitude. Gratitude has been shown to contribute not only to an increase in happiness, health, and other desirable life outcomes but also to a decrease in negative affect and problematic functioning, including in patients with neuromuscular disease, college students, hypertensives, patients with cancer, health care providers, and early adolescents (Cheng, Tsui, & Lam, 2015; Emmons & McCullough, 2003; Emmons & Stern, 2013; Froh, Sefick, & Emmons, 2008; Otto, Szczesny, Soriano, Laurenceau, & Siegel, 2016). Another study pinpointed gratitude as a protective factor against posttraumatic stress disorder (PTSD) symptoms (Israel-Cohen, Uzefovsky, Kashy-Rosenbaum, & Kaplan, 2015).

Gratitude differs considerably from other moral emotions such as empathy, sympathy, guilt, and shame. While empathy and sympathy can be understood primarily as a response to the distress of another person, and shame and guilt as responses to one's inability to meet moral standards, gratitude is the pleasant

http://dx.doi.org/10.1037/0000138-020
Positive Psychological Assessment: A Handbook of Models and Measures, Second Edition,
M. W. Gallagher and S. J. Lopez (Editors)

response of thankfulness to an outside agent after recognizing benefits received (Ellsworth & Smith, 1988; Weiner, 1986). From an evolutionary perspective, gratitude has been described to have evolved as an adaptive regulating mechanism for exchanging costly benefits among relatives (i.e., reciprocal altruism) and as a "pay it forward" form of distributing benefit to someone other than the benefactor (or "upstream reciprocity"; McCullough, Kimeldorf, & Cohen, 2008; Nowak & Roch, 2007). Furthermore, as a trait, gratitude is different from other positive traits. For example, trait gratitude is oriented toward noticing positive outcomes in life, whereas optimism is oriented toward expecting positive future outcomes (Wood, Froh, & Geraghty, 2010). Therefore, gratitude serves a distinctive function within the pantheon of human emotional experience.

FACETS OF GRATITUDE

Based on Rosenberg's (1998) hierarchical levels of affective experience, gratitude has been identified as a trait, emotion, and mood. The grateful disposition can be defined as a stable affective trait that would lower the threshold of experiencing gratitude (McCullough, Tsang, & Emmons, 2004) or as a characteristic self-reinforcing pattern (Rusk, Vella-Brodrick, & Waters, 2016). As an emotion, gratitude can be understood as an acute, intense, and relatively brief psychophysiological reaction to being the recipient of a benefit from another. Last, as a stable mood, gratitude has also been identified to have a subtle, broad, and longer duration impact on consciousness (McCullough et al., 2004).

These various meanings overlap the distinctions made by Lambert, Graham, and Fincham (2009) between *benefit triggered* and *generalized* gratitude. They defined the emotion that results from an interpersonal transfer of a benefit from a beneficiary to a benefactor as being *benefit-triggered* gratitude, or "grateful to" gratitude. The broader type of gratitude includes being grateful for all sorts of gifts in life, not just for particular benefits conferred by specific others. *Generalized* gratitude is the emotion or state resulting from an awareness and appreciation of that which is valuable and meaningful to oneself. Lay conceptions of gratitude encompass both meanings of the term as demonstrated in a series of studies (Lambert et al., 2009) in which they conclude that lay conceptions of gratitude are often broader than how the concept has been defined in prior research (Gulliford & Morgan, 2016).

REVIEW OF RESEARCH ON GRATITUDE AND ITS ASSESSMENT

Gratitude has been measured in a multitude of ways and forms. These previous measures of gratitude can be subsumed under the three categories of free response, attributions, and trait rating scales. In some studies, gratitude has been assessed as a dependent variable, a state whose intensity is influenced by other variables, whereas in other studies, gratitude has been treated as an independent variable that can influence various behavioral or cognitive–affective outcomes. Gratitude has also been looked at as a mediator, influencing the relationship between two variables.

Free Response

This category refers to research consisting of interviews or free-response answers to questions about gratitude. For example, Teigen (1997) had participants write about two instances in which they felt grateful: one when they were grateful to someone specifically and another where they were generally grateful, for instance, "grateful to life." Russell and Paris (1994) asked children to tell stories about protagonists who were feeling different emotions, including one story where the person felt "very grateful." Lambert, Graham, and Fincham (2009) asked participants to write down characteristics that come to mind when they hear the word *gratitude*. They derived 52 prototypical gratitude attributes from these free responses, which were then rated for their centrality to gratitude by another group of respondents. Biondo (2012) used a free-response method to elicit responses that were characteristic of natural and spontaneous gratitude, in contrast to resentment. Narrative accounts of grateful life experiences have also been collected (Lambert et al., 2009).

Gratitude frequency is one facet that is amenable to free responses. Okamoto and Robinson (1997) presented their participants with helping vignettes and asked them to write down what they would say or do in response to someone helping them. The frequency of participants' writing that they would say "thank you" depended on characteristics of the helper and the nature of the help (i.e., the level of imposition of the helper). The roles of the helper and the benefactor, and the relationship between them, have been explored in greater detail by Algoe, Kurtz, and Hilaire (2016). Sommers and Kosmitzki (1988) gave participants a list of emotions and asked them a number of questions using that list, including which emotions they experienced regularly and which emotions they thought were most constructive. Individuals often listed gratitude as one of the responses to these two questions. In addition, a variant of gratitude span has been measured by the Gallup Poll (1998), where researchers asked telephone interviewees to list two or three things for which they felt grateful. Although participants were not asked to list all the things they felt grateful for, this question tapped into the different types of benefits that people might feel grateful about (e.g., health, job/career, children, just being alive).

Attributional Measures

Gratitude also has been measured indirectly through attributions and behaviors. In one study, participants read and responded to scenarios depicting various helping events, in which indicators of helpers having autonomous or controlled (introjected) motivations were embedded (Weinstein, DeHaan, & Ryan, 2010).

Autonomous attributions predicted more gratitude and other positive recipient outcomes compared with controlled motivation, a finding consistent with a body of evidence demonstrating the benefit-triggered gratitude increases with perceived intentionality and cost to the benefactor. In another study (Froh et al., 2011), middle school classrooms (of 8–11-year-olds) were randomly assigned to an intervention that trained the appraisal of benefit exchanges (i.e., social-cognitive determinants of gratitude) or to a control condition. Three vignettes were created to measure the social-cognitive perceptions underlying gratitude (i.e., intent, cost, and benefit; Tesser, Gatewood, & Driver, 1968; Wood, Joseph, & Maltby, 2008). The vignettes depicted three helping situations in which the students were instructed to imagine that they were the main character in the stories. Following each story, students were asked four questions. The questions for each vignette were tailored to the respective benefactor (i.e., sister, friend, and parent) and situation (i.e., help studying, lending cleats to play soccer, and sharing a computer), and all three grateful cognitions across all three vignettes were measured. Using *sister* as an example, the questions were the following: "How much did your sister help you on purpose?" which aims to measure intent; "How much did your sister give up to help you?" which aims to measure cost; and "How much did your sister (quizzing) you help you?" which aims to measure benefit. Finally, attempting to gather preliminary construct validity of the vignettes as measures of grateful thinking, the last question for each vignette asked the student to rate how thankful he or she would feel toward the benefactor. For this question, students rated their responses using a 5-point Likert scale. The scale ranged from (1) *very slightly or not at all* to (5) *extremely*. In this sample, alphas for the benefit appraisal vignettes were .82 (pretest) and .86 (posttest). Alpha was computed across vignettes combining dimensions.

Dispositional Measures

By far, trait measures are the most widely used means for assessing gratitude. Three self-report measures of gratitude as a personality disposition have been constructed: the GRAT (Gratitude, Resentment, Appreciation Test; Watkins, Grimm, & Hailu, 1998), the Gratitude Questionnaire (GQ-6; McCullough, Emmons, & Tsang, 2002; see Appendix 20.1), and the Gratitude Adjective Checklist (GAC; McCullough et al., 2002). These individual difference measures emphasize both benefit-triggered gratitude and a generalized sense of gratitude. The GAC is the composite of three affect adjectives (grateful, appreciative, and thankful) and has been used to assess both state and trait indicators of grateful affect in repeated measures designs. The GAC can be used to measure gratitude as an emotion, mood, or disposition depending on the timeframe specified in the instructions. This measure evidenced strong psychometric properties in both early and late adolescent samples (Froh, Miller, & Snyder, 2007).

The 44-item GRAT form measures three dimensions of gratitude: resentment, simple appreciation, and appreciation of others (Watkins, Woodward, Stone, & Kolts, 2003). Some example items include "I basically feel like life has ripped me off," "Sometimes I find myself overwhelmed by the beauty of a musical piece," and "I feel deeply appreciative for the things that others have done for me in my life." Scores on the GRAT correlate positively and moderately with positive states and traits such as internal locus of control, intrinsic religiosity, life satisfaction, and a memory bias in favor of positive life events (Watkins, Grimm, & Kolts, 2004). Moreover, GRAT scores correlate negatively and moderately with negative states and traits such as depression, extrinsic religiosity, narcissism, and hostility (Watkins et al., 2004). The GRAT evidenced strong test–retest reliability, internal consistency, criterion-related validity, and sensitivity in adult samples (Froh et al., 2007).

The GQ-6 measures dispositional gratitude as a generalized tendency to recognize and emotionally respond with thankfulness, after attributing benefits received to an external moral agent (McCullough, Emmons, & Tsang, 2002). Items reflect gratitude intensity (e.g., "I feel thankful for what I have received in life"), gratitude frequency (e.g., "Long amounts of time can go by before I feel grateful to something or someone"), gratitude span (e.g., "I sometimes feel grateful for the smallest things"), and gratitude density (e.g., "I am grateful to a wide variety of people"). Each item is endorsed on a 7-point Likert-type scale (where 1 = *strongly disagree* and 7 = *strongly agree*).

McCullough et al. (2002) examined the validity of a one-factor solution for the six items via structural equation models with maximum likelihood estimation. Using three different fit indexes, the one-factor model provided an adequate fit to the data. Table 20.1 presents a summary of the descriptive statistics and acceptable internal consistencies of the GQ-6 across diverse samples. Alpha reliabilities have ranged from .67 to .94. The GQ-6 has been successfully validated across diverse populations such as U.S. high school youth, Taiwanese college students, Taiwanese athletes, U.S. older adults, business school graduate students, and veterans with PTSD (Andersson, Giacalone, & Jurkiewicz, 2007; Chen, Kee, Chen, & Tsai, 2008; Froh, Emmons, Card, Bono, & Wilson, 2010; Kashdan, Mishra, Breen, & Froh, 2009; Kashdan, Uswatte, & Julian, 2006). A study done by Jans-Beken, Lataster, Leontjevas, and Jacobs (2015) supports the validity of the GQ-6.

The grateful disposition has been found to be positively associated with personality traits reflecting well-being and positive social functioning. For example, in terms of the Big Five personality domains, gratitude has been found to be strongly associated with extraversion, openness, and agreeableness and negatively associated with resentment/hostility, depression, and vulnerability and materialistic attitudes and envy (McCullough et al., 2002, 2004; Wood, Joseph, & Maltby, 2008). Recent studies have even highlighted a relationship between gratitude and other surprising factors such as biology, sleep, and patience (Dickens & DeSteno, 2016; Jackowska, Brown, Ronaldson,

TABLE 20.1. Summary of Means, Standard Deviations, and Internal Consistencies for the GQ-6 Across Studies

Study	*N*	Sample	Alpha	*M*	SD
Andersson, Giacalone, and Jurkiewicz (2007)	603	Business school graduate students	.67	38.50	3.67
Breen, Kashdan, Lenser, and Fincham (2010)	140	U.S. college students	.91	35.62	5.25
Chen, Chen, Kee, and Tsai (2008)	608	Taiwanese college students	.80	28.55	5.25
Chen and Kee (2008), Study 1	169	Taiwanese senior high school athletes	.80	28.68	4.50
Chen and Kee (2008), Study 2	265	Taiwanese senior high school athletes	.78	27.54	4.56
Froh, Emmons, Card, Bono, and Wilson (2010)	1,035	U.S. high school students (14–19 years)	.76	33.17	5.43
Froh, Fan, Emmons, Bono, Huebner, and Watkins (2011)	1,405	U.S. high school students (10–19 years)	.76 to .85	28.08 to 30.44	4.32 to 5.11
Kashdan and Breen (2007)	144	U.S. college students	.77	36.68	5.13
Kashdan, Mishra, Breen, and Froh (2009), Study 2a	214	U.S. college students (*Female*)	.94	36.22	4.58
		U.S. college students (*Male*)		34.13	7.11
Kashdan et al. (2009), Study 2b	76	Older adults (*Female*)		36.98	4.75
		Older adults (*Male*)		35.76	4.05
Kashdan et al. (2009), Study 3	190	U.S. college students (*Female*)		.93	36.80
		U.S. college students (*Male*)	34.83	5.52	5.39
Kashdan, Uswatte, and Julian (2006)	75	PTSD group	.86	22.1	9.4
		Non-PTSD group		33.7	7.0
McCullough, Emmons, and Tsang (2002), Study 1	238	U.S. college students		35.52	5.28
McCullough et al. (2002), Study 2	1,228	Adult volunteers (age 18–75)	.82	36.9	4.92
McCullough et al. (2002), Study 3	156	U.S. college students		34.92	5.16
McCullough, Tsang, and Emmons (2004), Study 1	96	Adult volunteers (age 22–77)	.80 to .83	35.58	5.76
McCullough et al. (2004), Study 2	112	U.S. college students		37.86	3.90
Wood, Maltby, Stewart, Linley, and Joseph (2008), Study 1	156	British college students	Not reported	28.97 (T1) 29.57 (T2)	8.26 (T1) 8.71 (T2)
Wood, Maltby, Gillett, Linley, and Joseph (2008), Study 2	87	British college students	Not reported	35.13	4.40

& Steptoe, 2016). At the facet level, gratitude has been found to be most strongly associated with warmth, gregariousness, positive emotions, open actions, trust, altruism, tender-mindedness, and prosocial traits such as empathy, forgiveness, and willingness to help others (McCullough et al., 2002). Most important, the grateful disposition has been found to be independent of the Big Five and contributes uniquely to well-being (Goldberg & Saucier, 1998; Lin, 2014) above and beyond general positive affect (Bartlett & DeSteno, 2006).

Aside from numerous studies measuring gratitude among U.S. populations, the GQ-6 has increasingly been validated cross-culturally. It has been translated, adapted, and validated in Hungarian (Tamás, Magdolna, & Judit, 2016), Polish (Kossakowska & Kwiatek, 2012), and Dutch (Jans-Beken et al., 2015), among others. Across two cross-sectional studies, Chen and Kee (2008) examined the association between dispositional gratitude and well-being among Taiwanese athletes. The GQ was translated into Taiwanese. In the study 1,169 adolescent athletes (15–18 years old) were measured on the GQ-6 and other well-being measures. Dispositional gratitude strongly predicted more satisfaction with life, team satisfaction, and negatively predicted athlete burnout. After the GQ-6 was modified to orient gratitude in a sports setting (e.g., one of the GQ items was modified as "I have so much in my entire sport experience or endeavor to be thankful for"), sports-domain gratitude positively predicted team satisfaction and inversely predicted athlete burnout.

The grateful disposition has also been extensively examined as a buffer against stress (Wood et al., 2007). In one of the initial attempts to understand the stress buffering effects of gratitude, Vietnam War veterans with and without PTSD were examined for the effects of gratitude on well-being. In the PTSD group, though no differences were found for daily gratitude, dispositional gratitude significantly predicted greater daily positive affect, percent of pleasant days, intrinsically motivated activity, and self-esteem (Kashdan et al., 2006). The link between gratitude and PTSD has continued to be researched and expanded on (Israel-Cohen et al., 2015; Van Dusen, Tiamiyu, Kashdan, & Elhai, 2015). As an extension of this line of research, empirical attempts have been made to understand the link between dispositional gratitude and distinct coping styles. Wood et al. (2007) revealed that gratitude was associated with more approach styles of coping such as seeking more social support, positive interpretation, growth, active coping, and planning. Conversely, gratitude was negatively associated with behavior disengagement, self-blame, substance use, and denial. Across two longitudinal studies, Wood, Maltby, Stewart, Linley, and Joseph (2008) examined the association between dispositional gratitude, perceived social support, stress, and depression during a life transition. Study 1 revealed that dispositional gratitude significantly contributed to the development of social support during a life transition, reduced stress, and alleviated depression. Subsequently, these findings were replicated in Study 2 and revealed that dispositional gratitude contributed to well-being and social support beyond the Big Five personality traits.

INDUCING GRATITUDE: GRATITUDE JOURNALING AND RELATED INDUCTIONS

While gratitude has been studied as a trait, it has also been studied as an emotion—feeling grateful and equivalent states (appreciation, thankfulness). State gratitude has been experimentally activated through the self-guided exercise of journaling. In the first study examining the benefits of experimentally induced grateful thoughts on psychological well being in daily life, a gratitude induction was compared to a hassles and a neutral life events condition (Emmons & McCullough, 2003). The cultivation of grateful affect through daily and weekly journaling led to overall improved well-being, including fewer health complaints, and a more positive outlook toward life. Participants in the gratitude condition also reported more exercise and appraised their life more positively compared to participants in the hassles and neutral conditions. The impact of gratitude interventions on positive affect was recently replicated in a Spanish sample (Martínez-Martí, Avia, & Hernández-Lloreda, 2010). Results from another study (Froh et al., 2014) on gratitude intervention in youth indicated that children's awareness of the social-cognitive appraisals in receiving help from another can be strengthened and that this makes children more grateful and benefits their well-being. A weekly intervention obtained such effects up to 5 months later. A daily intervention produced these effects immediately (2 days later) and showed further that children expressed gratitude behaviorally more (i.e., wrote 80% more thank-you cards to their Parent–Teacher Association) and that their teachers even observed them to be happier.

In the past few years, a number of laboratory and research-based intervention studies have also examined the positive impact of gratitude-induced activities (e.g., the gratitude visit, gratitude letter) on psychological well-being, including happiness, depression, materialism, and relational satisfaction (Bono, Emmons, & McCullough, 2004; McCullough et al., 2004; Seligman, Steen, Park, & Peterson, 2005; Toepfer, Cichy, & Peters, 2012).

Extending the findings on personal well-being, there is empirical evidence that increasing short-term levels of gratitude promotes the formation and maintenance of interpersonal relationships (Koo, Algoe, Wilson, & Gilbert, 2008; Mikulincer, Shaver, & Slav, 2006). For example, a recent daily diary study examined daily gratitude and indebtedness in romantic relationships. Gratitude experienced as a result of the daily interactions between the romantic partners led to an increase in relationship connection and satisfaction the following day for both partners (Algoe, Gable, & Maisel, 2010; Algoe & Zhaoyang, 2016). Experiencing gratitude for the benefits derived from the romantic partner has strong implications for overall well-being, improvements in closeness in the relationship, and reducing interpersonal stress. Lambert and colleagues (Lambert, Graham, & Fincham, 2009) found that participants randomly assigned to express gratitude to a friend twice a week for 3 weeks reported more willingness to voice relationship concerns, had higher positive regard for the friend, and perceived greater communal strength than those in control conditions.

Considering the importance of examining the uniqueness of gratitude, in our laboratory we compared gratitude with two other psychological interventions. In a 14-day daily diary study, participants were randomly assigned to one of four conditions—gratitude, forgiveness, hope, or control. We found no major differences between the experimental conditions in terms of benefits to well-being. However, we observed gender differences on the GAC most strongly in the gratitude intervention condition. Women had higher levels of grateful emotions in the gratitude condition, indicating that women were more sensitive to the gratitude intervention. Maintaining a gratitude diary has also been shown to enhance school belonging and promote well-being (Diebel, Woodcock, Cooper, & Brignell, 2016).

MEASURING GRATITUDE IN YOUTH

Aside from several isolated studies that preceded current theorizing on gratitude (e.g., Baumgarten-Tramer, 1938; Becker & Smenner, 1986; Gleason & Weintraub, 1976; Russell & Paris, 1994), the study of gratitude in youth is in its infancy (for reviews, see Bono & Froh, 2009). Generally speaking, the emerging evidence mirrors the positive benefits found with adults. For instance, early adolescents (ages 11–13) who were more grateful reported more positive affect, optimism, social support from peer and family, and satisfaction with school, family, community, friends, and self (Froh, Yurkewicz, & Kashdan, 2009), compared with their less grateful counterparts. They also reported having fewer physical symptoms and giving more emotional support. Among late adolescents (ages 14–19), those who were more grateful reported greater life satisfaction, social integration, absorption in activities, and academic achievement and less envy, depression, and materialism. Longitudinal evidence also indicates links to greater psychological and social functioning up to 6 months later (Froh, Bono, & Emmons, 2010).

The most convincing evidence that gratitude can improve youth well-being comes from intervention studies (Froh, Sefick, & Emmons, 2008, Froh et al., 2009, 2014). Thus, gratitude is related to important indicators of psychological and social functioning in youth as it is in adults.

The aforementioned studies suggest advances in our understanding of gratitude in youth. Grateful youth appear to be happy youth, and the effects of gratitude interventions with children and adolescents mirror those with adults. As valuable as this research may be, psychologists must tread cautiously because the scales used in these studies were created for adults, not for youth. In other words, the validity of the research findings hinges on the assumption that these adult gratitude measures can validly measure youth gratitude.

Indeed, a major obstacle to gratitude research with youth is that no scale currently exists that was specifically designed to measure a grateful disposition that is still forming in development. Although psychologists may be tempted to use the adult scales previously discussed because they are readily accessible measures (as researchers have been doing for the past 3 years), caution should be used because the experience and expression of gratitude is different in adults than in children and adolescents (Bono & Froh, 2009).

The difficulty with evaluating gratitude in youth is further compounded by the uncertainty surrounding its developmental trajectory (Froh et al., 2007). Some scholars submit that the experience of gratitude increases as children mature (Baumgarten-Tramer, 1938; Graham, 1988). That is, older children report experiencing and expressing more gratitude compared to younger children. Therefore, measuring gratitude in infancy and early childhood may prove futile if gratitude emerges in middle childhood. But until a youth gratitude scale is created, one that is sensitive to the cognitive and emotional development of children and adolescents, psychologists are left with a choice to either not study gratitude or use the existing scales. Luckily for youth and those interested in studying gratitude on this population, a recent study was conducted on the psychometric properties of adult gratitude scales in children and adolescents.

Froh and colleagues (2011) asked an important question: Are the existing gratitude scales used with adults valid for use with youth? Based on a large youth sample (N = 1,405) with ages ranging from 10 to 19 years old, they examined the psychometric properties of scores of the GQ-6, the GAC, and the Gratitude Resentment and Appreciation Test (GRAT)—short form. Single-group and multiple-group confirmatory factor analyses indicated that the factor structures of these gratitude scales resemble those found with adults, and were invariant across age groups. Scores of all three gratitude scales revealed acceptable internal consistency estimates (i.e., > .70) across age groups. Results showed that while scores of all three gratitude scales were positively correlated with each other for 14- to 19-year-olds, GRAT-short form scores tended to display relatively low correlations (i.e., rs = .20–.35) with scores of the other two measures for younger children (10–13-year-olds). Further, the nomological network analysis showed that scores of all three gratitude scales were positively correlated with positive affect and life satisfaction scores across the age groups. The relationships with negative affect and depression scores, however, seemed dependent on the child's age.

Based on these results, Froh et al. (2011) offered several recommendations for those interested in studying gratitude in children and adolescents. First, the results suggest that the GQ-6, GAC, and GRAT-short form can be used with 14- to 19-year-olds, with one small exception: The GAC demonstrated lower correlations with negative affect; thus, caution should be used when using the GAC with this age group. Second, psychologists interested in using the GQ-6 to measure gratitude in youth should consider excluding item 6 ("Long amounts of time can go by before I feel grateful to something or someone") considering its low factor loading (.21 in their youth sample), and some youth reported it difficult to understand and abstract. Third, psychologists should not use the GRAT-short form with 10- to 13-year-olds. While the GQ-6 and GAC could be used with this age group, the results suggest that the GQ-6 is the more psychometrically sound scale. Nonetheless, they recommend that researchers attempting to measure gratitude in 10- to 13-year-olds should probably use both the GQ-6 and GAC, looking for convergent findings.

Emphasizing gratitude and building up positive anticipations should help youth sharpen goals and plans that directly augment their welfare and help coordinate efforts to meaningfully engage and educate them across the home, school, and community environments (Damon, 2008). If a comprehensive mission for schools is to turn youth into psychologically well, knowledgeable, responsible, socially skilled, physically healthy, caring and contributing citizens (Greenberg et al., 2003), then fostering gratitude in youth may be an essential aim. Pursuit of this ambitious mission, however, requires that researchers and school professionals first be confident in their assessments of gratitude in children and adolescents. This study provides initial support for the use of extant gratitude measures, with some exceptions, for research purposes.

APPENDIX 20.1
THE GRATITUDE QUESTIONNAIRE—SIX-ITEM FORM (GQ-6)

The Gratitude Questionnaire—Six-Item Form (GQ-6)

By Michael E. McCullough, PhD, Robert A. Emmons, PhD, Jo-Ann Tsang, PhD

Using the scale below as a guide, write a number beside each statement to indicate how much you agree with it.

1 = *strongly disagree*
2 = *disagree*
3 = *slightly disagree*
4 = *neutral*
5 = *slightly agree*
6 = *agree*
7 = *strongly agree*

____1. I have so much in life to be thankful for.
____2. If I had to list everything that I felt grateful for, it would be a very long list.
____3. When I look at the world, I don't see much to be grateful for.*
____4. I am grateful to a wide variety of people.
____5. As I get older I find myself more able to appreciate the people, events, and situations that have been part of my life history.
____6. Long amounts of time can go by before I feel grateful to something or someone.*

* Items 3 and 6 are reverse-scored.

Scoring Instructions:

1. Add up your scores for items 1, 2, 4, and 5.
2. Reverse your scores for items 3 and 6. That is, if you scored a "7," give yourself a "1"; if you scored a "6," give yourself a "2," etc.
3. Add the reversed scores for items 3 and 6 to the total from Step 1. This is your total GQ-6 score. This number should be between 6 and 42.

REFERENCES

Algoe, S., Gable, S. L., & Maisel, N. C. (2010). It's the little things: Everyday gratitude as a booster shot for romantic relationships. *Personal Relationships, 17,* 217–233. http://dx.doi.org/10.1111/j.1475-6811.2010.01273.x

Algoe, S. B., Kurtz, L. E., & Hilaire, N. M. (2016). Putting the "you" in "thank you": Examining other-praising behavior as the active relational ingredient in expressed gratitude. *Social Psychological & Personality Science, 7,* 658–666. http://dx.doi.org/10.1177/1948550616651681

Algoe, S. B., & Zhaoyang, R. (2016). Positive psychology in context: Effects of expressing gratitude in ongoing relationships depend on perceptions of enactor responsiveness. *The Journal of Positive Psychology, 11,* 399–415. http://dx.doi.org/10.1080/17439760.2015.1117131

Andersson, L. M., Giacalone, R. A., & Jurkiewicz, C. L. (2007). On the relationship of hope and gratitude to corporate social responsibility. *Journal of Business Ethics, 70,* 401–409. http://dx.doi.org/10.1007/s10551-006-9118-1

Bartlett, M. Y., & DeSteno, D. (2006). Gratitude and prosocial behavior: Helping when it costs you. *Psychological Science, 17,* 319–325. http://dx.doi.org/10.1111/j.1467-9280.2006.01705.x

Baumgarten-Tramer, F. (1938). "Gratefulness" in children and young people. *The Pedagogical Seminary and Journal of Genetic Psychology, 53,* 53–66. http://dx.doi.org/10.1080/08856559.1938.10533797

Becker, J. A., & Smenner, P. C. (1986). The spontaneous use of *thank you* by preschoolers as a function of sex, socioeconomic status, and listener status. *Language in Society, 15,* 537–546. http://dx.doi.org/10.1017/S0047404500012008

Biondo, C. (2012). Gratitude and resentment: An analysis using a free-description approach. *Dissertation Abstracts International, 72,* 5017.

Bono, G., Emmons, R. A., & McCullough, M. E. (2004). Gratitude in practice and the practice of gratitude. In P. A. Linley & S. Joseph (Eds.), *Positive psychology in practice* (pp. 464–481). Hoboken, NJ: John Wiley & Sons. http://dx.doi.org/10.1002/9780470939338.ch29

Bono, G., & Froh, J. J. (2009). Gratitude in school: Benefits to students and schools. In R. Gilman, E. S. Huebner, & M. Furlong (Eds.), *Handbook of positive psychology in schools* (pp. 77–88). New York, NY: Routledge.

Breen, W. E., Kashdan, T. B., Lenser, M. L., & Fincham, F. D. (2010). Gratitude and forgiveness: Convergence and divergence on self-report and informant ratings. *Personality and Individual Differences, 49,* 932–937. http://dx.doi.org/10.1016/j.paid.2010.07.033

Chen, L. H., Chen, M. Y., Kee, Y. H., & Tsai, Y. M. (2008). Relation of perfectionism with athletes' burnout: Further examination. *Perceptual and Motor Skills, 106,* 811–820. http://dx.doi.org/10.2466/pms.106.3.811-820

Chen, L. H., & Kee, Y. H. (2008). Gratitude and adolescent athletes' well-being. *Social Indicators Research, 89,* 361–373. http://dx.doi.org/10.1007/s11205-008-9237-4

Cheng, S. T., Tsui, P. K., & Lam, J. H. M. (2015). Improving mental health in health care practitioners: Randomized controlled trial of a gratitude intervention. *Journal of Consulting and Clinical Psychology, 83,* 177–186. http://dx.doi.org/10.1037/a0037895

Damon, W. (2008). *The path to purpose: Helping our children find their calling in life.* New York, NY: The Free Press.

Dickens, L., & DeSteno, D. (2016). The grateful are patient: Heightened daily gratitude is associated with attenuated temporal discounting. *Emotion, 16,* 421–425. http://dx.doi.org/10.1037/emo0000176

Diebel, T., Woodcock, C., Cooper, C., & Brignell, C. (2016). Establishing the effectiveness of a gratitude diary intervention on children's sense of school belonging. *Educational and Child Psychology, 33,* 117–129.

Ellsworth, P. C., & Smith, C. A. (1988). From appraisal to emotion: Differences among unpleasant feelings. *Motivation and Emotion, 12,* 271–302. http://dx.doi.org/10.1007/BF00993115

Emmons, R. A., & McCullough, M. E. (2003). Counting blessings versus burdens: An experimental investigation of gratitude and subjective well-being in daily life. *Journal of Personality and Social Psychology, 84,* 377–389. http://dx.doi.org/10.1037/0022-3514.84.2.377

Emmons, R. A., & Stern, R. (2013). Gratitude as a psychotherapeutic intervention. *Journal of Clinical Psychology, 69,* 846–855. http://dx.doi.org/10.1002/jclp.22020

Froh, J. J., Bono, G., & Emmons, R. A. (2010). Being grateful is beyond good manners: Gratitude and motivation to contribute to society among early adolescents. *Motivation and Emotion, 34,* 144–157. http://dx.doi.org/10.1007/s11031-010-9163-z

Froh, J. J., Bono, G., Fan, J., Emmons, R. A., Henderson, K., Harris, C., . . . Wood, A. M. (2014). Nice thinking! An educational intervention that teaches children to think gratefully. *School Psychology Review, 43,* 132–152.

Froh, J. J., Emmons, R. A., Card, N. A., Bono, G., & Wilson, J. A. (2010). Gratitude and the reduced costs of materialism in adolescents. *Journal of Happiness Studies, 12,* 89–102.

Froh, J. J., Fan, J., Emmons, R. A., Bono, G., Huebner, E. S., & Watkins, P. (2011). Measuring gratitude in youth: Assessing the psychometric properties of adult gratitude scales in children and adolescents. *Psychological Assessment, 23,* 311–324. http://dx.doi.org/10.1037/a0021590

Froh, J. J., Miller, D. N., & Snyder, S. (2007). Gratitude in children and adolescents: Development, assessment, and school-based intervention. *School Psychology Forum, 2,* 1–13.

Froh, J. J., Sefick, W. J., & Emmons, R. A. (2008). Counting blessings in early adolescents: An experimental study of gratitude and subjective well-being. *Journal of School Psychology, 46,* 213–233. http://dx.doi.org/10.1016/j.jsp.2007.03.005

Froh, J. J., Yurkewicz, C., & Kashdan, T. B. (2009). Gratitude and subjective well-being in early adolescence: Examining gender differences. *Journal of Adolescence, 32,* 633–650. http://dx.doi.org/10.1016/j.adolescence.2008.06.006

Gleason, J. B., & Weintraub, S. (1976). The acquisition of routines in child language. *Language in Society, 5,* 129–136. http://dx.doi.org/10.1017/S0047404500006977

Goldberg, L. R., & Saucier, G. (1998). What is beyond the Big Five? *Journal of Personality, 66,* 495–524. http://dx.doi.org/10.1111/1467-6494.00022

Graham, S. (1988). Children's developing understanding of the motivational role of affect: An attributional analysis. *Cognitive Development, 3,* 71–88. http://dx.doi.org/10.1016/0885-2014(88)90031-7

Greenberg, M. T., Weissberg, R. P., O'Brien, M. U., Zins, J. E., Fredericks, L., Resnik, H., & Elias, M. J. (2003). Enhancing school-based prevention and youth development through coordinated social, emotional, and academic learning. *American Psychologist, 58,* 466–474. http://dx.doi.org/10.1037/0003-066X.58.6-7.466

Gulliford, L., & Morgan, M. (2016). An empirical exploration of the normative dimensions of gratitude. In D. Carr (Ed.), *Perspectives on gratitude: An interdisciplinary approach* (pp. 199–214). New York, NY: Routledge.

Israel-Cohen, Y., Uzefovsky, F., Kashy-Rosenbaum, G., & Kaplan, O. (2015). Gratitude and PTSD symptoms among Israeli youth exposed to missile attacks: Examining the mediation of positive and negative affect and life satisfaction. *The Journal of Positive Psychology, 10,* 99–106. http://dx.doi.org/10.1080/17439760.2014.927910

Jackowska, M., Brown, J., Ronaldson, A., & Steptoe, A. (2016). The impact of a brief gratitude intervention on subjective well-being, biology and sleep. *Journal of Health Psychology, 21,* 2207–2217. http://dx.doi.org/10.1177/1359105315572455

Jans-Beken, L., Lataster, J., Leontjevas, R., & Jacobs, N. (2015). Measuring gratitude: A comparative validation of the Dutch Gratitude Questionnaire (GQ6) and Short Gratitude, Resentment, and Appreciation Test (SGRAT). *Psychologica Belgica, 55,* 19–31. http://dx.doi.org/10.5334/pb.bd

Kashdan, T. B., & Breen, W. E. (2007). Materialism and diminished well-being: Experiential avoidance as a mediating mechanism. *Journal of Social and Clinical Psychology, 26,* 521–539. http://dx.doi.org/10.1521/jscp.2007.26.5.521

Kashdan, T. B., Mishra, A., Breen, W. E., & Froh, J. J. (2009). Gender differences in gratitude: Examining appraisals, narratives, the willingness to express emotions, and changes in psychological needs. *Journal of Personality, 77,* 691–730. http://dx.doi.org/10.1111/j.1467-6494.2009.00562.x

Kashdan, T. B., Uswatte, G., & Julian, T. (2006). Gratitude and hedonic and eudaimonic well-being in Vietnam war veterans. *Behaviour Research and Therapy, 44,* 177–199. http://dx.doi.org/10.1016/j.brat.2005.01.005

Koo, M., Algoe, S. B., Wilson, T. D., & Gilbert, D. T. (2008). It's a wonderful life: Mentally subtracting positive events improves people's affective states, contrary to their affective forecasts. *Journal of Personality and Social Psychology, 95,* 1217–1224. http://dx.doi.org/10.1037/a0013316

Kossakowska, M., & Kwiatek, P. (2012, April). *Polish version of the GQ-6 to measure gratitude in research on spirituality.* Paper presented at the I International Conference "Science, Human Religiousness and Spirituality," Gdansk, Poland.

Lambert, N. M., Graham, S. M., & Fincham, F. D. (2009). A prototype analysis of gratitude: Varieties of gratitude experiences. *Personality and Social Psychology Bulletin, 35,* 1193–1207. http://dx.doi.org/10.1177/0146167209338071

Lin, C. (2014). A higher-order gratitude uniquely predicts subjective well-being: Incremental validity above the personality and a single gratitude. *Social Indicators Research, 119,* 909–924. http://dx.doi.org/10.1007/s11205-013-0518-1

Martínez-Martí, M. L., Avia, M. D., & Hernández-Lloreda, M. J. (2010). The effects of counting blessings on subjective well-being: A gratitude intervention in a Spanish sample. *The Spanish Journal of Psychology, 13,* 886–896. http://dx.doi.org/10.1017/S1138741600002535

McCullough, M. E., Emmons, R. A., & Tsang, J.-A. (2002). The grateful disposition: A conceptual and empirical topography. *Journal of Personality and Social Psychology, 82,* 112–127. http://dx.doi.org/10.1037/0022-3514.82.1.112

McCullough, M. E., Kimeldorf, M. B., & Cohen, A. D. (2008). An adaptation for altruism? The social causes, social effects, and social evolution of gratitude. *Current Directions in Psychological Science, 17,* 281–285. http://dx.doi.org/10.1111/j.1467-8721.2008.00590.x

McCullough, M. E., Tsang, J. A., & Emmons, R. A. (2004). Gratitude in intermediate affective terrain: Links of grateful moods to individual differences and daily emotional experience. *Journal of Personality and Social Psychology, 86,* 295–309. http://dx.doi.org/10.1037/0022-3514.86.2.295

Mikulincer, M., Shaver, P. R., & Slav, K. (2006). Attachment, mental representations of others, and interpersonal gratitude and forgiveness within romantic relationships. In M. Mikulincer & G. S. Goodman (Eds.), *Dynamics of romantic love* (pp. 190–215). New York, NY: Guilford Press.

Nowak, M. A., & Roch, S. (2007). Upstream reciprocity and the evolution of gratitude. *Proceedings. Biological Sciences, 274,* 605–610. http://dx.doi.org/10.1098/rspb.2006.0125

Okamoto, S., & Robinson, W. P. (1997). Determinants of gratitude expressions in England. *Journal of Language and Social Psychology, 16,* 411–433. http://dx.doi.org/10.1177/0261927X970164003

Otto, A. K., Szczesny, E. C., Soriano, E. C., Laurenceau, J. P., & Siegel, S. D. (2016). Effects of a randomized gratitude intervention on death-related fear of recurrence in breast cancer survivors. *Health Psychology, 35,* 1320–1328. http://dx.doi.org/10.1037/hea0000400

Rosenberg, E. L. (1998). Levels of analysis and the organization of affect. *Review of General Psychology, 2,* 247–270. http://dx.doi.org/10.1037/1089-2680.2.3.247

Rusk, R. D., Vella-Brodrick, D. A., & Waters, L. (2016). Gratitude or gratefulness? A conceptual review and proposal of the system of appreciative functioning. *Journal of Happiness Studies, 17,* 2191–2122.

Russell, J. A., & Paris, F. A. (1994). Do children acquire concepts for complex emotions abruptly? *International Journal of Behavioral Development, 17,* 349–365. http://dx.doi.org/10.1177/016502549401700207

Seligman, M. E. P., Steen, T. A., Park, N., & Peterson, C. (2005). Positive psychology progress: Empirical validation of interventions. *American Psychologist, 60,* 410–421. http://dx.doi.org/10.1037/0003-066X.60.5.410

Sommers, S., & Kosmitzki, C. (1988). Emotion and social context: An American-German comparison. *British Journal of Social Psychology, 27,* 35–49. http://dx.doi.org/10.1111/j.2044-8309.1988.tb00803.x

Tamás, M., Magdolna, G., & Judit, D. (2016). Introduction and psychometric properties of the Hungarian version of the Gratitude Questionnaire. *Mentálhigiéné és Pszichoszomatika, 15,* 203–214.

Teigen, K. H. (1997). Luck, envy, and gratitude: It could have been different. *Scandinavian Journal of Psychology, 38,* 313–323. http://dx.doi.org/10.1111/1467-9450.00041

Tesser, A., Gatewood, R., & Driver, M. (1968). Some determinants of gratitude. *Journal of Personality and Social Psychology, 9,* 233–236. http://dx.doi.org/10.1037/h0025905

Toepfer, S. M., Cichy, K., & Peters, P. (2012). Letters of gratitude: Further evidence for author benefits. *Journal of Happiness Studies, 13,* 187–201. http://dx.doi.org/10.1007/s10902-011-9257-7

Van Dusen, J. P., Tiamiyu, M. F., Kashdan, T. B., & Elhai, J. D. (2015). Gratitude, depression and PTSD: Assessment of structural relationships. *Psychiatry Research, 230,* 867–870. http://dx.doi.org/10.1016/j.psychres.2015.11.036

Watkins, P. C., Grimm, D. L., & Hailu, L. (1998, June). *Counting your blessings: Grateful individuals recall more positive memories.* Paper presented at the 11th Annual Convention of the American Psychological Society Convention, Denver, CO.

Watkins, P. C., Grimm, D. L., & Kolts, R. (2004). Counting your blessings: Positive memories among grateful persons. *Current Psychology: A Journal for Diverse Perspectives on Diverse Psychological Issues, 23,* 52–67. http://dx.doi.org/10.1007/s12144-004-1008-z

Watkins, P. C., Woodward, K., Stone, T., & Kolts, R. L. (2003). Gratitude and happiness: Development of a measure of gratitude, and relationships with subjective well-being. *Social Behavior and Personality, 31,* 431–451. http://dx.doi.org/10.2224/sbp.2003.31.5.431

Weiner, B. (1986). *An attributional theory of motivation and emotion.* New York, NY: Springer Verlag. http://dx.doi.org/10.1007/978-1-4612-4948-1

Weinstein, N., DeHaan, C. R., & Ryan, R. M. (2010). Attributing autonomous versus introjected motivation to helpers and the recipient experience: Effects on gratitude, attitudes, and well-being. *Motivation and Emotion, 34,* 418–431. http://dx.doi.org/10.1007/s11031-010-9183-8

Wood, A. M., Froh, J. J., & Geraghty, A. W. (2010). Gratitude and well-being: A review and theoretical integration. *Clinical Psychology Review, 30,* 890–905. http://dx.doi.org/10.1016/j.cpr.2010.03.005

Wood, A. M., Joseph, S., & Linley, P. A. (2007). Coping style as a psychological resource of grateful people. *Journal of Social and Clinical Psychology, 26,* 1076–1093. http://dx.doi.org/10.1521/jscp.2007.26.9.1076

Wood, A. M., Joseph, S., & Maltby, J. (2008). Gratitude uniquely predicts satisfaction with life: Incremental validity above the domains and facets of the five factor model. *Personality and Individual Differences, 45,* 49–54. http://dx.doi.org/10.1016/j.paid.2008.02.019

Wood, A. M., Maltby, J., Gillett, R., Linley, P. A., & Joseph, S. (2008). The role of gratitude in the development of social support, stress, and depression: Two longitudinal studies. *Journal of Research in Personality, 42*(4), 854–871. http://dx.doi.org/10.1016/j.jrp.2007.11.003

Wood, A. M., Maltby, J., Stewart, N., Linley, P. A., & Joseph, S. (2008). A social-cognitive model of trait and state levels of gratitude. *Emotion, 8,* 281–290. http://dx.doi.org/10.1037/1528-3542.8.2.281

21

Moral Judgment Maturity

From Clinical to Standard Measures

John C. Gibbs, Karen S. Basinger, Rebecca McDonald,
and Dasom Lee

Moral maturity is an integral aspect of positive individual and collective human life. In human development, the morally mature person evidences not only the courage to do what is right (see Chapter 11, this volume) and an empathic "connection" with others (see Chapters 14–17, this volume) but also a clear grasp in his or her moral judgment of the bases for interpersonal and societal norms of life, affiliation, contract or truth, property, law, and legal justice. "Clear grasp" can be interpreted as profound discernment of that which is intrinsically moral, unconfounded by extraneous considerations. "Moral judgment" refers to a reason-based and prescriptive evaluation of a value or decision pertaining to welfare and/or justice. Many researchers posit that moral judgment maturity is "constructed" through a cognitive process of social perspective taking and mental coordination that is distinguishable from traditional notions of identification or internalization in moral development (Gibbs, in press; see also neonativist views, e.g., Haidt & Kesebir, 2010). This chapter focuses on the history and construct validity of instruments that measure moral judgment maturity.

HISTORY: FROM CLINICAL TO STANDARD MEASURES

Measures of moral judgment maturity generally have derived from cognitive developmental theory and have evolved from clinical interviews into more standard measures of production and evaluation. Researchers who have

http://dx.doi.org/10.1037/0000138-021
Positive Psychological Assessment: A Handbook of Models and Measures, Second Edition,
M. W. Gallagher and S. J. Lopez (Editors)

developed measures of moral judgment maturity using the cognitive developmental approach have conceptualized moral judgment as a basic, cross-culturally discernible sequence of stages (Gibbs, 1995, in press; Gibbs, Basinger, Grime, & Snarey, 2007).

Piaget: The *Méthode Clinique*

Drawing from earlier work by James Mark Baldwin and others, Jean Piaget (1932/1965) innovated what became known as cognitive developmental theory in his classic work *The Moral Judgment of the Child.* In this exploratory work with children ages 6 through 13, Piaget viewed his young participants as active structurers of their experience. To identify basic age-typical cognitive structures, Piaget used task stimuli appropriate to children (e.g., pairs of simple stories describing a child's or a parent's acts in familiar situations) and, with the *méthode clinique,* asked the children to explain their responses. The *clinical method* is similar to diagnostic or therapeutic interviews, projective testing, and "the kind of informal exploration often used in pilot research throughout the behavioral sciences" (Flavell, 1963, p. 28). The trained clinical interviewer achieves "a middle course between systematization due to preconceived ideas and incoherence due to the absence of any directing hypothesis" (Piaget, 1929/1973, p. 20).

Through such interviews, Piaget (1932/1965) found that children's moral judgment develops from generally superficial or concrete impressions to a deeper understanding of the bases for moral decisions and values in interpersonal relationships. His interviews explored moral areas such as stealing, lying, retributive justice, "immanent" (naturally embedded) justice, distributive justice, reciprocity, and authority. For example, in the stealing area, he presented children with paired stories of transgressions and asked which story depicted the "naughtier" act and why. In one story pair, a story depicted a protagonist who accidentally breaks 15 cups on his (or, for female interviewees, her) way to dinner, and the other story depicted a protagonist who breaks one cup as he tries to sneak a treat out of the cupboard. The younger (6- and 7-year-old) participants were impressed by the "external, tangible" (p. 166) event of so many broken cups and often judged the coming-to-dinner child to be naughtier—even though that child was not the one with mischievous intentions.

Piaget's research design was criticized in subsequent literature (e.g., Miller, 2018) for its confounding of the intentionality variable and degree-of-damage variables. In fairness, however, the "confounding" was quite deliberate; Piaget's aim was not to investigate whether young children understand intentions (his research had established that they do) but rather to study whether and how children at different ages coordinate intentionality with external consequences. Given this aim, Piaget's juxtaposition of these variables was appropriate and indeed successful in documenting young children's vulnerability to superficial (concrete, external, tangible) moral judgment.

Damon and Enright: Distributive Justice

Since Piaget's innovative work, many cognitive developmentalists have used the clinical method to study both moral development in a broad sense (e.g., Kohlberg, discussed later in the chapter) and children's conceptual development in particular areas related to moral judgment development and maturity. These include not only the areas explored by Piaget (1932/1965) but also the topics of friendship (Selman, 1980; Youniss, 1980), interpersonal negotiation strategy (Selman & Shultz, 1990), prosocial behavior or altruism (Eisenberg, 1982; see also Chapter 16, this volume), and society or social institutions (Adelson, Green, & O'Neil, 1969; Furth, 1980). Among the areas originally studied by Piaget was distributive justice (i.e., the fair sharing of goods); William Damon (1977) examined this area more extensively using the clinical method to probe children's decisions concerning real-life as well as hypothetical distributive justice problems.

In the distributive justice area of moral development, measurement techniques evolved from the clinical method to more standard instrumentation (Enright et al., 1984; Enright, Franklin, & Manheim, 1980). Although skilled use of the clinical method permits developmental comparisons across interviewees (Damon, 1977), Robert Enright and colleagues (1980) noted that systematic use of the paired-item procedure in a fixed format promoted standardization of the assessment. Accordingly, Enright and colleagues (1980, 1984) developed the Distributive Justice Scale (DJS), which presents all possible paired comparisons to all participants. The DJS may be termed an "evaluation" (rating, recognition, objective) measure insofar as participants need only evaluate an item as preferred (e.g., identified as a reason the respondent would have produced). Evaluation or recognition measures are distinguished from "production" measures, such as Piaget's or Damon's, in which participants must produce reasons or justifications for their decisions or evaluations.

The DJS consists essentially of two distributive justice dilemma stories (represented in drawings) and a standardized forced-choice procedure for assessing respondents' stage. One story depicts children who have made pictures at a summer camp. The pictures are sold and paid for with a lot of nickels. How many nickels should each child get? Each drawing of a possible distribution of money includes four children: one bigger, one poor, one who made the most pictures, and one who simply wants more of the nickels. The drawing for an immature stage of moral development shows, for example, the most nickels going to the child who simply wanted to get the most. Representing a somewhat more advanced level is a drawing showing all the children getting the exact same number of nickels. Still more mature is a drawing depicting a compromise distribution: more nickels going to the more meritorious *and* the more needy children. Characteristics of the DJS are summarized in Table 21.1 along with the psychometric properties of other measures.

Kohlberg: The Moral Judgment Interview

The distributive justice research of Damon, Enright, and others represents an area in which assessment evolved from Piaget's clinical method to standard instrumentation. Although the distributive justice work has had some impact, by far the most influential methodological and theoretical evolution from Piaget's seminal work was initiated by Lawrence Kohlberg (1958). Kohlberg (1984) retained Piaget's relatively broad scope, or molar scale, of moral judgment—indeed, he described moral stages that cut across moral value areas—and Piaget's clinical method of interviewing. For the interview stimuli, however, Kohlberg replaced Piaget's story pairs with dilemmas, asking after each dilemma what the protagonist should do and why. The resulting format he called the Moral Judgment Interview (MJI). Kohlberg's scoring system for MJI responses was refined into the fixed format of standard issue scoring (Colby et al., 1987). As described by Colby and Kohlberg (1987), the MJI instrument includes "moral dilemmas . . . [that] focus on the two moral issues that were chosen to represent the central value conflict in that dilemma. For example, the familiar Heinz dilemma ["Should Heinz steal a drug to save his dying wife if the only druggist able to provide the drug insists on a high price that Heinz cannot afford to pay?"] is represented in Standard Scoring as a conflict between the value of preserving life and the value of upholding the law" (p. 41).

In addition to justifying their moral decisions in the hypothetical dilemmas, participants are asked to evaluate and justify the "issues" or values that have been "predefined" (Colby & Kohlberg, 1987, p. 41) for each dilemma. Thus, for the Heinz dilemma, participants produce reasons for the importance of saving a life and obeying the law, respectively. Many of the stage-scorable justifications of participants are prompted by these moral evaluation questions (Gibbs, Basinger, & Fuller, 1992).

The Standard Issue MJI was a mixed success (see Table 21.1). On one hand, the instrument evidenced good test–retest and interrater reliability and good theoretical construct validity (Colby, Kohlberg, Gibbs, & Lieberman, 1983). On the other hand, the Standard Issue Scoring System (SISS) was so demandingly intricate that Miller (2018) suggested "it may be *the* most complex scoring system in the psychological literature" (p. 305). Although good interrater reliability is possible, its attainment requires very extensive training of raters. Furthermore, optimal use of the MJI requires (especially for younger participants) time-consuming individual interviewing.

Production and Evaluation Alternatives to the MJI

Two main alternatives to the MJI—one a production measure and the other an evaluation measure—represent additional contributions to the development of standard assessments of moral judgment maturity (Miller, 2018, p. 305).

TABLE 21.1. Types and Characteristics of Moral Judgment Measures

Type and name of measure	Target age (years)	No. of items	Administration time (minutes)	Internal reliability	Construct validation
Production					
Moral Judgment Interview (MJI; Colby & Kohlberg, 1987).	10–100	15–33 (Form A)	30–60	.92–.96	Strong
Sociomoral Reflection Measure—Short Form (SRM-SF; Gibbs et al., 1992)	9–100	11	20	.92	Excellent
Evaluation/Recognition					
Distributive Justice Scale (DJS; Enright et al., 1980)	5–11	15–20	12–15	.51–.77	Excellent
Defining Issues Test (DIT; Rest et al., 1999)	15–100	72	50	.76–.78 (P index)	Strong
Sociomoral Reflection Objective Measure (SROM; Gibbs et al. 1984)	14–100	16	45	.77–.87	Strong
Sociomoral Reflection Objective Measure—Short Form (SROM-SF; Basinger & Gibbs, 1987)	16–100	12	20	.77–.75	Some support
Sociomoral Reflection Measure—Short Form Objective (SRM-SFO; Brugman, Basinger, & Gibbs, 2007)	10–100	10	10–15	.60–.80 (most studies)	Promising

Although less prominent than these two main alternatives, other measures are also noteworthy. All of the alternative measures are less complex and time-consuming to use than the MJI.

The Sociomoral Reflection Measure—Short Form

The main alternative production measure is the Sociomoral Reflection Measure—Short Form (SRM–SF; Gibbs et al., 1992; cf. Gibbs, Widaman, & Colby, 1982). As does the MJI, the SRM–SF elicits reasoning concerning moral values that are representative of the moral domain (e.g., life, law, affiliation, contract). Whereas the MJI uses moral dilemmas to stimulate moral reasoning, the SRM–SF uses 11 brief lead-in statements (e.g., "Let's say a friend of yours needs help and may even die, and you're the only person who can save him or her" or "Think about when you've made a promise to a friend of yours"). The lead-in statements are followed by evaluation and justification questions (see Appendix 21.1). The SRM–SF uses such evaluation/justification questions for all of the moral values the measure taps (rather than only a few of the moral values, as does the MJI). The omission of dilemmas streamlines the format and obviates dilemma-related methodological criticism (e.g., Boyes & Walker, 1988).

Cross-cultural studies have found acceptable levels of reliability (test–retest, internal consistency, interrater) and validity (concurrent, discriminant, construct) for the SRM–SF. For example, the measure correlates with theoretically relevant variables such as social perspective taking and prosocial behavior, but not with social desirability. The SRM–SF's discriminant validity is supported by its consistent identification of delinquent samples as developmentally delayed in moral judgment (see below). Relative to the MJI, the SRM–SF is group-administrable, takes less time to complete (see Table 21.1), requires less inferential scoring time (25 to 30 minutes vs. 30 to 60 minutes to score a transcribed MJI protocol), and is accompanied by adequate self-training materials. Hence, the SRM–SF is "far less time-consuming" than the MJI insofar as it enables "more efficient gathering and scoring of moral reasoning" (Berk, 2013, pp. 499–500).

In a cross-cultural review, Gibbs and colleagues (2007) noted the applicability of the SRM–SF to 23 diverse cultures. Studies were conducted in urban and rural areas as well as Western and non-Western countries, requiring translation into 16 languages other than English. Despite this cultural and linguistic diversity, the indicated moral values (life, contract, affiliation, property, etc.) were generally evaluated as important or very important. Also, protocol attrition (from unscorable justifications, etc.) in the studies was generally low (less than 10%). Trends in age-related stages of moral judgment development were found consistently across the countries. Evidently, moral values and moral judgment development are not entirely relative to particular cultures and socialization practices.

Use of the SRM–SF and Related Measures in Clinical Settings

The SRM–SF has been used (or adapted for use) with diverse populations in clinical settings. Senland and Higgins-D'Alessandro (2013, 2016) found good reliability and validity for SRM–SF among adolescents with high-functioning autism spectrum disorder. Good reliability and validity have also been found for the SRM–SF with men with intellectual disabilities (Langdon, Murphy, Clare, & Palmer, 2010). Hornsveld, Kraaimaat, and Zwets (2012) adapted the SRM–SF for use with forensic psychiatric patients and reported good reliability and validity. All three studies found moral developmental delay in their respective clinical groups. Whereas Langdon et al. (2010) found that the moral developmental delay among men with intellectual disabilities could be accounted for by generally lower intellectual functioning, Hornsveld et al. (2012) noted that moral developmental delay in their population correlated with psychopathic tendencies.

Prominent among the diverse populations studied in clinical or residential institutional settings have been offender groups. Researchers have investigated whether the SRM–SF and related measures discriminate between delinquents or juvenile offenders and nonoffender comparison groups (participants of equivalent chronological age in most studies, with verbal intelligence and/or socioeconomic status controlled in some studies). Moral judgment developmental delay among delinquent juveniles relative to comparison groups was evident in all countries where it was studied (see review by Gibbs et al., 2007; cf. meta-analysis by Stams et al., 2006). A U.S. study (Leeman, Gibbs, & Fuller, 1993; cf. van Stam et al., 2014) found that delinquent juveniles higher in moral judgment were less likely to recidivate at 12 months following release. In general, moral judgment developmental delay is evidently a risk factor for persistent antisocial behavior.

It should be emphasized that "developmental delay" in moral judgment pertains mainly to *reasons* or *justifications* for moral decisions or values. The first author (Gibbs) recalls discussing moral values and administering the SRM–SF with Joey, a 15-year-old at a specialized middle school in Columbus, Ohio, for juveniles with behavior problems. Joey seemed earnest and sincere when he emphatically affirmed the importance of moral values such as keeping promises, telling the truth, helping others, saving lives, not stealing, and obeying the law. "And why is it so important to obey the law or not steal?" Gibbs asked Joey.

"Because [pause], like, in a store, you may think no one sees you, but they could have cameras!" Joey's other explanations were generally similar: Keeping promises to others is important because if you don't, they might find out and get even; helping others is important in case you need a favor from them later; and so forth. The more Joey justified his moral evaluations, the less impressed Gibbs became with Joey's emphatic assertion of the importance of moral values.

Could Joey be trusted to live up to his moral values in situations in which his fear of observers and surveillance cameras would be less pronounced than his egocentric motives? Despite their evaluation of moral values as important, many antisocial juveniles are developmentally delayed in that they do not demonstrate a firm grasp of the deeper *reasons* or bases (selfishness, loss of trust, insecurity, chaos in the community, etc.) for the importance of those values and associated decisions.

The Defining Issues Test

The other main alternative to the MJI is an evaluation measure: the Defining Issues Test (DIT; King & Mayhew, 2002; Rest, 1979; Rest, Narvaez, Bebeau, & Thoma, 1999; Van den Enden, Boom, Brugman, & Thoma, in press). As does the MJI, the DIT uses moral dilemmas to elicit moral evaluations. The DIT requires participants to evaluate (rate and rank) the importance of stage-significant statements of moral reasoning (derived from an early MJI scoring manual) in the context of a set of six moral dilemmas. In connection with the Heinz dilemma, for example, participants evaluate the importance of moral reasoning appeals such as, "Isn't it only natural for a loving husband to care so much for his wife that he'd steal?" (indicative of Stage 3 moral judgment). Such evaluations identify the moral judgment "issues" that the participant sees as most relevant or definitive of the dilemma (hence the name "Defining Issues Test"). Differential patterns of evaluation permit developmentally relevant distinctions among performances. A participant who evaluates higher-stage statements as "most important" presumably has achieved greater moral judgment maturity than a participant whose highest evaluations go to lower-stage statements.

The DIT generally has "strong psychometric properties" and practical advantages (Lapsley, 1996, p. 100) relative to the MJI. The DIT's concurrent validity with the MJI is in the area of .60 to .70. The DIT can be administered to groups, requires less administration time, and is objectively or noninferentially scored. It has good test–retest and internal consistency reliability. The measure detects longitudinal development in moral judgment, is not contaminated with cohort or generational effects, and has good discriminant validity with regard to IQ, personality attributes, social attitudes, and other measures of cognitive development (see Rest, 1979; Rest et al., 1999). On the other hand, the DIT is of limited value for use with populations whose reading competence is low, such as children and delinquent youth (Gibbs et al., 1992).

Other Alternative Measures

Although not as widely known as the DIT, other alternative evaluation/recognition measures have been developed and are worthy of consideration (see Table 21.1). These measures include the Sociomoral Reflection Objective Measure (SROM; Gibbs et al., 1984), the Sociomoral Reflection Objective Measure—Short Form (SROM–SF; Basinger & Gibbs, 1987), and the Sociomoral Reflection Measure—Short Form Objective (SRM–SFO; Beerthuizen, Brugman, & Basinger, 2013; Brugman, Beerthuizen, Basinger, & Gibbs, 2017; cf. Wright, 2015; see also Lind, 1986). Of these measures, the SRM–SFO may be the most promising "for conceptual, practical, and empirical reasons" (Brugman et al., 2017).

CONSTRUCT VALIDITY ISSUES

As noted, most of the work assessing moral judgment maturity derives from cognitive developmental theory. Within that theoretical approach, most researchers have followed Colby and Kohlberg's (1987) argument that construct validity issues should be examined mainly in terms of whether a given measure "fits" or yields data consistent with the predictions or expectations of cognitive developmental theory. Two primary theoretical expectations follow from the claim that the basic age trend in moral judgment is best conceptualized as "an organization passing through an invariant developmental sequence" (p. 69) of stages (see also Miller, 2018): stage consistency and invariant sequence.

Stage Consistency and Invariant Sequence

The stage consistency and invariant sequence issues are related. The stage consistency expectation follows from the cognitive developmental approach: "If it makes sense to say that children are 'in' a particular stage, then their reasoning should consistently fall within this stage" (Miller, 2018, p. 305). But controversy has surrounded some of the longitudinal studies evaluating the construct validity expectation that the stages appear in a standard, consecutive order (invariant sequence). Stage inconsistency or mixture blurs the distinctness of invariant stage sequence. Mainly because of variability in stage use, Piaget suggested that immature and mature moral judgment, although "distinct" (p. 124), be understood not as "stages" (p. 126) but rather as "phases" (p. 317) that partially overlap (cf. Damon, 1980, p. 1017). Beyond Damon's 2-year longitudinal study, Kohlberg's longitudinal study of moral judgment lasted more than 20 years and involved periodic assessment every 3 to 4 years. The results were largely consistent with the expectations of an invariant, progressive sequence (no stage skipping; negligible stage regression, etc.; see Colby et al., 1983; cf. Boom, Brugman, & van der Heijden, 2001; cf. Walker, 1989).

Overall, the construct validity of cognitive developmental measures of moral judgment stage maturity is problematic in terms of Kohlberg's strong claims for stage consistency and invariant sequence but is reasonably good if one adopts the original Piagetian overlapping-phases model of moral judgment development. Piaget's model can be discerned in subsequent revisionist renditions of the nature of moral judgment stage development (e.g., Damon, 1980; Fischer, 1983). In fairness, Colby et al. (1983) themselves depicted the overlapping prevalence "curves" of stage development, "with earlier stages dropping out as later stages enter, such that the subject seems to be always in transition from one stage to the next" (p. 49).

The Moral Domain

Another construct validity issue is whether Kohlbergian cognitive developmental measures of moral judgment adequately represent the domain of morality. Elliott Turiel (1998; cf. Smetana, 2006) argued that morality in the Kohlbergian model is confounded with social conventional knowledge and accordingly should be reconceptualized to focus on justice in the strict sense. In contrast, Carol Gilligan (1982; Gilligan & Attanuci, 1988) argued that the Kohlbergian model needs expansion to include care-related concerns associated with the feminine "voice" in morality. In response to Turiel's works, Colby and Kohlberg

(1987) argued that morality and social convention are not after all "completely independent" (p. 15); in response to Gilligan, they pointed out that their Platonic conceptualization of justice includes "many or most moral concerns of care" (p. 24). In support of the Colby and Kohlberg defense are results from factor analysis indicating that the moral domain as defined and sampled in Kohlberg production measures is a unitary factor (Basinger, Gibbs, & Fuller, 1995; Colby et al., 1983; cf. Gibbs et al., 2007). Within that domain, female participants—although not prejudicially scored lower in stage assessment—do make more care-related appeals (Gibbs et al., 2007; cf. Walker, 1995).

The domain issues literature has not yielded new standard measures of moral judgment maturity. To illustrate his conception of judgment development in the moral domain, Turiel (1998) pointed mainly to distributive justice (the DJS measure described previously). Gilligan (1982; Gilligan & Belenky, 1980) posited from interview data three broad levels in "the feminine ethic," but the psychometric status of this typology "is unclear, since no scoring system [was] developed to assess such [levels] and they [were] omitted from her more recent presentations of the theory" (Walker, 1995, p. 86).

CONCLUSION

Various instruments have been developed for measuring moral judgment maturity. These instruments can be classified in different ways: clinical or standard; area-specific (mainly, distributive justice) or broad; and production or evaluation. For example, the DJS can be classified as standard, area-specific, and evaluation, whereas the MJI can be classified as evolving from clinical to standard (standard issue scoring), broad, and production. The SRM–SF and DIT (as well as the SROM and SRM–SFO) also are standard, broad measures, but the former assesses production responses and the latter measures assess evaluation responses exclusively.

These measures share the cognitive developmental view of moral judgment maturity as a profound moral understanding differentiated from extraneous considerations—that is, a grasp of that which is intrinsically moral, the product of a social cognitive growth beyond the superficial (Gibbs, in press). The extraneous considerations may be salient situational features, including impressive consequences or powerful authority figures (as in Piaget's clinical method of assessment); pragmatic or egocentric criteria (as in Damon's assessment work, Enright et al.'s DJS, or Gibbs et al.'s SRM–SF); or the social conventions of a group (as in Kohlberg's MJI, Rest et al.'s DIT, or Gibbs et al.'s SRM–SF in terms of "Moral Type B," or moral ideality). Some of the measures are age-targeted: The DJS may be optimal for an assessment of moral judgment development in the childhood years, whereas the DIT yields a range of moral judgment maturity scores for the adult years. The SRM–SF is the most broadly targeted, suitable for use with participants from the late childhood years through the adolescent and adult years. Measures of moral judgment maturity should be used with other measures of positive moral functioning, such as moral identity (e.g., Barriga, Morrison, Liau, & Gibbs, 2001), moral courage (Gibbs et al., 1986; see also Chapter 11, this volume), and empathy or related social variables (Chapters 14–17, this volume). In other words—as in Anne Colby and William Damon's (1992; Damon & Colby, 2015) case studies of moral exemplars—researchers should study and assess moral judgment maturity in the larger context of positive individual and collective social life.

APPENDIX 21.1
SRM-SF

1. Think about when you've made a promise to a friend of yours. How important is it for people to keep promises, if they can, to friends? Circle one:

   very important   important   not important

   WHY IS THAT VERY IMPORTANT / IMPORTANT / NOT IMPORTANT (WHICHEVER ONE YOU CIRCLED)? (This format is also used for the remaining questions.)

2. What about keeping a promise to anyone? How important is it for people to keep promises, if they can, even to someone they hardly know?
3. What about keeping a promise to a child? How important is it for parents to keep their promises to their children?
4. In general, how important is it for people to tell the truth?
5. Think about when you've helped your mother or father. How important is it for children to help their parents?
6. Let's say a friend of yours needs help and may even die, and you're the only person who can save him or her. How important is it for a person to save the life of a friend?
7. What about saving the life of anyone? How important is it for a person (without losing his or her own life) to save the life of a stranger?
8. How important is it for a person to live even if that person doesn't want to?
9. How important is it for people not to take things that belong to other people?
10. How important is it for people to obey the law?
11. How important is it for judges to send people who break the law to jail?

REFERENCES

Adelson, J., Green, B., & O'Neil, R. (1969). Growth of the idea of law in adolescence. *Developmental Psychology, 1*, 327–332. http://dx.doi.org/10.1037/h0027705

Barriga, A. K., Morrison, E. M., Liau, A. K., & Gibbs, J. C. (2001). Moral cognition: Explaining the gender difference in antisocial behavior. *Merrill-Palmer Quarterly, 47*, 532–562. http://dx.doi.org/10.1353/mpq.2001.0020

Basinger, K. S., & Gibbs, J. C. (1987). Validation of the Sociomoral Reflection Objective Measure—Short Form. *Psychological Reports, 61,* 139–146. http://dx.doi.org/10.2466/pr0.1987.61.1.139

Basinger, K. S., Gibbs, J. C., & Fuller, D. (1995). Context and the measurement of moral judgment. *International Journal of Behavioral Development, 18,* 537–556. http://dx.doi.org/10.1177/016502549501800309

Beerthuizen, A. G. C. J., Brugman, J., & Basinger, K. S. (2013). Oppositional defiance, moral reasoning, and moral value evaluation as predictors of self-reported juvenile delinquency. *Journal of Moral Education, 42,* 460–474. http://dx.doi.org/10.1080/03057240.2013.803955

Berk, L. E. (2013). *Child development* (9th ed.). Boston, MA: Pearson.

Boom, J., Brugman, D., & van der Heijden, P. G. M. (2001). Hierarchical structure of moral stages assessed by a sorting task. *Child Development, 72,* 535–548. http://dx.doi.org/10.1111/1467-8624.00295

Boyes, M. C., & Walker, L. J. (1988). Implications of cultural diversity for the universality claims of Kohlberg's theory of moral reasoning. *Human Development, 31,* 44–59. http://dx.doi.org/10.1159/000273203

Brugman, D., Basinger, K. S., & Gibbs, J. C. (2007). *The Sociomoral Reflection Measure—Short Form Objective (SRM–SFO).* Unpublished manuscript, University of Utrecht, Utrecht, Netherlands.

Brugman, D., Beerthuizen, M. G. C. J., Basinger, K. S., & Gibbs, J. C. (2017). *Measuring adolescents' moral judgment: An evaluation of the Sociomoral Reflection Measure—Short Form Objective.* Manuscript in preparation.

Colby, A., & Damon, W. (1992). *Some do care: Contemporary lives of moral commitment.* New York, NY: Free Press.

Colby, A., & Kohlberg, L. (1987). *The measurement of moral judgment: Theoretical foundations and research validation* (Vol. 1). Cambridge, England: Cambridge University Press.

Colby, A., Kohlberg, L., Gibbs, J. C., & Lieberman, M. (1983). A longitudinal study of moral judgment. *Monographs of the Society for Research in Child Development, 48* (1–2, Serial No. 200).

Colby, A., Kohlberg, L., Speicher, B., Hewer, A., Candee, D., Gibbs, J., & Power, C. (1987). *The measurement of moral judgment* (Vol. 2). Cambridge, England: Cambridge University Press.

Damon, W. (1977). *The social world of the child.* San Francisco, CA: Jossey-Bass.

Damon, W. (1980). Patterns of change in children's social reasoning: A two-year longitudinal study. *Child Development, 51,* 1010–1017. http://dx.doi.org/10.2307/1129538

Damon, W., & Colby, A. (2015). *The power of ideals: The real story of moral choice.* New York, NY: Oxford University Press.

Eisenberg, N. (1982). The development of reasoning regarding prosocial behavior. In N. Eisenberg (Ed.), *The development of prosocial behavior* (pp. 219–249). New York, NY: Academic Press. http://dx.doi.org/10.1016/B978-0-12-234980-5.50014-6

Enright, R. D., Bjerstedt, A., Enright, W. F., Levy, V. M., Lapsley, D. K., Buss, R. R., . . . Zindler, W. (1984). Distributive justice development: Cross-cultural, contextual, and longitudinal evaluations. *Child Development, 55,* 1737–1751. http://dx.doi.org/10.2307/1129921

Enright, R. D., Franklin, C. C., & Manheim, L. A. (1980). Children's distributive justice reasoning: A standardized and objective scale. *Developmental Psychology, 16,* 193–202. http://dx.doi.org/10.1037/0012-1649.16.3.193

Fischer, K. (1983). Illuminating the processes of moral development. In A. Colby, L. Kohlberg, J. Gibbs, & M. Lieberman (Eds.), *A longitudinal study of moral judgment. Monographs of the Society for Research in Child Development, 48*(1–2), 97–106.

Flavell, J. H. (1963). *The developmental psychology of Jean Piaget.* Princeton, NJ: D. Van Nostrand. http://dx.doi.org/10.1037/11449-000

Furth, H. G. (1980). *The world of grown-ups: Children's conceptions of society.* New York, NY: Elsevier.

Gibbs, J. C. (1995). The cognitive–developmental perspective. In W. M. Kurtines & J. L. Gewirtz (Eds.), *Moral development: An introduction* (pp. 27–48). Boston, MA: Allyn & Bacon.

Gibbs, J. C. (in press). *Moral development and reality: Beyond the theories of Kohlberg, Hoffman, and Haidt* (4th ed.). New York, NY: Oxford University Press.

Gibbs, J. C., Arnold, K. D., Morgan, R. L., Schwartz, E. S., Gavaghan, M. P., & Tappan, M. B. (1984). Construction and validation of a multiple-choice measure of moral reasoning. *Child Development, 55,* 527–536. http://dx.doi.org/10.2307/1129963

Gibbs, J. C., Basinger, K. S., & Fuller, D. (1992). *Moral maturity: Measuring the development of sociomoral reflection.* Hillsdale, NJ: Erlbaum.

Gibbs, J. C., Basinger, K. S., Grime, R. L., & Snarey, J. R. (2007). Moral judgment development across cultures: Revisiting Kohlberg's universality claims. *Developmental Review, 27,* 443–500. http://dx.doi.org/10.1016/j.dr.2007.04.001

Gibbs, J. C., Clark, P. M., Joseph, J. A., Green, J. L., Goodrick, T. S., & Makowski, D. G. (1986). Relations between moral judgment, moral courage, and field independence. *Child Development, 57,* 185–193. http://dx.doi.org/10.2307/1130650

Gibbs, J. C., Widaman, K. F., & Colby, A. (1982). Construction and validation of a simplified, group-administrable equivalent to the Moral Judgment Interview. *Child Development, 53,* 895–910. http://dx.doi.org/10.2307/1129126

Gilligan, C. (1982). *In a different voice: Psychological theory and women's development.* Cambridge, MA: Harvard University Press.

Gilligan, C., & Attanuci, J. (1988). Two moral orientations: Gender differences and similarities. *Merrill-Palmer Quarterly, 34,* 223–237.

Gilligan, C., & Belenky, M. F. (1980). A naturalistic study of abortion decisions. In R. Selman & R. Yandow (Eds.), *Clinical-developmental psychology* (pp. 69–90). San Francisco, CA: Jossey-Bass.

Haidt, J., & Kesebir, S. (2010). Morality. In S. T. Fiske, D. P. Gilbert, & G. Lindzey (Eds.), *Handbook of social psychology* (5th ed., Vol. 2, pp. 797–832). New York, NY: Wiley. http://dx.doi.org/10.1002/9780470561119.socpsy002022

Hornsveld, R. H. J., Kraaimaat, F. W., & Zwets, A. J. (2012). The adapted version of the Sociomoral Reflection Measure (SRM–AV) in Dutch forensic psychiatric patients. *The International Journal of Forensic Mental Health Services, 11,* 218–226. http://dx.doi.org/10.1080/14999013.2012.723667

King, P. M., & Mayhew, M. J. (2002). Moral judgment in higher education: Insights from the Defining Issues Test. *Journal of Moral Education, 31,* 247–270. http://dx.doi.org/10.1080/0305724022000008106

Kohlberg, L. (1958). *The development of modes of thinking and choices in the years from 10 to 16.* Unpublished doctoral dissertation, University of Chicago, Chicago, IL.

Kohlberg, L. (1984). *Essays on moral development: Vol. 2. The psychology of moral development.* San Francisco, CA: Harper & Row.

Langdon, P. E., Murphy, G. H., Clare, I. C. H., & Palmer, E. J. (2010). The psychometric properties of the Socio-Moral Reflection Measure—Short Form and the Moral Theme Inventory for men with and without intellectual disabilities. *Research in Developmental Disabilities, 31,* 1204–1215. http://dx.doi.org/10.1016/j.ridd.2010.07.025

Lapsley, D. K. (1996). *Moral psychology.* New York, NY: HarperCollins.

Leeman, L. W., Gibbs, J. C., & Fuller, D. (1993). Evaluation of a multi-component group treatment program for juvenile delinquents. *Aggressive Behavior, 19,* 281–292. http://dx.doi.org/10.1002/1098-2337(1993)19:4<281::AID-AB2480190404>3.0.CO;2-W

Lind, G. (1986). Cultural differences in moral judgment? A study of West and East European university students. *Behavior Science Research, 20,* 208–225. http://dx.doi.org/10.1177/106939718602000109

Miller, S. A. (2018). *Developmental research methods* (5th ed.). Thousand Oaks, CA: Sage.

Piaget, J. (1965). *The moral judgment of the child* (M. Gabain, Trans.). New York, NY: Free Press. (Original work published 1932)

Piaget, J. (1973). *The child's conception of the world* (J. Tomlinson & A. Tomlinson, Trans.). London, England: Paladin. (Original work published 1929)

Rest, J. R. (1979). *Development in judging moral issues.* Minneapolis: University of Minnesota Press.

Rest, J. R., Narvaez, D., Bebeau, M. J., & Thoma, S. J. (1999). *Postconventional moral thinking: A neo-Kohlbergian approach.* Mahwah, NJ: Erlbaum.

Selman, R. L. (1980). *The growth of interpersonal understanding: Developmental and clinical studies.* New York, NY: Academic Press.

Selman, R. L., & Shultz, L. H. (1990). *Making a friend in youth: Developmental theory and pair therapy.* Chicago, IL: University of Chicago Press.

Senland, A. K., & Higgins-D'Alessandro, A. (2013). Moral reasoning and empathy in adolescents with autism spectrum disorder: Implications for moral education. *Journal of Moral Education, 42,* 209–223. http://dx.doi.org/10.1080/03057240.2012.752721

Senland, A. K., & Higgins-D'Alessandro, A. (2016). Sociomoral reasoning, empathy, and meeting developmental tasks during the transition to adulthood in autism spectrum disorder. *Journal of Autism and Developmental Disorders, 46,* 3090–3105.

Smetana, J. G. (2006). Social-cognitive domain theory: Consistencies and variations in children's moral and social judgments. In M. Killen & J. Smetana (Eds.), *Handbook of moral development* (pp. 119–153). Mahwah, NJ: Erlbaum.

Stams, G. J., Brugman, D., Deković, M., van Rosmalen, L., van der Laan, P., & Gibbs, J. C. (2006). The moral judgment of juvenile delinquents: A meta-analysis. *Journal of Abnormal Child Psychology, 34,* 697–713. http://dx.doi.org/10.1007/s10802-006-9056-5

Turiel, E. (1998). The development of morality. In N. Eisenberg (Ed.), *Handbook of child psychology: Vol. 3. Social, emotional, and personality development* (pp. 863–932). New York, NY: Wiley.

Van den Enden, T., Boom, J., Brugman, D., & Thoma, S. (in press). Stages of moral judgment development: Applying item response theory to Defining Issues Test data. *Journal of Moral Education.*

Van Stam, M. A., van der Schuur, W. A., Tserkezis, S., van Vugt, E. S., Asscher, J. J., Gibbs, J. C., & Stams, G. J. J. M. (2014). The effectiveness of EQUIP on sociomoral development and recidivism reduction: A meta-analytic study. *Children and Youth Services Review, 38,* 44–51. http://dx.doi.org/10.1016/j.childyouth.2014.01.002

Walker, L. J. (1989). A longitudinal study of moral reasoning. *Child Development, 60,* 157–166. http://dx.doi.org/10.2307/1131081

Walker, L. J. (1995). Sexism in Kohlberg's moral psychology? In W. M. Kurtines & J. L. Gewirtz (Eds.), *Moral development: An introduction* (pp. 83–108). Boston, MA: Allyn & Bacon.

Wright, J. D. (2015). *An examination of the effects of moral maturity, propensity for moral disengagement, entitlement perception, and anomia on fraud behavior.* Unpublished doctoral dissertation. Chicago School of Professional Psychology, Chicago, IL.

Youniss, J. (1980). *Parents and peers in social development: A Sullivan–Piaget perspective.* Chicago, IL: University of Chicago Press.

V

MODELS AND MEASURES OF POSITIVE PROCESSES AND OUTCOMES

22

Measuring Religious Constructs

A Hierarchical Approach to Construct Organization and Scale Selection

Jo-Ann Tsang, Robert D. Carlisle, and Michael E. McCullough

Much recent research documents the importance of religion in predicting positive outcomes such as psychological health (e.g., Koenig, McCullough, & Larson, 2001; Rizvi & Hossain, 2017) and physical well-being (e.g., McCullough, Hoyt, Larson, Koenig, & Thoresen, 2000; Mishra, Togneri, Tripathi, & Trikamji, 2017; Rizvi & Hossain, 2017), as well as important social attitudes and behaviors (Tsang, Rowatt, & Shariff, 2015; Van Tongeren et al., 2016). Because of this potential, it may be worthwhile for researchers and practitioners to measure different aspects of religiousness. In this chapter, we discuss many important issues in the measurement of religion and spirituality and present a hierarchical model for conceptualizing the various aspects of religiousness that might be measured empirically.

GENERAL MEASUREMENT ISSUES

Gorsuch (1984) noted that measurement was both a bane and a boon to the psychology of religion. Specifically, the psychology of religion suffers from an abundance of scales and a lack of alternatives to self-report measures.

An Abundance of Scales

The duplication of scales in the psychology of religion is unnecessary given that psychometrically sound scales in similar content areas tend to produce similar

http://dx.doi.org/10.1037/0000138-022
Positive Psychological Assessment: A Handbook of Models and Measures, Second Edition,
M. W. Gallagher and S. J. Lopez (Editors)

results. Because of this, Gorsuch (1984) argued that religion researchers should refrain from constructing new scales without first doing a thorough literature review to locate an adequate existing scale. If a new scale is developed, psychologists should show that it adds new information. He maintained that researchers should shift their emphasis away from designing new measures and toward exploring relationships between the existing measures and other constructs.

Regrettably, Gorsuch's (1984) words of wisdom have gone largely unheeded in the past 35 years. Instead of creating new scales, psychologists would fare better to choose among the many preexisting religiousness measures. These measures have been reviewed repeatedly (e.g., Hill & Edwards, 2013; Hill & Hood, 1999; Koenig, Al Zaben, Khalifa, & Al Shohaib, 2015), so their psychometric properties and applications can be considered.

Is Self-Report the Only Answer?

The measurement design of choice overwhelmingly has been self-report questionnaires, at the expense of other forms of measurement (Gorsuch, 1984). This preference stems in part from ease of administration and scoring. However, the exclusive use of self-report measures is suboptimal because of social desirability biases (e.g., Sedikides & Gebauer, 2010; Trimble, 1997).

One alternative is to use peer reports of religiousness (e.g., Piedmont, 1999; Saroglou, Pichon, Trompette, Verschueren, & Dernelle, 2005), although peer ratings can also have social desirability biases (Pedregon, Farley, Davis, Wood, & Clark, 2012). Naumann, Vazire, Rentfrow, and Gosling (2009) presented a unique twist on peer reports by showing that observer ratings of full-body photographs predicted target religiousness above chance levels. Target participants were photographed and filled out self-reports of personality ratings, including religiousness. Observers, who did not know the targets, rated the targets on personality and religiousness based on the target photograph; accuracy was measured by comparing observer ratings with self- and informant-ratings. This suggests an interesting way for peers to judge participant religiousness through nonverbal behavior.

Behavioral measures of religiousness are another complement to self-reports. Theories applying costly signaling theory to religion (e.g., McCullough, Swartwout, Shaver, Carter, & Sosis, 2016; Sosis, 2003) suggest a number of possible behavioral indices such as church attendance, prayer, dietary restrictions, religious adornments, fasting, pilgrimages, and so on. The costly nature of many of these religious signals may help mitigate social desirability in assessment.

Implicit measures of religiousness are being used with increasing frequency. Implicit attitudes are largely unconscious and automatic, making them difficult to fake (Fiedler & Bluemke, 2005). Several researchers have made use of the Implicit Attitude Test (IAT; Greenwald, McGhee, & Schwartz, 1998) to create religious/spiritual IATs. The IAT measures the strength of the automatic association between target groups (e.g., self, other) and traits (e.g., religious, not religious) by measuring reaction times. Researchers have used the IAT to measure associations between religion and such target groups as self/other (Crescentini, Urgesi, Campanella, Eleopra, & Fabbro, 2014; LaBouff, Rowatt, Johnson, Thedford, & Tsang, 2010), positive/negative (e.g., Bassett et al., 2005), real/imaginary (Jong, Halberstadt, & Bluemke, 2012), the paranormal (Weeks, Weeks, & Daniel, 2008), and religious orientation (Wenger & Yarbrough, 2005). Single-target IATs (comparing only one target to two attributes) have been created to examine associations between religion and true/false words (Shariff, Cohen, & Norenzayan, 2008) as well as implicit attitudes about the soul and afterlife (Anglin, 2015). Researchers have also adapted the Go/No-Go Association task for use with religious constructs (Pirutinsky, Carp, & Rosmarin, 2017). The unconscious, automatic nature of implicit measures makes them one possible way to address social desirability concerns. The lack of concordance sometimes found between implicit and explicit measures (Anglin, 2015; Bassett et al., 2005; Jong et al., 2012; Pirutinsky, Siev, & Rosmarin, 2015) and their differential predictive validity (e.g., LaBouff et al., 2010) suggest that implicit and explicit religious measures may be assessing different constructs.

In summary, supplementing self-report measures of religiousness with other assessment techniques such as peer reports, behaviors, and implicit measures will help psychologists attain a broader, clearer picture of the character and consequences of religiousness.

STRATEGIES FOR SELECTING MEASURES

One important principle relevant to selecting a measure is whether religion consists of one general factor or many different factors. Gorsuch (1984) suggested that religion is a general factor that can be subdivided into other religious dimensions. He proposed that it would be appropriate to measure the general religious factor when it was being used to predict many other variables, whereas subdimensions should be used to predict exceptions to the rule. For example, when looking at broad variables such as age differences in religiousness, the use of a general religious factor is appropriate. When predicting a more specific variable such as prejudice, it is better to use subdimensions of religion to see the complete relationship.

A Hierarchical Model

Gorsuch's (1984) insights suggest viewing religiousness/spirituality as a hierarchically structured psychological domain. Higher levels of organization reflect broad individual differences in abstracted, trait-like qualities. At this higher level (Level I), the goal of measurement is to assess broad differences in religious tendencies so that one might asses how "religious" a person is. We call this the *dispositional* level of organization. Beyond individual differences in general religiousness, people manifest great diversity in religious experiences, motivations for being religious, and deployment of religion to solve problems. We call this second level (Level II) the *operational* level of organization.

Insights about religiousness and spirituality are complex because operational-level measures often contain dispositional-level variance. For instance, people who are inclined to religious coping (an operational concept) are probably more religious in general (a dispositional concept; Pargament, 1997). This overlap can be controlled in multivariate research. We propose that before researchers make conclusions about any operational religiousness factor, it is necessary to control for dispositional religiousness. Otherwise, researchers cannot know if their effects are a result of an operational variable rather than of general religiousness. Pargament (1997) provided good examples of the use of a hierarchical model in religious research. In their studies of religious coping (operational level), Pargament and colleagues typically use measures of general religiousness to control for individual differences at the dispositional level. This measurement strategy has allowed these investigators to make substantive conclusions about religious coping, while being careful not to confound such observations with the effects of general religiousness (e.g., Rosmarin, Pirutinsky, Greer, & Korbman, 2016).

In the remainder of this chapter, we use this hierarchical model for organizing religiousness and spirituality to review some of the more promising scales for assessing religiousness at both the dispositional and operational levels.

MEASURING RELIGIOUSNESS AT THE DISPOSITIONAL LEVEL

The dispositional level (Level I) assesses broad individual differences in people's religiousness or spirituality. How best to measure this general religiousness? We urge psychologists to eschew the use of the many single-item measures of general religiousness (see McCullough & Larson, 1999). Although single-item measures of attendance at religious services or self-rated religiousness have high face validity, their dependability is limited by the psychometric weaknesses that plague all single-item psychological measures. Assuming that the internal consistency of a single-item measure is .50 (which may be generous), then the associations of such a measure of religiousness with another construct would be attenuated by 29% relative to the true relation among the constructs in the population (Hunter & Schmidt, 1990). This level of attenuation is too high and completely unnecessary given the existence of many highly reliable multi-item measures of religiousness.

Instead, individual differences in Level I religiousness can be assessed easily by examining the common variance in a few items. Worthington et al. (2003) presented a brief measure of religious commitment, or the degree to which an individual integrates his or her religious beliefs and practices into daily life. Their Religious Commitment Inventory-10 is short enough to use easily in both research and counseling contexts and can be applied to a wide variety of religions. The scale showed very good internal consistency reliability ($\alpha = .93$), as well as test-retest reliability ($\alpha = .87$), and predicted religious activity attendance in Christians as well as Muslims, Hindus, Buddhists, and nonreligious individuals (Worthington et al., 2003).

A number of scales assess dispositional spirituality. Kapuscinski and Masters (2010) critically discussed scale development for 24 measures of spirituality, and recommended four of them as being of especially high-quality, including Piedmont's (1999) measure of Spiritual Transcendence and Underwood and Teresi's (2002) Daily Spiritual Experiences Scale.

Recent research has moved beyond the study of Christian religion to other religions and cultures. For instance, AlMarri, Oei, and Al-Adawi (2009) created a brief scale to measure Muslim religiousness. The Short Muslim Practice and Belief Scale was developed with a good balance of items measuring both religious actions and beliefs, and aimed to differentiate between dogmatic and more flexible ways of believing. The scale had good reliability ($\alpha = .83$) and predicted alcohol consumption or lack thereof. This was an important test of validity, as Islam forbids the drinking of alcohol in believers (see also Koenig et al.'s 2015 Muslim Religiosity Scale). Francis, Santosh, Robbins, and Vij (2008) created a scale of Hindu religiousness. Their measure assesses the affective component of attitudes, rather than beliefs or practices, in order to find items that transcended differences between various religious groups within Hinduism. Their unidimensional 19-item scale had good reliability ($\alpha = .83$), and scores on the scale significantly predicted the frequency of prayer and worship at home as well as public worship. (See Table 22.1 for references to these and several other measures of Level-1 religiousness and spirituality.)

MEASURING RELIGIOUSNESS AT THE OPERATIONAL LEVEL

The content of people's religiousness theoretically can be distinguished from the functions of religion in their lives (Gorsuch, 1984). Similarly, we suggest that the higher order, dispositional aspect of religion exists independently of the operational aspects of religion (where we might assess such differences in the *functions* or *experiences* of a person's religiousness). Two people who are

TABLE 22.1. Suggested Measures for Assessment of Dispositional Aspects of Religion and Spirituality

Reference	Scale name
AlMarri et al. (2009)	Short Muslim Practice and Belief Scale
Emavardhana and Tori (1997)	Buddhist Beliefs and Practices Scale
Francis et al. (2008)	Santosh-Francis Attitudes toward Hinduism Scale
Hood (1975)	Mysticism Scale
LaBouff et al. (2010)	Religiousness-Spirituality IAT
Piedmont (1999)	Spiritual Transcendence Scale
Plante and Boccaccini (1997)	Santa Clara Strength of Religious Faith Questionnaire
Rohrbaugh and Jessor (1975)	Religiosity Measure
Underwood and Teresi (2002)	Daily Spiritual Experiences Scale
Worthington et al. (2003)	Religious Commitment Inventory (RCI—10)

equally religious may have very different ways of experiencing and expressing their religiousness.

It would be impossible to describe all the different religious operations in one chapter. We focus on a few exemplars, including the motivations behind a person's religiousness, and the ways an individual might use religion in coping. In Table 22.2 we list published scales for assessing these and similar Level II constructs.

Religious Orientation

Despite several critiques (Kirkpatrick & Hood, 1990; Neyrinck, Lens, Vansteenkiste, & Soenens, 2010), Allport and Ross's (1967) distinction between intrinsic and extrinsic religious orientation is one of the most established and widely used Level II concepts in the psychology of religion. The extrinsically religious person uses religion as a means to another end, whereas the intrinsically religious person holds religion as an ultimate goal. Allport (1950) believed that extrinsically religious individuals used religion to buffer anxiety but did not take religion's lessons to heart. In contrast, the more mature intrinsically religious individuals represented the religious ideal: These individuals should be more helpful, more loving, and less prejudiced (e.g., Allport & Ross, 1967).

Reliabilities for Allport and Ross's (1967) Religious Orientation Scale (ROS) have ranged from .73 to .82 for the intrinsic and from .35 to .70 for the extrinsic scale (Trimble, 1997). Hoge's (1972) version of the intrinsic religiousness scale showed higher reliability (.90). Batson and his colleagues added an additional

TABLE 22.2. Suggested Measures for Assessment of Operational Aspects of Religion and Spirituality

Reference	Scale name
Religious orientation	
Allport and Ross (1967) Batson and Schoenrade (1991a, 1991b) Ghorbani, Watson, Ghramaleki, Morris, and Hood (2002)	Religious Orientation Scales: Intrinsic and Extrinsic Quest Religious Orientation
Hoge (1972) Ji and Ibrahim (2007)	Muslim-Christian Religious Orientation Scales Intrinsic Religious Motivation Scale Religious Life Inventory—Islamic Version
Coping	
Khan & Watson (2006)	Pakistani Religious Coping Practices Scale
Pargament et al. (1998)	Brief RCOPE
Pargament et al. (1988)	Religious Problem-Solving Scales
Phillips, Cheng, and Oemig-Dworsky (2014)	Buddhist Coping Scale
Rosmarin, Pargament, Krumrei, and Flannelly (2009)	Jewish Religious Coping Scale
Tarakeshwar, Pargament, and Mahoney (2003)	Hindu Religious Coping Scale
Anger at God, Spiritual Struggle	
Wood et al. (2010)	Attitudes Toward God Scale (ATGS-9)

dimension—religion as quest—to address limitations in intrinsic religious orientation scales regarding rigidity and dogmatism (e.g., Batson & Schoenrade, 1991a, 1991b). Quest was defined as a more complex, open-ended type of religious orientation that eschewed clear-cut religious answers.

The utility of the quest dimension becomes apparent in empirical differences between extrinsic, intrinsic, and quest religiousness. As Allport and Ross (1967) predicted, extrinsic religiousness is clearly associated with prejudice. Counter to Allport's (1950) theory, scores on intrinsic religiousness scales are related to decreased prejudice only on self-reports and when prejudice is condemned by the religious community (Batson, Schoenrade, & Ventis, 1993). Many studies using behavioral measures of prejudice (e.g., Batson, Floyd, Meyer, & Winner, 1999), or looking at prejudice that is not strictly prohibited by the church, such as prejudice against lesbians and gay men (e.g., Duck & Hunsberger, 1999), show intrinsic religiousness to be related to increased prejudice. Quest is the only religious orientation consistently related to decreased prejudice (Hall, Matz, & Wood, 2010).

The construct of religious orientation has shown that, in certain areas of psychology, differentiation among multiple religious dimensions is useful and necessary. In fact, an inaccurate picture is portrayed of the relationship between religion and other psychological concepts such as prejudice if Level II measurements such as religious orientation are not considered.

Religion and Coping

People often turn to the sacred in times of stress, particularly in situations of turmoil (Pargament, 1997). Whereas the concept of religious orientation helped explain the relationship between religion and negative concepts such as prejudice, the concept of religious coping can help clarify the relationship between religion and well-being.

The most widely used measure of religious coping is the Brief RCOPE (Pargament, Smith, Koenig, & Perez, 1998). Pargament et al. (1998) developed the 14-item Brief RCOPE to assess positive and negative religious coping. They provided some evidence that positive religious coping was positively related to mental and physical health, whereas the opposite was generally true for negative religious coping. Pargament, Koenig, Tarakeshwar, and Hahn (2004) demonstrated that negative religious coping (or *religious struggle*) is related to mortality among medically ill older adults. Another way of examining religious coping has been pioneered by Exline and her colleagues, who have found complex relationships between personality, religious and spiritual struggles, and well-being (e.g., Wilt, Grubbs, Exline, & Pargament, 2016).

CONCLUSION

The availability of so many measures of religiousness can pose challenges. We have attempted to simplify the process by classifying religious and spiritual psychological concepts into a two-level hierarchical structure. At the superordinate level are dispositional measures of general religiousness, which assess religiousness as broad individual differences in the tendency toward religious interests and sentiments. At a subordinate level of organization are operational measures of religiousness, which assess how particular aspects of religion function. Examples of operational measures include religious orientation and religious coping. The specific religious concept that a psychologist chooses to measure must be driven by theory. In addition, psychologists interested in Level II religious operations should concurrently assess Level I religiousness. Without Level I measures, a researcher might mistakenly attribute effects to operational variables when they are actually caused by general religiousness.

Similar to others before us, we also recommend the use of alternative measurement techniques to supplement self-report questionnaires of religiousness and spirituality. Many of the relationships between religiousness and other concepts are subject to socially desirable responding or may be of limited validity in some applications. Use of alternatives such as peer reports, interviews, behavioral measures, and implicit attitude tests can provide us with a richer notion of religiousness and spirituality and a broader understanding of its associations with other domains of human functioning.

As Gorsuch (1984) noted more than 3 decades ago, measurement is the boon of the psychology of religion. From the perspective of positive psychology, certain forms of religiousness show promising associations with physical and mental health, the promotion of tolerance and prosocial behavior, and positive interpersonal relationships, to name a few. Because of the pervasiveness of religiousness and spirituality around the world and religion's potential to influence individual lives in a positive way, positive psychology would do well to continue to integrate religious and spiritual concepts into its perspective.

REFERENCES

Allport, G. W. (1950). *The individual and his religion: A psychological interpretation*. New York, NY: Macmillan.

Allport, G. W., & Ross, J. M. (1967). Personal religious orientation and prejudice. *Journal of Personality and Social Psychology, 5*, 432–443. http://dx.doi.org/10.1037/h0021212

AlMarri, T. S. K., Oei, T. P. S., & Al-Adawi, S. (2009). The development of the Short Muslim Practice and Belief Scale. *Mental Health, Religion & Culture, 12*, 415–426. http://dx.doi.org/10.1080/13674670802637643

Anglin, S. M. (2015). On the nature of implicit soul beliefs: When the past weighs more than the present. *British Journal of Social Psychology, 54*, 394–404. http://dx.doi.org/10.1111/bjso.12094

Bassett, R. L., Smith, A., Thrower, J., Tindall, M., Barclay, J., Tiuch, K., . . . Monroe, J. (2005). One effort to measure implicit attitudes toward spirituality and religion. *Journal of Psychology and Christianity, 24*, 210–218.

Batson, C. D., Floyd, R. B., Meyer, J. M., & Winner, A. L. (1999). "And who is my neighbor?" Intrinsic religion as a source of universal compassion. *Journal for the Scientific Study of Religion, 38*, 445–457. http://dx.doi.org/10.2307/1387605

Batson, C. D., & Schoenrade, P. A. (1991a). Measuring religion as quest: 1. Validity concerns. *Journal for the Scientific Study of Religion, 30*, 416–429. http://dx.doi.org/10.2307/1387277

Batson, C. D., & Schoenrade, P. A. (1991b). Measuring religion as quest: 2. Reliability concerns. *Journal for the Scientific Study of Religion, 30,* 430–447. http://dx.doi.org/10.2307/1387278

Batson, C. D., Schoenrade, P., & Ventis, W. L. (1993). *Religion and the individual.* New York, NY: Oxford University Press.

Crescentini, C., Urgesi, C., Campanella, F., Eleopra, R., & Fabbro, F. (2014). Effects of an 8-week meditation program on the implicit and explicit attitudes toward religious/spiritual self-representations. *Consciousness and Cognition, 30,* 266–280. http://dx.doi.org/10.1016/j.concog.2014.09.013

Duck, R. J., & Hunsberger, B. (1999). Religious orientation and prejudice: The role of religious proscription, right-wing authoritarianism and social desirability. *International Journal for the Psychology of Religion, 9,* 157–179. http://dx.doi.org/10.1207/s15327582ijpr0903_1

Emavardhana, T., & Tori, C. D. (1997). Changes in self-concept, ego defense mechanisms, and religiosity following seven-day Vipassana meditation retreats. *Journal for the Scientific Study of Religion, 36,* 194–206. http://dx.doi.org/10.2307/1387552

Fiedler, K., & Bluemke, M. (2005). Faking the IAT: Aided and unaided response control on the Implicit Association Tests. *Basic and Applied Social Psychology, 27,* 307–316. http://dx.doi.org/10.1207/s15324834basp2704_3

Francis, L. J., Santosh, Y. R., Robbins, M., & Vij, S. (2008). Assessing attitude toward Hinduism: The Santosh-Francis Scale. *Mental Health, Religion & Culture, 11,* 609–621. http://dx.doi.org/10.1080/13674670701846469

Ghorbani, N., Watson, P. J., Ghramaleki, A. F., Morris, R. J., & Hood, R. W., Jr. (2002). Muslim-Christian religious orientation scales: Distinctions, correlations, and cross-cultural analysis in Iran and the United States. *International Journal for the Psychology of Religion, 12,* 69–91. http://dx.doi.org/10.1207/S15327582IJPR1202_01

Gorsuch, R. L. (1984). The boon and bane of investigating religion. *American Psychologist, 39,* 228–236. http://dx.doi.org/10.1037/0003-066X.39.3.228

Greenwald, A. G., McGhee, D. E., & Schwartz, J. L. K. (1998). Measuring individual differences in implicit cognition: The implicit association test. *Journal of Personality and Social Psychology, 74,* 1464–1480. http://dx.doi.org/10.1037/0022-3514.74.6.1464

Hall, D. L., Matz, D. C., & Wood, W. (2010). Why don't we practice what we preach? A meta-analytic review of religious racism. *Personality and Social Psychology Review, 14,* 126–139. http://dx.doi.org/10.1177/1088868309352179

Hill, P. C., & Edwards, E. (2013). Measurement in psychology of religiousness and spirituality: Existing measures and new frontiers. In K. I. Pargament, J. J. Exline, & J. W. Jones (Eds.), *APA handbook of psychology, religion, and spirituality* (Vol. 1, pp. 51–77). Washington, DC: American Psychological Association. http://dx.doi.org/10.1037/14045-003

Hill, P. C., & Hood, R. W., Jr. (Eds.). (1999). *Measures of religiosity.* Birmingham, AL: Religious Education Press.

Hoge, D. R. (1972). A validated intrinsic religious motivation scale. *Journal for the Scientific Study of Religion, 11,* 369–376. http://dx.doi.org/10.2307/1384677

Hood, R. W., Jr. (1975). The construction and preliminary validation of a measure of reported mystical experience. *Journal for the Scientific Study of Religion, 14,* 29–41. http://dx.doi.org/10.2307/1384454

Hunter, J. E., & Schmidt, F. L. (1990). *Methods of meta-analysis: Correcting error and bias in research findings.* Thousand Oaks, CA: Sage.

Ji, C.-H. C., & Ibrahim, Y. (2007). Islamic doctrinal orthodoxy and religious orientations: Scale development and validation. *International Journal for the Psychology of Religion, 17,* 189–208. http://dx.doi.org/10.1080/10508610701402192

Jong, J., Halberstadt, J., & Bluemke, M. (2012). Foxhole atheism, revisited: The effects of mortality salience on explicit and implicit religious belief. *Journal of Experimental Social Psychology, 48,* 983–989. http://dx.doi.org/10.1016/j.jesp.2012.03.005

Kapuscinski, A. N., & Masters, K. S. (2010). The current status of measures of spirituality: A critical review of scale development. *Psychology of Religion and Spirituality, 2,* 191–205. http://dx.doi.org/10.1037/a0020498

Khan, Z. H., & Watson, P. J. (2006). Construction of the Pakistani Religious Coping Practices Scale: Correlations with religious coping, religious orientation, and reactions to stress among Muslim university students. *International Journal for the Psychology of Religion, 16,* 101–112. http://dx.doi.org/10.1207/s15327582ijpr1602_2

Kirkpatrick, L. A., & Hood, R. W. (1990). Intrinsic-extrinsic religious orientation: The boon or bane of contemporary psychology of religion? *Journal for the Scientific Study of Religion, 29,* 442–462. http://dx.doi.org/10.2307/1387311

Koenig, H. G., Al Zaben, F., Khalifa, D. A., & Al Shohaib, S. (2015). Measures of religiosity. In G. J. Boyle & D. H. Saklofske (Eds.), *Measures of personality and social psychological constructs* (pp. 530–561). Chennai, India: Elsevier. http://dx.doi.org/10.1016/B978-0-12-386915-9.00019-X

Koenig, H. G., McCullough, M. E., & Larson, D. B. (2001). *Handbook of religion and health.* New York, NY: Oxford University Press. http://dx.doi.org/10.1093/acprof:oso/9780195118667.001.0001

LaBouff, J. P., Rowatt, W. C., Johnson, M. K., Thedford, M., & Tsang, J. (2010). Development and initial validation of an implicit measure of religiousness-spirituality. *Journal for the Scientific Study of Religion, 49,* 439–455. http://dx.doi.org/10.1111/j.1468-5906.2010.01521.x

McCullough, M. E., Hoyt, W. T., Larson, D. B., Koenig, H. G., & Thoresen, C. (2000). Religious involvement and mortality: A meta-analytic review. *Health Psychology, 19,* 211–222. http://dx.doi.org/10.1037/0278-6133.19.3.211

McCullough, M. E., & Larson, D. B. (1999). Religion and depression: A review of the literature. *Twin Research, 2,* 126–136. http://dx.doi.org/10.1375/twin.2.2.126

McCullough, M. E., Swartwout, P., Shaver, J. H., Carter, E. C., & Sosis, R. (2016). Christian religious badges instill trust in Christian and non-Christian perceivers. *Psychology of Religion and Spirituality, 8,* 149–163. http://dx.doi.org/10.1037/rel0000045

Mishra, S. K., Togneri, E., Tripathi, B., & Trikamji, B. (2017). Spirituality and religiosity and its role in health and diseases. *Journal of Religion and Health, 56,* 1282–1301. Retrieved from https://link.springer.com/content/pdf/10.1007%2Fs10943-015-0100-z.pdf

Naumann, L. P., Vazire, S., Rentfrow, P. J., & Gosling, S. D. (2009). Personality judgments based on physical appearance. *Personality and Social Psychology Bulletin, 35,* 1661–1671. http://dx.doi.org/10.1177/0146167209346309

Neyrinck, B., Lens, W., Vansteenkiste, M., & Soenens, B. (2010). Updating Allport's and Batson's Framework of Religious Orientations: A reevaluation from the perspective of self-determination theory and Wulff's social cognitive model. *Journal for the Scientific Study of Religion, 49,* 425–438. http://dx.doi.org/10.1111/j.1468-5906.2010.01520.x

Pargament, K. I. (1997). *The psychology of religion and coping: Theory, research, practice.* New York, NY: Guilford Press.

Pargament, K. I., Kennell, J., Hathaway, W., Grevengoed, N., Newman, J., & Jones, W. (1988). Religion and the problem-solving process: Three styles of coping. *Journal for the Scientific Study of Religion, 27,* 90–104. http://dx.doi.org/10.2307/1387404

Pargament, K. I., Koenig, H. G., Tarakeshwar, N., & Hahn, J. (2004). Religious coping methods as predictors of psychological, physical and spiritual outcomes among medically ill elderly patients: A two-year longitudinal study. *Journal of Health Psychology, 9,* 713–730. http://dx.doi.org/10.1177/1359105304045366

Pargament, K. I., Smith, B. W., Koenig, H. G., & Perez, L. (1998). Patterns of positive and negative religious coping with major life stressors. *Journal for the Scientific Study of Religion, 37,* 710–724. http://dx.doi.org/10.2307/1388152

Pedregon, C. A., Farley, R. L., Davis, A., Wood, J. M., & Clark, R. D. (2012). Social desirability, personality questionnaires, and the "better than average" effect. *Personality and Individual Differences, 52,* 213–217. http://dx.doi.org/10.1016/j.paid.2011.10.022

Phillips, R. E., III, Cheng, C. M., & Oemig-Dworsky, C. (2014). Initial evidence for a brief measure of Buddhist coping in the United States. *International Journal for the Psychology of Religion, 24,* 215–227. http://dx.doi.org/10.1080/10508619.2013.808867

Piedmont, R. L. (1999). Does spirituality represent the sixth factor of personality? Spiritual transcendence and the Five-Factor Model. *Journal of Personality, 67,* 985–1013. http://dx.doi.org/10.1111/1467-6494.00080

Pirutinsky, S., Carp, S., & Rosmarin, D. H. (2017). A paradigm to assess implicit attitudes toward God: The positive/negative God associations task. *Journal of Religion and Health, 56,* 305–319. http://dx.doi.org/10.1007/s10943-016-0303-y

Pirutinsky, S., Siev, J., & Rosmarin, D. H. (2015). Scrupulosity and implicit and explicit beliefs about God. *Journal of Obsessive-Compulsive and Related Disorders, 6,* 33–38. http://dx.doi.org/10.1016/j.jocrd.2015.05.002

Plante, T. G., & Boccaccini, M. T. (1997). The Santa Clara Strength of Religious Faith Questionnaire. *Pastoral Psychology, 45,* 375–387. http://dx.doi.org/10.1007/BF02230993

Rizvi, M. A. K., & Hossain, M. Z. (2017). Relationship between religious belief and happiness: A systematic literature review. *Journal of Religion and Health, 56,* 1561–1582. http://dx.doi.org/10.1007/s10943-016-0332-6

Rohrbaugh, J., & Jessor, R. (1975). Religiosity in youth: A personal control against deviant behavior. *Journal of Personality, 43,* 136–155. http://dx.doi.org/10.1111/j.1467-6494.1975.tb00577.x

Rosmarin, D. H., Pargament, K. I., Krumrei, E. J., & Flannelly, K. J. (2009). Religious coping among Jews: Development and initial validation of the JCOPE. *Journal of Clinical Psychology, 65,* 670–683. http://dx.doi.org/10.1002/jclp.20574

Rosmarin, D. H., Pirutinsky, S., Greer, D., & Korbman, M. (2016). Maintaining a grateful disposition in the face of distress: The role of religious coping. *Psychology of Religion and Spirituality, 8,* 134–140. http://dx.doi.org/10.1037/rel0000021

Saroglou, V., Pichon, I., Trompette, L., Verschueren, M., & Dernelle, R. (2005). Prosocial behavior and religion: New evidence based on projective measures and peer ratings. *Journal for the Scientific Study of Religion, 44,* 323–348. http://dx.doi.org/10.1111/j.1468-5906.2005.00289.x

Sedikides, C., & Gebauer, J. E. (2010). Religiosity as self-enhancement: A meta-analysis of the relation between socially desirable responding and religiosity. *Personality and Social Psychology Review, 14,* 17–36. http://dx.doi.org/10.1177/1088868309351002

Shariff, A. F., Cohen, A. B., & Norenzayan, A. (2008). The devil's advocate: Secular arguments diminish both implicit and explicit belief. *Journal of Cognition and Culture, 8,* 417–423. http://dx.doi.org/10.1163/156853708X358245

Sosis, R. (2003). Why aren't we all hutterites? Costly signaling theory and religious behavior. *Human Nature, 14,* 91–127. http://dx.doi.org/10.1007/s12110-003-1000-6

Tarakeshwar, N., Pargament, K. I., & Mahoney, A. (2003). Initial development of a measure of religious coping among Hindus. *Journal of Community Psychology, 31,* 607–628. http://dx.doi.org/10.1002/jcop.10071

Trimble, D. E. (1997). The Religious Orientation Scale: Review and meta-analysis of social desirability effects. *Educational and Psychological Measurement, 57,* 970–986. http://dx.doi.org/10.1177/0013164497057006007

Tsang, J., Rowatt, W. C., & Shariff, A. F. (2015). Religion and prosocial behavior. In D. Schroeder & R. Graziano (Eds.), *Handbook of prosocial behavior* (pp. 609–625). Oxford, England: Oxford University Press.

Underwood, L. G., & Teresi, J. A. (2002). The daily spiritual experience scale: Development, theoretical description, reliability, exploratory factor analysis, and preliminary construct validity using health-related data. *Annals of Behavioral Medicine, 24,* 22–33. http://dx.doi.org/10.1207/S15324796ABM2401_04

Van Tongeren, D. R., Hakim, S., Hook, J. N., Johnson, K. A., Green, J. D., Hulsey, T. L., & Davis, D. E. (2016). Toward an understanding of religious tolerance: Quest religiousness and positive attitudes toward religiously dissimilar others. *International Journal for the Psychology of Religion, 26,* 212–224. http://dx.doi.org/10.1080/10508619.2015.1039417

Weeks, M., Weeks, K. P., & Daniel, M. R. (2008). The implicit relationship between religious and paranormal constructs. *Journal for the Scientific Study of Religion, 47,* 599–611. http://dx.doi.org/10.1111/j.1468-5906.2008.00429.x

Wenger, J. L., & Yarbrough, T. D. (2005). Religious individuals: Evaluating their intrinsic and extrinsic motivations at the implicit level of awareness. *The Journal of Social Psychology, 145,* 5–16. http://dx.doi.org/10.3200/SOCP.145.1.5-16

Wilt, J. A., Grubbs, J. B., Exline, J. J., & Pargament, K. I. (2016). Personality, religious and spiritual struggles, and well-being. *Psychology of Religion and Spirituality, 8,* 341–351. http://dx.doi.org/10.1037/rel0000054

Wood, B. T., Worthington, E. L., Jr., Exline, J. J., Yali, A. M., Aten, J. D., & McMinn, M. R. (2010). Development, refinement, and psychometric properties of the Attitudes Toward God Scale (ATGS-9). *Psychology of Religion and Spirituality, 2,* 148–167. http://dx.doi.org/10.1037/a0018753

Worthington, E. L., Jr., Wade, N. G., Hight, T. L., Ripley, J. S., McCullough, M. E., Berry, J. W., . . . O'Connor, L. (2003). The Religious Commitment Inventory—10: Development, refinement, and validation of a brief scale for research and counseling. *Journal of Counseling Psychology, 50,* 84–96. http://dx.doi.org/10.1037/0022-0167.50.1.84

23

Vocational Psychology Assessment

Positive Human Characteristics Leading to Positive Work Outcomes

Christine Robitschek and Matthew W. Ashton

Work can play many roles in a person's life: It can be a way of earning money for survival or to support a chosen lifestyle, a pathway on which a person progresses (e.g., earns promotions and recognition), or a mechanism by which one expresses purpose in life and self-concept (Super, 1963; Wrzesniewski, McCauley, Rozin, & Schwartz, 1997). Work provides benefits to both the individual engaging in the work and to society (e.g., Gerstel & Gross, 1987), which reflects positive psychology's shared emphases on personal and societal well-being (Seligman & Csikszentmihalyi, 2000). If workers are to strive for positive outcomes for themselves and society, however, they must possess or develop positive human characteristics and behaviors. This chapter addresses these positive characteristics, behaviors, and outcomes.

Because of space limitations, this chapter does not cover the breadth of constructs or perspectives in the work domain. A few examples of relevant topics that the reader may find interesting but that are not covered are Savickas's (2000) taxonomy of human strengths, which is derived from vocational theory and can be applied across life domains; Wrzesniewski et al.'s (1997) assessment of work as job, career, or calling; and Sympson's (1999) operationalization of hope in the work domain. Given the expertise of the authors, this chapter focuses on the assessment of constructs found in the vocational psychology literature.

The following sections describe assessment of good career decision making, the role of work in our lives, adaptability within the career role, and areas for

http://dx.doi.org/10.1037/0000138-023
Positive Psychological Assessment: A Handbook of Models and Measures, Second Edition,
M. W. Gallagher and S. J. Lopez (Editors)

future assessment efforts. Although 12 assessments are described, many more remain unmentioned. The reader is directed to Kapes, Mastie, and Whitfield (1994), Seligman (1994), and Levinson, Ohlers, Caswell, and Kiewra (1998) for descriptions of many other measures.

HOW PEOPLE MAKE "GOOD" CAREER DECISIONS

The bulk of vocational psychology literature deals with the way in which human beings go about making decisions within and about their careers. Phillips and Jome (2005) summarized the vocational literature about career decision making, noting that the "best" career choices may be defined by either (a) an individual's selecting the "best" option for him or her, or (b) an individual's engaging in the "best" decision-making process regardless of what alternative is selected. We discuss the different constructs and processes that have been most prominently connected to making "good" career decisions and the assessment instruments that measure them.

Career Exploration

Most current theories of career development and choice highlight the importance of *career exploration*, defined as behavior that increases individuals' understanding of themselves or their environment with the aim of choosing or progressing within an occupation (Jordaan, 1963). Exploratory behaviors are beneficial at predictable developmental stages (i.e., adolescence and emerging adulthood) characterized by work-related experimentation (Super, Savickas, & Super, 1996) and during career transitions in which the behaviors assist the person with important decisions. This traditional view of career exploration is similar to *exploration in breadth*, which is gathering information about a variety of options to be used in making decisions (Luyckx, Goossens, Soenens, & Beyers, 2006). *Exploration in depth* is also important. This involves exploring one's current work commitments (Luyckx et al., 2006), which is an important behavior as people reevaluate their commitments, for example, as a job or work environment changes. Given these perspectives, assessment of career exploration should address exploration of the self and the work environment as well as exploration in breadth and exploration in depth.

Career Exploration Survey

The Career Exploration Survey (CES; Stumpf, Colarelli, & Hartman, 1983) is a 59-item instrument that is administered and scored by the researcher or practitioner. Test takers answer items in the context of the 3 months before taking the CES, responding to each item on a 5-point scale, with anchors that vary to match item content. For example, 1 = *little* or *not satisfied* and 5 = *a great deal* or *very satisfied*. Results yield scores on 16 dimensions of career exploration. Several dimensions are aspects of the exploration process: environmental exploration, self-exploration, number of occupations considered, intended-systematic exploration, frequency (of exploratory behavior), amount of information, and focus. Three dimensions are aspects of reactions to exploration: satisfaction with information, explorational stress, and decisional stress. Six dimensions are aspects of beliefs: employment outlook, certainty of career exploration outcome, external search instrumentality, internal search instrumentality, method instrumentality, and importance of obtaining preferred position. The CES provides a multidimensional perspective on exploration. (See Stumpf et al., 1983, for psychometric information.)

Vocational Identity Status Assessment

The Vocational Identity Status Assessment (VISA; Porfeli, Lee, Vondracek, & Weigold, 2011) is a 30-item measure of work-related identity status. The VISA assesses two broad dimensions of identity formation: career exploration and career commitment. Within career exploration, there are two subscales: In-Breadth Career Exploration and In-Depth Career Exploration. Each subscale comprises five items with response options ranging from 1 (*strongly disagree*) to 5 (*strongly agree*). Subscale scores are calculated by averaging item scores for that subscale. The measure and psychometric information are available in Porfeli et al. (2011).

Vocational Interests

Many current vocational theories emphasize the importance of vocational interests as a foundation for making career decisions. Interests can be an indicator of a person's vocational strengths—that is, areas in which the person is likely to be motivated to learn and perform at a high level. Holland's (1959) vocational theory is perhaps the most widely used theory for categorizing vocational interests. Holland posited a hexagonal model of interests, which he viewed as personality types. These six types (with examples of typical interests) are (a) realistic (e.g., mechanics, agriculture, and sports); (b) investigative (e.g., science and scholarly pursuits); (c) artistic (e.g., visual or culinary arts, creative writing, and drama); (d) social (e.g., teaching, counseling, and other helping professions); (e) enterprising (e.g., selling products, services, or ideas); and (f) conventional (e.g., typing, filing, and accounting). A person's profile of interests can be expressed by scores on relatively independent scales measuring these six types. Profiles, arranged into what are known as Holland codes, typically consist of the three highest scores among these six types, although some people can best be described in fewer or greater numbers of types. In this section, we present two widely used measures of vocational interests based on Holland's model of interests.

Self-Directed Search

The Self-Directed Search, fifth edition (SDS; Holland & Messer, 2013), is administered (25–35 minutes) and scored (10 minutes) by the test taker. It is administered via paper and pencil (available from Psychological Assessment

Resources) or online at www.self-directed-search.com. Results yield Holland codes for "activities" (things the test taker would like to do), "competencies" (things the test taker already can do well), "occupations" (things in which the test taker has interest or finds appealing), and "self estimates" (self-ratings of abilities compared with other people). The test taker calculates a composite Holland code that includes all of these areas. There are several forms of the SDS: (a) Form R is the most commonly used form and is appropriate for ages 11 to 70, (b) Form E is written at a fourth-grade level for people with limited reading skills, and (c) Career Explorer is for junior high school and middle school students. Other forms are available in several languages. The SDS is used in conjunction with the *You and Your Career* booklet, which provides information about Holland's hexagonal model and assistance with career exploration; *Occupations Finder*, a booklet with a wide variety of occupations, listed by Holland code, as a means for test takers to compare their codes with the codes of occupations; and the *Educational Opportunities Finder*, *Veterans and Military Occupations Finder*, and *Leisure Finder*, which are used in similar ways. The online version of the SDS yields a Client Interpretive Report. Reliability and validity information is available in Holland, Fritzche, and Powell (1994).

Strong Interest Inventory

The Strong Interest Inventory, revised edition (SII; Consulting Psychologists Press, 2012), is a 291-item instrument that is administered by the researcher or practitioner and scored by the publisher, CPP. Test takers use a 5-point scale ranging from *strongly like* to *strongly dislike* to rate items in the five areas of occupations, school subjects, activities, leisure activities, and types of people. Test takers also mark the extent to which additional items identify their characteristics with response options on a 5-point scale ranging from *strongly like me* to *strongly unlike me*. Three sets of scores, related to Holland types, are provided in the results. General Occupational Themes are composite Holland codes. Basic Interest scales are subscales of the Holland codes. Occupational scales compare the test taker's profile with the profiles of people who are successfully employed in specific occupations.

The SII also yields scores on five bipolar Personal Style scales, which describe aspects of how the test taker prefers to interact with the world around him or her. The scales are work style, learning environment, leadership style, risk taking/adventure, and team orientation. Readers are directed to Donnay, Thompson, Morris, and Schaubhut (2004) and Herk and Thompson (2012) for reliability and validity information for the revised SII.

These two measures of vocational interests have different strengths. The SDS is useful in examining discrepancies among an individual's Holland codes as indicated by the different areas measured by the SDS. Areas include things I would like to do, things I already do well, things I find appealing, and self-ratings of my abilities compared to other people. The SII is particularly useful because it divides the test taker's Holland codes into the basic interest scales, which can help tease apart unexpected results. Also, the SII gives test takers direct comparisons of their profiles with people in a wide range of occupations. In contrast, *Occupations Finder* of the SDS relates clients' Holland codes with the codes of occupations.

Work Needs and Values

Individuals vary in the things they need or want from work. One way to conceptualize these needs is in terms of basic psychological needs (e.g., needs identified in self-determination theory; Ryan & Deci, 2000) that may be satisfied through work settings and experiences. Ryan and Deci (2000) posited that the basic psychological needs of autonomy, competence, and relatedness are universal and inherent in human beings. When these basic needs are met in the workplace, people experience greater engagement in work and job satisfaction, more affective commitment to their work, and protection against burnout and job strain (see Van den Broeck, Ferris, Chang, & Rosen, 2016, for a review).

A second way of conceptualizing needs is in terms of *work values*, which are beliefs about the qualities of life that are considered important and desirable specifically in one's vocational pursuits (Hartung, 2009). Super (1990) viewed work values as acquired adaptations transmitted through proximal and distal cultural influences. When work environments are congruent with our work values, outcomes are similar to when our basic psychological needs are met. See, for example, greater job satisfaction (e.g., Feather & Rauter, 2004) and job commitment (e.g., Rounds, 1990).

Given these multiple conceptualizations of work needs and values, various measures serve different purposes in research and practice.

Work-Related Basic Need Satisfaction

The Work-Related Basic Need Satisfaction Scale (W-BNS; Van den Broeck, Vansteenkiste, De Witte, Soenens, & Lens, 2010) assesses the extent to which the needs for competence, autonomy, and relatedness are met in one's current work situation. The W-BNS has 16 items that the test taker rates on a Likert scale ranging from 1 (*totally disagree*) to 5 (*totally agree*). The three scale scores (each measuring one of the needs) are calculated by averaging the item scores for that scale. Psychometric information can be found in Van den Broeck and colleagues (2010). Although there is considerable research on self-determination theory and the importance of basic psychological need fulfillment across domains, only in recent years have we seen measures of work-related basic psychological needs, such as the W-BNS, with strong psychometric evidence. Also, we were unable to locate literature describing use of these measures in applied situations. Thus, although the W-BNS is useful in research, its utility in practice remains undetermined.

Super's Work Values Inventory—Revised

Super's Work Values Inventory—Revised (SWVI–r; Suen, 2015) is a 72-item instrument that is administered by the researcher or practitioner and scored by the scale publisher (Kuder). Test takers indicate the level of importance for each item on a 5-point scale ranging from 1 (*Not important at all. Not a factor in my job selection.*) to 5 (*Crucial. I would not consider a job without it.*). Results yield scores on 12 scales (i.e., achievement, coworkers, creativity, income, independence, lifestyle, challenge, prestige, security, supervision, variety, and workplace). Reliability and validity information is summarized in Suen (2015). The SWVI–r has been used extensively in practice and research to aid in understanding how values can manifest in the work domain.

Work Values Inventory

The Work Values Inventory (WVI; Santa Cruz County Regional Occupational Program, n.d.) is a self-administered, self-scored, and self-interpreted assessment of work values. The WVI comprises four brief sections that assess core values in one's life (e.g., honesty and power), values related to work environments (e.g., flexible and high earnings), values related to coworker interactions (e.g., competition and diversity), and valuing types of work activities (e.g., creative and public contact). For each item with these four sections, respondents rate each item as *Always important, Sort of important,* or *Not important.* A fifth section of the WVI asks respondents to identify their top five values among the values they rated as *Always important.* Respondents then identify the section (e.g., core values, coworker interactions) each of these top values is from. Identifying the sections provides information regarding differential importance of broad domains of values for the respondent. A final section of the WVI asks respondents to "write a paragraph describing how you see your top 5 values being important in your work" (p. 3). This story helps the person to situate their work values specifically within their work experiences and goals. We were unable to locate any information regarding the psychometric properties of the WVI. However, in our experience, the WVI and similar assessments of work values are the assessments most commonly used in applied settings. These assessments are transparent to the test taker and are quickly administered and interpreted, without any need to submit the assessment elsewhere for scoring. This suggests a possible disconnect between research and practice in the assessment of work values and needs. Addressing this disconnect and conducting research on assessment of work values and needs that are connected to practice are warranted.

Job/Work Satisfaction

Assessing satisfaction with work in general or the current job a person holds continues to be a challenging task. A multitude of measures have been used in research. Yet it is not clear why researchers have opted to reinvent the wheel each time they want to measure satisfaction with work. Despite the plethora of measures with little evidence of reliability or validity, two measures that serve different purposes have seen some repeated use, the Minnesota Satisfaction Questionnaire (Weiss, Dawis, England, & Lofquist,

1967) and the Overall Job Satisfaction Scale (Judge, Locke, Durham, & Kluger, 1998).

Minnesota Satisfaction Questionnaire

The Minnesota Satisfaction Questionnaire (MSQ; Weiss et al., 1967) is administered and scored by the researcher or practitioner. The measure is available in the public domain from the publisher (Vocational Psychology Research, University of Minnesota–Minneapolis). Three forms are available: two versions of the 100-item long form (1967; 1977) and a 20-item short form (1977). The MSQ measures the degree to which test takers are satisfied with 20 aspects of their current job, such as recognition, security, advancement, and variety. Item responses on the 1967 long form are on a unidirectional 5-point scale ranging from *not satisfied* to *extremely satisfied*. The 1977 long and short forms use revised response options, a balanced 5-point scale ranging from *very satisfied* to *very dissatisfied*. Psychometric information is available in Weiss et al. (1967) and in the MSQ manual (Weiss et al., 1967).

Overall Job Satisfaction Scale

The Overall Job Satisfaction Scale (OJS; Judge et al., 1998) is administered and scored by the researcher or practitioner and is available in the public domain. The five items are based on a longer measure by Brayfield and Rothe (1951) and can be found in Judge et al. (1998). Item responses range from *strongly disagree* to *strongly agree*. Researchers and practitioners should use the OJS if they are interested in job satisfaction as a unitary construct. Users should consider the MSQ if they are interested in multidimensional work satisfaction.

ROLE SALIENCE AND BALANCE

Super (1980) put forth these constructs from a vocational perspective. *Role salience* refers to the absolute and relative importance of various life roles. *Role balance* refers to the extent to which a person is comfortable with the amount of time and energy put into each role in relation to other life roles. Our most salient life roles (referred to as *core* roles) are more critical to our life satisfaction than more peripheral life roles (Super et al., 1996). Therefore, if a core life role is demanding more time and energy than usual, we are able to sacrifice time and energy in peripheral life roles with limited effect on life satisfaction. Conversely, if peripheral roles demand more time and energy and core roles suffer as a result, this will have a negative impact on life satisfaction (Super et al., 1996).

Salience Inventory

The Salience Inventory (SI; Nevill & Super, 1986) is a 170-item instrument that is administered and scored by the researcher or practitioner, and it is available free of charge to researchers and practitioners through www.vocopher.com. Item responses are on a 4-point scale from *never or rarely/little or none* to *almost always or always/a great deal.* Results yield scores for five life roles: student, worker, homemaker (including parenting and partner roles), leisurite, and citizen. Within each life role, three aspects of salience are tapped (yielding a total of 15 subscale scores: three aspects of salience for each of five life roles). These three aspects of salience are participation (i.e., what the test taker actually does in this life role), commitment (i.e., attitudinal and affective importance of the life role), and value expectations (i.e., the degree to which the life role is expected to fulfill the test taker's values and needs). Thus, the SI informs about not only which roles are most important but also the extent to which test takers actually are engaged in activities (participation) that are important (commitment) and meet their needs (values expectations). Reliability and validity information is available in Nevill and Super (1986).

Life-Career Rainbow

The Life-Career Rainbow (Super, 1980) is a qualitative way to assess role salience, among other constructs. Construction of the Rainbow can be completed by the individual being assessed after thorough instructions are given or by this individual in conjunction with the researcher or practitioner. The lifespan is represented by the length of the Rainbow, with the left and right ends representing birth and death, respectively. Each band of the Rainbow represents a different life role. The width of each band at any given point in the life span represents the salience of that life role at that point in time. For example, the "worker" band of the Rainbow likely would be empty for most people until sometime in the teenage years, at which point it might be fairly narrow (compared with other bands) if the worker role has minimal salience. In the adult years, the worker band might be wide, if, for example, the individual is employed full-time, outside the home, in a job that has meaning and purpose for the worker. This band is likely to narrow again or end completely after retirement depending on whether the person quits work altogether or continues to work in some part-time capacity after formally retiring. A cross section of the Rainbow at any point in the lifespan provides a picture of the life space (i.e., a comprehensive view of the multiple life roles a person plays at any one time).

Although the Life-Career Rainbow might be of limited utility to researchers, particularly those involved in quantitative research, it is very useful to practitioners and their clients. Similar to the SI, the Rainbow can help clients understand the relative importance of various life roles and how these roles might interact. In contrast to the SI, however, the Rainbow adds the life-span dimension, which allows people to explore how the importance of these roles, and even the presence or absence of each role, has changed over time. Furthermore, the Rainbow allows people to be planful about how they will structure their life space and balance their life roles in the future.

HOW INDIVIDUALS ADAPT AND CHANGE

The world of work is rapidly changing. A *typical* career path now involves multiple changes in job, employer, and often location over one's time in the workforce. Although many of these changes are instigated by the worker, many are not. Factors such as technological advances, abrupt economic recessions, outsourcing, and organizational mergers can result in vocational upheaval ranging from job restructuring to layoffs. Workers must be adaptive in their careers to cope successfully with these rapid changes (Murphy, Blustein, Bohlig, & Platt, 2010).

Career adaptability is an individual's readiness to handle both predictable and unexpected career changes and challenges across the lifespan (Super & Knasel, 1981). Here we present the most recent assessment of career adaptability, the Career Adapt-Abilities Scale (CAAS; Savickas & Porfeli, 2012).

The CAAS is a 24-item instrument available in Appendix 2 of Savickas and Porfeli (2012). The CAAS assesses four components of career adaptability: *Concern* about the future of one's career; taking *Control* and preparing for one's career; *Curiosity* about how one's career and self might be in the future; and *Confidence* in one's ability to achieve career goals. Response options range from 1 (*not strong*) to 5 (*strongest*). Scores are calculated by averaging item scores on each subscale. Initial psychometric information for the assessment is available in Savickas and Porfeli (2012). Additional psychometric information specific to each of 13 countries is available in multiple articles compiled in a special issue of the *Journal of Vocational Behavior* (Vol. 80, Issue 3).

MEASUREMENT ISSUES AND FUTURE DEVELOPMENTS

Considerable evidence indicates solid reliability and validity for the instruments discussed in this chapter. Readers are directed to the references mentioned throughout for test-specific measurement issues. In recent years, however, several themes have emerged questioning the breadth of utility for these measures. First, the majority of the psychometric evidence is for primarily White, non-Hispanic Americans. We need to devote considerable effort and resources to determine not only whether the assessments themselves are psychometrically sound for diverse populations but also whether the theoretical propositions underlying these assessments are culturally appropriate for people with diverse identities (Hardin, Robitschek, Flores, Navarro, & Ashton, 2014).

A second theme involves the changing world of work. Many of today's jobs did not exist 30 years ago (e.g., web designer or Transportation Security Administration baggage screener), when many of the assessments described here were first developed. We also have seen dramatic changes in economic globalization, movement further into a postindustrial economy, and tremendous advances in technology resulting in enormous reductions in the number of jobs for unskilled and semiskilled workers (DeBell, 2006). Yet most vocational assessments have not kept pace with these dramatic changes in the world of work. Most vocational measures could benefit from modernization to reflect new jobs, new organizational structures, and new individual work patterns within the world of work.

Finally, future developments in vocational assessment need to address the distinction between "what is" and "what might be" in a person's work life. Unfortunately, this has changed little since the first edition of this book was published. As Krumboltz (e.g., Mitchell & Krumboltz, 1996) pointed out, we do a disservice to people if vocational assessment limits their choices to options to which they already have been exposed. Vocational assessment, particularly in the context of positive psychology, should open doors and increase the range of options that people perceive in the world of work. Current vocational assessment tools do an excellent job of assessing "what is." We now need to add to these tools to include "measures of the possible."

REFERENCES

Brayfield, A. H., & Rothe, H. F. (1951). An index of job satisfaction. *Journal of Applied Psychology, 35,* 307–311. http://dx.doi.org/10.1037/h0055617

Consulting Psychologists Press. (2012). *The Strong Interest Inventory* (Rev. ed.). Sunnyvale, CA: Author.

DeBell, C. (2006). What all applied psychologists should know about work. *Professional Psychology: Research and Practice, 37,* 325–333. http://dx.doi.org/10.1037/0735-7028.37.4.325

Donnay, D. A., Thompson, R. C., Morris, M. L., & Schaubhut, N. A. (2004). *Technical brief for the newly revised Strong Interest assessment: Content, reliability and validity.* Mountain View, CA: Consulting Psychologists Press.

Feather, N. T., & Rauter, K. A. (2004). Organizational citizenship behaviors in relation to job status, job insecurity, organizational commitment and identification, job satisfaction and work values. *Journal of Occupational and Organizational Psychology, 77*(1), 81–94. http://dx.doi.org/10.1348/096317904322915928

Gerstel, N., & Gross, H. E. (Eds.). (1987). *Families and work.* Philadelphia, PA: Temple University Press.

Hardin, E. E., Robitschek, C., Flores, L. Y., Navarro, R. L., & Ashton, M. W. (2014). The cultural lens approach to evaluating cultural validity of psychological theory. *American Psychologist, 69,* 656–668. http://dx.doi.org/10.1037/a0036532

Hartung, P. J. (2009, June). *Why work: The story of values in vocational psychology.* Invited address given at the Ninth Biennial Meeting of the Society for Vocational Psychology, St. Louis, MO.

Herk, N. A., & Thompson, R. C. (2012). *Strong Interest Inventory manual supplement: Occupational scales update 2012.* Mountain View, CA: Consulting Psychologists Press.

Holland, J. L. (1959). A theory of vocational choice. *Journal of Counseling Psychology, 6,* 35–45. http://dx.doi.org/10.1037/h0040767

Holland, J. L., Fritzche, B. A., & Powell, A. B. (1994). *Technical manual for the Self-Directed Search.* Odessa, FL: Psychological Assessment Resources.

Holland, J. L., & Messer, M. A. (2013). *Self-directed search* (5th ed.). Lutz, FL: Psychological Assessment Resources.

Jordaan, J. P. (1963). Exploratory behavior: The formation of self- and occupational concepts. In D. E. Super & Associates (Eds.), *Career development: Self-concept theory* (pp. 42–78). New York, NY: College Entrance Examination Board.

Judge, T. A., Locke, E. A., Durham, C. C., & Kluger, A. N. (1998). Dispositional effects on job and life satisfaction: The role of core evaluations. *Journal of Applied Psychology, 83,* 17–34. http://dx.doi.org/10.1037/0021-9010.83.1.17

Kapes, J. T., Mastie, M. M., & Whitfield, E. A. (Eds.). (1994). *A counselor's guide to career assessment instruments* (3rd ed.). Alexandria, VA: National Career Development Association.

Levinson, E. M., Ohlers, D. L., Caswell, S., & Kiewra, K. (1998). Six approaches to the assessment of career maturity. *Journal of Counseling & Development, 76,* 475–482. http://dx.doi.org/10.1002/j.1556-6676.1998.tb02707.x

Luyckx, K., Goossens, L., Soenens, B., & Beyers, W. (2006). Unpacking commitment and exploration: Preliminary validation of an integrative model of late adolescent identity formation. *Journal of Adolescence, 29,* 361–378. http://dx.doi.org/10.1016/j.adolescence.2005.03.008

Mitchell, L. K., & Krumboltz, J. D. (1996). Krumboltz's learning theory of career choice and counseling. In D. Brown & L. Brooks (Eds.), *Career choice and development* (3rd ed., pp. 233–280). San Francisco, CA: Jossey-Bass.

Murphy, K. A., Blustein, D. L., Bohlig, A. J., & Platt, M. G. (2010). The college-to-career transition: An exploration of emerging adulthood. *Journal of Counseling & Development, 88,* 174–181. http://dx.doi.org/10.1002/j.1556-6678.2010.tb00006.x

Nevill, D. D., & Super, D. E. (1986). *The Salience Inventory: Theory, application and research.* Palo Alto, CA: Consulting Psychologists Press.

Phillips, S. D., & Jome, L. M. (2005). Vocational choices: What do we know? What do we need to know? In W. B. Walsh & M. L. Savickas (Eds.), *Handbook of vocational psychology* (3rd ed., pp. 127–153). Mahwah, NJ: Erlbaum.

Porfeli, E. J., Lee, B., Vondracek, F. W., & Weigold, I. K. (2011). A multi-dimensional measure of vocational identity status. *Journal of Adolescence, 34,* 853–871. http://dx.doi.org/10.1016/j.adolescence.2011.02.001

Rounds, J. D. (1990). The comparative and combined utility of work value and interest date in career counseling with adults. *Journal of Vocational Behavior, 37,* 32–45. http://dx.doi.org/10.1016/0001-8791(90)90005-M

Ryan, R. M., & Deci, E. L. (2000). Self-determination theory and the facilitation of intrinsic motivation, social development, and well-being. *American Psychologist, 55,* 68–78. http://dx.doi.org/10.1037/0003-066X.55.1.68

Santa Cruz County Regional Occupational Program. (n.d.). *Work Values Inventory.* Unpublished instrument. Retrieved from http://www.rop.santacruz.k12.ca.us/resources/career_planning/index.htm

Savickas, M. L. (2000, August). Building human strength: Career counseling's contribution to a taxonomy of positive psychology. In W. B. Walsh (Chair), *Fostering human strength: A counseling psychology perspective.* Symposium presented at the annual meeting of the American Psychological Association, Washington, DC.

Savickas, M. L., & Porfeli, E. J. (2012). Career Adapt-Abilities Scale: Construction, reliability, and measurement equivalence across 13 countries. *Journal of Vocational Behavior, 80,* 661–673. http://dx.doi.org/10.1016/j.jvb.2012.01.011

Seligman, L. (1994). *Developmental career counseling and assessment* (2nd ed.). Thousand Oaks, CA: Sage.

Seligman, M. E. P., & Csikszentmihalyi, M. (2000). Positive psychology. An introduction. *American Psychologist, 55,* 5–14. http://dx.doi.org/10.1037/0003-066X.55.1.5

Stumpf, S. A., Colarelli, S. M., & Hartman, K. (1983). Development of the Career Exploration Survey (CES). *Journal of Vocational Behavior, 22,* 191–226. http://dx.doi.org/10.1016/0001-8791(83)90028-3

Suen, H. K. (2015). *Super's Work Values Inventory—Revised (SWVI–r)* [Technical Brief]. Retrieved from https://www.kuder.com/research/technical-briefs/supers-work-values-inventory-r/

Super, D. E. (1963). Self-concepts in vocational development. In D. E. Super, R. Starshevsky, N. Matlin, & J. P. Jordaan (Eds.), *Career development: Self-concept theory* (pp. 17–32). New York, NY: College Entrance Examination Board.

Super, D. E. (1980). A life-span, life-space approach to career development. *Journal of Vocational Behavior, 16,* 282–298. http://dx.doi.org/10.1016/0001-8791(80)90056-1

Super, D. E. (1990). A life-span, life-space approach to career development. In D. Brown & L. Brooks (Eds.), *Career choice and development* (2nd ed., pp. 197–261). San Francisco, CA: Jossey-Bass.

Super, D. E., & Knasel, E. G. (1981). Career development in adulthood: Some theoretical problems and a possible solution. *British Journal of Guidance & Counselling, 9,* 194–201. http://dx.doi.org/10.1080/03069888108258214

Super, D. E., Savickas, M. L., & Super, C. M. (1996). The life-span, life-space approach to careers. In D. Brown & L. Brooks (Eds.), *Career choice and development* (3rd ed., pp. 121–178). San Francisco, CA: Jossey-Bass.

Sympson, S. (1999). *Validation of the Domain Specific Hope Scale: Exploring hope in life domains* (Unpublished doctoral dissertation). University of Kansas, Lawrence.

Van den Broeck, A., Ferris, D. L., Chang, C.-H., & Rosen, C. C. (2016). A review of self-determination theory's basic psychological needs at work. *Journal of Management, 42,* 1195–1229. http://dx.doi.org/10.1177/0149206316632058

Van den Broeck, A., Vansteenkiste, M., De Witte, H., Soenens, B., & Lens, W. (2010). Capturing autonomy, competence, and relatedness at work: Construction and initial validation of the Work-related Basic Need Satisfaction scale. *Journal of Occupational and Organizational Psychology, 83,* 981–1001. http://dx.doi.org/10.1348/096317909X481382

Weiss, D. J., Dawis, R. V., England, G. W., & Lofquist, L. H. (1967). Manual for the Minnesota Satisfaction Questionnaire. *Minnesota Studies in Vocational Rehabilitation, XXI.* Minneapolis: University of Minnesota.

Wrzesniewski, A., McCauley, C., Rozin, P., & Schwartz, B. (1997). Jobs, career, and callings: People's relations to their work. *Journal of Research in Personality, 31,* 21–33. http://dx.doi.org/10.1006/jrpe.1997.2162

24

Measuring Satisfaction and Meaning at Work

Michael F. Steger, Bryan J. Dik, and Yerin Shim

What makes work worth doing? Work provides a means of making a living, a way to occupy one's time, and a forum to satisfy achievement needs. However, from a positive psychological perspective, the answer to the question of why work is worthwhile goes far beyond these reasons. Instead, we should anticipate that the best work experiences add value to people's lives and are an important part of their personal and communitarian flourishing. Ideally, work also is enjoyable, provides a desirable sense of challenge, and both cultivates and makes use of people's strengths. At its best, work also contributes to the health and equity of organizations, communities, and societies.

There is a substantial volume of research on job satisfaction, the most widely studied topic in organizational behavior research (Spector, 1997) and long a focal construct in both industrial–organizational and vocational psychology (Lent & Brown, 2006). Our PsycINFO search with the keyword "job satisfaction" revealed 19,865 articles since 2000, and high-quality measures of the constructs abound. Research on meaning at work, on the other hand, is relatively new, and finding appropriate instruments to assess work meaning can be challenging. In part, this is because research frequently has used proxy measures. In this chapter, our focus is on measures designed to assess job satisfaction, meaningful work, and perceptions of work as a calling.

Whereas happiness has often served as a shorthand term and public face for positive psychology (e.g., Diener & Biswas-Diener, 2008; Lyubomirsky, 2006; Seligman, 2003), happiness per se has not made many inroads into the world

http://dx.doi.org/10.1037/0000138-024
Positive Psychological Assessment: A Handbook of Models and Measures, Second Edition,
M. W. Gallagher and S. J. Lopez (Editors)

of work. In fact, we were unable to locate any measures of work happiness with even adequate psychometric support. Therefore, we begin with a review of job satisfaction measures, which have provided a critical, although incomplete, contribution to our understanding of work-related well-being. We proceed to review measures of work meaning and perceptions of work as a calling, two other constructs that overlap with work happiness. We close with observations and recommendations for future measurement of this aspect of positive human functioning.

ASSESSING JOB SATISFACTION

Job satisfaction refers to how well people like their jobs, or more formally, an emotional state emerging from a cognitive appraisal of job experiences (Fritzsche & Parrish, 2005). Most definitions of job satisfaction focus on its affective component, although most measures of the construct place a greater emphasis on the cognitive aspects of the construct (Fisher, 2000). Job satisfaction has been measured predominantly using self-report instruments that can be divided into two categories: (a) facet measures, which assess satisfaction with specific aspects of a job such as job security, coworkers, working conditions, company policies, and opportunities for achievement, accomplishment, and advancement (Weiss, Dawis, England, & Lofquist, 1967); and (b) global measures, which focus on overall appraisals of a job. As Fritzsche and Parrish (2005) noted, no theory is available to guide selection of which facets are most important under which circumstances. Furthermore, global job satisfaction does not equal the sum of the facet scores (Highhouse & Becker, 1993; Scarpello & Campbell, 1983).

Facet Measures

The most popular facet measures of job satisfaction are the Job Descriptive Index (JDI; Smith, Kendall, & Hulin, 1969), the Job Satisfaction Survey (JSS; Spector, 1985), and the Minnesota Satisfaction Questionnaire (MSQ; Weiss et al., 1967). The JDI is a 72-item scale in which respondents evaluate adjectives and phrases according to the extent to which each describes their job using the anchors *yes*, *no*, and *uncertain* (represented by "?"). Item responses are summed to provide scores on satisfaction with Work, Pay, Promotions, Supervision, and Coworkers. Internal consistency reliabilities for JDI facets are in the .8s, and mean test–retest reliability coefficients averaged across multiple studies range from .56 to .67 across the facets. Meta-analytic evidence also supports the convergent and discriminant validity of JDI subscale scores, with facet scores correlating in predicted directions with criterion variables, conforming to a nomological net of job satisfaction relations (Kinicki, Mckee-Ryan, Schriesheim, & Carson, 2002).

The shorter JSS uses 36 items with a 6-point scale (*strongly agree–strongly disagree*) to assess nine facets (Pay, Promotion, Supervision, Fringe Benefits,

Contingent Rewards, Operating Procedures, Coworkers, Nature of Work, and Communication). Internal consistency reliabilities reported by Spector (1985) for the facets range from .60 (Coworkers) to .82 (Supervision), with a value of .91 for the total score and 18-month test–retest coefficients ranging from .37 to .71. A multitrait-multimethod matrix analysis using JSS and JDI facet scales supported their construct validity (Spector, 1985).

Finally, the MSQ has 100-item and 20-item (5-point scale ranging from *not satisfied* to *extremely satisfied*) versions that assess a total of 20 job satisfaction facets, providing a comprehensiveness that many researchers find desirable. The scale scores have median internal consistency reliability coefficients above .8, median 1-week test–retest correlations of .83, convergent and discriminant correlations that conform to hypotheses, and concurrent validity evidence from group differences in satisfaction (e.g., Dawis, Pinto, Weitzel, & Nezzer, 1974; Dunham, Smith, & Blackburn, 1977; Weiss et al., 1967).

Global Measures

One frequently used measure of global job satisfaction is the Job in General Scale (JIG; Ironson, Smith, Brannick, Gibson, & Paul, 1989), an 18-item scale designed for use in tandem with the JDI, serving as a "more global, more evaluative, and longer in time frame" (p. 195) measure. JIG items consist of adjectives or short phrases paired with the same response scale as the JDI. Internal consistency estimates range from .91 to .95, with convergent correlations of .66 to .80 with other global satisfaction scales. Many researchers opt for very short measures of global job satisfaction, particularly when job satisfaction is a secondary focus in a study. For example, Chen and Spector (1991) used a three-item scale that yielded an alpha of .85 and correlated in predicted directions with convergent and discriminant criterion variables. Often even one-item scales are used (e.g., "All and all, how satisfied would you say you are with your job?" Quinn & Staines, 1979). One-item scales frequently are criticized, but Wanous, Reichers, and Hudy (1997) demonstrated in a meta-analytic study that the corrected mean correlation between single-item and multi-item satisfaction measures was $r = .67$, and the minimum estimated test–retest reliability for single-item scales was $r = .70$.

Summary

Apart from the lack of theory available to guide selection of the facets in facet instruments, and the fact that scales emphasize cognitive rather than affective aspects of the construct, the measurement of job satisfaction is a strength of research in organizational and vocational psychology. The most popular job satisfaction instruments are well designed and supported by strong evidence of reliability and validity. Yet from a positive psychology perspective, questions can be raised regarding the comprehensiveness of construct. Job satisfaction is a useful criterion for those interested in how favorably people view particular aspects of their jobs, or their jobs overall, but as typically assessed, job satisfaction focuses mainly on hedonic well-being and, to a lesser extent, personal fulfillment. This overlaps with definitions of work meaning and perceptions of work as a calling, but meaning and calling emphasize eudaimonic aspects of well-being (e.g., a sense of purpose, contribution, and prosocial attitudes) that, if addressed by existing job satisfaction scales at all, are usually peripheral considerations.

MEASURING MEANINGFUL WORK

Meaningful work can be considered an umbrella term that subsumes a range of constructs, including work meaning, work meaningfulness, and the positive connotations associated with the meaning of work. A narrower definition of meaningful work refers broadly to the amount of significance people perceive to exist in their work (Rosso, Dekas, & Wrzesniewski, 2010). Others have argued that, as in the broader psychological tradition of meaning in life, work is meaningful not only when it is judged to be significant but also when it is viewed as having a distinct purpose or point (Steger & Dik, 2009). A closely related term is *calling*. The idea of work serving as a calling has deep historical and religious roots. However, in modern parlance, a distinction has been made between neoclassical conceptualizations of calling that emphasize, duty, destiny, and a transcendent summons (Bunderson & Thompson, 2009; Dik & Duffy, 2009) and "modern" conceptualizations that frame calling as an inner drive to do fulfilling and self-actualizing work (Baumeister, 1991; Hall & Chandler, 2005).

We review scholarly definitions of calling in a later section. First, we examine the ways in which meaningful work has been defined and operationalized. Two trends have dominated meaningful work assessment. The first is the guiding influence of an early definition of meaningful work. The second is the deployment of ad hoc, single-use measures of meaningful work.

Job Diagnostics Survey

Currently, only a handful of measures of meaningful work are available in the published domain. The earliest example of assessing meaningful work comes from groundbreaking research on job design. The Job Characteristics Model (Hackman & Oldham, 1976) proposed a set of important job qualities, a set of psychological mediators that linked these job characteristics to outcomes, and a set of valued personal and work outcomes. Meaningful work was seen as an important psychological state that mediates between the job characteristics of skill variety, task identity, and task significance and the outcomes of internal (intrinsic) work motivation, work performance, satisfaction with work, and absenteeism and turnover (Hackman & Oldham, 1976). To test their model, Hackman and Oldham (1975) developed the Job Diagnostics Survey (JDS), which defines *experienced meaningfulness of the work* as "the degree to which the employee experiences the job as one which is generally meaningful, valuable, and worthwhile" (p. 162). Although this definition could be considered overly vague (e.g., what do employees consider meaningful?), it has been monumentally influential. Subsequent efforts to understand meaningful work have almost uniformly adopted this definition, or very similar definitions.

The JDS uses two pairs of items to assess experienced meaningfulness of work. The first pair refers to respondents' personal feelings: "Most of the things I have to do on this job seem useless or trivial" (reverse-scored) and "The work I do on this job is very meaningful to me." The second pair refers to other people in the respondents' organization: "Most people on this job feel that the work is useless or trivial" (reverse-scored) and "Most people on this job find the work very meaningful." Hackman and Oldham (1975) reported initial internal consistency reliability was acceptable (α = .76), and a later review confirmed this general range of reliability estimates (.74–.81; Fried & Ferris, 1987). Although we were unable to locate more recent reviews, the Job Characteristics Model, by bracketing meaningful work with job characteristics and work and personal outcomes, anticipated a trend that emerged in the 2000s. Researchers began using proxy measures for meaningful work rather than measuring meaningful work itself. There are studies in which specific job characteristics, such as task identity and task significance, were used as proxies for meaningful work (e.g., Piccolo & Colquitt, 2006), and others in which a haphazard array of variables was assembled and labeled as meaningful work (e.g., Britt, Dickinson, Moore, Castro, & Adler, 2007). It may be the case that these proxy measures were directed at filling a vacuum in meaningful work measurement. Although the JDS scale has fine reliability, the fact that half of its items require judgments about other people's attitudes toward a job shifts the focus away from an individual's personal convictions that his or her own job is meaningful. Yet, to discard these items leaves only two items remaining.

For the past several decades, ad hoc measures of meaningful work appeared in isolated efforts to explore other constructs, as in Spreitzer's (1995) study of empowerment at work. Spreitzer used three items to assess a meaning dimension of empowerment: "The work I do is very important to me," "My job activities are personally meaningful to me," and "The work I do is meaningful to me." The influence of the Job Characteristics Model's definition of meaningful work is apparent in these items. In fact, one of the items is a JDS item with a couple of words omitted. Although these three items demonstrated good internal consistency reliability (α = .87), little additional psychometric development was attempted.

May and Colleagues' Meaningful Work Scale

A somewhat more developed example of creating meaningful work measures for the purposes of testing ideas about other constructs comes from May, Gilson, and Harter (2004). In their investigation of engagement in work, May and colleagues pulled together items from other sources to more fully capture meaningful work. They used all three of the items Spreitzer (1995) developed as well as one item from Hackman and Oldham (1980), which itself was a modified version of an item from the JDS: "The work I do on this job is worthwhile." Finally, two items were drawn from an unpublished dissertation by Tymon (1988): "My job activities are significant to me" and "I feel that the work I do on my job is valuable." Again, it is worth pointing out that all of these items are subtle variations on the definition (and, indeed, items) of meaningful work first delineated by Hackman and Oldham (1975). May and colleagues reported good reliability for scores on the scale formed by these items ($\alpha = .90$). There has, however, been very little further psychometric development of this scale.

Arnold and Colleagues' Meaningful Work Scale

The unfortunate gravitation toward ad hoc measurement utilization is probably the dominant trend in how meaningful work has been operationalized. The measure(s) of meaningful work published by Arnold, Turner, Barling, Kelloway, and McKee (2007) does not snap that streak. However, in Arnold and colleagues' research of the mediating role of meaningful work in the relationship of transformational leadership and psychological well-being, a new definition of meaningful work appears. Meaningful work was defined as "finding a purpose in work that is greater than the extrinsic outcomes of the work" (Arnold et al., 2007, p. 195). Curiously, two different measures were assembled to assess meaningful work in the two studies they conducted with different samples. In only one of the studies did Arnold and colleagues use a measure that derived from their definition. In the study with funeral directors and dental hygienists, Arnold et al. developed four items to measure meaningful work: "The work I do in this job is fulfilling," "The work I do in this job is rewarding," "I do not achieve important outcomes from the work I do in this job" (reverse-scored), and "I am able to achieve important outcomes from the work I do in this job." Internal consistency of this measure in this sample was good ($\alpha = .84$).

Workplace Spirituality Scale

Arnold and colleagues (2007) used six items taken from a subscale of Ashmos and Duchon's (2000) Workplace Spirituality Scale (WSS). The original subscale used seven items to assess meaningful work as an important component of workplace spirituality. The WSS measures workplace spirituality at three different levels: (a) individual, (b) work unit, and (c) organizational. One of the subscales directed at individual-level workplace spirituality is labeled "meaning at work." The seven items were not driven using a particular definition of the construct but rather by a recognition that "employees want to be involved in work that gives meaning to their lives" (Ashmos & Duchon, 2000, p. 136). This conceptualization is vague, yet it subtly shifts the focus away from workplace activities to the overall contribution of work to the entirety of people's lives. In this sense, the WSS Meaning at Work subscale may come closer to capturing a positive psychological perspective of meaningful work than the other measures reviewed so far. Three of the items offer a perspective of meaningful work that resonates with Seligman's (2003) ideas about meaning consisting of connecting with endeavors larger than one's self. These items are: "The work I do is connected to what I think is important in life," "I see a connection between my work and the larger social good of my community," and "I understand what gives my work personal meaning." However, the remaining items appear fairly riddled with extraneous item content like joy ("I experience joy in my work"), energy ("My spirit is energized by my work"), and diffuse positive feelings about work ("I look forward to coming to work most days"). The final item seems to aim at measuring perceptions of one's work contributing to some good: "I believe others experience joy as a result of my work." The internal consistency of the WSS subscale was good in the original sample ($\alpha = .86$), and with the six-item version used by Arnold et al. ($\alpha = .84$; 2007).

Comprehensive Meaningful Work Scale

As a response to the increased use of ad hoc measures of meaningful work, Lips-Wiersma and Wright (2012) developed a dynamic multidimensional measure based on a theoretical framework of meaningful work that emerged from their qualitative data. The Comprehensive Meaningful Work Scale (CMWS) is a 28-item measure that consists of four content dimension subscales, including Developing the Inner Self ($\alpha = .72$), Unity with Others ($\alpha = .90$), Expressing Full Potential ($\alpha = .83$), and Serving Others ($\alpha = .83$), and three process dimension subscales, including Balancing Tensions ($\alpha = .85$), Reality ($\alpha = .79$), and Inspiration ($\alpha = .89$). All subscales and the total scale ($\alpha = .92$) showed high internal consistency and 2-month test–retest reliability ($\alpha = .80$). In relation to other existing constructs relevant to meaningful work, the authors found that the total scores on the CMWS were positively associated with constructs such as meaning in life, work engagement, intrinsic rewards, intrinsic motivation, and calling and negatively correlated with burnout and depression. These initial validation data appear to indicate the potential of this scale in measuring meaningful work. The unique strength of this measure is that it grasps the ongoing process of search for meaning in work and the dynamic interactions between various dimensions of meaningful work. However, it is unclear whether these dimensions represent a broad range of individuals' experience of meaningful work and thus requires further validation with diverse samples.

Work and Meaning Inventory

In an effort to provide a theoretically driven measure of meaningful work, Steger, Dik, and Duffy (2012) developed a brief measure that captures three primary dimensions that emerged in a literature review of meaningful work.

The Work and Meaning Inventory (WAMI), which is included in Appendix 24.1, uses subscales for Positive Meaning, Meaning-Making Through Work, and Greater Good Motivations to create a composite Meaningful Work score. Initial reliability (alphas from .82 to .89 for subscale scores and .93 for total scores), validity, and factor structure estimates are solid, and this may be a promising measure. In validating the WAMI, Steger and colleagues found that total and subscale scores correlated in expected directions with measures of well-being, job satisfaction, work motivation, withdrawal intentions, organizational commitment, and days absent from work. The Meaningful Work total score explained unique variance in job satisfaction, above and beyond withdrawal intentions, organizational commitment, and calling. This score also explained unique variance in number of days absent from work above and beyond job satisfaction, withdrawal intentions, organizational commitment, and calling. This latter result is particularly important because it shows that meaningful work is a better predictor of absenteeism than the widely used variable *job satisfaction*, cementing its key role in people's investment in their work. Initial research with an earlier version of the WAMI found that Meaningful Work scores were positively correlated with using one's strengths at work and with job satisfaction (Littman-Ovadia & Steger, 2010).

Summary

Several decades of research on meaningful work has yielded few advances beyond the initial efforts within the Job Characteristics Model (Hackman & Oldham, 1976), which stressed personal meaningfulness and importance. As measures gained items, they retained good reliability but began to subsume other constructs (including fulfillment, joy, optimism, and energy) on a seemingly ad hoc basis. Emerging efforts have begun to focus on developing more theoretically sound measures.

MEASURING CALLING

Efforts to measure calling emerged a couple of decades after efforts to measure meaningful work. However, these efforts have been more systematic overall.

University of Pennsylvania Work-Life Questionnaire

Wrzesniewski, McCauley, Rozin, and Schwartz (1997) were among the first researchers who attempted to measure calling. Although an earlier effort by Davidson and Caddell (1994) used a vignette approach to assess the construct, Wrzesniewski et al. appealed to theory by applying this strategy to well-known conceptual distinctions between perceptions of work as a job, career, or calling that had been proposed in a best-selling book by Bellah, Madsen, Sullivan, Swidler, and Tipton (1985). Specifically, they asked participants to read each of three paragraphs designed to capture these three work orientations and indicate how much they were like each description using a 4-point scale (3 = *very much,* 2 = *somewhat,* 1 = *a little,* 0 = *not at all like me*). Eighteen true–false items that were related to the three dimensions of job, career, and calling also were included to measure participants' behaviors and feelings related to work. Examples of items related to calling were: "I would choose my current work life again if I had the opportunity," "If I was financially secure, I would continue with my current line of work even if I was no longer paid," and "My work is one of the most important things in my life."

Vocation Identity Questionnaire

Dreher, Holloway, and Schoenfelder's (2007) Vocation Identity Questionnaire (VIQ) was developed to measure people's sense of calling. Dreher et al. used *vocation* interchangeably with *calling* and defined it as people's attitudes toward work such that "whether paid or unpaid, when work is a vocation, people use their time and talents in meaningful ways, finding fulfillment, building community, and making personal contributions to the world" (pp. 103–104). The VIQ consists of nine items with two factors of Intrinsic Motivation and Meaning (six items) and Joy and Satisfaction (three items) and uses a 5-point scale (1 = *strongly disagree,* 5 = *strongly agree*) to rate the responses. The internal consistency of the total scale was $\alpha = .84$, and those of the two subscales were $\alpha = .82$ and $\alpha = .59$, respectively.

The Calling Scale

The Calling Scale (CS; Dobrow & Tosti-Kharas, 2011) was designed to measure the degree to which participants perceive a "consuming, meaningful passion people experience toward a domain" (p. 1001). The instrument consists of 12 items, which use a 7-point response scale ranging from *strongly disagree* to *strongly agree.* Using four different samples of participants representing music, arts, business, and management domains, Dobrow and Tosti-Kharas found scores to have strong internal consistency reliability (alphas of .88–.94) and test–retest reliability (e.g., .90 at 1.5 months, .61 at 7 years). The items loaded on a single factor, resulting in a unidimensional scale. Construct validity was evident in positive correlations between CS scores and scores on measures of work engagement, job involvement, intrinsic and extrinsic motivation, religiosity, domain satisfaction, career-related self-efficacy, career insight, and professional association achievement.

Multidimensional Calling Measure

The Multidimensional Calling Measure (MCM; Hagmaier & Abele, 2012) was designed to measure the degree to which participants view their career as one that they strongly identify with, that contributes to a sense of meaning, and that is guided by a transcendent force. The instrument consists of nine items that use a 6-point scale ranging from *strongly disagree* to *strongly agree.*

Scores can be calculated for three subscales: Identification and Person–Environment Fit, Transcendent Guiding Force, and Sense of Meaning and Value-Driven Behavior. Development of the MCM began with a qualitative study that established core features of a calling, then used three other studies to quantify the core categories, examine the dimensionality of the items, and establish convergent and criterion-related validity evidence using German and U.S. samples. Scores on all three subscales correlate positively with job satisfaction, negatively with burnout, and positively with scores on the Brief Calling Scale (BCS).

Brief Calling Scale

Dik and Steger (2006) developed a brief scale measuring the presence of and search for calling. *Calling* was defined in the BCS instructions as "a person's belief that she or he is called upon to do a particular kind of work" (Dik, Eldridge, Steger, & Duffy, 2012). The BCS consists of four items with two subscales, Presence of Calling (two items) and Search for Calling (two items). The responses are rated on a 5-point scale ranging from 1 = *not at all true of me* to 5 = *totally true of me*. The correlation between the two items of BCS-Presence was reported by Duffy and Sedlacek (2007) as $r = .81$, and $r = .75$ for BCS-Search items; scores on the scale correlate in predicted directions and magnitudes with self-efficacy, outcome expectations, materialism, spirituality, and sense of calling assessed using the career development strivings strategy (Dik, Sargent, & Steger, 2008).

Calling and Vocation Questionnaire

Recognizing the need for a theoretically based and psychometrically sound measure of calling, Dik et al. (2012) developed the Calling and Vocation Questionnaire (CVQ), which is a multidimensional scale based on Dik and Duffy's (2009) definition of calling as

> a transcendent summons, experienced as originating beyond the self, to approach a particular life role in a manner oriented toward demonstrating or driving a sense of purpose or meaningfulness and that holds other-oriented values and goals as primary sources of motivation. (p. 427)

The scale comprises 24 items that uses a 4-point scale (1 = *not at all true of me*, 7 = *absolutely true of me*) to measure the presence of calling (CVQ-P) and search for calling (CVQ-S), as well as six subscales measuring "presence of" and "search for" each of the three dimensions in Dik and Duffy's (2009) definition: Transcendent Summons, Purposeful Work, and Prosocial Orientation. Initial validation results with college students show that CVQ subscale scores have a high internal consistency ranging from $\alpha = .85$ to $\alpha = .92$ and high 1-month test–retest reliability for CVQ-P ($r = .75$) and CVQ-S ($r = .67$). Construct and criterion-related validity evidence was supported in the scale development sample and by convergent and discriminant correlations in a multitrait-multimethod matrix study using self-report and informant-report scores (Dik et al., 2012).

Career Calling Scale

Praskova, Creed, and Hood (2015) developed a 15-item scale specifically for emerging adults (i.e., individuals 18–25 years of age). Conceptualizing calling as "a salient career goal that is personally meaningful and oriented toward helping others" (p. 91), their Career Calling Scale (CCS) contains three subscales, Other-Oriented Meaning, Personal Meaning, and Active Engagement. Items used a 6-point scale ranging from *strongly disagree* to *strongly agree*, and internal consistently reliabilities for the subscale scores were high (all above $\alpha = .80$). A confirmatory factor analysis supported the three-factor structure, and scores correlated in predicted directions with BCS scores and with general career indecision and life satisfaction.

Summary

Early calling measures gravitated toward a broad "personal meaningfulness" interpretation of calling. More recent efforts have focused on some components that are specific to classical and neoclassical views of calling that, however, include the sense that people were summoned or destined to fulfill a certain kind of work. Like one of the meaningful work scales (Work and Meaning Inventory), many calling scales also consider the capacity for work to contribute to some larger good. In the only study to directly compare the psychometric properties of multiple measures of calling, Duffy, Autin, Allan, and Douglass (2015) found that the CS, MCM, BCS, and CVQ were each reliable and had strong 3-month test–retest reliability in a sample of U.S. working adults. They found that the BCS and CVQ were the best predictors of responding "yes" to the question "Do you have a calling?" but that the CS and MCM were stronger predictors of work outcomes.

APPLICATIONS OF MEANINGFUL WORK MEASUREMENT

Most of the measures reviewed in this chapter were designed with research in mind. One implication of this is that they typically do not yield cut-off scores indicating that one person has "meaningless work" and the next "meaningful work." Measures of job satisfaction, especially, have been used in workplaces, usually to gain an idea of the current working climate of an organization. However, the best measures reviewed here hold untapped potential for application with individuals, as tools to help clients understand their work experience, track growth and decline in meaning and satisfaction over time and across jobs, and make tangible the impact of positive (and negative) work experiences on the rest of people's lives. Coaches working with workers, executives, leaders, managers, and entrepreneurs can use measures of meaningful work, calling, and job satisfaction to stimulate conversation about why their clients are working, and why they have been investing so much in their work, or perhaps divesting themselves from it. Clinicians working with people struggling with psychological distress can use these generally brief measures to explore with clients the carry-over from working life to personal life. Organizational consultants can use these measures to help their corporate clients gauge whether employees are resonating with their mission, culture, and social environment at work, particularly if the organizations are concerned with corporate social responsibility or serve multiple bottom lines. We use a brief case to exemplify one way to work with measures of meaningful work. It is a familiar situation of someone gaining more pay and responsibility but trading away at least some of what they loved about work.

Shawna had worked as a physical therapist (PT) in a clinic that was part of a large hospital. She was very well regarded by her coworkers and active in creating a warm, collegial, and effective work environment. Her positive impact on the clinic—and the excellent reputation the clinic had within the larger hospital organization—was noticed at the organizational level. Shawna was encouraged to apply for a manager-level job in which she would be responsible for the clinic and all of the physical therapists, occupational therapists, speech-language pathologists, and support staff working there. She pursued the job and was hired as the clinic manager. It meant greater pay, access, and influence within the organization. However, Shawna sought counseling, telling her therapist that she felt "stressed out," "empty," and "depressed." The stresses of her managerial role quickly became apparent in session. Initially, the pace and volume of work and personality clashes with other managers seemed to be sources of Shawna's misery. The therapist asked Shawna to fill out the WAMI. Her Meaningful Work total score was a depressing 13. She rated nearly every item a 1. The only exceptions were the three items on the Greater Good Motivations subscale. The therapist then asked Shawna to complete the WAMI for her previous position as a PT. Her total score was significantly higher, 44 out of 50, although her Greater Good Motivations subscale score was still the highest. The only item that was not rated a 4 or 5 was "I view my work as contributing to my personal growth," which was rated a 3. When Shawna was asked about this item, she said that she felt like things had become somewhat routine in her physical therapy work and that she wanted new challenges. When she was offered the management job, it seemed like a perfect way to grow. Further conversation helped Shawna conclude that she missed seeing a positive impact on people that she had achieved daily as a PT and that she missed doing what had resonated so deeply with her personal values of helping and being with people. Later sessions explored how Shawna could reconnect with meaningful work while identifying and engaging in new challenges. In Shawna's case, the conventional answer to positive work outcomes—promotions, responsibility, and pay raises—left meaningful work behind.

CONCLUSION

Depending on whether researchers and practitioners are interested in relatively simple feelings of satisfaction at work (in general or with respect to multiple facets) or more complex perceptions of personal meaning or a sense of calling, numerous measurement options are available. We believe that all three of these constructs capture different elements of the work experience, although they probably overlap considerably on an empirical basis. In particular, we point to the distinction between meaningful work—perceptions of personal significance, understanding, and impact at work—and calling—meaningful work toward which one feels summoned or destined and which benefits a greater good. The terms often are used interchangeably, without consideration of their differing theoretical and conceptual histories and articulations.

APPENDIX 24.1
THE WORK AND MEANING INVENTORY (WAMI)

Please indicate how well the following statements apply to you and your work and/or career. Please try to answer as truthfully as you can.

	Absolutely untrue		Neither true nor untrue/can't say		Absolutely true
1. I have found a meaningful career.	1	2	3	4	5
2. I view my work as contributing to my personal growth.	1	2	3	4	5
3. My work really makes no difference in the world.	1	2	3	4	5
4. I understand how my work contributes to my life's meaning.	1	2	3	4	5
5. I have a good sense of what makes my job meaningful.	1	2	3	4	5
6. I know my work makes a positive difference in the world.	1	2	3	4	5
7. My work helps me better understand myself.	1	2	3	4	5
8. I have discovered work that has a satisfying purpose.	1	2	3	4	5
9. My work helps me make sense of the world around me.	1	2	3	4	5
10. The work I do serves a greater purpose.	1	2	3	4	5

Scoring the WAMI: Responses for Items 1, 4, 5, and 8 can be summed for the Positive Meaning subscale score. Responses for Items 2, 7, and 9 can be summed for the Meaning-Making Through Work subscale score. Item 3 is a reverse-scored item. Responses for Item 3 can be subtracted from 6, then added to responses for Items 6 and 10 for the Greater Good Motivations subscale score. The scores from the Positive Meaning, Meaning-Making Through Work, and Greater Good Motivations subscales can be summed for the Meaningful Work total score.

REFERENCES

Arnold, K. A., Turner, N., Barling, J., Kelloway, E. K., & McKee, M. C. (2007). Transformational leadership and psychological well-being: The mediating role of meaningful work. *Journal of Occupational Health Psychology, 12,* 193–203. http://dx.doi.org/10.1037/1076-8998.12.3.193

Ashmos, D. P., & Duchon, D. (2000). Spirituality at work: A conceptualization and measure. *Journal of Management Inquiry, 9,* 134–145. http://dx.doi.org/10.1177/105649260092008

Baumeister, R. F. (1991). *Meanings in life.* New York, NY: Guildford Press.

Bellah, R. N., Madsen, R., Sullivan, W. M., Swidler, A., & Tipton, S. M. (1985). *Habits of the heart.* Berkeley: University of California Press.

Britt, T. W., Dickinson, J. M., Moore, D., Castro, C. A., & Adler, A. B. (2007). Correlates and consequences of morale versus depression under stressful conditions. *Journal of Occupational Health Psychology, 12,* 34–47. http://dx.doi.org/10.1037/1076-8998.12.1.34

Bunderson, J. S., & Thompson, J. A. (2009). The call of the wild: Zookeepers, callings, and the double-edged sword of deeply meaningful work. *Administrative Science Quarterly, 54,* 32–57. http://dx.doi.org/10.2189/asqu.2009.54.1.32

Chen, P. Y., & Spector, P. E. (1991). Negative affectivity as the underlying cause of correlations between stressors and strains. *Journal of Applied Psychology, 76,* 398–407. http://dx.doi.org/10.1037/0021-9010.76.3.398

Davidson, J. C., & Caddell, D. P. (1994). Religion and the meaning of work. *Journal for the Scientific Study of Religion, 33,* 135–147. http://dx.doi.org/10.2307/1386600

Dawis, R. V., Pinto, P. P., Weitzel, W., & Nezzer, M. (1974). Describing organizations as reinforcer systems: A new use for job satisfaction and employee attitude surveys. *Journal of Vocational Behavior, 4,* 55–66. http://dx.doi.org/10.1016/0001-8791(74)90092-X

Diener, E., & Biswas-Diener, R. (2008). *The science of optimal happiness.* Boston, MA: Blackwell. http://dx.doi.org/10.1002/9781444305159

Dik, B. J., & Duffy, R. D. (2009). Calling and vocation at work: Definitions and prospects for research and practice. *The Counseling Psychologist, 37,* 424–450. http://dx.doi.org/10.1177/0011000008316430

Dik, B. J., Eldridge, B. M., Steger, M. F., & Duffy, R. D. (2012). Development and validation of the Calling and Vocation Questionnaire (CVQ) and Brief Calling Scale (BCS). *Journal of Career Assessment, 20,* 242–263. http://dx.doi.org/10.1177/1069072711434410

Dik, B. J., Sargent, A. M., & Steger, M. F. (2008). Career development strivings: Assessing goals and motivation in career decision-making and planning. *Journal of Career Development, 35,* 23–41. http://dx.doi.org/10.1177/0894845308317934

Dik, B. J., & Steger, M. F. (2006, July). *Work as a calling: Randomized trial of a calling-based career development workshop.* Paper presented at the National Career Development Association Global Conference, Chicago, IL.

Dobrow, S. R., & Tosti-Kharas, J. (2011). Calling: The development of a scale measure. *Personnel Psychology, 64,* 1001–1049. http://dx.doi.org/10.1111/j.1744-6570.2011.01234.x

Dreher, D. E., Holloway, K. A., & Schoenfelder, E. (2007). The Vocation Identity Questionnaire: Measuring the sense of calling. *Research in the Social Scientific Study of Religion, 18,* 99–120. http://dx.doi.org/10.1163/ej.9789004158511.i-301.42

Duffy, R. D., Autin, K. L., Allan, B. A., & Douglass, R. P. (2015). Assessing work as a calling: An evaluation of instruments and practice recommendations. *Journal of Career Assessment, 23,* 351–366. http://dx.doi.org/10.1177/1069072714547163

Duffy, R. D., & Sedlacek, W. E. (2007). The presence of and search for a calling: Connections to career development. *Journal of Vocational Behavior, 70,* 590–601. http://dx.doi.org/10.1016/j.jvb.2007.03.007

Dunham, R. B., Smith, F. J., & Blackburn, R. S. (1977). Validation of the Index of Organizational Reactions with the JDI, the MSQ, and Faces Scales. *Academy of Management Journal, 20,* 420–432.

Fisher, C. D. (2000). Mood and emotions while working: Missing pieces of job satisfaction? *Journal of Organizational Behavior, 21,* 185–202. http://dx.doi.org/10.1002/(SICI)1099-1379(200003)21:2<185::AID-JOB34>3.0.CO;2-M

Fried, Y., & Ferris, G. R. (1987). The validity of the job characteristics model: A review and meta-analysis. *Personnel Psychology, 40,* 287–322. http://dx.doi.org/10.1111/j.1744-6570.1987.tb00605.x

Fritzsche, B. A., & Parrish, T. J. (2005). Theories and research on job satisfaction. In R. Brown & R. Lent (Eds.), *Career development and counseling: Putting theory and research to work* (pp. 180–202). Hoboken, NJ: Wiley.

Hackman, J. R., & Oldham, G. R. (1975). Development of the Job Diagnostic Survey. *Journal of Applied Psychology, 60,* 159–170. http://dx.doi.org/10.1037/h0076546

Hackman, J. R., & Oldham, G. R. (1976). Motivation through the design of work: Test of a theory. *Organizational Behavior & Human Performance, 16,* 250–279. http://dx.doi.org/10.1016/0030-5073(76)90016-7

Hackman, J. R., & Oldham, G. R. (1980). *Work redesign.* Reading, MA: Addison-Wesley.

Hagmaier, T., & Abele, A. E. (2012). The multidimensionality of calling: Conceptualization, measurement and a bicultural perspective. *Journal of Vocational Behavior, 81,* 39–51. http://dx.doi.org/10.1016/j.jvb.2012.04.001

Hall, D., & Chandler, D. (2005). Psychological success: When the career is a calling. *Journal of Organizational Behavior, 26,* 155–176. http://dx.doi.org/10.1002/job.301

Highhouse, S., & Becker, A. S. (1993). Facet measures and global job satisfaction. *Journal of Business and Psychology, 8,* 117–127. http://dx.doi.org/10.1007/BF02230397

Ironson, G. H., Smith, P. C., Brannick, M. T., Gibson, W. M., & Paul, K. B. (1989). Construction of a Job in General scale A comparison of global, composite, and specific measures. *Journal of Applied Psychology, 74,* 193–200. http://dx.doi.org/10.1037/0021-9010.74.2.193

Kinicki, A. J., Mckee-Ryan, F. M., Schriesheim, C. A., & Carson, K. P. (2002). Assessing the construct validity of the Job Descriptive Index: A review and meta-analysis. *Journal of Applied Psychology, 87,* 14–32. http://dx.doi.org/10.1037/0021-9010.87.1.14

Lent, R. W., & Brown, S. D. (2006). Integrating person and situation perspectives on work satisfaction: A social-cognitive view. *Journal of Vocational Behavior, 69,* 236–247. http://dx.doi.org/10.1016/j.jvb.2006.02.006

Lips-Wiersma, M., & Wright, S. (2012). Measuring the meaning of meaningful work: Development and validation of the Comprehensive Meaningful Work Scale (CMWS). *Group & Organization Management, 37,* 655–685. http://dx.doi.org/10.1177/1059601112461578

Littman-Ovadia, H., & Steger, M. F. (2010). Character strengths and well-being among volunteers and employees: Towards an integrative model. *The Journal of Positive Psychology, 5,* 419–430. http://dx.doi.org/10.1080/17439760.2010.516765

Lyubomirsky, S. (2006). Is it possible to become lastingly happier? Lessons from the modern science of well-being. *Vancouver Dialogues* (pp. 53–56). Vancouver, British Columbia, Canada: Truffle Tree.

May, D. R., Gilson, R. L., & Harter, L. M. (2004). The psychological conditions of meaningfulness, safety and availability and the engagement of the human spirit at work. *Journal of Occupational and Organizational Psychology, 77,* 11–37. http://dx.doi.org/10.1348/096317904322915892

Piccolo, R. F., & Colquitt, J. A. (2006). Transformational leadership and job behaviors: The mediating role of core job characteristics. *Academy of Management Journal, 49,* 327–340. http://dx.doi.org/10.5465/amj.2006.20786079

Praskova, A., Creed, P. A., & Hood, M. (2015). The development and initial validation of a Career Calling Scale for emerging adults. *Journal of Career Assessment, 23,* 91–106. http://dx.doi.org/10.1177/1069072714523089

Quinn, R. P., & Staines, G. L. (1979). *The 1977 Quality of Employment Survey.* Ann Arbor, MI: Institute for Social Research.

Rosso, B. D., Dekas, K. H., & Wrzesniewski, A. (2010). On the meaning of work: A theoretical integration and review. *Research in Organizational Behavior, 30,* 91–127. http://dx.doi.org/10.1016/j.riob.2010.09.001

Scarpello, V., & Campbell, J. P. (1983). Job satisfaction: Are all the parts there? *Personnel Psychology, 36,* 577–600. http://dx.doi.org/10.1111/j.1744-6570.1983.tb02236.x

Seligman, M. P. (2003). Positive psychology: Fundamental assumptions. *The Psychologist, 16*(3), 126–127.

Smith, P. C., Kendall, L. M., & Hulin, C. L. (1969). *The measurement of satisfaction in work and retirement.* Chicago, IL: Rand McNally.

Spector, P. E. (1985). Measurement of human service staff satisfaction: Development of the Job Satisfaction Survey. *American Journal of Community Psychology, 13,* 693–713. http://dx.doi.org/10.1007/BF00929796

Spector, P. E. (1997). *Job satisfaction: Application, assessment, causes, and consequences* (Vol. 3). Thousand Oaks, CA: Sage.

Spreitzer, G. M. (1995). Psychological empowerment in the workplace: Dimensions, measurement, and validation. *Academy of Management Journal, 38,* 1442–1465.

Steger, M. F., & Dik, B. J. (2009). If one is looking for meaning in life, does it help to find meaning in work? *Applied Psychology: Health and Well-Being, 1,* 303–320. http://dx.doi.org/10.1111/j.1758-0854.2009.01018.x

Steger, M. F., Dik, B. J., & Duffy, R. D. (2012). Measuring meaningful work: The Work and Meaning Inventory (WAMI). *Journal of Career Assessment, 20,* 322–337. http://dx.doi.org/10.1177/1069072711436160

Tymon, W. G., Jr. (1988). *An empirical investigation of a cognitive model of empowerment* (Unpublished doctoral dissertation). Temple University, Philadelphia, PA.

Wanous, J. P., Reichers, A. E., & Hudy, M. J. (1997). Overall job satisfaction: How good are single-item measures? *Journal of Applied Psychology, 82,* 247–252. http://dx.doi.org/10.1037/0021-9010.82.2.247

Weiss, D. J., Dawis, R. V., England, G. W., & Lofquist, L. H. (1967). *Manual for the Minnesota Satisfaction Questionnaire.* Minnesota Studies in Vocational Rehabilitation (Vol. 22). Minneapolis: University of Minnesota, Industrial Relations Center.

Wrzesniewski, A., McCauley, C., Rozin, P., & Schwartz, B. (1997). Jobs, careers, and callings: People's relations to their work. *Journal of Research in Personality, 31,* 21–33. http://dx.doi.org/10.1006/jrpe.1997.2162

25

Defining, Measuring, and Applying Subjective Well-Being

Jeana L. Magyar and Corey L. M. Keyes

Social scientists have been researching well-being since the mid-1900s. This research, aimed at tapping into how individuals perceive their existence, has resulted in a multitude of ways to define and measure well-being. For quite some time, however, health and well-being had been equated to the absence of disease, disorder, or problems. Contemporary research suggests that well-being is not simply the absence of malfunction; rather, well-being consists of the presence of assets, strengths, and other positive attributes (Frisch, 2000; Keyes, 1998).

Although there is still some debate in the field, the two most common lines of well-being research have focused on well-being as the presence of something positive versus the absence of something negative and have included defining well-being in terms of positive feelings or in terms of positive functioning. More specifically, well-being that is defined by the degree of positive feelings (e.g., happiness) experienced and by one's perceptions of his or her life overall (e.g., satisfaction) constitute the first line of research on *hedonic well-being* and is referred to as *emotional well-being* (Diener, Suh, Lucas, & Smith, 1999; Gurin, Veroff, & Feld, 1960). The second stream of well-being research is based on *eudaimonic well-being* and includes dimensions of *positive functioning*, which are experienced when one realizes his or her human potential in terms of psychological well-being (e.g., autonomy and personal growth; Jahoda, 1958; Keyes, 1998; Ryff, 1989b; Ryff & Keyes, 1995) and social well-being (e.g., social integration and social contribution; Keyes, 1998). Essentially, those who

http://dx.doi.org/10.1037/0000138-025
Positive Psychological Assessment: A Handbook of Models and Measures, Second Edition,
M. W. Gallagher and S. J. Lopez (Editors)

are high in terms of emotional well-being feel good about life, whereas those high in psychological and social well-being function well in life.

Subjective well-being consists of a combination of these two broad lines of research on positive emotions and positive functioning (e.g., Ryan & Deci, 2001; Waterman, 1993). Hence, those who are high in subjective well-being report both feeling good and functioning well. The components of subjective well-being are further elucidated in the following sections, and information regarding ways to measure well-being and how to use information regarding well-being for client conceptualization and treatment planning purposes are provided. Additional applications of subjective well-being are explored.

POSITIVE EMOTIONS (AKA EMOTIONAL WELL-BEING)

Emotional well-being consists of one's perceptions of declared happiness and satisfaction with life and the ratio of positive to negative affect experienced (Bryant & Veroff, 1982; Lucas, Diener, & Suh, 1996; Shmotkin, 1998). Emotional well-being differs from happiness in that *happiness* is based on spontaneous reflections of pleasant and unpleasant feelings in one's immediate experience, whereas emotional well-being adds the life satisfaction component, which represents a long-term assessment of one's life (Keyes & Magyar-Moe, 2003).

The threefold structure of emotional well-being that consists of life satisfaction, the presence of positive affect, and the absence of negative affect has been confirmed in numerous studies (e.g., Bryant & Veroff, 1982; Lucas et al., 1996; Shmotkin, 1998). A debate over the structure of positive and negative affect, however, continues to this day and creates some confusion around the emotional well-being construct (for several scholarly debates on this topic, see Barrett, 2017; Green & Salovey, 1999; Russell & Carroll, 1999; Tellegen, Watson, & Clark, 1999a, 1999b; Watson & Tellegen, 1999). More specifically, the debate is over whether positive and negative affect are on opposite ends of a single continuum (i.e., highly negatively correlated) or whether these feelings are relatively independent and therefore better understood as existing on their own separate continua (i.e., modestly negatively correlated). Evidence has supported both the unidimensional (Barrett, 2017; Feldman Barrett & Russell, 1998; Russell & Carroll, 1999) and bidimensional (Diener & Emmons, 1984) models. Nevertheless, the coupling of satisfaction and affect serves as a meaningful and measurable conceptualization of well-being.

A variety of brief measures of emotional well-being are available, including single-item measures of life satisfaction that use Cantril's (1965) Self-Anchoring Scale. These single-item measures require respondents to "rate their life overall these days" on a scale ranging from 0 *(the worst possible life overall)* to 10 *(the best possible life overall)*. Variants of Cantril's (1965) measure have been used extensively and applied to the measurement of avowed happiness with life (Andrews & Withey, 1976). Multi-item scales of life satisfaction and happiness also have been developed and are used extensively (for a list of measures of positive affect and emotional well-being, see Diener, 1984, p. 546, and Chapter 12, this volume).

Most measures of positive and negative affect tap the frequency with which a respondent reports experiencing the symptoms of these affects. For example, using the scale "all," "most," "some," "a little," or "none of the time," individuals often are asked to indicate how much of the time during the past 30 days they have felt six types of negative and six types of positive indicators of affect. Symptoms of negative affect usually include feeling (a) so sad nothing could cheer you up, (b) nervous, (c) restless or fidgety, (d) hopeless, (e) that everything was an effort, and (f) worthless. Symptoms of positive affect usually involve feeling (a) cheerful, (b) in good spirits, (c) extremely happy, (d) calm and peaceful, (e) satisfied, and (f) full of life (Keyes, 1998; Mroczek & Kolarz, 1998.)

Estimates of internal reliability of the multi-item scales of life satisfaction (Diener, 1994; Diener, Emmons, Larsen, & Griffin, 1985; Pavot & Diener, 1993) and positive and negative affect (e.g., Mroczek & Kolarz, 1998) usually exceed .80; single-item indicators of well-being are less reliable. In addition, researchers have found that social desirability is not a major confound in the well-being literature and that ratings of life satisfaction tend to be more stable than reports of positive and negative affect (Diener, 1984; Larsen, Diener, & Emmons, 1985).

POSITIVE FUNCTIONING (AKA PSYCHOLOGICAL AND SOCIAL WELL-BEING)

Positive functioning consists of the multidimensional constructs of psychological well-being and social well-being (Keyes, 1998; Ryff, 1989a). Like emotional well-being, the focus of psychological well-being remains at the individual level, whereas relations with others and the environment are the primary foci of social well-being. Ryff's (1989a) model of psychological well-being and Keyes's (1998) model of social well-being are delineated in the following subsections.

Psychological Well-Being

Elements of psychological well-being are descended from the Aristotelian theme of *eudaimonia*, which suggests that the highest of all goods achievable by human action is happiness derived from lifelong conduct aimed at self-development (Waterman, 1993). Thus, many aspects of psychological well-being are subsumed in such concepts as self-actualization (Maslow, 1968), full functioning (Rogers, 1961), individuation (Jung, 1933; Von Franz, 1964), maturity (Allport, 1961), and successful resolution of adult developmental stages and tasks (Erikson, 1959; Neugarten, 1973).

The variety of concepts from personality, developmental, and clinical psychology that have been synthesized as criteria for psychological well-being (Ryff, 1989a) also have been defined as criteria of mental health (Jahoda, 1958).

More specifically, Ryff's (1989a) six-dimensional model of psychological well-being encompasses a breadth of wellness areas inclusive of positive evaluations of oneself and one's past life, a sense of continued growth and development as a person, the belief that one's life is purposeful and meaningful, the experience of quality relations with others, the capacity to manage effectively one's life and surrounding world, and a sense of self-determination (Ryff & Keyes, 1995). (See Table 25.1 for detailed definitions of the distinct wellness dimensions of Ryff's [1989a] psychological well-being model.) Each of the six dimensions of psychological well-being includes challenges that individuals encounter as they strive to function fully and realize their unique talents (see Keyes & Ryff, 1999; Ryff, 1989a, 1989b; Ryff & Keyes, 1995).

Social Well-Being

Information regarding social wellness originates from sociological research on anomie and alienation that indicates a host of problems that can arise when there is a breakdown of social norms and values within a society (Mirowsky & Ross, 1989; Seeman, 1959). Within this scholarship, issues related to the creation and disillusionment of human solidarity and on social regulation and order are explored. Drawing on these theoretical roots, Keyes (1998) developed a multidimensional model of social well-being inclusive of social integration, social contributions, social coherence, social actualization, and social acceptance. Each of these five dimensions of social well-being, defined in Table 25.1, includes challenges that people face as social beings. These dimensions provide information about whether and to what degree individuals are functioning well in their social world (e.g., as neighbors, as coworkers, as citizens; Keyes, 1998; Keyes & Shapiro, 2004).

Whereas psychological well-being is conceptualized as a primarily private phenomenon that focuses on the challenges encountered by adults in their private lives, social well-being represents a primarily public phenomenon that focuses on the social tasks encountered by adults in their social structures and communities (Keyes & Magyar-Moe, 2003).

MEASUREMENT OF SUBJECTIVE WELL-BEING IN ADULTS

Taken together, emotional well-being and positive functioning converge to create a comprehensive model of subjective well-being that takes into consideration multiple aspects of both the individual and his or her functioning in society. In total, subjective well-being includes elements of perceived happiness and life satisfaction, the ratio of positive to negative affects, psychological well-being, and social well-being.

The Mental Health Continuum—Long Form (MHC–LF; Keyes, 2002, 2005b) is a 35-item measure of the three components of subjective well-being. The measure and scoring information can be found in Appendix 25.1. All 35 items are summed together to produce a total well-being score ranging

TABLE 25.1. Dimensions of Psychological and Social Well-Being

Dimensions of Ryff's (1989a) psychological well-being model	Dimensions of Keyes's (1998) social well-being model
Self-acceptance is the criterion toward which adults must strive to feel good about themselves. Such self-acceptance is characterized by a positive attitude toward the self and acknowledging and accepting multiple aspects of self, including unpleasant personal aspects. In addition, self-acceptance includes positive feelings about past life.	*Social integration* is the evaluation of the quality of one's relationship to society and community. Integration is therefore the extent to which people feel they have something in common with others who constitute their social reality (e.g., their neighborhood) as well as the degree to which they feel that they belong to their communities and society.
Positive relations with others consist of the ability to cultivate the presence of warm, trusting, and intimate relationships with others. Concern for the welfare of others and the ability to empathize, cooperate, and compromise are aspects of this wellness dimension.	*Social contribution* is the evaluation of one's value to society. It includes the belief that one is a vital member of society with something of value to give to the world.
Autonomy reflects the seeking of self-determination and personal authority or independence in a society that sometimes compels obedience and compliance. The abilities to resist social pressures so as to think or behave in certain ways and to guide and evaluate behavior based on internalized standards and values are crucial in this domain.	*Social coherence* is the perception of the quality, organization, and operation of the social world, social coherence includes a concern for knowing about the world. Social coherence is analogous to meaningfulness in life (Mirowsky & Ross 1989; Seeman 1959, 1991) and involves appraisals that society is discernable, sensible, and predictable.
Environmental mastery includes the ability to manage everyday affairs, control a complex array of external activities, make effective use of surrounding opportunities, and choose or create contexts suitable to personal needs. A sense of mastery results when individuals recognize personal needs and desires, and also feel capable of and permitted to take an active role in getting what they need from their environments.	*Social actualization* is the evaluation of the potential and trajectory of society. This is the belief in the evolution of society and the sense that society has potential that is being realized through its institutions and citizens.
Purpose in life consists of one's aims and objectives for living, including the presence of life goals and a sense of directedness. Those with high purpose in life see their daily lives as fulfilling a direction and purpose, and therefore view their present and past life as meaningful.	*Social acceptance* is the construal of society through the character and qualities of other people as a generalized category. Individuals must function in a public arena that consists primarily of strangers. Individuals who illustrate social acceptance trust others, think that others are capable of kindness, and believe that people can be industrious. Socially accepting people hold favorable views of human nature and feel comfortable with others.
Personal growth reflects the continuous pursuit of existing skills, talents, and opportunities for personal development and for realizing one's potential. In addition, personal growth includes the capacity to remain open to experience and to identify challenges in a variety of circumstances.	

Note. Data from Ryff (1989a) and Keyes (1998).

from 39 to 271; higher scores indicate higher levels of well-being. The overall emotional well-being subscale consists of two items, and scores range from 6 to 40; the overall psychological well-being subscale consists of 18 items, and scores range from 18 to 126; and the overall social well-being subscale consists of 15 items, and scores range from 15 to 105. As with the total score, higher scores on the subscales also represent higher well-being levels.

The scales of psychological well-being and social well-being in the MHC–LF are the reduced three-item scales (see Ryff [1989b] for the full 20-item scales of psychological well-being and Keyes [1998] for the full 10-item scales of social well-being) for use in large studies that often include an extensive assessment schedule (Ryff & Keyes, 1995). Indeed, the MHC–LF grew out of the 1995 MacArthur Foundation's National Study of Successful Midlife Development in the United States (MIDUS; for details regarding the exemplary MIDUS study, which was the first national study to measure all facets of subjective well-being, see Keyes, 1998, and Mroczek & Kolarz, 1998).

The reduced-item scales of psychological and social well-being possess moderate internal reliabilities that range from 0.40 to 0.70. When the scales are summed to form scales of overall psychological well-being and overall social well-being, the internal reliabilities are very good at 0.80 or higher (Keyes & Ryff, 1998). The scales of social well-being correlated approximately −0.30 with a measure of dysphoric symptoms (Keyes, 1998). Keyes and Lopez (2002) also reported an average correlation (−0.50) between the scales of psychological well-being and standard measures of depression (i.e., the Center for Epidemiologic Studies–Depressed Mood Scale [CES-D; Radloff, 1977] and the Self-Rating Depression Scale [Zung, 1965]). Measures of life satisfaction and quality of life correlated, on average, around −0.40 with these depression scales. Confirmatory factor analyses of the CES-D subscales and the psychological well-being scales in the United States (as well as South Korea) have shown that a two-factor model consisting of a mental illness and a mental health latent factor provided the best fit to the data (Keyes & Ryff, 2003; see also Keyes, 2005b). In that same study, the overall CES-D and psychological well-being scales were negatively correlated (−0.68) in the United States.

Several studies using community and nationally representative samples have supported the theories of the factor structure of social and psychological well-being. Confirmatory factor models have revealed that the proposed five-factor conceptualization of social well-being is the best-fitting model (Keyes, 1998), and the proposed six-factor theory of psychological well-being is the best fitting model (Ryff & Keyes, 1995). Moreover, elements of positive functioning (i.e., social and psychological well-being) are empirically distinct. The scales of social and psychological well-being correlated as high as 0.44, and exploratory factor analysis revealed two correlated ($r = 0.34$) factors with the scales of social well-being loading on a separate factor from the items measuring happiness, satisfaction, and the overall scale of psychological well-being (Keyes, 1996).

Measures of social well-being also are factorially distinct from traditional measures of emotional well-being (Keyes, 1996). In addition, measures of emotional well-being (i.e., positive and negative affect, life satisfaction) are factorially distinct from measures of psychological well-being (Keyes, Shmotkin, & Ryff, 2002). McGregor and Little's (1998) factor analysis yielded two distinct factors that revealed an underlying emotional factor (including depression, positive affect, and life satisfaction) and an underlying psychological functioning factor (including four of the psychological well-being scales: personal growth, purpose in life, positive relations with others, and autonomy).

Keyes (2005b) also developed the Mental Health Continuum—Short Form (MHC–SF). As elucidated in Appendix 25.2, this measure contains 14 items, three of which tap into emotional well-being, five of which measure social well-being, and six of which assess psychological well-being. In a study of more than 1,000 Setswana-speaking adults in the North West province of South Africa, Keyes et al. (2008) found that the three-factor structure of emotional, psychological, and social well-being found in U.S. samples using the MHC–LF was replicated using the MHC–SF. The internal reliability of the overall MHC–SF scale was 0.74. The total score on the MHC–SF correlated 0.52 with the Affectometer Positive Affect Scale (Kammann & Flett, 1983), 0.39 with the Generalized Self-Efficacy Scale (Schwarzer & Jerusalem, 1993), 0.37 with the Satisfaction With Life Scale (Diener et al., 1985), 0.34 with the N-Cope Coping Strategies Scale (Van der Walt, 2007), 0.32 with the Sense of Coherence Scale (Antonovsky, 1987), and 0.30 with the Community Collective Efficacy Scale (Carroll, Rosson, & Zhou, 2005). Confirmatory factor analysis supported the hypothesized two-continua model of mental health and mental illness found in the United States.

MEASUREMENT OF SUBJECTIVE WELL-BEING IN YOUTHS

Most of the available research on subjective well-being has been conducted using adult populations. The majority of well-being research with youth populations is limited to the assessment of emotional well-being or positive feelings. Keyes (2006) began to explore the measurement of well-being in youths to determine if the three-factor model of adult subjective well-being applies to youth populations.

Keyes (2006) administered a 12-item measure of subjective well-being (see Appendix 25.3), adapted from the MHC–LF, to a nationally representative sample of almost 3,000 youths between the ages of 12 and 18 years. Results indicated that subjective well-being in youths can be characterized in terms of distinct dimensions of emotional, psychological, and social well-being. The youth subjective well-being measures exhibited construct validity, correlating highly with the Global Self-Concept Scale (0.44–0.54; Marsh, 1990); a scale of self-determination (0.35–0.46, Keyes, 2006); and a school integration scale (0.37–0.42, Keyes, 2006). The youth subjective well-being measures also correlated modestly (−0.23 to −0.33) with the Children's Depression Inventory (Kovacs, 1992) and a measure of self-rated overall health (0.25–0.27), and weakly with perceived math and reading skills (Keyes, 2006).

Findings from this research also revealed that within youth samples, levels of emotional well-being were highest, followed by psychological well-being, and then social well-being (Keyes, 2006). In general, the youths reported that they experienced social well-being about once a week during the past month. In other words, about once a week, America's youths felt that they had something to contribute to the world, felt liked they belonged, and felt that society made sense, that society was becoming a better place, and that people in society were basically good. In contrast, youths reported that they experienced psychological well-being (i.e., management of responsibilities, trusting relationships with other youths, growth-producing experiences, and confidence to express ideas) about two or three times a week during the past month (Keyes, 2006).

UTILITY AND APPLICATIONS OF SUBJECTIVE WELL-BEING

Since Aristotle, well-being—particularly happiness—has been deemed a summum bonum of life. As one of life's highest goods, well-being is an end rather than a means in life because its consummation could quench desire and motivation. and its accomplishment could render individuals complacent and unproductive. From this perspective, the utility of well-being is that it is the proverbial carrot at the end of life's stick that maintains individuals' motivations to be productive and ethical citizens. Alternatively, well-being may be conceptualized as a means rather than solely an end in life. If the objective of life is the process of living a healthy and productive life, then well-being may unleash human potential in terms of creativity, productivity, and community involvement (Keyes & Magyar-Moe, 2003).

Social scientific evidence has suggested that well-being is a means to a better, more productive, and mentally healthy life. The elements of subjective well-being may contribute to quality-adjusted life years. Indeed, in the global burden of disease study, Murray and Lopez (1996) found that unipolar depression ranked second only to ischemic heart disease as the most potent cause of reduced healthy years of life for adults of all ages. Furthermore, unipolar depression was the leading cause of disability life years among adults under the age of 44 in developed and developing countries. Depression reduces productivity in society, amounting to billions in costs through health care and employment absence (Keyes & Lopez, 2002). Moreover, mood disorders are associated with nearly a third of all suicides (Rebellon, Brown, & Keyes, 2000; U.S. Department of Health and Human Services, 1998). These findings suggest that increasing subjective well-being may serve to offset or decrease symptoms of mental illness and to potentially buffer individuals from such problems in the first the place. Indeed, increased social well-being, as defined by high levels of relationship satisfaction in couples, has been shown to buffer against adverse psychological effects of 12 key life stressors, such as unemployment, financial strain, physical health problems, and pregnancy (Røsand, Slinning, Eberhard-Gran, Røysamb, & Tambs, 2012). Takebayashi, Tanaka, Sugiura, and Sugiura (2017) found that the purpose in life and autonomy dimensions of psychological well-being buffer the negative effects of fear of anxiety and negative beliefs about worry on increased generalized anxiety in young adults. They concluded that interventions focused on enhancing these dimensions of psychological well-being may be effective in preventing generalized anxiety disorders.

The role of subjective well-being in relation to mental health status, client conceptualization, treatment planning, and therapy outcomes as well as physical health status and outcomes, and workplace functioning and outcomes are briefly reviewed in the following sections.

Mental Health

Although there are many potential applications of information regarding subjective well-being within counseling and psychotherapy, the role of subjective well-being may be most prominent when it comes to client conceptualization and treatment planning. For many years, mental health had been equated with the absence of mental illness; however, more recently, scholars and practitioners are realizing that the absence of mental illness does not necessarily result in the presence of mental health. As a result, the complete state model of mental health (Keyes & Lopez, 2002) was developed; it defines mental health and mental illness as existing on two separate continuums. As such, clients must be assessed and understood according to the degree of symptoms of mental illness they are experiencing (high to low) as well as the degree of symptoms of well-being they are experiencing (high to low).

When combining these continua of symptoms of mental illness and symptoms of subjective well-being together, a client can be conceptualized as (a) completely mentally healthy or flourishing (low symptoms of mental illness and high symptoms of well-being), (b) completely mentally ill or floundering (high symptoms of mental illness and low symptoms of well-being), (c) incompletely mentally healthy or languishing (low symptoms of mental illness and low symptoms of well-being), or (d) incompletely mentally ill or struggling (high symptoms of mental illness and high symptoms of well-being; Keyes & Lopez, 2002).

Based on the complete state model, therapists are able to see for themselves as well as share with their clients where each client falls and to discuss with the client his or her therapy outcome goals. For example, a client who is floundering may have come to therapy simply hoping to decrease his or her symptoms of mental illness thereby leading to a label of languishing. However, when he or she is able to see that there is more to life than just being free of symptoms of pathology, the client's goal may become twofold, namely, to not only decrease symptoms of mental illness but to also purposefully increase symptoms of well-being, ultimately leading him or her to the flourishing category (Magyar-Moe, 2009; Magyar-Moe, Owens, & Conoley, 2015, Magyar-Moe, Owens, & Scheel, 2015; Owens, Magyar-Moe, & Lopez, 2015).

The connection between the complete state model of mental health and optimal therapy outcomes is illustrated in Figure 25.1. Whereas many therapists and clients consider therapy to be successful when clients have reached a baseline level of functioning, the complete state model of mental health (Keyes

FIGURE 25.1. The Connection Between the Complete State Model of Mental Health and Optimal Therapy Outcomes

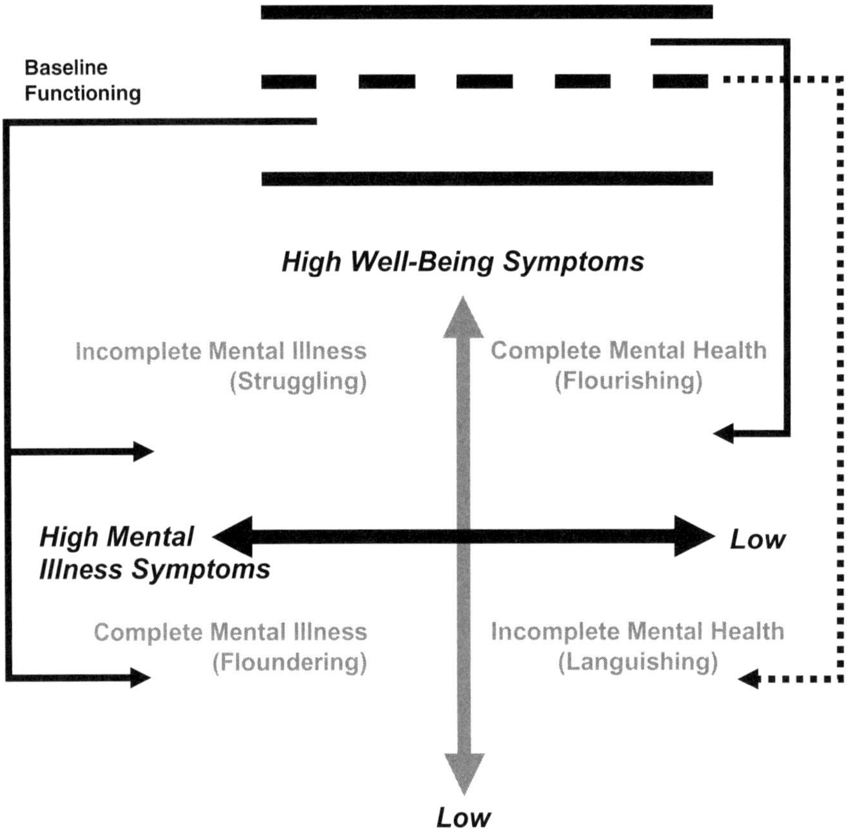

From *Therapist's guide to positive psychological interventions* (p. 25), by J. L. Magyar-Moe, 2009, San Diego, CA: Elsevier/Academic Press. Copyright 2009 by Elsevier/Academic Press. Reprinted with permission.

& Lopez, 2002) reveals that there is more that can be done to help people achieve optimal functioning. Indeed, therapy that results in baseline functioning for those who started below the baseline should be considered successful because it has reduced deficits in client functioning. However, such therapy stops short given that there is much more to life than just feeling neutral or functioning at the baseline. For many, functioning beyond the baseline can or should be the marker of therapeutic success. For those with unrelenting mental illness, complete mental health may not be possible, but rather than simply accepting that life will include ongoing issues related to pathology, he or she can be assisted to see that despite this, a life that is inclusive of symptoms of well-being is still possible (Magyar-Moe, 2009; Owens et al., 2015).

A worksheet designed to help clinicians document where clients fit within the complete state model of mental health can be found in Appendix 25.4 (Magyar-Moe, 2009). Having clients complete a measure of symptoms of mental illness (e.g., the Outcome Questionnaire–45.2, which assesses subjective discomfort, interpersonal relations, and social role performance; Lambert et al., 1996) and a measure of symptoms of subjective well-being (e.g., the MHC–LF), and then plotting the scores from these measures on the appropriate continua produce a visual picture of a client's levels of mental health and mental illness (Magyar-Moe, 2009). In addition, gathering client data according to the balanced diagnostic impressions model of positive psychological assessment also is recommended (see Owens et al., 2015, for a detailed review of this model for use in clinical psychology settings).

A variety of positive psychological interventions can be used to augment traditional forms of counseling and therapy, such that both symptoms of pathology and well-being are addressed in treatment. Examples of positive psychological interventions include quality of life therapy (Frisch, 2006), well-being therapy (Fava, 1999), hope therapy (Cheavens, Feldman, Gum, Michael, & Snyder, 2006; Lopez et al., 2004), and positive psychotherapy (Seligman, Rashid, & Parks, 2006; Rashid, 2008). (For more details on these and other positive psychological interventions, see Magyar-Moe, 2009.)

Health

A growing body of evidence has linked subjective well-being to all-cause mortality. The bulk of this research has focused exclusively on the contribution of emotional well-being to predicting mortality. Several meta-analyses have concluded that lower levels of positive emotions, such as joy and happiness, and lower levels of satisfaction with life are associated with increased risk of all-cause mortality in healthy populations (Chida & Steptoe, 2008; Diener & Chan, 2011; Howell, Kern, & Lyubomirsky, 2007; Pressman & Cohen, 2005) and in populations with preexisting physical illnesses (Chida & Steptoe, 2008; Howell et al., 2007). For example, in their review of 49 longitudinal studies, Howell and colleagues (2007) found an overall effect size of .14 for mortality between individuals with high and low emotional well-being (i.e., positive affect, life satisfaction, or both).

Many fewer studies have investigated the influence of psychological or social well-being on physical health. However, what has been published has suggested that the dimensions of psychological well-being, such as purpose in life, and dimensions of social well-being, such as social coherence and a sense of contribution to society, also are predictive of mortality. Adults with higher levels of purpose in life (Boyle, Barnes, Buchman, & Bennett, 2009; Krause, 2009; Sone et al., 2008); who find life more meaningful, manageable, and predictable (Surtees, Wainwright, Luben, Khaw, & Day, 2003; Wainwright et al., 2008); and who feel more useful to other people (Gruenewald, Karlamangla, Greendale, Singer, & Seeman, 2007) have reported lower adjusted risk of all-cause mortality.

Research also has suggested that subjective well-being may be a protective factor against physical illness in older adults (Ostir, Markides, Black, & Goodwin, 2000; see also Penninx et al., 1998). In a sample of Hispanic adults between the ages of 65 and 99 who had no limitations of daily life at the start of the study,

Ostir et al. (2000) found that adults with high emotional well-being were half as likely as adults with low emotional well-being to have died or to have acquired limitations of daily activities 2 years later. These results were found even when controlling for sociodemographic variables, functional physical status, lifestyle indicators (i.e., smoking and drinking), and negative affect scores at baseline.

Subjective well-being also has been established as a protective factor against cardiovascular diseases. More specifically, in a study of more than 3,000 adults in the United States, cardiovascular disease was found to be lowest among flourishing adults and increased as mental well-being decreased, and the absence of subjective well-being was a distinct risk factor along with major depressive episodes for cardiovascular diseases (Keyes, 2004).

Research further has indicated that chronic physical conditions, such as migraines, back pain, arthritis, high blood pressure, and gastrointestinal problems, are lowest among adults who are flourishing and increase with age as mental well-being declines. At all ages, completely mentally healthy adults reported the fewest chronic conditions, suggesting that subjective well-being may act as a protective factor in aging (Keyes, 2005a).

Work

A growing body of research has suggested that facets of subjective well-being are associated with a host of positive business outcomes. Employees who reported more satisfaction with life and their jobs were more cooperative and more helpful to their colleagues, more punctual and time efficient, showed up for more days of work, and stayed with a company longer than employees who reported low levels of life satisfaction (Spector, 1997). Investigation of the happy–productive worker clearly links emotional well-being with management evaluations of work performance. Employees who reported experiencing a greater ratio of positive emotional symptoms over negative emotional symptoms received higher performance ratings from supervisors than employees who reported feeling more negative than positive emotions (Wright & Bonett, 1997; Wright & Cropanzano, 2000).

Meta-analyses of the relations between employee satisfaction with their workplace and their perceptions of personal development at and through work (i.e., whether they have close friendships at work) are reliably correlated with positive business-level outcomes. Businesses with more employees who have high levels of employee well-being also have tended to report greater customer satisfaction and loyalty, greater profitability, more productivity, and lower rates of turnover (Harter & Schmidt, 2000; Harter, Schmidt, & Keyes, 2003; Keyes, Hysom, & Lupo, 2000). Utility analyses have conservatively estimated that companies with the most employees with high levels of well-being have reported dramatically higher monetary returns than companies in the lowest quartile of employee well-being (Harter & Schmidt, 2000; Harter et al., 2003). Companies such as the Gallup Organization are developing techniques for promoting well-being in the workplace, for example, through the design and implementation of a strengths-based approach to business and management (see Buckingham & Clifton, 2001; Buckingham & Coffman, 1999; Clifton &

Nelson, 1995), suggesting the potential for productive collaborations between employers and employees.

CONCLUSION

The research reviewed in this chapter indicates that there are internally reliable and accurate measures of emotional well-being, psychological well-being, and social well-being for adult and youth populations. Although this research documents a consistent dimensional structure within each domain of subjective well-being, there has been less research on the overall structure of subjective well-being. Given the many implications and applications of subjective well-being to a variety of mental health, physical health, and workplace outcomes, additional research is warranted.

Indeed, the social utility of subjective well-being thus far has been established in terms of measures of business profitability, productivity, and employee retention (Harter et al., 2003); delayed onset of physical disability and mortality in older adults (Ostir et al., 2000); the expression and experience of emotional states that facilitate and improve cognition and immune system function (Fredrickson, 1998; Salovey, Rothman, Detweiler, & Steward, 2000); and as a protective factor against depression (Lewinsohn, Redner, & Seeley, 1991) and risk of suicide (Weerasinghe & Tepperman, 1994). Studies further show the role of subjective well-being in association with civic responsibility, the provision of emotional and material supports to others, higher levels of generativity (i.e., intergenerational transmission of skills and resources), and local community involvement and volunteering (Keyes, 1996; Keyes & Ryff, 1998).

Although research on subjective well-being in youths has begun only more recently, the available findings suggest that America's youths regularly feel happy but only rarely feel that they have experiences that challenge them to grow and become better people, and infrequently feel that they have something important to contribute to society. It appears that more should be done to enhance the subjective well-being of youths because emotional well-being is only one component of overall well-being. Indeed, most parents hope they can raise children who are happy and who go on to become happy adults; however, parents most likely also aspire to raise children who are psychologically and socially healthy human beings. A comprehensive approach to the assessment of youth subjective well-being can provide a more detailed picture of the strengths and weaknesses of our youths and their experiences. Such an approach will suggest directions for future programmatic initiatives related to the enhancement of subjective well-being for youths (Keyes, 2006).

Finally, this chapter highlighted the role of subjective well-being in understanding mental health as more than merely the absence of mental illness. Measures of subjective well-being provide vital information regarding mental health status and can be used in the study and promotion of mental health. This material can augment the wealth of information and measures already available for the study and treatment of mental illness, all for the purpose of promoting complete states of mental health.

APPENDIX 25.1
MENTAL HEALTH CONTINUUM—LONG FORM

EWB1. <u>During the past 30 days</u>, how much of the time did you feel . . .

	All the time	Most of the time	Some of the time	A little of the time	None of the time
a. . . . cheerful?	1	2	3	4	5
b. . . . in good spirits?	1	2	3	4	5
c. . . . extremely happy?	1	2	3	4	5
d. . . . calm and peaceful?	1	2	3	4	5
e. . . . satisfied?	1	2	3	4	5
f. . . . full of life?	1	2	3	4	5

EWB2. Using a scale from 0 to 10 where 0 means "the worst possible life overall" and 10 means "the best possible life overall," how would you rate your life overall these days?

WORST										BEST
0	1	2	3	4	5	6	7	8	9	10

PWB. Please indicate how strongly you agree or disagree with each of the following statements.

	Agree				Disagree		
	Strongly	Some what	A little	Don't know	A little	Some what	Strongly
1. I like most parts of my personality.	1	2	3	4	5	6	7
2. When I look at the story of my life, I am pleased with how things have turned out so far.	1	2	3	4	5	6	7
3. Some people wander aimlessly through life, but I am not one of them.	1	2	3	4	5	6	7
4. The demands of everyday life often get me down.	1	2	3	4	5	6	7
5. In many ways I feel disappointed about my achievements in life.	1	2	3	4	5	6	7
6. Maintaining close relationships bas been difficult and frustrating for me.	1	2	3	4	5	6	7

	Agree				Disagree		
	Strongly	**Some what**	**A little**	**Don't know**	**A little**	**Some what**	**Strongly**
7. I live life one day at a time and don't really think about the future.	1	2	3	4	5	6	7
8. In general, I feel I am in charge of the situation in which I live.	1	2	3	4	5	6	7
9. I am good at managing the responsibilities of daily life.	1	2	3	4	5	6	7
10. I sometimes feel as if I've done all there is to do in life.	1	2	3	4	5	6	7
11. For me, life has been a continuous process of learning, changing, and growth.	1	2	3	4	5	6	7
12. I think it is important to have new experiences that challenge how I think about myself and the world.	1	2	3	4	5	6	7
13. People would describe me as a giving person, willing to share my time with others.	1	2	3	4	5	6	7
14. I gave up trying to make big improvements or changes in my life a long time ago.	1	2	3	4	5	6	7
15. I tend to be influenced by people with strong opinions.	1	2	3	4	5	6	7
16. I have not experienced many warm and trusting relationships with others.	1	2	3	4	5	6	7
17. I have confidence in my own opinions, even if they are different from the way most other people think.	1	2	3	4	5	6	7

(*table continues*)

	Agree				Disagree		
	Strongly	Some what	A little	Don't know	A little	Some what	Strongly
18. I judge myself by what I think is important, not by the values of what others think is important.	1	2	3	4	5	6	7

SWB. Please indicate how strongly you agree or disagree with each of the following statements.

	Agree				Disagree		
	Strongly	Some what	A little	Don't know	A little	Some what	Strongly
1. The world is too complex for me.	1	2	3	4	5	6	7
2. I don't feel I belong to anything I'd call a community.	1	2	3	4	5	6	7
3. People who do a favor expect nothing in return.	1	2	3	4	5	6	7
4. I have something valuable to give the world.	1	2	3	4	5	6	7
5. The world is becoming a better place for everyone.	1	2	3	4	5	6	7
6. I feel close to other people in my community.	1	2	3	4	5	6	7
7. My daily activities do not create anything worthwhile for my community.	1	2	3	4	5	6	7
8. I cannot make sense of what's going on in the world.	1	2	3	4	5	6	7
9. Society has stopped making progress.	1	2	3	4	5	6	7
10. People do not care about other people's problems.	1	2	3	4	5	6	7
11. My community is a source of comfort.	1	2	3	4	5	6	7

	Agree				Disagree		
	Strongly	Some what	A little	Don't know	A little	Some what	Strongly
12. I try to think about and understand what could happen next in our country.	1	2	3	4	5	6	7
13. Society isn't improving for people like me.	1	2	3	4	5	6	7
14. I believe that people are kind.	1	2	3	4	5	6	7
15. I have nothing important to contribute to society.	1	2	3	4	5	6	7

SCORING INSTRUCTIONS

Emotional Well-Being (section EWB items):
Positive Affect Scale = Reverse code items EWB1a through EWB1f, then sum items.

Psychological Well-Being (section PWB items):
Reverse code the following items: 1, 2, 3, 8, 9, 11, 12, 13, 17, 18.

Self-Acceptance Scale = Sum items 1, 2, 5.
Purpose in Life Scale = Sum items 3, 7, 10.
Environmental Mastery Scale = Sum items 4, 8, 9.
Positive Relations With Others Scale = Sum items 6, 13, 16.
Personal Growth scale = Sum items 11, 12, 14.
Autonomy Scale = Sum items 15, 17, 18.

Social well-being (section SWB items):
(Reverse code the following items: 3, 4, 5, 6, 11, 12, 14)

Social Coherence Scale = Sum items 1, 8, 12.
Social Integration Scale = Sum items 2, 6, 11.
Social Acceptance Scale = Sum items 3, 10, 14.
Social Contribution Scale = Sum items 4, 7, 15.
Social Actualization Scale = Sum items 5, 9, 13.

APPENDIX 25.2
MENTAL HEALTH CONTINUUM—SHORT FORM (MHC-SF) FOR ADULTS

Please answer the following questions are about how you have been feeling and how you have been functioning during the past two weeks. Place a check mark in the box that best represents how often you have experienced or felt the following:

During the past two weeks, how often did you feel . . .	Never	Once or twice	About once a week	About 2 or 3 times a week	Almost every day	Every day
1. happy?						
2. interested in life?						
3. satisfied?						
4. that you had something important to contribute to society?						
5. that you belonged to a community (like a social group or your neighborhood)?						
6. that our society is becoming a better place for people?						
7. that people are basically good?						
8. that the way our society works makes sense to you?						
9. that you liked most parts of your personality?						
10. good at managing the responsibilities of your daily life?						
11. that you had warm and trusting relationships with others?						
12. that you had experiences that challenged you to grow and become a better person?						

During the past two weeks, how often did you feel . . .	Never	Once or twice	About once a week	About 2 or 3 times a week	Almost every day	Every day
13. confident to think or express your own ideas and opinions?						
14. that your life has a sense of direction or meaning to it?						

Symptom Clusters and Dimensions:

Cluster 1; Items 1–3 = *Hedonic*, Emotional Well-Being

Cluster 2; Items 4–8 = *Eudaimonic*, Social Well-Being
Item 4 = Social Contribution; Item 5 = Social Integration; Item 6 = Social Actualization (i.e., Social Growth); Item 7 = Social Acceptance; Item 8 = Social Coherence (i.e., Social Interest)

Cluster 3; Items 9–14 = *Eudaimonic*, Psychological Well-Being
Item 9 = Self-Acceptance
Item 10 = Environmental Mastery
Item 11 = Positive Relations With Others
Item 12 = Personal Growth
Item 13 = Autonomy
Item 14 = Purpose in Life

APPENDIX 25.3
ITEMS FROM THE SUBJECTIVE WELL-BEING MEASURE FOR YOUTHS

How often in the past month have you felt . . .	Never	Once or twice	About once a week	About 2 or 3 times a week	Almost every day	Every day
1. happy?						
2. interested in life?						
3. satisfied?						
4. that you had something important to contribute to society?						

(*table continues*)

How often in the past month have you felt . . .	Never	Once or twice	About once a week	About 2 or 3 times a week	Almost every day	Every day
5. that you belonged to a community, like a social group, your school, or your neighborhood?						
6. that our society is becoming a better place for people?						
7. that people are basically good?						
8. that the way our society works makes sense to you?						
9. good at managing the responsibilities of your daily life?						
10. that you had warm and trusting relationships with other kids?						
11. that you had experiences that challenged you to grow or become a better person?						
12. confident to think or express your own ideas and opinions?						

Note. Purpose in life and self-acceptance were not measured in the CDS (Child Development Supplement)-II study because self-esteem, a closely related measure of self-acceptance, was already part of the CDS, and purpose in life did not seem to be a pertinent question for pre-high school youths, and the study was designed to obtain measures on all youths between the ages of 12 and 18 (Keyes, 2006).

APPENDIX 25.4
PLOTTING CLIENT FUNCTIONING ON THE COMPLETE STATE MODEL OF MENTAL HEALTH

To document where a client fits within the complete state model of mental health (Keyes & Lopez, 2002), determine his or her total score on the OQ-45.2 (see Magyar-Moe, 2009) and plot it on the horizontal axis. Next, determine his or her score on the MHC–LF (Keyes, 2002, 2005b; see Appendix 25.1) and plot

FIGURE 25A.1. Plotting Client Functioning on the Complete State Model of Mental Health Using the Outcome Questionnaire-45.2 (OQ-45.2) and Mental Health Continuum-Long Form (MHC-LF) Scores

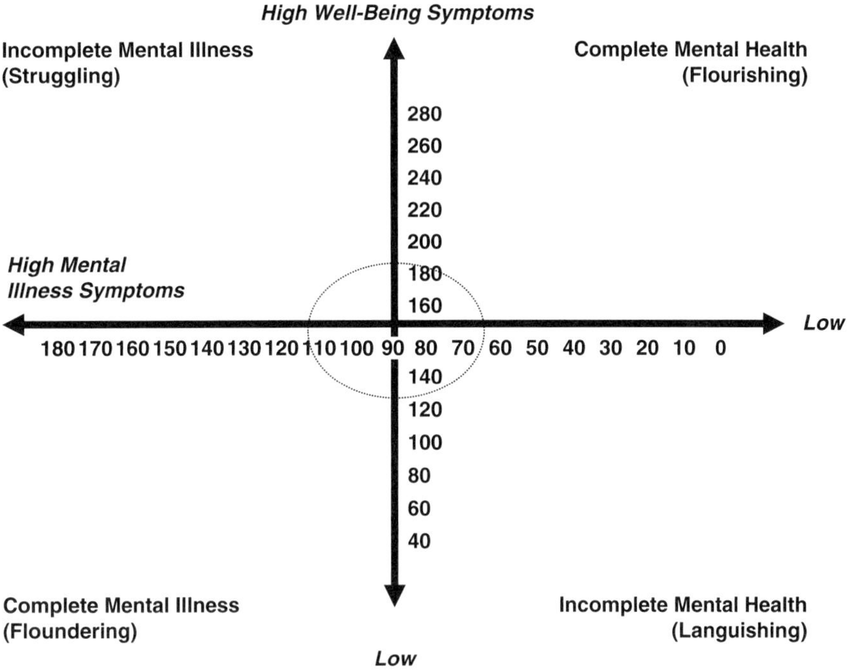

it on the vertical axis. Then connect the two points to determine which of the four categories best describes the client. In addition, scores on each of the subscales of both measures can be plotted on the appropriate continua to determine individual areas of poor functioning that may need extra attention or areas of strength that can be built on in treatment planning. Scores closer to the center of the axes are less representative than those that fall outside the center circle (Magyar-Moe, 2009).

From *Therapist's Guide to Positive Psychological Interventions* (p. 34), by J. L. Magyar-Moe, 2009, San Diego, CA: Elsevier/Academic Press. Copyright 2009 by Elsevier/Academic Press. Adapted with permission.

REFERENCES

Allport, G. W. (1961). *Pattern and growth in personality*. Oxford, England: Holt, Rinehart & Winston.

Andrews, F. M., & Withey, S. B. (1976). *Social indicators of well-being: Americans' perceptions of life quality*. New York, NY: Plenum Press. http://dx.doi.org/10.1007/978-1-4684-2253-5

Antonovsky, A. (1987). *Unraveling the mystery of health: How people manage stress and stay well*. San Francisco, CA: Jossey-Bass.

Barrett, L. F. (2017). *How emotions are made: The secret life of the brain*. New York, NY: Houghton Mifflin Harcourt.

Boyle, P. A., Barnes, L. L., Buchman, A. S., & Bennett, D. A. (2009). Purpose in life is associated with mortality among community-dwelling older persons. *Psychosomatic Medicine, 71,* 574–579. http://dx.doi.org/10.1097/PSY.0b013e3181a5a7c0

Bryant, F. B., & Veroff, J. (1982). The structure of psychological well-being: A socio-historical analysis. *Journal of Personality and Social Psychology, 43,* 653–673. http://dx.doi.org/10.1037/0022-3514.43.4.653

Buckingham, M., & Clifton, D. O. (2001). *Now, discover your strengths.* New York, NY: The Free Press.

Buckingham, M., & Coffman, C. (1999). *First, break all the rules.* New York, NY: Simon & Schuster.

Cantril, H. (1965). *The pattern of human concerns.* New Brunswick, NJ: Rutgers University Press.

Carroll, J. M., Rosson, M. B., & Zhou, J. (2005). Collective efficacy as a measure of community. In W. Kellogg & S. Zhai (Conference Chairs), *CHI '05: Proceedings of the SIGCHI Conference on Human Factors in Computing Systems,* April 2–7, 2005, Portland, Oregon (pp. 1–10). http://dx.doi.org/10.1145/1054972.1054974

Cheavens, J. S., Feldman, D. B., Gum, A., Michael, S. T., & Snyder, C. R. (2006). Hope therapy in a community sample: A pilot investigation. *Social Indicators Research, 77,* 61–78. http://dx.doi.org/10.1007/s11205-005-5553-0

Chida, Y., & Steptoe, A. (2008). Positive psychological well-being and mortality: A quantitative review of prospective observational studies. *Psychosomatic Medicine, 70,* 741–756. http://dx.doi.org/10.1097/PSY.0b013e31818105ba

Clifton, D. O., & Nelson, P. (1995). *Soar with your strengths.* New York, NY: Dell.

Diener, E. (1984). Subjective well-being. *Psychological Bulletin, 95,* 542–575. http://dx.doi.org/10.1037/0033-2909.95.3.542

Diener, E. (1994). Assessing subjective well-being: Progress and opportunities. *Social Indicators Research, 31,* 103–157. http://dx.doi.org/10.1007/BF01207052

Diener, E., & Chan, M. Y. (2011). Happy people live longer: Subjective well-being contributes to health and longevity. *Applied Psychology: Health and Well-Being, 3,* 1–43. http://dx.doi.org/10.1111/j.1758-0854.2010.01045.x

Diener, E., & Emmons, R. A. (1984). The independence of positive and negative affect. *Journal of Personality and Social Psychology, 47,* 1105–1117. http://dx.doi.org/10.1037/0022-3514.47.5.1105

Diener, E., Emmons, R. A., Larsen, R. J., & Griffin, S. (1985). The Satisfaction With Life Scale. *Journal of Personality Assessment, 49,* 71–75. http://dx.doi.org/10.1207/s15327752jpa4901_13

Diener, E., Suh, E. M., Lucas, R. E., & Smith, H. L. (1999). Subjective well-being: Three decades of progress. *Psychological Bulletin, 125,* 276–302. http://dx.doi.org/10.1037/0033-2909.125.2.276

Erikson, E. H. (1959). Identity and the life cycle. *Psychological Issues, 1,* 18–164.

Fava, G. A. (1999). Well-being therapy: Conceptual and technical issues. *Psychotherapy and Psychosomatics, 68,* 171–179. http://dx.doi.org/10.1159/000012329

Feldman Barrett, L., & Russell, J. A. (1998). Independence and bipolarity in the structure of current affect. *Journal of Personality and Social Psychology, 74,* 967–984. http://dx.doi.org/10.1037/0022-3514.74.4.967

Fredrickson, B. L. (1998). What good are positive emotions? *Review of General Psychology, 2,* 300–319. http://dx.doi.org/10.1037/1089-2680.2.3.300

Frisch, M. B. (2000). Improving mental and physical health care through quality of life therapy and assessment. In E. Diener & D. R. Rahtz (Eds.), *Advances in quality of life theory and research* (pp. 207–241). Dordrecht, Netherlands: Kluwer Academic Press. http://dx.doi.org/10.1007/978-94-011-4291-5_10

Frisch, M. B. (2006). *Quality of life therapy: Applying a life satisfaction approach to positive psychology and cognitive therapy.* Hoboken, NJ: Wiley.

Green, D. P., & Salovey, P. (1999). In what sense are positive and negative affect independent? A reply to Tellegen, Watson, and Clark. *Psychological Science, 10*, 304–306. http://dx.doi.org/10.1111/1467-9280.00158

Gruenewald, T. L., Karlamangla, A. S., Greendale, G. A., Singer, B. H., & Seeman, T. E. (2007). Feelings of usefulness to others, disability, and mortality in older adults: The MacArthur study of successful aging. *Journals of Gerontology: Series B, 62*, P28–P37. http://dx.doi.org/10.1093/geronb/62.1.P28

Gurin, G., Veroff, J., & Feld, S. (1960). *Americans view their mental health*. New York, NY: Basic Books.

Harter, J. K., & Schmidt, F. L. (2000). *Validation of a performance-related and actionable management tool: A meta-analysis and utility analysis* (Gallup Technical Report). Lincoln, NE: Gallup Organization.

Harter, J. K., Schmidt, F. L., & Keyes, C. L. M. (2003). Well-being in the workplace and its relationship to business outcomes: A review of the Gallup studies. In C. L. M. Keyes & J. Haidt (Eds.), *Flourishing: Positive psychology and the life well-lived* (pp. 205–224). Washington, DC: American Psychological Association. http://dx.doi.org/10.1037/10594-009

Howell, R. T., Kern, M. L., & Lyubomirsky, S. (2007). Health benefits: Meta-analytically determining the impact of well-being on objective health outcomes. *Health Psychology Review, 1*, 83–136. http://dx.doi.org/10.1080/17437190701492486

Jahoda, M. (1958). *Current concepts of positive mental health*. New York, NY: Basic Books. http://dx.doi.org/10.1037/11258-000

Jung, C. G. (1933). *Modern man in search of a soul* (W. S. Dell & C. F. Baynes, Trans.). New York, NY: Harcourt, Brace & World.

Kammann, R., & Flett, R. (1983). Affectometer 2: A scale to measure current levels of general happiness. *Australian Journal of Psychology, 35*, 259–265. http://dx.doi.org/10.1080/00049538308255070

Keyes, C. L. M. (1996). Social functioning and social well-being: Studies of the social nature of personal wellness. *Dissertation Abstracts International: Section B. Sciences and Engineering, 56*(12-B), 7095.

Keyes, C. L. M. (1998). Social well-being. *Social Psychology Quarterly, 61*, 121–140. http://dx.doi.org/10.2307/2787065

Keyes, C. L. M. (2002). The mental health continuum: From languishing to flourishing in life. *Journal of Health and Social Behavior, 43*, 207–222. http://dx.doi.org/10.2307/3090197

Keyes, C. L. M. (2004). The nexus of cardiovascular disease and depression revisited: The complete mental health perspective and the moderating role of age and gender. *Aging & Mental Health, 8*, 266–274. http://dx.doi.org/10.1080/13607860410001669804

Keyes, C. L. M. (2005a). Chronic physical conditions and aging: Is mental health a potential protective factor? *Ageing International, 30*, 88–104. http://dx.doi.org/10.1007/BF02681008

Keyes, C. L. M. (2005b). Mental illness *and/or* mental health? Investigating axioms of the complete state model of health. *Journal of Consulting and Clinical Psychology, 73*, 539–548. http://dx.doi.org/10.1037/0022-006X.73.3.539

Keyes, C. L. M. (2006). The subjective well-being of America's youth: Toward a comprehensive assessment. *Adolescent & Family Health, 4*, 3–11.

Keyes, C. L. M., Hysom, S. J., & Lupo, K. (2000). The positive organization: Leadership legitimacy, employee well-being, and the bottom line. *Psychologist-Manager Journal, 4*, 143–153. http://dx.doi.org/10.1037/h0095888

Keyes, C. L. M., & Lopez, S. J. (2002). Toward a science of mental health: Positive directions in diagnosis and intervention. In C. R. Snyder & S. J. Lopez (Eds.), *Handbook of positive psychology* (pp. 26–44). New York, NY: Oxford University Press.

Keyes, C. L. M., & Magyar-Moe, J. L. (2003). The measurement and utility of adult subjective well-being. In S. J. Lopez & C. R. Snyder (Eds.), *Positive psychological assessment: A handbook of models and measures* (pp. 411–425). Washington, DC: American Psychological Association. http://dx.doi.org/10.1037/10612-026

Keyes, C. L. M., & Ryff, C. D. (1998). Generativity in adult lives: Social structural contours and quality of life consequences. In D. McAdams & E. de St. Aubin (Eds.), *Generativity and adult development: Perspectives on caring for and contributing to the next generation* (pp. 227–263). Washington, DC: American Psychological Association. http://dx.doi.org/10.1037/10288-007

Keyes, C. L. M., & Ryff, C. D. (1999). Psychological well-being in midlife. In S. L. Willis & J. D. Reid (Eds.), *Life in the middle: Psychological and social development in middle age* (pp. 161–180). San Diego, CA: Academic Press. http://dx.doi.org/10.1016/B978-012757230-7/50028-6

Keyes, C. L. M., & Ryff, C. D. (2003). Somatization and mental health: A comparative study of the idiom of distress hypothesis. *Social Science & Medicine, 57,* 1833–1845. http://dx.doi.org/10.1016/S0277-9536(03)00017-0

Keyes, C. L. M., & Shapiro, A. D. (2004). Social well-being in the United States: A descriptive epidemiology. In C. D. Ryff, R. C. Kessler, & O. G. Brim, Jr. (Eds.), *A portrait of midlife in the United States* (pp. 350–372). Chicago, IL: University of Chicago Press.

Keyes, C. L. M., Shmotkin, D., & Ryff, C. D. (2002). Optimizing well-being: The empirical encounter of two traditions. *Journal of Personality and Social Psychology, 82,* 1007–1022. http://dx.doi.org/10.1037/0022-3514.82.6.1007

Keyes, C. L. M., Wissing, M., Potgieter, J. P., Temane, M., Kruger, A., & van Rooy, S. (2008). Evaluation of the Mental Health Continuum—Short Form (MHC–SF) in Setswana-speaking South Africans. *Clinical Psychology & Psychotherapy, 15,* 181–192. http://dx.doi.org/10.1002/cpp.572

Kovacs, M. (1992). *Children's Depression Inventory manual.* North Tonawanda, NY: Multi-Health Systems.

Krause, N. (2009). Meaning in life and mortality. *Journal of Gerontology: Series B, 64B,* 517–527. http://dx.doi.org/10.1093/geronb/gbp047

Lambert, M. J., Hansen, N. B., Umpress, V., Lunnen, K., Okiishi, J., Burlingame, G. M., & Reisinger, C. W. (1996). *Administration and scoring manual for the OQ-45.2 (Outcome Questionnaire).* Salt Lake City, UT: American Professional Credentialing Services.

Larsen, R. J., Diener, E., & Emmons, R. A. (1985). An evaluation of subjective well-being measures. *Social Indicators Research, 17,* 1–17. http://dx.doi.org/10.1007/BF00354108

Lewinsohn, P. M., Redner, J. E., & Seeley, J. R. (1991). The relationship between life satisfaction and psychosocial variables: New perspectives. In F. Strack, M. Argyle, & N. Schwarz (Eds.), *Subjective well-being: An interdisciplinary perspective. International series in experimental social psychology* (Vol. 21, pp. 141–169). Elmsford, NY: Pergamon Press.

Lopez, S. J., Snyder, C. R., Magyar-Moe, J. L., Edwards, L. M., Pedrotti, J. T., Janowski, K., . . . Pressgrove, C. (2004). Strategies for accentuating hope. In P. A. Linley & S. Joseph (Eds.), *Positive psychology in practice* (pp. 388–404). Hoboken, NJ: Wiley.

Lucas, R. E., Diener, E., & Suh, E. (1996). Discriminant validity of well-being measures. *Journal of Personality and Social Psychology, 71,* 616–628. http://dx.doi.org/10.1037/0022-3514.71.3.616

Magyar-Moe, J. L. (2009). *Therapist's guide to positive psychological interventions.* San Diego, CA: Elsevier/Academic Press.

Magyar-Moe, J. L., Owens, R. L., & Conoley, C. W. (2015). Positive psychology interventions in counseling: What every counseling psychologist should know. *Counseling Psychologist, 43,* 508–557. http://dx.doi.org/10.1177/0011000015573776

Magyar-Moe, J. L., Owens, R. L., & Scheel, M. J. (2015). Applications of positive psychology in counseling psychology: Current status and future directions. *Counseling Psychologist, 43,* 494–507. http://dx.doi.org/10.1177/0011000015581001

Marsh, H. (1990). *Self-description questionnaire manual.* Macarthur, Canberra: University of Western Australia.

Maslow, A. (1968). *Toward a psychology of being* (2nd ed.). New York, NY: Van Nostrand.

McGregor, I., & Little, B. R. (1998). Personal projects, happiness, and meaning: On doing well and being yourself. *Journal of Personality and Social Psychology, 74,* 494–512. http://dx.doi.org/10.1037/0022-3514.74.2.494

Mirowsky, J., & Ross, C. E. (1989). *Social causes of psychological distress.* New York, NY: Aldine.

Mroczek, D. K., & Kolarz, C. M. (1998). The effect of age on positive and negative affect: A developmental perspective on happiness. *Journal of Personality and Social Psychology, 75,* 1333–1349. http://dx.doi.org/10.1037/0022-3514.75.5.1333

Murray, C. J. L., & Lopez, A. D. (Eds.). (1996). *The global burden of disease: A comprehensive assessment of mortality and disability from diseases, injuries, and risk factors in 1990 and projected to 2020.* Cambridge, MA: Harvard School of Public Health.

Neugarten, B. L. (1973). Personality change in late life: A developmental perspective. In C. Eisdorfer & M. P. Lawton (Eds.), *The psychology of adult development and aging* (pp. 311–335). Washington, DC: American Psychological Association. http://dx.doi.org/10.1037/10044-012

Ostir, G. V., Markides, K. S., Black, S. A., & Goodwin, J. S. (2000). Emotional well-being predicts subsequent functional independence and survival. *Journal of the American Geriatrics Society, 48,* 473–478. http://dx.doi.org/10.1111/j.1532-5415.2000.tb04991.x

Owens, R. L., Magyar-Moe, J. L., & Lopez, S. J. (2015). Finding balance via positive psychological assessment and conceptualization: Recommendations for practice. *Counseling Psychologist, 43,* 634–670. http://dx.doi.org/10.1177/0011000015584956

Pavot, W., & Diener, E. (1993). Review of the satisfaction with life scale. *Psychological Assessment, 5,* 164–172. http://dx.doi.org/10.1037/1040-3590.5.2.164

Penninx, B. W. J. H., Guralnik, J. M., Simonsick, E. M., Kasper, J. D., Ferrucci, L., & Fried, L. P. (1998). Emotional vitality among disabled older women: The women's health and aging study. *Journal of the American Geriatrics Society, 46,* 807–815. http://dx.doi.org/10.1111/j.1532-5415.1998.tb02712.x

Pressman, S. D., & Cohen, S. (2005). Does positive affect influence health? *Psychological Bulletin, 131,* 925–971. http://dx.doi.org/10.1037/0033-2909.131.6.925

Radloff, L. S. (1977). The CES–D scale: A self-report depression scale for research in the general population. *Applied Psychological Measurement, 1,* 385–401. http://dx.doi.org/10.1177/014662167700100306

Rashid, T. (2008). Positive psychotherapy. In S. J. Lopez (Ed.), *Positive psychology: Exploring the best in people* (Vol. 4, pp. 187–217). Westport, CT: Praeger.

Rebellon, C., Brown, J., & Keyes, C. L. M. (2000). Mental illness and suicide. In C. E. Faupel & P. M. Roman (Eds.), *The encyclopedia of criminology and deviant behavior* (Vol. 4, pp. 426–429). London, England: Taylor & Francis.

Rogers, C. R. (1961). *On becoming a person.* Boston, MA: Houghton Mifflin.

Røsand, G.-M., Slinning, K., Eberhard-Gran, M., Røysamb, E., & Tambs, K. (2012). The buffering effect of relationship satisfaction on emotional distress in couples. *BMC Public Health.* Advance online publication. http://dx.doi.org/10.1186/1471-2458-12-66

Russell, J. A., & Carroll, J. M. (1999). On the bipolarity of positive and negative affect. *Psychological Bulletin, 125,* 3–30. http://dx.doi.org/10.1037/0033-2909.125.1.3

Ryan, R. M., & Deci, E. L. (2001). On happiness and human potentials: A review of research on hedonic and eudaimonic well-being. *Annual Review of Psychology, 52,* 141–166. http://dx.doi.org/10.1146/annurev.psych.52.1.141

Ryff, C. D. (1989a). Beyond Ponce de Leon and life satisfaction: New directions in quest of successful ageing. *International Journal of Behavioral Development, 12,* 35–55. http://dx.doi.org/10.1177/016502548901200102

Ryff, C. D. (1989b). Happiness is everything, or is it? Explorations on the meaning of psychological well-being. *Journal of Personality and Social Psychology, 57,* 1069–1081. http://dx.doi.org/10.1037/0022-3514.57.6.1069

Ryff, C. D., & Keyes, C. L. M. (1995). The structure of psychological well-being revisited. *Journal of Personality and Social Psychology, 69,* 719–727. http://dx.doi.org/10.1037/0022-3514.69.4.719

Salovey, P., Rothman, A. J., Detweiler, J. B., & Steward, W. T. (2000). Emotional states and physical health. *American Psychologist, 55,* 110–121. http://dx.doi.org/10.1037/0003-066X.55.1.110

Schwarzer, R., & Jerusalem, M. (1993). *Measurement of perceived self-efficacy: Psychometric scales for cross-cultural research.* Berlin, Germany: Freie Universität.

Seeman, M. (1959). On the meaning of alienation. *American Sociological Review, 24,* 783–791. http://dx.doi.org/10.2307/2088565

Seeman, M. (1991). Alienation and anomie. In J. P. Robinson, P. R. Shaver, & L. S. Wrightsman (Eds.), *Measures of personality and social psychological attitudes* (Vol. 1, pp. 291–371). San Diego, CA: Academic Press.

Seligman, M. E. P., Rashid, T., & Parks, A. C. (2006). Positive psychotherapy. *American Psychologist, 61,* 774–788.

Shmotkin, D. (1998). Declarative and differential aspects of subjective well-being and implications for mental health in later life. In J. Lomranz (Ed.), *Handbook of aging and mental health: An integrative approach* (pp. 15–43). New York, NY: Plenum Press. http://dx.doi.org/10.1007/978-1-4899-0098-2_2

Sone, T., Nakaya, N., Ohmori, K., Shimazu, T., Higashiguchi, M., Kakizaki, M., . . . Tsuji, I. (2008). Sense of life worth living (*Ikigai*) and mortality in Japan: Ohsaki study. *Psychosomatic Medicine, 70,* 709–715. http://dx.doi.org/10.1097/PSY.0b013e31817e7e64

Spector, P. E. (1997). *Job satisfaction: Application, assessment, cause, and consequences.* Thousand Oaks, CA: Sage.

Surtees, P., Wainwright, N., Luben, R., Khaw, K.-T., & Day, N. (2003). Sense of coherence and mortality in men and women in the EPIC–Norfolk United Kingdom prospective cohort study. *American Journal of Epidemiology, 158,* 1202–1209. http://dx.doi.org/10.1093/aje/kwg272

Takebayashi, Y., Tanaka, K., Sugiura, Y., & Sugiura, T. (2017). Well-being and generalized anxiety in Japanese undergraduates: A prospective cohort study. *Journal of Happiness Studies, 19,* 917–937.

Tellegen, A., Watson, D., & Clark, L. A. (1999a). Further support for a hierarchical model of affect: Reply to Green and Salovey. *Psychological Science, 10,* 307–309. http://dx.doi.org/10.1111/1467-9280.00159

Tellegen, A., Watson, D., & Clark, L. A. (1999b). On the dimensional and hierarchical structure of affect. *Psychological Science, 10,* 297–303. http://dx.doi.org/10.1111/1467-9280.00157

U.S. Department of Health and Human Services. (1998). *Suicide: A report of the surgeon general.* Rockville, MD: Author.

Van der Walt, C. (2007). *Validation of a coping scale in an African context* (Unpublished master's thesis). North-West University, Potchefstroom, South Africa.

Von Franz, M. L. (1964). The process of individuation. In C. G. Jung (Ed.), *Man and his symbols* (pp. 158–229). New York, NY: Doubleday.

Wainwright, N. W. J., Surtees, P. G., Welch, A. A., Luben, R. N., Khaw, K. T., & Bingham, S. A. (2008). Sense of coherence, lifestyle choices and mortality. *Journal of Epidemiology and Community Health, 62,* 829–831. http://dx.doi.org/10.1136/jech.2007.066464

Waterman, A. S. (1993). Two conceptions of happiness: Contrasts of personal expressiveness (eudaimonia) and hedonic enjoyment. *Journal of Personality and Social Psychology, 64,* 678–691. http://dx.doi.org/10.1037/0022-3514.64.4.678

Watson, D., & Tellegen, A. (1999). Issues in dimensional structure of affect—Effects of descriptors, measurement error, and response formats: Comment on Russell and

Carroll (1999). *Psychological Bulletin, 125*, 601–610. http://dx.doi.org/10.1037/0033-2909.125.5.601

Weerasinghe, J., & Tepperman, L. (1994). Suicide and happiness: Seven tests of the connection. *Social Indicators Research, 32,* 199–233. http://dx.doi.org/10.1007/BF01078685

Wright, T. A., & Bonett, D. G. (1997). The role of pleasantness and activation-based well-being in performance prediction. *Journal of Occupational Health Psychology, 2,* 212–219. http://dx.doi.org/10.1037/1076-8998.2.3.212

Wright, T. A., & Cropanzano, R. (2000). Psychological well-being and job satisfaction as predictors of job performance. *Journal of Occupational Health Psychology, 5,* 84–94. http://dx.doi.org/10.1037/1076-8998.5.1.84

Zung, W. W. (1965). A self-rating depression scale. *Archives of General Psychiatry, 12,* 63–70. http://dx.doi.org/10.1001/archpsyc.1965.01720310065008

VI

LOOKING AHEAD

26

The Future of Positive Psychological Assessment

Making a Difference

Matthew W. Gallagher, Shane J. Lopez, and C. R. Snyder

Thirty-five years ago, an article titled "Uncovering Hidden Resources" was published, and in the introduction, the authors (Wright & Fletcher, 1982) stated,

> It has been recognized that when the assessment of client problems did not sufficiently incorporate positive aspects of client functioning or the role of the environment, the assessment was seriously deficient. Yet this deficiency persists, and we add our voices to those who have already urged that positives as well as negatives be systematically examined with respect to both *the* person and the environment. (p. 229)

We add our voices to this call for a more balanced, comprehensive assessment. We do this because we believe that the uncovering of hidden resources can make a difference in the lives of people. That is our omnibus hypothesis.

In this final chapter, we specify hypotheses that need to be tested to further clarify the extent to which positive psychological assessment can make a positive difference in the pursuit of some of life's fulfillments: education, meaningful work, and mental health; whether positive psychology can influence the training, practice, and research of counselors and psychologists; and whether the lessons and benefits of positive psychology can be extended worldwide and not limited to any one country or culture. Tremendous progress has been made in these areas in recent years as the field of positive psychology continues to grow. There are now multiple taxonomies of human strength that have been developed and have shown great promise (Peterson & Seligman, 2004; Rath, 2007), and measures of well-being and positive characteristics

http://dx.doi.org/10.1037/0000138-026
Positive Psychological Assessment: A Handbook of Models and Measures, Second Edition, M. W. Gallagher and S. J. Lopez (Editors)

have now been incorporated into widely used public databases of recommended psychosocial assessment tools, such as the NIH Toolbox (National Institutes of Health, 2017) or Patient-Reported Outcomes Measurement Information System (PROMIS; Cella et al., 2010) Furthermore, as highlighted throughout this handbook, our understanding of how to conceptualize and assess hope, courage, well-being, and many other aspects of positive functioning continues to progress. We contend that much remains to be done, however, and we reaffirm that the quests for negative and positive information are complementary. Also, we provide the basic foundation of a model explaining the connections between positive personal and environmental characteristics and aspects of the good life.

THE NEGATIVES AND POSITIVES IN US ALL

Beatrice Wright, a founder of rehabilitation psychology, has framed many of the ideas associated with positive psychological assessment. In this subsequent vignette (originally presented in Wright, 1991, and reprinted in Wright & Lopez, 2009), she emphasized the importance of finding the negatives and positives in us all:

> A counselor, seeking consultation concerning the rehabilitation of a delinquent youth, presented the case of 14-year-old John. . . . The following 10 symptoms were listed: assault, temper tantrums, stealing (car theft), fire setting, self-destructive behavior (jumped out of a moving car), threats of harm to others, insatiable demand for attention, vandalism, wide mood swings, and underachievement in school. On the basis of these symptoms, the diagnosis on Axis I of the *Diagnostic and Statistical Manual of Mental Disorders* . . . was conduct disorder, undersocialized, aggressive, and with the possibility of a dysthymic disorder; on Axis II, passive aggressive personality. No physical disorders were listed on Axis III. The psychosocial stressors, rated as extreme on Axis IV, noted the death of his mother when John was a baby and successive placement with various relatives and homes. On Axis V, John's highest level of healthy functioning was rated as poor.
>
> Following perusal of this dismal picture, Wright asked the counselor whether John had anything going for him. The counselor then mentioned that John kept his own room in order, took care of his personal hygiene, liked to do things for others (although on his own terms), liked school, and had an IQ of 140. Notice how quickly the impression of John changes once positives in the situation are brought out to share the stage with the problems. Before that, the fundamental negative bias reigned supreme. Whereas the fact of John's delinquency had led to the detection of all sorts of negatives about John's conduct and situation, the positives remained unconsidered. Is this case atypical? Only in its extreme neglect of strengths, we venture to say. . . .
>
> Notice, also, that the positives in John's case had been neglected with respect to both personal characteristics and significant environments. (Wright & Lopez, 2009, p. 73)

This vignette demonstrates that, despite the surface presentation of weakness, this person has resources (i.e., personal and environmental) that change the overall impression. As such, finding strengths and assessing positive aspects of functioning more broadly make a difference.

POSITIVE CHARACTERISTICS, POSITIVE LIVES: TOWARD A MODEL OF HEALTHY PSYCHOLOGICAL GROWTH

Operationalizing strengths and environmental resources has received increasing attention in recent years because of an increasing awareness of the potential benefits of assessing and understanding positive aspects of human functioning. The second edition of this handbook is but one example of this "movement." Now, more scholarly efforts are needed to define and measure qualities of a positive life—fulfillments of the good life (e.g., love, lasting joy, meaningful work, civic pride). Scholars must consider any associated value judgments when identifying aspects of a positive life; failure to do so could result in scholarship's suggesting the "right way to live" rather than a healthy way to live (see Pedrotti, Edwards, & Lopez, 2009).

Without a doubt, the interconnections between strengths, resources, healthy processes, and fulfillments are complex. Yet, if each and every set of psychological variables were well operationalized, associations could be elucidated more easily. Indeed, if more scholarly efforts were devoted to refining measures of strengths, to creating new measures of healthy processes (e.g., resiliency), to validating existing measures (e.g., coping), and to developing and validating measures of fulfillments, then the anatomy of the "good life" would become clearer.

Although scholars currently are drafting models to explain how "vital living" is achieved, there is not yet a comprehensive theoretical model with robust empirical support that articulates how strengths, healthy processes, and fulfillments all reverberate and interact with one another to produce good living. We do, however, have ideas about how this may happen (see Figure 26.1). Notice that the model represented by the delta and the arrows is embedded in an environmental context; thus, all evaluations of strengths and healthy processes, and their interplay, should be contextualized (i.e., considering environmental and cultural variables).

An Assumption About Strength

All people have psychological strengths and the capacity to attain optimal mental health. Our model of healthy psychological growth is grounded in this assumption. Furthermore, as the model suggests, we believe that strengths are essential for growth; they are the springboards for healthy processes and life fulfillments. Without human strength, healthy processes may not develop and human fulfillments may not be attained. To borrow a comment on one strength from past (e.g., Publius Terentius Afer [Terence], Marcus Tullius Cicero) and recent (Menninger, Mayman, & Pruyser, 1963) scholars, "Where there is hope there is life" (Menninger et al., 1963, p. 417).

The Role of Healthy Processes

Healthy processes (e.g., coping) may be most effective if they are congruent with and build on an individual's strengths. For example, it is possible that

FIGURE 26.1. A Model of Healthy Psychological Growth

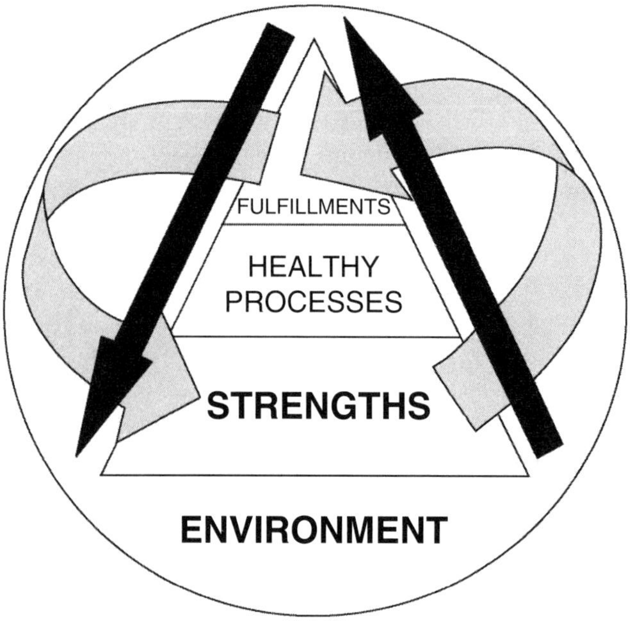

individuals who cope best with adversity possess more potent strengths before the adversity or cope with adversity in a manner that leverages their strengths most effectively. Healthy processes that do not take advantage of human strengths may facilitate "psychological survival" but may be insufficient for achieving optimal mental health. For example, a person with little hope may cope with the daily stressors of life fairly well but not realize flourishing mental health. A hopeful person, however, may cope with daily insults to well-being in the same manner and turn the successful coping into increased agency for goal pursuits. Furthermore, even in the aftermath of traumatic events, we know that humans have a remarkable capacity for resilience, and it may be that the presence of wisdom, courage, hope, or other character strengths may play an important role in minimizing symptoms of posttraumatic stress disorder and maximizing the experience of posttraumatic growth following traumatic incidents. Given the mounting evidence that mental health is more than just the absence of mental illness and that components of positive mental health uniquely predict various aspects of functioning (e.g., Keyes, 2007), it is incumbent on us as a field to identify individual and environmental characteristics that promote flourishing rather than just target the absence of mental illness as the goal.

Toward a Fulfilling Life

We believe that people who have a repertoire of potent strengths and active healthy processes will create fulfilling lives for themselves. Those people will find meaning in their relationships and work; moreover, they will find benefits in adversity and face challenges with vigor. In essence, individuals who cultivate strengths and refine healthy processes may realize fulfilling lives during good times and bad.

The Interplay Between Strengths, Healthy Processes, and Fulfillments

As indicated by the arrows in Figure 26.1, there are many paths to healthy psychological growth. The straight arrow to the right of the delta (signifying change and growth) represents direct and indirect relationships between strengths, healthy processes, and fulfillments. That is, strengths may be used to develop and engage in healthy processes, and these effective processes then lead to fulfillment (or healthy processes mediate or moderate the association between strengths and fulfillments). An alternative path is represented by the curved arrow pointing up (at the right of the delta). The arrow links strength and fulfillment directly, suggesting that strength may, at times, manifest itself as meaning, love, or satisfaction.

The arrows to the left of the delta reflect our views of how strengths and healthy processes are maintained. The straight arrow indicates that those who are fulfilled adapt better and, in turn, retain or develop new strengths. The curved arrow indicates that fulfillments may build a person's repertoire of strengths directly. This model does not account for the complexity of all of the relationships between strengths, healthy processes, and fulfillments, but we do believe that this type of theorizing needs to be undertaken. This is our current best guess, and it should be revised and refined by the field of positive psychology as our understanding of psychological growth expands.

OMNIBUS HYPOTHESIS: POSITIVE PSYCHOLOGICAL ASSESSMENT MAKES A DIFFERENCE

Our omnibus hypothesis—positive psychological assessment makes a difference—is based on two assumptions: (a) Data about the negative and the positive aspects of human nature can be gathered about every person, and (b) all people have psychological strengths and the capacity to attain optimal functioning. Identifying and measuring human strengths, healthy processes, and fulfillments may have a positive effect on people. Testing this hypothesis directly may be difficult given the broad definition of the independent variable (i.e., positive psychological assessment) and the dependent variable (i.e., making a difference). Nevertheless, many specific hypotheses follow from our omnibus hypothesis related to aspects of positive psychological assessment and measurable positive outcomes that can be clearly specified and examined empirically.

Hypothesis 1: Identifying and Enhancing Strengths Improves Achievement

Adjunctive K–12 school programs often focus on academic remediation (e.g., reading programs designed to bring students up to "standard") and on prevention of psychosocial problems (e.g., psychoeducational programs designed to prevent bullying and other forms of violence). Recently, however, enhancement programs have been developed and administered in our nation's schools. The Gallup Student Poll (Gallup, n.d.) is an applied measure built on the foundation of positive psychology research that is free to administer and has now been used to measure the hope, engagement, and well-being of more than 4 million American students. This tool has helped parents, teachers, and schools better understand how to build resilience and promote academic success in youths from diverse backgrounds and is a great example of the potential benefits of integrating the science and practice of positive psychology within education.

Hypothesis 2: Measuring Strengths Leads to Meaningful, Productive Work

Analysts at the Gallup organization have conducted millions of interviews of leaders of all types (e.g., CEOs, activists, exemplary teachers). During construction of this monumental data set, Gallup analysts determined that "each person's talents are enduring and unique" and "each person's greatest room for growth is in the areas of the person's greatest strength" (Buckingham & Clifton, 2001, p. 215). In their book *Now, Discover Your Strengths* (Buckingham & Clifton, 2001), Marcus Buckingham, a Gallup senior analyst, and former CEO Donald Clifton outlined aspects of a strategic approach for managing according to strengths. They offered the following directives that continue to be relevant and increasingly are supported by empirical evidence:

> You should spend a great deal of time and money selecting people properly. You should focus performance by "legislating" outcomes rather than forcing people to pursue one type of successful outcome. You should focus training time and money on educating people about strengths and figuring out ways to build on these strengths rather than on plugging "skill gaps." You should devise individualized ways to help people "grow" their career without necessarily promoting them *up* the corporate ladder and *out* of areas of strengths. (Buckingham & Clifton, 2001, pp. 7–8)

In the years following these recommendations, substantial work has further explored how best to conceptualize strengths in a way that can be applied effectively in the workplace, how doing so can improve workplace satisfaction and productivity of employees in many different fields, and how organizations that support the identification and promotion of strengths observe clear benefits both in terms of employee satisfaction and retention, and financial outcomes. What has become clear is that applying this type of management style requires the careful measurement of human strength and an individualized management plan. It also requires operationalization of numerous outcomes that reflect what meaningful, productive work means to each and every employee of a team, company, or government. Given the individualized nature of the expected results of managing for strengths, a variety of methodologies have been used and should continue to be used for testing the hypothesis regarding the effects of positive psychological assessment and enhancement in the workplace, but the relevance of positive psychology to the workplace is increasingly clear.

Hypothesis 3: Measuring and Enhancing Strengths Improves Mental Health

Seligman (1998) asserted that "we have discovered that there is a set of human strengths that are the most likely buffer against mental illness: courage, optimism, interpersonal skill, work ethic, hope, honest and perseverance." This assertion most certainly evokes many testable hypotheses. Akin to but a significant departure from Seligman's assertion is the hypothesis that strengths serve to improve mental health. The distinction between mental illness and mental health is becoming clearer as positive psychology scholars develop theories and conduct research illustrating how illness and health are related yet orthogonal dimensions (Keyes, 2007). We have made great strides in the past 15 years in our understanding of how best to conceptualize and assess different facets of positive mental health (e.g., subjective well-being, eudaimonic well-being, social well-being), but much remains to be done to understand how best to measure and promote mental health.

To test our hypothesis, it would be necessary to start by measuring human strength. Then the routes to strengths enhancement would have to be chosen—there are many. Universal applications (shared with all members of a team or school) of general strength-enhancement programs have been implemented. In these programs, all participants learn to be strong, but particular strengths are not targeted for enhancement. Universal programs designed to enhance one strength have been used—these often are brief and focused. Programs targeting individuals low in a particular strength also may be appropriate in certain situations. Therefore, the nature of the treatment variable (i.e., type of treatment: universal vs. targeted or general strength vs. specific strengths) needs to be well defined, and empirically pitting two or more of these treatments against each other needs to be considered a viable means of testing this hypothesis.

Hypothesis 4: Training in Positive Assessment Improves Practice and Research

We teach what we believe, as suggested by our colleague Thomas Krieshok (1999). We continue to believe that positive psychological assessment provides the information we need to be more helpful in clinical practice and to conduct meaningful, positive psychological research. Our students pick up on this belief and run with it. Thus, our students (and the readership of this handbook) serve as the most appropriate target population for examination of this hypothesis.

Our work with our graduate students, many of whom have contributed to this handbook and to positive psychology articles and books, is the intervention; their good deeds (in scholarly and practice realms) are the outcomes of interest. Testing our hypothesis (i.e., training in positive psychological assessment improves practice and research conducted by our students and others) might involve examining the extent to which our students have indoctrinated and applied the positive psychological assessment approach (i.e., independent variable). The variability in indoctrination and application would have to be determined, and then students' contributions to practice and research (i.e., dependent variable) would have to be quantified and qualified. This is an area in which there has not been as much progress in the intervening years since the first edition of this handbook, but examination of training outcome would help us to further understand the effects of positive psychological assessment and practice.

Hypothesis 5: Universally Sharing the Benefits of Assessing Strengths

As stated earlier, a fundamental premise and assumption of this handbook is that all individuals have strengths and that we can measure and potentially promote strengths and other positive outcomes in all individuals. A question that naturally follows from this premise is whether the scientific study and intervention efforts of positive psychology are being shared worldwide so that individuals of all backgrounds can benefit equally. Early studies in positive psychology often were conducted with convenience samples that were relatively homogenous racially, but in recent years, there has been increasing awareness of and focus on the importance of examining positive psychology outcomes and interventions in diverse samples (e.g., Chapter 4, this handbook; Pedrotti et al., 2009). We believe that it is crucial for the field to continue this examination so that whether it is country of origin, culture, gender, age, race/ethnicity, sexual orientation, disability, or any facet of diversity, the assessment and benefits of positive psychological assessment are more fully understood and more widely disseminated. The translation of many of the measures discussed in this handbook to many different languages has advanced substantially in recent years, but it will be important to extend these efforts and to do fundamental work on the examination of measurement invariance of strengths, well-being, and other positive psychology constructs, whether the relationships between positive psychological factors and functioning outcomes are consistent across culture and other individual differences, and whether the same strategies and interventions are equally efficacious in promoting these outcomes across diverse contexts. In doing so, we, as a field, can best ensure that the lessons and benefits of positive psychology are shared by individuals of all backgrounds.

CONCLUSION

"First you need to measure their strengths!" This is the impassioned reply that Don Clifton (personal communication, October 1999) gave when asked how to better manage, educate, or counsel people. He believed that measuring and enhancing strengths is what makes a difference in the lives of people—all people.

The research and assessment tools reviewed in this handbook represent the tremendous efforts and progress that have been made in improving our understanding of the assessment of positive psychology constructs. We continue to believe that use of positive psychological assessment will help us to broaden psychology and to explore fascinating new clinical and research hypotheses. These hypotheses lead us and the people we teach and counsel to discoveries about healthy processes and human fulfillment. At the heart of our "making a difference" pursuits are the discoveries about the best in all of us.

REFERENCES

Buckingham, M., & Clifton, D. O. (2001). *Now, discover your strengths.* New York, NY: The Free Press.

Cella, D., Riley, W., Stone, A., Rothrock, N., Reeve, B., Yount, S., . . . Hays, R. (2010). The Patient-Reported Outcomes Measurement Information System (PROMIS) developed and tested its first wave of adult self-reported health outcome item banks: 2005–2008. *Journal of Clinical Epidemiology, 63,* 1179–1194. http://dx.doi.org/10.1016/j.jclinepi.2010.04.011

Gallup. (n.d.). *Gallup Student Poll* [Measurement instrument]. Retrieved from https://www.gallup.com/175316/gallup-student-poll-methodology.aspx

Keyes, C. L. (2007). Promoting and protecting mental health as flourishing: A complementary strategy for improving national mental health. *American Psychologist, 62,* 95–108. http://dx.doi.org/10.1037/0003-066X.62.2.95

Krieshok, T. S. (1999). We teach what we believe. *Career Planning and Adult Development Journal, 15,* 13–21.

Menninger, K., Mayman, M., & Pruyser, P. (1963). *The vital balance: The life process in mental health and illness.* New York, NY: Viking Press.

National Institutes of Health and Northwestern University. (2017). *NIH Toolbox* [Measurement instrument]. Retrieved from http://www.healthmeasures.net/images/nihtoolbox/NIH_Toolbox_brochure_June_2017.pdf

Pedrotti, J. T., Edwards, L. M., & Lopez, S. J. (2009). Positive psychology within a cultural context. In S. J. Lopez & C. R. Snyder (Eds.), *The handbook of positive psychology* (2nd ed., pp. 49–58). New York, NY: Oxford University Press.

Peterson, C., & Seligman, M. E. P. (2004). *Character strengths and virtues: A handbook and classification.* New York, NY: Oxford University Press.

Rath, T. (2007). *StrengthsFinder 2.0.* New York, NY: Gallup Press.

Seligman, M. E. P. (1998). *Building human strength: Psychology's forgotten mission.* https://nonopp.com/ar/Psicologia/00/pres.htm

Wright, B. A. (1991). Labeling: The need for greater person–environment individuation. In C. R. Snyder & D. R. Forsyth (Eds.), *Handbook of social and clinical psychology: A health perspective* (pp. 469–487). New York, NY: Pergamon Press.

Wright, B. A., & Fletcher, B. L. (1982). Uncovering hidden resources: A challenge in assessment. *Professional Psychology, 13,* 229–235. http://dx.doi.org/10.1037/0735-7028.13.2.229

Wright, B. A., & Lopez, S. J. (2009). Widening the diagnostic focus: A case for including human strengths and environmental resources. In S. J. Lopez & C. R. Snyder (Eds.), *Handbook of positive psychology* (2nd ed., pp. 71–88). New York, NY: Oxford University Press.

INDEX

A

F

I

J

K

L

M

N

Q

R

S

U

V

W

ABOUT THE EDITORS

Matthew W. Gallagher, PhD, is an associate professor in the Department of Psychology and Texas Institute for Measurement, Evaluation, and Statistics at the University of Houston. Dr. Gallagher received his PhD in clinical and quantitative psychology from the University of Kansas. He completed a postdoctoral fellowship at the Center for Anxiety and Related Disorders at Boston University and was previously a staff research psychologist in the Behavioral Science Division of the National Center for PTSD. His research interests include understanding how positive thinking (e.g., hope, optimism, self-efficacy) promotes well-being and provides resilience to anxiety and stress disorders, identifying mechanisms of change of empirically supported treatments, evaluating the efficacy of transdiagnostic treatments for anxiety and stress disorders, and the development and validation of measures of positive psychological characteristics and emotional disorder symptomatology. His research has been funded by the National Institute of Mental Health, the National Institute of Drug Abuse, the National Institute of Alcohol Abuse and Alcoholism, and the Department of Defense. His research has won awards from the Association for Psychological Science and the Society for Multivariate Experimental Psychology. Dr. Gallagher is the author of more than 100 articles, chapters, and books, including the *Oxford Handbook of Hope* (with Shane J. Lopez), and is a licensed psychologist.

Shane J. Lopez, PhD, was a Gallup Senior Scientist and research director of the Clifton Strengths Institute. Dr. Lopez received his doctorate in counseling psychology from the University of Kansas and was previously a faculty member in the Counseling Psychology Program at the University of Kansas. He was a fellow of the American Psychological Association and the International Positive Psychology Association. His research focused on developing and disseminating hope and strengths promotion programs in schools, examining the impact of hope on engagement and well-being across the life span, and refining a model and measures of psychological courage. He was the chief architect of the Gallup Student Poll, a measure that has been used to assess the hope, engagement, and well-being of more than 5 million students. He published more than 100 articles and chapters, and wrote or edited more than a dozen books, including *Making Hope Happen: Create the Future You Want for Yourself and Others*, *The Oxford Handbook of Hope*, *The Oxford Handbook of Positive Psychology*, and *Positive Psychology: The Scientific and Practical Explorations of Human Strengths*. He won multiple awards for teaching and mentoring and was a licensed psychologist.